E-Commerce Adoption and Small Business in the Global Marketplace:
Tools for Optimization

Brychan Thomas
University of Glamorgan, UK

Geoff Simmons
University of Ulster, UK

BUSINESS SCIENCE REFERENCE

Hershey · New York

Director of Editorial Content:	Kristin Klinger
Director of Book Publications:	Julia Mosemann
Publishing Assistant:	Sean Woznicki
Typesetter:	Carole Coulson, Sean Woznicki
Quality Control:	Jamie Snavely
Cover Design:	Lisa Tosheff
Printed at:	Yurchak Printing Inc.

Published in the United States of America by
Business Science Reference (an imprint of IGI Global)
701 E. Chocolate Avenue
Hershey PA 17033
Tel: 717-533-8845
Fax: 717-533-8661
E-mail: cust@igi-global.com
Web site: http://www.igi-global.com/reference

Library of Congress Cataloging-in-Publication Data

E-commerce adoption and small business in the global marketplace : tools for optimization / Brychan Thomas and Geoff Simmons, editors.
     p. cm.

 Includes bibliographical references and index.
 Summary: "This book focuses on isolating what determines the adoption of e-commerce applications that will optimize potential opportunities presented to small businesses through adoption"--Provided by publisher.

 ISBN 978-1-60566-998-4 (hardcover) -- ISBN 978-1-60566-999-1 (ebook) 1.
Electronic commerce. 2. Small business. I. Thomas, Brychan, 1955- II.
Simmons, Geoff, 1971-
  HF5548.32.E217 2009
  658.8'72--dc22
                          2009045586

British Cataloguing in Publication Data
A Cataloguing in Publication record for this book is available from the British Library.

All work contributed to this book is new, previously-unpublished material. The views expressed in this book are those of the authors, but not necessarily of the publisher.

Marta Raus, *ETH Zurich, Switzerland*

Noor Azuan Hashim, *Sheffield University Management School, UK*

Audrey Gilmore, *University of Ulster, UK*

Guangming Cao, *University of Ulster, UK*

Laura Galloway, *Heriot-Watt University, UK*

Harry Matlay, *Birmingham City University, UK*

Roman Boutellier, *ETH Zurich, Switzerland*

Table of Contents

Section 1
E-Commerce Trading and Small Business

Section 2
E-Commerce and Small Business in Different Countries and Regions

Section 3
Internet Marketing and Small Business

Section 4
The International Dimension of ICT, Websites and E-Commerce for Small Business

Chapter 15

Detailed Table of Contents

Section 1
E-Commerce Trading and Small Business

Marta Raus, ETH Zurich, Switzerland
Roman Boutellier, ETH Zurich, Switzerland

International trade conducted electronically is seen as a major driver of globalisation. It is argued that the development of international electronic trade might grow faster if adequate governmental regulations support it. Based on a literature review and EU/OECD reports, the chapter demonstrates how legislation is important for the success of international e-commerce. In particular, there is focus on EU e-customs regulations and related IT systems. It is shown how e-customs systems might be used as a tool for e-commerce adoption facilitation.

Paul Jones, University of Glamorgan, UK
Gary Packham, University of Glamorgan, UK
David Pickernell, University of Glamorgan, UK
Paul Beynon-Davies, Cardiff University, UK

This study profiles an empirical study of E-Commerce trading patterns of SMEs. It is noted that academic debate continues to espouse the importance of the SME community in engendering economic prosperity and enhanced economic development although the sector also remains categorised by high failure rates. The strategic adoption of information technology offers the opportunity for increased competitiveness and enhanced profitability. Evidence suggests, however, that SMEs, particularly the smaller SME classifications, are not effectively exploiting E-business, with limited recorded examples of successful adoption.

Section 2
E-Commerce and Small Business in Different Countries and Regions

Chapter 3

While many strategies for improving e-commerce have been suggested, the focus has mainly been on economic and technological factors and less on human and social aspects such as compliance behaviours. This has resulted in the development of e-commerce systems that do not incorporate regulatory requirements. Consequently, the level of exposure to cyber-risks and legal liabilities has increased and market competitiveness compromised. This chapter examines the factors influencing compliance with IT regulations and e-security and how these impact on e-commerce optimization in South African SMEs. It also provides some useful frameworks and checklists SME managers can use to evaluate their compliance behaviours and security practices in order to make improvement to their e-commerce activities.

Chapter 4

Small and medium-sized enterprises (SMEs) in Malaysia have been slow in the uptake of e-commerce. This chapter explores the extent of e-commerce use by SMEs, and provides some empirical evidence of how internal factors of firm and owner are influencing e-commerce adoption among smaller businesses in Malaysia. The methodology and results of this study may be applicable to other developing countries. Findings confirm the low level of participation in e-commerce by SMEs. The age of enterprise, as well as the owner's gender and education were found to be significant in determining the level of e-commerce adoption.

Chapter 5

A region where e-commerce will have a particular impact for SMEs over the next few years is South East Wales (SEW). In response to this a survey was undertaken to assess the e-commerce activity of firms within the SEW area. Results from the survey demonstrated that nearly all firms used some form of ICT. The results also highlighted that a significant proportion of the sample (77%) were currently using a Web site to increase trade or improve opportunities for e-commerce. Furthermore, it was observed that firms in the personal services, distribution and transport industries were less likely to utilise a Web site than firms in the manufacturing, business services and hospitality industries. Despite the large proportion of firms that had a Web site, only 11% of businesses reported that their site enabled customers to order and pay for products online although 42% of respondents considered e-commerce to be important for their business' future.

Section 3
Internet Marketing and Small Business

Chapter 6

John Sanders, Heriot-Watt University, UK
Laura Galloway, Heriot-Watt University, UK
David Deakins, University of the West of Scotland, UK

This chapter explores the uses and effectiveness of private and public/charity managed and funded internet portals on rural SMEs' e-commerce activities. Specifically, the study investigated whether there were differences in how rural SMEs used and perceived the effectiveness of each type of internet portal. Hypotheses were drawn from qualitative results carried out. Ninety-six rural SMEs spread across the two types of rural internet portals were interviewed via telephone to gain their perceptions. Cross-tabulations using chi square testing discovered that in the main there were no perceived differences between the uses and effectiveness of private and public/charity funded internet portals on rural SMEs' e-commerce activities. However, testing did discover that rural SME users of public/charity funded internet portals were more likely to be charged a fee for membership. The main preoccupation of rural SMEs was representation on an internet portal to help facilitate their e-commerce activities, not how it was owned or operated.

Chapter 7

Daniel John Doiron, University of New Brunswick, Saint John Campus, Canada

The chapter presents and supports the hypothesis that SMEs should stop investing in their web site's design and functionality and start investing in efforts to market their web sites online, no matter how *lousy* their web site may be in comparison to today's standards. With the support of two case studies, illustrating the successful utilization of internet marketing by two very different SMEs, the chapter relates how a SME can effectively market their web site online. Tools and techniques available to help an SME successfully begin a journey of internet marketing are discussed.

Section 4
The International Dimension of ICT, Websites and E-Commerce for Small Business

Chapter 8

Robert Williams, NEO, UK
Gary P. Packham, University of Glamorgan, UK
Brychan C. Thomas, University of Glamorgan, UK
Piers Thompson, University of Wales Institute, UK

This chapter investigates the level of SME website adoption and functionality and how this relates to growth aspirations, specifically the geographical expansion of customer bases. One potential explanation for this slow uptake of true e-commerce is a lack of employees with basic and advanced IT skills. The possibility that IT skills shortages could explain the gap between the Internet's potential and the extent of involvement by a vast majority of UK SMEs is explored. Discussion within the chapter is complemented with analysis of data from a large survey of SMEs.

Chapter 9

Ingrid Wakkee, VU University Amsterdam, The Netherlands
Peter van der Sijde, VU University Amsterdam, The Netherlands

This study looks into the process by which an opportunity scenario unfolds in the context of global start-ups and links theoretical insights on opportunity recognition to theoretical insights on international entrepreneurship and of ICT-supported communication. Insights are utilised from cases previously published in the global start-up literature to illustrate and conceptualize how entrepreneurs virtually embed themselves and use IT to interact with international contacts throughout this process.

Section 5
E-Business and E-Marketing among Small Business Enterprises

Chapter 10

Martin Beckinsale, Leicester Business School, UK

This chapter examines and reviews the existing body of literature on Ethnic Minority Businesses (EMBs) and ICT. Secondly, EMB cases that have developed ICT to a degree where they are engaging in e-business activity are analysed and discussed. The findings provide a number of options and guidance for EMB owners. Finally, the recommendations point to the need for improved ICT awareness, better business support provision nationally and the importance of generation and education as key drivers.

The chapter depicts the current findings of an ongoing longitudinal study pertaining to e-business and the graphic design industry. The research problem can be described as being: to identify the extent of engagement by graphic designers with e-business. The location of the study is Industrial South Wales: Cardiff, Newport, Swansea and the South Wales Valleys with the particular focus being Small and Medium Size Enterprises (SMEs). For the purpose of the study, the European Commission definitions relating to SMEs have been utilised (last revised 2005).

It is posited that by exploring the components of e-customer relations management (e-CRM) in the unique context of SME business and marketing practice that a natural synergy exists between e-CRM and SME marketing in the creation of value propositions. Specifically this is addressed through the two contributing constructs of SME marketing; namely entrepreneurial marketing and network marketing.

The chapter builds on the current body of knowledge in the field of e-marketing through a survey and systematic review of the published work related to the Technology Acceptance Model (TAM), Innovation Diffusion Theory (IDT) and E-Marketing adoption by small business enterprises. Furthermore, the chapter illustrates that although many e-marketing adoption factors are driven from the literature of e-marketing, as well as the technology adoption theories like TAM and IDT, only some of these factors are found to significantly affect the adoption of e-marketing by small business enterprises.

Section 6
Small Business and Electronic Retailing

Chapter 14

Daniela Andreini, University of Bergamo, Italy

This chapter studies the multi channel integration strategies for small and medium retailers, formulating a multi channel integration codification scheme and explaining the barriers and related solutions under these strategic decisions.

Chapter 15

Simon McCarthy, University of Glamorgan, UK
Brychan Thomas, University of Glamorgan, UK
Geoff Simmons, University of Ulster, UK

The last chapter of the book introduces the importance of the e-fulfilment industry for offshore centres and in particular the small business and economic policy implications. The extant concepts, research, and experiences the chapter builds on is the literature concerning the e-fulfilment industry. It argues that the key results, evidence, and experience, from the models that have been developed and the specific model formulated for this work, indicate reasons for the development of e-fulfilment in offshore centres.

Foreword

I have worked for many years with small businesses. Whilst such businesses are hugely heterogeneous with diverse focus and purpose dictated by their unique market circumstances, they do have some common characteristics regardless of market position.

All small businesses are characterised by the fact they are small and as such have severe limitations in what they can do, particularly in the domain of business development and marketing. All small businesses have limitations of resources, not least cash, limitations of expertise, particularly in any specialised area and limitations in their market impact, because of these limitations and, because they are a small pebble in the big pond of most markets.

Over the past decade there have been many who have argued that the world wide web can enable small business to do global business. The emergence of E-Commerce has been seen by some to be a panacea for small business growth and success. Few have fully recognised how the small business limitations eluded to here impact upon small business E-commerce.

This text of readings, in my opinion, is the first to address the notion of small business adoption of E-Commerce in a realistic, interesting and usable way. Congratulations are due to the editors in compiling a comprehensive range of topics covering a truly global span of topics that are of interest to any scholar of small business and also to small business owner managers. Chapters not only present meaningful insights into E-Commerce in the small business context but also acknowledge the difficulties small businesses have in simply developing their business.

I commend this text to students, researchers and scholars of small business and to small business owner managers interested in setting their own problems and challenges in the context of similar circumstances of other small businesses.

David Carson
Professor of Marketing
University of Ulster

__David Carson__ is President of the Academy of Marketing UK, the foremost representative body of marketing academics in the UK and Ireland. He is also a Fellow of the Chartered Institute of Marketing (CIM) and Honorary President of CIM Ireland. He has wide experience in middle and senior management training in service industries including organisations such as Walt Disney World and Cadogan Holidays. Also, he has worked with hundreds of SMEs in Ireland and elsewhere and has published widely in SME and Entrepreneurial Marketing and research methodologies.

Preface

At an international level, the use of information and communications technologies (ICT) is seen as critical in relation both to capabilities within firms and to the innovative role that small businesses are expected to play in the emerging knowledge economy (EC, 2005; BERR, 2008). In addition, it is argued that the effective use of ICT is often considered to be a prerequisite for small business survival (Packham, 2002; Packham et al., 2005). There are few signs however that Europe, and the UK in particular, have caught up let alone overtaken the US in reaping the productivity gains from the effective production, implementation and optimisation of ICT applications (Vaitilingam, 2004; Timmer & van Ark, 2005; Havik et al., 2008).

The importance of the small business sector to economic growth has long been recognised. For example, the Ministerial Declaration at the OECD Conference held in Istanbul, 2004, attended by representatives from all major EU, US, Asian and South American trading block partners, reaffirmed the need for international focus on small business access to international markets; information and communication technologies (ICT); and e-commerce expertise.

The Declaration stated within this context that small business assistance and development programmes should be based on sound research, empirical evidence, public/private dialogue and partnerships, and evaluated regularly for effectiveness and efficiency; and, be able to enhance small business ability to take full advantage of information and communication technologies

The significant opportunities offered to small businesses through ICT adoption, plus an awareness of the barriers to the implementation of ICT applications, have led researchers to concentrate on the factors that determine adoption (Poon & Swatman, 1999; Parasuraman, 2000; Raymond, 2001; Houghton & Winklehofer, 2002; Pfughoeft et al., 2003; Jones et al., 2003; Fillis et al., 2003; Fillis & Wagner, 2005; Bengtsson et al., 2007; Simmons et al., 2007, 2008). However, apart from in specialised R&D-intense sectors, there has been little success in linking the determinants of ICT adoption in small businesses with expected outcomes – such as innovation, productivity-improvements, competitiveness, business-model transformation and the ultimate commercial success of adoption. Various studies have focused on these issues introducing stage models that often focus on ICT-adoption issues rather than business transformation effects (Earl, 2000; Rayport & Jaworski, 2002; Rao et al., 2003; Gray, 2006a). Others, viewing these as inadequate, have proposed broader multi-dimensional frameworks to take account of varying business operating contexts (Tagliavani et al., 2001; Levy & Powell, 2003; Mendo & Fitzgerald, 2005). Despite some value, however, these concepts do not present a specific means of ascertaining the optimisation of ICT implementation in small businesses. Indeed, with the near universal adoption of computers and the Internet by all but the smallest businesses, research interest has shifted from adoption issues and a focus on e-commerce (Internet-mediated trading) and a wider and more advanced use of ICT applications in business processes and business growth (e-business). Optimisation introduces a new concept into small business ICT adoption research, providing opportunities for research to be more focused on specific tools/applications that make the most of small business ICT adoption in value chains and markets.

It is clear from official statistics and many academic studies that only an active, motivated and capable minority of small businesses have sufficient resources, knowledge and strategic intention to contribute significantly to the optimised ICT adoption in small businesses that will renovate economies and transform society (FSB, 2006; FSB 2008; Wiseman et al., 2006; Gray, 2006a). It is these small businesses with their above average *absorptive capacity* - the experience, knowledge and skills base plus the knowledge creation and sharing processes in a firm (Cohen & Levinthal, 1990; Zahra & George, 2002; Gray, 2006b) - plus their effective use of networking and more optimised use of ICT applications that are the focus of this book. Previous studies suggest that small businesses that are early adopters of more advanced ICT applications and first movers in transforming their firms into e-businesses tend to be (1) early-adopters in previous and subsequent ICT applications; (2) more entrepreneurial in their growth strategies; and (3) core opinion-formers in their networks (Gray, 2006b). In addition, it is likely that they conduct more R&D or adaptation of ICT applications to their own requirements than other small businesses. It is hoped that this book will provide greater understanding of these propositions.

The 2007 Quarterly Survey of Small Business in Britain confirmed, despite almost universal use of personal computers and rapidly increased use of the internet and websites by small businesses there have been few improvements in the participation rates of these businesses in the 'digital economy'. The 2006 Federation of Small Business (FSB) survey of its members revealed that only one third of respondents engaged in any form of e-commerce – ranging from 37% in London to 25% in Northern Ireland. This was mainly generating sales from their own website. Of those who did trade on the Internet, their e-commerce represented less than 10% of overall sales turnover. The main reasons cited for not engaging in e-commerce were lack of relevance (37%), costs of developing and maintaining a website (24%), risk of fraud (19%) and lack of relevant ICT skills inside the firm (18%), which was a particular problem in Wales, Scotland and Northern Ireland (FSB, 2006).

More recently, the FSB (2008) survey identified that nearly 28% of businesses did not have a website and for owner-only businesses this increased to over 35%. Within these businesses however, only 36% used the web for advertising and 14% sold products and services online. In fact, the FSB (2008) survey revealed that only a minority of small firms (less than 2%) actually utilised e-commerce to link to suppliers.

The research also highlights that firms employing 5 or more people are more likely to have developed websites for advertising and facilitating online sales. Unsurprisingly, businesses with higher turnover were also more likely to (1) have a website presence and (2) utilise the website to advertise and sell products online. Similarly businesses that had seen an increase in turnover were more likely to utilise their websites to advertise and/or sell online. (43%) when compared with businesses that had experienced a decline in turnover (34%).

Across the UK, there were considerable variances in the number of businesses with websites with London the highest (78%) and Northern Ireland having the lowest (68%). Website use in Wales (69%) and Scotland (70%) were also below the UK average of 72%. In terms of differences across different business sectors, industries reporting the highest use of websites to advertise and sell online were wholesale and retail (23%) and hotel and restaurant businesses (16%). In contrast the lowest users were found in the mining and construction (35%) and motor vehicle sales and repair (5%) sectors.

Surveys conducted for *e-skills UK* (the ICT industry sector skills training board) reveal that there is still a huge need to upgrade small business knowledge of existing ICT applications (e-Skills, 2008). In addition, there is a need to develop this knowledge base in order to benefit from future ICT applications and for small businesses to play a full role in the creation and sustaining of Britain's knowledge economy. At the organisational level, this increases pressures on entrepreneurial firms to have the right capabilities and effective linkages with other firms and stakeholders.

The e-commerce focus of small businesses is likely to be on applications that deliver cost savings or access to new markets. Appropriate ICT applications increase the internal capacity to outsource efficiently (Tapscott, 2002), connect and communicate more effectively (Merisavo & Raulas, 2004; Andrews & Boyle, 2008), acquire and manage knowledge and achieve productivity gains (Phippen, 2004, Evans & Mathur, 2005; Harrigan et al. 2008) which is also helped by decreases in sourcing, production and delivery costs and lead times (Graham & Hardaker, 2000; Porter, 2001). However, e-commerce has to be managed effectively in a customer-oriented way and it is not a time for experimentation. At the managerial level, there is a need to improve the effective use of resources and capabilities of small firm, linkages with other firms and organisations (networks) and penetration of wider markets: regional, European and global (Simmons et al., 2008). In fact, it is contended that for a firm to achieve a business platform from which it can secure survival and the potential for growth it must accumulate the necessary resources and develop the ability to manage and allocate resources effectively (Packham, 2002). The acquisition and creation of knowledge in organisations is essentially a social process and one that needs to span the traditional boundaries of firms, big and small. In difficult times, effective networking offers small businesses a way of overcoming their capacity and knowledge constraints by providing opportunities of scope in sharing some of their resources, capabilities and information while also offering opportunities of scale through collaborative work – with e-commerce adoption a critical potential facilitator (Jones et al., 2003).

Small businesses are represented in all different communities on the global stage. While the self-employed and micro firms (<10 employees) often provide the best employment opportunities for marginalised groups, it is the small firms (in EU and UK definitions, 10-50 employees) that offer the best scope for innovation, effective use of ICT and consequent productivity gains. Even so, the 2006 FSB survey concluded 'closer inspection of the statistics reveals the existence of a small number of genuine 'new economy' businesses, predominantly micro businesses that derive most, if not all, of their sales over the Internet and in many cases are trading internationally. This is an interesting group of businesses for further analysis.' (FSB, 2006, p 60). Furthermore, the latest FSB (2008) survey confirms that small firms employing 5 or more people are more likely to utilise the internet to advertise and sell products and services online.

The EU Research Advisory Board has produced a useful typology (EURAB, 2004). There are four basic categories based on the level of use and the amount of related R&D conducted: (1) *basic* – the 70% or so of all small businesses that undertake no or little R&D and under-utilise the potential of ICT applications; (2) *technology adopting* – around 20% that adapt existing technologies and are low innovative businesses; (3) *leading technology users* – less than 10% that develop or combine existing technologies on an innovative level and optimise their use of ICT applications; and (4) *technology pioneers* – less than 3% that conduct high level research activities. The shift from basic into technology adoption mode is a well researched field while the technology pioneers are an interesting but rather specialised niche. Research is primarily interested in the shift from category 2 into category 3 and the characteristics of category 3 small businesses (especially those with potential and inclination to shift into category 4). There is also the need to identify the pathways into and the distinctive characteristics of leading technology users (optimised adoption) as they survive and maintain their critical market edge.

ORGANIZATION OF THE BOOK

The book contains fifteen chapters grouped into six sections based upon the themes of each chapter. Section I consists of two chapters relating to e-commerce trading and small business. This section presents factors facilitating e-commerce adoption and trading patterns.

Chapter 1 introduces the finding that international trade conducted electronically is seen as a major driver of globalisation. It is argued that the development of international electronic trade might grow faster if adequate governmental regulations support it. Based on a literature review and EU/OECD reports, the chapter demonstrates how legislation is important for the success of international e-commerce. In particular, there is focus on EU e-customs regulations and related IT systems. It is shown how e-customs systems might be used as a tool for e-commerce adoption facilitation.

Chapter 2 profiles an empirical study of E-Commerce trading patterns of SMEs. It is noted that academic debate continues to espouse the importance of the SME community in engendering economic prosperity and enhanced economic development although the sector also remains categorised by high failure rates. The strategic adoption of information technology offers the opportunity for increased competitiveness and enhanced profitability. Evidence suggests, however, that SMEs, particularly the smaller SME classifications, are not effectively exploiting E-business, with limited recorded examples of successful adoption.

Section 2 comprises three chapters relating to e-commerce and small business in different countries and regions. This includes e-security and non-compliance with government regulations on IT and the determinants of e-commerce among small and medium-sized enterprises.

Chapter 3 reports that while many strategies for improving e-commerce have been suggested, the focus has mainly been on economic and technological factors and less on human and social aspects such as compliance behaviours. This has resulted in the development of e-commerce systems that do not incorporate regulatory requirements. Consequently, the level of exposure to cyber-risks and legal liabilities has increased and market competitiveness compromised. This chapter examines the factors influencing compliance with IT regulations and e-security and how these impact on e-commerce optimization in South African SMEs. It also provides some useful frameworks and checklists SME managers can use to evaluate their compliance behaviours and security practices in order to make improvement to their e-commerce activities.

Chapter 4 relates that small and medium-sized enterprises (SMEs) in Malaysia have been slow in the uptake of e-commerce. This chapter explores the extent of e-commerce use by SMEs, and provides some empirical evidence of how internal factors of firm and owner are influencing e-commerce adoption among smaller businesses in Malaysia. The methodology and results of this study may be applicable to other developing countries. Findings confirm the low level of participation in e-commerce by SMEs. The age of enterprise, as well as the owner's gender and education were found to be significant in determining the level of e-commerce adoption.

Chapter 5 recounts that one region where e-commerce will have a particular impact for SMEs over the next few years is South East Wales (SEW). In response to this a survey was undertaken to assess the e-commerce activity of firms within the SEW area. Results from the survey demonstrated that nearly all firms used some form of ICT. The results also highlighted that a significant proportion of the sample (77%) were currently using a Web site to increase trade or improve opportunities for e-commerce. Furthermore, it was observed that firms in the personal services, distribution and transport industries were less likely to utilise a Web site than firms in the manufacturing, business services and hospitality industries. Despite the large proportion of firms that had a Web site, only 11% of businesses reported that their site enabled customers to order and pay for products online although 42% of respondents considered e-commerce to be important for their business' future.

Section 3 focuses on internet marketing and small business. How effective internet portals are for rural business owners and internet marketing by SMEs are considered.

Chapter 6 explores the uses and effectiveness of private and public/charity managed and funded internet portals on rural SMEs e-commerce activities. Specifically, the study investigated whether there were differences in how rural SMEs used and perceived the effectiveness of each type of internet portal. Hypotheses were drawn from qualitative results carried out. Ninety-six rural SMEs spread across the two types of rural internet portals were interviewed via telephone to gain their perceptions. Cross-tabulations using chi square testing discovered that in the main there were no perceived differences between the uses and effectiveness of private and public/charity funded internet portals on rural SMEs e-commerce activities. However, testing did discover that rural SME users of public/charity funded internet portals were more likely to be charged a fee for membership. The main preoccupation of rural SMEs was representation on an internet portal to help facilitate their e-commerce activities, not how it was owned or operated.

Chapter 7 presents and supports the hypothesis that SMEs should stop investing in their web site's design and functionality and start investing in efforts to market their web sites online, no matter how *lousy* their web site may be in comparison to today's standards. With the support of two case studies, illustrating the successful utilization of internet marketing by two very different SMEs, the chapter relates how a SME can effectively market their web site online. Tools and techniques available to help an SME successfully begin a journey of internet marketing are discussed.

Section 4 tackles the international dimension of ICT, web sites and e-commerce for small business. Small business sales growth and internationalisation links to website functions and ICT opportunities are investigated.

Chapter 8 investigates the level of SME website adoption and functionality and how this relates to growth aspirations, specifically the geographical expansion of customer bases. One potential explanation for this slow uptake of true e-commerce is a lack of employees with basic and advanced IT skills. The possibility that IT skills shortages could explain the gap between the Internet's potential and the extent of involvement by a vast majority of UK SMEs is explored. Discussion within the chapter is complemented with analysis of data from a large survey of SMEs.

Chapter 9 looks into the process by which an opportunity scenario unfolds in the context of global start-ups and links theoretical insights on opportunity recognition to theoretical insights on international entrepreneurship and of ICT-supported communication. Insights are utilised from cases previously published in the global start-up literature to illustrate and conceptualize how entrepreneurs virtually embed themselves and use IT to interact with international contacts throughout this process.

Section 5 discusses e-business and e-marketing among small business enterprises. E-business among ethnic minority businesses, the 'knock-on' effect of e-business upon graphic design SMEs, electronic customer management and SME marketing practice and understanding the factors affecting the adoption of e-marketing by small business enterprises are explored.

Chapter 10 examines and reviews the existing body of literature on Ethnic Minority Businesses (EMBs) and ICT. Secondly, EMB cases that have developed ICT to a degree where they are engaging in e-business activity are analysed and discussed. The findings provide a number of options and guidance for EMB owners. Finally, the recommendations point to the need for improved ICT awareness, better business support provision nationally and the importance of generation and education as key drivers.

Chapter 11 depicts the current findings of an ongoing longitudinal study pertaining to e-business and the graphic design industry. The research problem can be described as being: to identify the extent of engagement by graphic designers with e business. The location of the study is Industrial South Wales: Cardiff, Newport, Swansea and the South Wales Valleys with the particular focus being Small and Medium Size Enterprises (SMEs). For the purpose of the study, the European Commission definitions relating to SMEs have been utilised (last revised 2005).

Chapter 12 posits that by exploring the components of e-customer relations management (e-CRM) in the unique context of SME business and marketing practice that a natural synergy exists between e-CRM and SME marketing in the creation of value propositions. Specifically this is addressed through the two contributing constructs of SME marketing; namely entrepreneurial marketing and network marketing.

Chapter 13 builds on the current body of knowledge in the field of e-marketing through a survey and systematic review of the published work related to the Technology Acceptance Model (TAM), Innovation Diffusion Theory (IDT) and E Marketing adoption by small business enterprises. Furthermore, the chapter illustrates that although many e-marketing adoption factors are driven from the literature of e-marketing, as well as the technology adoption theories like TAM and IDT, only some of these factors are found to significantly affect the adoption of e-marketing by small business enterprises.

Section 6 examines small business and electronic retailing. This includes multi channel integration for small and medium retailers and e-fulfilment and offshore centres involving economic policy implications for small business.

Chapter 14 studies the multi channel integration strategies for small and medium retailers, formulating a multi channel integration codification scheme and explaining the barriers and related solutions under these strategic decisions.

Chapter 15, the last chapter of the book, introduces the importance of the e-fulfilment industry for offshore centres and in particular the small business and economic policy implications. The extant concepts, research, and experiences the chapter builds on is the literature concerning the e-fulfilment industry. It argues that the key results, evidence, and experience, from the models that have been developed and the specific model formulated for this work, indicate reasons for the development of e-fulfilment in offshore centres.

REFERENCES

Andrews, L., & Boyle, M. (2008). Consumers' accounts of perceived risk online and the influence of communication sources. *Qualitative Market Research: An International Journal*, 11(1), 59-75.

Bengtsson, M., Boter, H., & Vanyushyn, V. (2007). Integrating the Internet and marketing operations: A study of antecedents in firms of different size. *International Small Business Journal*, 25(2), 27-48.

Carter, S., Mason, C., & Tagg, S. (2006). *Lifting the Barriers to Growth in UK Small Businesses*. London: Federation of Small Business.

Cohen, W., & Levinthal, D. (1990). Absorptive Capacity: A New Perspective on Learning and Innovation. *Administrative Science Quarterly,* 35(1), 128-152.

Department for Business, Enterprise and Regulatory Reform (BERR). (2008). *Business Plan 2008–2011.* June. London.

Earl, M.J. (2000). Evolving the e-business. *Business Strategy Review*, 11(2), 33-38.

e-skills UK. (2008). *Technology Counts: IT and Telecoms Insights 2008.* September, London, UK.

EURAB. (2004). *SMEs and ERA (European Research Area).* EURAB 04.028-final. Brussels

European Commission (2005). Implementing the Community Lisbon Programme – Modern SME Policy for Growth and Employment. (COM(2005) 551 final. November. Brussels.

Evans, J.R., & Mathur, A. (2005). The value of online surveys. *Internet Research*, 15(2), 195-219.

Fillis, I., Johanson, U., & Wagner, B. (2003). E-business development: a conceptual model of the smaller firm. *Journal of Small Business and Enterprise Development*, 10(3), 336-345.

Fillis, I., & Wagner, B. (2005). E-business development: An exploratory investigation of the small firm. *International Small Business Journal*, 23(12), 604-634.

Graham, G., & Hardaker, G. (2000). Supply-chain management across the internet. *International Journal of Physical Distribution & Logistics Management*, 30(3/4), 340-352.

Gray C. (2006a). Stage models of ICT adoption in small firms. In S. Zappala & C. Gray (Eds.), *Impact of e-Commerce on Consumers and Small Firms* (pp. 3-20). Aldershot, UK: Ashgate.

Gray C. (2006b). Absorptive capacity, knowledge management and innovation in entrepreneurial small firms. *International Journal of Entrepreneurial Behaviour & Research,* 12(6), 345-360.

Harrigan, P., Ramsey, E., & Ibbotson, P. (2008). e-CRM in SMEs: an exploratory study in Northern Ireland. *Marketing Intelligence and Planning*, 26(4), 385-404.

Havik, K., McMorrow, K., Wand, R., & Turrini, A. (2008 September). The EU-US total factor productivity gap: An industry perspective. *European Economy*. Economic Papers 339.

Houghton, K.A., & Winklhofer, H. (2002). Internet adoption in exportings: Development of a conceptual model. *American Marketing Association*, Conference Proceedings, Chicago, 13, 504.

Jones, P., Beynon-Davies, P., & Muir, E. (2003). E-business Barriers within the SME sector. *Journal of Systems and Information Technology*, 7(1), 1–26.

Levy, M., & Powell, P. (2003). Exploring SME internet adoption: towards a contingent model. *Electronic Markets*, 13(2), 173-181.

Mendo, F.A., & Fitzgerald, G. (2005). A multidimensional framework for SME e-business progression. *Journal of Enterprise Information Management*, 18(6), 678-696.

Merisavo, M., & Raulas, M. (2004). The impact of e-mail marketing on brand loyalty. *Journal of Product and Brand Management*, 13(7), 498-505.

OECD. (2005). *Small to Medium-Sized Business (SME) and Entrepreneurship Outlook*. OECD. Paris.

Open University. (2007). *Quarterly Survey of Small Business in Britain,* 23(2).

Packham, G., Brooksbank, D., Miller, C., & Thomas, B. (2005). Climbing the Mountain: Management Practice Adoption in Growth Oriented Firms in Wales. *Small Business and Enterprise Development,* 12, 482-497.

Packham, G. (2002). Competitive Advantage and Growth: The Challenge For Small Firms. *International Journal of Management and Decision-Making,* 3, 165-179

Parasuraman, A. (2000). Technology Readiness Index (TRI), a multiple-item scale to measure readiness to embrace new technologies. *Journal of Service Research,* 2, 397-329.

Pflughoeft, K.A., Ramamurthy, K. Soofi, E. S., Yasai-Ardekani, M., & Fatemah, M. (2003). Multiple conceptualizations of SME Web use and benefit. *Decision Sciences,* 34(3), 467-513.

Phippen, A.D. (2004). An evaluative methodology for virtual communications using web analytics. *Campus-Wide Information Systems,* 21(5), 179.

Poon, S., & Swatman, P. (1999). An exploratory study of SME Internet commerce issues. *Information and Management,* 35(1), 9-18.

Porter, M.E. (2001). Strategy and the Internet. *Harvard Business Review,* 79(3), 63-78.

Raymond, L. (2001). Determinants of Web site implementation in SMEs. *Internet Research, 11*(5), 411-423.

Rao, S.S., Metts, G., & Mora Monge, C.A. (2003). Electronic commerce development in small and medium sized enterprises; a stage model and its implications. *Business Process Management, 9*(1), 11-32.

Rayport, J.F., & Jaworski, B.J. (2001). *E-Commerce.* New York: McGraw-Hill/Irwin.

Sydney Rogers, E.M. (1995). *Diffusion of Innovations.* New York: Free Press.

Simmons, G.J, Durkin, M.G., McGowan, P., & Armstrong, G.A. (2007). Determinants of internet adoption by SME agri-food companies. *Journal of Small Business and Enterprise Development, 14*(4), 620-640.

Simmons, G.J., Armstrong, G.A., & Durkin, M.G. (2008). A conceptualization of the determinants of small business Website adoption: Setting the research agenda. *International Small Business Journal, 26*(3), 351-389.

Tagliavini, M., Ravarini, A., & Antonelli, A. (2001). An evaluation model for electronic commerce activities within SMEs. *Information Technology and Management, 2*(2), 211-230.

Tapscott, D. (2002). Rethinking strategy in a networked world. *Harvard Business Review,* 24, 1-8.

Timmer, L. P., & Van Ark, B. (2005). Does information and communication technology drive EU-US productivity growth differentials? *Oxford Economic Papers,* 57(4), 693-716.

Vaitilingam, R. (2004). *The UK's Productivity Gap: What research tells us and what we need to find out.* ESRC Seminar Series: Mapping the public policy landscape. Swindon: ESRC.

Wiseman, J., Roe, P., & Elliott, J. (2006). *Annual Survey of Small Businesses: UK 2004/05.* London: Small Business Service.

Zahra, S., & George, G. (2002). Absorptive capacity: A review, reconceptualization and extension. *Academy of Management Review*, 27(2), 185–203.

Zappala, S., & Gray, C. (2006). *Impact of e-Commerce on Consumers and Small Firms*. Aldershot, UK: Ashgate.

Acknowledgment

The publication of this book would not have been possible without the assistance of a number of people and institutions to whom we are grateful. We are indebted to the Welsh Enterprise Institute and the Centre for Enterprise at the University of Glamorgan and to the Department of Marketing, Entrepreneurship and Strategy at the University of Ulster, for their support in the course of editing this book. We are also grateful to all the chapter authors, for their hard work and contributions to the book and to the reviewers of the book chapters for their helpful comments and advice. Special thanks go to IGI Global and its publishing team, in particular Christine Bufton, for helping us to keep to schedule. Finally, we would like to make a special thank you to Anne and Fiona for their support and encouragement.

Dr. Brychan Thomas and Dr. Geoff Simmons
Cardiff and Belfast
June 2009

Section 1
E–Commerce Trading and Small Business

Chapter 1
Facilitating E-Commerce Adoption:
An Electronic Customs System

Marta Raus
ETH Zurich, Switzerland

Roman Boutellier
ETH Zurich, Switzerland

ABSTRACT

International trade conducted electronically is seen as a major driver of globalisation. We argue that the development of international electronic trade might grow faster if adequate governmental regulations support it. Based on a literature review and EU/OECD reports, we demonstrate how legislation is important for the success of international e-commerce. In particular, we focus on EU e-customs regulations and related IT systems. We show how e-customs systems might be used as a tool for e-commerce adoption facilitation. As an example we consider Switzerland as a non-EU country having to adapt its regulations to be EU compliant and therefore facilitate international trade for local companies. We analyse the situation of small and medium-sized enterprises (SMEs) in Switzerland, and study eight factors that can change after e-customs implementation and possible advantages yielded by such implementations. Finally, we propose factors related to e-customs implementation: increased control of the customs office, less entry errors, electronic notice of VAT assessment, data and communication standardisation, declaration possible 24 hours a day and more transparent export process; as well as three EU customs regulations: Integrated Tariff of the European Communities, Modernised Customs Code, and Community Customs Code that can enhance e-commerce adoption.

INTRODUCTION

In the last eight years, i.e., from 2000 to 2008, Internet usage grew tremendously worldwide. According to data provided by Internet World Stats (2008), 384 Mio Europeans use the Internet. Internet population penetration among the 27 member states has already reached 48%. In actual fact, during the mentioned time period, European Internet usage grew by an astonishing 266%.

Internet diffusion changed the way of doing business in general and commerce in particular. The

DOI: 10.4018/978-1-60566-998-4.ch001

Figure 1. Internet penetration by firm size class, 2006 (Adapted from OECD, 2007a)

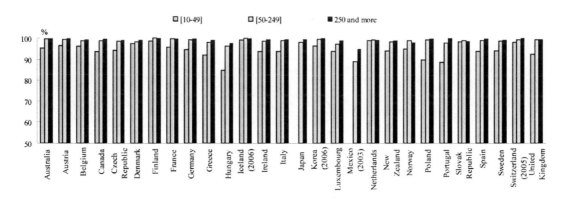

quick growth of e-commerce has already been noted by many authors towards the end of the 1990s (Cheung, 1998; Froehlich, Hoover, Liew, & Sorenson, 1999; Leebaert, 1998; Maes, Guttman, & Moukas, 1999). According to OECD statistics (OECD, 2007a), Internet penetration in different businesses all over the world reached almost 100% as early as 2006. In the same year, selling and purchasing through the Internet became a reality for many industry groups in several countries. For example in Germany, the wholesale and retail industry reached 18.2% for selling and 48.3% for purchasing, respectively (OECD, 2007b). Not only big enterprises but also small and medium-sized enterprises use Internet for their business (see Figure 1). We refer to small and medium-sized enterprises (SMEs) according to the definition given by the European Commission in Article 2 of the Annex of Recommendation 2003/361/EC (European Commission, 2003, p. 4): *'The category of micro, small and medium-sized enterprises is made up of enterprises which employ fewer than 250 persons and which have an annual turnover not exceeding € 50 million, and/or an annual balance sheet total not exceeding € 43 million'.*

SMEs represent a large share of the business sector economy and generate most of business turnover. According to an OECD study that took place in 2002, SMEs represent between 96% and 99% of the total number of enterprises in most economies (OECD, 2002). Despite this high percentage, which highlights the importance of SMEs in the world market, SMEs are under-represented in world trade (OECD, 2005). However, SMEs show willingness to go international and already have a differentiated approach to internationalisation. Indeed, SMEs try to optimise their international competitiveness by exporting new business opportunities in the value chain, encouraging trade, cross-border clustering and collaboration, alliances or subsidiaries, branches, and joint ventures abroad. Participating in international markets can offer a range of opportunities to firms, for example new niche markets or possibilities to lower costs and access finance. A study of the European Commission (2004) identified seven motivators for the internationalisation of SMEs: (1) Access to know-how and technology; (2) High production costs on the domestic market; (3) Access to new and larger markets for products/services; (4) Strict laws and regulations on the domestic market; (5) Additional production capacity; (6) Access to capital; (7) Access to labour. However, SMEs face many barriers to their internationalisation: the high costs of the internationalisation process, e.g., adaptation of products to foreign markets, travel expenses, or business and financial risks; existing law and regulations; product standards; intellectual property rights protection; lack of capital or finance; lack of support and advice; cultural and language differences; lack of information.

Over the last few years, technological advances in Information and Communication Technologies (ICTs) and in particular the Internet, e.g., web-based sales, Internet marketing, or communication networks, have facilitated information flows and made it easier for SMEs to participate in the international economy. Therefore, e-commerce is an even more important instrument for SMEs' international growth.

Froehlich et al. (1999) confirmed that e-commerce is not just the substitution of paper-based business through the use of computers; indeed, it implies more, such as using non-proprietary open networks, not requiring client software, and services available 24 hours a day, 7 days a week. The authors also stated that e-commerce enables customers and suppliers to be geographically distributed worldwide. This also includes goods' cross-border.

E-commerce implies new legislations that regulate international trade handled electronically; for this reason, governmental involvement is needed. Governments usually encourage e-commerce development through legislation and directives designed to support and regulate online business transactions (Blakeley & Matsuura, 2001). Blakeley & Matsuura emphasised that the government itself is changing its viewpoint, i.e., from being a regulator to becoming a player. Governments are thus interested in adopting legislations and regulations that will facilitate their own online activities. In this way, i.e., by providing rules that ease governments' e-transactions, governments also help to facilitate the growth of industrial e-commerce transactions.

E-CUSTOMS

An example of how governments may help e-commerce transactions by developing new concepts, which also ease governmental tasks, is given by the introduction of electronic customs. In the European Union, national electronic customs declaration systems are already used in many countries, e.g., Atlas in Germany, Aida in Italy or Sagitta Entry in the Netherlands. However, a common standardised electronic customs system is still missing but it is topic of research promoted by the EU. The goal of a common customs system is to overcome interface barriers between national systems. The EU has already started the implementation of standardised systems (European Commission, 2007a); together with the already existing Community Customs Code (European Commission, 1992), this implementation will facilitate European trade. The implementation is composed of four key stages:

1. The first stage builds on existing work; namely the New Computerised Transit System (NCTS) and risk management tools. It creates the foundation for an electronic customs declaration environment by adding systems for Import (ICS) and Export (ECS), applying the International Road Transport Convention for Transit (NCTS-TIR), and including the Economic Operators Registration and Identification System;

2. The second stage is seen as providing aspects of the electronic customs vision which primarily addresses trader concerns: the Economic Operators Registration and Identification System and the Authorised Economic Operator, together with the Common Customs Information Portal and the Single Electronic Access Point;

3. The third stage is based on the Modernised Customs Code concept (European Commission, 2007b) and is focused on more ambitious aspects of the electronic environment. These projects would lead to the completion of a fully Automated Export and Import System (AES and AIS), as well as the completion of the Common Customs

Tariff and Integrated Tariff of the European Communities (Taric), which came into force in 1987 (European Commission, 1987);

4. The fourth stage is related to the Single Window project as described in the Council's proposal for a paperless environment for customs and trade (European Commission, 2006).

The goal of the EU customs project is to enable a paperless environment for customs and trade, i.e., to develop a common standardised e-customs system. The envisioned e-customs system will be based on Single Window (SW) and Authorised Economic Operator (AEO). Single Window is a methodology for standardised business processes and business information exchange; in Recommendation no. 33, the United Nations Centre for Trade Facilitation and Electronic Business, defines a single window as '*a facility that allows parties involved in trade and transport to lodge standardised information and documents with a single entry point to fulfil all import, export, and transit-related regulatory requirements. If information is electronic, then individual data elements should only be submitted once. This may also provide a platform for coordinating controls among the agencies involved and payment of relevant duties, taxes, and fees*' (United Nations Economic Commission for Europe, 2005, p. 3). Authorised Economic Operator is a certification given by the customs office of a European country that enables an industry to simplify trade. Legislation stipulates that customs authorities shall grant to European reliable traders the status of 'authorised economic operator' (WCO, 2006). The idea is to grant the AEO status to reliable operators including those that are also compliant with respect to security and safety standards and can, therefore, be considered as 'secure' traders. Those traders should have a specific status, which would grant them the status of secure members

of the supply chain and would identify them as the most reliable trading partners.

In this work we consider the phenomenon of e-customs, arguing that it is a driver for e-commerce adoption that facilitates SMEs' internationalisation. We analyse the customs situation in Europe paying particular attention to Switzerland. We focus on the specific case of Switzerland since it is a country with a high potential of e-commerce diffusion for three main reasons:

1. It is a small country: according to the European Commission (2004), smaller countries are more internationalised and therefore more prone to use e-commerce than others;
2. The percentage of Swiss SMEs with foreign suppliers or exports is high: according to the European Commission (2004), 28% and 54% of Swiss SMEs export and have foreign suppliers, respectively. Therefore, e-commerce can bring many advantages to Swiss SMEs, such as, e.g., time optimisation;
3. Switzerland is a country with a very high Internet penetration: according to Figure 1, 98% of SMEs with 10-49 employees and 99% of SMEs with 50-249 employees already use Internet.

In the following, we first provide an overview on e-commerce and its use by SMEs emphasising the role of European directives in the diffusion of e-commerce among EU member states. We further concentrate on e-customs giving an overview of existing European regulations. We thus focus on Switzerland presenting firstly its e-customs initiative and secondly a case study. The case study took place in October 2008 and involved 36 Swiss SMEs. As a result of the case study, we will provide a set of changes that e-customs will bring and their related benefits. In a discussion section we summarise our findings and propose a set of six factors related to e-customs implementation and describe three EU customs regulations that can facilitate e-commerce adoption. A particular section is dedicated to future research. The conclusion follows in the last section.

BACKGROUND: E-COMMERCE AND E-CUSTOMS LEGISLATIONS

Many researchers have already studied the e-commerce phenomenon in respect to its penetration into SMEs daily businesses. For example Taylor, McWilliam, England, & Akomode (2004) highlighted that various factors may affect e-commerce development and adoption. They built a skill set that, according to their research, is required for e-commerce projects in the SMEs sector. This set comprises of both technical and business viewpoints: design, programming, testing, linking website to database, website promotion, security, content management, business terminology, and legislation. They argued that legislation is an important requirement from a business viewpoint. Based on Turban, Lee, King, & Chung's (2000) statements, they affirmed that there is a potential wide range of legal issues related to e-commerce. Because legislations and regulations are promoted by government, government may directly influence development of e-commerce. After an empirical study that took place in Shanghai and involved 1,211 firms, Zhang, Cui, Huang, & Zhang (2007) confirmed that government IT-related policies affect firm's IT usage positively, and therefore e-commerce, as long as e-government initiatives help firms to improve their IT usage.

In Europe two main directives regulate e-commerce: the Electronic Commerce Directive (European Commission, 2000b) and the Digital Signature Directive (European Commission, 2000a). In Article 1.2 of the Electronic Commerce Directive, a set of harmonised rules is established in relation to internal market, establishment of service providers, commercial communications,

electronic contracts, liability of intermediaries, codes of conduct, dispute settlements, court actions, and cooperation between member states. The Electronic Commerce Directive is the first European mandatory transnational recognition of electronic contracts. In addition to this, the Digital Signature Directive establishes the requirements for electronic signature certificates throughout the European Union including mechanisms for cooperation with third countries on the basis of mutual recognition of certificates, bilateral, and multilateral agreements.

Despite all the regulations mentioned above, according to a report of the European Commission, the proportion of online consumers shopping cross-border has not increased since 2006, while the proportion of online retailers selling cross-border has declined (European Commission, 2008c). The report of the European Commission states that if harmonised consumer regulations were put in place across the European Union, only 41% of the retailers would choose not to sell cross-border. This would be a significant improvement compared with the 75% not selling cross-border. Many (60%) retailers who are not selling cross-border are concerned about varying fiscal regulations, compliance with varying national laws, cross-border delivery, and the increased risk of fraud. The biggest concern relates to the higher risk of fraud and non-payments in cross-border sales. More than two-thirds (68%) of retailers not selling cross-border see this as an important obstacle.

Therefore, in some cases companies do not trust e-commerce because of different national laws and regulations. Specifically, although SMEs increasingly use information systems for a variety of commercial and production-related purposes, there is generally a lack of awareness of e-commerce so that trust and transaction security remain two big barriers. Additionally, according to OECD (2002), the major part of electronic transactions is dominated by established networks among medium-sized and large firms in which few small suppliers or micro firms participate; for this reason, the volume of electronic transactions over the Internet is very small even in countries where e-commerce is considered to be fast growing.

In the past few years several researchers paid attention to e-commerce adoption and involvement of SMEs considering specific countries, such as, e.g., the US (Karagozoglu & Lindell, 2004), Sweden and Australia (MacGregor & Vrazalic, 2005), or UK (Simpson & Docherty, 2004). The authors stated that e-commerce adoption among SMEs could be promoted in different ways, e.g., by analysing successful strategies to follow for providing a more suitable environment. Accordingly, the government is one important player since it could facilitate SMEs' e-commerce adoption by offering a better economic and legislative environment. According to declarations of the World Trade Organisation (WTO), governments may help development and adoption of e-commerce among SMEs, by building a triangular partnership for performance that includes customs, banks, and SMEs (Labbé, 2007). However, customs duties and regulations are often difficult to understand and may impede e-commerce; indeed, e-commerce often takes place in regional markets only, excluding potential international consumers, since it is not clear how international e-commerce is regulated and how much it costs the consumer (Boyd, Hobbs, & Kerr, 2003). A study of the European Commission (2008c) confirmed that online consumers continue to be more confident shopping in their own country than abroad.

Thus, customs regulations play a key role not only in international trade but also in international e-commerce. Already in 1987 the EU was aware of the importance of common customs regulations and developed the so called Combined Nomenclature that is the tariff and statistical nomenclature of the Customs Union (European Commission, 1987). The Common Customs Tariff is the external tariff applied to products imported into the Union. The *Integrated Tariff of the Euro-*

pean Communities is referred to as Taric, which incorporates all Community and trade measures applied to goods imported into and exported out of the community. It is managed by the Commission, which publishes a daily updated version on the official Taric website. Furthermore, in 1992, the EU promoted the Community Customs Code that comprises of the rules, arrangements, and procedures applicable to goods traded between the European Community and non-member countries (European Commission, 1992).

More recently, in order to facilitate customs systems, the EU started in 2004 a customs initiative that aims to achieve a paperless trade using IT systems, i.e., electronic customs systems. According to the European Commission (2008b), the electronic customs initiative essentially involves three pieces of legislation: two proposals and an existing regulation.

The first proposal regards a decision on the paperless environment for customs and trade, Electronic Customs Decision (European Commission, 2008a), and sets the basic framework and major deadlines for the electronic customs projects. The second proposal is related to the modernisation of the European Customs Code (European Commission, 2007b); this should lead to the completion of the computerisation of customs. The existing regulation is the Security and Safety Amendment to the Customs Code (European Commission, 2005): it is a regulation which came into force in May 2005 and provides full computerisation of all procedures related to security and safety. A detailed description of the two proposals and the existing regulation follows.

Electronic customs decisions. It aims to establish secure, interoperable electronic customs systems for the exchange of data in order to: (1) Facilitate import and export procedures; (2) Reduce compliance and administrative costs; (3) Improve clearance times; (4) Coordinate the approach to the control of goods and application of the legislation; (5) Ensure proper collection of Community duties and charges; (6) Enable a seamless flow of data between the parties involved and allow re-use of data.

Modernised customs code. A political agreement was reached by the European Council of Ministers on 25 June 2007 on a Modernised Community Customs Code, which will simplify legislation and streamline customs process and procedures for the benefit of both customs authorities and traders. The agreement needs to be confirmed by the European Parliament in a second reading which is expected to come in 2009. The Modernised Customs Code will focus on four different tasks: (1) To introduce electronic lodging of customs declarations and accompanying documents as the rule; (2) To provide exchange of electronic information between national customs and other competent authorities; (3) To promote the concept of 'centralised clearance', under which authorised traders will be able to declare goods electronically and pay their customs duties at the place where they are established, irrespective of the member state through which the goods will be brought in or out of the EU customs territory or in which they will be consumed; (4) To offer a basis for the development of the 'single window' and 'one-stop-shop' concepts, under which economic operators give information on goods to only one contact point ('single window'), even if the data should reach different administrations/ agencies, so that controls on them for various purposes (e.g., customs, sanitary) are performed at the same time and at the same place ('one-stop-shop' concept).

Security and safety amendment to the customs code. Regulation (EC) 648/2005 and its implementing provisions require pre-arrival and pre-departure information (in form of summary declarations lodged before the goods are brought into or out of the Community customs territory) to be filed electronically and envisage exchange and sharing of the information between the member states administrations, when possible.

All these changes aroused the interest of several researchers, such as, e.g., Baida, Liu, & Tan (2007), Baida, Rukanova, Liu, & Tan (2007), Bjørn-Andersen, Razmerita, & Henriksen (2007), Boyd, Hobbs, & Kerr (2003), Henriksen, Rukanova, & Tan (2008), Kuiper (2007), and Raus, Flügge, & Boutellier (2008). In these articles the authors present the e-customs situation in different European countries emphasising problems, best-practices, and diffusion processes of e-customs systems.

Besides the 27 EU member states, Switzerland also aims to have an electronic customs system. Indeed, in order to be compliant to EU regulations and specifically to the e-customs initiative, Switzerland started in June 2007 a project called IDEE (IDEE = Ideale elektronische Exporteurlösung, ideal solution for exporters). According to this project, promoted by the Swiss Federal Customs Administration, from 1st July 2009, Swiss companies have the possibility to declare their exports electronically. This change will especially affect SMEs since big companies are already used to use e-customs systems. In order to understand how this change will affect small and medium firms, we interviewed 36 SMEs. In the next section, the Swiss e-customs initiative is described and the case study is presented and discussed.

SWISS E-CUSTOMS INITIATIVE

Because of political, legal, technological, and economic developments of the past years, the Swiss Federal Customs Administration has nowadays a very broad palette of services, all of which have the same objective: the customs clearance of goods. These services include diverse form-based and IT-based solutions for import, transit, and export of goods. This multiplicity of customs clearance systems increasingly results in service offerings that are perceived by both clients and the Swiss Federal Custom Administration as too broad and thus difficult to use. In addition, the offered customs clearance systems are often isolated solutions that are not sufficiently harmonised. This

Figure 2. E-dec Export process (Adapted from Swiss Federal Customs Administration, 2008b)

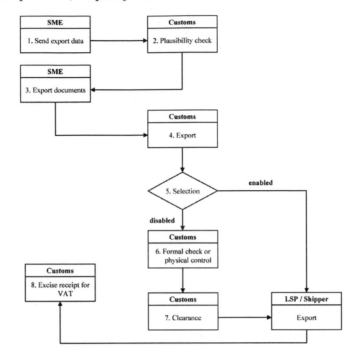

leads to efficiency deficits and higher costs for all parties involved. For these reasons and in order to be compliant to EU regulations (new customs code), the Swiss Federal Customs Administration launched the IDEE project. Switzerland has big interests to be EU compliant and to trade with it in an efficient way because of the considerable Swiss-EU goods traffic: in 2006 it amounted to about € 155,000 million; € 70,000 million in exports and € 85,000 million in imports (Swiss Federal Customs Administration, 2008c).

The goal of this project is to introduce a new electronic customs system called e-dec that is going to replace the old customs system, the VAR system (VAR = Vereinfachte Ausfuhrregelung, a simplified set of export rules). With e-dec, the Swiss Federal Customs Administration is developing a central system for customs clearance that will gradually replace existing solutions, such as the electronic customs clearance system M90 and the form-based transit procedure. E-dec has a modular structure so that the Swiss Federal Customs Administration aims to offer the clients

the possibility of performing electronic clearance of import, transit, and export goods using largely uniform guidelines. Thus, more uniform and streamlined processes are created for both parties, resulting in lower costs. E-dec is the outcome of two projects carried out by the Swiss Federal Customs Administration. These projects are named IgVV (Computer-Aided Common/ Community Transit Procedure) and RM90. E-dec Import is being developed within the RM90 project. The IgVV project covers the Transit and Export Modules (Swiss Federal Customs Administration, 2008a). E-dec Export relies on Export Control System (ECS) and Automated Export System (AES). It allows electronic signatures that confirm the authentication of e-documents and e-invoices.

The e-dec Export process is composed of eight steps. Since we aim to analyse the particular situation of SMEs, we adapted the e-dec Export process to SMEs. Based on the guidelines provided by the Swiss Federal Customs Administration (2008b), the eight steps are (Figure 2):

1. **Send export data:** The SME has to send the export data to the customs office by e-mail or using web-services provided by the Swiss Federal Customs Administration;
2. **Plausibility check:** The IT system of the Swiss Federal Customs Administration conducts a plausibility check of the data and sends back to the SME an export list with bar codes in form of a XML or PDF document;
3. **Export documents:** The validity of the export list is limited, i.e., the SME has to export the declared goods within 30 days. If this does not occur, the export documents will be cancelled and the SME has to start the process anew (back to step 1);
4. **Export:** By exporting goods out of Switzerland, the SME exhibits the export documents to the customs office at the border. The customs office reads the document with a bar code reader. After reading the provided export documents, the customs office at the border states whether the export declaration fulfils all requirements or not. This process is called 'selection' so that the export can be set as either enabled or disabled;
5. **Selection:** If the selection results to be positive, the customs office at the border prints out a delivery document which certificates that the export declaration has been enabled and the goods can leave Switzerland;
6. **Formal check or physical control:** If the selection results to be negative the customs office states the export declaration to be disabled. As a consequence of this, the custom office controls all export accompanying documents and usually checks the goods physically;
7. **Clearance:** After the formal and physical control, the customs office at the borders approves the export and inserts the corresponding data in the IT system. Thus, the goods can leave Switzerland;

8. **Excise receipt for VAT:** After the clearance has taken place, the corresponding excise receipt is certificated electronically (XML and PDF) so that other authorised organisations, such as the trade statistics office, can use it for their purpose.

In order to understand how small and medium-sized firms perceive the e-dec Export initiative; an online survey was conducted involving 36 Swiss SMEs. The SMEs were asked to answer several questions regarding their willingness to adopt the new e-customs system and their perceived benefits. Additionally, we interviewed face to face a big Swiss logistics provider and a customs agent. The case study took place in October 2008. Next sub-section is dedicated to the case study and its results.

Case Study

34 of the 36 interviewed SMEs have not yet implemented e-dec Export. This outcome was anticipated as full implementation is not expected to be completed until the end of June 2009. 30 of the 34 SMEs, which did not implement e-dec Export yet, declared the intention to implement it at the beginning of 2009 while only four SMEs planned to delegate the export process to a logistics provider. According to this result, all interviewed SMEs will have implemented e-dec Export by the end of June 2009. Most of the interviewees not only export to European countries but also to Asia (89%), Africa (53%), the US (86%), and Australia (61%), declaring about 100 exports every day.

Table 1 shows what SMEs currently think about the changes that the new e-customs system will implicate. The eight analysed factors are: (1) Time needed to complete export declarations; (2) Number of daily export declarations; (3) Price of an export declaration; (4) Waiting time at the borders; (5) Control of the customs office; (6) Number of entry errors; (7) Transparency between SMEs and customs office; (8) Control of the goods along the

Table 1. Changes after e-dec export implementation

Factor	Will increase	Will decrease	Will not change	n.s.
Time needed to complete export declarations	39%	3%	6%	52%
Number of daily export declarations	6%	0%	56%	38%
Price of an export declaration	28%	0%	11%	61%
Waiting time at the borders	11%	38%	11%	40%
Control of the customs office	27%	6%	14%	53%
Number of entry errors	0%	31%	17%	52%
Transparency between **SMEs** and customs office	28%	0%	11%	61%
Control of the goods along the supply chain	19%	0%	22%	59%

supply chain. The SMEs were asked to estimate whether the mentioned factors will increase, decrease, or remain unchanged. Since these questions required more estimation and some interviewees were not able to answer, n.s. (not specified) was included as a possible option.

Based on these data, most of the SMEs do not know how the e-dec Export implementation will affect the export process and cannot make a prediction since they have not implemented it yet. For this reason, many interviewees chose the option 'not specified'. However, some SMEs gave their opinion enabling the formulation of first statistics. In order to fulfil this gap, we further interviewed face-to-face one big Swiss logistics provider and one customs agent.

1. In respect to the *time needed to complete export declarations*, 39% of the SMEs think that it will increase. The idea of an electronic system is to reach the opposite, i.e., to decrease the time needed to complete export declarations. However, it is predictable that in the first months SMEs employees have to get used to the new system and have to learn how to use it. For this reason, a time increase during the first implementation period is expected. A decrease in time will occur when the employees begin to understand how to use the system and get familiar with it. In order to get deeper understanding of this

factor, we further conducted a face-to-face interview with a Swiss customs agent. The interviewed customs agent stated that two or three months are necessary for employees to understand how to use the e-dec Export system in a proper and efficient way. We can therefore deduce that the 3%, who answered that the time needed to complete export declarations will decrease, are already familiar with the system or have had similar experiences with other IT implementations: therefore they can judge the time investment of the introduction of e-dec Export.

2. The *number of daily export declarations* does not seem to be affected by the introduction of the e-dec Export system since 56% of the interviewed SMEs think that it will not change. This contrasts the expectation of the Swiss Federal Customs Administration, which believes the number of daily declarations will significantly increase. In order to get more information about these data, we additionally interviewed a big Swiss logistics provider that already implemented e-dec Export a year ago. In effect, the logistics provider stated that the number of daily export declarations increased in a considerable manner: before 1990, only 15 export declarations a day were accomplished; after the introduction of M90, an electronic system introduced in 1990 and already mentioned

in the beginning of this section, it was possible to declare 100 exports daily; nowadays, e-dec enables 1000 export declarations per day. The interviewed logistics provider affirmed that five minutes are needed in order to electronically fulfil the export data (step 1). After fulfilling the export data, the logistics provider sends it to the IT system of the Swiss Federal Customs Administration for plausibility check (step 2). The IT system of the Swiss Federal Customs Administration sends the export documents back to the logistics provider after a maximum of ten minutes after receipt of the export data (step 3). It has to be noted that a big logistics provider, such as the interviewed one, is usually more specialised in exports than a SME. For this reason, we can deduce that the interviewed SMEs still have to become more familiar with the system in order to reach a faster export process execution. In addition, according to the online survey, most SMEs do less than 100 export declarations a day. However, this is not caused by the declaration system but by their export volume. Therefore, even if the new electronic system would enable 1000 daily export declarations, SMEs would not perceive this as an important change as there are no more than 100 exports to be declared a day; in other words, the number of daily declarations would essentially not change for SMEs.

3. The *price of an export declaration* that a SME has to pay depends on who is going to be engaged in it. If a SME decides to delegate the export process to a logistics provider, the price that the SME has to pay will increase in respect to the actual price. Indeed, logistics providers have imposed the so called 'e-dec fee', i.e., 10-15 Swiss Francs (ca. € 6-10) per declaration, in order to amortise the IT implementation investments of e-dec Export. In this case a SME avoids the e-dec Export

implementation investment but it pays every single export declaration.

4. According to the interview with the logistics provider, the truck is able to leave the borders within a few minutes. The truck driver does not even have to leave the truck as long as the bar code reading of the export documents at the borders fulfils all the needed requirements. Therefore, the *waiting time at the borders* is decreasing. This is also confirmed by the opinion of most of the interviewees (38%).

5. According to 27% of the interviewees, the *control of the customs office* will increase. The customs office will indeed conduct a more accurate control through the IT system. This is possible since the export data can be reviewed by the customs office up to five years after the export took place. Using an IT system this control will be easier and faster since the needed data are stored in a database.

6. The *number of entry errors* should decrease but not in a considerable manner. According to the data provided by the interviewed logistics provider, entry errors do not constitute a major issue since they do not occur frequently. For this reason, their reduction is not perceived as a considerable change. Despite of this, 31% of the interviewed SMEs recognised that entry errors may be reduced.

7. The *transparency between SMEs and the customs office* will increase (opinion of 28% of the participants). Every export declaration is stored in a database: customs office and SMEs can access to it whenever needed. In this way, both parties can check the actions of the other party and view the export declaration status or location.

8. Because of security issues, *control of the goods along the supply chain* is a factor that concerns all exporters. The interviewees had

Table 2. Advantages of E-dec export implementation

Factor	It is an advantage	It has no influence	n.s.
Electronic notice of VAT assessment	28%	34%	38%
No media breaks	31%	19%	50%
Data and communication standardisation	53%	20%	27%
Declaration possible 24 hours a day	45%	33%	22%
Unique data collection	42%	28%	30%
Export certificate also used for internal controls	34%	39%	27%
More transparent export process	44%	33%	23%
Elimination of the monthly export list	45%	27%	28%

different opinions about how the control of the goods will change: 19% think that the control will increase while 22% believe that it will not change. An electronic customs system can improve goods' control along the supply chain since it enables the electronic registration of exported goods at the point of origin, the borders, and the delivery point in a foreign country. We already illustrated the export process from the point of origin to the Swiss borders. From the Swiss borders, the goods are transported to the delivery point: the data are registered again and the information is given to the national customs office of the import country. The customs office of import sends a notification to the Swiss customs office confirming the delivery of the goods. Nowadays, this advice is not sent by a common IT system, since Switzerland and the 27 EU member states do not possess a common electronic customs system; resolving this is the goal of the EU customs initiative cited before.

After reflecting the changes that e-dec Export implementation will bring, SMEs were asked to think about potential advantages. The questions were formulated based on factors that were stated by the Swiss Federal Customs Administration to be advantages for exporters. The SMEs had to give their opinion about the proposed factors

indicating whether they think them to be advantageous or without influence (Table 2). The eight analysed factors are: (1) Electronic notice of VAT assessment; (2) No media breaks; (3) Data and communication standardisation; (4) Declaration possible 24 hours a day; (5) Unique data collection; (6) Export certificate also used for internal control; (7) More transparent export process; (8) Elimination of the monthly export list.

1. E-dec Export enables the *electronic notice of VAT assessment*. 28% of the interviewed participants think that this change will be an advantage. After the clearance of the goods, the VAT assessment is generated automatically (step 8) so that errors are avoided. Indeed, nowadays the exports data for the VAT declaration have to be provided separated from the export, often resulting in inconsistency between the VAT declaration and the effectively exported goods. However, 34% think that the electronic notice will not have any influence on the efficiency of the export process while 38% do not know how to judge it.

2. The old customs system, the VAR system, has already celebrated its 30th birthday. Due to its simplicity, it is a successful solution. However, it has become too old and its structure no longer complies with new EU standards, such as NCTS. For this reason, a

media break occurs if exporters still use the VAR system. On the contrary, the electronic customs solution proposed by IDEE makes it possible to avoid media breaks (*no media breaks*). 31% of the participants think that this is an advantage since it avoids possible manual entry errors caused by the transition from system to system and it makes export process execution faster.

3. Thus, also the *exchanged data* and the *communication* between the exporters and the customs office will be *standardised*. In other words, the exporters directly insert their data into a system which is the same system used by the customs office. Indeed, the goal of the Swiss Federal Customs Office is to achieve complete electronic goods traffic before the end of 2010 so that each exporter uses the same IT system. Thanks to this system, inconsistencies between different IT solutions or difficulties due to different standards will not occur anymore. 53% of the participants affirmed this to be a factor that will increase the efficiency and speed up the export process.

4. The new electronic system enables the exporters *to declare 24 hours a day*. 45% of the interviewees declared this to be an advantage since it gives them more flexibility. Flexibility plays an important role along the export process for two main reasons. First of all, the exporters do not depend on the opening time of the customs office. Secondly, the exporters can be easily compliant to the new European regulation regarding the prior notification; following the terror attacks of 11th September 2001 and subsequent efforts by the US and the World Customs Organisation (WCO) to enhance the security of the supply chain, the European Union decided to require prior notification of goods crossing its external borders as of 1st July 2009. This involves both imports

and exports. The prior notification period is 24 hours for goods crossing by sea, two hours for rail transport, and one hour for road transport; the provided data of notification have to have an electronic format and be compliant to EU standards. If the summary declaration is not lodged in electronic format the prior notification period is at least four hours. Therefore, the e-dec Export system can avoid the slowdown of export processes and enable the completion of the prior notification 24 hours a day.

5. E-dec Export will enable a *unique data collection*. Nowadays, exporters have to provide the same data three times: to the customs office for the export declaration, to the finance department for the VAT assessment, and to the department of statistics for the corresponding statistics. Entry errors may occur and fraud is possible. E-dec Export will provide a unique database so that exporters have to submit the same data only once. 48% of the interviewees considered it as an advantage for two main reasons: it reduces fraud and it enables the exporters to save time since they have to provide the data to a unique system.

6. The e-dec Export certificate can also be used for *internal controls*. Exporters can use it, e.g., for inventory control and warehouse management. This factor is not seen as a big improvement since the majority of the participants think that it is not influent to their daily tasks and processes. However, 34% think this to be an advantage while 27% remain without an opinion to this question.

7. As mentioned before, the *export process will be more transparent*. This is seen as an improvement by 44% of the 36 interviewed SMEs. However, at this stage it is not possible to quantify how much more transparent the process will be. For this reason, 23%

of the interviewees did not know what to answer and 33% do not consider it as an advantage.

8. The last analysed factor is the *elimination of the monthly export list*. Nowadays, exporters have to send an export list to the customs office in Bern by the end of a month with all export details of the month. This will not be needed anymore since the customs office will collect export details automatically in the IT system. Nearly half (45%) of the participants judge the elimination of the monthly list to be an improvement since they do not have to spend additional time for its compilation.

After presenting the results of the study, we can draw some conclusions that show how e-solutions are accepted. First, most of the SMEs do not know how the new e-dec Export implementation will affect their daily business. They cannot give estimation of concrete data related to the execution of the export process, such as, e.g., time needed for an export declaration or waiting time at the borders. However, we have to take into consideration that the case study took place in October 2008 when only two SMEs had already implemented e-dec Export, since the full implementation is foreseen to be done by the end of June 2009. Therefore, it is to be expected that most of the interviewed SMEs do not know how their business will change.

Second, although only two SMEs have already implemented e-dec Export, it is common opinion that at least four factors will not decrease but either increase or remain unchanged: number of daily export declarations, price of an export declaration, transparency between SMEs and customs office, and control of the goods along the supply chain.

Last but not least, although the majority of the participants could not give a consistent opinion about potential changes, most of the SMEs expect advantages of the new e-solution.

DISCUSSION

In the introduction and background section, we learned that potential e-commerce adopters, especially SMEs, do not trust in e-commerce because of security and legislation deficiency. Based on the Swiss examples, we can identify six e-customs factors related to security increase and legislation improvement: (1) Increased control of the customs office; (2) Less entry errors; (3) Electronic notice of VAT assessment; (4) Data and communication standardisation; (5) Declaration possible 24 hours a day; (6) More transparent export process. All these improvements can therefore ease e-commerce implementation. If exporters felt more confident in the export process and e-commerce could be regulated by electronic customs, e-commerce could be taken into account as a valid option to traditional trade.

In the introduction section, it was mentioned that 60% of online retailers, who are not selling cross-border, worry about varying fiscal regulations, compliance with varying national laws, cross-border delivery and the increased risk of fraud (European Commission, 2008c). Thanks to e-customs it is possible to overcome obstacles to cross-border sales. Based on the findings of the Swiss case study and on EU customs regulations, we relate the obstacles to online cross-border sales to the improvements that e-customs will bring in order to understand if these improvements will also affect cross-border online activities.

1. The first obstacle mentioned by 60% of the retailers corresponds to the *varying fiscal regulations* in different European countries. Taric, described in the background section, comprises all customs duty rates and Community rules applicable to Community's external trade. It allows goods clearance by the EU member states. It also provides the best means of collecting, exchanging, and publishing data on community external trade statistics. Taric does not solve the problem

of different fiscal regulations of the member states but makes possible to understand which tariff will be applied to exported goods since the nomenclature is harmonised and standardised. Another regulation that could help in overcoming this first obstacle is the suggested Modernised Customs Code. In this regulation the EU proposes the concept of a 'centralised clearance' so that exporters could be able to declare goods electronically and pay the customs duties in the country where they are established (European Commission, 2007b).

2.   The second issue that worries exporters is the *compliance with varying national laws*. In fact, EU countries have different laws. However, the Community Customs Code codifies Community customs law. It replaces many acts of law, improving transparency. It entered into force in 1992 and mainly concerns: general provisions on people's rights and obligations with regard to customs legislation, import and export duties, customs tariff, tariff classification of goods and their origin, presentation of goods to customs, customs declaration, non-Community goods which are moved under a transit procedure, customs-approved treatment or use, introduction of goods into a free zone or free warehouse, re-export, destruction of goods and their abandonment to the exchequer. In particular, the amendments added in 2005 are aimed at tightening security requirements for movements of goods across international frontiers. Economic operators are now required to provide the customs authorities with details of goods before they are imported into the EU or exported from it. This will entail the setting up of a one-stop shop for importers and exporters. The new concept of Authorised Economic Operator (AEO) simplifies trade. The EU member states may grant AEO status to any economic operator meeting common

criteria. These criteria concern control systems, financial solvency and operator's track record in complying with the rules. The code therefore helps exporters so that common customs regulations are into force among the EU member states.

3.   The third issue concerns *delivery problems* that exporters could experience. These problems are related, e.g., to delivery errors so that the delivery could take place with delay or even not take place at all. A more transparent process can therefore help exporters to have a better overview on the export process and more control on the whole supply chain. Delays could also be avoided or reduced by the possibility to declare 24 hours a day: exporters can deliver as soon as they have the goods ready to leave, i.e., when they have gotten the permission from the customs office. The standardisation of the data and the communication between exporters and customs offices could also avoid or reduce delivery errors since the export declaration will be standardised and therefore misunderstandings could be overcome.

4.   The last factor that exporters recognised to be an obstacle to cross-border delivery is the *risk of fraud*. Increased controls of customs offices together with the increased export process' transparency could reduce this risk. The Community Customs Code takes into consideration security and fraud issues. Therefore a joint collaboration of EU member states could lead to a reduction of fraud. For this reason, it could be more difficult to defraud. The electronic notice of VAT assessment will also reduce frauds with regards to VAT payment. This is related to exporters or importers with respect to their VAT declarations to the tax and customs office so that attempts to defraud could be reduced and the correct VAT amount will be paid.

Table 3. E-customs and e-commerce

Obstacles to e-commerce	E-customs improvements
Varying fiscal regulations	• *Taric*: It helps to understand which tariffs will be applied on exported goods; • *Modernised Customs Code*: It will promote the concept of 'central clearance' so that exporters will pay customs duties in the country where they are located.
Compliance with varying national laws	• *Community Customs Code*: It helps exporters so that customs regulations are into force among the **EU** member states.
Cross-border delivery	• *More transparent process*: It helps exporters to have a better overview on the export process so that delivery errors can be reduced; • *Declaration possible 24 hours a day*: It gives the exporters the flexibility to deliver without waiting too long for customs approval; • *Data and communication standardisation*: It reduces delivery errors since all data are interpreted by all export players in the same way.
Risk of fraud	• *Increased control of the customs office*: It helps to reduce the risk of fraud since the export process will be controlled more efficiently; • *More transparent process*: It helps to reduce the risk of fraud since exporters have a better overview on the whole export process; • *Less entry errors*: The elimination of media breaks makes more difficult attempts to defraud; • *Electronic notice of VAT assessment*: It helps the tax and customs office to receive the correct VAT amount.

Table 3 summarises the results giving an overview on how e-customs systems can help in overcoming obstacles to cross-border online sales, i.e., to e-commerce.

FUTURE RESEARCH DIRECTIONS

Future research is needed. In this work we gave a detailed overview on European e-commerce regulations but we did not consider worldwide legislations. Therefore, it is necessary to further analyse the connection between e-commerce adoption and related worldwide directives. In addition to a worldwide study, special attention has to be paid to new EU member states; a study on new member states' e-commerce adoption and their regulations can clarify if e-commerce implementation is impeded by legislations issues or other related problems, such as, e.g., low Internet penetration or infrastructures' deficiency.

SMEs are the core of worldwide trade and therefore it is vital to support their international growth. We state e-commerce to be a tool for SMEs internationalisation. We analysed a particular field, e-customs, which can enhance e-commerce and therefore SMEs internationalisation. Studies of SMEs e-commerce adoption are needed in order to give best practices not only to academic researchers but also to industrial stakeholders. Further case studies on e-customs applications and their related SMEs benefits could clarify whether the factors provided in this study can be validated. Especially, future studies could take this work into consideration in order to analyse the customs situation in other countries. Factors which can increase the trust in security and legislations can be analysed more deeply based on other case studies. This could lead to an extended and more detailed set of advantages, which can facilitate e-commerce adoption.

CONCLUSION

E-commerce is all about selling goods and services via the Internet. The trader and customer do not deal face to face at any point conducting business remotely, regardless of location. A number of legislative initiatives regulate and influence business conducted online. Legislations aim to ensure that online contracts are legally binding. However, legislations can be complex and confuse e-commerce traders impeding rapid e-commerce diffusion. On the contrary, simplified legislations can push e-commerce adoption. In order to support this statement, in this work we analysed how facilitating legislations and especially customs procedures can help international e-commerce, based on the European example and by focusing on the Swiss situation. Switzerland may be exemplary in showing the importance of facilitated legislations and e-customs systems since it is a small non-EU country inside the EU and therefore needs customs regulations for every trade within Europe. Based on European and Swiss regulations, OECD reports and statistics, e-commerce best practices reports, and case studies, in this contribution we studied how Switzerland is adapting its procedures and customs policies to European regulations in order to bring forward Swiss companies trading internationally. Since big companies often find a solution by themselves, e.g., opening a subsidiary enterprise in the EU, we focused on SMEs. Based on the Swiss examples and EU declarations, we identified six factors related to e-customs implementation and three EU customs regulations that can enhance e-commerce adoption.

The Swiss analysis showed that e-customs systems implementation will bring a set of changes, such as, e.g., the decrease of the time needed for export declarations or the reduction of entry errors. This research also confirmed the assertion of the Swiss Federal Customs Administration that stated e-customs will bring a set of advantages to Swiss companies, such as, e.g., electronic notice of VAT assessment or data and communication standardisation.

Finally, this study shows how governments can positively influence e-commerce adoption and diffusion among SMEs by providing a facilitated legislative environment contributing to the large e-commerce adoption research giving a new perspective on the importance of legislations and procedures.

REFERENCES

Baida, Z., Liu, J., & Tan, Y.-H. (2007). Towards a methodology for designing e-government control procedures. *Electronic Government, 4646*, 56-67. Berlin/Heidelberg: Springer.

Baida, Z., Rukanova, B., Liu, J., & Tan, Y. H. (2007, June 3-6). Rethinking EU trade procedures - The beer living lab. In *Proceedings of the 20th Bled eConference: eMergence*. Bled, Slovenia.

Bjørn-Andersen, N., Razmerita, L. V., & Henriksen, H. Z. (2007). The streamlining of cross-border taxation using IT: The Danish eExport solution. In J. Makolm & G. Orthofer (Eds.), *E-Taxation: State & perspectives: E-government in the field of taxation: Scientific Basis, Implementation Strategies, Good Practice Examples* (pp. 195-206). Linz, Austria: Trauner Verlag.

Blakeley, C. J., & Matsuura, J. H. (2001). E-Government: An Engine to Power e-Commerce Development. In *Proceedings of the European Conference on e Government, Trinity College; Dublin, Ireland,* September 27-28.

Boyd, S. L., Hobbs, J. E., & Kerr, W. A. (2003). The impact of customs procedures on business to consumer e-commerce in food products. *Supply Chain Management: An International Journal, 8*(3), 195–200. doi:10.1108/13598540310484591

Cheung, W. (1998). The use of the World Wide Web for commercial purposes. *Industrial Management & Data Systems, 98*(4), 172–177. doi:10.1108/02635579810219345

European Commission. (1987). Council Regulation (EEC) No 2658/87 of 23 July 1987 on the Tariff and Statistical Nomenclature and on the Common Customs Tariff [Electronic Version]. *Official Journal of the European Communities, L256*. Retrieved April 8, 2009, from http://www.eugbc.net/files/52_129_447309_23.07.1987-CombinedNomenclature.pdf

European Commission. (1992). Council Regulation (EEC) No 2913/92 of 12 October 1992 establishing the Community Customs Code [Electronic Version]. *Official Journal of the European Communities, L253*. Retrieved April 8, 2009, from http://eur-lex.europa.eu/LexUriServ/LexUriServ.do?uri=CONSLEG:1992R2913:20070101:EN:PDF

European Commission. (2000a). Directive 1999/93/EC of the European Parliament and of the Council of 13 December 1999 on a Community framework for electronic signatures [Electronic Version]. *Official Journal of the European Communities, L13/12*. Retrieved April 8, 2009, from http://eur-lex.europa.eu/LexUriServ/LexUriServ.do?uri=OJ:L:2000:013:0012:0020:EN:PDF

European Commission. (2000b). Directive 2000/31/EC of the European Parliament and of the Council of 8 June 2000 on certain legal aspects of information society services, in particular electronic commerce, in the Internal Market (Directive on electronic commerce) [Electronic Version]. *Official Journal of the European Communities, L178/1*. Retrieved April 8, 2009, from http://eur-lex.europa.eu/LexUriServ/LexUriServ.do?uri=OJ:L:2000:178:0001:0016:EN:PDF

European Commission. (2003). Commission Recommendation 2003/361/EC of 6 May 2003 Concerning the Definition of Micro, Small and Medium-Sized Enterprises [Electronic Version]. *Official Journal of the European Union, L 124*, 36. Retrieved April 8, 2009, from http://eur-lex.europa.eu/LexUriServ/LexUriServ.do?uri=OJ:L:2003:124:0036:0041:EN:PDF

European Commission. (2004). Internationalisation of SMEs [Electronic Version]. *Obervatory of European SMEs 2003, 4*. Retrieved April 9, 2009, from http://ec.europa.eu/enterprise/enterprise_policy/analysis/doc/smes_observatory_2003_report4_en.pdf

European Commission. (2005). Regulation (EC) No 648/2005 of the European Parliament and of the Council of 13 April 2005 amending Council Regulation (EEC) No 2913/92 establishing the Community Customs Code [Electronic Version]. *Official Journal of the European Union, L 117*. Retrieved April 8, 2009, from http://eur-lex.europa.eu/LexUriServ/LexUriServ.do?uri=CELEX:32005R0648:en:HTML

European Commission. (2006). *Annex to the Proposal on the Community Programme Customs 2013 – Impact Assessment*. Retrieved February 10, 2009, from http://ec.europa.eu/taxation_customs/resources/documents/Customs2013_impact.pdf.

European Commission. (2007a). *Electronic Customs Multi-Annual Strategic Plan, 2007 Yearly Revision (MASP 8)*. Retrieved March 16, 2009, from http://ec.europa.eu/taxation_customs/resources/documents/customs/policy_issues/e-customs_initiative/MASP_rev7.pdf.

European Commission. (2007b). *Proposal for a Regulation of the European Parliament and of the Council laying down the Community Customs Code (Modernized Customs Code)*. Retrieved February 10, 2009, from http://ec.europa.eu/taxation_customs/resources/documents/customs/procedural_aspects/general/community_code/mccc_en.pdf.

European Commission. (2008a). Decisions Adopted Jointly by the European Parliament and the Council: Decision No 70/2008/EC of the European Parliament and the of the Council of 15 January 2008 on a paperless environment for customs and trade [Electronic Version]. *Official Journal of the European Union, L 23/21 - L23/26*. Retrieved April 8, 2009, from http://eur-lex.europa.eu/LexUriServ/LexUriServ.do?uri=OJ:L:2008:023:0021:0026:EN:PDF

European Commission. (2008b). *Legislation Proposed or Adopted*. Retrieved February 10, 2009, from http://ec.europa.eu/taxation_customs/customs/policy_issues/electronic_customs_initiative/electronic_customs_legislation/index_en.htm.

European Commission. (2008c). *Synthesis Report on Consumer and Business Attitudes to Cross-Border Sales and Consumer Protection in the Internal Market*. Retrieved February 10, 2009, from http://ec.europa.eu/consumers/strategy/docs/eurobar_298_synthrep_oct2008_en.pdf.

Froehlich, G., Hoover, H. J., Liew, W., & Sorenson, P. G. (1999). Application framework issues when evolving business applications for electronic commerce. *Information Systems, 24*(6), 457–473. doi:10.1016/S0306-4379(99)00027-7

Henriksen, H. Z., Rukanova, B., & Tan, Y.-H. (2008). Pacta Sunt Servanda but where is the agreement? The complicated case of eCustoms. In M. A. Wimmer, H. J. Scholl & E. Ferro (Eds.), *EGOV 2008* (pp. 13-24). Berlin Heidelberg: Springer Verlag.

Internet World Stats. (2008). *Internet usage statistics*. Retrieved February 10, 2009, from http://www.internetworldstats.com/stats.htm

Karagozoglu, N., & Lindell, M. (2004). Electronic commerce strategy, operations, and performance in small and medium-sized enterprises. *Journal of Small Business and Enterprise Development, 11*(3), 290–301. doi:10.1108/14626000410551555

Kuiper, E. J. (2007). *Convergence by cooperation in IT – The EU's customs and fiscalis programmes* [Electronic Version]. Master's Thesis, Delft University of Technology. Retrieved April 8, 2009, from http://www.itaide.org/forms/document.asp?Q=7771

Labbé, M. (2007). The role of government in the promotion of e-commerce [Electronic Version]. *Workshop on Potential of e-Commerce*. Retrieved February 10, 2009, from http://www.intracen.org/e-trade/docs/trainiran/ITC_IROST_e-government_JUN07v3.ppt#257,2,Putting EC into perspective

Leebaert, D. (1998). *The future of electronic market place*. Cambridge, MA, USA: MIT Press.

MacGregor, R. C., & Vrazalic, L. (2005). A basic model of electronic commerce adoption barriers: A study of regional small businesses in Sweden and Australia. *Journal of Small Business and Enterprise Development, 12*(4), 510–527. doi:10.1108/14626000510628199

Maes, P., Guttman, R., & Moukas, A. (1999). Agents that buy and sell. *Communications of the ACM, 42*(3), 81–91. doi:10.1145/295685.295716

OECD. (2002). *OECD small and medium enterprise outlook - 2002 Edition*. Paris: OECD Publishing.

OECD. (2005). *OECD SME and entrepreneurship outlook - 2005 Edition*. Paris: OECD Publishing.

OECD. (2007a). *Key ICT indicators: Internet penetration by size class*. Retrieved February 10, 2009, from http://www.oecd.org/dataoecd/20/23/37442795.xls

OECD. (2007b). *Key ICT indicators: Internet selling and purchasing by industry*. Retrieved February 10, 2009, from http://www.oecd.org/dataoecd/20/22/34083121.xls

Raus, M., Flügge, B., & Boutellier, R. (2008). Innovation steps in the diffusion of e-customs solutions. In S. A. Chun, M. Janssen & J. R. Gil-Garcia (Eds.), *ACM International Conference Proceeding Series* (Vol. 289, pp. 315-324). Montréal, Canada: Digital Government Society of North America.

Simpson, M., & Docherty, A. J. (2004). E-commerce adoption support and advice for UK SMEs. *Journal of Small Business and Enterprise Development, 11*(3), 315–328. doi:10.1108/14626000410551573

Swiss Federal Customs Administration. (2008a). *E-dec*. Retrieved February 10, 2009, from http://www.ezv.admin.ch/themen/00476/00494/index.html?lang=en

Swiss Federal Customs Administration. (2008b). *IDEE - Handbuch für Kunden / Firmen*. Retrieved February 10, 2009, from http://www.ezv.admin.ch/themen/00476/02278/02376/index.html?lang=de&download=M3wBPgDB/8ull6Du36Wen ojQ1NTTjaXZnqWfVpzLhmfhnapmmc7Zi6rZ nqCkkIN4fn97bKbXrZ6lhuDZz8mMps2gpKfo &typ=.pdf

Swiss Federal Customs Administration. (2008c, May, 2008). *Talks with the EU on amending the agreement on the carriage of goods (24-hour rule)*. Retrieved February 10, 2009, from http://www.ezv.admin.ch/zollinfo_firmen/verzollung/02302/index.html?lang=en

Turban, E., Lee, J., King, D., & Chung, H. (2000). *Electronic commerce: A manager's perspective*. Upper Saddle River, NJ, USA: Prentice Hall.

United Nations Economic Commission for Europe. (2005). *Recommendation and guidelines on establishing a single window - recommendation No. 33*. Retrieved March 16, 2009, from http://www.unece.org/cefact/recommendations/rec33/rec33_trd352e.pdf

WCO. (2006). *Authorized economic operator*. Retrieved February 10, 2009, from http://www.ifcba.org/UserFiles/File/SP0218E1(2).doc.

Zhang, C., Cui, L., Huang, L., & Zhang, C. (2007). Exploring the role of government in information technology diffusion: An empirical study of IT usage in Shanghai Firms. In *Organizational dynamics of technology-based innovation: Diversifying the research agenda* (vol. 235/2007, pp. 393-407). Boston: Springer.

ADDITIONAL READING

Bakry, S. H. (2004). Development of e-Government: a STOPE View. *International Journal of Network Management, 14*(5), 339–350. doi:10.1002/nem.529

Burn, J., & Robins, G. (2003). Moving towards e-government: A case study of organisational change process. *Logistics Information Management, 16*(1), 25–35. doi:10.1108/09576050310453714

Carina, I., Monika, M., Ada, S., & Virpi Kristiina, T. (2003). SME barriers to electronic commerce adoption: Nothing changes-everything is new. In *Managing IT in government business & communities* (pp. 147-163). Hershey, PA, USA: IGI Publishing.

Chau, P. Y. K. (2001). Determinants of small business EDI adoption: An empirical investigation. *Journal of Organizational Computing and Electronic Commerce, 11*(4), 229–252. doi:10.1207/S15327744JOCE1104_02

European Commission. (1999). Directive 1993/93/EC of the European parliament and of the Council [Electronic Version]. *Official Journal of the European Communities, L13/12*. Retrieved April 8, 2009, from http://portal.etsi.org/esi/Documents/e-sign-directive.pdf

European Commission. (2006). *Authorized economic operators*. Retrieved March 16, 2009, from http://www.ifcba.org/UserFiles/File/SP0218E1(2).doc

Evans, D., & Yen, D. C. (2006). E-government: Evolving relationship of citizens and government, domestic, and international development. *Government Information Quarterly, 23*(2), 207–235. doi:10.1016/j.giq.2005.11.004

Folstand, A., Jorgensen, H. D., & Krogstie, J. (2004). User involvement in e-government development projects. In *Proceedings of the Third Nordic Conference on Human-Computer Interaction* (Vol. 82, pp. 217-224). New York: ACM.

Hamel, G. (2000). *Leading the revolution.* Boston: Harvard Business School Press.

Hempell, T. (2006). Diffusion of information and communication technology. In U. Schmoch, C. Rammer & H. Legler (Eds.), *National systems of innovation in comparison* (pp. 169-184). New York: Springer.

Henriksen, H. Z., & Rukanova, B. (2008, April 23-25). Barriers and drivers of ecustoms implementation: Never mind IT. In *Proceedings of the 6th Eastern European eGovernment Days*, Prague, Czech Republic.

Jarillo, J. C. (1995). *Strategic networks: Creating the borderless organization.* Woburn, MA: Butterworth-Heinemann.

Kalakota, R., Oliva, R. A., & Donath, B. (1999). Move Over, e-Commerce. *Marketing Management, 8*(3), 22–32.

Keen, P. (1999). E-commerce: Chapter 2. *Computerworld, 33*(37), 48.

Keller, W. (2004). International technology diffusion. *Journal of Economic Literature, 42*(3), 752–782. doi:10.1257/0022051042177685

Kumar, V., Maheshwari, B., & Kumar, U. (2002). ERP systems implementation: Best practices in canadian government organizations. *Government Information Quarterly, 19*(2), 147–172. doi:10.1016/S0740-624X(02)00092-8

Lee, C. B. P., & Lei, U. L. E. (2007). Adoption of e-government services in Macao. In *ACM International Conference Proceeding Series* (Vol. 232, pp. 217-220). New York: ACM.

Niitamo, V. P., Kulkki, S., Eriksson, M., & Hribernik, K. A. (2006). State-of-the-art and good practice in the field of living labs. In *Proceedings of the 12th International Conference on Concurrent Enterprising: Innovative Products and Services through Collaborative Networks*, Milan, Italy, June 26-28.

Porter, M. E. (2001). Strategy and the Internet. *Harvard Business Review, 79*(3), 63–78.

Raus, M., Flügge, B., & Schumacher, R. (2008). Neue Zollabwicklung in der Schweiz. *Swiss Export, 4. Quartal, 2008*, 39–41.

Raus, M., Kipp, A., & Boutellier, R. (2008). Diffusion of e-government IT innovation: A case of failure? In P. Cunningham & M. Cunningham (Eds.), *Collaboration and the knowledge economy: Issues, applications, case studies.* Amsterdam: IOS Press.

Rogers, E. M. (Ed.). (2003). *Diffusion of innovations* (5th ed.). New York: The Free Press.

Shackleton, P., Fisher, J., & Dawson, L. (2004, January 5-8). Evolution of local government e-services: The applicability of e-business maturity models. In *Proceedings of the 37th Annual Hawaii International Conference on System Sciences*, Waikoloa, Big Island, HI.

Taylor, M. J., McWilliam, J., England, D., & Akomode, J. (2004). Skills required in developing electronic commerce for small and medium enterprises: Case based generalization approach. *Electronic Commerce Research and Applications, 3*(3), 253–265. doi:10.1016/j.elerap.2004.04.001

Teofilovic, N. (2002). The reality of innovation in government. *Innovation Journal*, 1-30.

Thomas, F. (2002). Business: Oriented testing in e-commerce. In *Software Quality and Software Testing in Internet Times* (pp. 117-137). New York: Springer-Verlag Inc.

Yildiz, M. (2007). E-government research: Reviewing the literature, limitations, and ways forward. *Government Information Quarterly, 24*(3), 646–665. doi:10.1016/j.giq.2007.01.002

Zhu, K., Kraemer, K., & Xu, S. (2003). Electronic business adoption by European firms: A cross-country assessment of the facilitators and inhibitors. *European Journal of Information Systems, 12*(4), 251–268. doi:10.1057/palgrave.ejis.3000475

Chapter 2
E–Commerce Trading Patterns within the SME Sector:
An Opportunity Missed?

Paul Jones
University of Glamorgan, UK

Gary Packham
University of Glamorgan, UK

David Pickernell
University of Glamorgan, UK

Paul Beynon-Davies
Cardiff University, UK

ABSTRACT

This study profiles an empirical study of E-Commerce trading patterns of SMEs in Wales. Academic debate continues to espouse the importance of the SME community in engendering economic prosperity and enhanced economic development although the sector also remains categorised by high failure rates. The strategic adoption of information technology offers the opportunity for increased competitiveness and enhanced profitability. Evidence suggests, however, that SMEs, particularly the smaller SME classifications, are not effectively exploiting E-business, with limited recorded examples of successful adoption. Within this study, E-Commerce trading practices are therefore contrasted against traditional non E-Commerce trading activity and conclusions are drawn on the behaviour adopted by SME Owner/ Managers. The conclusions will inform Owner/Managers, policy makers, practitioners, researchers and educators involved in E-Commerce deployment in the SME sector.

INTRODUCTION

Academic literature has long highlighted the importance of the small and medium enterprise (SME) community in engendering economic prosperity and enhancing economic development (Baldwin, Lymer & Johnson, 2000). Currently the SME sector exhibits high business failure rates (SBS, 2005), a situation exacerbated by the present economic climate in the United Kingdom (UK). Understanding this context,

DOI: 10.4018/978-1-60566-998-4.ch002

therefore, it is particularly important to note that the Internet was described by Fillis and Wagner (2005) as providing a new paradigm for business, and that effective strategic adoption of information communication technology (ICT) by businesses offers the opportunity for increased competitiveness, efficiency, enhanced profitability and the opportunity to create a competitive advantage (Simmons, Armstrong & Durkin, 2008).

Existing emergent evidence, however, suggests that SMEs, particularly the smaller sized SME classifications, are not effectively exploiting ICT, with minimal examples of successful adoption (Love, Irani, Standing, Lin & Burn, 2005). This chapter therefore profiles E-Commerce trading patterns in the SME community within a regional UK context, the study focusing on Wales specifically. Empirical data is presented which contrasts E-Commerce trading performance against traditional non E-Commerce trading activity and conclusions are drawn on the behaviour and practices adopted by SME Owner/Managers towards E-Commerce. These conclusions will inform Owner/Managers, policy makers, practitioners and the academic community involved in E-Commerce deployment in the SME sector.

BACKGROUND

The activity within electronic markets is typically referred to as electronic business (E-Business) or electronic commerce (E-Commerce) (Turban, Lee, King & Chung, 2000). E-Business can be viewed as an all organisation transformation concept in relation to ICT, with the capability of connecting business processes, enterprise applications and influencing organisation structure (Al-Qirim, 2003). Kalakota and Whinston (1996: 1) define E-Commerce as the:

...buying and selling of information, products and services via computer networks.

Sterrett and Shah (1998) and Stockdale and Standing (2004) have argued that micro-sized enterprises could compete with larger-sized enterprises by using the Internet, as their smaller size enabled them to be more adaptable and responsive to changing market conditions. Effective ICT usage provides an opportunity to achieve increased competitiveness and operational efficiency (Piris, Fitzgerald & Serrano, 2004). For effective E-Commerce utilisation to occur within an enterprise, Lederer and Sethi, (1988) and Blili and Raymond, (1993) state the need to integrate strategy, structure and systems with people and processes.

Further, Blackburn and Athayde (2000) recommended three strategies to assist the SME sector, namely developing E-Business aptitude awareness raising initiatives (Iacovou, Benbasat & Dexter, 1995), provision of training to enhance IT/IS skills (Pollard & Hayne, 1998) and utilisation of consulting services to assist transfer of business practices to the Internet (Zalud, 1999). To enable this process to occur Schneider and Perry (2001), Lockett and Brown (2003), Gibbs and Kraemer (2004) and Galloway and Mochrie (2005) also suggest SMEs' Owner/Managers require significant support from government and support agencies to enable this transition. Gibbs and Kraemer (2004) identify the provision of a positive legal environment and specific incentives as necessary to encourage E-Business adoption, whilst Pavic, Koh, Simpson and Padmore, (2007) posit that governments needed to take a long-term view, with the provision of extensive telecommunications networks and a proactive regulatory framework of particular importance. Before policy can be put in place, however, it is first necessary to determine the extent to which E-Commerce is currently being deployed, and in what ways, particularly the trading markets.

DOMAIN OF THE STUDY: WALES

Wales was selected as the area of investigation of this study for several reasons. Firstly, uptake and usage of E-Commerce within Wales remained largely unreported outside government-related sources (Jones, Beynon-Davies & Muir, 2003). This indicated the need for further research to enhance the extant knowledge. Secondly, the poor uptake of E-Commerce technologies within Wales (eCIC, 2005), in comparison to the rest of the UK (DTI, 2004), was significant and warranted further investigation and explanation. Previously, the Welsh economy was based upon agriculture, and the primary extraction industries such as iron, steel and the coal mining industries (Beynon-Davies, Evans & Owens, 2000). The last four decades however, have witnessed a massive decline in the primary and secondary sectors within Wales, due to increased global competition and falling demand, especially in the coal extraction and metals production industries (Jones-Evans, 2001). The coal industry can now be considered a minority employer and the metals processing industry concentrated in two integrated steel plants whose future and ownership remain uncertain (WERU, 2005) especially in light of the current global recession.

The National Economic Development Strategy (NEDS) (2001) identifies the key contributors to poor economic performance in Wales as a weak indigenous business base, low activity rates, depleted added value production, too few enterprises exporting and an underdeveloped service sector. Other areas of weakness identified, were a lack of high technology, knowledge-driven industries with insufficient research and development, minimal exploitation of ICT, low wages, deprived levels of entrepreneurship, inferior business birth rates, high business failure rates, meagre growth rates from SMEs to Public Limited Companies and underdeveloped potential within the tourism industry (NEDS, 2001). Wales lags behind other British regions, with a rate for business start-up 30% below average (NEDS, 2001). These are significant factors that contribute to the low levels of Internet use for business purposes.

Levels of E-Business Utilisation in Wales

Analysis of fifteen academic and public sector reports in Wales revealed the major E-Business performance trends in Wales since 2000. The DTI (2004) survey enabled comparison between Wales E-business performances in twenty-two areas, against 11 other UK regions. Wales was ranked 12th out of 12 in six of these areas, 11th in five areas and 10th in four areas. Wales only achieved 6 top 6 ratings and an average overall ranking of ninth against other UK regions. This analysis placed Wales as the worst but one performing region, with only Northern Ireland (NI) ranked lower. Wales performed poorly in access to the Internet, use of e-mail, online trading, online ordering, paying for goods online and enabling customers to pay online. In terms of barriers to implementing E-business, set up cost was identified as the most significant inhibitor with 51%, an increase of 16% on 2003. Other key barriers were identified as running costs (35%), limited time and resources (19%) and insufficient IT skills (13%). Access to the Internet in Wales had decreased, from 93% in 2002 to 88% in 2004. Local area network (LAN) usage had decreased from 74% in 2003 to 70% in 2004. Wales and NI had the lowest proportion of SMEs with internal network technologies. The trend for SMEs with e-mail (85%) had declined by 2% since 2002. By contrast, enterprise usage of websites had increased to 79%, a growth of 7% since 2003, and wide area networks (WAN) uptake had increased by 8% to 53%. Enterprise usage of intranets has increased from 38% in 2002 to 51% in 2004.

Levels of basic E-business technologies such as Internet usage had increased from 46% (NOP, 2000) to 59% in 2006 (eCIC, 2006). Broadband access had continued to increase with 78% of all enterprises utilising this connection method (eCIC, 2006). Website usage had increased to 72% (eCIC, 2006) up from 20% in NOP (2000) and e-mail from 20% (NOP, 2000) to 58% (eCIC, 2005). Uptake of more sophisticated E-business technologies in the eCIC (2005) survey revealed minimal uptake and even decline of technologies such as intranets (4%) and extranets (2%). Contrastingly eCIC (2006) suggested Intranet (18%) and extranet (7%) usage had increased dramatically. Use of information technology (IT) was more prevalent in the larger sized SME classifications with employees (eCIC, 2006). The eCIC (2006) study reported 69% of SMEs paying for goods and services online a healthy increase of 20% since 2005. Customers paying online (7%) demonstrated a decrease of 3% since 2004. The latest eCIC (2006) study identified 18% of connected businesses with employees reported that they sold goods or services on-line which again reflected a significant decrease of 11% since 2004. Use of customer relationship management (17.5%), supply chain management (6.7%) and enterprise resource planning (7.1%) systems demonstrated greater prominence than prior surveys but deployment remained limited especially within the smaller sized classified enterprises. eCIC (2005) identified that drivers to E-business differed between existing and new users. SMEs that were not connected to the Internet identified the desire to attract new customers (27%) and improve efficiency (26%). Existing E-business users identified drivers as the desire to attain further customers (18%), more efficient internal processes (16%), staying ahead of competitors (15%) and attaining increased customer satisfaction (13%).

This evidence suggests that the perceived drivers of E-business become more sophisticated with increased usage. However, 23% of SME Owner/Managers connected to the Internet, identified no specific drivers to E-business, suggesting a limited awareness. Lewis and Cockrill (2002) differentiated between direct and indirect benefits attained.

Indirect benefits were identified as access to new markets and customers. Direct benefits were identified as cost and time savings. The FSB (2004) and eCIC (2005) studies identified that SMEs had obtained inquiries and sales and new business opportunities from the UK and overseas. The eCIC (2005) study identified efficiency gains from internal processes. However, over 20% of SMEs Owner/Managers in eCIC (2005) identified no benefits obtained from E-business utilisation.

Sterrett and Shah (1998) and Stockdale and Standing (2004) have argued that micro-sized SMEs can compete with larger organisations through E-Commerce as their size enabled them to be more adaptable and responsive to changing conditions. Effective E-Commerce deployment means that enterprises are no longer restricted by geographical locations and able to compete in new national and global markets, both for customers and suppliers (Damanpour, 2001; Dholakia and Kshetri, 2004). However, Jones and Mohon, (2005) and Fink and Disterer, (2006) recognised that there was minimal research reporting the implementation of E-Commerce in the SME sector. Furthermore, Barry and Milner (2002) and MacGregor and Vrazalic (2005) suggested that SME Owner/Managers were not enthusiastic or proficient about adopting E-Commerce technologies and their advanced deployment remained low. Levy et al., (2004) recounted that only half the SMEs they surveyed believed that E-Commerce was important or essential. Schneider and Perry (2001) and Galloway and Mochrie (2005) suggest that SME Owner/Managers require support from government and support agencies to enable an effective transition in mindset. Blackburn and Athayde (2000) recommended three strategies to assist SMEs in developing E-Commerce aptitude, namely awareness raising initiatives (Iacovou et al, 1995), training provision to enhance IT skills (Pollard and Hayne, 1998) and utilisation of consulting services to assist transfer of business practices to the Internet (Zalud, 1999). Pavic et al., (2004) suggested that governments needed to take a long-term view, with the provision of extensive telecommunications networks and a proactive regulatory framework. Gibbs and Kraemer (2004) identified providing a positive legal environment and incentives to encourage usage. The picture that is apparent in Wales is one of basic utilisation of E-business technology, especially in the smaller sized micro SME classifications. Higher levels of organisational utilisation are restricted by a number of inhibitors, which delay initial adoption and inhibit further growth (Jones et al, 2003).

Overall, Wales' unique economic circumstances and inferior economic performance contrasted significantly with other UK regions. The Welsh economy has suffered from a large number of inherent weaknesses including low skills, minimal exploitation of E-Commerce within industry and high business failure rates. To improve these factors, the SME sector has become the focus of regeneration strategies by the Welsh Assembly Government (WAG) (WAG, 2005). The WAG represents the devolved government for Wales's administration and legislature set up in 1999. This process was initiated by a raft of new strategies and policy declarations from the WAG, to encourage business start-ups and enable growth within existing SMEs (WAG, 2003). The ability of individual SMEs to effectively deploy E-Commerce technologies and its subsequent impact upon enterprise turnover and sustainability is assessed within this chapter.

Focus of the Study: The Importance of SMEs in Wales

Analysis of available secondary statistics concerning SME performance reinforces the importance of SMEs in Wales and the UK. SMEs in the UK generated 48% of all private sector employment, but this rose to 75% within Wales (SBS 2005a). There is, however, also strong evidence regarding the specific economic importance of "Sole-Proprietor" micro-sized classified enterprises, to both Wales and the UK economies (SBS, 2005a). Within

the UK economy, SMEs accounted for 99.8% of all UK enterprises, whilst in Wales they account for 99.9% of total Welsh enterprises. Moreover, the "Sole-Proprietor" enterprises - those made up of sole traders without employees (Fielden, Davidson & Makin, 2000; Gray & Lawless, 2000; SBS, 2005a) - accounted for 70% of all UK enterprises. Contrastingly, medium sized (50 to 249 employees) and non-SME classified enterprises (greater than 250 employees) comprised only 0.7% and 0.2% of total UK enterprises, respectively. Such statistics therefore emphasise the reliance of the Welsh economy on a buoyant and thriving SME community.

METHODOLOGY

The study involved a questionnaire analysis of SMEs usage of E-Commerce within national, European and global trading markets. The survey utilised both self-completion (mailed questionnaires and personal delivery) and interview techniques (telephone questionnaires). The combined usage of several data collection methods within a survey was previously reported in Jobber (1991), Dillman (2000) and Koh and Maguire (2004). The survey instrument itself utilised two forms of closed questions, namely list and category style questions. The questionnaire was sequenced to initially consider the enterprise's use of IT and thereafter increasingly sophisticated E-Commerce technologies and their levels of deployment. SMEs were randomly selected using business directories from 14 unitary authorities within Wales. The selected authorities represented the diverse geographical and economic regions within Wales, e.g. urban (e.g. Swansea), rural areas (e.g. Carmarthenshire), areas of high unemployment and social deprivation (e.g. Blaenau Gwent) (Palvia and Palvia, 1999; NOP, 2000). All SMEs details were recorded in a database by the research team to ensure there was no replication in enterprises surveyed.

Table 1. SME groupings by number of employees

SME Size Classification	Grouping	Number of Employees
Sole-Proprietor	Micro	None
1-9	Micro	Between 1-9
10-49	Small	Between 10-49
50-249	Medium	Between 50-249

SME Defined

In terms of enterprise size classifications, this study employed a hybrid definition of the European Commission (EC) classification (Table 1). The rationale behind this decision was first to enable categorisation of SMEs into the three recognised sized groups namely micro (0-9), small (10-49) and medium (50-249) and the widespread use of the European union definition deployed within prior studies (Gray, 2004a). There was a need however, to further categorise the micro-sized SME group to denote the "Sole-Proprietor" enterprises, as they represented over 70% of all SMEs within Wales and the UK (SBS, 2005a). Hay and Kamshad (1994), Hisrich and Peters (1998) and Jones (2004) noted that such enterprises often remained constant in size as their existence provided lifestyle advantages for Owner/Managers. These enterprises typically had minimal ambition beyond maintaining their current operations and providing their products and services within existing markets (Levy, Powell & Worrall, 2005). Such enterprises use of E-Commerce therefore warranted further investigation given their limited existing literature (Fink and Disterer, 2006).

Survey Response Rates and Representativeness

The three data collection methods were utilised concurrently over a six-month period, to achieve a survey response of 500 respondents. The rationale for this target was cost, time, comparison with surveys previously undertaken in Wales (Remenyi et al, 1998; Lehmann, 1989). Table 2 illustrated the response rate achieved from each collection method. The most effective method in terms of response proved to be personnel delivery (85%), whereby the interviewer would visit an enterprise and await completion of the questionnaire. The main drawback with this method proved to be the time scale required to visit each enterprise individually. As a result, it only contributed 21% of all survey returns. The telephone collection method (38%) proved to be the second most successful data collection method and achieved the highest number of returns, 211 (42% of total sample). This response rate was within the range suggested by Remenyi, Williams, Money and Swartz (1998) as acceptable. Telephone proved an effective method of contacting enterprises, although there was a high occurrence of redundant numbers in the sources utilised namely local telephone directories and local authority databases. Postal returns provided the least efficient method of data collection in terms of respondent response rates (21%), although still contributed 37% of total survey responses. The postal response rate of 21% was disappointing in contrast to prior studies such as Love et al., (2005) (52%) and Mitchell and Clark (1999) (42%) although, it was superior to Ramsey et al., (2003) (11%) and Lau and Voon (2004) (16%). The overall sample return rate of 32% (Table 1) reflected the reluctance of Owner/Managers, especially the "Sole-Proprietor" sector, to commit time with no potential of reward for their efforts. All questionnaires were coded and input into SPSS software. This study employed a 95% confidence level for the survey data (Field, 2005).

When the survey was analysed by business type, the "Sole-Proprietor" size sector represented 34.4% of the total respondent population. The "1-9" sized classification proved the most significant sector, contributing 44.4%, followed by the "10-49" small (14%) and the "50-249" medium-sized enterprises (7.2%) category (Table

Table 2. Questionnaire response by delivery method as a percentage

Data collection method	Returned f	Total sample F	% of data collection Method	% of total Sample
Postal	185	872	21	37
Personnel Delivery	104	122	85	21
Telephone	211	549	38	42
Total	n=500	1543	32	

3). In terms of representation of industrial activity (IA) against SME size classification, Table 3 provided a breakdown of respondents. The "Sole-Proprietor" (SP) sized classification most significant IA proved to be Services/Transport (32%), followed by the Retail/Repair (21%) sector. The "1-9" sized classification main contributors proved to be the Manufacturing (18%) and Services/Transport sectors (18%). Similarly, the "10-49" group was predominantly populated by the Manufacturing (26%) and Services/Transport (15%) sectors. The respondents within the largest SME sized category, "50-249" were dominated by the Manufacturing (39%) and Services/Transport sectors (28%). Overall, in terms of IA, the Services/Transport sector (26%) provided the most respondents, followed by Manufacturing (22%) and Retail/Repair (17%).

The survey therefore provided a broad and adequate representation of the Welsh SME community in terms of size classification and IA with no non-SMEs classified enterprises included. There was a marginal over-representation of the larger-sized SME "50-249" classification within the survey sample in contrast to the UK population, although this was useful for comparative purposes. Overall 93% of survey respondents' were within the "0-49" SME size category,

Table 3. Industry activity by SME size categorisation by percentage

Industrial Sector	SME Size by Employee Number					
	Total f	SP %	1-9 %	10-49 %	50-249 %	As a % of all sample
Agriculture/Forestry/ Fishing	11	2.4	2.7	1.4	0.0	2.0
Construction	50	14.1	8.1	9.7	2.8	10.0
Manufacturing	110	14.1	23.9	26.4	38.9	22.0
Communications/ Computing	17	1.8	5.0	2.8	2.8	3.0
Wholesaler	28	5.3	4.1	9.7	8.3	6.0
Retail/Repair	84	21.2	17.6	9.7	5.6	17.0
Finance/Insurance/ Real Estate/Legal	38	3.5	10.4	9.7	5.6	8.0
Services/Transport	129	32.4	23.9	15.3	27.8	26.0
Education	4	0.6	0.5	2.8	0.0	1.0
Health/Medical	3	0.6	0.9	0.0	0.0	1.0
Other	26	4.1	3.2	12.5	8.3	5.0
Total	N=500	34.0	44.4	14.4	7.2	100

which equated to the latest SBS statistics for the UK small business population (2005). All the IA sectors were present in the survey, with the most significant returns a representative approximation of the main UK sectors, such as Manufacturing, Construction, Services/Transport and Retail/ Repair (SBS, 2003).

Data Analysis

To analyse the data, a number of univariate statistical methods were utilised to enable comparison with prior surveys to identify data trends. Several statistical techniques were employed to evaluate, compare and contrast the results, including reporting frequencies, percentages, ranking, means, cross-tabulations (two-way and three-way) and standard deviations (Mustaffa and Beaumont, 2002). Frequency counts of the survey population were undertaken to identify summarised individual responses to questions. Cross-tabulations and measures of central tendency were utilised to allow comparison between subcategories of variables. Similarly, measures of dispersion, such as standard deviation were utilised to evaluate levels of variance from the mean. The data was analysed and contrasted throughout by SME size and industry activity (IA) classification.

Survey respondents were asked to identify their "traditional" trading markets in terms of geographical location within each of the following geographical areas:

• In Wales only
• Outside Wales but in United Kingdom
• Outside the UK but in the European Union
• Outside the European Union within a global market
• No E-Commerce trade
• Don't know

Responses were calculated in terms of contribution to total sales turnover in the previous 12 months expressed as a percentage. "Traditional" sales turnover referred to turnover attained through channels without the usage of E-Commerce technologies. Thereafter, survey respondents were asked to identify the level of income obtained from E-Commerce trading activity within the same geographical trading markets identified above in the previous twelve months as a percentage. As the questionnaire contained mainly categorical data, this limited the type and extent of statistical analysis that could be deployed. Wherever possible, and to increase the comparability of

Figure 1. Chart identifying traditional business market within Wales as a percentage of total trade

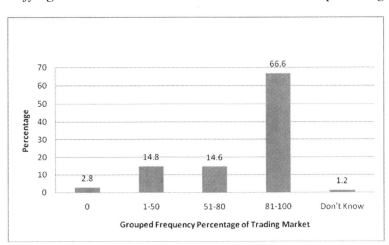

the data, the SME size classification and IA were cross tabulated as base comparators throughout the analysis.

FINDINGS

The following sections evaluate trading behaviour in traditional and E-Commerce trading markets.

Traditional Trading Market

Survey respondents were requested to identify their traditional trading markets without the influence of E-Commerce trading. Overall 67% of survey respondents indicated that between 80-100% of their trade occurred within Wales only, whilst 81.2% identified that over 50% of their turnover was within traditional markets in Wales (Figure 1). The mean revealed a strong reliance on Wales as a trading market for SMEs, with an average of 81% and a standard deviation of 29.9%. Such a large standard deviation suggests a wide diversity of practice.

When the Welsh trading market was cross tabulated by SME size classification, several trends were apparent (Figure 2). First micro-sized groupings placed a heavy reliance on this market, with 74% of "Sole-Proprietor", 73.9% of "1-9" and 51.4% of "10-49" sized SMEs undertaking between 80-100% of their trade only within Wales. By combining the grouped frequencies categories, further trends emerged. Analysis revealed that 82.5% of "Sole-Proprietor", 88.3% of "1-9" and 81.9% of "10-49" SME size classifications did more than 50% of their trading only within Wales.

By contrast, the largest SMEs size classification the "50-249" sector was less reliant on this traditional market, with only 31% of this sector trading 100% within Wales. Indeed, 34.5% of the "50-249", SME size sector surveyed undertook less than 50% of their trade within Wales and 17.2% none whatsoever. The results revealed that the majority of all SMEs (50.1%) only traded within Wales. Further, 89% of all respondents identified less than 50% of all trade was outside Wales within a UK market (Figure 3). A mean of 15.7% and a

Figure 2. Chart of traditional trading market in Wales cross tabulated by SME size classification by percentage

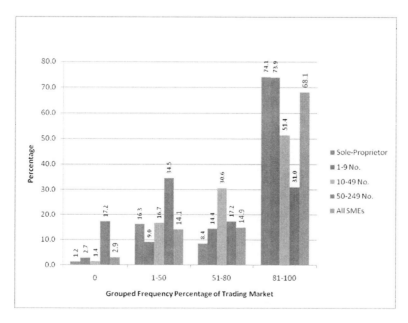

standard deviation of 25.5%, again suggested a wide range of trading performance in this market. Micro-sized Welsh SMEs, for example, were not trading extensively within a UK market. For example, 61.7% of "Sole-Proprietor", 55.3% of "1-9", 29.9% of "10-49" and 15.2% of "50-249" of SMEs undertook no trade in the UK outside Wales. Overall, only 13.2% of "Sole-Proprietor", 5.1% of "1-9" and 9.1% of "10-49" identified undertaking over 50% of their total trade within a UK market outside Wales. Contrastingly, the

"50-249" sector was extremely proactive in this market, with 42.4% undertaking over 50% of their trade, and only 15.2% not trading, in a UK market (Figure 3).

Analysis of trade for all respondents within a European union market, revealed minimal exploitation, with 88.1% of respondents identifying that they did not trade within this market and only 11.9% identified that up to 50% of their trade came from this geographical region (Figure 4). When grouping cumulative frequencies by SME size

Figure 3. Chart of traditional market in UK cross tabulated by SME size classification by percentage

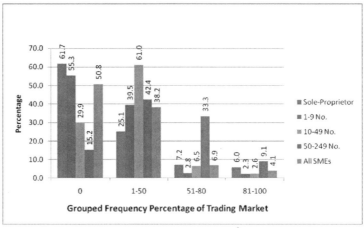

Figure 4. Chart by percentage of traditional market in European Union cross tabulated by SME size classification

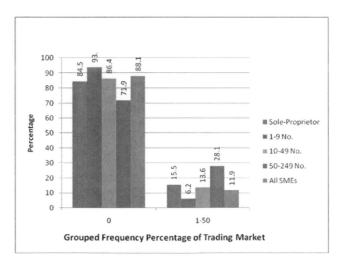

classification only 15.5% of "Sole-Proprietor", 6.2% of "1-9" identified undertaking up to 50% of their total trade within European union markets. The "50-249" sector demonstrated the highest level of trade within the European union, with 28.1% identifying trade of up to 50% of overall sales in this region.

Analysis of trade outside the European union, within a global market (Figure 5), revealed that 94.2% of all SMEs noted a zero level of global trade. In terms of SME size classification, 96.3% of the "Sole-Proprietor", 95.7% of "1-9", 78.1% of "10-49" and 78.1% of the "50-249" identified zero global trade outside Europe. Only 15.6% of the "10-49" and the "50-249" sectors identified that global trade accounted for up to 50% of their overall sales (Figure 5). Thus it was apparent that there were higher levels of trading in the larger sized SMEs than smaller sized SMEs within global markets

When the trading market was then analysed using a grouped frequency cross-tabulation against IA, the following trends emerged (see Table 4). Table 4 displays levels of dependence on geographical trading markets by industrial classifica-

tion. The table identifies both extremes of trading activity namely a zero level of activity and a 100% maximum commitment. Seventy-six per cent of all the Construction and 73% of Agriculture/Forestry/Fishing enterprises surveyed undertook all their trade within Wales. The Communications/Computing and Manufacturing sectors were least reliant on trade within Wales, with 23% and 6% respectively undertaking no trade within this region. In terms of UK trade outside Wales, 50% of the Finance/Insurance/Real Estate/Legal and 17% of the manufacturing sector identified that over 50% of their trade occurred within this market.

Other sectors performed poorly in terms of UK trade outside Wales, including the majority of the Agriculture/Forestry/Fishing (72%), Construction (76%) and Retail/Repair (66%) sectors, which identified no trade within this market. In terms of European union trade, all industry sectors performed poorly, with high levels of zero trade apparent in several IAs (see Table 4). High levels of activity were minimal, with only 6% of the Communications/Computing sector reporting 100% of its trade in the European union. Evidence of global trade was also insignificant,

Figure 5. Chart by percentage of traditional market in global market cross tabulated by SME size classification

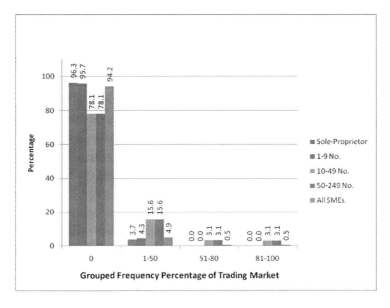

Table 4. Dependence on traditional trading market by industrial activity classification

Sector Classification	Wales		UK		EU		Global Market	
	0%	100%	0%	100%	0%	100%	0%	100%
Agriculture/Forestry/ Fishing	0.0	72.7	72.7	0.0	81.8	0.0	100.0	0.0
Construction	0.0	76.0	76.0	0.0	100.0	0.0	100.0	0.0
Manufacturing	6.4	36.4	37.3	1.8	78.2	0.0	87.3	0.0
Communications/ Computing	23.5	35.3	47.1	5.9	76.5	5.9	94.1	5.9
Wholesaler	0.0	50.0	50.0	0.0	89.3	0.0	96.4	0.0
Retail/Repair	1.2	65.5	66.7	1.2	90.5	0.0	98.8	0.0
Finance/Insurance/ Real Estate/Legal	0.0	50.0	50.0	0.0	92.1	0.0	92.1	0.0
Services/Transport	0.8	43.2	44.0	0.0	81.6	0.0	88.8	0.8
Education	0.0	25.0	25.0	0.0	50.0	0.0	50.0	0.0
Health/Medical	0.0	66.7	100.0	0.0	100.0	0.0	100.0	0.0
Other	4.2	29.2	29.2	4.2	79.2	0.0	87.5	0.0
Total	2.8	49.4	50.6	1.0	85.0	0.2	92.1	0.4

* The 0% column identifies where there was zero trading activity within the industrial activity classification displayed as a percentage.

**The 100% column identifies where there was a 100% level of trading activity within the industrial activity classification displayed as a percentage.

with several sectors identifying no trade presence. As previously the Communications/Computing sector was the only notable presence in a global market with 6% undertaking 100% of its sales within this sector.

E-COMMERCE TRADING MARKETS

When the SME Owner/Managers were asked to identify the level and location of their E-Commerce trade, this elicited a limited detailed response from only 71 (14.2% of total survey respondents) of the surveyed enterprises. A further 79 (15.8%) of respondents indicated that they were unaware of which trading market their E-Commerce sales, if any, occurred within. Such a low response rate reflected the limited utilisation of E-Commerce within the SME sector (see Figure 6) as previously suggested in the literature. This evidence therefore confirms limited deployment and suggests limited understanding and evaluation of E-Commerce

behaviour and trading performance, negligible market intelligence and overall a high level of ignorance exhibited by SME Owner/Managers.

Respondent replies suggested reluctance to trade through E-Commerce markets in different geographical areas. In Wales, 17 out of 71 respondents, (24% or 3.4% of all survey) identified that they did not trade electronically in Wales. Moreover, 37% (26 out of 71) of respondents to the E-Commerce trading enquiry indicated they did not trade within the UK outside Wales. This trend continued in the other potential markets although it magnified in intensity. For example (51 out of 70) of respondent enterprises (73%) did not utilize E-Commerce for European union trade and (52 out of 70) (74%) global trade. This suggests that the opportunity offered by E-Commerce in potentially accessing and exploiting new markets is being under-utilized.

Actual E-Commerce trading performance was limited (see Figure 6) when considered as a percentage of all enterprises surveyed. E-Commerce

Figure 6. Comparative chart by percentage of e-commerce markets

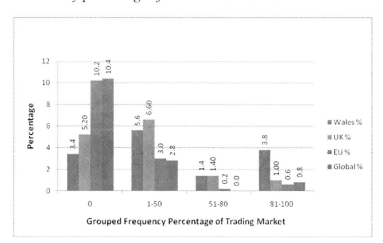

trade was marginally more prevalent within Wales than the other potentially newer and more lucrative markets. For example 5.6% of enterprises identified up to 50% of their sales occurred within Wales. Contrastingly, 3.8% of enterprises surveyed identified that between 81-100% of their turnover was within Wales only. Aside from this result it was apparent from Figure 6 that exploitation of UK, European Union and global markets was minimal. In a UK market outside Wales, 6.60% of respondents identified that between one and 50% of their E-Commerce sales occurred in this geographical region. E-Commerce sales in a European union market were marginal with 3% of respondents identifying that up to 50% of sales occurred in this region. E-Commerce sales in a global market were disappointing with only 2.8% of survey participants undertaking up to 50% of their E-Commerce trading in this region.

When E-Commerce trading activity was considered by main business activity the most active sectors by presence were Communications/Computing (59%), Manufacturing (28%) and Services (12%). The most productive in terms of E-Commerce trading was the Communications/Computing sector whereby 24% of such enterprises achieved 100% of their sales. By way of contrast, 49% (35 out of 71) of question

respondents indicated that they thought over 40% of their E-Commerce trade was located within local trading markets in Wales although this only equated to 7% of the total survey population. Using the same comparative measure of number of enterprises achieving 40% of their E-Commerce trade there was less reliance on UK outside Wales (29.6% or 4.2% of the full survey), European union (5.7% or 0.8%) and global markets (11.4% or 1.6%).

When the E-Commerce trading performance is analysed by market performance it can be seen that the large sized SME exhibit the higher levels of E-Commerce activity. In the Welsh market (see Figure 7) it was apparent that overall there was a limited utilisation of E-Commerce with only 10.8% of surveyed enterprises identifying trading activity). There was greater deployment of E-Commerce trading within the larger sized SME categories ("10-49" 20.8% and "50-249" 22.2%) in comparison to the smaller sized enterprises ("Sole-Proprietor" 5.3% and "1-9" 10.8%).

Overall levels of E-Commerce activity in Wales were disappointing (Figure 7). In total, 5.2% of all enterprises identified over 50% of their turnover was achieved through E-Commerce trading. The "50-249" SME size category identified higher levels of E-Commerce trading activity with 22.2%

Figure 7. Chart by percentage of e-commerce market in Wales cross tabulated by SME size classification

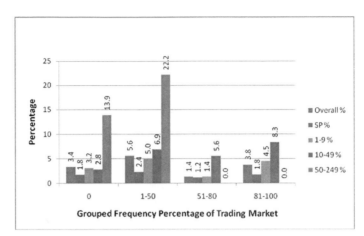

identifying that up to 50% of their sales occurred through electronic trading. The "50-249" SME category identified no enterprises achieving E-Commerce sales above 51% of their total turnover. The smaller SME categories ("Sole-Proprietor" 3%, "1-9" 5.9% and "10-49" 11%) did suggesting pockets of effective E-Commerce utilisation in local trading markets Moreover 8.3% of the "10-49" grouping identified that between 81-100% of their trade occurred within Wales.

In the UK market (see Figure 8) overall there was a limited utilisation of E-Commerce trading which contributed to increased turnover (14%). As within the Wales trading market, there was greater awareness of the E-Commerce trading position in the larger sized SME categories ("10-49"= 20.8% and "50-249"= 36.1%) in comparison to the smaller sized enterprises ("Sole-Proprietor" =7.1% and "1-9" =14%). Even within those enterprises which were able to identify their level of their E-Commerce activity in the previous trading year, a proportion of all size categories recorded a zero level of trade (e.g. "50-249"= 11.1%). In terms of E-Commerce trade in the UK outside Wales, 2.4% of all enterprises identified that over 50% of their trading turnover was achieved through E-Commerce trading activity. The "50-249" SME size category was able to identify higher levels

of E-Commerce trading activity with 11.1% of this category identifying that between 51-100% of their sales were achieved through this market. Such a performance was markedly inferior in the "Sole-Proprietor" (1.2%), "1-9" (2.3%) and "10-49" (1.4%) sectors.

Figure 9 displays the E-Commerce trading performance by SME size classification within the European Union market. In the European union market there was a limited overall utilisation of E-Commerce (14%) with higher levels of utilisation in the larger SME size categories ("10-49"= 19.4% and "50-249"= 36.1%) in contrast to the smaller SME classifications ("Sole-Proprietor" =7.1% and "1-9" =14%). However, even within those enterprises which were able to identify their level of their E-Commerce trading activity in the previous trading year, a proportion of all size categories (10.2%) recorded a zero level of trade overall ("Sole-Proprietor" 4.7%, "1-9" 12.6%). "10-49"= 12.5% and "50-249"= 16.7%). This result suggests a previous level of trade has occurred within a European market which has not been sustained. In terms of intensity levels of E-Commerce trade within the European union, activity was minimal, with 0.8% of all SMEs identified that over 50% of their trading turnover was achieved through E-Commerce utilisation. Only the "50-249" SME

Figure 8. Chart by percentage of e-commerce market in UK cross tabulated by SME size classification

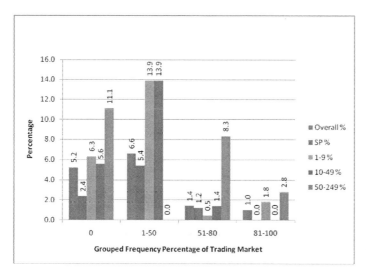

size classification was able to identify any notable levels of E-Commerce trading activity with over 5% of this category identifying over 51% of their sales achieved through this market.

Figure 10 displays the E-Commerce trading performance cross tabulated by SME size classification within a global market. In this trading market (Figure 10) there was a limited overall utilisation of E-Commerce (14%) with higher levels of utilisation in the larger size categories ("10-49"= 19.4% and "50-249"= 36.1%) in contrast to the smaller SME classifications ("Sole-

Figure 9. Chart by percentage of e-commerce market in European Union cross tabulated by SME size classification

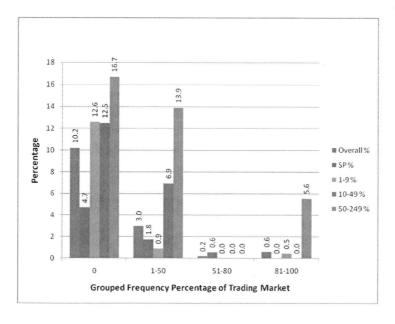

Figure 10. Chart by percentage of e-commerce market in UK cross tabulated by SME size classification

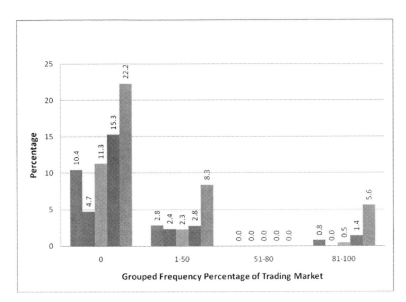

Proprietor" =7.1% and "1-9" =14%). However, even within those enterprises which were able to identify their level of their E-Commerce activity in the previous trading year, a proportion of all size categories recorded a zero level of trade overall 10% ("Sole-Proprietor" 4.7%, "1-9" 11.3%, "10-49" 15.3% and "50-249" 22.2%). This again suggests a previous level of trade has occurred within a global market which has not been retained. Intensity levels of global trade were minimal, with 0.8% of all SMEs identified that over 50% of their trading turnover was achieved through E-Commerce trading. Only the "50-249" SME size classification was able to identify any notable levels of E-Commerce trading activity with over 5.6% of this category identifying over 51% of their sales achieved through this market.

Further analysis of means supported this statistic, with the Welsh E-Commerce trading market achieving an average rating of 43%. Thereafter there was noticeably less reliance on the UK outside Wales (28%), European Union outside the UK (9%) and global trade (11%). Furthermore, these groupings reported notable variances within standard deviations (20% plus), suggesting wide

extremes of E-Commerce utilisation between individual enterprises. A three-way cross-tabulation of SME size classification against website cost and income revealed minimal data of significance. It was apparent that website investment of over £5,000 only created an income in excess of £5,000 in three instances (two "50-249" and one "1-9" sized enterprise). A website investment of up to £100 generated an income of over £5,000 for six enterprises (two "Sole-Proprietor", two "1-9", one "10-49" and one "50-249"), thus providing limited evidence of the potential of E-Commerce to enhance revenue. These findings also reflect the high levels of ignorance, limited understanding, evaluation and ambition towards adoption of E-Commerce trade within SMEs' existing business practices.

DISCUSSION

The global credit crunch has increased pressure on the SME community to compete and survive in times of a global economic depression. Effective E-Commerce deployment provides opportunity to achieve increased, profitability and operational efficiency (Piris, Fitzgerald & Serrano, 2004). The literature review identified the necessity to explore SME E-Commerce trading markets and practices. The analysis of SME traditional trading behaviour as opposed to E-Commerce activity provides some noteworthy conclusions.

The majority of traditional trading patterns of the SME community within Wales were dominated by excessive reliance on local and regional trading markets, with minimal exploitation of the UK, EU and global markets. This trend was particularly prevalent within "Sole-Proprietor" and "1-9" SME micro-sized classifications. Within industry sectors, the more traditional primary and manufacturing type industries, such as Construction and Agriculture/Forestry/Fishing, demonstrated the weakest performance in terms of exploitation of markets outside Wales. Only the Communications/Computing sector was able to demonstrate any noticeable activity within EU and global markets. In addition, the largest SME size classifications demonstrated higher level of trade within European and global markets, although this was very much the exception rather than the rule.

The E-Commerce trading performance of surveyed SMEs in Wales was extremely disappointing with minimal levels of exploitation especially within the context of UK national, European and global markets. E-Commerce sales intensity (Table 5) generally declined the larger

Table 5. SME e-commerce trading market intensity by region achieving greater than 51% of sales

Trading Region	Overall %	SP %	1-9 %	10-49%	50-249%
Wales	5.2	2.9	5.9	11.1	0.0
UK	2.4	1.2	2.3	1.4	11.1
European Union	0.8	0.6	0.5	0.0	5.6
Global	0.8	0.0	0.5	1.4	5.6

** Table denotes proportion of SMEs achieving greater than 51% of their total sales turnover in specified trading markets

the market. These results suggest a limited Owner/Manager awareness towards the technology and high level of ignorance regarding the potential that E-Commerce offers the SME.

It was apparent that SMEs trading behaviour was dominated by excessive reliance on local and regional markets with minimal exploitation of UK national, European and global markets in either traditional or E-Commerce trading behaviour. This was disappointing to note, suggesting that the majority of SME Owner/Managers were not deploying E-Commerce strategically but instead were mirroring their selling behaviour in traditional markets although on a significantly smaller scale. It must be noted that there was limited E-Commerce trading activity within the surveyed population. Overall only 14.2% of the survey population were able to confirm a level of E-Commerce trading activity whilst a further 15.8% were unaware of their level of E-Commerce trade. Thus, the evidence from the survey highlighted that Welsh SME deployment of E-Commerce trading practices remained embryonic, with the majority not participating in sophisticated, large scale trading. Lewis and Cockrill (2002) noted a similar trend in a prior study of E-Commerce trading practices in Welsh SMEs.

The survey response produced limited examples of innovative SMEs that were evolving their business model as a consequence of E-Commerce trading practices as similarly reported within Loebbecke & Schäfer, (2001). The norm in the sector suggested E-Commerce trading was regarded as an additional practice to enhance business turnover at a minimal risk which typically occurred in conjunction with existing traditional trading practices. Thus SME Owner/Managers typically looked to further penetrate local and national trading markets through E-Commerce as opposed to seeking new national, European and global market opportunities. Prior surveys in Wales (NOP, 2000; eCIC 2005) have suggested similar trends. This suggests a limited understanding and awareness of E-Commerce trading activity amongst the SME

Owner/Manager community in Wales. Indeed a high proportion of Owner/Managers were unaware regarding the level and locality, if any, of E-Commerce trading activity.

It was also apparent that the smaller sized SME classifications ("Sole-Proprietor" and "1-9") were more susceptible to trading in local markets for both traditional and E-Commerce transactions as opposed to UK, European Union and global markets. This confirms the extant literature suggesting that smaller sized SMEs are more growth adverse with a tendency to remain as small lifestyle enterprises (Hisrich & Peters, 1998; Jones, 2004). Perhaps unsurprisingly, the primary and manufacturing industries such as Construction and Agriculture/Forestry/Fishing demonstrated less involvement in trading markets outside Wales in both traditional and E-Commerce trading markets.

CONCLUSION

In Wales and the rest of the UK, the SME sector continues to struggle with ongoing business closures and redundancies. It is evident that there is a need to inform and educate the Welsh SME Owner/Manager community in terms of the business benefits offered by successful E-Commerce deployment as existing practices are deficient and potential new trading markets ignored. The process of E-Commerce trading in an SME must be a strategically managed process by the Owner/Manager and not an extension of existing trading activity otherwise the potential of the new media is not being maximised. Key actions would need to be undertaken through a cohesive inclusive manner through the coordinated action of policy makers throughout Wales as represented in Figure 1

Within this model, the WAG would coordinate the actions of key groups such as Higher and Further Education (FE) providers, trade bodies and enterprise support agencies. In addition, the WAG must create effective legislation and policy to encourage new business start-up, entrepreneurial growth and an effective infrastructure for business development. This role will involve liaison and effective management with the media, the IT/IS industry and telecommunications industry. The WAG needs to use the media to inform and highlight best practice within the SME sector, which should encourage the business and start-up community in the use of E-Commerce. Furthermore, the WAG must ensure a consistent and long term vision of network support agencies with no overlap in provision.

The Higher Education (HE) and FE sectors must be at the forefront of the WAG policy to develop high class graduates with the appropriate range of knowledge and skills to support and develop a knowledge economy underpinned by E-Commerce technology. This would involve the HE sector producing undergraduate and postgraduate graduates in a variety of disciplines, including business, computing, engineering, technology, arts and the media that would benefit the economy through the creation of SMEs which exploit niche markets and enable the development of a knowledge economy. Similarly, the FE community must encourage students to attain a range of vocational skills and knowledge through the completion of relevant qualifications such as trades which any economy requires. Within both the HE and FE sectors, there is a need to ensure students acquire an effective range of IT/IS skills and knowledge of the business start-up process and the concept of entrepreneurialism. If this is achieved, then the educational sector will be producing a pool of expertise that has the potential to undertake the business start-up process or work within a small business community. To ensure effective utilisation of new technology within the new business start-ups, the telecommunications and IT/IS industry must liaise and work in close partnership with the WAG, HE, FE bodies and trade associations. This process will encourage the creation of new and appropriate businesses by individuals with the appropriate skills and knowledge to be

Figure 11. The support framework required for an effective SME e-commerce community

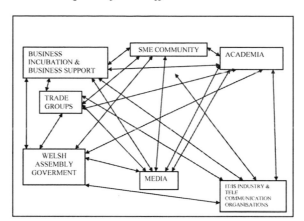

successful entrepreneurs and identify, understand and utilise E-Commerce effectively.

In addition, the WAG must encourage the existing SME community to become more efficient and to potentially grow through the usage of E-Commerce technologies. This will again involve the presence of a supporting legislature and the coordination of key bodies such as enterprise support agencies, trade groups, educational providers and the use of the media to enhance knowledge and understanding. There is a need for support groups such as enterprise support agencies and networks to liaise with the SME community on a micro level to understand the individual adoption position. It is critical that the WAG encourages the SME community to adopt new E-Commerce technologies such as customer relationship management software as they become more affordable and available, as they could provide the enabler to increased organisational efficiency and growth. Similarly, the existing entrepreneurial community requires ongoing and coordinated support and encouragement from all the key bodies identified in Figure 1. The existing SME community requires effective support from all the identified bodies to encourage sustainability, increased efficiency and business growth through the effective utilisation of E-Commerce.

SME Owner/Managers require ongoing education and information on the benefits of E-Commerce regarding increased efficiency, effectiveness and sustainability to encourage adoption and ongoing usage. Such education is the responsibility of the WAG, to enable coordinated actions of academic institutions, trade groups and business support agencies to provide suitable and effective training. WAG must also encourage the IT/IS and telecommunications providers to work closely with academic and business communities, to ensure that their services and products meets the requirements of the SME sector.

In conclusion, to ensure the further adoption of E-Commerce within the SME sector, it is critical that key groups encourage long term usage by enhancing Owner/Manager knowledge and understanding of the technology and its benefits. Within the context of Wales, this would involve the WAG and academia taking a central role in encouraging and monitoring participation. In addition, the media must play a role in the positive portrayal of E-business usage. The telecommunication industry must insure that a robust IS/IT infrastructure is provided that is accessible and affordable for the SME community. The activities of trade organisations, business networks and professional bodies must support and underpin all these actions. Reliance on short-termism adoption strategies, including fixed term funded European projects, must be avoided. The critical success factor remains the education of the SME Owner/

Managers to ensure that they acquire the relevant knowledge, understanding to develop long term strategic management and evaluation skills of their key business process including E-Commerce.

FURTHER RESEARCH

Whilst the results of the study are representative of the Welsh SME population further research is required to investigate whether they are generalisable to other regions of the UK or particular to that area. The Welsh SME community's use of E-Commerce undoubtedly suffers from its higher proportion of smaller sized enterprises and the diverse nature of its economic trading activity. Moreover, further research is required to explore and understand the attitudes of Owner/Managers towards E-Commerce adoption.

REFERENCES

Al-Qirim, N. (2003). A framework for electronic commerce research in small to medium-sized enterprises. In: N. Al-Qirim, N. (Ed.), *Electronic commerce in small to medium-sized enterprises: Frameworks, issues and implications* (pp. 1-16). Hershey, PA: IGI Global Publishing.

Baldwin, A., Lymer, A., & Johnson, R. (2000). Business impacts of the Internet for small and medium-sized enterprises. In B. Hunt & S. Barnes (Eds.), *E-commerce and v-business: business models for global success* (pp. 103-120). Oxford, UK: Butterworth-Heinemann.

Beynon-Davies, P., Evans, S., & Owens, I. (2000). Electronic commerce and small and medium enterprises. In *Proceedings of 10th Business Information Technology Conference (BIT)*, Manchester Metropolitan University, UK.

Blackburn, R., & Athayde, R. (2000). Making the connection: the effectiveness of Internet training in small businesses. *Education and Training, 42*(4/5), 289–299. doi:10.1108/00400910010373723

Blili, S., & Raymond, L. (1993). Information technology: Threats and opportunities for small and medium sized enterprises. *International Journal of Information Management, 13*(6), 439–448. doi:10.1016/0268-4012(93)90060-H

Dillman, D. (2000) *Mail and Internet surveys: The tailored design method* (2nd Ed.). New York: John Wiley and Sons.

DTI. (2004). *Business in the information age, international benchmarking study 2004.* A report prepared by Booz, Allen, Hamilton. eCIC (2005). *eCommerce in Welsh SMEs: The State of the Nation report 2005/6.* eCommerce Innovation Centre, Cardiff Business School, Cardiff University.

Field, A. (2005) *Discovering Statistics Using SPSS* (2nd Ed.). London: Sage Publications.

Fielden, S., Davidson, M., & Makin, P. (2000). Barriers encountered during micro and small business start-up in North West England. *Journal of Small Business and Enterprise Development, 7*(4), 295–304. doi:10.1108/EUM0000000006852

Fillis, I., & Wagner, B. (2005). E-Business Development. *International Small Business Journal, 23*(6), 603–634. doi:10.1177/0266242605057655

Fink, D., & Disterer, G. (2006). International case studies – To what extent is ICT infused into the operations of SMEs? *Journal of Enterprise Information Management, 19*(6), 608–624. doi:10.1108/17410390610708490

Galloway, L., & Mochrie, R. (2005). The use of ICT in rural firms: a policy orientated literature review. *Info, 7*(3), 33–46. doi:10.1108/14636690510596784

Gibbs, J., & Kraemer, K. (2004). A Cross-country investigation of the determinants of scope of E-Commerce use: an institutional approach. *Electronic Markets, 14*(2), 124–137. doi:10.1080/10 1967804 10001675077

Gray, C. (2004a). Entrepreneurship: Links between growth, ICT-adoption and innovation. In *Proceedings of the 27th ISBA Conference*, Newcastle, Gateshead.

Gray, C., & Lawless, N. (2000). Innovations in the distance development of SME management. *European Journal of Open and Distance Learning*. Retrieved May 16, 2002, from http://www1.nks.no/eurodl/shoen/Gray.html

Hay, M., & Kamshad, K. (1994). Small firm growth: intentions, implementation and impediments. *Business Strategy Review, 5*(3), 49–68. doi:10.1111/j.1467-8616.1994.tb00166.x

Hisrich, R., & Peters, M. (1998). *Entrepreneurship* (4th Ed.). Boston: McGraw Hill.

Iacovou, C., Benbasat, I., & Dexter, A. (1995). Electronic data interchange and small organisations: Adoption and impact of technology. *MIS Quarterly, 19*(4), 465–485. doi:10.2307/249629

Jobber, D. (1991). Choosing a survey method in management research. In N.G. Smith, & P. Dainty (Eds.), *The management research handbook* (pp. 174-179). London: Routledge.

Jones, J. (2004). Training and development, and business growth: A study of Australian manufacturing small-medium sized enterprises. *Asia Pacific Journal of Human Resources, 42*(1), 96–121. doi:10.1177/1038411104041535

Jones, P., Beynon-Davies, P., & Muir, E. (2003). E-business barriers within the SME sector. *The Journal of Systems and Information Technology, 7*(1), 1–26.

Jones-Evans, D. (2001). Creating an entrepreneurial Wales – Growing our indigenous enterprises. *The Gregynog papers, Institute of Welsh Affairs, 3*(1). Cardiff: Welsh Academic Press.

Kalakota, R., & Whinston, A. (1996). *Frontiers of electronic commerce*. London: Addison-Wesley.

Koh, S., & Maguire, S. (2004). Identifying the adoption of e-business and knowledge management within SMEs. *Journal of Small Business and Enterprise Development, 11*(3), 338–348. doi:10.1108/14626000410551591

Lau, G. T., & Voon, J. (2004). Factors affecting the adopting of electronic commerce among small and medium enterprises in Singapore. *Journal of Asian Business., 20*(1), 1–26.

Lederer, A., & Sethi, A. (1988). The implementation of strategic information systems planning methodologies. *MIS Quarterly, 12*(3), 445–461. doi:10.2307/249212

Levy, M., Powell, P., & Worrall, L. (2005). Strategic intent and e-business in SMEs: Enablers and inhibitors. *Information Resources Management Journal, 18*(4), 1–20.

Lockett, N., & Brown, D. (2003b). *The investigation of e-business engagement by SMEs with reference to strategic networks and aggregation: The dairy farming industry*. Lancaster University Management School Working Paper, 19.

Love, P., Irani, Z., Standing, C., Lin, C., & Burn, J. (2005). The enigma of evaluation: benefits, costs and risks of IT in Australian small-medium-sized enterprises. *Information & Management, 42*(7), 947–964. doi:10.1016/j.im.2004.10.004

Mitchell, S., & Clark, D. (1999). Business adoption of information and communications technologies in the two tier rural economy: some evidence from South Midlands. *Journal of Rural Studies, 15*(4), 447–455. doi:10.1016/S0743-0167(99)00012-1

Mustaffa, S., & Beaumont, N. (2002). The Effect of Electronic Commerce on Small Australian Enterprises. *Technovation, 24*(2), 85–95. doi:10.1016/S0166-4972(02)00039-1

National Economic Development Strategy (NEDS). (2001). *A Winning Wales – the National Economic Development strategy of the Welsh Assembly Government.* Retrieved December 10, 2005, from http://www.wales.gov.uk/themes-budgetandstrategic/content/neds/awinningwales-0302-e.pdf

NOP. (2000). *Small Business in Wales – An NOP study in the ICT and advice needs of SMEs based on their market orientation and attitude towards growth.* NOP research group.

Palvia, P., & Palvia, S. (1999). An examination of the IT satisfaction of small-business users. *Information & Management, 35*(3), 127–137. doi:10.1016/S0378-7206(98)00086-X

Pavic, S., Koh, S., Simpson, M., & Padmore, J. (2007). Could e-business create a competitive advantage in UK SMEs? *Benchmarking: An International Journal, 14*(3), 320–351. doi:10.1108/14635770710753112

Piris, L., Fitzgerald, G., & Serrano, A. (2004). Strategic motivators and expected benefits from E-Commerce in traditional organisations. *International Journal of Information Management, 24*(6), 489–506. doi:10.1016/j.ijinfomgt.2004.08.008

Pollard, C., & Hayne, S. (1998). The changing face of information systems issues in small firms. *International Small Business Journal, 16*(3), 70–87. doi:10.1177/0266242698163004

Ramsey, E., Ibbotson, P., Bell, J., & Gray, B. (2003). E-opportunities of service sector SMEs an Irish cross border study. *Journal of Small Business and Enterprise Development, 10*(3), 250–264. doi:10.1108/14626000310489709

Remenyi, D., Williams, B., Money, A., & Swartz, E. (1998). *Doing research in business and management – An introduction to process and method.* London: Sage Publications.

Schneider, G., & Perry, J. (2001). *Electronic commerce* (2nd Ed.). Andover: Thomson.

Simmons, G., Armstrong, G., & Durkin, M. (2008). A conceptualisation of the determinants of small business Website adoption. *International Small Business Journal, 26*(3), 351–389. doi:10.1177/0266242608088743

Small Business Service (SBS). (2005a). *SME statistics 2004 UK.* Retrieved October 16, 2005, from http://www.sbs.gov.uk/SBS_Gov_files/researchandstats/SMEStatsUK2004.xls.

Sterrett, C., & Shah, A. (1998). Going global on the information super highway. *S.A.M. Advanced Management Journal, Winter, 63*(1), 43-47.

Stockdale, R., & Standing, C. (2004). Benefit and barriers of electronic marketplace participation: an SME perspective. *The Journal of Enterprise Information Management, 17*(4), 301–311. doi:10.1108/17410390410548715

Turban, E., Lee, J., King, D., & Chung, H. (2000). *Electronic commerce: A managerial perspective.* Upper Saddle River, NJ: Prentice-Hall, Inc.

Welsh Assembly Government (WAG). (2003). *Wales for innovation – The Welsh assembly government's action plan for innovation.* Retrieved February 5, 2006, from http://www.wda.co.uk/resources/action-e.pdf

Welsh Assembly Government (WAG). (2005). *Wales: A vibrant economy, the Welsh assembly government's strategic framework for economic development.* Consultation Document, November. Retrieved December 10, 2005, from http://www.wales.gov.uk/subitradeindustry/content/wave/wave-report-e.pdf

Welsh Economic Research Unit (WERU). (2005). *The Welsh economy*. Retrieved October 17, 2005, from http://www.weru.org.uk/economy.html

Zalud, B. (1999). E-commerce obstacles, solutions for small businesses. *Security Distributing and Marketing, January*.

Section 2
E–Commerce and Small Business in Different Countries and Regions

Chapter 3
E-Crime and Non-Compliance with Government Regulations on E-Commerce:
Barriers to E-Commerce Optimization in South African SMEs

M.E. Kyobe
University of Cape Town, South Africa

ABSTRACT

E-commerce is critical to national development. Small and Medium sized organizations (SMEs) are encouraged to adopt it to address poverty, improve competitiveness and productivity. However, the escalation in electronic crime (e-crime) and lack of compliance with e-commerce regulations threaten e-commerce success in South Africa. While many strategies for improving e-commerce have been suggested, the focus has mainly been on economic and technological factors and less on human and social aspects such as compliance behaviors. This has resulted in the development of e-commerce systems that do not incorporate regulatory requirements. Consequently, the level of exposure to cyber-risks and legal liabilities has increased and SME market competitiveness compromised (Kyobe, 2009). This chapter examines the factors influencing compliance with e-commerce regulations and e-security requirements and how these impact on e-commerce optimization in South African SMEs. It also provides some useful frameworks and checklists SME managers can use to evaluate their compliance behaviors and security practices in order to make improvement to their e-commerce activities.

INTRODUCTION

E-commerce plays a key role in the development of nations. Many Small and Medium sized organizations (SMEs) are encouraged by governments and economist to adopt it in order to address pov-erty, improve market competitiveness and increase productivity. In terms of South Africa's National Small Business Act 102 of 1996 (amended 2003), Small, Micro and Medium Enterprises (SMMEs) are organizations with less or equal to 200 full-time equivalent of paid employees (The Presidency, 2003).

DOI: 10.4018/978-1-60566-998-4.ch003

While e-commerce can provide such benefits, the escalating rate of electronic crime (e-crime) Upfold and Sewry (2005) and lack of compliance with government regulations on e-commerce have resulted in high levels of insecurity and lack of trust in digital transactions. These problems present major barriers to e-commerce optimization in many SMEs today (Sengupta, Mazumdar & Barik, 2005; Seldon, 2004; Sunday Times, 2002). "E-crime" is defined here as the offences where a computer or other Information Technologies are used as a tool to commit an offence and "Compliance" as the state of being in accordance with established rules, guidelines or regulations.

Strategies for enhancing e-commerce effectiveness have traditionally been dominated by economic (e.g. cost reduction, revenue increase and pricing) and technological considerations (e.g. visibility, functionality, web design, etc). Social and human aspects of ecommerce have received limited attention (Keen et al., 2004; Meziane & Kasiran, 2008). In the SME field, for instance, there have been limited scientific studies into compliance behaviors and security attitudes of business managers and how these affect e-commerce utilization. Effort to improve e-commerce has often been frustrated by lack of regulatory compliance and poor security. This leads to system implementations that do not incorporate regulatory requirements, increased cyber-attacks on organizations and their business partners, increased liabilities and compromised market positions (Kyobe, 2009).

Understanding the factors that influence compliance with e-commerce regulations and e-security (defined here as the process of ensuring the confidentiality, integrity, and availability of electronic information and protecting it against malicious attacks), is crucial to ensuring effective utilization of e-commerce in SMEs. Research conducted in the field of entrepreneurship confirms that personal characteristics or behaviors of managers moderate the process of e-commerce

adoption and utilization (Wejnert, 2002). In their study of SME regulatory compliance in South Africa, SBP (2003) also maintains that factors influencing compliance with regulations must be understood clearly if effective solutions to SME challenges are to be provided

The objectives of this chapter is to create better understanding of the factors influencing compliance with e-commerce regulations and e-security and show how these have impacted on e-commerce optimization in South African SMEs. It also aims to provide frameworks and checklists SME managers can use to evaluate their compliance and security behaviors; identify the impediments to e-commerce; and make appropriate improvements to e-commerce activities.

The chapter begins with a brief introduction to e-commerce in South Africa (SA). This is followed by a review of e-commerce related regulations and reported incidents of non-compliance with these regulations in SA. Theories explaining why organizations and individuals fail to comply with regulations and good practices are presented, and the importance of identifying and evaluating compliance and security impediments in SMEs shown. Two evaluation frameworks and checklists SME managers can use to determine their compliance and security behaviors are then presented. Finally, results of studies conducted to validate these frameworks are discussed and useful recommendations made at the end of this chapter.

BACKGROUND: E-COMMERCE IN SOUTH AFRICA

Internet based connections began in late 80's in South Africa (Zantsi & Eloff, 2003). The country is still lagging the world in internet usage with 9.02 percent of the population having internet access (Jourbert & Van Belle, 2004). On-line retail in South Africa however grew by 20 percent in 2005, down from 25 percent in 2004 (Ibls, 2007). Total spending on online goods however increased to R5.14m in 2005 and was expected to increase by 20 percent in the following years (Ibls, 2007).

SME and e-commerce sector have experienced grown rapid over the last five years, thanks to better Telkom communication links, government effort, electronic and m-banking (Warden & Motjolopane, 2007). Purchases done online usually include groceries, apparel, books, flowers, gifts, food, beverage, and online airline tickets. The Airline Company Kulula.com appears to be the largest revenue-generating B2C business in South Africa, while 1 time Airline claims 75% of online travel transactions (Warden & Remenyi, 2005).

Several barriers to e-commerce adoption have also been identified. These include negative attitudes, lack of knowledge, resistance to change, lack of management commitment, gaps between online shopping and the physical experience, ability to judge quality and ease of buying locally, lack of privacy, lack of security and fraud (Jourbert & Van Belle, 2004; Warden & Remenyi, 2005), and non-compliance with the regulations (Kyobe, 2009).

Lack of security, fraud and non-compliance with regulations are causing much concern today (Computer Business Review, 2004; Elc, 2003). Recent reports show, for instance, that there were 2388 incidents of identity theft in the first quarter of 2008 alone and that the SA government was defrauded of R199 million through electronic crime in the same year (PublicTechnology.net, 2008; Engelbrecht, 2008). These incidents erode customer confidence in e-commerce in South Africa and have lead to the establishment of regulatory measures by the government.

E-Commerce Regulation in South Africa

In order to address e-crime challenges; the imbalances of the past; the inconsistencies in South African law with international best practices; and to increase consumer trust in e-commerce, several regulations and legislations affecting the use of computers and electronics facilities have been introduced in South Africa. These include: the new Company bill; FICA; The Electronic Communication & Transactions (ECT Act, 2002); and the Value Added Tax (VAT Act), 1991 (amended 2008).

In this chapter we will examine some crucial provisions of the ECT and VAT Acts of South Africa and show how non-compliance with these Acts has impacted on e-commerce in South African SMEs. These South African law chapters (i.e. III, VII, VIII and XIII) stipulate some crucial requirements for conducting business on-line and provide useful guidance on dealing with several compliance and security issues raised in SME literature recently (Elc, 2003; Mullon, 2006; Upfold and Sewry, 2005).

The Electronic Communication and Transactions (ECT Act, 2002) of South Africa

The ECT Act of 2002 is a wide legislation dealing with any form of electronic communication (e.g. by email, the internet or SMS) and other issues relating to cyber inspectors, service provider liability and domain names (Michalson et al, 2005, p.3). It aims to provide for the facilitation and regulation of electronic communication and transactions; provide for the development of a national e-strategy; promote universal access to electronic communications and transactions and the use of electronic transactions by SMMEs; provide for human resource development in electronic transactions; prevent abuse of information systems; encourage the use of e-government services and other related matters. According to Michalson et al (2005) one does not have to comply with the entire Act but with sections relating to incorporation by reference; electronic signatures; electronic evidence; production of information; record retention; automated transactions; website architecture and content; contract formation; cryptography service providers; secure payment systems; SPAM and protection of critical data (i.e. South African law chapters III, V, VI, VII, IX, XII and XIII). A person who contravenes these sections would be guilty of an offence and liable on conviction to a fine or imprisonment.

As indicated above, this chapter focuses on South African law chapters III, VII, VIII and XIII and some of the requirements of the VAT Act.

Electronic Evidence and Record Retention (Part 1, Chapter III of the ECT Act)

This section of the Act provides legal recognition of electronic documents (e.g., contracts, typed or an image of hand written signature, etc) just like paper based counterparts. Special types of electronic signatures would however be required in situations where the law requires a signature. Minimum requirements for transactions on the web where signatures are not required by parties may be an expression of intent e.g. (by clicking on an "I agree" button). The Act also permits the retention of electronic data for statutory record retention purposes. It makes provision for integrity as key to ensuring proper evidentiary weight of electronic evidence. Records can be kept in electronic form provided a reliable and auditable process is implemented (Michalson, 2005, p.3). Contracts can now be performed by machines functioning as electronic agents for parties to an electronic transaction. This section also makes presumptions as to the time and place of receipt of information.

However organizations need to take some precautions when communicating electronically. For instance, by merely showing intent in an email, a company can be legally bound by such intent. It is also important to verify the validity of the certificate utilized to digitally sign (e.g. email orders) and to exercise caution when forming on-line contract. Some compliance problems with this provision have been reported in South Africa.

Mybroadband (2008) report that in a study conducted by Mimecast SA which involved over 300 IT professionals, over 80% of the businesses were unable to prevent confidential information leaving their premises via email, 46% left employees to store and delete their emails and 68% were unable to present a full forensic audit and repudiation data for an email sent three years ago.

Consumer Protection/ Website Content (Chapter VII of the ECT Act of South Africa)

One major reason for the slowdown in e-commerce has been lack of trust. To build this trust, customers need to have confidence in the accuracy of representations made regarding the goods and services offered online. There are various statutes providing consumer protection in South Africa – Usury Act, the Credit Agreements Act, the competition Act, the consumer affairs (unfair business practices) Act and the ECT Act.

The consumer protection section of the ECT Act requires that the following information be provided on the website: the price of products, contact details and the right to withdraw from an electronic transaction before completion (Michalson et al (2005, p. 2). In certain circumstances, consumers are also entitled to a "cooling off" period within which they may correct mistakes or withdraw from the transaction without incurring any penalty. The Act also places on businesses trading on-line the responsibility of ensuring that sufficiently secure payment systems are used. If a payment system is breached, the supplier must reimburse the consumer for any loss suffered.

Consumers also have a right not to be bound to unsolicited communications (SPAM) offering goods and services. Under section 45, a merchant who sends unsolicited electronic communication must provide the consumer with the option to cancel its subscription to the mailing list and must identify the source from which that merchant obtained such customer's personal information.

It is an offense to continue to send unsolicited communications after having been advised that they are not welcome. No agreement may be concluded if the consumer has not responded to the SPAM.

E-Billing/E-Invoicing Regulation and Issues Involved

As indicated in the previous section, the introduction of the concept of functional equivalent of paper and data messages into the South African law made e-invoicing and other electronic documents part of the financial and legal practices of an organization. Further e-invoicing requirements are set out in the Value Added Tax (VAT) Act of 1991 (ruling 28/3/1-25) of South African Revenue Services (SARS) and other publications (Elc, 2003). These rules also facilitate effective auditing of electronic invoices and ensure that there is conformity between paper and electronic invoices.

According to Elc (2003, p.1), there are two important issues raised in the VAT Act of South Africa. The first one concerns the validity of the electronic delivery process as a replacement for the traditional print and post process. While an invoice must be presented as a 'document', it does not necessarily have to be physically printed onto paper. An electronic invoice is a valid document.

The second issue relates to the format of this electronic invoice document. According to SARS, a legal electronic tax invoice should meet the following requirements: First, it must contain the following mandatory information: the name, address and VAT registration number of the biller; the name and address of the customer; a unique invoice number; the date; the words "tax invoice"; a description of the goods/services supplied; the number of units, mass or volume of goods; the amount due and the VAT charged; or a statement that VAT is included in the price, as well as the rate of VAT charged. Similar requirements are

also stipulated for other documents (e.g. credit and debit notes).

The second requirement concerns the security of the electronic document in transit (between the sender and the recipient). In order to be valid, documents must be transmitted using encryption with a key length of at least 128-bits or contain an electronic signature, which means that the software used to create and send electronic invoices must have encryption capability. In addition, the recipient must have a means of decoding the document.

Thirdly, SARS requires that the recipient of an electronic bill must submit written confirmation (electronic or otherwise) that they will accept electronic invoices for the purposes of claiming VAT. A further requirement is that the electronic invoice be treated as the original (assuming no paper version), and that any copies printed by the recipient bear the words "copy tax invoice". The biller and the recipient are also required to retain the documents in a readable and encrypted format for a period of five years from the date of issue.

There are many indications that South African firms are not compliant with the consumer protection requirements of the regulations. Technews (2004) report that 81% of the websites surveyed did not have legal notices. Some had simply adopted notices and disclaimers from foreign websites which never addressed South African legal requirements. These have been attributed to high website development expenses, limited understanding of legal requirements and misinformation about legal compliance. Similar observations were made by Burrows (2004).

In their investigation of adherence to the internationally accepted privacy principles by the top 100 South African E-commerce sites, Jourbert & Van Belle (2004) also found that 42% of the websites did not comply with half of the provisions of the ECT Act. The websites were least compliant with those provisions that specify the manner and period within which consumers can access and maintain a full record of the transaction. Over 32% of the websites did not allow the consumer to withdraw from the transaction once payment details are submitted and there was lack of adequate communication to enable consumers to make informed decisions regarding potential purchases. Another serious problem on South African websites relates to security.

Personal Information and Privacy Protection (Chapter VIII of the ECT Act)

Privacy related complaints include those about unsolicited email, identity theft, harassing phone calls, and selling of data to third parties (Mithal, 2000). Privacy is regulated in South Africa by the constitution, common law and other regulations such as the regulation of interception of communication and provision of communication, and the ECT Act, 2002. The legislations that demand effective storage of email include the ECT Act, the regulation of interception of communications and provision of communications-related information Act (interception Act), the financial advisory and intermediary services (FAIS), national archives of South Africa Act and the companies Act. The King II report also requires companies to identify and mitigate data risk.

According to the ECT Act, 2002, personal information includes any information capable of identifying an individual such as information relating to race, gender, pregnancy, marital status, national, ethnic or social origin, color, sexual orientation, age, physical or mental health, well-being, etc (Michalson et al., 2005, p.2). The challenges involved in ensuring the protection of such information are vast and usually include the cost of storing millions of emails in a way that does not erode the integrity of the mail, the infrastructure to retrieve and archive the emails and the people to manage it all.

Section 51 of the ECT Act requires that collectors of such information must have the express written permission of the consumer for the collection, collation, processing or disclosure of any

personal information on that consumer. Information obtained must be used for the lawful purpose for which it was obtained and the collectors are expected to subscribe to a set of universally accepted data protection principles.

Joubert & Van Belle (2004) allege that Internet users in South Africa have limited knowledge of who else shares their personal information on the Web. They found that the top 100 South African economic sites had not implemented appropriate information protection principles. They also report that just under a quarter (24%) of sites that collect personal identifying information, say anything about what specific personal information is collected.

Illegal Activities and Offences (Cyber Crime – Chapter XIII of the Ect Act)

This chapter makes statutory provisions on cyber crime in South African jurisprudence. It introduces statutory criminal offenses relating to unauthorized access to data (e.g. through hacking), interception of data (e.g. tapping into data flows or denial of service attacks), interference with data (e.g. viruses) and computer related extortions, fraud and forgery. They also state that a person aiding those involved in these crimes will be guilty as an accessory. The Act prescribes the penalties for these offences.

On their part, however, SMEs have been criticized for shunning good security practices and often considering electronic crime to be an issue for large organizations only (Zorz, 2003; US-CERT, 2004; Kyobe, 2009). According to Allan et al (2003), the adoption of security technologies such as firewall, authentication systems and intrusion detection systems is not extensive among small firms. It is also widely reported that because of their false sense of security, small business managers are complacent about cyber-attacks and often shun good security systems and practices (BBC, 2002; Zorz, 2003). Management of security in e-commerce has also been complicated by the highly dynamic electronic environment and technologies. Furthermore, the security measures applied in these systems are increasingly visible to the customers (Barlette & Fomin, 2008). This means that customers are more and more aware of the effectiveness of their partners' security systems which may influence their choice of whom they deal with.

There is no doubt that non-compliance with the law and lack of good security practices impact on e-commerce activities in many organisations. If appropriate solutions to these problems are to be found, it is imperative that managers understand those specific factors causing these barriers in their organisation and deal with them. Theories provide insight into potential causes of problems. In the following section, the author will examine some of fundamental theories of compliance behaviors of organizations and individuals.

COMPLIANCE THEORIES AND STRATEGIES

Compliance is a state in which someone or something is in accordance with established guidelines, specifications, or legislation. Two fundamental theories of compliance examined in this section are: the rationalist model and normative model (Grossman et al., 2005).

The rationalist model posits that regulated individuals act rationally to maximize their economic self-interest (e.g., by calculating the costs and benefits involved). Small firms for instance evade tax because of heavy tax burdens (Mayne, 2006). There are also firms that deliberately decline to comply once they realize that the cost of potential penalties is much lower than that of compliance. In such a case, provision is made for potential liabilities. Proponents of the rationalist model emphasize enforcement and deterrence as measures to change the individual's economic perceptions.

However, enforcement of the law is difficult to effect in a digital environment where criminals cover their tracks or remain anonymous (Lynch, 2005). Cheating in online auctions (e.g. shill bidding), for instance, leaves no direct evidence of its occurrence to validate the facts (Jenamani, Zhong & Bhargava, 2007). In addition, the rationalist model does not consider social action based on values, beliefs or emotions. Value is restricted to utility measured in economic terms. Furthermore, the model assumes certainty in present and future evaluations of consequences. This may not always be true especially in the present environment characterized by rapid changes in demand, technology and legislations. This model also fails to explain the issue of conflict. While compliance is conceptualized as an economic transaction in which both parties benefit from the relationship, in reality there may be conflicts and resistance when one party gains from a transaction and the other does not (Coleman, Fararo & Zey, 1993).

The normative perspective on compliance held by the sociology literature is that laws that are developed and implemented fairly should be followed and that individuals and firms will comply if they believe the rules are legitimate and fairly applied (Tyler, 1990; Grossman et al., 2005). Research in psychology and sociology emphasizes the importance of cognitive and social learning processes (Kohlberg, 1969). Here compliance with rules is perceived to depend very much on the individual's capabilities and ability to address environmental influences. They maintain that non-compliance will occur mainly in situations where the regulated entity lacks capacity (e.g. knowledge of the rules, financial abilities and technological abilities) and commitment. Psychological and sociological theories therefore call for a more cooperative approach, increased dissemination of information, technological assistance and adequate inspections. This approach has recently been adopted by the South African Revenue Authority to encourage SMEs to pay taxes.

One major limitation of the normative model is that it implicates an environment where there is adequate information flow and interactions between stakeholders (e.g. owner, manager, employees, etc). This may not always be the case in smaller organizations.

Other Models and Strategies

Strategic management research also shows that structural and organizational components of the firm influence compliance behavior (Malloy, 2003; Henriques & Sadorsky, 1996). Large firms have many characteristics that encourage compliance (e.g. size, resources, skills, public image, etc) although greater coordination and monitoring costs may affect their ability to comply. On the other hand, small firms have limited capital to invest in up-to-date technology and often use cheaper alternatives e.g. pirate software which is insecure. Compliance can also be enforced through adoption of good practices, professional or international standards (Kalember, 2004; Mullon, 2006; Elc,2003).

Compliance can also be enforced through capacity building and use of technology. Usually regulated entities fail to comply because they lack awareness of the law and its implications, lack necessary skills and resources and technological capabilities (Upfold & Sewry, 2005; Allan et al., 2003). Technologies can facilitate planning, analysis, monitoring (e.g. automated audit processes). Modern applications such as Microsoft Exchange 2007 have tools and templates that could be used to draw contracts, archive e-mails, update documents and notices required for legal compliance. These cost less than the legal fees.

In summary, this review suggests that compliance with legislation is influenced by various factors. These include: economic factors (e.g. potential legal/illegal gains, cost of compliance); psychological factors (e.g. cognitive capabilities, learning, previous interactions, individual capabilities, ability to address environmental influences); sociological factors (e.g. what is perceived to be moral, fair or equitable, norms of the groups involved and trust); the industry (professional standards, ethics, good practice); technological factors (e.g. IT skills, IT resources, content and complexity of electronic information) and business related factors (such as type, size and location).

Managers need to identify these factors in order to build appropriate solutions to ecommerce challenges. Models available to guide this process are however not comprehensive enough to capture many of these factors. Researchers recommend that a comprehensive framework should be used in this investigation (Black, 2001; Brown, 1994). The author developed such framework and validated it in an empirical study as explained in the following section.

Assessment of Compliance Behaviors and E-Security Practices in SMEs

You cannot manage what you have not measured.

Researchers maintain that assessment or evaluation of business operations can enable effective control of projects, better change management, communication improvement, better resource allocation and utilisation, enhanced motivation and effective systems planning (Hedman & Borrell, 2005). Strassmann (1985: p.100) argues that you cannot tell whether you have improved something unless you measure or evaluate its performance. Citing the work of Remenyi (1991), Costello et al (2007) also contend that it is only through effective IS assessment that organizations can reach maturity in the use of their IS resources.

Since the crash of the Dot Coms, evaluation of e-commerce has become increasingly important. There are very few capital firms today willing to invest in e-commerce properties that cannot justify or show a well developed discipline for

Figure 1. Framework for measuring SME compliance with e-commerce regulations

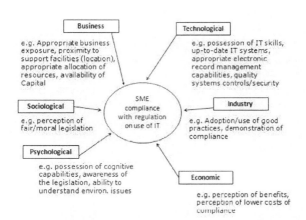

evaluating investments in e-commerce (Hahn & Kauffman, 2003). Porter (2001) maintains that no organization should undertake an ecommerce project without understanding the costs and performance issues involved. Roztocki & Weistroffer (2006) found that companies possessing reliable cost management systems such as Activity Based Costing (ABC) are less likely to make expensive mistakes when investing in IT and are better able to single out those IT projects which positively impact competitiveness. Furthermore, Onwubiko & Lenaghan (2007) also argue that swift management of threats and vulnerabilities requires better understanding of security issues, concepts and practices. Such understanding can assist SMEs in implementing the right mix of protection controls to mitigate threats and vulnerabilities.

It is therefore imperative that organizations conduct assessments of their e-commerce activities in order to identify and deal with potential impediments. However, this assessment should not only focus on economic and technological barriers (cost and risks, website design, infrastructure) as suggested above. There is need to examine as well social, human, psychological or cultural barriers to e-commerce. Weaknesses in human behaviors (e.g. non-compliance with regulations

and poor attitude towards security) often present serious barriers to e-commerce development and utilization in SMEs. Personal characteristics or behaviors of small business managers have been found to moderate the process of e-commerce adoption and utilization (Wejnert, 2002). The author argues that e-commerce in SMEs can be enhanced through understanding of compliance behaviors and attitude towards security, and how these impact on organizations and their business partners. With this understanding, it can then be possible to minimize e-commerce risks; costs; and potential legal liabilities and build the much needed customer confidence and trust. Two frameworks are therefore proposed in the following section to guide this assessment. These frameworks were validated in two separate empirical studies conducted in South Africa (Kyobe, 2008; 2009) and are presented below.

Framework for Measuring Compliance with E-Commerce Regulation

The framework in Figure 1 represents various factors influencing regulatory compliance in an organization. These factors are used to determine the extent to which an SME is compliant with e-commerce regulations.

Table 1. Checklist 1 - List of items used to measure compliance

i. Awareness of the electronic communication and transaction (ECT Act, 2002)
ii. Adherence to professional standards such as 1SO 17799, SANS 15801 (or possess a certificate of good practice).
iii. Perception of the costs of compliance (e.g. is it high or low?)
iv. Demonstration of compliance e.g. through security audits
v. Availability of a specific person responsible for ensuring compliance in the organization (the new South African company bill requires that companies must have a compliance person. The presence of such a person also ensures that compliance is taken more seriously)
vi. Possession of policies on compliance and record retention. (e.g. policy issues relating to e-invoicing, electronic storage of invoices, cross-border communication, signature policy, etc)
vii. Possession of an automated compliance process (e.g. does the organization use automated application tools to ease or enhance the compliance process?)
viii. Possession of adequate system security measures or controls
ix. Conducting regular backup and archiving of emails, e-invoices, etc
x. Participation in compliance and security education or training programmes
xi. Availability of sufficient IT resources (and funds) for ensuring compliance
xii. Perception of the ECT Act (e.g. is it just and fair?)

In this framework, compliance is determined by evaluating the possession and perceptions of SMEs of certain compliance factors identified in the literature review above (e.g. economic; psychological; sociological; industry; technological; and business related factors). Statements relating to each factor were formulated and managers were requested to indicate their opinion (or agreement/disagreement) with these statements. Checklist 1 presents a list of the items used to measure these factors. For instance, in the case of the technological factor, if an organization possesses adequate security controls (item viii) and effectively manages its electronic records (item ix, Checklist 1), this would indicate compliance with technological requirements stipulated in chapters III, VIII and XIII of the ECT Act. On the other hand, for the sociological dimension, if respondents perceive the Act to be unfair or immoral (item xii in Checklist 1 – see Table 1), chances of compliance with the Act would be slim.

The compliance framework was validated with a sample of 80 SME respondents from different provinces and industries in South Africa. Figure 2 and 3 present summaries of the results obtained from SMEs in different industries and located in both urban and rural areas. Items in figure 2 were measured on a Likert scale of 1 – 5 (1=strong disagreement, 5 strong agreement). In figure 3 the items were measured on a scale of 1 – 2 (1= disagreement, 2=Agreement).

Industries:

1. Manufacturing & Production
2. Retail and Wholesale
3. Property Management
4. Finance
5. Tourism
6. Agriculture
7. Marketing
8. Construction
9. Education and Training

Figures 2 and 3 reveal differences in compliance behaviors of SME managers and the challenges involved in the implementation of the regulations. The findings reveal that most SMEs lack awareness of the law and its penalties for non-compliance and many have not adopted good practices. There were disparities in the levels of awareness between urban and rural respondents and between industries. A few SMEs aware of

Figure 2. Mean scores on compliance measures by different SME industries (scale =1-5)

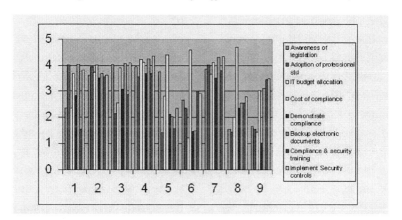

the Act mainly came from the manufacturing, finance and marketing sectors and are located in urban areas where government support is readily available. Some of these SMEs indicated that they were forced to work towards compliance by their business partners (e.g. banks & auditors) and had adopted standards such as SANS 17799, ITIL and SANs 15849. Others complied because they understood and feared the consequences of non-compliance. Most rural SMEs were not aware of the Act and as such know little about its requirements or penalties. There were also those least interested in the Act arguing that such legislations were not meant for small firms.

The lack of awareness and compliance appears to be escalating due to the failure by these organizations to engage in compliance and security training (see Figure 3). This problem is also

revealed in the designs of some South African websites. Most of those examined by the author were poorly designed and did not offer adequate payment services. In addition, information about legal requirements governing e-business transactions, enforcement and redress is hardly provided. This means consumers have limited assurance of their protection (e.g. in case of a dispute). Limited knowledge of the regulations results in poor system implementation, exposure of business partners to security risks and eventually, loss of consumer confidence.

The cost of compliance was found to be high by almost all respondents (see Figure 2). Such perception of high costs makes SMEs reluctant to make substantial investments in secure technologies. Rural SMEs in particular possess out-dated hardware, software and poor security controls.

Figure 3. Mean scores on compliance measures by different SME industries (scale =1-2)

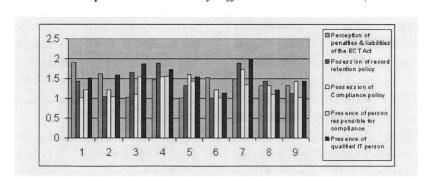

Such systems increase the risk of cyber-attacks; make access to websites or internet problematic; and the data stored or transmitted on these systems may be easily compromised.

Figure 3 shows that the perceptions of the penalties and liabilities of the Act are generally negative. One manager alleged that they were not involved in drafting of the Act and as such did not believe in it. He felt that such penalties were detrimental to the development of small businesses. In addition, not many of the SME possessed policies relating to (e.g., security, e-invoicing, and signatures) and few had people with IT skills or responsible for ensuring compliance (as required by the new company bill). This provides limited assurance to the consumer regarding the security of their personal information, business transaction and quality of goods and services to be provided.

Such level of non-compliance puts most SMEs in South Africa and their business partners at risk. As revealed in the following study, this situation has impacted negatively on the confidence consumers have in SMEs. SMEs and policy-makers need to work together to address these problems if e-commerce is to be optimized.

Framework for Evaluating E-Security within SMEs

The level of electronic abuse committed in South Africa threatens the economic growth and market competitiveness of its business sector including that of the SMEs (Upfold and Sewry, 2005; PublicTechnology.net, 2008; Engelbrecht, 2008). SMEs are struggling to manage their investment in IT and according to Van Niekerk and Labuschagne (2005), information protection and evaluation continue to be problem areas in this sector.

In order to address this problem, the author developed a framework (see figure 4 below) that can be used to identify e-security weaknesses which impact negatively on the SMEs' ability to optimize e-commerce operations. This framework

allows for a more comprehensive assessment of information security across all stages of data processing; examines in more simplified ways the effectiveness of the security measures in place; and the impact of the security situation on the trust and confidence of consumers.

Adapted from McConnell's (1994) NSTISSC model, and enhanced by adding a dimension to measure the impact of security on the organisation's competitiveness, this framework evaluates the following aspects of security: the vulnerabilities to Confidentiality, Integrity and Availability (CIA) across different states of information (storage, processing and transmission); the security measures in place and their effectiveness (technology, policy and education) and the impact of the security systems on the organization.

On dimension Y are the critical aspects of information security: Confidentiality, Integrity and Availability (CIA). Confidentiality is the assurance that only authorized users have access to information. Integrity is the quality or state of being whole, complete or uncorrupted. Availability is the characteristic of information that enables users to access information without interference or obstruction. All these three attributes of security must be preserved since loss of one or more leads to system threats and vulnerabilities.

Dimension X makes a distinction of the three states of information: storage, processing and transmission. This distinction is fundamental since it emphasizes the need to ensure security in all the states of information. In addition, it also indicates that as information changes states, specific security controls may be required. For instance an e-invoice would require secure measures during its preparation to ensure the details are accurate and that the invoice numbers are sequential (no gaps); secure processing to ensure that no information is lost and appropriate encryption to ensure safe transmission.

Dimension Z(a) reflects three security measures ((i) Technology (ii) Policy, procedures (e.g. full documentation and auditing), standards and

Figure 4. Information security evaluation model

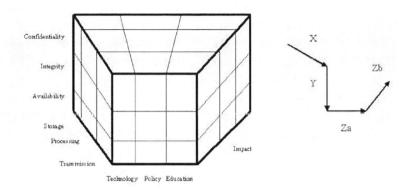

regulations and (iii) Education (training, awareness)), which must be implemented (or enforced) to maintain the critical characteristics of information (CIA). Technology plays a critical role in ensuring CIA and the protection of information in all its states. This contributes to e-commerce optimization in various ways. If people feel secure about the website, their level of trust is greatly increased. Provision of secure access controls and legal information about e-transactions are effective ways of locking in customers.

However, use of technology should be guided by security policies, standards or legislative requirements. Hence, there is a need for a signature policy, cross-border communication policy, contract enforcement policy, e-invoicing rules, and other policies. Furthermore, in order to ensure better understanding of security principles and proper application and use of technology based on policies, it is essential to educate, train and create security awareness.

Dimension Z(b) measures the impact of the security status on the organization. This impact may be positive or negative and may be, for instance: the satisfaction of customers and partners or users; the trust and confidence in the security system, digital transactions or the organization in general; the potential social and legal liabilities; resulting market position, loss of reputation, loss of customers or loss of accreditation of industry

standard. Numerous studies show that security and privacy are major reasons people do not buy on the web.

Once the information states within the system are identified (X), the evaluator then works down the vertical path of the three critical information characteristics (Y) analyzing threats and vulnerabilities. For each of the vulnerabilities discovered, existing security measures (Za) are examined to determine their effectiveness in ensuring CIA and the impact (Zb) this may have on the organization. This framework therefore captures more comprehensively the many possible weaknesses in security management in SMEs and provides managers with relevant information to inform the assessment of their systems.

For this framework to be effective, it should also minimize on the difficulties and uncertainties involved in the measurement or estimation of its inputs. Managers in SMEs usually have difficulties working with available complex economic and accounting models and this difficulty is compounded by lack of proper records keeping, skills, financial resources and willingness to disclose actual figures (Ang et al., 2001: p.161). Some measures are also difficult to obtain or compare. For instance, there are no reliable methods for estimating vulnerability since its value depends on many factors e.g. the changing threat landscape, the architecture of the system, nature of target, etc. In the same way, technologies used have different specifications (e.g. size, power, etc). In order to address this problem, data can be captured by measuring managers' subjective assessment or perceptions of the various security issues outlined in the framework. For instance, data on vulnerabilities can be captured by asking straight forward questions about the number of times (in a year) the system is unavailable due to computer attacks. This then allows the framework to work best for managers without getting bogged down in complex calculations. It also enables the application of the framework to different industries, SMEs or business organizations. This approach is widely used in many IT related studies. A questionnaire was therefore developed and the framework was then validated empirically in 84 rural and urban SMEs. Checklist 2 (see Table 2) represents a list of items used to evaluate the dimensions of the security framework. Apart from the general information, the rest of the items were measured on a 5 point Likert scale (1=strongly disagree, 5=strongly agree).

The results of the security study conducted by the author are presented in figure 5. With the Security framework presented above, it was possible to establish various security challenges facing SMEs which impede the effective development of e-commerce in this sector.

Industries in Figure 5:

1. Manufacturing & Production
2. Retail & Wholesale
3. Property Management

Table 2. Checklist 2 – List of items used to evaluate information security in SMEs

General Information: - G1-Respondent's years of computer/Internet/Buziness experience - G2-Number of years the organization has been engaged in e-commerce
C1 – Signing of confidentiality/non-disclosure agreements by systems users
C2 – Authorization of users to access data and computing resources
I1- Protection of data from corruption during storage, processing & transmission
I2- Confirmation of receipt of electronic transmissions (e.g. email, e-invoices)
A1-Availability of system (e.g. for business operations)
A2- Financial loss suffered due to unavailability of online information
T1-Up-to-datedness of software and Hardware used
T2-Use of anti-virus and/or anti-spyware software
T3-Use of passwords
T4-Use of firewall & data encryption measures (e.g. encryption of e-invoices)
P1-Use of security frameworks e.g. ISO17799,COBIT,ITIL
P2-Possession of a security policy (including signature policy)
P3-Compliance with the ECT Act
P4-Conducting of security Audits
P5-Documentation of security activities
P6-Reporting of security incidents to law enforcement agencies
E1-Training of staff on information security risks and measures
E2-Awareness by employees of social engineering techniques used by hackers
E3- Awareness of the ECT Act requirements & penalties
IMP1-The level of trust customers, sellers or partners have in the organization's system security
IMP2-User satisfaction with the organisation's system security

4. Finance
5. Tourism
6. Agriculture
7. Marketing
8. Mining
9. Textile (No responses obtained from the Education & Construction industries)

Figure 5 indicates that SMEs are vulnerable to electronic attacks. Most firms (except for those in marketing and finance sectors) do not ensure confidentiality and integrity of the data. This poses a major obstacle to online buying and selling and could have serious legal implications for these organisations. Many respondents also indicated that they had experienced some form of loss or interruptions in business operations resulting from unavailability of information systems. Furthermore, they also indicated that their information system security did not build customer trust nor enhance business reputation. The researcher run a correlation analysis which indicated a positive and significant association between IMP1 (trust) and the critical aspects of information security (C1, I1 and A1). This confirms earlier observations by Kathmandu (2000) that lack of buyers' confidence is a major impediment to e-commerce development in developing countries.

Further analysis of T1 (Use of up-to-date software and hardware) indicated that 68% of the respondents did not use up-to-date technologies and 60% were not certain whether they had firewalls or data encryption technologies. Firms in the marketing, finance and tourism sectors again appear to have implemented satisfactory IT systems than their counterparts in the production sector. This could perhaps be explained by the fact that they had more years of Internet experience. It could also be due to the nature of the products traded online. Service firms usually trade in virtual (rather than physical) products or services which are more susceptible to e-crime. The evaluation also revealed that firms in rural areas are struggling to achieve compliance with security and legal

requirements. Some rural managers felt that they have been abandoned by the government since they hardly received financial, legal and technical assistance to deal with these problems.

This study also confirms earlier observations by Jourbert & Van Bella (2004) that SME websites are not fully functional nor are they updated regularly. While some of the websites surveyed were labelled "proudly South African", accreditation as trustworthy by an independent third party could not be established. Poor publicity (security incidents), difficulties experienced in establishing online payment systems, and disparities in the quality of security and compliance between rural and urban SMEs are major concerns creating unfavourable perception of South African SMEs.

FUTURE RESEARCH DIRECTIONS

This study has established several human factors contributing to the failure to optimise e-commerce in SMEs. The author has not however established scientifically whether these are indeed causal factors. Future research can test the causality of these factors.

The disparities in compliance and security quality between industrial sectors and also between rural and urban SMEs need to be investigated further. While the government in the past has adopted a blanket policy towards SME development, it may be necessary to examine the possibility of providing interventions focused on specific organisational needs. The findings of such a study may provide useful information needed for ecommerce policy development.

This study also focused on one main regulation – the ECT Act. There are other regulations in South Africa which impact on the use of electronic facilities (e.g. the new Company bill; FICA; the Value Added Tax Act, 1991 (amended 2008), etc). The impact of these on e-commerce in SMEs needs to be understood. Furthermore, the fact that SMEs are expected to comply with

Figure 5. Information security evaluation – Average responses by industry

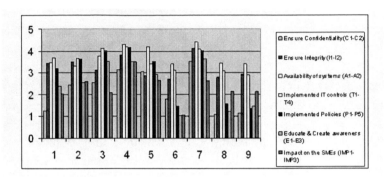

many of these regulation causes much concern and confusion and raise the costs of compliance in many organisations. These problems need to be investigated further with a view to find solutions that will lead to economic growth and development in those firms engaged in e-commerce.

Finally, this study examined the perceptions of SME business managers regarding customer satisfaction, trust and confidence. It would be interesting to know the views of the customers regarding security, online payment methods, and compliance. This would provide more accurate assessment of trust and competitiveness than is the case when such information is obtained from SME managers. It is also equally important to know the perceptions of other stakeholders. Interesting insight into e-commerce impediments could be provided by IT personnel or managers, Internet service providers and system users.

CONCLUSION

The objectives of this chapter were to create better understanding of the factors influencing compliance with e-commerce regulations and e-security requirements, and provide some useful frameworks and checklists SME managers can use to identify compliance and security barriers to e-commerce optimisation. The findings reveal several impediments to e-commerce resulting from

managers' own behaviors. In addition, there are also concerns about lack of government support and poor implementation of regulations. This article emphasizes the need to address human and social factors if optimal e-commerce activities are to be achieved in SMEs.

SME managers need to understand that consumers are particularly concerned about the security of their personal data; quality of services rendered on the Web; security of their money and how they can resolve issues in case of disputes. There is also great need for government support in ensuring that cheaper but up-to-date hardware & software are made available to SMEs (especially in the rural areas), in order to reduce costs and improve security. Training and education on aspects of electronic law, technology and security is necessary for proper development of a compliance and security culture that can sustain customer trust and confidence in these organisations.

The burdens of security and regulatory compliance are especially challenging for SMEs. These organizations often do not have the expertise and resources to recognize and address the above challenges. Simpler and less costly means are necessary to enable SMEs identify those factors that impede their ability to comply with regulatory and security requirements. Literature suggests that several factors combine to influence compliance behaviors in SMEs. The checklists (1 and 2) specify several requirements of the e-commerce regulations and good security practices. They ensure a more comprehensive assessment of managers' compliance behaviors by examining various economic, psychological, sociological, industry, business and technological factors. The questions in these checklists are easy to understand and use and managers can pinpoint quickly any potential risks or liabilities that may require interventions. These checklists therefore act as effective measures, benchmarks and reference guides for ensuring regulatory compliance and quality security in SMEs.

REFERENCES

Allan, C., Annear, J., Beck, E., & Beveren, J. (2003). *A framework for the adoption of ICT and security technologies by SMEs.* Retrieved January 11, 2005, from http://www.cecc.com.au/programs/resource_manager/accounts/seaanz_papers/62AnnearetalFinal.pdf

Ang, C., Davies, M., & Finlay, P. (2001). An empirical model of IT usage in the Malaysian public sector. *The Journal of Strategic Information Systems, 10*, 159–174. doi:10.1016/S0963-8687(01)00047-6

Barlette, Y., & Fomin, V. (2008). Exploring the suitability of IS security management standards for SMEs. In *Proceedings of the 41ˢᵗ Hawaii International Conference on System Sciences, 2008.* Retrieved May 24, 2008, from http://csdl2.computer.org/comp/proceedings/hicss/2008/3075/00/30750308.pdf

Black, J. (2001). *Managing discretion.* Unpublished manuscript, London School of Economics, UK.

Brown, R. (1994). Theory and practice of regulatory enforcement: Occupational health and safety regulation in British Colombia. *Law & Policy, 16*, 63–71. doi:10.1111/j.1467-9930.1994.tb00117.x

Burrows, T. (2004). Making Web site compliance easy. *ITWeb.* Retrieved September 4, 2005, from http://www.itweb.co.za/sections/internet/2004/0409 220806.asp?A=COV&S=Cover

Buys. (2007). *Records management guide,* Buys IT Law Consulting (Pty) Ltd. Retrieved October 14, 2008, from http://www.buys.co.za/gbDownloads.asp?field=file&RID=517

Coleman, S., Fararo, T., & Zey, M. (1993). Rational choice theory: Advocacy and critique. *Social Forces, 72*(1), 273–275. doi:10.2307/2580174

Computer Business Review. (2004). Website compliance survey. *Computer business review.* Retrieved September 20, 2006, from http://www.cbr.co.za/article.aspx?pklArticleId=3246&pklCategoryId=384

Costello, P., Sloane, A., & Moreton, R. (2007). IT evaluation frameworks – Do they make a valuable contribution? A critique of some of the classic models for use by SMEs. *Electronic Journal of Information systems . Evaluation, 10*(1), 57–64.

ECT Act (2002). Electronic Communications and Transactions Act. 2002. *Acts Online.* Retrieved March 30, 2005, from http://www.acts.co.za/ect_act/

ELC. (2003). Legalising electronic communications - electronic billing. *Electronic Law Consultancy.* Retrieved February 24, 2006, from http://elc.co.za/article.php?subaction=showfull&id=1052909342&archive=&start_from=&ucat=3&.

Engelbrecht, L. (2008, April 18). Fraud flies in Q1 2008. ITWeb 2008. Retrieved April 20, 2008 from http://www.itweb.co.za/sections/business/2008/0804181100.asp

Grossman, D., & Zaelke, D. 2005. An introduction to theories of why states and firms do (and do not) comply with law. INECE Conference Proceedings. *INECE*. Retrieved September 10, 2006, from www.inece.org/conference/7/vol1/index.html.

Hahn, J., & Kauffman, R. (2003). Measuring what you could never measure: A new science of Web site design performance evaluation. In *Revolutionary Strategies and Tactics in Research Design and Data Collection for E-Business Management Research Workshop in association with the International Conference on Electronic Commerce (ICEC 2003)*, Pittsburgh, PA, September 2003.

Hedman, J., & Borell, A. (2005). Broadening information systems evaluation through narratives. *Electronic Journal of Information Systems Evaluation, 8*(2), 115–122.

Henriques, I., & Sadorsky, P. (1996). The determinants of an environmentally responsive firm: An empirical approach. *Journal of Environmental Economics and Management, 30*, 381–384. doi:10.1006/jeem.1996.0026

Hudson, J. (2003). RIAS and private sector development: Some thoughts from the South African context. *Centre on Regulation and Competition*. Retrieved January 4, 2007, from http://www.competition-regulation.org.uk/conferences/mcrria03/conf8.pdf.

Ibls -Internet Business Law. (2007). *Overview of e-commerce in South Africa*. Retrieved January 20, 2008, from http://www.ibls.com/internet_law_news_portal_view.aspx?s=sa&id=1098

Jenamani, M., Zhong, Y., & Bhargava, B. (2007). Cheating in online auction – Towards explaining the popularity of English auction. *Electronic Commerce Research and Applications, 6*, 53–62. doi:10.1016/j.elerap.2005.12.002

Jensen, J. (2004). *Issues facing SMEs in their adoption of electronic commerce*. Retrieved February 24, 2005, from http://www.crf.dcita.gov.au/papres03/jensenpaper12final.pdf

Joubert, J., & Van Belle, J. P. (2004). *Compliance of South African E-Commerce Websites with Legislation to protect consumer rights*. Retrieved March 14, 2007, from http://www.commerce.uct.ac.za/InformationSystems/Staff/PersonalPages/jvbelle/pubs/IBIMA04.doc

Kalember, R. (2004). *Compliance Essentials: standard method of fulfilling requirements,* storage & security journal. Retrieved September 20, 2006 from World Wide Web: http://issj.sys-con.com/47516.htm

Kathmandi. (2000). *Commerce and LDCs – challenges for enterprises and governments*. Retrieved January 12, 2007 from http://r0.unctad.org/ecommerce/event_docs/kathmandu_background.pdf

Keen, C. A., Wetzels, M. B., De Ruyter, c., & Feinberg, D. R. (2004). Marketing on the web - behavioural, strategy and practices and public policy: E-tailers versus retailers, which factors determine consumer preferences. *Journal of Business Research, 57*(7), 685–695. doi:10.1016/S0148-2963(02)00360-0

Kohlberg, L. (1969). *Stage and sequence: the cognitive-development approach to socialization.* In Goslin, DA. (Ed.), Handbook of Socialisation Theory and Research, Rand McNally, New York, NY

Kyobe, M. E. (2008, November 5-7) Evaluating information security within SMEs engaged in e-commerce in South Africa. In *Proceedings of the 31st Institute for Small Business & Entrepreneurship Conference,* Belfast, N. Ireland.

Kyobe, M. E. (2009). Factors influencing SME compliance with government regulation on use of IT. *Journal of Global Information Management, 17*(2), 30–59.

Lynch, J. (2005). Identity theft in cyberspace: Crime control methods and their effectiveness in combating phishing attacks. *Berkeley Technology Law Journal, 20,* 259–300.

Malloy, T. F. (2003). Compliance and the firm. *Temple Law Review, 76,* 451–457.

Mayne, M. (2006). How are businesses facing up to the compliance challenge? *SC Magazine Australia.* Retrieved November 30, 2006, from http://www.scmagazine.com.au/feature/how-are-businesses-facing-up-to-the-compliance-challenge.aspx

McConnell, J. (1994). *National Training Standard for Information System Security.* Retrieved March 12 2007, from http://sccurity.isu.edu/pdf/4011.pdf

Meziane, F., & Kasiran, M. (2008). Evaluating trust in electronic commerce: A study based on information provided on merchant's Websites. *The Journal of the Operational Research Society, 59*(4), 464–472. doi:10.1057/palgrave.jors.2602430

Michalson, L., & Hughes, B. (2005). Guide to the ECT Act, *Michalsons Attorneys.* Retrieved September 20, 2006, from http://www.michalson.com

Mithal, M. (2000). Illustrating B2C complaints in the online environment. In *The Joint Conference of the OECD, HCOPIL, ICC: Building Trust in the Online Environment: Business to Consumer Dispute Resolution, The Hague.* Retrieved from http://www1.oecd.org/dsti/sti/it/secur/act/online_trust/presentations.htm

Mullon, P. (2006). The six elements of legally acceptable electronic documents. *Computer Business Review, Technews.* Retrieved December 05, 2006, from http://cbr.co.za/article.aspx?pklArticleId=3972&pklIssueId=447&pklCategoryId=384

MyBroadband. (2008). *South Africa's email risk.* Retrieved December 20, 2008, from http://mybroadband.co.za/news/General/6355.html

Nicol, C. (2003). ICT Policy: *A beginner's handbook. The Association for Progressive Communications (APC). South Africa.* Internet and ICT for Social Justice and Development.

Onwubiko, C., & Lenaghan, A. (2007). Managing security threats and vulnerabilities for small to medium enterprises. In *5th IEEE International Conference on Intelligence and Security Informatics, IEEE ISI 2007,* IEEE Press, May, New Jersey, USA.

Orford, J., Herrington, M., & Wood, E. (2004). *South African Report Global Entrepreneurship Monitor.* Retrieved January 22, 2005, from www.gsb.uct.ac.za/gsbwebb/userfiles/GEM_ 2004.pdf

Porter, M. E. (2001). Strategy and the internet. *Harvard Business Review,* (March): 63–78.

PublicTechnology.net. (2008). *Cybercrime syndicate scoops millions from South African government.* Retrieved June 13, 2008, from http://www.publictechnology.net/modules.php?op=modload&name=News&file=article&side=16110

Review, S. M. M. E. 2003. (2004). *Annual Review of Small Business in South Africa– 2003.* Retrieved January 18, 2007, from http://www.tips.org.za/2003/SMMEReviewSCREENFINAL.pdf

Roztocki, N., & Weistroffer, H. (2006). Stock Price Reaction to Investments in Information Technology: The Relevance of Cost Management Systems. *The Electronic Journal Information Systems Evaluation, 9*(1), 27–30.

SBP – Strategic business partnership for growth in Africa (2003). *Is South Africa a good place to do business?* SME Alert. Retrieved January, 15, 2006, from World Wide Web: http://www-za.sbp.org.za/docs/SME_Alert_Nov_2003.pdf

Seldon, A. (2004). E-business in South Africa, a matter of trust. *Netdotwork*. Retrieved February, 20, 2006, from http://netdotwork.co.za/article.aspx?pklArticleId=3081

Sengupta, A., Mazumdar, C., & Barik, M. S. (2005). E-commerce security: A life cycle approach, in Sadhana. *Journal of the Indian Academy of Sciences, 30*(2 & 3), 119–140.

Strassmann, P. A. (1985). *Information Payoff: The Transformation of work in electronic age.* New York: Free Press.

Sunday Times. (2002). Dozens of threats beset your data. *Sunday Times Surveys*. Retrieved October 5, 2004, from http://www.sundaytimes.co.za/business/surveys/internet/survey10.asp

Technews. (2004). 2004 Website compliancy survey. *Computer Business Review*. Retrieved January 15, 2005, from http://cbr.co.za/article.aspx

The Presidency. (2003). No 26 of 2003: National Small Business Amendment Act, 2003, South Africa. Retrieved March 30, 2005, from http://www.info.gov.za/view/DownloadFileAction?id=68002

Tyler, T. R. (1990). *Why people obey the Law.* New Haven, CT: Yale University Press.

Upfold, C. T., & Sewry, D. A. (2005). *An investigation of Information security in small and medium enterprises (SMEs) in Eastern Cape.* Retrieved September 20, 2006, from http://icsa.cs.up.ac.za/issa/2005/Proceedings/Research/082_Article.pdf

US-CERT. (2004). *US-CERT Technical Cyber Security Alert TA04-2939A 2004.* Retrieved December 12, 2004, from http://www.us-cert.gov/cas/techalerts/TA04-2939A

Van Niekerk, L., & Labaschagne, L. (2005). The Peculium Model: Information security risk management for the South African SMME. In *ISSA Conference*, Gauteng, South Africa, June 29th – 1 July, 2005. Retrieved January 14, 2007 from http://icsa.cs.up.ac.za/issa/2006/Proceedings/Full/12_Paper.pdf

Warden, S., & Motjolopane, I. M. (2007). E-commerce adoption factors: supporting cases from South Africa. In *Information Resource management Association conference*, Vancouver, Canada. Retrieved from http://www.stuartwarden.com/Warden_Motjolopane_eCommerceAdoptionFactors_IRMA2007.pdf

Warden, S., & Remenyi, D. (2005). *E-commerce in an SME. A case study of a South African low cost or "no frills" airline".* Paper delivered at ZA-WWW (World Wide Web) 2005 Conference, Cape Town, South Africa 29 to 31 August.

Wejnert, B. (2002). Integrating models of diffusion of innovations: A conceptual framework. *Annual Review of Sociology, 28,* 297–326. doi:10.1146/annurev.soc.28.110601.141051

Zantsi, N., & Eloff, M. (2003). *Guide to South African Law.* Retrieved 20 February, 2007, from http://icsa.cs.up.ac.za/issa/2003/Publications/001.doc

Zorz. (2003). Small firms 'shun' PC security, *BBC NEWS*. Retrieved October 15, 2004, from http://www.net_security.org/news:php?id=2650

Chapter 4
Determinants of E-Commerce Adoption among Small and Medium-Sized Enterprises in Malaysia

Sim Chia Hua
Swinburne University of Technology, Malaysia

Modapothala Jashua Rajesh
Swinburne University of Technology, Malaysia

Lau Bee Theng
Swinburne University of Technology, Malaysia

ABSTRACT

With a major proportion of research on Electronic Commerce (EC) undertaken on large corporations, and focused primarily on developed countries, little is known about the determinants of EC in Small and Medium-sized Enterprises (SMEs) of developing nations. This chapter explores the extent of EC use by SMEs, and provides some empirical evidence of how internal factors of firm and owner are influencing EC adoption among smaller businesses in Malaysia. The methodology and results of this study may be applicable to other developing countries. Findings confirm the low level of participation in EC by SMEs. The age of enterprise, as well as the owner's gender and education were found to be significant in determining the level of EC adoption. Though some of the results contradict those of previous studies, they may have a greater implication for government authorities in drawing up guidelines, approaches, and formulating more effective frameworks to promote EC use among SMEs in developing countries.

INTRODUCTION

The Small and Medium-sized Enterprise (SME) sector plays an important role in the economic development of many countries (Curran & Blackburn, 2001; Simpson & Docherty, 2004). As a major source of income and provider of employment, SMEs account for more than 95 per cent of businesses, generate two thirds of private sector employment (Organisation for Economic Coop-

DOI: 10.4018/978-1-60566-998-4.ch004

eration and Development [OECD], 2005), and contribute between 30 per cent and 70 per cent of the Gross Domestic Product (GDP) of most nations (OECD, 1997). In the United Kingdom, for example, 99.9 per cent of the private sector enterprises are SMEs and they account for 59 per cent of employment in the country (Department for Business Enterprise & Regulatory Reform [BERR], 2007). Similarly, in Malaysia, SMEs form a significant part of the economy, and have evolved to become key suppliers and service providers over the years (United Nations Development Programme [UNDP], Malaysia, 2007). More than 90 per cent of enterprises in Malaysia are SMEs which generate employment for more than half of the work force in the country, and contribute 32 per cent to the GDP (Department of Statistics Malaysia, 2005).

With the evolution and widespread use of the Internet, the capability and competitiveness of SMEs have greatly increased. Electronic commerce (EC), in particular, allows buying and selling of products, services, information via computer networks including the Internet (Turban, King, Lee, & Viehland, 2004). Through the use of web sites, email services and web browsers, EC facilitates communication and enables access to large amounts of information. With increased connectivity and flexibility, EC offers new exciting opportunities for firms to improve their business performance (see for example, Tetteh & Burn, 2001). In fact, SMEs are increasingly finding a web presence to be important in building brand/product awareness, and enhancing company image (Gribbins & King, 2004). Others concur that EC brings numerous advantages to firms in terms of lower costs, reduced remittance time, and improved customer service (Wen, Chen, & Hwang, 2001). Through a virtual interactive environment that promotes communication between trading parties, EC also provides SMEs with an effective mechanism for competing with larger organizations worldwide. Hoi, Shim, and Yin (2003) observe that SMEs perceive EC to be beneficial

in improving their international exposure and responsiveness. With increased diffusion, EC is expected to remove barriers of culture and national boundaries, leading towards a more unified and globalised economy (Sagi, 2004).

In Malaysia, the SMEs are aware of the importance of Information and Communication Technologies (ICTs) in improving their productivity and business performance (Lim, 2006). However, a review of the literature shows that SMEs in Malaysia have been slow in the uptake of ICTs and EC in particular (Alam, Ahmad, Abdullah, & Ishak, 2007; Alam & Ahsan, 2007; Bolongkikit, Obit, Asing, & Tanakinjal, 2006; Hashim, 2006). In a survey of 12,000 SMEs in the country, only 16 per cent of the firms indicated that they had a web presence, compared to 80 per cent of similar enterprises in Europe and North America (Patrick, cited in UNDP, Malaysia, 2007). Research shows that the slow development of ICTs among Malaysian SMEs may be explained by factors related to technical expertise (Lim, 2006), and security issues (Tan, Chong, Lin, & Eze, 2009). Smaller businesses generally perceive the implementation of ICTs to be risky and technically challenging. Liew (2002) in a study on SMEs concurs that the implementation and maintenance of EC are restricted due to hindrances related to organization, infrastructure and technology.

With limited resources to draw upon, owner-managers of SMEs often inhabit a very different world from that of their counterparts in larger enterprises (Beaver, 2007). Due to the dominance of a single owner-manager and factors such as resource constraints, SMEs have their own unique characteristics, and are not simply scaled-down versions of large organizations (Shrader, Mulford, & Blackburn 1989). In many ways, they behave in a distinctly different fashion from their larger counterparts (Hansemark, 1998). However, in the past, considerable research on EC has been conducted on large enterprises or those that are dot.com players. Most of the studies have focused predominantly on SMEs in developed countries.

A review on eBusiness/EC research by Parker and Castleman (2007) shows that over half of the journal articles from 2003 to 2006 investigated SMEs in the United Kingdom, United States of America, Australia, Canada and New Zealand. This suggests that there is a need for further study on eBusiness/EC adoption among SMEs in developing countries. While it is important to understand EC in the context of advanced countries, issues faced by SMEs in developing countries may be different from those encountered by their counterparts in developed nations (Elbeltagi, 2007; Sarosa & Underwood, 2005). It is therefore relevant to investigate the issue of EC adoption from the perspective of SMEs in developing economies like Malaysia. In particular, this study aims to fill the knowledge gaps in EC research by attempting to identify some internal factors that are influential in explaining adoption of EC among SMEs in the country.

BACKGROUND

Electronic Commerce

The definitions of E-commerce (EC) are many and varied. The World Trade Organization (WTO) defines EC as "the production, distribution, marketing, sale or delivery of goods and services by electronic means" (Baker & McKenzie, 2001). This basically involves the use of digital devices for gathering information, conducting business communication and ultimately trading with business partners. The electronic media involved both 'open' and 'closed' networks like the Internet, the World Wide Web, electronic data interchange (EDI) and intranet. In other words, EC is a concept covering any form of business communication or transaction conducted using ICTs (European Strategic Program on Research in Information Technology, 1997). For the purposes of this study, we have adopted the definition provided by Turban, McLean and Wetherbe (2004) who describe EC

as "the process of buying, selling, transferring, or exchanging products, services, and/or information via computer networks, including the Internet". EC is thus not limited to buying and selling of products or services over electronic networks, but is also concerned with transferring or exchanging information and funds such as making orders and payments online.

Small and Medium-sized Enterprises (SMEs)

There is no one universal definition of an SME. The two common ways of defining SMEs are based on: (i) the financial turnover, and (ii) the number of employees (Curran & Blackburn, 2001). The main criterion that OECD countries use for statistical purposes is the number of persons employed (OECD, 2004). This criterion is considerably more transparent, and objective (Curran & Blackburn, 2001). As in the European Union, the most frequent upper limit designating an SME is 250 employees (OECD, 2005). In Malaysia, SMEs are also defined based on the annual sales turnover and number of full-time employees (National SME Development Council [NSDC], 2005). In general, the Small and Medium Industries Development Corporation (SMIDEC) of Malaysia defined SMEs as enterprises with annual sales turnover not exceeding MYR25 million[1], and full-time employees not more than 150 (cited in UNDP, Malaysia, 2007). For the purposes of this study, the number of employees was adopted as the basis for the definition of an SME, in line with small business research (Analoui & Karami, 2003; Cragg & King, 1993; Smith, 1998). An SME is hereby identified as a firm employing not more than 150 full-time employees, and registered under the Malaysian Companies Act 1965 (NSDC, 2005).

RESEARCH OBJECTIVES

The literature shows that there is a number of overlapping divergent models that have been used to predict the decision by SMEs to adopt Internet/EC in Malaysia. Most of the prior studies have attempted to examine the perceived characteristics of the innovation that can potentially explain the Internet/EC adoption rate in the country. For example, perceived usefulness, perceived ease of use, and social influence have been identified as influential in explaining the decision to adopt broadband Internet in Malaysia (Dwivedi, Selamat, Abd Wahab, Mat Samsudin, & Lal, 2008). Other studies found relative advantage, compatibility, complexity, observability, and security issues to be significant in predicting internet-based ICT adoption among SMEs in the country (Tan et al., 2009). In another research to examine the factors affecting EC adoption among electronic manufacturing companies, results suggest that relative advantage and compatibility have significant positive impact on EC adoption in Malaysia, whereas complexity and security were reported to have negative effects (Alam, Khatibi, Sayyed Ahmad, & Ismail, 2007). This is confirmed by Hussin and Mohamad Noor (2005) in a study on CEOs/managers of Malaysian SMEs in the manufacturing sector. Results concur that perceived relative advantage, complexity, and observability significantly affect the adoption of EC. In addition, the study found evidence that the CEO's commitment towards Information Technology (IT) impacted the decision to adopt EC.

Other studies have examined the influence of owner characteristics in explaining the decision to adopt technology in the country. Ramayah, Dahlan, Mohamad, and Siron (2002) used the Technology Acceptance Model (TAM) along with demographic variables such as gender and educational level of owner-managers to examine technology usage among SME owner-managers in Malaysia. In another study, Jantan, Ismail, Ra-

mayah, and Mohamed Salehuddin (2001) analysed how CEO's characteristics affect the adoption of Advanced Manufacturing Technology among small and medium scale manufacturing industries in the country. Further, Dahlan, Ramayah, and Koay (2002) investigated how individual demographic variables like gender influence the level of data mining readiness within the Malaysian banking industry. Other similar research conducted in the South East Asian region include Teo (2001) who examined the impact of motivational and demographic variables (such as age, gender and education level) on Internet usage.

As this chapter represents a preliminary study of a series of research on the determinants, perceived benefits and barriers of EC use by SMEs, no emphasis is given to the technical aspects or detailed issues surrounding EC adoption. Instead, this study focuses on investigating organisational issues and characteristics of owners involved in the introduction and use of EC. In short, it is an attempt to provide a broader view of the effect of owner and firm characteristics on EC deployment, in the context of SMEs in a developing country.

Alzougool and Kurnia (2008) in a review of EC determinants among SMEs identified various factors that have been studied in developed and developing countries, and classified them into different categories. The review shows that the impact of owner's characteristics such as gender, age and educational level have been investigated in the developed world (Chuang, Nakatani, Chen, & Huang, 2007), but not in the developing countries. For SMEs, the decision whether to adopt EC is usually made by the owner-manager, who is often the founder of the firm. As pointed out by Beaver (2007), there is little separation of ownership and control in smaller businesses, and that all corporate and functional strategies are the concerns of the founder and owner-manager of the enterprise. This is confirmed by Thong and Yap (1995) that CEO's characteristics are important factors in predicting IT adoption by small businesses. It is therefore

Table 1. EC adoption by SMEs: Contradictory findings on organisational factors (Adapted from Alzougool & Kurnia, 2008)

		Significant findings	Insignificant findings
Organisational size & business category	Developed countries	Ling (2001) Zhu & Kraemer (2005) Zhu, Kraemer, & Xu (2003)	Al-Qirim (2007) Chuang, Nakatani, Chen, & Huang (2007) Sparling, Toleman, & Cater-Steel (2007)
	Developing countries	Huy & Filiatrault (2006)	Jeon, Han, & Lee (2006)
Business age	Developed countries		Chuang, Nakatani, Chen, & Huang (2007)
	Developing countries	Hinson & Abor (2005)	

relevant to investigate how owners' characteristics are influencing adoption of EC among SMEs in a developing economy.

On the other hand, the effects of business attributes like organisational size, category and business age have been studied in both developed and developing nations, but no consistent findings reported (Table 1).

MacGregor and Vrazalic (2008) in another review summarized the business characteristics which have been shown to have an impact on the adoption of EC by SMEs (see Table 2).

From the literature on the effects of business characteristics on EC and prior research on how demographic variables of owner can possibly influence the usage of technology, several determinants are proposed, and arguments provided

as to why these variables might play a role in explaining the decisions to adopt EC. Specifically, this study aims to explore the current level of EC adoption by SMEs, and identify which of the attributes of firm and owner is/are influential in explaining the adoption of EC among SMEs in the country.

RESEARCH HYPOTHESES

Business Attributes

The introduction of EC into an SME could be affected by features of the firm itself such as its age, size, and nature of business. Prior research shows that the adoption of innovative information

Table 2. Business characteristics affecting EC adoption by SMEs (Adapted from MacGregor & Vrazalic, 2008)

Business characteristics	Reported by
Business size (number of employees)	Blackburn & Athayde (2000) Fallon & Moran (2000) Matlay (2000)
Age of the business (length of time in operation)	Kai-Uwe Brock (2000) MacGregor, Vrazalic, Carlsson, Bunker, & Magnusson (2002)
Business sector	BarNir & Smith (2002) Blackburn et al. (2000) MacGregor et al. (2002) Matlay (2000) Schindehutte & Morris (2001)

systems by an SME in a developing economy is heavily dependent on organisational characteristics such as firm size (Dasgupta, Agarwal, Ioannidis, & Gopalakrishnan, 1999). Teo and Tan (1998) in another study on Internet adoption in Singapore also note that technology adoption can be analyzed according to the physical characteristics of a business. This is supported by Blackburn and Athayde (2000) who show that the adoption of EC technology is associated with business characteristics such as firm size and business type. On the other hand, other studies found contradictory results. Seyal and Rahman (2003) in a research on EC adoption among SMEs in a South East Asian country concluded that organizational characteristics do not have an influential impact on EC adoption. Others noted that firm size had no bearing on implementation of Internet Commerce/EC by SMEs in South Italy (Scupola, 2003), and Canada (Sparling, Toleman, & Cater-Steel, 2007).

Nature of business: Firms in different business sectors have different information processing needs, which in turn affect the adoption of technology (Yap, Soh, & Raman, 1992). It appears that industries with higher information content (such as services) are more likely to adopt IT than those with less information content (such as mining or manufacturing) (Yap, 1990). The impact of business type is expected to affect EC in a similar manner as with other technologies. Blackburn and Athayde (2000), and Matlay (2000) show that the nature of the business in which a firm operates is significantly associated with EC adoption. These studies conclude that service organisations tend to adopt EC more than any other industries. It can therefore be predicted that a tourism enterprise, for example, is more likely to employ EC in its business process than is a firm in cement manufacturing or coal mining. Given that EC adoption might be affected by the nature of business activities, it is hypothesized that (H1): the degree to which SMEs adopt EC differs across business sectors.

Size of enterprise: Firm size has often been viewed as one of the important determinants affecting the adoption of new technologies. Prior studies consistently show significant links between business size and the adoption of IT (Chuang, Rutherford & Lin, 2007; Frambach & Schillewaert, 2002; Tiessen, Wright, & Turner, 2001), and the Internet (Fallon & Moran, 2000; Teo & Tan, 1998). Research suggests that as firm size grows, coordination becomes more complicated, and the need for information processing increases. Hence, firms with larger scale of operations are more likely to use IT than smaller firms (Yap, 1990). The impact of firm size is expected to affect EC use in a similar manner as with other technologies. As shown by Huy and Filiatrault (2006), size of the enterprise affects the adoption of EC among SMEs in Vietnam, whereas Matlay (2000) concurs that smaller businesses in the British economy are less likely to adopt EC than larger SMEs. Given that EC applications involve substantial investment in financial, human resource and technological aspects, larger firms which tend to be more resourceful, are more likely to adopt the technology. Small enterprises, on the other hand, often lack resources and face financial constraints (Thong, 1999); therefore they tend to be more cautious with technology adoption. Hence, it is hypothesized that (H2): the extent of EC deployment varies depending on the size of the SMEs.

Age of enterprise: Studies have also shown that EC adoption may be affected by the age of the business (Blackburn & Athayde, 2000; Schindehutte & Morris, 2001). As noted by Daniel, Wilson, and Myers (2002), SMEs which had been in business for a longer period of time were less likely to use EC. The reason might lie with the fact that EC is an innovation to a business. Older businesses with long established rules, procedures and practices tend to be more resistant to change. The long-accepted work norms in established organizations are likely to result in conservative ideas and traditional approaches, and this prohibits the widespread use of EC in business operations. Hence, it is hypothesized that (H3): the involvement of SMEs in EC differs with regards to the age of the enterprise.

Demographic Features of Owners

It is well established that research on SMEs includes an analysis on the roles of the owner-manager. This is attributable to the unique characteristics of SMEs where the business is mostly controlled by a small management team with strong owner influence and centralized power (Reynolds, Savage, & Williams, 1994). As the decision maker, the owner-manager of a SME is inevitably the key person to recognize the relevance and potentials of EC and to adopt it. Bunker and MacGregor (2000) confirm that IT decisions in SMEs are usually made by the owner (cited in MacGregor, 2004). Other research on small businesses also identified a significant link between the gender of the CEO and the level of EC adoption (Mazzarol, Volery, Doss, & Thein, 1999). Age and level of education of the CEO, however, were found to be unrelated.

- **Age of owner:** Prior research has shown that the elderly have a tendency to resist change (Baggozi & Lee, 1999), including changes in work situations and relocation (Kasteler, Gay, & Caruth, 1968; Pollman & Johnson, 1974). Other studies further confirm that the elderly tend to resist adoption of innovation or new technologies (Robertson, 1971; Uhl, Anrus, & Poulson, 1970). This resistance to change could be attributable to the risk-taking attitudes of an individual. Wiersema and Bantel (1992) argue that people's flexibility may decline, and rigidity increase, as they age. Hence, risk-taking propensity is likely to be lower among older owner-managers. In fact, Xiao, Alhabeeb, Hong, and Haynes (2001) show that age has an impact on risk-taking

attitudes and behavior among business owners. In strategic choices made by CEOs, it is observed that the younger ones tend to pursue risky and innovative strategies (Grimm & Smith, 1991; Hambrick & Mason, 1984), and are more positive toward EC (Hunter & Kemp, 2004). Further, research shows that the young to middle-aged have an advantage with respect to technology adoption (Hoffman, Novak, & Schlosser, 2000). Compared to the older generation, young owner-managers tend to be equipped with better education and technical knowledge (Bantel & Jackson, 1989), and hence are more likely to appreciate the potential of innovations like EC. It is therefore proposed that (H4): the extent of EC adoption differs significantly according to the age of the owner-managers.

- **Gender of owner:** Research indicates that gender affects the use of technology like the Internet (Sexton, Johnson, & Hignite, 2002), and EC (Uzoka, Seleka, & Khengere, 2007). Men were reported to make more frequent use of technological products than women (Hoffman et al., 2000). For example, male and female Internet users engage in online activities at different rates. Despite increased awareness and popularity of the Internet, Akhter (2003) observes that men, as consumers, are still more likely to use the Internet for shopping than women. The rationale might lie with the fact that significant differences exist between men and women with respect to the aversion or propensity to risk (Slovic, 1966), and technology in general (Brunner & Bennett, 1998). It is generally believed that risk-averse behavior of women is likely to result in lower rates of technology adoption, especially in developing countries although Ogunlana (2004) argues that women easily adopt innovations that can enhance their economic status. As EC is a special application of IT, it is hypothesized that (H5): the adoption of EC differs significantly according to the gender of the owner-managers.

- **Education level of owner:** The level of formal education attained by the owner-managers has also been identified to be associated with IT adoption by SMEs (Chuang, Rutherford, & Lin, 2007). Owner-managers with some forms of higher education are likely to generate more creative and innovative solutions in business operations. Hoffman et al. (2000) note that the adopters of IT products like computers and electronic banking tend to have higher levels of education. Hambrick and Mason (1984) add that insufficient education can be an important hindrance to the adoption of new technology. It is believed that owner-managers with some form of higher education tend to have more awareness and understanding of the potential and value of innovations like EC. This is supported by Tabor (2005) who notes that skills beyond simple IT experience are required for successful implementation of EC. Hence, it is proposed that (H6): a firm's involvement in EC varies with the education level of the owner-managers.

METHODOLOGY

Data Collection

The samples of this study were selected from the business directory of the SME Info Portal, which is accessible through the website of the Small and Medium Industries Development Corporation (SMIDEC) of Malaysia. Eight hundred firms were randomly selected from the directory to be surveyed. A questionnaire-based survey of local SMEs was carried out. The questionnaire was checked for content validity with the as-

sistance of academics from both business and IT disciplines. This led to revising and rewording of some items. The revised questionnaire was pilot tested on a sample group. Recommended changes were incorporated into the survey before final distribution. Data collection was performed in two stages. The owner-managers of the selected firms were identified from the directory, and contacted via telephone. To give the subjects a clear understanding of the survey, they were provided with a simplified definition of EC, and an overview of the research aims and design of the survey instrument. Upon receiving the consent from the owner-manager, a cover letter and the questionnaire were sent to them by fax or email. In total, three hundred and thirty four questionnaires were obtained, yielding a response rate of 41 per cent. The response rate is comparable to similar Information Systems (IS) studies on how business characteristics influence adoption of Internet technology (Goode & Stevens, 2000). Due to incomplete data in some questionnaires, only three hundred and twenty nine fully completed responses were used for analysis.

Design of Instrument

The questionnaire consisted of three sections. Section A collects the data about the demographic profile of an SME, covering organizational characteristics, i.e. type, size and age of the business. Business type was categorized in accordance with the definition of the National SME Development Council of Malaysia which groups SMEs into manufacturing, mining and quarrying, services, construction and primary agriculture. As mentioned earlier, the number of employees was used as a measure for the size of an enterprise. The age of a firm was determined using the number of years since the business was in existence. Section B consisted of questions on the managerial profile, i.e. the owner's gender, age in years and education level. Section C measured the extent of EC adoption by SMEs. As identified by Price-

Table 3.EC Capabilities of an SME

Level 1	SME with very basic or no EC capabilities
Level 2	SME with a website but does not carry out online transactions
Level 3	SME takes orders and provides customer service on its website
Level 4	SME completes transactions and receives payment via its website

waterhousecoopers (PWC) at the Asia Pacific Economic Cooperation forum (PWC, 1999), the EC capabilities of an SME were measured in four levels as in Table 3.

RESULTS

Sample Characteristics

Results indicated that the majority of the respondents (82 per cent) were from the service industry. This is consistent with the conclusion of Normah (2006) that most of the SMEs in Malaysia are in the service sector, accounting for 86 per cent of total businesses in the country. In terms of size, slightly more than three-fifths (62 per cent) of the respondents were from businesses that had 5 to 50 full-time employees, which are rather small-sized SMEs. In relation to the length of time in business, slightly more than half (52 per cent) of the firms surveyed indicated that they had been operational for more than 10 years. This suggests that the SMEs in this study were more experienced businesses. Only 18 per cent of the firms surveyed were young enterprises which had been operational for less than 5 years.

In terms of owners' characteristics, about three-fifths (58 per cent) of the respondents indicated that they were 45 years or above. Only 14 per cent of them were young entrepreneurs aged below 35. Despite a random selection of sample, the great majority of owner-managers were reported to be male (81 per cent). This suggests that females in the country are not playing a key role in owning and managing businesses; or that males tend to show more positive response in IS survey than females. As for the level of education of the owner-managers, about two-thirds (69 per cent) of the owner-managers surveyed had some form of professional qualification. Of this, slightly more than half were bachelor degree or postgraduate degree holders, while another half were professional certificate or diploma holders. This indicates that the results throughout this study were made by 'informed' respondents.

Analysis and Discussion

Slightly more than three quarters of the respondents (77 percent) indicated that they use computers and Internet connection in daily business operation. Of this, nearly half (47 percent) owned a website but less than one quarter (22 per cent) of them took orders, completed transactions and received payment on their websites. The findings confirm the low level of participation in EC by local SMEs. Instead, SMEs in the country place greater preference on the more familiar regional and international trade shows (UNDP, Malaysia, 2007) to promote their products and services, rather than on EC which could further enhance their competitiveness in the global market. An analysis of ANOVA showed that each level of the EC adoption differs significantly from the total of extent of adoption (Table 4). None of these stages overlapped with one another; hence the model chosen for the study proved satisfactory. This is confirmed by the graphs depicted in Figure 1. In particular, Figure 1(d) is a clear inverse replica of Figure 1(a) with no graphical

Table 4. ANOVA

	F	Sig.
Level 1	4843.909	.000*
Level 2	282.728	.000*
Level 3	273.776	.000*
Level 4	1665.475	.000*

*significant at 0.05 level

overlapping between the varying levels and the total of extent of adoption.

Further, correlation was performed to measure the relationship between the total extent of EC adoption with each stage of EC adoption. The total of extent of EC adoption in relation to each stage is highly correlated (Table 5). Overall, the results indicate the greater the degree of adoption, the greater the relationship is (+0.07), i.e., the correlation (*r*) increased from level 1 to level 2, and dropped only marginally in level 3.

Business Attributes

When analysed with the Chi-square test, the hypothesis (H1) that EC adoption differs across business sectors is supported (p = .09). Among the different types of businesses, the service sector was found to be more likely to adopt EC than manufacturing or agriculture-based SMEs. The result supports the findings of prior research that the decision to adopt EC is significantly associated with the nature of business activities

Figure 1.

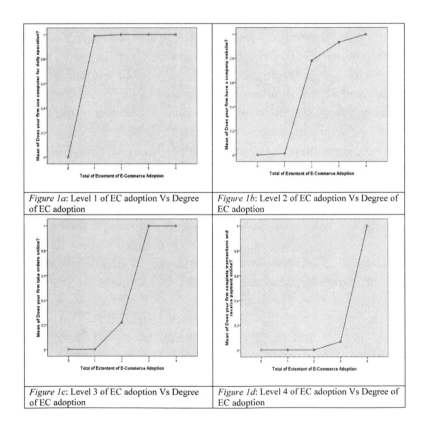

Figure 1a: Level 1 of EC adoption Vs Degree of EC adoption	*Figure 1b*: Level 2 of EC adoption Vs Degree of EC adoption
Figure 1c: Level 3 of EC adoption Vs Degree of EC adoption	*Figure 1d*: Level 4 of EC adoption Vs Degree of EC adoption

Table 5. Level of EC adoption vs. total of extent of EC adoption

	Correlation
Does your firm use the computer and internet for daily operations?	.682**
Does your firm have a company website?	.796**
Does your firm take orders online?	.794**
Does your firm complete transactions and receive payment online?	.725**

** Significant at 0.10 level

(Matlay, 2000; Schindehutte & Morris, 2001). It is, however, contrary to the findings of Seyal and Rahman (2003); Sparling et al., 2007) who concluded that type of business had no bearing on the adoption of EC. The significant impact of business type on EC adoption could be due to the fact that 21 per cent of the respondents were operating in the mining/construction sector. As compared to services and manufacturing firms, owner-managers in the mining and construction industries might not have perceived the relevance and value of EC as highly as their counterparts in the other two industries do.

The Chi-square test also shows that the size of enterprise (H2) is significant at the 0.10 level ($\chi2$ = 19.061, d.f = 12, p-value <.087). The result is line with some of the prior research in EC adoption (Huy & Filiatrault, 2006; Uzoka et al., 2007), but contradicts others (Scupola, 2003; Seyal & Rahman, 2003). The finding shows that the degree of EC adoption was greater for larger-sized SMEs. It supports the rationale that having more resources leads to greater EC utilisation. Further, results indicate that the age of the enterprise (H3) is significant at the 0.05 level ($\chi2$ = 26.683, d.f = 16, p-value <.045). The findings support earlier studies (Blackburn & Athayde, 2000; Schindehutte & Morris, 2001) that business age plays an influential role in the decision to adopt EC. The degree of EC adoption was lower for firms which had been in business for 20 years or more. This suggests that older businesses with long established rules, procedures and practices might be more resistant to change, which in turn, prohibits the widespread use of EC. The results of Chi-square tests are summarized in Table 6.

Demographic Features of Owners

The hypothesis regarding the effect of owner's age (H4) on the extent of EC adoption is not supported. This result confirmed the findings of Chuang, Nakatani, et al. (2007) that owner's age does not influence the extent of EC adoption in

Table 6. EC adoption – Chi-square results

Influence of variables on the extent of EC adoption	Chi-square (p-value)
Nature of Business	.09**
Size of enterprise	.087**
Age of enterprise	.045*
Owner's Age	N.S.
Owner's Education Level	.000*

* Significant at 0.05 level
** Significant at 0.10 level
N.S. Not significant

SMEs. It is, however, contrary to the finding of Morris and Ventakesch (2000) that age plays an important role in influencing technology adoption. In this study, there was no significant difference between the older and younger entrepreneurs in terms of EC employment. This could be due to the growing popularity and awareness of EC among various age groups. When the perceived benefits outweigh the cost, owners opt to employ the technology regardless of their age, hence lessening the effect of the variable on the extent of EC adoption.

In contrast, an analysis with the T-test reveals that the owner's gender (p-value = 0.089) is significant on the extent of EC employment. The mean score indicates that greater preference of EC comes from male owners. This supports Hypothesis 5 that males are more open to EC as business owners because they are more willing to adopt the technology as consumers (Akhter, 2003). The findings concur with those of earlier research that that gender affects technology usage (Venkatesh & Morris, 2000; Teo & Lim, 2000), and the intention and ability to adopt EC (Uzoka et al., 2007). On the other hand, the Chi-square test shows that the owner's education level (H6) is significant at 0.05 level ($\chi 2 = 46.722$, d.f = 16, p<.00) (see Table 6). The result is consistent with the finding of Chuang, Rutherford, and Lin (2007) that owner's education is a significant predictor of IT adoption in SMEs. However, it contradicts with MacGregor and Vrazalic (2008) who found no associations between the level of the CEO's education and EC adoption in SMEs. In this study, owner-managers with a diploma or degree demonstrated a greater extent of EC employment in their business. This supports the rationale that owner-managers with some form of higher education are more likely to recognize and appreciate the values of EC.

CONCLUSION

This study is the first step in a series of research projects that aim at understanding and predicting the adoption of EC technology by SMEs in Malaysia. Owner-managers in this study were informed respondents, with two-thirds of them holding some form of higher qualification. The great majority of them were male, and nearly three-fifths of the respondents were mature and experienced owner-managers aged 45 years and above. They were from the more experienced businesses, which had been operational for more than 10 years. The great majority of the firms surveyed operated in the service industry, with full-time employees not exceeding 50. It was found that three quarters of the firms possessed basic EC applications such as computers and internet connection. However, less than one quarter of them took orders, completed transactions and received payment electronically. The findings confirm the low level of participation in EC by Malaysian SMEs.

Further, the study provides some empirical evidence of the effects of firm and owner attributes on EC adoption by SMEs in the country. Findings on organizational attributes conformed to the features of a developing economy. The age of the enterprise significantly influenced EC employment. The degree of EC adoption was lower for older businesses which had been operational for 20 years or more, implying that older firms with long established rules, procedures and practices might be more resistant to change, which in turn, prohibits the widespread use of EC. Additionally, the degree of EC adoption was greater for larger-sized SMEs. This lends support to the rationale that big firms which tend to be more resourceful are more likely to adopt EC. The findings further confirmed that firms in the service industry were more likely to adopt EC than manufacturing or agriculture-based enterprises. On the influence of owner's attributes, results suggest that gender of owner-manager significantly influenced the extent of EC adoption. A greater preference for EC came from male owner-managers, implying that they might be more open to EC compared to their female counterparts. Additionally, the owner's education level had a significant influence on adoption of EC. Owner-managers with some form of higher qualification seemed to appreciate the value of EC more, and demonstrated a greater deployment of EC in their business. Contrary to prior research, owner's age did not influence the extent of EC adoption. No significant difference was found between the older and younger entrepreneurs in terms of EC employment.

LIMITATIONS OF STUDY

The study focuses on analysing the adoption of E-commerce by SMEs. However, no single definition exists that is universally acceptable for the terms 'E-commerce' or 'SME'. The lack of a single definition for both E-commerce and SME makes comparisons with other studies difficult. Further, the measure of E-commerce adoption extent was created based on the 'Four levels of SME E-commerce capabilities' model (PWC, 1999). With the evolving nature of technology, this model may not be the most accurate reflection of E-commerce behaviour among SMEs. In an exploratory case study using the same staged model, Scupola (2003) argues that the model does not incorporate some of the issues confronting firms as they proceed to higher levels of E-commerce capability/activity. In particular, it does not take into consideration changes in a firm's capabilities and business processes as it progresses from one stage to the next stage of EC activity (Scupola, 2003). Further, the study is conducted through a survey, and only those interested in the study were likely have responded (Sohal & Ng, 1998). As data was gathered across various business industries, it is not possible to make any sector-specific conclusions.

IMPLICATIONS AND FUTURE RESEARCH

It is hoped that the findings of the study would enrich the IS adoption literature, and provides more insights into EC adoption by SMEs in developing countries. The results may have a greater implication for government authorities responsible in promoting EC adoption and utilization. Given the unique context of SMEs, such an understanding could be useful for governments in drawing guidelines, approaches, and formulating more effective frameworks to promote SME-EC development. It appears that owner's attribute like education drive the adoption and utilisation of EC among smaller businesses in the country. Government agencies, for example, could intensify their efforts to organise seminars or training courses to better equip owner-managers with knowledge of EC, and create a more innovative culture among smaller firms. IT consultants and vendors can direct their marketing efforts at firms which are more likely to adopt EC such as younger enterprises and those operating in the service industry. Future studies may place greater emphasis on developing countries to examine SMEs in different geographic areas, and provide some insights on the factors influencing EC adoption from a cross-country perspective. More comprehensive, prescriptive research could be conducted on a longitudinal approach in terms of case studies.

REFERENCES

Akhter, S. H. (2003). Digital divide and purchase intention: Why demographic psychology matters? *Journal of Economic Psychology, 24*(3), 321–327. doi:10.1016/S0167-4870(02)00171-X

Alam, S. S., Ahmad, I., Abdullah, Z., & Ishak, N. A. (2007). ICT usage in SMEs: Empirical study of service sectors in Malaysia. In *Proceedings of the 4th SMEs in a Global Economy Conference,* Shah Alam, Malaysia.

Alam, S. S., & Ahsan, M. N. (2007). ICT adoption in Malaysian SMEs from services sectors: Preliminary findings. *Journal of Internet Banking and Commerce, 12*(3). Retrieved May 12, 2009, from http://www.arraydev.com/commerce/jibc/2007-12/Syed_accepted.pdf

Alam, S. S., Khatibi, A., Sayyed Ahmad, M. I., & Ismail, H. (2007). Factors affecting e-commerce adoption in the electronic manufacturing companies in Malaysia. *International Journal of Commerce and Management, 17*(1/2), 125–139. doi:10.1108/10569210710776503

Alzougool, B., & Kurnia, S. (2008). Electronic commerce technologies adoption by SMEs: A conceptual study. In *Proceedings of the 19th Australasian Conference on Information Systems,* Christchurch, New Zealand.

Analoui, F., & Karami, A. (2003). *Strategic management in SMEs.* London: Thomson Learning.

Baggozi, R., & Lee, K. H. (1999). Consumer resistance to, and acceptance of, innovations. *Advances in Consumer Research. Association for Consumer Research (U. S.), 26,* 218–225.

Baker & McKenzie. (2001). *Doing e-commerce in Europe.* Hong Kong: Baker and McKenzie.

Bantel, K. A., & Jackson, S. E. (1989). Top management and innovations in banking: Does the composition of the top management team make a difference? *Strategic Management Journal, 10,* 107–124. doi:10.1002/smj.4250100709

Beaver, G. (2007). The strategy payoff for smaller enterprises. *The Journal of Business Strategy, 28*(1), 11–17. doi:10.1108/02756660710723161

Blackburn, R., & Athayde, R. (2000). Making the connection: The effectiveness of Internet training in small business. *Education and Training, 42*(4/5), 289–299. doi:10.1108/00400910010373723

Bolongkikit, J., Obit, J. H., Asing, J. G., & Tanakinjal, G. H. (2006). An exploratory research of the usage level of e-commerce among SMEs in the West Coast of Sabah, Malaysia. *Journal of Internet Banking and Commerce, 11*(2).

Brunner, C., & Bennett, D. (1998). Technology perceptions by gender. *Education Digest,* (February): 56–58.

Chuang, T. T., Nakatani, K., Chen, J. C. H., & Huang, I. L. (2007). Examining the impact of organisational and owner's characteristics on the extent of e-commerce adoption in SMEs. *Int. J. Business and Systems Research, 1*(1), 61–80. doi:10.1504/IJBSR.2007.014770

Chuang, T. T., Rutherford, M. W., & Lin, B. (2007). Owner/manager characteristics, organisational characteristics and IT adoption in small and medium enterprises. *International Journal of Management and Enterprise Development, 4*(6), 619–634. doi:10.1504/IJMED.2007.014985

Cragg, P. B., & King, M. (1993). Small-firm computing: motivators and inhibitors. *MIS Quarterly, 17*(1), 47–60. doi:10.2307/249509

Curran, J., & Blackburn, R. A. (2001). *Researching the small enterprise.* SAGE Production, London.

Dahlan, N., Ramayah, T., & Koay, A. H. (2002). Data mining in the banking industry: An exploratory study. In *Proceedings of the International Conference, Internet Economy and Business,* Kuala Lumpur, Malaysia.

Daniel, E. M., Wilson, H., & Myers, A. (2002). Adoption of e-commerce by SMEs in the UK: Towards a stage model. *International Small Business Journal, 20*(3), 253–270. doi:10.1177/0266242602203002

Dasgupta, S., Agarwal, D., Ioannidis, A., & Gopalakrishnan, S. (1999). Determinants of information technology adoption: An extension of existing models to firms in a developing country. *Journal of Global Information Management, 7*(3), 30–40.

Department for Business Enterprise & Regulatory Reform of UK. (2007). *Small and medium enterprise statistics for the UK and regions*. Retrieved May 8, 2009, from http://stats.berr.gov.uk/ed/sme/

Department of Statistics Malaysia. (2005). *Census of establishments and enterprises 2003*. The Secretariat, Research & Development Division, Department of Statistics, Federal Government Administrative Centre, Putrajaya, Malaysia.

Dwivedi, Y. K., Selamat, M. H., Abd Wahab, M. S., Mat Samsudin, M. A., & Lal, B. (2008). Examining factors influencing the behavioral intention to adopt broadband in Malaysia. In León, G., Bernardos, A., Casar, J., Kautz (Eds), *Open IT-based innovation: Moving towards cooperative IT transfer and knowledge diffusion* (pp. 325-342). Boston: Springer.

Elbeltagi, I. (2007). E-commerce and globalization: An exploratory study of Egypt. *Cross Cultural Management: An International Journal, 14*(3), 196–201. doi:10.1108/13527600710775748

European Strategic Program on Research in Information Technology. (1997). *ESPRIT and ACTS projects related to Electronic Commerce*. Retrieved May 8, 2009, from http://cordis.europa.eu/esprit/src/ecomproj.htm

Fallon, M., & Moran, P. (2000). Information Communications Technology (ICT) and manufacturing SMEs. In *Proceedings of the 2000 Small Business and Enterprise Development Conference*, University of Manchester (pp. 100–109).

Frambach, R., & Schillweaert, N. (2002). Organizational innovation adoption: A multi-level framework of determinants and opportunities for future research. *Journal of Business Research, 55*(2), 163–176. doi:10.1016/S0148-2963(00)00152-1

Goode, A., & Stevens, K. (2000). An analysis of the business characteristics of adopters and non-adopters of World Wide Web technology. *Information Technology and Management, 1*, 129–154. doi:10.1023/A:1019112722593

Gribbins, M., & King, R. (2004). Electronic retailing strategies: A case study of small businesses in the gifts & collectibles industry. *Electronic Markets, 14*(2), 138–152. doi:10.1080/10196780410001675086

Grimm, C. M., & Smith, K. G. (1991). Management and organizational change: a note on the railroad industry. *Strategic Management Journal, 12*, 557–562. doi:10.1002/smj.4250120708

Hambrick, D. C., & Mason, P. A. (1984). Upper echelons: The organization as a reflection of it's top managers. *Academy of Management Review, 9*, 193–206. doi:10.2307/258434

Hansemark, O. C. (1998). The effects of an entrepreneurship programme on need for achievement and locus of control of reinforcement. *International Journal of Entrepreneurial Behaviour and Research, 4*(1), 28–50. doi:10.1108/13552559810203957

Hashim, N. A. (2006). E-commerce adoption issues in Malaysian SME. In *Proceedings of International Conference on E-commerce (ICoEC)*, Penang, Malaysia.

Hoffman, D. L., Novak, T. P., & Schlosser, A. E. (2000). The evolution of the digital divide: How gaps in Internet access may impact Electronic commerce. *Journal of Computer-Mediated Communication, 5*(3).

Hoi, J., Shim, J. P., & Yin, A. (2003). Current progress of e-commerce adoption: SMEs in Hong Kong. *Communications of the ACM, 46*(9).

Hunter, K., & Kemp, S. (2004). The personality of e-commerce investors. *Journal of Economic Psychology, 25*(4), 529–537. doi:10.1016/S0167-4870(03)00050-3

Hussin, H., & Mohamad Noor, R. (2005). Innovating business through e-commerce: Exploring the willingness of Malaysian SMEs. Retrieved: March 3, 2009, from http://www.it-innovations.ae/iit005/proceedings/articles/I_4_IIT05_Hussin.pdf

Huy, L. V., & Filiatrault, P. (2006). The adoption of e-commerce in SMEs in Vietnam: A study of users and prospectors. *In Proceedings of the 10th Pacific Asia Conference on Information Systems,* Kuala Lumpur, Malaysia (pp. 1335-44).

Jantan, M., Ismail, N., Ramayah, T., & Mohamed Salehuddin, A. H. (2001). The CEO and AMT adoption in Malaysian small and medium scale manufacturing industries. In *Proceedings of the International Conference on Information Technology,* Lausanne, Switzerland.

Kasteler, J. M., Gay, R. M., & Caruth, M. J. (1968). Involuntary relocation of the elderly. *The Gerontologist, 8*(4), 276–279.

Liew, V. K. (2002). *The prospect of e-commerce for the small and medium enterprises in Malaysia.* Kuala Lumpur: University of Malaya.

Lim, T. M. (2006). *Outsourcings to ensure successful ICT systems implementation and maintenance.* School of Information Technology, Monash University. Retrieved March 20, 2008, from http://www.infotech.monash.edu.my/news/media.html

MacGregor, R. C. (2004). The role of small business strategic alliances in the adoption of E-commerce in small-medium enterprises (SMEs). Retrieved June 6, 2008, from http://ro.uow.edu.au/cgi/viewcontent.cgi?article=1303&context=theses

MacGregor, R. C., & Vrazalic, L. (Eds.). (2008). *E-commerce in regional small to medium enterprises.* Hershey, PA: IGI Global Publishing.

Matlay, H. (2000). Training in the small business sector of the British economy. In S. Carter & D. Jones (Eds.), *Enterprise and small business: Principles, policy, and practice.* London: Addison Wesley Longman.

Mazzarol, T., Volery, T., Doss, N., & Thein, V. (1999). Factors influencing small business start-ups. *International Journal of Entrepreneurial Behaviour and Research, 5*(2), 48–63. doi:10.1108/13552559910274499

Morris, M., & Ventakesch, V. (2000). Age differences in technology adoption decisions: Implications for a changing work force. *Personnel Psychology, 53*(2), 375–403. doi:10.1111/j.1744-6570.2000.tb00206.x

National SME Development Council of Malaysia. (2005). *Definitions for small and medium enterprises in Malaysia.* Secretariat to National SME Development Council, Bank Negara Malaysia, Kuala Lumpur. Retrieved May 3, 2009, from http://www.smeinfo.com.my/pdf/sme_definitions_ENGLISH.pdf

Normah, M. A. (2006). *SMEs: Building blocks for economic growth.* Paper presented at the National Statistical Conference, Kuala Lumpur, Malaysia.

Ogunlana, E. A. (2004). The technology adoption behavior of women farmers: The case of alley farming in Nigeria. *Renewable Agriculture and Food Systems, 19,* 57–65. doi:10.1079/RAFS200057

Organisation for Economic Co-operation and Development. (1997). *Globalisation and small and medium enterprises (SMEs).* Paris, France: OECD Publications Service.

Organisation for Economic Co-operation and Development. (2004). *SME statistics: Towards a more systematic statistical measurement of SME behaviour.* Background report for the 2nd OECD Conference of Ministers Responsible for Small and Medium Enterprises (SMEs), Istanbul, Turkey. Retrieved May 3, 2009, from http://www.oecd.org/dataoecd/6/6/31919286.pdf

Organisation for Economic Co-operation and Development. (2005). *OECD SME and Entrepreneurship Outlook - 2005 Edition.* Paris, France: OECD Publications Service. Retrieved May 3, 2009, from http://www.oecd.org/document/15/0,2340,en_2649_33956792_35096847_1_1_1_1,00.html

Parker, C., & Castleman, T. (2007). New directions for research on SME-eBusiness: Insights from an analysis of journal articles from 2003-2006. *Journal of Information Systems and Small Business, 1*(1), 21–40.

Pollman, A., W., & Johnson, A. C. (1974). Resistance to change, early retirement and managerial decisions. *Industrial Gerontology, 1*(1), 33–41.

Pricewaterhousecoopers (1999). *Asia Pacific Economic Cooperation (APEC): SME Electronic Commerce Study - Final Report September 24, 1999.* Retrieved May 12, 2009, from http://www.apec.org/apec/publications/free_downloads/1999.MedialibDownload.v1.html?url=/etc/medialib/apec_media_library/downloads/workinggroups/telwg/pubs/1999.Par.0001.File.v1.1

Ramayah, T., Dahlan, N., Mohamad, O., & Siron, R. (2002). Technology usage among owners/managers of SME's: The role of demographic and motivational variables. In *Proceedings of the 6th Annual Asian-Pacific Forum for Small Business on Small and Medium Enterprises Linkages, Networking and Clustering*, Kuala Lumpur, Malaysia.

Reynolds, W., Savage, W., & Williams, A. (1994). *Your own business: A practical guide to success.* New York: Thomson Learning Nelson.

Robertson, T. S. (1971). *Innovative behavior and communication.* New York: Holt, Rinehart and Winston, Inc.

Sagi, J. (2004). ICT and business in the new economy: Globalization and attitudes towards eCommerce. *Journal of Global Information Management, 12*(3), 44–65.

Sarosa, S., & Underwood, J. (2005). Factors affecting IT adoption within Indonesian SMEs: manager's perspectives. In *Proceedings of the 9th Pacific Asia Conference on Information Systems*, Bangkok, Thailand.

Schindehutte, M., & Morris, M. H. (2001). Understanding strategic adaptation in small firms. *International Journal of Entrepreneurial Behaviour and Research, 7*(3), 84–107. doi:10.1108/EUM0000000005532

Scupola, A. (2003). The adoption of Internet commerce by SMEs in the South of Italy: An environmental, technological and organizational perspective. *Journal of Global Information Technology Management, 6*(1), 52–71.

Sexton, R. S., Johnson, R. A., & Hignite, M. A. (2002). Predicting Internet/EC use. *Internet Research: Electronic Networking Application and Policy, 12*(5), 402–410. doi:10.1108/10662240210447155

Seyal, A. H., & Rahman, M. N. A. (2003). A preliminary investigation of e-commerce adoption in small & medium enterprises in Brunei. *Journal of Global Information Technology Management, 6*(2), 6–26.

Shrader, C., Mulford, C., & Blackburn, V. (1989). Strategic and operational planning, uncertainty, and performance in small firms. *Journal of Small Business Management, 27*(4), 45–60.

Simpson, M., & Docherty, A. J. (2004). E-commerce adoption support and advice for UK SMEs. *Journal of Small Business and Enterprise Development, 11*(3), 315–328. doi:10.1108/14626000410551573

Slovic, P. (1966). Risk-taking in children: Age and sex difference. *Child Development, 37*, 169–176. doi:10.2307/1126437

Smith, J. A. (1998). Strategies for start-ups. *Long Range Planning, 31*(6), 857–872. doi:10.1016/S0024-6301(98)80022-8

Sohal, A. S., & Ng, L. (1998). The role and impact of information technology in Australian Business. *Journal of Information Technology, 13*, 201–217. doi:10.1080/026839698344846

Sparling, L., Toleman, M., & Cater-Steel, A. (2007). SME Adoption of e-Commerce in the Central Okanagan Region of Canada. *In Proceedings of the 18ᵗʰ Australasian Conference on Information Systems*, Toowoomba, Australia (pp. 1046-1059).

Tabor, S. W. (2005). Achieving significant learning in e-commerce education through small business consulting projects. *Journal of Information Systems Education, 16*(1).

Tan, K. S., & Chong, S., C., Lin, B., & Eze, U. C. (2009). Internet-based ICT adoption: Evidence from Malaysian SMEs. *Industrial Management & Data Systems, 109*(2), 224–244. doi:10.1108/02635570910930118

Teo, T. S. H. (2001). Demographic and motivational variables associated with Internet usage activities. *Internet Research: Electronic Networking Applications and Policy, 11*(2), 125–137. doi:10.1108/10662240110695089

Teo, T. S. H., & Lim, V. K. G. (2000). Gender differences in Internet usage and task preferences. *Behaviour & Information Technology, 19*(4), 283–295. doi:10.1080/01449290050086390

Teo, T. S. H., & Tan, M. (1998). An empirical study of adopters and non-adopters of Internet in Singapore. *Information & Management, 34*, 339–345. doi:10.1016/S0378-7206(98)00068-8

Tetteh, E., & Burn, J. (2001). Global strategies for SME-business: Applying the SMALL framework. *Logistics Information Management, 14*(1-2), 171–180. doi:10.1108/09576050110363202

Thong, J. Y. L. (1999). An integrated model of information systems adoption in small businesses. *Journal of Management Information Systems, 15*(4), 187–214.

Thong, J. Y. L., & Yap, C. S. (1995). CEO characteristics, organizational characteristics and information technology adoption in small business. *Omega . International Journal of Management Science, 23*(4), 429–442.

Tiessen, J., Wright, R., & Turner, I. (2001). A model of E-commerce use by internationalizing SMEs. *Journal of International Management, 7*, 211–233. doi:10.1016/S1075-4253(01)00045-X

Turban, E., King, D., Lee, K. J., & Viehland, D. (2004). *Electronic commerce: A managerial perspective*. New Jersey: Pearson Prentice Hall.

Turban, E., McLean, E., & Wetherbe, J. (2004). *Information technology for management: Transforming organizations in the digital economy*. Hoboken, NJ: John Wiley & Sons.

Uhl, K., Anrus, R., & Poulson, L. (1970). How are laggards different? An empirical inquiry. *JMR, Journal of Marketing Research, 7*, 51–54. doi:10.2307/3149506

United Nations Development Programme. Malaysia. (2007). *Small and medium enterprises: Building an enabling environment*. Retrieved May 12, 2009, from http://www.undp.org.my/uploads/UNDP_SME_Publication.pdf

Uzoka, F. M. E., Seleka, G. G., & Khengere, J. (2007). E-commerce adoption in developing countries: A case analysis of environmental and organizational inhibitors. *International Journal of Information Systems and Change Management, 2*(3), 232–260. doi:10.1504/IJISCM.2007.015598

Venkatesh, V., & Morris, M. G. (2000). Why don't men ever stop to ask for directions? Gender, social influence, and their role in technology acceptance and usage behavior. *MIS Quarterly, 24*(1), 115–139. doi:10.2307/3250981

Wen, H. J., Chen, H. G., & Hwang, H. G. (2001). E-commerce Web site design: Strategies and models. *Information Management & Computer Security, 9*(1), 5–12. doi:10.1108/09685220110366713

Wiersema, M. F., & Bantel, K. A. (1992). Top management team demography and corporate strategic change. *Academy of Management Journal, 35*, 91–121. doi:10.2307/256474

Xiao, J. J., Alhabeeb, M. J., Hong, G. S., & Haynes, G. W. (2001). Attitude toward risk and risk-taking behavior of business-owning families. *The Journal of Consumer Affairs, 35*(2), 307–325.

Yap, C. S. (1990). Distinguishing characteristics of organizations using computers. *Information & Management, 18*(2), 97–107. doi:10.1016/0378-7206(90)90056-N

Yap, C. S., Soh, C. P. P., & Raman, K. S. (1992). International systems success factors in small business. *Omega International of Management Science, 5*(6), 597–609. doi:10.1016/0305-0483(92)90005-R

ENDNOTE

[1] In June 2009, the exchange rate for the Malaysian Ringgit (MYR) is approximately MYR3.54 to USD1.00.

Chapter 5
E–Commerce and Small and Medium–Sized Enterprises in S.E. Wales

Brychan Thomas
University of Glamorgan, UK

Geoff Simmons
University of Ulster, UK

Gary Packham
University of Glamorgan, UK

Christopher Miller
University of Glamorgan, UK

ABSTRACT

One region where e-commerce will have a particular impact for small and medium-sized enterprises (SMEs) over the next few years is South East Wales (SEW). In response to this a survey was undertaken by the Welsh Enterprise Institute (WEI) in collaboration with the Open University Business School and Rennes ESC in Brittany to assess the e-commerce activity of firms within the SEW area. The survey was conducted using a database of 3,000 members provided by the Cardiff Chamber of Commerce, Trade and Industry and a survey form was sent to the sample as a postal questionnaire. Results from the survey demonstrated that nearly all firms used some form of Information Communication Technologies (ICT). The results also highlighted that a significant proportion of the sample (77%) were currently using a Web site to increase trade or improve opportunities for e-commerce. Furthermore, it was observed that firms in the personal services, distribution and transport industries were less likely to utilise a Web site than firms in the manufacturing, business services and hospitality industries. Despite the large proportion of firms that had a Web site, only 11% of businesses reported that their site enabled customers to order and pay for products online although 42% of respondents considered e-commerce to be important for their business' future. This chapter therefore argues that these results clearly underpin the necessity for an e-commerce policy in SEW for the future competitiveness of the area. There are real opportunities to develop and diversify the SEW economy through e-commerce.

DOI: 10.4018/978-1-60566-998-4.ch005

INTRODUCTION

It has already been recognised that e-commerce is revolutionising business transactions. In fact, e-commerce is changing the way businesses of all sizes operate in terms of their interaction with customers and suppliers. In addition, it is contended that the rapid adoption of e-commerce by many firms is also providing the catalyst for societal change. Through e-commerce it is possible to market products and services to customers around the World. It continues however, to present a significant challenge to regional and central governments alike in terms of policies and programmes. In this sense, it is argued that businesses will need to adopt a proactive approach if they are to benefit from this new medium. Moreover, it is submitted that unless firms develop their own procedures and systems to keep pace with electronic developments, they are likely to be left behind and fall by the wayside as the 'e-economy' gathers momentum.

Due to there being no internationally accepted definition of e-commerce, according to MacGregor and Hodgkinson (2007), there are nearly as many e-commerce definitions as contributions to the literature and they highlight the following:

Any 'net' business activity that transforms internal and external relationships to create value and exploit market opportunities driven by new rules of the connected economy. (Damanpour, 2001, p. 18)

Functions of information exchange and commercial transaction support that operate on telemcommunications networks linking business partners (typically customers and suppliers). (Raymond, 2001, p. 411)

An emerging concept that describes the process of buying, selling or exchanging services and information via computer networks. (Turban et al, 2002, p.4)

Small and medium-sized enterprises (SMEs) have exhibited considerable evolutionary change. From the perspective of SMEs, global challenges and opportunities are being intertwined with the increasing business potency of the Internet. The contemporary small business landscape is presenting SMEs with tantillising and testing possibilities within the Internet context (Fillis & Wagner, 2005; Matlay & Westhead, 2005; Bengtsson et al., 2007). Despite the widespread acceptance of Internet use in corporate environments, the extent of Internet use continues to vary widely among small businesses (Sadowski et al., 2002). The opportunities presented by e-commerce participation for SMEs, relate to the leveraging of inherent strengths to create competitive advantage. The size of SMEs enables them to be more adaptable and responsive to changing conditions than larger organizations and to further benefit from the speed and flexibility that the electronic environment offers (Stockdale & Standing, 2004). However, for SMEs the Internet is also viewed by other researchers as posing significant challenges. For most SMEs Internet based e-commerce is manifested through Website adoption (Simmons et al., 2007; Simmons et al., 2008). Many small businesses initially adopt the Internet for business use as a tool for email and surfing the World Wide Web. However, Website adoption takes this Internet adoption to a higher level by requiring the SME to register a URL and develop a Website, which can be accessed by visitors globally (Simmons et al., 2008). Within this context, the proliferation of Websites is making it more difficult for SMEs, compared to their larger counterparts, to attract visitors and convert them to customers. Auger (2005) states that this can be due to factors such as a lack of brand recognition, lack of advertising resources, and limited Website development and maintenance budgets.

BACKGROUND

SMEs are adopting e-commerce for marketing, promoting, buying and selling of goods and ser-

Figure 1. Internet usage growth 1996-2006(Source: Internet World Stats, 2007)

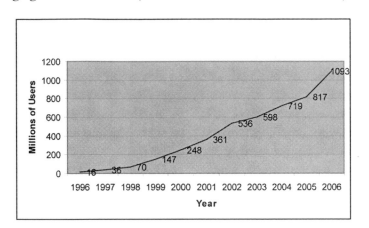

vices electronically. In particular, this is carried out as a new way of transacting business and encompasses various aspects of Internet use. This involves virtual store fronts that are sites for shopping and making purchases and business-to-business, b2b, business-to-consumer, b2c, exchange of data and e-mail. There is also business-to-business buying and selling and the need for the security of data handling and transactions (Van Ketel & Nelson, 1998, 2003). In these terms Forrester Research (1998), an independent research firm, defines e-commerce as 'the trading of goods and services in which the final order is placed over the Internet'. According to Forrester Research (2007) 'while e-commerce sales continue to grow at a rapid pace, unmet customer opportunities abound in the areas of Web site purchasing, Web site operations and fulfilment'. It is evident that a growing number of SMEs are accessing the Internet for their business and to reach new customers. Although online sales are growing e-commerce only represents a small amount of SMEs' use of the Internet. Consequently, more research is required into the barriers to e-commerce. Nearly all areas of business are beginning to use e-commerce to reach customers more effectively, plan production, streamline logistics and inventories, manage multiple relationships and as a means of cost saving on purchasing (USDoC, 1998, 2002).

As a consequence, this medium is experiencing considerable growth. Figure 1 illustrates Internet usage growth from 1996 to 2006.

Internet adoption for SMEs is not a standardized process, with a wide variety of Websites being adopted in the level of sophistication and relevance they have for target customers and company value. Indeed, Houghton and Winklhofer (2002) believe there are several reasons behind the need to understand what determines Internet adoption more clearly. Firstly, initial adoption by a SME does not necessarily imply continued and increasingly sophisticated use of the medium. Individual determinants will result in the sophistication and relevance of Internet adoption. Secondly, knowledge of the determinants of SME Internet adoption will assist in more focused efforts to stimulate adoption in SMEs. The lack of coherence and integration within the SME Internet adoption literature has been a concern (Pflughoeft et al., 2003; Downie, 2003; Fillis et al., 2003; Martin & Matlay, 2003; Simmons et al., 2007). However, recent work by Simmons et al. (2008) has created a new research agenda, with a specific focus on the central Internet adoption context of Websites.

Three phases of Internet adoption which SMEs go through as their Internet involvement develops are described as connectivity, customer

Figure 2. Phases in the development of e-commerce for SME Web sites (Adapted from von Goeler, 1998)

Phases	Information exchange	Web site development
Connectivity	Product/Service and Enterprise Information Customer Feedback Forms	Brochure-ware sites
Customer Connections	Online catalogue	Pre E-Commerce sites
E-Commerce	Online ordering Online payment	Simple E-Commerce sites

relations and commerce (YG, 1998, 2002; Ng et al, 1998). 'Web-based applications are commonplace today. Tens of millions use Internet commerce and information sites daily, and corporations are increasingly choosing to use Web architectures and applications across the enterprise.' (YG, 2002) The three phases are seen as the 'building blocks of e-commerce' (Williams & Phillips, 1999) as shown in Figure 2 (based on von Goeler, 1998).

The three phases towards e-commerce can be described as follows:

- **Brochure-ware sites:** Enterprises use their Web sites for product/service advertisement and gather information and improve services through customer feedback forms. Such enterprises need to install electronic technology to sell goods over the World Wide Web.
- **Pre-commerce sites:** Enterprises are able to provide information on price for immediate orders from their Web sites. But they do not carry out online point-of-sale transactions although they keep their site current.
- **Simple e-commerce sites:** Enterprises accept orders and payments over the Web.

Customers have developed a behavioural sequence to online shopping. Indeed, Forrester Research (1998, 2007) has divided the online retail market into the three categories of convenience items, replenishment goods and research purchases. Convenience items are low cost discretionary items such as books, clothes and music. Replenishment goods are medium cost high frequency purchases like groceries. Research purchases are information driven and cost more than the other two categories and include planned purchases such as cars, computers and airline tickets. The Forrester Research study (1998) found that first time buyers usually bought convenience items and that it took around one year for online shoppers to move to a further category. Internet sales are showing a fast growth in books, cars, computers and software (USDoC, 1998, 2002). Important players in this growth are online entrepreneurs (Simons, 1998).

Whereas some SMEs have been early adopters of e-commerce others have lagged behind in establishing the ability to sell their products and services over the Internet (Simmons et al., 2007). In fact, SMEs have been slower than large businesses in embracing e-commerce (Sadowski et al., 2002; Simmons et al., 2008). Even though the number of SMEs using the Internet is rising there are a number of obstacles to their use of e-commerce. These include cost features, customer service requirements, security problems and technical expertise (Van Smith & Webster, 2000; Lewis & Cockrill, 2002; Jones et al., 2003; Fillis et al., 2005).

SMEs rely on knowing customer needs and build business processes and quality control around communications. A major concern is that the loss of customer contact may lead to a lower quality of service and there may be customer resistance to product price at the point of transaction. However, the contention of most authors is that Internet adoption will be a critical component of SME survival into the future (Fillis & Wagner, 2005; Matlay & Westhead, 2005; Bengtsson et al., 2007). It is the proposition of this chapter that due to the future importance for indigenous SMEs to sell their products and services over the Internet it is necessary for an e-commerce policy in regions like South East Wales (SEW) for the future competitiveness of the area.

The cost of building and maintaining an e-commerce site is seen as the largest restriction to online selling with the lack of technical expertise, site security and the cost of building transactions based sites as other barriers (Simmons et al., 2008; Grunert & Ramus, 2005; Van Smith & Webster, 2000; Lewis & Cockrill, 2002). Quayle (2001), who explores the awareness and level of implementation of e-commerce, has eloquently described the e-commerce challenge for Welsh SMEs. Results of a survey of 298 small firms were used to identify barriers faced by these enterprises and he suggests paths, which might be followed in seeking to achieve best in class performance for e-commerce.

RESEARCH METHODOLOGY

The research concerning e-commerce and SMEs in SEW, reported in this chapter, was carried out as part of the 'Effects of E-Commerce on Small and Medium Enterprises in Britain and France' (E-CoSME) survey (Brooksbank et al, 2001). The sample for SEW was composed of firms who were members of Cardiff Chamber of Commerce, Trade and Industry. The survey form, agreed by E-CoSME partners, was sent to the sample as a postal questionnaire at the same time as the Chamber Quarterly Economic Survey to be returned by freepost or fax. The Chamber of Commerce conducted the survey using their database of members.

The Chamber database included 3,000 current members in the SEW area and questionnaire forms were sent during November to be returned before Christmas. 157 replies were received giving a response rate of 5%, similar to the E-CoSME Devon and Cornwall study. Although this is a low response it appears sufficient for this study. Since the response included ten large companies as well as SMEs the findings are analysed according to the whole return and also for SMEs specifically for the analysis.

E-CoSME Survey of South East Wales

The questionnaire returns received for the E-CoSME survey of SEW demonstrate that nearly all firms use computers (only one respondent company did not use a computer although they were anticipating obtaining one within a year). Three quarters of the firms are networked and this finding is similar for the whole return in SEW and SMEs specifically. Table 1 illustrates the differences between industries for SMEs and large companies (LCs) and the split between networked and non-networked computers.

Table 2 provides the differences between industries for SMEs specifically. The results show only slight adjustments to the data from Table 1 for the 10 large companies (LCs) that are excluded.

About three-quarters of respondents had networked computers. The areas of manufacturing had more than 80% of companies with networked computers, business services 88%, personal services 62.5%, building/construction 53%, distribution and transport 70% and 70.5%

Table 1. Computer usage by type of industry (SMEs and LCs)

	No	No, but will within a year	Yes, Non-networked/ Standalone computer(s)	Yes, Networked computers	Total	%
Manufacturer – finished goods	0	0	3	22	25	16
Manufacturer – components	0	0	3	14	17	11
Business services	0	0	5	40	45	29
Personal services	0	0	3	5	8	5
Building/construction	0	0	7	8	15	9
Distribution/transport	0	0	6	14	20	13
Hospitality	0	1	5	3	9	6
Other	0	0	6	12	18	11
Total	0	1	38	118	157	
%	0	1	24	75		

for others. Only hospitality had more companies with non-networked/standalone computers (55%), 33% networked and 1 company without a computer at the moment.

A significant determinant of e-commerce is the use of a company Web site. Similar to Devon and Cornwall the SEW study exhibits an unbalanced split between the use of Web sites (77%) and companies without Web sites 23%, as illustrated in Table 3.

Table 4 shows the split between companies with Web sites and those without for SMEs specifically.

Again, the results show only slight adjustments to the data from Table 3 for the 10 large companies (LCs) that are excluded.

Some 76% of SMEs who responded had a Web site and 24% did not. Those industries where around 40% of the respondents did not have a Web site were personal services and distribution and transport. Alternatively, the manufacturing, business services, hospitality and 'other' had high Web site usage. Only 11% of businesses reported that their Web site allowed customers to order and pay for products online. For those respondents with

Table 2. Computer usage by type of industry (SMEs)

	No	No, but will within a year	Yes, Non-networked/ Standalone computer(s)	Yes, Networked computers	Total	%
Manufacturer – finished goods	0	0	3	17	20	14
Manufacturer – components	0	0	3	13	16	11
Business services	0	0	5	37	42	29
Personal services	0	0	3	5	8	5
Building/construction	0	0	7	8	15	10
Distribution/transport	0	0	6	14	20	14
Hospitality	0	1	5	3	9	6
Other	0	0	5	12	17	11
Total	0	1	37	109	147	
%	0	1	25	74		

Table 3. Website usage by type of industry (SMEs and LCs)

	No	No, but intend to within a year	Yes	Total	%
Manufacturer – finished goods	2	1	22	25	16
Manufacturer – components	1	5	11	17	11
Business services	4	1	40	45	29
Personal services	3	0	5	8	5
Building/construction	4	1	10	15	9
Distribution/transport	5	4	11	20	13
Hospitality	0	2	7	9	6
Other	2	1	15	18	11
Total	21	15	121	157	
%	13	10	77		

Web sites 18% updated them frequently (daily or weekly – the same percentage as for Devon and Cornwall), 15% once a month and 45% did not update their Web site more frequently than three months and often longer.

Most respondents were connected to the Internet with only 5% not connected. The most common connection was ISDN (42%) and there were 33% with fixed-line, 20% cable modem, 10% for ADSL and leased line and 4% using a WAP connection. 43% of businesses with a business plan had an 'ICT plan' and 42% of respondents considered e-commerce to be very necessary for their business. Only 5% did not feel that e-commerce

was important. With regard to ICT skills 50% of respondents reported that they acquired these in-house, 36% on a formal course, 43% said that staff learn these on the job as they go along, 8% recruit skills and 3% through other means.

FUTURE RESEARCH DIRECTIONS

It is planned by the authors to undertake future research through 'follow-up' surveys of the adoption of e-commerce by SMEs not only in S.E. Wales but also in other areas of the UK. This will enable an inter-regional longitudinal study

Table 4. Website usage by type of industry (SMEs)

	No	No, but intend to within a year	Yes	Total	%
Manufacturer – finished goods	2	1	17	20	14
Manufacturer – components	0	5	11	16	11
Business services	4	1	37	42	28
Personal services	3	0	5	8	5
Building/construction	4	1	10	15	10
Distribution/transport	5	4	11	20	14
Hospitality	0	2	7	9	6
Other	2	1	14	17	12
Total	20	15	112	147	
%	14	10	76		

to be developed over a number of years and will shed light on the e-commerce activities of SMEs during times of differing economic conditions. By undertaking research in a number of regions, including Northern Ireland and S.E. Wales, it will be possible to make further regional comparisons to those that have already been made in the present study. It is anticipated by some researchers that even in a situation where there is negative economic growth e-commerce may still be relatively resilient on the basis that during a recession people will not stop spending but will spend more carefully. This can be beneficial for SME e-commerce web sites since if people can find cheaper products and services online they are more likely to make online purchases. There will be a number of reasons for this including the fact that customers can make informed decisions online by comparing prices, they can save on travel and time, there can be increased customer trust through improved online transaction security, and there may also be advantages due to environmental factors, convenience, improved product imaging and product reviews. It is also possible for SMEs to reduce overhead costs through e-commerce web sites and this will be important in order to survive in a recession. Future research directions will therefore investigate reasons for people buying products and services online from SMEs during varying economic conditions and it will be possible to make temporal and regional comparisons that will be of significance not only to an understanding of e-commerce adoption by SMEs and small business, and the tools for optimisation, but also to the overall e-commerce activity of the economy.

CONCLUSION AND POLICY IMPLICATIONS

The E-CoSME study shows that about 75% of respondents have networked computers in South East Wales. The areas of manufacturing have more than 80% of companies with networked computers, business services 88%, personal services 62.5%, building/construction 53%, distribution and transport 70% and 70.5% for others. Only hospitality has more companies with non-networked/standalone computers (55%), 33% networked and 1 company without a computer at the moment. A significant determinant of e-commerce is the use of a company Web site. Similar to Devon and Cornwall the South East Wales study exhibits an unbalanced split between the use of Web sites (77%) and companies without Web sites (23%).

It is apparent that 76% of SMEs who responded have a Web site and 24% do not. Industries where around 40% of the respondents do not have a Web site are personal services and distribution and transport. Manufacturing, business services, hospitality and 'other' have high Web site usage. 11% of businesses report that their Web site allows customers to order and pay for products online. For those with Web sites 18% update them frequently (daily or weekly – the same percentage as Devon and Cornwall), 15% once a month and 45% do not update their Web site more frequently than three months and often longer.

Generally, respondents are connected to the Internet with only 5% not connected. ISDN (42%) is the most common connection and there are 33% with fixed-line, 20% cable modem, 10% for ADSL and leased line and 4% using a WAP connection. Some 43% of businesses with a business plan have an 'ICT plan' and 42% of respondents consider e-commerce to be necessary for their business. Only 5% do not feel that e-commerce is important. With regard to ICT skills 50% of respondents report that they acquire these in-house, 36% on a formal course, 43% say that staff learn these on the job as they go along, 8% recruit skills and 3% through other means.

Based upon these findings the aim for the Wales Assembly Government should be to improve affordable access to a high bandwidth communications infrastructure for SMEs and to provide practical, accessible support for these firms, to encourage and enable them to make successful use of e-commerce opportunities. By implementing this policy it is envisaged that the proportion of businesses in SEW using e-commerce will increase and eventually converge on the UK average. Sufficient attention to date has not been given to bringing together all the various programmes in Wales involving e-commerce into a high profile and coherent strategy as exemplified by other governments (IoMG, 2000).

ACKNOWLEDGMENT

The authors would like to acknowledge Professor Colin Gray, Head of the SME Research Unit, Open University Business School, for inviting the WEI to participate in the ECoSME study, and to Professor David Brooksbank, Director of Enterprise, Cardiff School of Management, University of Wales Institute Cardiff and the late Professor Michael Quayle, Director of the Business School, University of Glamorgan, for their support for the project in South East Wales.

REFERENCES

Andersen, A., & National Small Business United. (1998). *Survey of Small and Medium-sized Businesses*.

Auger, P. (2005). The impact of interactivity and design sophistication on the performance of commercial websites for small businesses. *Journal of Small Business Management*, *43*(2), 119–137.

Bengtsson, M., Boter, H., & Vanyushyn, V. (2007). Integrating the Internet and marketing operations. *International Small Business Journal*, *25*(1), 27–48. doi:10.1177/0266242607071780

Brooksbank, D., Morse, L., & Thomas, B. (2000). *Learning Chamber Report 'Towards a Learning Strategy*. Cardiff: Cardiff Chamber of Commerce, 92. Retrieved from http://www.cardiffchamber.co.uk/

Brooksbank, D., Quayle, M., & Thomas, B. (2001). Project looks at the effects of e-commerce on SMEs. *The Western Mail*, Wednesday, September 19.

Damanpour, F. (2001). E-business e-commerce evolution: perspective and strategy. *Managerial Finance*, *27*(7), 16–33. doi:10.1108/03074350110767268

Downie, G. (2003). Interactive marketing and SMEs. *Management Services*, *47*(7), 8.

Dun & Bradstreet. (1998, February 19). *17 Annual D&B small business study*. Retrieved from http://www.dnb.com/newsview/0217news4.htm

Fillis, I., Johanson, U., & Wagner, B. (2003). E-business development: a conceptual model of the smaller firm. *Journal of Small Business and Enterprise Development*, *10*(3), 336–345. doi:10.1108/14626000310489808

Fillis, I., & Wagner, B. (2005). E-business development: an explanatory investigation of the small firm. *International Small Business Journal*, *23*(6), 604–634. doi:10.1177/0266242605057655

Fillis, I., & Wagner, B. (2005). E-business development: an exploratory investigation of the small firm. *International Small Business Journal*, *23*, 604–634. doi:10.1177/0266242605057655

Forrester Research. (1998, November 19). *Growth spiral in online retail sales will generate $108 billion in revenues by 2003*. Retrieved from http://www.forrester.com.

Forrester Research. (2007, May 11). *Five immediate opportunities for ecommerce improvement*. Retrieved from http://www.forrester.com.

Grunert, K. G., & Ramus, K. (2005). Consumers' willingness to buy food through the internet. *British Food Journal, 107*(6), 381–403. doi:10.1108/00070700510602174

Hill, S. (2000). *Changing Wales Report*. Cardiff, Wales.

Houghton, K. A., & Winklhofer, H. (2002). Internet adoption in exporting SMEs: development of a conceptual model. *American Marketing Association, Conference Proceedings, Chicago, 13*, 504.

Inland Revenue. (1998). Chapter 1 - Encouraging the growth of e-commerce, *Electronic Commerce: The UKs Taxation Agenda*. http://www.inlandrevenue.gov.uk/taxagenda/ecom1.htm.

International Data Corporation (IDC). (1998). *Small business embraces the Internet.* http://www.idc.com/F/HNR/071398.htm.

Internet World Stats. (2007). *Internet usage growth*. Retrieved from http://www.internetworldstats.com

Isle of Man Government. (IoMG) (2000, July, 25). *E-commerce strategy – A report by the council of ministers*. Douglas, Isle of Man.

Jones, C., Hecker, R., & Holland, P. (2003). Small firm internet adoption: opportunities forgone, a journey not begun. *Journal of Small Business and Enterprise Development, 10*(3), 287–298. doi:10.1108/14626000310489763

Lewis, R., & Cockrill, A. (2002). Going global—remaining local: the impact of e-commerce on small retail firms in Wales. *International Journal of Information Management, 22*(3), 195–209. doi:10.1016/S0268-4012(02)00005-1

MacGregor, R. C., & Hodgkinson, A. (2007). *Small business clustering technologies: Applications in marketing, management, IT and economics.* Hershey, PA: Idea Group Inc (IGI).

Martin, L., & Matlay, H. (2003). Innovative use of the internet in established small firms: the impact of knowledge management and organisational learning in accessing new opportunities. *Qualitative Market Research, 6*(1), 18–26. doi:10.1108/13522750310457348

Matlay, H., & Westhead, P. (2005). Virtual teams and the rise of e-entrepreneurship in Europe. *International Small Business Journal, 23*(3), 279–302. doi:10.1177/0266242605052074

Mehling, H. (1998). Survey Says: E-commerce is crucial to success - Small businesses are eager to sell wares on the Web. *Computer Reseller News,* May 4, 787.

Ng, H.-I., Pan, Y. G., & Wilson, T. D. (1998). Business use of the World Wide Web: A report on further investigations. *International Journal of Information Management, 18*(5), 291–314. doi:10.1016/S0268-4012(98)00021-8

Pflughoeft, K. A., Ramamurthy, K., Soofi, E. S., Yasai-Ardekani, M., & Fatemah, M. (2003). Multiple conceptualizations of small business Web use and benefit. *Decision Sciences, 34*(3), 467–513. doi:10.1111/j.1540-5414.2003.02539.x

Pricewaterhouse Coopers (1998, November 3). Economic outlook appears bright for technology businesses, especially smaller ones. *Trendsetter Barometer Report.*

Quayle, M. (2001). *E-commerce: The challenge for Welsh small and medium size enterprises.* Business Week in Wales Lecture, Cardiff. *Cardiff International Arena, 16*(May), 14.

Raymond, L. (2001). Determinants of Web site implementation in small business. *Internet Research, 11*(5), 411–424. doi:10.1108/10662240110410363

Roberts, V. (1999). Information technology sector to lead US economy's continuing growth in 1999. *Economic Outlook*, January 27(17). http://www.newsstand.k-link.com/.

Sadowski, B. M., Maitland, C., & Van Dongen, J. (2002). Strategic use of the Internet by small- and medium-sized companies: an exploratory study. *Information Economics and Policy, 14*(1), 75–93. doi:10.1016/S0167-6245(01)00054-3

Simmons, G. J., Armstrong, G. A., & Durkin, M. G. (2008). A conceptualization of the determinants of small business Website adoption: Setting the research agenda. *International Small Business Journal, 26*(3), 351–389. doi:10.1177/0266242608088743

Simmons, G. J., Durkin, M. G., McGowan, P., & Armstrong, G.A. (2007). Determinants of Internet adoption by SME agri-food companies. *Journal of Small Business and Enterprise Development, 14*(4), 620–640. doi:10.1108/14626000710832730

Simons, J. (1999, January 26). States chafe as Web shopper ignore sales taxes. *The Wall Street Journal*, B1.

Stockdale, R., & Standing, C. (2004). Benefits and barriers of electronic marketplace participation: an SME perspective. *Journal of Enterprise Information Management, 17*(4), 301–311. doi:10.1108/17410390410548715

Tax Foundation (1998). Mismatch between old tax and new E-commerce has Governments scrambling. *Tax Features, 42*(10), 4,8.

Turban, E., Lee, J., King, D., & Chung, H. M. (2002). *Electronic commerce: A managerial perspective*. Englewood Cliff, NJ: Prentice-Hall International Inc.

United States Department of Commerce (USDoC). (1998). *The emerging digital economy*. Washington, DC: USDOC.

United States Department of Commerce (USDoC). (2002). *A nation online: How Americans are expanding their use of the Internet*. Washington, DC: USDOC.

Van Ketel, M., & Nelson, T. D. (1998 May 18). *E-commerce*. Retrieved from http://www.whatis.com/

Van Ketel, M., & Nelson, T. D. (2003). *E-commerce, USA*, http://searchcio.techtarget.com/.

Van Smith, J., & Webster, L. (2000). The knowledge economy and SMEs: A survey of skills requirements. *Business Information Review, 17*(3), 138–146. doi:10.1177/0266382004237656

von Goeler, K. (1998, November 8). *Internet commerce by degrees: Small business early adopters*. Retrieved from http://instat.com

Williams, V., & Phillips, B. D. (1999). *E-commerce: Small businesses venture online*. Report, Office of Advocacy, US Small Business Administration, Washington, DC, July. Retrieved from http://www.sba.gov/advo/stats/e_comm.pdf

Yankee Group (YG). (1998, November 17). Yankee group finds small and business market missing the Internet commerce opportunity: Market unsatisfied with current Internet solution provider offerings. *YG Communication*.

Yankee Group (YG). (2002, January 1). Application Infrastructure and Software Platforms. *YG Communication*.

ADDITIONAL READING

Al-Qirim, N. A. Y. (Ed.). (2004). *Electronic commerce in small to medium-sized enterprises: Frameworks, issues and implications*. Hershey, PA: IGI Global Publishing.

Zappala, S., & Gray, C. (Eds.). (2006). *Impact of e-commerce on consumers and small firms*. Aldershot: Ashgate.

Zhao, F. (Ed.). (2008). *Information technology entrepreneurship and innovation*. Hershey, PA: Information Science Reference.

KEY TERMS AND DEFINITIONS

B2B (Business to Business): E-commerce involving the exchange of information, services and products from business to business over the Web.

B2C (Business to Consumer): E-commerce involving the exchange of information, services and products from business to consumer over the Web.

E-Commerce: Buying and selling goods and services over the Internet.

Information and Communication Technology (ICT): The use of computer based information systems (ISs) and communication systems (CSs) to process, transmit and store information and data.

Internet: The worldwide network of networks that use the TCP/IP communications protocol.

Network: A computer network that is a group of computers or devices connected together to share resources and exchange data.

Portal: A website giving access to a range of services and resources.

Software: Computer programming code providing a computer with instructions to perform tasks.

APPENDIX

LIST OF ABBREVIATIONS

ADSL - Asymmetric Digital Subscriber Line
B2B - Business to Business (E-commerce)
B2C - Business to Consumer (E-commerce)
E-CoSME - E-Commerce and Small and Medium-sized Enterprises (Project)
ICT - Information and Communication Technology
ISDN - Integrated Services Digital Network
LCs - Large Companies
SMEs - Small and Medium-sized Enterprises
SEW - South East Wales
URL - Uniform Resource Locator
WAP - Wireless Application Protocol
WEI - Welsh Enterprise Institute

Section 3
Internet Marketing and Small Business

Chapter 6

The Effectiveness of Internet Portals on the E-Commerce Activities of Rural SME Business Owners:
A Study of Rural SMEs in Scotland

John Sanders
Heriot-Watt University, UK

Laura Galloway
Heriot-Watt University, UK

David Deakins
University of the West of Scotland, UK

ABSTRACT

This chapter explores the uses and effectiveness of private and public/charity managed and funded internet portals on rural SMEs e-commerce activities in Scotland. Specifically, the study investigated whether there were differences in how rural SMEs used and perceived the effectiveness of each type of internet portal. Hypotheses were drawn from qualitative results carried out by Deakins et al. (2003) and Galloway et al. (2008, November). Ninety-six rural SMEs spread across the two types of rural internet portals were interviewed via telephone to gain their perceptions. Cross-tabulations using chi square testing discovered that in the main there were no perceived differences between the uses and effectiveness of private and public/charity funded internet portals on rural SMEs e-commerce activities. However, testing did discover that rural SME users of public/charity funded internet portals were more likely to be charged a fee for membership. The main preoccupation of rural SMEs was representation on an internet portal to help facilitate their e-commerce activities, not how it was owned or operated.

DOI: 10.4018/978-1-60566-998-4.ch006

INTRODUCTION

Within the small business literature a major issue is what constitutes a small and medium-sized enterprise (SME). Some authors use annual sales and total assets; while others utilise a firm's method of production or legal status. The multiplicity of definitions employed reflects the diverse character of the SME sector. For the purpose of this chapter an uncomplicated and popular definition of SMEs will be used. The source of this definition is from the United Kingdom's Department for Business, Enterprise and Regulatory Reform (BERR) and it simply classifies firms by their employee numbers. BERR (2009) define a small business as having 0 to 49 employees, whilst medium-sized businesses employ between 50 and 249 employees.

Small business research has in the main concentrated on the experiences and issues confronting urban rather than rural SMEs. As the literature review will explain, rural SMEs have unique needs which must be addressed and understood if they are going to fulfill their potential. For instance, rural SMEs face limited access to business services, shortage of labour and inadequate transport links.

Certainly many authors view e-commerce as an important means for assisting rural SMEs to surmount the aforementioned difficulties. Wigand (1997) describes e-commerce as "the seamless application of information and communication technology from its point of origin to its end point along the entire value chain of business processes conducted electronically and designed to enable the accomplishment of a business goal. These processes may be partial or complete and may encompass business-to-business, as well as business-to-consumer and consumer-to-business transactions" (p.5). Stifling SME owners/managers e-commerce endeavours is a lack of computer/internet literacy and website expertise. A positive development to remedy rural SMEs information technology deficiencies is the emergence of local internet portals run either by dedicated private individuals or via not-for-profit organisations like local charities or government authorities. The authors define internet portals as a collective activity using the internet to present businesses via a common brand, most often industry or location-specific.

Rural firms have been found in various studies to use portals. There is evidence of collective action amongst rural business owners through local area marketing of rural locations, for example in Scotland (Galloway et al., 2004); industry-focused marketing such as tourism (Pease, et al., 2005, August); and combinations of these, notably agri-food, for example in Greece (Baourakis et al., 2002; Vakoufaris et al., 2007) and Wales (Thomas, et al. 2002). Such strategies can benefit member firms that may not have a direct internet presence: as Pease and Rowe (2005, July) note, in many cases, particularly in rural locations, "the premise…is the realisation that on its own an SME is not able to cope with the increasingly complex [internet] environment…nor does it possess the skills and expertise needed to compete in that environment". The aim of this chapter is to report findings from a survey of rural firms in Scotland which make use of internet portals. The implications of these findings are then discussed for policy-makers in terms of optimising e-commerce activities for rural SMEs.

The remainder of this chapter includes a literature review that briefly examines some of the major trends and issues surrounding rural SME owners and entrepreneurs. A further element of the literature review will address the usage of e-commerce by rural SMEs. Following this discussion the impact of internet portals on rural SMEs is reported. The authors believe internet portals are an important vehicle for optimising rural SMEs e-commerce efforts. Certainly the expertise offered by internet portal operators can pave the way for rural SMEs to more rapidly improve their e-commerce activities than might otherwise happen. In support of this belief, two qualitative studies investigating the characteristics and effectiveness of internet portals are discussed. Next, six hypotheses are presented which were formulated from the two aforementioned studies. The method used by the authors to test the hypotheses is subsequently outlined. After the method section, results are detailed followed by discussion and conclusion sections. Finally, avenues for future research are detailed.

Literature Review

In the developing literature on rural business owners and entrepreneurs, it is claimed that there are a number of characteristics of rural entrepreneurship, compared to entrepreneurship in urban areas that determine its distinctiveness. It is now well established that rural areas have relatively more self-employment and business ownership than urban areas, and that in many areas the rural economy is increasingly supported by the small firms and self-employment sectors, as agriculture and traditional industry decline (e.g., Roberts, 2002). Despite greater proportions of independent economic activity, however, businesses in rural areas tend to be smaller in size, and are less likely to be classifiable as growth firms, resulting in part in the rural business environment being characterised as less volatile and exhibiting less 'business churn' relative to urban areas (e.g., Smallbone et al. 2002). Other characteristics of the rural business environment include that there can be shortages of skilled labour, providing difficulties in recruitment (Patterson and Henderson, 2003) due in part to net outward migration of younger ages of the population (Courtney and Brydon, 2001, November). Other issues include reliance on local markets to a greater extent than in urban areas (Galloway and Mochrie, 2006), caused in part by remoteness from extended markets (Huggins and Izushi, 2002), and limited numbers and density of business networks (ibid). Further, Galloway and Mochrie (2006) found also that there is a high proportion of family-owned businesses in the rural economy and a business advice

and support premium, due to the more spatially dispersed pattern and lack of business networks. More recently, the Small Business Service confirm that these issues and characteristics of the rural small businesses economy prevail in England (Telford, 2006, October), and it is likely that this can be generalised to the British and European contexts at least.

Rural Business and E-Commerce

The benefits, real and potential, associated with e-commerce adoption for businesses are many, and they have been extensively reported elsewhere in the literature. It is not the intention here to reiterate these in detail, however, a summary of now established principles includes access to extended markets (e.g., Lawson et al., 2003); increased trading hours (e.g., Buhalis and Main, 1998); product/ service refinement and more efficient market targeting as a result of communications with and information from customers (e.g., Baourakis et al., 2002); improved business to business dealings including supply chains (e.g., Bharadwaj and Soni, 2007); more efficient transaction arrangements as a result of online payment facilities (e.g., Leatherman, 2000); and supplementary networking channels (e.g., Swan et al., 1999).

Despite these well-documented benefits, several studies have identified that rural firms have been relatively slow to take-up innovation and technology, including e-commerce use, and rural SMEs have been presented as being slow to understand the benefits of internet adoption (e.g., Smallbone et al., 2002). These types of findings have been identified as surprising by those who have theorised that since rural firms have more to gain from the benefits of the e-commerce, especially access to extended markets (due to the issues associated with rurality and peripherality, already outlined), they would be more, and not less, likely to engage in e-commerce activities than urban firms (Vaessen and Keeble, 1995). It may be the case that where there was lag, this was characteristic of early use of the internet for business, as the study from which the current research builds found that in fact far from being laggards in the take-up of internet activity, levels of adoption can be high, but the full utilisation of the benefits of it may be more limited (Deakins et al., 2003). This has been supported by other more recent research such as Dwelly et al. (2005) and recent analysis of the Small Business Service's annual small business survey, in which was found, for example, that "for almost all purposes, businesses in rural areas with dispersed dwellings are significantly more likely than those in other types of area to use ICT" (Telford, 2006). Forman et al. (2005) go some way to explain this more recent reportage of high levels of internet activity amongst rural firms. Based on empirical testing of US data they found that current variation in internet technology up-take and use between urban and rural businesses comprises a concentration of innovative and enhanced technology use in urban firms in order to provide internal advantage, while common internet technologies are introduced more often and to greater advantage in rural firms in their pursuit of the benefits associated with participating in the external business environment.

The reported reticence of rural firms to adopt internet technologies in the late 1990's and early 2000's was undoubtedly associated with erratic roll-out of internet technologies appropriate for business use, such as broadband (Galloway, 2007). Additionally, information failures among potential users were implicated. Recent UK government commitment to technology solutions for rural and remote locations, most often in the form of subsidised ADSL provision is likely to have dispatched with the first of these issues (DTI, 2004). The issue of demand failure as a symptom of information deficit amongst potential users, however, has inherent the implication that gaps in knowledge can be filled though the provision of fuller information, training support and dissemination of good practice. It may be that policy promotion has encouraged the take-up of e-commerce activity

amongst rural entrepreneurs, or there may now be more generally an increased awareness of the benefits of it in rural areas.

Internet Portals

In theory an internet portal is an additional resource that can add to the entrepreneurial capital of rural SMEs. Supporting this argument is a growing research literature exploring the characteristics and benefits of internet portals for rural SMEs. Some of this emergent research has investigated how rural internet portals have benefited a regional wine industry cluster in Australia (Sellitto and Burgess, 2007), local African communities (Adomi, 2007), marketing local tourism in Australia (Rowe et al., 2007), and assisting e-commerce adoption within rural SMEs in Aberdeen, Scotland (Fulford, 2007). Related exploratory research by Deakins et al. (2003) and Galloway et al. (2008, November) has also investigated the structure, operations and strategy of internet portals in rural localities. Specifically, Deakins et al. (2003) investigated six rural internet portals (referred to as forums at that time) and found that SMEs used portals for getting started on the internet (most portal operators provided a website building service), reaching extended markets, raising their profile, and there was some evidence that networking and access to support and advice were being facilitated also. It was also found that those individuals involved in portal operation anticipated a significant contribution to economic activity in the rural area. The earliest of these portals were found to be privately created and operated, the rationale being that profit for firms resulting from effectiveness of the portal would reap profit for the portal operator as a service supplier. Indeed, the anticipation of the contribution portals could make to the rural economy was such that public and charity-funded portals were developed, and these too were represented in the original study. The study also concluded that where the remit of the founding organisation was too broad, lack of focus was likely to result in the portal being less effective. Conversely, those that were highly focused on business objectives would be most successful.

In a follow-up study to Deakins et al. (2003), Galloway et al. (2008, November) re-investigated five years on, the same rural portals to see whether they were sustainable, the effect they were having on business and economic development in the rural locations they catered for, and identified the characteristics of successful portal operation. Four of the portals sampled in the previous study were included along with a further two portals not previously studied in order to increase the sample and afford additional comparison. Of the six portals investigated, three were publicly funded, and three were privately owner-managed. Following the rationale outlined in Yin (2003), case studies were conducted for all portals included in the research, including in-depth interviews with portal operators or owners, and triangulation by analysis of the portal itself in terms of extent and type of content, availability of services for firms, and amount of local business representation.

From the above two studies six hypotheses were generated to further develop an understanding of rural internet portals. Specifically, these hypotheses would determine if there were differences in user perceptions of rural internet portals effectiveness and their manner of operation. Galloway et al. (2008, November) found that two distinct forms of ownership structure exist and broadly these are determined by their funding status: private, where the owner leads and manages activity; or not-for-profit, where either hired part-time staff or employed volunteer staff to operate the portal. The study also found that portal content, use, aims and effectiveness varied between these two ownership structures. The degree of this variation is outlined below.

Portal Content and Use

The privately owned (PO) portals demonstrated a higher degree of content richness, fullness of the services offered, and the extent of community and local business usage. In contrast, the not-for-profit owned (NFPO) portals suffered from limited content and a narrow selection of services, some political infighting, low employee commitment, and modest community and business usage. Based on the above findings from Galloway et al. (2008, November) it was believed that if you compared the rural SME users' level of web-site involvement within each internet portal type that differences in the amount of content and services offered would be observed. It was considered that the enthusiasm, greater user participation, wide range of services and fullness of content linked to PO portals would inspire its users to provide higher levels of content. In other words, the extent of choices available to rural SME users of PO internet portal would enhance their own web-site and e-commerce content. Three surrogate measures were used to indicate the richness of the users' web-site content. These surrogate measures were directory, web-link and advertising usage. Based on the aforementioned discussion it was hypothesised that:

H1: *A greater amount of web-site content and functions will be employed by PO portal users, rather than NFPO portal users.*

Corresponding to the aforementioned hypothesis, it was considered that more outside assistance in web-site construction and maintenance would be obtained by users of PO internet portals to assist with the higher-levels of web-site content and e-commerce functions observed. Again it was felt that the higher levels of content found in PO portals would inspire its users to enhance their own web-sites via the input of outside professionals. Therefore it was hypothesised that:

H2: *The greater sophistication of PO portals will encourage its rural SME users to demonstrate higher utilisation of outside professionals from the outset to construct their web-sites and e-commerce functions, than NFPO portal users.*

Finally, it was believed that rural SME users of PO portals would seek more outside professional assistance in web-site construction and maintenance to assist with the higher-levels of web-site content and e-commerce functions observed. Again it was felt that the higher levels of content found in PO portals would inspire its rural SME users to enhance their own web-sites via the input of outside professionals. Therefore it was hypothesised that:

H3: *The greater sophistication of PO portals will encourage its rural SME users to demonstrate greater utilisation of outside professionals to maintain their web-site and e-commerce functions, than NFPO portal users.*

Portal Aims

Deakins et al. (2003) concluded that where the founding remit of a portal was too broad, this lack of focus would result in its operations being less effective. Specifically, for the rural portals studied by Deakins et al. (2003), those NFPO with remits that included, for example, economic development through business provision, community engagement in the internet, provision of local internet services, provision of community information, and other community aims such as contributing to employability skills amongst the population by using the portal as a trainer and employer of those without jobs, would result in least effective achievement of the aims of the portal. Conversely, those that were highly focused on business objectives would be most successful.

Certainly Galloway et al. (2008, November) reinforced the aforesaid argument that the PO portals were highly focused and applied good business practices to the management and operation of their portals. Moreover, these owners believed that the application of business principles had ensured portal survival. Given that PO portals have a greater focus and business orientation to ensure the efficiency of their operations, it can be assumed that they probably emphasis financial viability as well. Consequently it was hypothesised that:

H4: *PO portals higher degree of business focus or orientation will result in them exerting greater efforts to gather revenue from there users, than NFPO portals.*

Furthermore it was supposed that PO portals greater focus and business orientation would make them much more active in contacting and attracting potential users to increase their web-site portal membership. Specifically, the PO internet portals would better appreciate the productivity and efficiency gains that could be obtained via an increased membership, i.e. economies of scale, market share and reputation. Thus it was therefore hypothesised that:

H5: *PO portals higher degree of business focus or orientation will result in them exercising greater effort to increase their web-site portal membership, than NFPO portals.*

Portal Effectiveness

Galloway et al. (2008, November) ascertained that operators of both types of portals are convinced that they are worthwhile endeavours. The existence of portals, rural and otherwise, in itself demonstrates that economic contribution or development is anticipated, whether direct (as a result of affording access to markets) or indirect (in terms of including and encouraging firms to exist online at

Table 1. Characteristics of the Internet portals

Portal	Age	Funding status	Change in funding status	Operation	In 2003 study
A	12	Charitable status (training organisation)	Yes Was originally privately operated	One person responsible as part of overall duties of employment with training organisation	No
B	10	Public (LEC and tourist organisation)	No	Two part-time staff who operate it as part of duties for the LEC.	Yes
C	6	Charitable status (part of greater charitably funded regeneration activity)	Yes Was previously funded through consultancy firm by public sector grants	One person as part of overall regeneration duties	Yes
D	7	Private	No	One person	No
E	9	Private	No	One person	Yes
F	12	Private	No	One person	Yes

a time where the internet is becoming established as an essential for all firms). As previously stated Galloway et al. (2008, November) established that PO portals demonstrated higher amounts of content, services and community and local business involvement. On the contrary, the NFPO portals had lower amounts of content, services, community and local business interest. Additionally, the study revealed that NFPO portals suffered from political infighting amongst stakeholders and low employee commitment. These results indicated that PO portals were more effective. From the preceding discussion it was believed that users of each internet portal type would perceive their effectiveness as being markedly different due to the disparity in content, services, management and commitment offered. Therefore it was hypothesised that:

H6: *The perceived e-commerce benefits of being a rural SME user of a PO portal will be higher than a NFPO portal.*

Methods

In April 2008, ninety-six rural SME users of six rural internet portals within Scotland were surveyed via telephone to determine whether any

operational characteristics and perceived differences in effectiveness existed between internet portal types. Table 1 provides some details about the six internet portals that were included in the research.

The study found that the six internal portals could be evenly divided into PO (n=3) and NFPO (n=3) portals due to their structural characteristics and ownership type. Rural SME user respondents from each of the six rural internet portals were identified from the portal site, and only those with a presence that included either web-pages on the portal site, or their own web pages available via click-throughs on the portal site were included in the survey. Potential respondents that met the aforesaid conditions were then alphabetically listed and uniquely numbered. Through a random sampling selection process the respondents to contact were then identified; beginning with the first individual on the list, every second individual was selected until the sample size was achieved (Saunders, Lewis and Thornhill, 2000). The distribution of respondents across the six internet portals is shown in Table 2. The sample contained fifty-three and forty-three private and publicly-funded internet portal respectively. Semi-structured telephone interviews were conducted with the ninety-six respondents, representing an

Table 2. Number of rural small firm respondents by Internet portal

Portal	A	B	C	D	E	F
No of firms n = 96	11	19	13	15	18	20
Total members = 197	38	30	21	36	36	36
Response rate = 49%	29%	63%	62%	42%	50%	56%

overall response rate of 49%, this varied across the six portals, reaching over 60% for two of the portals.

The purpose of this study was to statistically test whether the responses of the business users would differ between the aforementioned internet portal types, i.e. whether the structural characteristics of PO portals were perceived as being more effective by rural SME users, than NFPO portal users. To facilitate the comparison between rural SME users and internet portal types, hypotheses were formulated in the main from the Galloway et al. (2008, November) study, which investigated six internet portals. Due to the nature of the data collected (i.e. categorical) cross-tabulations were performed using chi-square testing.

RESULTS

Analysis of the data involved comparing experiences between rural SME users of PO and NFPO internet portals. The study also provides informa-

tion about how rural SME users included in the survey have benefited or otherwise.

Portal Content and Use

It was hypothesised that users with higher-levels of web-site content and functions will be associated with PO portals, rather than NFPO portals. Table 3 shows that directory use by PO portal users was 47 (55.3%), while it was 38 (44.7%) for NFPO portal users. A Chi Square test was performed to determine if PO or NFPO portals were distributed differently in their utilisation of directories. The test failed to indicate a significant difference, χ^2 (1, N=88) = 0.026, p = 0.872 (an alpha level of 0.05 was adopted for this and all subsequent statistical tests. In addition, the Yates' Correction for Continuity value was used for each chi square test because 2 by 2 tables were employed).

In addition, the utilisation of web-links was investigated to see whether their usage differed between PO portals and NFPO portals. Like directories the usage of web-links would help to illustrate

Table 3. Directory use, by Internet portal type

			Directory		
			no	yes	Total
Internet Portal type	Private	Count	1	47	48
		% within Directory	33.3%	55.3%	54.5%
	Public	Count	2	38	40
		% within Directory	66.7%	44.7%	45.5%
	Total	Count	3	85	88
		% within Directory	100.0%	100.0%	100.0%

Table 4. Web-link use, by Internet portal type

			Web-link		
			no	yes	Total
Internet Portal type	Private	Count	11	35	46
		% within Web-link	47.8%	60.3%	56.8%
	Public	Count	12	23	35
		% within Web-link	52.2%	39.7%	43.2%
	Total	Count	23	58	81
		% within Web-link	100.0%	100.0%	100.0%

whether rural SME users with higher-levels of web-site content and functions will be associated with PO portals, rather than NFPO portals. Table 4 shows that web-link use by PO portal users was 35 (60.3%), while it was 23 (39.7%) for NFPO portal users. A Chi Square test was performed to determine if PO or NFPO internet portals were distributed differently in their utilisation of web-links. The test failed to indicate a significant difference, χ^2 (1, N=81) = 0.604, p = 0.437.

The final approach to demonstrate whether users of PO portals employed higher-levels of web-site content and functions was the employment of advertising. Table 5 reveals that advertising handling by PO portal users was 13 (52%), while it was 12 (48%) for NFPO portal users. A Chi Square test was performed to determine if PO or NFPO portals were distributed differently in their utilisation of advertising. The test failed to indicate a significant difference, χ^2 (1, N=79) = 0.131, p = 0.718.

The last hypothesis investigating portal content and use considered the provision of outside assistance in the original construction of the web-site. It was hypothesised that users of PO portals would make greater use of outsiders to assist with their web-site content and functions. However, the data collected did not support this hypothesis that the greater sophistication of PO portals will encourage its users to make much greater use of outsiders to construct and maintain the appearance and functions of their web-sites, than NFPO portals. Indeed the chi square test failed to confirm a significant difference, χ^2 (1, N=66) = 0.063, p = 0.801. Table 6 indicates that an outsider as the original Web-site contractor on a PO portal was 21 (63.6%), while it was 12 (36.4%) for NFPO portal users.

The remaining method to test the provision of outside assistance to increase the sophistication of PO or NFPO portals was to discover who monitored and maintained the user's website.

Table 5. Advertising use, by Internet portal type

			Advertising		
			no	yes	Total
Internet Portal type	Private	Count	32	13	45
		% within Advertising	59.3%	52.0%	57.0%
	Public	Count	22	12	34
		% within Advertising	40.7%	48.0%	43.0%
	Total	Count	54	25	79
		% within Advertising	100.0%	100.0%	100.0%

Table 6. Origin of Web-site contractor, by Internet portal type

			Origin of Web-site contractor		
			I built it	external firm built it	Total
Internet Portal type	Private	Count	19	21	40
		% within Origin of Web-site contractor	57.6%	63.6%	60.6%
	Public	Count	14	12	26
		% within Origin of Web-site contractor	42.4%	36.4%	39.4%
	Total	Count	33	33	66
		% within Origin of Web-site contractor	100.0%	100.0%	100.0%

The data collected did not support the hypothesis that there would be a difference between the two internet portal types in who they used to regularly maintain their web-site and functions, χ^2 (1, N=69) = 0.616, p = 0.433. Table 7 reveals that regular maintenance of their web-site by an external firm for PO portal was 12 (52.2%), while it was 11 (47.8%) for NFPO portal users.

Portal Aims

Two hypothesis were constructed to test whether there was perceived differences in the aims of PO and NFPO portals users. First, it was hypothesised that PO portals higher degree of business focus or orientation will result in them exerting greater efforts to gather revenue from there users, than NFPO portals. Table 8 indicates that payment for portal representation by users on PO portal was 16 (36.4%), while it was 28 (63.6%) for NFPO portal users. A Chi Square test was performed to determine if users of PO or NFPO portals were distributed differently in their requirement for payment for portal representation. The test undertaken indicated that there was a significant difference, χ^2 (1, N=86) = 9.257, p = 0.002. However, this result was contrary to the hypothesis supposing that PO portals would be more likely to charge a fee for representation; instead it was NFPO portals, which demonstrated a significant preference for requiring payment.

Second, a hypothesis was constructed that stated PO portals higher degree of business focus or orientation will result in them exercising greater

Table 7. Regular maintenance of Web-site, by Internet portal type

			Regular maintenance of web-site		
			me	external firm	Total
Internet Portal type	Private	Count	30	12	42
		% within Regular maintenance of web-site	65.2%	52.2%	60.9%
	Public	Count	16	11	27
		% within Regular maintenance of web-site	34.8%	47.8%	39.1%
	Total	Count	46	23	69
		% within Regular maintenance of web-site	100.0%	100.0%	100.0%

Table 8. Payment for portal representation, by Internet portal type

			Payment for portal representation		
			no	yes	Total
Internet Portal type	Private	Count	30	16	46
		% within Payment for portal representation	71.4%	36.4%	53.5%
	Public	Count	12	28	40
		% within Payment for portal representation	28.6%	63.6%	46.5%
	Total	Count	42	44	86
		% within Payment for portal representation	100.0%	100.0%	100.0%

effort to increase their web-site portal membership, than NFPO portals. Table 9 illustrates that PO portals approached 24 (63.2%) users to join, while 14 (36.8%) NFPO portal users were approached. A Chi Square test was performed to determine if users of PO or NFPO internet portals were distributed differently in how they were approached to join. The results of the data do not support the hypothesis, χ^2 (1, N=79) = .711, p = 0.399.

Portal Feasibility and Effectiveness

It was hypothesised that users of PO portals would be more likely to perceive greater benefits from their membership than those represented on a NFPO portal (Table 10). Among the PO portals

users interviewed 41 (59.4%) stated that their inclusion within the portal had been worthwhile, while 28 (40.6%) of NFPO portal users had thought it was worthwhile. The results of the data do not support the hypothesis, χ^2 (1, N=88) = 2.220, p = 0.136.

DISCUSSION

The authors hypothesised after studying the work of Deakins et al. (2003) and Galloway et al. (2008, November) that PO, rather than NFPO, internet portals offered the optimum membership choice for rural SMEs making use of e-commerce activities. However, as Table 11 indicates internet portal

Table 9. How rural SME user approached to join, by Internet portal type

			How user approached to join		
			I approached them	they approached me	Total
Internet Portal type	Private	Count	21	24	45
		% within How user approached to join	51.2%	63.2%	57.0%
	Public	Count	20	14	34
		% within How user approached to join	48.8%	36.8%	43.0%
	Total	Count	41	38	79
		% within How user approached to join	100.0%	100.0%	100.0%

Table 10. Perceived benefits of membership, by Internet portal type

			Perceived benefits of membership		
			no	yes	Total
Internet Portal type	Private	Count	7	41	48
		% within Perceived benefits of membership	36.8%	59.4%	54.5%
	Public	Count	12	28	40
		% within Perceived benefits of membership	63.2%	40.6%	45.5%
		% of Total	13.6%	31.8%	45.5%
	Total	Count	19	69	88
		% within Perceived benefits of membership	100.0%	100.0%	100.0%

type does not make a difference to rural SMEs e-commerce choices or activities. Hypotheses H1, H2 and H3 examined portal content and use. The results for these hypotheses did not support the view that the sophistication of the internet portal web-site content and functions influences respondent usage of outside experts or amount of content they employ on their own sites. Level of web-site sophistication and use of expert assistance by rural SMEs is more likely to be influenced by other competing resource priorities than portal membership.

Hypotheses H4 and H5 investigated how organised and business-like the aims of the two internet portal types were in terms of collecting membership fees and recruiting new users. The study found that the business-like PO portals were rated similarly in their attempts to recruit new users as NFPO portals. Surprisingly NFPO portals were more likely to charge a membership fee, than PO portals. This result probably indicates the increasing need for not-for-profit agencies to demonstrate accountability and responsibility for their financial dealings. Since the NFPO portals are responsible to others for how efficiently they spend and/or recover monies, they will be under greater scrutiny than the operators of the PO portals in this study. The final hypothesis, H6, considered whether rural SME users perceived membership

to be beneficial to their e-commerce activities. The resulted demonstrated that rural SME users perceived that membership to either type of portal as beneficial to their e-commerce efforts.

What Does This Mean for Optimising the E-Commerce Activities of Rural SMEs?

From a policy-making perspective to optimise the e-commerce efforts of rural SMEs it would be ideal if local/central government or charitable organisations worked alongside private initiatives, rather than organising and managing local portals themselves. Dedicated private individuals appear to be the ideal mechanism for optimising e-commerce activity for rural SMEs. However, in the absence of these local champions from specific rural locations, it is essential for rural SMEs that either central/local government or charitable organisations establish internet portals to facilitate their e-commerce efforts. A NFPO portal might not be the optimal method for developing rural SME e-commence efforts, but it is better than nothing. Certainly each portal type has developed and evolved according to the available resources and needs of its local area or community. In this regard local/central government or charitable organisations are fulfilling one of their prime roles,

Table 11. Summary of hypotheses and findings

H#	Hypothesis	Supported?
H1	A greater amount of web-site content and functions will be employed by PO portal users, rather than NFPO portal users.	No
H2	The greater sophistication of PO portals will encourage its rural SME users to demonstrate higher utilisation of outside professionals from the outset to construct their web-sites and e-commerce functions, than NFPO portal users.	No
H3	The greater sophistication of PO portals will encourage its rural SME users to demonstrate greater utilisation of outside professionals to maintain their web-site and e-commerce functions, than NFPO portal users.	No
H4	PO portals higher degree of business focus or orientation will result in them exerting greater efforts to gather revenue from there rural SME users, than NFPO portal users.	No
H5	PO portals higher degree of business focus or orientation will result in them exercising greater effort to increase their web-site portal membership, than NFPO portals.	No
H6	The perceived e-commerce benefits of being a rural SME user of a PO portal will be higher than a NFPO portal.	No

intervening due to market or community resource deficiencies or failure. Currently, the portal aims and their level of sophistication and content are not critical to rural SMEs. What is critical for rural SMEs is that their local area has an internet portal that can support their e-commerce efforts.

CONCLUSION

Generally the findings across the three research themes including portal content and use, portal aims, and portal feasibility and effectiveness demonstrated no significant difference between the two types of rural internet portals. Therefore, rural SME users do not perceive differences in their membership of either type of rural internet portal. These results should not be surprising

given that most rural SME users for both types of rural internet portals perceive them as being a worthwhile resource. Certainly for rural SME users of either type of internet portal membership is perceived to be a valuable resource for gaining an improved market presence, which would be difficult to achieve independently of the portal. Additionally from the rural SME users perspective the positives of membership nullify any of the idiosyncratic operating practices or ownership structures that are part of each type of portal. Rural SME users appear to be simply concerned with the practicality of gaining a presence that will positively associate them with a location or community of interest.

SUGGESTIONS FOR FUTURE RESEARCH

The results of this study suggest several possible areas of future research. First, this study examined rural SME users and internet portals in Scotland. It would be important to expand the study to other regions of the United Kingdom to see if the results obtained are generalisable. Second, a qualitative study examining in detail the characteristics of rural SME users and how they employ e-commerce would provide valuable new insights into the key factors that need to be present to ensure success. A final possibility is to undertake a longitudinal study of rural SME users that utilise e-commerce via internet portals and those that do not. This research would investigate whether internet portals offer performance benefits to rural SME users' e-commerce activities and to the community in general.

REFERENCES

Adomi, E. E. (2007). African Web portals. In A. Tatnall (Ed.), *Encyclopedia of portal technologies and applications,* (Vol. 1, pp. 41-46). Hershey, PA: Information Science Publishing.

Baourakis, G., Kourgiantakis, M., & Migdalas, A. (2002). The impact of e-commerce on agro-food marketing: The case of agricultural co-operatives, firms and consumers in Crete. *British Food Journal, 104*(8), 580–590. doi:10.1108/00070700210425976

BERR. (2009). *Enterprise directorate analytical unit frequently asked questions.* Retrieved May 4, 2009, from http://www.berr.gov.uk/whatwedo/enterprise/enterprisesmes/research-and-statistics/statistics/page38573.html

Bharadwaj, P. N., & Soni, R. G. (2007). E-commerce usage and perception of e-commerce issues among small firms: Results and implications from an empirical study. *Journal of Small Business Management, 45*(4), 501–521. doi:10.1111/j.1540-627X.2007.00225.x

Buhalis, D., & Main, H. (1998). Information technology in peripheral small and medium hospitality enterprises: Strategic analysis and critical factors. *International Journal of Contemporary Hospitality Management, 10*(5), 198–202. doi:10.1108/09596119810227811

Chen, S. (2005). *Strategic management of e-business* (2nd ed.). Chichester, UK: John Wiley & Sons.

Courtney, P., & Brydon, J. (2001, November). *Differential economic performance: Experience from two Scottish regions.* Paper presented at RICS Research Foundation Rural Research Conference, London.

Deakins, D., Galloway, L., & Mochrie, R. (2003). *The use and effect of ICT on Scotland's rural business community.* Scotecon Report.

DTI. (2004) *UK National Broadband Strategy.* Retrieved April 24, 2005, from http://www.dti.gov.uk/industry_files/pdf/uknational_broadband_strategy.pdf

Dwelly, T., Maguire, K., & Truscott, F. (2005). *Under the radar: Tracking and supporting rural home based businesses.* Live Network Report to the Commission for Rural Communities.

Forman, C., Goldfarb, A., & Greenstein, S. (2005). How did location affect adoption of the commercial internet? Global village vs. urban leadership. *Journal of Urban Economics, 58,* 389–420. doi:10.1016/j.jue.2005.05.004

Fulford, H. (2007). A local community web portal and small business. In A. Tatnall (Ed.), *Encyclopedia of portal technologies and applications.* (Vol. 1, pp. 559-563). Hershey, PA: Information Science Publishing.

Galloway, L. (2007). Can broadband access rescue the rural economy? *Journal of Small Business and Enterprise Development, 14*(4), 641–653. doi:10.1108/14626000710832749

Galloway, L., Deakins, D., & Sanders, J. (2008, November). *The use of Internet portals by Scotland's rural business community.* Paper presented at Institute for Small Business & Entrepreneurship Conference, Belfast, Northern Ireland.

Galloway, L., & Mochrie, R. (2006). Entrepreneurial motivation, orientation and realisation in rural economies: A study of rural Scotland. *International Journal of Entrepreneurship and Innovation, 7*(3), 173–184.

Galloway, L., Mochrie, R., & Deakins, D. (2004). ICT-enabled collectivity as a positive rural business strategy. *International Journal of Entrepreneurial Behaviour and Research, 10*(4), 247–259. doi:10.1108/13552550410544213

Huggins, R., & Izushi, H. (2002). The digital divide and ICT learning in rural communities: Examples of good practice service delivery. *Local Economy, 17*(2), 111–122. doi:10.1080/02690940210129870

Lawson, R., Alcock, C., Cooper, J., & Burgess, L. (2003). Factors affecting adoption of electronic commerce technologies by SMEs: An Australian study. *Journal of Small Business and Enterprise Development, 10*(3), 265–276. doi:10.1108/14626000310489727

Leatherman, J. C. (2000). Internet-based commerce: Implications for rural communities. *Reviews of Economic Development Literature and Practice*, 5. US Economic Development Administration, Washington, USA.

Patterson, H., & Henderson, D. (2003). What is really different about rural and urban firms? Some evidence from Northern Ireland. *Journal of Rural Studies, 19*(4), 477–490. doi:10.1016/S0743-0167(03)00027-5

Pease, W., & Rowe, M. (2005, July). *Use of information technology to facilitate collaboration and co-opetition between tourist operators in tourist destinations.* Paper presented at the Technology Enterprise Strategies: Thriving and Surviving in an Online Era Conference, Melbourne, Australia.

Pease, W., Rowe, M., & Cooper, M. (2005, August). *Regional tourist destinations – The role of information and communications technology in collaboration amongst tourism providers.* Paper presented at the ITS Africa-Asia-Australasia Regional Conference, Perth, Australia.

Porter, M. E. (2001). Strategy and the Internet. *Harvard Business Review, 79*(3), 63–78.

Roberts, S. (2002). *Key drivers of economic development and inclusion in rural areas.* Initial scoping study for the socio-economic evidence base for DEFRA.

Rodgers, J. A., Yen, D. C., & Chou, D. C. (2002). Developing e-business: A strategic approach. *Information Management & Computer Security, 10*(4), 184–192. doi:10.1108/09685220210436985

Rowe, M., Pease, W., & McLeod, P. (2007). Web portals as an exemplar for tourist destinations. In A. Tatnall (Ed.), *Encyclopedia of portal technologies and applications,* (Vol. 2, pp. 1157-1160). Hershey, PA: Information Science Publishing.

Saunders, M. N. K., Lewis, P., & Thornhill, A. (2000). *Research methods for business students* (2nd ed.). Harlow, UK: Pearson Education Limited.

Sellitto, C., & Burgess, S. (2007). A study of a wine industry internet portal. In A. Tatnall (Ed.), *Encyclopedia of portal technologies and applications* (Vol. 2, pp. 979-984). Hershey, PA: Information Science Publishing.

Smallbone, D., North, D., Baldock, R., & Ekanem, I. (2002). *Encouraging and supporting enterprise in rural areas*. Centre for Enterprise and Economic Development Research, Middlesex University Business School, London, Report to the Small Business Service.

Swan, J., Newell, S., Scarbrough, H., & Hislop, D. (1999). Knowledge management and innovation: networks and networking. *Journal of Knowledge Management, 3*(4), 262–275. doi:10.1108/13673279910304014

Telford, R. (2006, October). *Small businesses in rural areas – How are they different?* Paper presented at the 26th ISBE Conference, Cardiff, Wales.

Thomas, B., Sparkes, A., Brooksbank, D., & Williams, R. (2002). Social aspects of the impact of information and communication technologies on agri-food SMEs in Wales. *Outlook on Agriculture, 31*(1), 35–41.

Turban, E., & King, D. Lee, J. & Viehland, D. (2004). *Electronic commerce 2004: A managerial perspective*. Upper Saddle River, NJ: Pearson Education Inc.

Vaessen, P., & Keeble, D. (1995). Growth-oriented SMEs in unfavourable regional environments. *Regional Studies, 29*, 489–505. doi:10.1080/00343409512331349133

Vakoufaris, H., Spilanis, I., & Kizos, T. (2007). Collective action in the Greek agrifood sector: Evidence from the North Aegean region. *British Food Journal, 109*(10), 777–791. doi:10.1108/00070700710821322

Wigand, R. T. (1997). Electronic commerce: Definition, theory, and context. *The Information Society, 13*(1), 1–16. doi:10.1080/019722497129241

Yin, R. (2003). *Case study research: Design and methods* (3rd ed.). Thousand Oaks, CA: Sage Publications.

Chapter 7
Internet Marketing and SMEs

Daniel John Doiron
University of New Brunswick, Saint John Campus, Canada

ABSTRACT

Small and medium enterprises (SMEs) have been adopting the internet at a feverish pace. Recent studies have shown that up to 85% of SMEs in industrialized countries have web sites, yet less than half are utilizing these web sites to securely transact with their customers. Consumer media consumption is moving away from traditional media, like newspapers, to the internet. These revelations coupled with the growth of tools and techniques available to support online marketing, make it a perfect time for SMEs to market their web sites and ultimately succeed online. In this chapter we will present and support the hypothesis that SMEs should stop investing in their web site's design and functionality and start investing in efforts to market their web sites online, no matter how lousy their web site may be in comparison to today's standards. With the support of two case studies, illustrating the successful utilization of internet marketing by two very different SMEs, we will relate how a SME can effectively market their web site online. We will also discuss the tools and techniques available to help an SME successfully begin a journey of internet marketing.

INTRODUCTION

Internet marketing can be simply described as marketing or advertising a web site online. This is accomplished through the use of a number of tools and techniques, which are readily available on the internet. These tools tend to be relatively inexpensive

DOI: 10.4018/978-1-60566-998-4.ch007

and fairly easy to use for any business no matter its size or stature. Why then, aren't more SMEs actively marketing their web sites? The answer partially lies in understanding what motivates an SME to venture into the realm of the internet in the first place, or more importantly, what factors are inhibiting them from initiating this journey. Recent research is shedding important light on this question. With this information in hand, we can more readily discuss how SMEs should approach the tremendous opportunity of internet marketing. One thing we know for sure is that the internet is going to play an increasingly important role for all enterprises, big or small, in the way they market their products or services, given the rapid rate at which consumers are transitioning away from traditional media. In fact, media consumption is moving to the internet from more traditional channels at an unprecedented pace. This is good news for SMEs as they are not as disadvantaged when it comes to marketing online, as they have been with more traditional mediums, like television.

Once there is an appreciation that SMEs need to be fully engaged in internet marketing, the question shifts to how they should approach this opportunity. SMEs tend to lean towards spending their limited resources in making more attractive, more functional web sites under the notion that "if my web site is *better* than my competitors then it will attract more potential customers." The pressure to do this can be enormous, driven primarily by the seemingly endless advances in internet (or HTML) technology. This approach bears little fruit and often increases the mystic of internet marketing when few gains are achieved. We will present and support a hypothesis suggesting SMEs should spend all their resources marketing their current web sites, before they undertake any efforts to update or add functionality to their online presence.

We will look at some of the most popular tools and techniques available to help SMEs market their web sites. This will include discussing analytics, search engine optimization, search engine advertising, e-mail and social media marketing.

Throughout the chapter we will reinforce the notion that SMEs need to look at internet marketing from a strategic point of view. Implementing tactical internet marketing initiatives can indeed have short term positive results, but it will be highlighted that a strategic approach to internet marketing is the only way to achieve sustained, long term results.

After reviewing this chapter the reader will better understand why internet marketing can be so attractive to SMEs, how they should approach their engagement with it, and which tools and techniques are available for them to utilize on this transformational journey. Finally, much of what a SME puts into place with regards to its internet marketing must be strategically planned and critically evaluated to achieve the desired result of business growth.

BACKGROUND

Davis et al (2004, 2005) in their studies of Atlantic Canadian SMEs in both 2004[1] & 2005[2] showed, among other things, that SMEs are adopting the internet at a record pace. However, they identified a large gap in the number of SMEs who have web sites and the number of SMEs who are actually securely transacting on those web sites. Other recent studies of SMEs and internet adoption would support these findings and also suggest that *facilitators* play a primary role in moving SMEs to the internet or to use advanced internet technology. This seems to be true with internet marketing as well. It could even be suggested that Google, in fact, sees their role as *the* facilitator of internet marketing. Google, while profit motivated, has, nonetheless, been primarily responsible for enabling the SME market to engage in internet marketing through the introduction of tools and services like Google Analytics ™ and Google Adwords ™.

There is no better time than the present for SMEs to close this gap. Media consumption is moving to the internet at a rapid pace, while at the same time the tools and techniques available to help a small business market their web site online are relatively inexpensive to use and increasingly accessible and abundant online.

OPENING CASE STUDY: AIDEN'S DEEP SEA FISHING[3] (WWW.PEIFISHING.COM)

When a family business that is steeped in 50 years of proud history trials a progressive, modern-day internet marketing strategy, new opportunities for growth come to light that can position the company for another 50 years of business success. Aiden's Deep Sea Fishing of North Rustico PEI, Canada is successfully defying a two-year, 25% downturn in the provincial tourism industry by creating a new market of customers through their Google Adword™ advertising campaign. While competitors are forced to cancel tours, or send their boats out without a full complement of customers, Aiden's two boats continue to sail three tours a day, many times at or near capacity.

Aiden's Deep Sea Fishing is owned and operated by Paul and Colleen Doiron, who, in 2005, invested in the development of a website to profile the business, like many other tour operators around the province. Given that Paul's father Aiden, the company founder, was credited with pioneering the deep sea fishing industry in PEI, the company enjoys a solid business reputation amongst the over 40 competitors throughout the province. However, in an effort to attract customers, service or product differentiation in the industry is very difficult, and as such, marketing plays a key role to ensure maximum boat capacity for each of the day's scheduled tours. The competition is stiff: within 20 miles of North Rustico, there are twelve competitors, four of whom offer tours from the same location along the picturesque wharf of North Rustico's inner harbour. The company's reputation serves them well, but a competitive advantage would also provide a critical edge over the competition.

During the website development, the company was able to secure the URL *peifishing.com,* a desirable address that could attract many visitors to their site when searching for a "PEI fishing" experience. While searches amongst MSN and Yahoo portals provided a top-ten search ranking for the company, inquiries on the most popular search engine, Google, did not bring up the new site. In an effort to get Google working for them, the company made the decision to trial one of Google's own offerings – Google Adwords™. The strategy was straight forward: a Google Adwords™ advertisement could drive traffic to their site by giving them a "virtual" number one ranking when customers search one of over 20 keyword phrases. Among other advantages, this will also enable the Google spiders to notice the increased activity to the URL and a higher search engine ranking may be achieved. Today, even when the Adwords™ campaign is paused during the off season, Aiden's Deep Sea Fishing enjoys a "first page" ranking on a Google search for deep sea fishing.

In 2007, the company celebrated its 50th Anniversary, and to mark the occasion, Aiden's offered a prize package promotion to every customer who sailed with them during the season. In completing the ballot, customers responded to the question "Where did you hear about us?" and were asked to include their email address. Valuable insight from the customers' responses was gained. With 39% of customers indicating that a referral was their primary reason for choosing Aiden's, there is no doubt that the business relies on this traditional means of promotion. However, after their first full season with a Google Adword Campaign, 11% of the customer base indicated that they had they had found the company through the internet. This customer segment was an important driver to helping Aiden's succeed in a down market. Given the total cost of the Adword Campaign was less than $200, yet supported a rate of 11% of customers converting to purchase, a significant opportunity exists to expand the customer base and maximize revenues through this highly cost effective, targeted and less labour-intensive effort than some traditional marketing channels.

Aiden's marketing efforts have typically focused on print advertising in a variety of tourism brochures, the selective distribution of their own brochure though partnerships with local accommodation providers and the effective visibility of their onsite signage at the wharf. Road and highway signage, some radio advertising and a link to the provincial tourism website is also a part of the marketing mix. However, like many small businesses, measuring the effectiveness of any individual marketing strategy proves to be difficult, and as such, advertising expenditures are made on some anecdotal information and intuition. During the tourism season of 2007, Aiden's took another step toward better understanding their market by turning on Google Analytics capability within their website. This is a free service offered by Google. The data that is available to Aiden's from tracking its website traffic allows for detailed information such as the number of new and previous customers that are accessing the site, what information customers are most interested in reading, and the hometown from where they are making the inquiry. By their own admission, Paul and Colleen have yet to fully utilize the power and information available through their Google Analytics reports, but through future evaluation, Aiden's will be able to target a prospective new customer base, and even support the level of referrals to the business which represents their largest group of customers. They have already made changes to their website to more efficiently push their prospective customers to their "reservation" page. By setting goals within Analytics they will be able to better understand how users are finding their way to this page.

They started the 2008 tourism season off with an email newsletter campaign which drove a number of online bookings prior to the season opening. Although 2008 was another down year in tourism for PEI, Aiden's saw their online orders almost double. The effectiveness of their internet marketing activities was really starting to pay off. At the end of 2008 they implemented a "fishing blog" and are excited by the prospect of extending their reach to increase their referral business.

Aiden's Deep Sea Fishing has successfully adopted a progressive internet marketing strategy that has provided them with a competitive edge during negative market conditions, which will position them for future seasons of maximum growth in this competitive industry.

THE INTERNET AS A MARKETING TOOL

Many SMEs in today's marketplace have adopted web sites to market their products or services. In fact, in some industrialized countries, up to 85%[4] of SMEs currently have functioning web sites (Davis et al., 2005). The sad anecdote to this, however, is that very few of them are actually transacting online. For the most part, SME's web sites are not really working as sales and marketing tools. One set of benchmark studies in Atlantic Canada, taken from 2004 through to 2007[5] (Davis et al, 2004; Davis et al., 2005; Fleet, 2007), would suggest that only 35% of SMEs currently provide the capability to execute secure transactions online. While this has been climbing at a rate of approximately 10% per year, the overall low adoption of this capability is indicative of how these SMEs view their web sites; as electronic brochures and not as a true opportunity to sell products or services through secure online transactions. Further, the research indicates that only 58.8% of SMEs with web sites are not treating the internet as a true marketing channel. Most SMEs would disagree and suggest the reason they have a web site is to market their products or services and their web sites are functionally designed for this purpose. What, then, does this statement really suggest?

To explore this apparent division in intent versus reality, we would like to propose a simple hypothesis, which is aimed at uncovering the underlying issues and challenges facing SMEs as they attempt to leverage the internet.

SMEs should not spend their efforts and resources enhancing their web site designs or even on enhancements for enabling secure online transactions. Instead, they should spend their efforts and the associated costs on MARKETING their current web sites, no matter the current design.

This notion immediately raises a number of concerns and objections when presented to SMEs. For one, most businesses would think that a *"lousy"* or old web site will not be appealing to their target customers and thus the argument for updating their web sites frequently. Clearly, this argument is strengthened with the move to a more interactive web (Web 2.0) and the popular theory that the internet is changing quickly and businesses have to change with it.

However, there is a powerful argument for another, better approach, whose foundation rests in one of the basic tenants of marketing – understanding your customers! If businesses don't understand their customers' reactions to their web site, how will they know what is or isn't working, and more importantly, what will work. A second driver for this approach is that web sites need to be part of a marketing mix, not an adjunct advertising channel. This notion has not been overwhelmingly adopted in the business community and even less so in the SME sector. Most SMEs do not have a detailed marketing strategy, treating all advertising channels equally as incremental opportunities to sell products or build awareness. SMEs rarely measure the incremental effectiveness of the money spent on advertising and their web sites are no exception. For the most part, web sites are knee jerk reactions to the opportunity to sell products or services outside of traditional selling territory, a way to circumvent traditional distribution channels or utilized because their competitors are also online. The irony is that web sites and customers' interaction with them are infinitely measurable. In fact, understanding customer's interaction with web sites is remarkably easy and for the most part, free. Yes that is right, free! Marketing a web site

is relatively inexpensive and this has been made possible by the explosion of internet marketing capabilities, services and tools, for which any small or large business should thank Google.

The approach which supports the hypothesis is actually quite simple. It goes something like this – promote your web site, regardless of how bad it is against today's current standards, measure what potential customers who respond to this marketing do on the web site, regardless of how much or little time they spend on it, then and only then, make adjustments to the site to *incrementally* improve its effectiveness. The notion of "incrementality" is critical to understand and is somewhat analogous to a "virtual flywheel". The momentum created by a flywheel as it begins to spin is fed back into the underlying propulsion system, which in turn allows it to drive the flywheel even faster. The net effect of this is to use the energy created to create and sustain even more energy. By measuring how customers interact with a web site, any SME can introduce incremental changes based on what they learn and then implement further changes as customer interactions dictate. Through this iterative process any SME can dramatically improve the effectiveness of their web site, as it relates to their business goals; in effect creating a virtual flywheel.

As simple as it sounds, this approach is a hard sell to SMEs. And, to be fair, this approach would not even have been possible a few years ago, given the state of the tools and capabilities available on the internet to market and measure web site effectiveness. However, now is a great time to execute this approach, due mainly to the accessibility of cost effective tools that are exploding at an exponential pace. This has turned the traditional marketing equation on its head and provided a strong argument that if SMEs don't adopt internet marketing as part of their marketing mix, they will quickly fall behind and lose ground to competitors. If you buy into this notion, then the hypothesis isn't really a hypothesis at all; it is a fact of doing business in an internet enabled world.

Figure 1. U.S. Media Spend[6] (©2007, UNB Saint John. Used with permission.)

	2006	2007	2008	2009
Newspapers	21.4	19.8	18.1	16.8
TV	22.1	20.8	21.2	19.1
Cable Network Television	10.1	10.5	10.5	10.4
Branded Ent. /Product Placement	2.4	3.2	3.9	4.9
Videogame Advertising	0.1	0.2	0.5	0.7
Cinema Advertising	0.3	0.3	0.3	0.4
Terrestrial Radio	9.4	9	8.6	8
Satellite Radio	0.1	0.1	0.2	0.2
Magazines (consumer and business)	18.4	19.3	19.2	19.3
Online / Internet	6.2	7.2	8.4	10.5
Out-of-Home/Place-Based (excl. Cinema)	2.9	3	3.1	3.1
Mobile Advertising	0.2	0.2	0.4	1
Yellow Pages-Print	6.4	6.3	5.8	5.5

There is however, one fundamental tenant which all SMEs must embrace prior to setting out on this journey. It is the creation of a well defined marketing plan, or in the very least, a set of goals and objectives which will drive their internet marketing activities.

INTERNET MARKETING AS PART OF SMES MARKETING MIX?

The 4 P's of marketing, product, pricing, promotion and placement (or distribution) are evolving in today's internet world as a more complex, internet-centric model. This is being driven, in part, by the effectiveness of the internet as a marketing and promotion channel. We need only look at recent trends to better understand what the future holds.

The internet today represents the second most popular media in terms of consumption. In the United States, 21% of "media" consumption currently takes place on the internet, with television at 50% and radio at 20%[3]. With the first internet-savvy generation about to take over the workplace, one can only assume media consumption will continue to move in the internet's favor. The irony is that ad spending in the United States has the internet projected to be a paltry 10.5% in 2009 as noted in figure 1; half of its current con-

Figure 2. Communications model evolution[7] (Adapted from Jarboe, 2007. © 2007, UNB Saint John. Used with permission.)

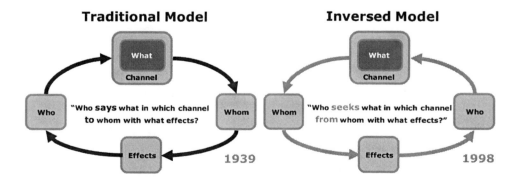

Figure 3. Old vs. digital media

Old Media	Digital Media
One-to-many communication model	One-to-one or many-to-many communication model
Mass-marketing push model	Individualized marketing or mass customization (pull model for web)
Monologue	Dialogue
Branding	Communication
Supply-side thinking	Demand-side thinking
Customer as a target	Customer as a partner
Segmentation	Communities

sumption. However, the rapid decline of relative advertising spending in more traditional channels, like newspapers, is indicative of the inevitable shift to the internet. Plainly, consumers are using it. For businesses, the potential reach of internet advertising solves the traditional richness vs. reach conundrum and most importantly, customer interaction and reactions are measurable and directly attributable to sales.

One way to exemplify the changes the internet is driving is to look at the extreme shift it has imposed on traditional communication models. Figure 2 highlights this shift.

Essentially, communication models have evolved from a push model with the advertisers in control to a pull model with consumers in control.

The fundamental differences in these models are highlighted in figure 3.

All of this would suggest that internet marketing should be included in a firm's marketing mix. However, a more appropriate way to think about the changes being driven by the capacity of internet marketing is that the marketing mix itself needs to evolve to reflect the new marketing realities brought about by the internet. This is best reflected in figure 4.

The new marketing mix will take into consideration the broader notions of interactivity and individualization, along with leveraging the new communities of interest that are available only on the internet. The power of communicating with interactive communities, made possible by sites

Figure 4. Evolution of the marketing mix[8] (© 2007, UNB Saint John. Used with permission)

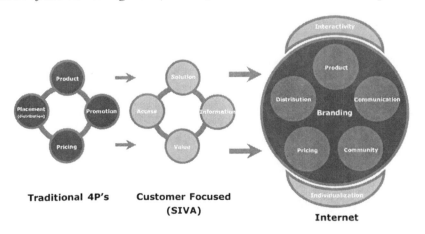

like *Facebook*, exemplifies this notion. *Twitter* is a more recent phenomenon which takes this notion of communities of interest to a real time standard. Imagine launching a product in real time to an expressed group of interested or passionate customers or stakeholders!

An example of the power of utilizing this evolved marketing mix can be illustrated through the case presented at the start of the chapter, Aiden's Deep Sea Fishing. Through a traditional promotion, Aiden's found that 39% of their customers found them through referrals. How could they leverage this new found knowledge? A traditional marketing approach would have led them to a rather expensive promotion or referral program: refer customers and earn a chance to win a prize or a free trip. These kinds of programs are often difficult to execute, where the expensive component isn't the prize, its promoting the promotion.

A SME's marketing plan that embraces an internet marketing mix would address this opportunity differently. In our example, Aiden's would purchase digital cameras for each of their boats and the captain or crew would take pictures of the customers catching their fish and having fun, much like the photos in Figure 5.

On completion of the trip they would post these pictures on their blog, which is free to build (and host) and linked to their web site. They would encourage their customers to visit their web site and blog to view and download pictures from the trip. This will create an opportunity for their customers to refer their friends, relatives and colleagues to Aiden's through what is called "e-mail viral marketing"- a fancy way of saying they will send an e-mail with a link to the blog to all their friends suggesting they "look at the huge fish my son caught during our visit to PEI!". This is a very effective means of building a rich referral network by taking full advantage of the interactivity of the internet at no cost to the business as your customers are promoting your products or services for you! This represents the evolved internet marketing mix. The incremental costs of this program would be two digital cameras, which have a pay back of one referral. Everything else is free; as it should be on the internet.

The simple message this example highlights is that a marketing mix for an SME needs to properly allow for the opportunities the internet represents. Later in this chapter we will discuss the importance of maintaining a strategic view of these activities. Even internet marketing activities fizzle out quickly if they are not executed in the broader context of a marketing strategy.

SMES AND INTERNET ADOPTION

As noted earlier in this chapter, SMEs have adopted the internet at a frenzied pace, although only 35% have evolved their online activities to include

Figure 5. Fishing and fun with Aiden's Deep Sea Fishing[9]

transacting with their customers in a secure on-line fashion. The question of why the majority of SMEs have not been more successful in growing their business via the internet can be more easily answered by studying those who have been successful. A study in Atlantic Canada, by Davies & Vladica in 2004, provides some important clues to help answer this question. In this study, they contacted over 450 SMEs through an extensive questionnaire, with the intent to understand the factors affecting e-business adoption. When the data was analyzed for the causal factors affecting success, it presented some startling findings. The measure for success was defined as an SME successfully utilizing e-business, which was more broadly defined as selling online and/or using internet based tools to drive productivity within their businesses. The two most surprising findings of the study were:

1. Having a broadband or high speed internet link into the business had zero causal effect on successful e-business adoption
2. Having a web site had zero causal effect on successful e-business adoption

This research suggests that the adoption of a web site or broadband link are not enabling factors in moving SMEs to the next level of e-business effectiveness. This is truly surprising as most industry stakeholders push for the universal availability of these capabilities. Governments around the world are spending billions of dollars to make high speed internet universal, and a consistent part of the argument is associated with driving efficiencies and competitiveness into the SME sector. It is often thought that internet adoption is a sequential, step by step process that starts with SMEs using the internet to communicate more effectively (via email, MSN or an equivalent) to source products or services the business uses or sells. They then invest in a web site to promote their products or services, and when traffic begins to flow to the web site or inquiries are generated

through it, they then evolve to implement the functionality to transact online. Finally, businesses begin to utilize the internet as a core productivity tool through the use of an intranet or CRM system. Well, this sequential process does not hold. It seems there is no link to having a web site and then moving on to more complex e-business type applications.

To better understand this we need to explore the third and most revealing finding from the research:

3. The one major defining factor in driving e-business success, by far, was the presence of a "facilitator"

Facilitators played the defining factor in enabling these SMEs to adopt e-business in their firms. When Davies et al dug a little deeper they found that facilitators are more loosely defined by the SMEs as "someone, from within or outside the firm, who is trusted and understands this crazy internet stuff". A facilitator could be a front desk employee who embraces the internet, a relative with an internet background, or they could be the consultant who helped build the company's web site. The important factor is facilitators are a *trusted* source of knowledge and posses the capability to help the SME wade through the complexity of the internet.

This is an extraordinary piece of information to understand why, or more importantly how, SMEs move to the next level of internet activity. We also believe facilitators to be important catalysts when it comes to helping SMEs build and execute internet marketing strategies as well. This was true in the case of Aiden's Deep Sea Fishing as the owners didn't implement all the internet marketing activities discussed, their cousin did. He was not associated with the business; he and his family owned a cottage nearby where they spent the summer months and they loved to go fishing!

LEVELING THE PLAYING FIELD WITH INTERNET MARKETING

Internet marketing represents a significant opportunity for SMEs, primarily due to the fact that it levels the playing field and in some cases, provides an advantage over larger competitors. So why aren't more SMEs succeeding on the internet today, especially when up to 85% of them have web sites?

One of the challenges for a SME utilizing the internet is the inherent belief that if the site is there, customers will find you. This is the internet communication model discussed earlier; consumers are in control, they instigate finding the business, and if they choose, interact with the company.. However, the complexity starts with how the consumer approaches finding a business. The internet is a very crowded place with more and more businesses turning to it as a marketing and promotion channel, coupled with the fantastic growth of social media. However, this growth area can be a double edge sword. If consumers are spending all of their time on Facebook™, they are not looking for your web site, and thus, SMEs must spend energy and resources attracting customers to their site. This is really what internet marketing is all about. Once a potential customer has found a website, the SME must work diligently in the opportunity to build a relationship with them and eventually close a sale.

The good news surrounding internet marketing, as exemplified in the case studies presented in this chapter, is that it can be inexpensive and very effective. The best and cheapest way to have a potential customer find an SME's web site is through effective search placement, which is the practice of ensuring the SME's website appears on the first page of a Google search. If the company's web site can achieve this kind of search placement against the important key words for their product or service, they will drive traffic to their web site. While this is ideal, it is also very hard to achieve. Search Engine Optimization is an art

and a very complex one at that. An easier way to drive traffic to a web site is through pay-per-click (PPC) advertising. Google's PPC product is called Adwords™. This tool entails paying for small text based ads which typically present on the right hand side of a search page. This service offering is the bread and butter of Google's $21.8B U.S.[10] in revenue and represents the majority of internet marketing spending by companies ("Google Investor Relations," 2008). The good news for SMEs is that the service is simple to engage and very cost effective as Google only charges for the click-throughs[11] to a business's web site that were generated from the advertisement. As such, the SME is effectively only paying for a somewhat qualified lead.

Once a customer "finds" a SME's web site, the focus should be to convert them to a paying customer. The most important tool to help achieve this is the deployment of *analytics*. This is the art of measuring what customers are doing on a web site. Google's product, called Google Analytics™, is free and discussed at greater length later in this chapter.

These tools support the hypothesis presented at the beginning of the chapter, that SMEs should essentially spend all of their available resources directing potential customers to their web site and then measure what they are doing on the site, prior to making adjustments. Studying customer usage and behavior patterns will allow SMEs to make informed decisions as to what changes will be most effective for their website.

The important message here is that internet marketing is not difficult to execute, it is relatively inexpensive and in some cases free. This gives SMEs an opportunity to more directly compete with larger competitors. Historically, this was not possible within the confines of traditional media, as only the large companies could afford to fund media placement in channels such as television for example. SMEs were effectively shut out of this marketing channel, or those that tried, did so with relatively poor results; remember those

Figure 6. Internet marketing at a glance[13] (© 2007, UNB Saint John. Used with permission.)

- **Search engine marketing**
- **Search engine optimization**
- **Social media marketing**
- **Display advertizing**
- **E-Mail marketing**
- **Blog marketing**
- **Mobile marketing**
- **In-game (in-world) marketing**
- **Widget marketing**
- **Viral marketing (Word-of-mouse)**
- **Online PR**

car dealer commercials of yesteryear! Thus, only larger companies had access to powerful marketing channels with broad reach that deployed rich messages while SMEs were relegated to newspaper, radio or direct mail advertising and promotions. This is all changing as media consumption moves to the internet. SMEs can now promote their services as effectively as large companies, by using the internet. In fact, due to their size, they can in most cases move more quickly to engage in new opportunities, like Twitter or Adwords™ campaigns.

The playing field is leveling, or as Thomas Friedman so eloquently put it, "*the world is flattening*" [12] (Friedman, 2005), and internet marketing is not exception to this new reality.

INTERNET MARKETING TOOLS

The execution of an internet marketing strategy is really a function of utilizing one or multiple tools and techniques available on the internet through providers like Google. As mentioned earlier, these tools are being developed at a tremendous pace with some defining this pace as "internet time". Samples of key internet marketing tools are highlighted in figure 6.

It is fairly straight forward for an SME to utilize these tools and achieve positive results. However, without strategic forethought it is difficult to achieve sustained long term results over time. The notion of strategic internet marketing will be discussed further in the next section of this chapter.

A brief overview of five of the most common internet marketing tools and techniques will follow. These are:

1. Analytics
2. Search engine advertising (SEA)
3. Search engine optimization (SEO)
4. Email marketing
5. Social media marketing

Analytics

If you don't measure it, you can't manage it! This is a common phrase, often heard in management circles and goes hand-in-hand with the earlier hypothesis. Promote the web site to attract customer visits, measure what they are doing on the site, and make adjustments accordingly. The measurement is made possible through analytics. Google offers a tremendous analytics tool, which is free to use. Google understands the value in offering

Figure 7. Google analytics HTML tracking code[14]

```
<script type="text/javascript">
var gaJsHost = (("https:" == document.location.protocol) ?
"https://ssl." : "http://www.");
document.write(unescape("%3Cscript src='" + gaJsHost +
"google-analytics.com/ga.js'
type='text/javascript'%3E%3C/script%3E"));
</script>

<script type="text/javascript">
try{
var pageTracker = _gat._getTracker("UA-xxxxxx-x");
pageTracker._trackPageview();
} catch(err) {}
</script>
```

this free service as it helps to drive AdWords™ revenue. Turning on analytics is the first step in journeying into the world of internet marketing. It is straight forward only requiring three simple steps. First, an SME needs to create a Google account and register their web site for analytics. Secondly, the SME needs to attach a "tag" or tracking code to the bottom of each page of their web site. Tags are essentially HTML commands; shown in figure 7. It should take a web designer less than 15 minutes to make this modification to a typical SME web site.

The final step is to submit the web site to Google. This is an option available to anyone with a Google account. Once a web site is submitted, it may take a few hours or days for the Google Analytics to start working effectively, so a little patience is required.

Setting up analytics is the easy part. SME's then need to begin to utilize the plethora of information Google Analytics provides. Some important highlights are:

Visits and Bounce Rate

Visits to a web site are fairly self explanatory and represent the number of people who open the site whether for the first time or as a repeat visitor. Bounce rate represents a percentage of visitors who come to a web site and then leave the site immediately from the entry page without clicking through to another page. The assumption in this case is that nothing really caught their eye or the site was not what they were looking for. Bounce rate is a key measure within internet marketing. Clearly, if SMEs are going to spend a fair amount of effort attracting potential customers to a web site, they do not want them "bouncing". The other important thing to understand is that bounce rate is a relative measure, where some industries have extremely high bounce rates and others are relatively low. Bounce rates can be more easily understood by benchmarking a web site against others in the SME's sector. Google Analytics allows you to do this.

Traffic Sources

Analytics will capture where traffic to a site originates from; either by the customer typing in the URL directly, from a search engine, a referring site or from a search engine ad if the SME is running an AdWords™ campaign. While it is optimal to have potential customers find a web site directly through a search engine, this will not always be the case and successful internet marketing will attract traffic through a combination of these and other sources. Analyzing traffic sources and how they are changing or evolving over time is essential to effective internet marketing.

Goals

Setting goals within analytics (which may be, as an example, the desire to create an order page on the web site) allows an SME to understand how potential customers either find their way to a goal page - or not. Setting goals and then managing the effectiveness of the web site to achieve these goals is paramount to effective internet marketing. Analytics offers a tremendous amount of information to help an SME manage to their goals.

Key Words

Analytics will also highlight the key words that are being used to find their web sites (Figure 8). This makes good sense for Google as it will enhance the effectiveness of their AdWords™ system by driving more focused and presumably successful, AdWords™ advertising. By analyzing what words potential customers are using in their searches to find a web site, SME's are then able to turn around and advertise against those words with the goal of driving more traffic to their web site.

Analytics is clearly a critical first step in adopting internet marketing. Used correctly it can help drive small, incremental changes to a web site which can have a material impact on a firm's bottom line via online originated sales. An important rule of thumb with the deployment of analytics is that it is an investment in human capital first and foremost and technology second. This will be an ongoing investment of time spent digesting information about the site and then acting upon it. Analytics helps an SME understand their customer's behavior and gives them the opportunity to react to it in near real time.

Search Engine Advertising (SEA)

Search engine advertising is the most utilized internet marketing technique available. Adwords™, Google's primary search engine advertising service, is the bread and butter of Google's success. SEA has a number of key features of which a SME should be aware. First and foremost, the company only pays for click-throughs. Unlike more traditional media, where payment is based on *potential* exposure to an ad, the internet allows for a more targeted, measurable service. By paying for click-throughs the SME is ensured of an opportunity to turn a visitor into a customer. In other words, it is in their hands once the potential customer hits their web site.

One little known fact about Google Adwords™ is the logic behind how Google sets the rate for a click-through. One of the defining factors is Google's view of how successful the web site will be in turning a potential customer into a sale. They will analyze a web site for its effectiveness and set the click-through rate accordingly. The more effective they view the web site to be, the cheaper the rate. The less effective they consider the web site in their conversion to sales, the higher the rate. Obviously, they want successful customers for their Adwords™ service who will continue to use this means of internet marketing. Another interesting factor is that the SME chooses how much they want to spend and against which key words. Google takes this information and displays the Adwords™ message based on these criteria. If a lower spending limit is indicated, the ad will not be shown every time a key word is searched, thus balancing the amount of advertising spend against the broader number of searches on a desired set of keywords. Setting up an SEA account with Google is quite simple; a menu pick within a Google account.

Figure 8. Google analytics dashboard[15]

Search Engine Optimization (SEO)

A highly desirable result for any company is to appear on the first page of a search against relevant key words. This is effective search engine placement and is accomplished through search engine optimization. If this can be achieved, then the requirement to use Adwords™ for example diminishes and internet marketing becomes much cheaper. But SEO is an art as much as a science and is best left to the experts. SEO is more generally defined as:

a structured approach used to increase the position of a company or its products in natural or organic search engine results listings for selected keywords or phrases.

In a nutshell, effective SEO can be broken down into two distinct categories:

- On the page (inherent in the SME's site)
  - ○ Optimization and coding standards
  - ○ Relevant content, keyword phrases and cross-links

- Off the page (recognized affiliations with other sites)
  - ○ Link building strategy

It is the art of building web pages which are searchable against certain keywords and building content and links which meet certain search criteria. Links are extremely important in Google's world, and the nature of links represents the very foundation for which Google built their search engine. Changing content is also an important aspect of successful SEO and one reason why more and more web sites are building in blogs. Blogs represent user-based, dynamically changing content, and Google likes that. Some of the common mistakes and related best practices for effective search engine optimization are listed in Table 1. In part, this is meant to illustrate the complexities in effective SEO and why it is best left to the professionals.

E-Mail Marketing

E-mail marketing is a form of direct marketing that uses electronic mail to build relationships

Table 1. Search engine optimization – Avoiding the common mistakes[16] (© 2007, UNB Saint John. Used with permission.)

Common Mistakes	Best Practices
Same title, meta description and keywords on every page	Cerate standardized but unique titles for every page Use distinct but relevant description and keyword phrases on every page
Insufficient or poor body content	No content = no ranking Be relevant and proofread content
Poor cross-linking	Add relevant cross-links (body and image links, secondary navigation, bread-crumbs, site maps, etc) Avoid link over kill
Inexistent or poor incoming links	No incoming links = no ranking Create a link strategy based on context, relevancy and quality of placement Avoid link farms, link networks, poorly ranked or banned sites
Duplicate content	Avoid duplicate body content Avoid multiple domain names for same site Avoid circular navigation and inconsistent cross-linking Exclude duplicate pages
Un-crawlable navigation	Avoid problematic technologies (Flash, JavaScript, DHTML) if possible Add a second navigation schemes
Invalid HTML	Fix the errors! Validate to standards
No site map	Create one! (Google site map makes it easy)
No alt text on images	Add alt text to images
Improper link anchor text	Be relevant Avoid generic "click here"
No use of heading tags	Use H1, H2 . . . H6 properly
No exclusions	Robots.txt is a must Exclude the appropriate pages
Over optimization	Design for users, not search engines
Mass submission	Avoid using automated submission services Don't manually submit to crawlers

with current and prospective customers, increase sales and improve customer retention. Put another way, e-mail marketing represents an important step in internet marketing and can be the delivery engine behind effective database marketing. Building a database of users, through online and more traditional means and then effectively communicating with them, on their terms, is central to good marketing. A key understanding here is the notion that e-mail communication needs to be offered on the customer's terms and is not all about sales. It can strengthen an SME's database

marketing and can be used to engage customers across the entire customer life cycle as depicted in Figure 9.

E-mail marketing engines are readily available, inexpensive and can be quite effective. One thing to look for in an e-mail marketing tool is the reporting ability which allows the SME to know, among other things, *who opened what e-mail when*. Most e-mail marketing tools also include "opt out" capability for customers and will report on which links (assuming there are multiple links in the message) the customers choose.

Figure 9. Customer life cycle and engagement tactics[17] (© 2007, UNB Saint John. Used with permission.)

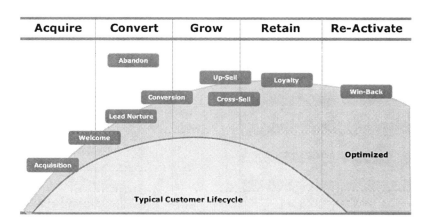

Social Media Marketing

Social Media Marketing (SMM) is the form of internet marketing which seeks to achieve branding and marketing communication goals through the participation in various social media networks and online communities by encouraging brand feedback and dialogue. Some SMEs may question "Why does it matter?" The simple answer, which is highlighted in Figure 10, is that more and more on-line time is spent on "user-generated" sites, like Facebook™, MySpace™ and LinkedIn™. Internet evolution seems to be moving at the fastest speed within these social media networks.

SMEs who engage in social media sites and product/service specific blogs have, in some cases, shown a tremendous ability to engage with customers and ultimately drive sales. The important nuance of social media marketing is it has to be indirect. This approach takes a fair amount of patience, something that SMEs cannot always afford in terms of their development. Slapping up a Facebook™ site is not effective social media marketing. Engaging in discussion forums, bringing product expertise to relative blog sites, working to build an online reputation and understanding the issues facing potential customers are all facets of social media marketing. Undoubtedly, social media marketing will consume a significant amount of the entrepreneurs' time. The closing case study of Abbyshot Clothiers effectively illustrates the potential of social media marketing.

There are many other and evolving forms of internet marketing but the commonality is such that results are measurable and can be immediate, and one reason why internet marketing is growing at an accelerated pace. However, a caution flag needs to be raised surrounding the longer term implications of effective internet marketing. Internet marketing tactics left alone are just that, tactics. They will be copied, lose relevance and essentially become less effective over time. Internet marketing tactics executed within the context of a strategic marketing plan can, however, have long lasting effects.

STRATEGIC INTERNET MARKETING

Internet marketing, when guided by fundamental marketing practices, can provide desirable, extraordinary results over long periods of time. It is the integration and focused execution of multiple internet marketing tactics which, when driven by a broader set of objectives and goals, can lead to great results. Our case study at the beginning of the chapter on Aiden's Deep Sea Fishing, exemplifies this very notion.

Figure 10. Why does it matter? (© 2007, eMarketer.com, Used with permission.)

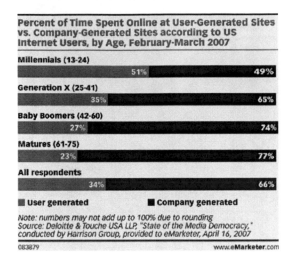

In summary, Aiden's customer database drives e-mail campaigns which helps customers learn of their fishing blog, driving voluntary, customer-originated viral e-mail marketing which may enhance customer referrals. These tactics are tied to the effective use of analytics to understand key word search and goal conversion, ultimately driving an increasingly more effective spend in search engine advertising. All of this activity is focused on the goal of growing the strength of their referral-originated business, which currently represents just under half of their total customers with online-originated new customers more than doubling annually. The irony is the referral business is measured by asking the simple question – *How did you find out about us?* – at dockside when customers show up to go fishing. This exemplifies, in a simple way, how Aiden's is tying old marketing techniques, with new internet marketing tactics, to leverage their current strengths in their market and deal with challenging market conditions. Aiden's started their internet marketing journey by running a simple Adwords™ campaign and turning on Google Analytics which was quickly copied by their prime competitor in the region, and represents a key downfall of internet marketing. In its simplest forms it can be easily replicated, yet when woven into a broader marketing approach can become more strategic, less tactical and much harder to copy.

When building a marketing mix to leverage the power of the internet, it is important to build in the notions of interactivity, measurability, community and communication. This expanded view of the four P's will set the stage for an internet marketing strategy designed to be sustainable over the long run. The challenge for SMEs, as with more traditional marketing, will be to take the time and effort to set their goals and objectives properly; ones which are reflective of the opportunities facing them and realistic as to the challenges of their particular markets.

FUTURE RESEARCH DIRECTIONS

Further benchmark research needs to be conducted to provide an understanding of the adoption rates of internet marketing in the global SME market. This research should also focus on the factors driving internet adoption and the use of internet marketing. A strong understanding of these driving factors can help policy makers and internet marketing providers make informed decisions as to the most effective way to build adoption of internet technologies and internet marketing efforts within the SME sector. Through these policy and commercial efforts, SMEs can become comfortable in adopting the internet in greater numbers, which will result in leveling the playing field with their larger competitors and reaching out to a broader set of global growth opportunities. Internet marketing is the future marketing engine of the SME sector, the sooner, and better we understand the factors affecting successful adoption of internet marketing and related technologies the sooner we can help this sector use this understanding to grow and thrive in a global marketplace.

CONCLUSION

In this chapter we learned how small and medium sized businesses can utilize internet marketing to level the playing field with their larger competitors. And, that internet marketing must come before web site changes or renewal. We took the view that long term success with internet marketing is predicated on a more integrated strategic approach, versus a non-integrated tactical approach. Two small businesses were profiled that used various internet marketing tools and techniques to successfully build online sales and referral programs. We have a better sense of a number of key internet marketing tools, like analytics, search engine advertising, search engine optimization, email marketing and social media marketing and we understand how cost effective and thus attractive these tools can be to the SME sector.

We better understand why it is an opportune and encouraging time for SMEs to engage in internet marketing, with media consumption moving quickly away from traditional media outlets and over to the internet. Finally, we have also gained a sense of how the internet is changing the marketing mix with the introduction of measurable interactivity and accessible communities of interest.

CLOSING CASE STUDY: ABBYSHOT CLOTHIERS – A DEEP APPRECIATION FOR THEIR CUSTOMERS (WWW. ABBYSHOT.COM)[18]

What happens when a smash hit movie creates a loyal, if not cult-like following? A niche market for screen accurate, movie inspired clothing is created. Armed with the basic premise that fans would crave the likeness of their favorite movie character, independent web consultant Adam Bragg and classically trained seamstress Bonnie Cook, created AbbyShot Clothiers.

From the beginning, this creative team had the intuitive sense to present their website as a customer-focused interface, catering to the response and feed back of their clients. The humble, single item clothing line which was presented on a single-page site in 2002, has grown to become an eight-page site featuring 41 product items with sales in over 28 countries around the globe. Their successful growth is attributable to the carefully cultivated customer relationships that have been a function of segmenting their customer base and having a rich understanding of their customer profile.

Appreciate Your Customer Demographic

Fans are a dedicated and "fanatical" bunch. Across sporting, music or movie genres, you can find the subculture of on-line communities where fans gather. Adam was a fan of the original 1999 Matrix movie that spurred the entire business concept for Abbyshot. While surfing the net, he came across others who were enthralled with the movie, and who, would even like to wear the same coat as their favorite movie character. His research revealed that "no one else on the planet" was offering these unique, customized overcoats. In that moment he saw an opportunity.

Initially, Abbyshot would visit the fan websites and movie review sites, posting comments about their company, soliciting feedback. "We knew that to connect with the fans of the movie, we would want to express interest in their "fandom" and let them know that we like it too, and are willing to invest in their interests." Within 3 months they had added 4 more styles to their product offering and in their first year of business exceeded $150,000 in revenues.

Reviewing the source material (such as the movies or hit shows) is important for product development, but even more so is understanding the inherent differences that exist between the "fandoms" and keeping up to speed with their customers. Abbyshot continues to visit the fan discussion forums of the various movies which serve as the catalysts for their screen-accurate wares. This provides valuable insight into potential customer preferences, and also ensures that they can talk sensibly about the products they consider producing. From these forums, different opportunities for each product may arise. One on-line fan community allowed them to promote their products to their membership, where another supported a "peer review" prior to a product's release. "The fans will know if a lapel is 3 degrees off-center, and they are telling us!"

Create a Dialogue with Your Customer

It became evident that customers in this niche market would willingly offer direction, create demand, and support the venture. The key would be to continue to manage the customer relationship, engaging knowledgeable fans, their customers, in dialogue which would support their business.

A primary tool of their customer engagement is their company newsletter. In 2002, it was a simple, text-based email announcement of new product releases to a very small distribution list of a few hundred. If recipients clicked on the link, they would land on the website. With the addition of product photography to their newsletter, the response rate, as measured by click-throughs and open rates began to grow. The addition of a "subscribe now!" button captured even more names and contributed to growing the distribution list. Finally, embedding their newsletter within the format of the email message has successfully garnered a 30% open rate and a click-through rate as high as 40%. Today, Abbyshot engages a newsletter management service enabling them to track statistics and generate reports which reflect who is opening it, how quickly upon receipt, and what articles or areas in the newsletter are of interest. There is now an appreciation for the increase

in the click-through rate when their newsletter announces a product debut. Understanding their customer from all angles is the cornerstone of their marketing strategy.

The solid relationship and dialogue that Abbyshot has created with its customers has also provided leads to broader markets through other websites that Abbyshot has not been aware of. It is market information directed by their customers. However, lessons are to be learned in the process, and customer comments and suggestions also require a degree of management and evaluation. In early 2007, the company closed its own customer forum as it started to become less of a product development tool, and more of a chat room with less useful product information provided by fans and customers. This has prompted the creation of a blog to augment the company's efforts to speak to its customer base.

Manage Your Customer Relationship for Future Growth

Of course, new movie releases, sequels, DVD and video game launches provide ongoing product development opportunities and a shot in the arm for revenue for the company. However, it has been Abbyshot's commitment to profiling and engaging their customer base that has reaped the rewards. With only 6-7,000 customers within their current niche market, the company relies on the constant "back and forth" with their customers, valuing their comments and suggestions, and enjoying a healthy 30% "second" purchase rate amongst customers who have already invested in one of Abbyshot's products.

The company so values the relationships created with the "fandoms" that have become their customer base, that they have donated garments for charity fundraisers to the fan clubs. The mutual respect has been established, and fandoms link to Abbyshot as well.

While the company's first five years were intensely product-quality focused given the savvy fan knowledge, Abbyshot now looks forward to continued growth as their reputation has been established as the leading world-wide producer of screen-accurate movie clothing. With over 9,000 unique views per month, and total revenues having grown by 100% in five years, to over $300,000/ year, Abbyshot will continue to closely follow its customers' direction, expand its newsletter reach, and begin to focus more closely on targeting website visitors to ensure maximum sales are achieved. Abbyshot Clothiers believes in its own credo that "No longer are we using marketing to attract customers, our marketing strategies should support what the customer demands from the company. Ignore at your peril!"

ACKNOWLEDGMENT

I would like to acknowledge all the contributors to this chapter, including the UNB Saint John Electronic Commerce Research and Training Center for their willingness to share information from their *Marketing on the Internet* training seminar, with special thanks to Louis Philippe Gauthier for his expertise, knowledge and passion for internet marketing. I would also like to acknowledge Catherine Connolly for her editing help and of course Jackie for her support and patience throughout the learning and writing process.

REFERENCES

Davis, C., Lin, C., & Vladica, F. (2005). *State of e-Business in SMEs in Atlantic Canada in 2005.* Paper presented at the annual Atlantic Schools of Business conference, Halifax, N.S., Canada.

Davis, C., & Vladica, F. (August 2004). *Adoption of Internet technologies and e-business solutions by small and medium enterprises (SMEs) in New Brunswick.* Saint John, Canada: University of New Brunswick Saint John, Electronic Commerce Centre.

Dev, C.S., & Schultz, D.E. (2005, January/February). In the mix: A customer focused approach can bring the current marketing mix into the 21st century. *Marketing Management, 14*(1).

Electronic Commerce Research & Training Centre (ECRTC). (2008). *Marketing on the Internet training program.* University of New Brunswick Saint John, Saint John, N.B., Canada.

Fleet, G. (November 2008). *Export and the role of the Internet for SMEs in Atlantic Canada.* Paper presented at the International Council for Small Business (ICSB) 2008 World Conference, Halifax, N.S., Canada.

Friedman, T. (April 2005). *The world is flat: A brief history of the 21st century.* New York: Farrar, Straus & Giroux.

Google investor relations – Financial tables. (2008). Retrieved March 18, 2009, from http://investor.google.com/fin_data.html

Jack Myers media business report: US advertising forecast. (November 2007). Retrieved November 2008 from http://www.jackmyers.com

Jarboe, G. (March 16, 2007). *Boosting PR results with SEO and RSS.* Retrieved March 18, 2009 from www.ipressroom.com/pr/SchwartzmanPR/info/document/JarboeBulldogChicago2007.ppt

McCarthy, E. J. (1960). *Basic marketing: A managerial approach.* Homewood, IL: Irwin.

ENDNOTES

1. Davis, Vladica (2004)
2. Davis, Lin, Vladica (2005)
3. This case was built for the UNBSJ Electronic Commerce Research & Training Centre *Marketing on the Internet* training program by Catherine M. Connolly, L. Philippe Gauthier and the author.
4. Davis, Lin, Vladica (2005)

5   Including the two studies from Davis et al in 2004 & 2005, plus the subsequent study by Fleet in 2007

6   Information retrieved from Jack Myers Media Business Report (November 2007)

7   Greg Jarboe (March 16, 2007). Illustration created by L. Philippe Gauthier for the UNBSJ Marketing on the Internet training seminar.

8   Information sourced from McCarthy E.J., & Dev, C. S., Schultz, D.E. Illustrated by L. Philippe Gauthier for the UNB Saint John *Marketing on the Internet* training program.

9   Photos provided with permission from the author.

10   Google Investor Relations – 2008 earnings report.

11   Click-through's refer to when an ad is clicked on and the user is brought to the company's web site

12   Friedman, T. *The World is Flat*

13   Compliments of the UNBSJ Marketing on the Internet training seminar

14   Tracking html code information sourced from www.google.com

15   Take from the authors Google account.

16   Sourced from UNB Saint John *Marketing on the Internet* training program. This table was compiled for UNB Saint John by L. Philippe Gauthier.

17   Adapted from information on Bronto. com – List Management essential to Email marketing (2007). Illustrated for the UNB Saint John *Marketing on the Internet* training seminar by L. Philippe Gauthier.

18   This case study was written for the UNBSJ *Marketing on the Internet* training program by Catherine Connolly and L. Philippe Gauthier.

19   Radian6 is a social media monitoring company

APPENDIX A

ADDITIONAL READING

A significant amount of information on the world of internet marketing and its implications is available through traditional published sources and of course, on the internet. If you like to read, I would suggest the following:

- *Web analytics: An hour a day* (Avinash Kaushik & Jim Sterne)
- *33 Million people in a room: How to create, influence, and run a successful business with social networking* (Juliette Powell)
- *Creative marketing for SMEs* (Ian Fillis)
- *Internet marketing: Integrating online and offline strategies* (Mary Lou Roberts)

   Not to be overlooked is the immediate, real time way to capture insight on this topic: engage with Twitter. If this is of interest, a first step could be to ask Radian6[19] to allow you to follow them into the world of real time social media marketing; a fantastic way to relish the possibilities that are present within the scope of internet marketing.

- *Purple cow: Transform your business by being remarkable* (Seth Godin)
- *The world is flat* (Thomas Friedman)
- *Ultimate guide to Google AdWords: How to access 100 million people in 10 minutes* (Perry Marshal and Bryan Todd)

Section 4
The International Dimension of ICT, Websites and E–Commerce for Small Business

Chapter 8
Small Business Sales Growth and Internationalization Links to Web Site Functions in the United Kingdom

Robert Williams
NEO, UK

Gary P. Packham
University of Glamorgan, UK

Brychan C. Thomas
University of Glamorgan, UK

Piers Thompson
University of Wales Institute, UK

ABSTRACT

The potential of the Internet to both geographically expand customer bases and provide a source of growth has led to a rapid embracement of the Internet by a majority of small businesses in the United Kingdom. However, many studies suggest that much of this adoption takes the form of simple websites representing little more than an electronic brochure. Although theories and models have been proposed suggesting adoption and development of e-commerce takes a staged process, with firms moving to more complex e-commerce processes after first mastering simpler forms of website, studies have found mixed evidence with regard to this. This chapter investigates the level of Small and Medium Enterprise (SME) website adoption and functionality and how this relates to growth aspirations, specifically the geographical expansion of customer bases. One potential explanation for this slow uptake of true e-commerce is a lack of employees with basic and advanced IT skills. The possibility that IT skills shortages could explain the gap between the Internet's potential and the extent of involvement by a vast majority of UK SMEs is explored. Discussion within the chapter is complemented with analysis of data from a large survey of SMEs.

DOI: 10.4018/978-1-60566-998-4.ch008

INTRODUCTION

The increasing accessibility of the Internet has led to a massive increase in the level of e-commerce in the UK in recent years, with sales over the Internet rising from £3.2 billion in 2002 to 38.8 billion in 2007 (ONS, 2008). This is not just a reflection of customers becoming familiar and comfortable with accessing the websites of large established businesses within the UK, but also the increasing number of smaller businesses which have taken advantage of the potential of the Internet to cheaply advertise and sell their products to a wide range of customers (O'Keefe et al., 1998). As well as more traditional business models being augmented with the addition of a website there are new businesses reliant entirely on the Internet for their sales although many of these collapsed when the dot.com bubble burst in the early 2000s (Drew, 2003). Again Web only activity has not just been restricted to the larger, now household names, such as Amazon. Relatively low fixed costs and perceived risk has led to an explosion of entrepreneurial activity by individuals often alongside other economic activity such as salaried employment (O'Keefe, et al., 1998). There is an extensive literature examining the possible determinants for firms choosing to develop websites which includes not only the opportunities created (Stockdale and Standing, 2004), but also the threats that Internet usage brings (Kleindl, 2000). Whatever the driving forces by the beginning of the present century the unavoidability of the Web meant that e-commerce in its broadest sense has become an imperative rather than an alternative (Wen et al., 2001).

Whilst a vast majority of firms have or will develop their own Web presences, there is a greater variation in the speed, depth and form that involvement will take (Wen et al., 2001). It has also been suggested that website development is a staged process often driven by the availability of resources, particularly knowledge (Levy and Powell, 2003; Rao et al., 2003; Lee, 2004). Not all researchers are convinced of the merit of simpler stages models given the existence of early adopters and heterogeneity of small businesses (Martin and Matlay, 2001; Alonso Mendo and Fitzgerald, 2005a).

This study concentrates on the functions included in the websites of UK SMEs, and how these different levels of functionality relate to the perceived benefits of the Internet in providing growth potential and in particular access to markets beyond their local core market (Lawson et al., 2003). This would mean that greater adoption of e-commerce would lead to higher sales growth (Raymond et al., 2005), even providing a relatively cheap method of internationalizing client bases (Kula and Tatoglu, 2003). These opportunities are particularly pertinent to SMEs who often may operate in niche markets, relying on a thinly but widely distributed customer base (Napier et al., 2001; Galloway et al., 2008). Whether, UK SMEs can fully take advantage of the opportunities open to them seems questionable given that their websites are often little more than product brochures (Levy and Powell, 2003; Crespi et al., 2004).

Given the potential of the Internet to not only grow the firm, but also to simply allow the firm to compete in a rapidly globalizing marketplace, it seems strange that studies have found little sign of true e-commerce adoption. One explanation comes from those studies examining the choice to adopt, which find a link to the perceived ease of use (Grandon and Pearson, 2004). Therefore potential skills shortages for owners/managers and their staff could clearly hold back greater functionality of websites (Mehrtens et al., 2001; Mirchandani and Motwani, 2001; Robertson et al., 2007).

When discussing the issues raised by UK SME website functionality analysis of data from the Federation of Small Business (FSB) 'Lifting the Barriers to Growth' survey is used to complement discussion of existing literature. The next section discusses studies that have examined the decision to adopt and develop a Web presence and what role growth plays in this decision. Since one of the main potentials for growth from the internet for SMEs is to break out of their traditional markets, attention is then turned to the possibility of geographical expansion and internationalization through website functions. The role IT skills shortages play in low website functionality is explored in the fourth section before considering future routes for research, and drawing conclusions in the last section.

GROWTH, WEBSITE ADOPTION AND FUNCTIONALITY

The latter part of the 20th century saw a reduced importance of large corporations in western economies in terms of output and employment, and a greater emphasis on small and medium enterprises (SMEs). Explanations proposed for the rapid resurgence of small business activity in the form of a 'third industrial revolution' (Audretsch and Thurik, 2001), are: emergence of new industries, such as software and biotechnology; deregulation and privatization of many sectors; greater emphasis on concentrating on core competences by large firms; new demand for more varied products; greater prosperity leading to a greater desire for self-realization from work; and finally a greater emphasis on services (Carree et al., 2002). Given the increasing need for flexibility and reduced scale, advances in information and communications technology (ICT) such as e-commerce become essential tools for remaining competitive in the modern economy (Fillis et al., 2004).

As the Internet has become more widely accessed by the world's population its commercial potential has exploded. Although, both stock and order models of technology adoption suggest that the benefits of adoption decline with the number of firms already using the technology and the order in which firms adopt technology, the adoption

rate is positively related to the expected number of future users (Crespi et al., 2004). This means that given the potential for further expansion of the Internet there is still a strong incentive for SMEs to set up their own websites. In addition, access to a larger variety of suppliers and ease of comparison mean positive network externalities exist, generating more online sales for both firms creating new and those with existing Web presences (Elliot and Fowell, 2000). This means that a presence on the Internet is becoming more and more of a competitive necessity, if only to keep up with competitors (Wen et al., 2001). This is reflected in the FSB data with 77.3 per cent of firms responding that they have a website of some kind (see the data appendix for greater explanation of the FSB data and website functionality measures).

The probability of developing a website has been found to vary greatly between different groups of SMEs with certain firm characteristics either increasing the benefits of adoption or reducing the barriers that need to be overcome. One such characteristic is firm size, with larger firms generally deemed to have the resources to pursue adoption at all stages of website development (Dutta and Evrard, 1999; Love and Irani, 2004). Some studies on the other hand have found no significant connection between firm size and website development (Daniel et al., 2002). These conflicting results may reflect higher levels of adoption positively influenced by the greater flexibility of smaller firms but also by the superior resource availability of larger firms. Using the FSB data to provide insights into those characteristics associated with the decision to adopt a Website, a logit regression is run with presence of a firm website as the dependent variable. Clearly the availability of resources plays an important role with larger firms both in terms of employment and turnover significantly more likely to have a website (Table 1). While only 72.1 per cent of businesses with turnover of less than £100,000 a year have a website, of those reporting turnover greater than £1 million this figure rises to 90.2 per cent. Employment shows a similar pattern with 69.6 per cent of those with no employees having a website compared to 88.8 per cent of those employing ten or more people. The relationship between employment and website presence is perhaps the most telling as those businesses with fewer employees are more likely to have to draw on outside expertise to develop and maintain a website (Cragg and Zinatelli, 1995).

Clearly the importance of a Web presence will vary between firms operating in different industry sectors, with service industries suggested to benefit more from closer relationships to their clients (O'Keefe, 1998). The tourist trade has been isolated as being one industry where the Web could play a valuable role in generating a competitive edge (Kierzkowski et al., 1996). The reliance of the business on the tourist trade understandably increases the probability of having a website as sales are more likely to be non-repeat sales and therefore greater market presence will be required.

The age of the firm is likely to have a complicated relationship with website adoption. Given that studies suggest there is may be a minimum level of resources required to produce a website, this may prevent adoption by the youngest firms (Dutta and Evard, 1999). A pattern apparent in the FSB data. Equally though older and larger established firms that have been successfully trading may not see the fit with their existing business models (Fariselli et al., 1999; Darch and Lucas, 2002), explaining why firms in the FSB data over 9 years of age are no more likely to have websites than those just formed.

Even after controlling for industry sectors and size, UK SMEs are not homogeneous, but also differ greatly in terms of their aims, objectives and cultures. Whilst it is difficult if not impossible to produce a strong understanding of all these potential influences through a survey instrument, the central figure of a majority of SMEs is the owner-manager. Whilst imperfect the

characteristics of the owner-manager are likely to be strongly related to the business's raison d'être. For instance the age of the entrepreneur themselves is likely to have major influence on the strategic aims of a business, with businesses owned by older entrepreneurs perhaps less likely to seek growth and expansion, which will obviously impact on Web presence. The entrepreneur's age may also have an important role to play in terms of knowledge relating to website technology. As such the owner-manager's knowledge and attitude towards IT innovations is found to be highly influential in an SME's adoption decision relating to new technologies (Eurostat, 1996). Fundamentally the more knowledgeable and comfortable the owner-manager is with IT in general and the Internet specifically (Iacovou et al., 1995) the more likely the firm is to have a website. It is clear that younger entrepreneurs brought up using the Web will be more likely to push their firms to greater adoption and better integration of websites, although this is likely to lead to higher levels of business failure where untried entrepreneurs combine with untested business models (Howcroft, 2001). The FSB data confirms this where firms owned by the youngest group of business owners (aged under 35 years) are significantly more likely to have websites.

Owner-managers with higher levels of education are more likely to have firms with websites, although this represents a crude measure of IT skill and usage, higher formal education qualifications may indicate an ability to understand and foresee the potential of website facilities for achieving growth. This coming from a greater familiarity with the Internet from their studies and previous work experience, thus increasing the owner-managers' perceived capability levels (Dutta and Evrard, 1999).

Whilst a large body of work has examined the differences between male and female entrepreneurs (Carter and Bennett, 2006), work looking at the impact of gender on SME adoption of the Web is relatively sparse (Chuang et al., 2007). A

Table 1. Logit of Website usage and active Website usage

		Website		Active Website	
Employment (Base category – owner only)	2 - 4 Employees	**0.2468**	(0.020)	0.1852	(0.164)
	5 - 9 Employees	**0.4384**	(0.003)	0.0722	(0.668)
	10 - 19 Employees	**0.7244**	(0.000)	0.1405	(0.499)
	20+ Employees	**0.7819**	(0.003)	0.1018	(0.681)
Turnover (Base category – less than £25,000)	£25K - £50K	0.0874	(0.576)	0.1106	(0.556)
	£500k - £100K	0.1156	(0.457)	-0.1284	(0.504)
	£100K - £200K	**0.3747**	(0.024)	0.0354	(0.857)
	£200K - £300K	**0.3923**	(0.040)	0.0941	(0.672)
	£300K - £500K	**0.5675**	(0.005)	0.2637	(0.246)
	£500K - £1m	**0.7877**	(0.000)	0.1839	(0.429)
	£1 million	**1.3001**	(0.000)	0.4720	(0.071)
Tourist Trade (Bc – no involvement)	Direct Tourist Trade	**1.1470**	(0.000)	**0.4021**	(0.015)
	Indirect Tourist Trade	0.2291	(0.078)	0.2062	(0.110)
Firm Age (Base category – less than 3 years old)	4 - 9 years	**0.4661**	(0.004)	**0.4202**	(0.017)
	10 to 19 years	0.1442	(0.416)	**0.4677**	(0.014)
	20 or more years	-0.2313	(0.235)	**0.4814**	(0.025)
Entrepreneur's Age (Base category – younger than 35 years)	35 to 44 years old	**-0.5419**	(0.014)	0.1952	(0.330)
	45 to 54 years old	**-0.5612**	(0.009)	0.0043	(0.983)
	55 to 64 years	**-0.6134**	(0.006)	0.1346	(0.513)
	Over 65 years old	**-0.6605**	(0.010)	0.1577	(0.517)
Entrepreneur's educational attainment (Base category A-levels)	Postgraduate	**0.3777**	(0.024)	0.1853	(0.279)
	Bachelors Degree	**0.2839**	(0.039)	0.0632	(0.667)
	Professional Qualifications	-0.0265	(0.839)	-0.0856	(0.557)
	GCSE/O level	-0.2198	(0.123)	0.0981	(0.532)
	Vocational Qualifications	**0.3803**	(0.027)	-0.0185	(0.932)
	No Formal Qualifications	-0.0768	(0.686)	0.1570	(0.454)
Gender of owners (Bc – equal male & female)	Male Majority	-0.0018	(0.983)	-0.0906	(0.351)
	Female Majority	**-0.2947**	(0.019)	-0.1283	(0.366)
Hours committed to business (Bc – 30 to 48 hours)	Less than 30 hours	**-0.5236**	(0.002)	0.1851	(0.368)
	49 to 60 hours	-0.0987	(0.288)	0.0722	(0.495)
	More than 60 hours	-0.1032	(0.377)	0.1010	(0.424)
Change in sales volume over last 12 months (base category – decreased by 0% to 5%)	Decreased by 20%+	0.2805	(0.140)	0.0231	(0.919)
	Decreased by 10%-20%	0.1672	(0.355)	-0.1411	(0.511)
	Decreased by 5%-10%	-0.0358	(0.844)	0.1119	(0.602)
	Increased by 0%-5%	-0.0118	(0.937)	-0.0515	(0.778)
	Increased by 5%-10%	0.1748	(0.263)	-0.1396	(0.454)
	Increased by 10%-20%	0.0961	(0.563)	-0.0771	(0.683)
	Increased by 20%+	0.2817	(0.111)	0.2325	(0.232)

continued on the following page

Table 1. continued

Objectives for business over next two years (base category – remain same size)	Grow turnover 20%+	**0.9703**	(0.000)	**0.6440**	(0.000)
	Expand up to 20%	**0.6795**	(0.000)	**0.3229**	(0.010)
	Downsize business	-0.0292	(0.883)	0.2118	(0.444)
	Sell or close business	-0.0540	(0.701)	0.1896	(0.308)
	Hand on business	0.4367	(0.145)	0.5220	(0.123)
N		5089		3938	
R^2		0.204		0.2368	
Hosmer-Lemeshow		12.46	(0.132)	10.61	(0.225)

Notes: p-values in parenthesis

number of studies have suggested that the motivations and measures of success differ considerably between male and female business owners with non-pecuniary factors playing a more important role for women (Walker and Brown, 2004). For example, the greater autonomy of self-employment can make it attractive to women looking for the flexible employment required for childcare and other domestic chores which they traditionally bear the greatest burden of (Carter and Allen, 1997). Given this it is perhaps of little surprise that the FSB data indicates that those firms majority owned by women are less likely to have websites. Emphasizing this, those firms in which, a lower level of hours are committed by the owner, are also less likely to have websites.

Having taken account of some of the factors that increase or decrease the rate of adoption it would still be expected that the desire to grow will drive website development (Levy et al., 2002). The FSB data suggests that actual growth of firms is not connected to the decision to adopt a website. Turning attention towards those firms which are intending to grow their businesses over the next two years there is more likely to be a website present. As indicated by Raymond et al. (2005) the strategic position of a firm substantially changes the likelihood of a firm having a website, so that those intending to expand rapidly is two

and half times that of those intending to maintain turnover at current levels (odds ratio of 2.633), while those intending to grow turnover by up to 20 per cent are twice as likely to have a website as those taking a more conservative approach (odds ratio of 1.973). Clearly the desire to grow the firm has a strong influence on website adoption. Whether this is sustaining existing growth (85.4 per cent adoption), or new growth (81.9 per cent adoption) the proportion of SMEs adopting a website is much higher than for those firms not intending to grow in the future, whether growth was previously present (68.5 per cent adoption), or the firm has no intention to grow and has not previously grown (64.8 per cent adoption).

It is worth noting that those firms included in the FSB data are primarily traditional bricks and mortar SMEs. This means that the drive of growth may be under-estimated due to a possible under-representation of pure play Web-based firms, as these firms may be more focused on expansion than their traditional counterparts.

Clearly the Internet has potential to provide the next opportunities for economic growth and expansion for those small businesses embracing new business practices based around the Internet. However, for all its potential only 7.7% of UK sales of non-financial business take place through the Internet, although this has risen rapidly from 1.1%

in 2002 (ONS, 2008), with business to business usage likely to be an even smaller proportion of total activity. One explanation for the conflicting facts of high UK SME website adoption and relatively low e-commerce sales is that many websites take the form of simple brochures. These simple websites without functions for interaction do not fully exploit the potential of a Web presence (Levy and Powell, 2003; Crespi et al., 2004). The FSB data indicates that when considering those firms with websites nearly one in four have nothing more than basic contact information available (24.3 per cent). In addition, an even larger proportion is found in the next level up with just information provided to advertise their products (49.3 per cent). This means that roughly only a quarter of those firms with websites utilize their websites in an active manner. It is found that 21.3 per cent of firms have websites providing facilities to sell their products online to customers. A much smaller proportion of firms use their websites as a method of connecting with their suppliers alone (1.5 per cent), although a further 3.6 per cent of firms with websites use these as tools to interact with both suppliers and customers.

This low level of active website development may be driven by a number of issues. Included within these are: resource restrictions; complementarities of available website and software solutions with the firms' businesses; and security issues. Although the Internet has often been seen as having the potential to provide a level playing field for SMEs to compete with large firms (Howcroft, 2001), the limited time SMEs have to spend on future business development can result in under exploitation of opportunities presented by technological developments (Irani et al., 1997; Levy et al., 1998). Use of resources such as management time can see indirect costs of adoption increasing rapidly (Cohen and Kallirol, 2006). In terms of website development this leads to the 'bare minimum' brochure website being developed to allow customers to contact the firm, but little more. Daniel and Wilson (2002) also find

that the highest rated motivations for adoption of e-commerce relate to keeping up with competitors. This means that adoption decisions are taken with a desire to not fall behind rather than consideration of what needs to be undertaken to ensure any ITC investment is value adding. Where benefits are considered these are not necessarily considered in relation to existing organization goals marginalizing the e-commerce as a sideshow of the firm (Lin et al., 2007).

Studies find that where managers possess greater IT skills the more likely a firm is to have a sophisticated interactive website (Damanpour, 1991; Fichman and Kemerer, 1997). However, one problem can often exist is that while top management is enthusiastic about new technology they do not consider the desires and preferences of their staff. The extent that innovations are embraced by those who use them is may influence the level of adoption, so where enthusiastic managers that do not consult their work forces this may result in lower development of websites (Lin et al., 2007).

Most enterprise software, however, has been designed for and marketed to, the larger organizations, who have the budgets, processes and technical skills required to deploy it. One of the key issues has been that SMEs come in all shapes and sizes which presents one of the numerous problems suppliers face in developing e-commerce software for the SME sector. The high cost of marketing to and then servicing hundreds of thousands of small companies rather than a small number of very large clients means the SME sector is neglected. The SME sector is also unique in terms of its business style, with higher risk awareness, plus a lack of confidence and trust in new technologies, also there is often a lack of relevant experience, education and understanding of the e-commerce opportunities available (Kadlec and Mareš, 2003).

The security of those transactions undertaken through websites also forms a barrier to greater website development, with both SMEs and their

Table 2.

Step	Title	Description
0	**Not started yet**	The business does not have Internet access.
1	**E-Mail**	Accesses information and services on-line and uses e-mail. Does not have web-site, or surfs the Web, but has an efficient internal and external communications structure.
2	**Web-site**	Business has web-site but contains only basic information about business, relies on customer initializing contact for further information. Can buy services and supplies on-line.
3	**E-Commerce**	Customers have access to more information (catalogue) about products/services. On-line ordering and payment (store) system. Reduced costs and higher levels of accessibility and speed. Web-site not linked to internal systems and orders are processed manually.
4	**E-Business**	Have integrated supply chain, ordering, manufacture, delivery, accounts and marketing to other business systems (seamless processing). Minimum (reduction of) waste regarding resources between supply chain stages.
5	**Transformed Organizations**	Open information systems for customers, suppliers and partners. Internet technology drives both external and internal processes more effectively and efficiently (enabled). Based on networking between firm and other organizations/individuals.

Adapted from: Cisco led Information Age study on E-commerce and Small Business (Martin and Matlay, 2001)

customers displaying a degree of distrust towards online payments (Yeung and Lu, 2004). In fact although not sufficient to ensure success of a website, security and trust are necessary conditions for development of a successful website (Liu and Arnett, 2000).

All these factors mean that the adoption processes relating to IT within SMEs is different from that in larger businesses. The limited resources of SMEs available for managing the IT adoption process mean, SMEs need to be more conservative in their IT investment. Investment decisions have to pass through a number of stages. The process therefore consists of: assessing the SME's IT requirements (step 1), assessment of organization's IT maturity (step 2), evaluation of available IT solutions in the market (step 3), matching the available solutions with the SME's IT requirements and SME's IT maturity and readiness (step 4), implementation of the selected IT solution (step 5), and post adoption evaluation (step 6). Even though the guidelines appear to be a sequential process, it is possible to use the guidelines as an iterative process (Sarosa and Zowghi, 2003).

In combination these barriers to website development mean that SMEs level of adoption is restricted by the availability of resources within the firm. These resources take the form of time, capital and knowledge. This has led to a number of models being developed with website and e-commerce development occurring in stages as enough resources are acquired to move to the next stage. To an extent this implies website development is a natural process which gradually takes place over time. Firms making the decision to develop websites will automatically add further facilities to their websites as time passes. For example, Daniel et al. (2002) identify four clusters of firms moving from development of e-commerce tools, to communication through email, through informative non-interactive websites, to the adoption of true e-commerce tools of online selling in the final cluster. The adoption ladder (Table 2) developed under the UK Department for Trade and Industry, provides an alternative hierarchy of stages of ITC adoption and integration within SMEs.

Ultimately, this assumes that the website decisions of business owners, takes the form of two distinct and sequential decisions (Daniel et al., 2002; Rao et al., 2003). Initially the decision to develop a Web presence is taken. At a later date a decision is taken to develop e-commerce facilities within the webpage of increasing complexity as time progresses.

Under the stages models firms over time learn the skills required to add additional features to the website, gradually progressing up a hierarchy of interactivity and functionality (Daniel et al., 2002). Obviously this progression is associated with acquired knowledge from experience of Web presence, rather than business experience in general (Levy and Powell, 2003; Rao et al., 2003; Lee, 2004). Even so it would be expected that newer firms would be at lower levels of website functionality. An ordered logit using website functionality as the dependent variable finds this to be the case for the FSB data, although additional business maturity beyond 9 years is not associated with a higher probability of movement up the hierarchy (Table 3). A multi-nominal logit specification confirms that age of the firm has a significant influence on the development of an active website rather than simple brochure style website (Table 4). Staged models have been criticized as unrealistic given the existence of early adopters and heterogeneity of small businesses (Martin and Matlay, 2001; Alonso Mendo and Fitzgerald, 2005a). This has led to the development of a number of alternative models examining the e-commerce adoption process of SMEs from a number of perspectives, although the decisions made are likely to require a combination of many models to truly do justice to the adoption process (Alonso Mendo and Fitzgerald, 2005b).

As well as acquiring knowledge about Web technologies it would be natural to expect as Arnott and Bridgewater (2002) find that larger firms have more sophisticated websites in terms of their informational, relationship and transactional functions, due to the various resources available to them. This is supported by both a logit of active versus non-active websites (Table 1) and the ordered logit of website functionality (Table 3). However, models such as a probit model incorporating a Heckman (1979) selection model (Van de Ven and Van Praag, 1981) as shown in Table

5 which separate the decisions indicate that it is the adoption decision that drives this relationship. This perhaps represents the resource in shortest supply for SMEs, time, of which website development is particularly hungry (McConville, 2009). Direct involvement in the tourist trade increases the probability of having an active rather than non-active website, as customers will frequently be at distance from the firm's base and is identified as a tool capable of expanding such businesses' reach (Lituchy and Rail, 2000).

Interestingly the characteristics of the business owner have little further influence on the probability of website functionality. This is quite striking given the role that age and education played in initial website adoption. Whilst a young dynamic entrepreneur may see the benefits of a Web presence and may even know enough to develop a basic website this may be the point that the skills of the owner and his workforce are restricted to. Any further work will involve bringing in talent from outside, either as new employees, training of existing employees, or outside contractors. The alternative suggested by the stages models will require experience to be acquired gradually over time, with no shortcuts available. However, there could be communication problems between the owner-manager and the other employees, so that information is hoarded rather than disseminated throughout the workforce. Where managers take this approach Martin (2005) finds firms struggle to reach higher levels of e-commerce adoption.

Raymond et al. (2005) find that those firms with more aggressive strategies towards new markets are more likely to be utilizing e-commerce. This is reflected in the FSB data with those firms intending to grow moderately are around forty per cent more likely to have active rather than non-active websites than those not intending to grow their firms (odds ratio = 1.381). Those with the strongest growth ambitions encompassing those intending to expand turnover by more than 20 per cent a year are approaching twice as likely to have active websites (odds ratio = 1.904). This is further

Table 3. Ordered logit of Website facilitation

		Model 1		Model 2	
Employment (Base category – owner only)	2 - 4 Employees	**0.2490**	(0.004)	**0.2521**	(0.003)
	5 - 9 Employees	**0.3217**	(0.004)	**0.3240**	(0.004)
	10 - 19 Employees	**0.4786**	(0.001)	**0.4956**	(0.000)
	20+ Employees	**0.4581**	(0.008)	**0.4447**	(0.009)
Turnover (Base category – less than £25,000)	£25K - £50K	0.0732	(0.562)	0.0953	(0.445)
	£500k - £100K	-0.0150	(0.905)	-0.0163	(0.896)
	£100K - £200K	0.1882	(0.152)	0.1902	(0.142)
	£200K - £300K	0.2341	(0.120)	0.2269	(0.126)
	£300K - £500K	**0.3880**	(0.013)	**0.3971**	(0.009)
	£500K - £1m	**0.4637**	(0.004)	**0.4772**	(0.003)
	£1 million	**0.8127**	(0.000)	**0.8111**	(0.000)
Tourist Trade (Bc – no involvement)	Direct Tourist Trade	**0.7854**	(0.000)	**0.7474**	(0.000)
	Indirect Tourist Trade	**0.2287**	(0.018)	**0.2693**	(0.005)
Firm Age (Base category – less than 3 years old)	4 - 9 years	**0.4449**	(0.000)	**0.4470**	(0.000)
	10 to 19 years	**0.2609**	(0.046)	0.2443	(0.059)
	20 or more years	0.0685	(0.643)	0.0942	(0.520)
Entrepreneur's Age (Base category – younger than 35 years)	35 to 44 years old	-0.1138	(0.423)	-0.1059	(0.444)
	45 to 54 years old	-0.2044	(0.142)	-0.1837	(0.176)
	55 to 64 years	-0.1826	(0.208)	-0.1444	(0.307)
	Over 65 years old	-0.2272	(0.194)	-0.1712	(0.318)
Entrepreneur's educational attainment (Base category A-levels)	Postgraduate	**0.2911**	(0.015)	**0.2921**	(0.013)
	Bachelors Degree	**0.2312**	(0.023)	**0.2280**	(0.023)
	Professional Qualifications	-0.0331	(0.740)	-0.0398	(0.686)
	GCSE/O level	-0.1088	(0.324)	-0.1184	(0.276)
	Vocational Qualifications	**-0.3111**	(0.027)	**-0.3153**	(0.024)
	No Formal Qualifications	-0.0367	(0.804)	-0.0314	(0.830)
Gender of owners (Bc – equal male & female)	Male Majority	-0.0628	(0.344)	-0.0710	(0.278)
	Female Majority	**-0.2435**	(0.013)	**-0.2265**	(0.019)
Hours committed to business (Bc – 30 to 48 hours)	Less than 30 hours	**-0.2741**	(0.046)	**-0.2737**	(0.044)
	49 to 60 hours	-0.0324	(0.647)	-0.0227	(0.745)
	More than 60 hours	-0.0383	(0.660)	-0.0411	(0.632)
Change in sales volume over last 12 months (base category – decreased by 0% to 5%)	Decreased by 20%+	0.2392	(0.114)	0.2351	(0.115)
	Decreased by 10%-20%	0.0646	(0.653)	0.0622	(0.661)
	Decreased by 5%-10%	0.0488	(0.740)	0.0664	(0.648)
	Increased by 0%-5%	-0.0071	(0.953)	-0.0017	(0.988)
	Increased by 5%-10%	0.0856	(0.489)	0.0876	(0.474)
	Increased by 10%-20%	0.0751	(0.559)	0.0856	(0.500)
	Increased by 20%+	**0.3058**	(0.022)	**0.3258**	(0.013)

continued on the following page

Table 3. continued

Objectives for business over next two years (base category – remain same size)	Grow turnover 20%+	**0.8246**	(0.000)	**0.8284**	(0.000)
	Expand up to 20%	**0.5533**	(0.000)	**0.5456**	(0.000)
	Downsize business	0.0060	(0.972)	-0.0064	(0.970)
	Sell or close business	0.0197	(0.869)	0.0109	(0.927)
	Hand on business	**0.5516**	(0.019)	**0.5387**	(0.020)
N		5089		5089	
R^2		0.1843		0.1702	
Cut Point 1		-0.380		-0.359	
Cut Point 2		3.141		3.159	
Cut Point 3		n/a		5.706	

Notes: p-values in parenthesis

Table 4. Multinominal logit of non-active and active Website

		Website		Active Website	
Employment (Base category – owner only)	2 - 4 Employees	**0.2210**	(0.040)	**0.4086**	(0.008)
	5 - 9 Employees	**0.4352**	(0.003)	**0.4815**	(0.018)
	10 - 19 Employees	**0.7093**	(0.000)	**0.7946**	(0.003)
	20+ Employees	**0.7652**	(0.004)	**0.8525**	(0.011)
Turnover (Base category – less than £25,000)	£25K - £50K	0.0749	(0.637)	0.1921	(0.382)
	£500k - £100K	0.1351	(0.390)	0.0266	(0.905)
	£100K - £200K	**0.3823**	(0.023)	0.4300	(0.064)
	£200K - £300K	**0.3902**	(0.044)	0.4713	(0.075)
	£300K - £500K	**0.5376**	(0.008)	**0.8232**	(0.003)
	£500K - £1m	**0.7761**	(0.000)	**0.9873**	(0.001)
	£1 million	**1.2535**	(0.000)	**1.7628**	(0.000)
Tourist Trade (Bc – no involvement)	Direct Tourist Trade	**1.0960**	(0.000)	**1.4774**	(0.000)
	Indirect Tourist Trade	0.1956	(0.142)	0.4416	(0.008)
Firm Age (Base category – less than 3 years old)	4 - 9 years	**0.3944**	(0.017)	**0.7843**	(0.000)
	10 to 19 years	0.0670	(0.708)	**0.5105**	(0.031)
	20 or more years	-0.3262	(0.099)	0.1557	(0.556)
Entrepreneur's Age (Base category – younger than 35 years)	35 to 44 years old	**-0.5687**	(0.010)	-0.3931	(0.160)
	45 to 54 years old	**-0.5553**	(0.011)	**-0.5805**	(0.035)
	55 to 64 years	**-0.6248**	(0.005)	-0.5378	(0.058)
	Over 65 years old	**-0.6744**	(0.009)	-0.5318	(0.105)

continued on the following page

Table 4. continued

	Postgraduate	**0.3502**	(0.038)	**0.5503**	(0.013)
	Bachelors Degree	0.2704	(0.053)	0.3571	(0.053)
Entrepreneur's educational attainment (Base category A-levels)	Professional Qualifications	-0.0247	(0.852)	-0.0829	(0.644)
	GCSE/O level	-0.2470	(0.089)	-0.0582	(0.762)
	Vocational Qualifications	-0.3929	(0.025)	-0.3070	(0.219)
	No Formal Qualifications	-0.1079	(0.577)	0.1250	(0.627)
Gender of owners (Bc – equal male & female)	Male Majority	0.0160	(0.858)	-0.1039	(0.389)
	Female Majority	**-0.2773**	(0.031)	**-0.3764**	(0.029)
Hours committed to business (Bc – 30 to 48 hours)	Less than 30 hours	**-0.5568**	(0.001)	-0.3578	(0.126)
	49 to 60 hours	-0.1059	(0.260)	-0.0377	(0.771)
	More than 60 hours	-0.1145	(0.333)	-0.0236	(0.881)
	Decreased by 20%+	0.2705	(0.161)	0.3353	(0.209)
	Decreased by 10%-20%	0.1951	(0.288)	0.0786	(0.757)
Change in sales volume over last 12 months (base category – decreased by 0% to 5%)	Decreased by 5%-10%	-0.0558	(0.764)	0.0536	(0.833)
	Increased by 0%-5%	-0.0054	(0.972)	-0.0541	(0.800)
	Increased by 5%-10%	0.1809	(0.252)	0.0812	(0.714)
	Increased by 10%-20%	0.0973	(0.564)	0.0499	(0.828)
	Increased by 20%+	0.2346	(0.191)	**0.4841**	(0.044)
	Grow turnover 20%+	**0.8844**	(0.000)	**1.4624**	(0.000)
Objectives for business over next two years (base category – remain same size)	Expand up to 20%	**0.6502**	(0.000)	**0.9384**	(0.000)
	Downsize business	-0.0349	(0.862)	0.0570	(0.854)
	Sell or close business	-0.0757	(0.598)	0.1257	(0.548)
	Hand on business	0.3691	(0.228)	**0.8646**	(0.035)
N		5089			
R^2		0.221			
Hosmer-Lemeshow					

Notes: p-values in parenthesis

emphasized with higher website functionality in the ordered logits associated with those owner-manager characteristics which are generally associated with greater growth ambitions, youth and higher levels of education. Where other objectives are likely to play a more important role such as in female majority ownership and businesses run on a part-time basis, these firms are found to be lower down the functionality hierarchy.

Again it is the ambition to grow which is more strongly linked to website functionality rather than the growth itself. A resource-based explanation for the lack of connection between website functionality and growth achieved is that it is not the presence of e-commerce tools that is important in improving firm performance, but rather the performance of the firm's e-commerce strategy which is important. E-commerce performance success requires the presence of complementary business resources without these e-commerce resources will not guarantee e-commerce success (Zhuang and Lederer, 2006).

Drew's (2003) finding that e-business was seen as important to supporting major growth thrusts of firms in the East of England using active websites, is backed up by models such as the multinominal logit (Table 4) or a probit model with selection (Table 5) which separate the adoption and development decisions. In both cases more rapid growth of turnover over the previous two years was significantly linked to development of websites with greater functionality.

Table 5. Probit of active Website usage with selection

		Website		Active Website	
Employment (Base category – owner only)	2 - 4 Employees	0.1115	(0.053)		
	5 - 9 Employees	**0.2115**	(0.007)		
	10 - 19 Employees	**0.3286**	(0.002)		
	20+ Employees	**0.4069**	(0.003)		
Turnover (Base category – less than £25,000)	£25K - £50K	0.0293	(0.733)	0.0680	(0.471)
	£500k - £100K	0.0259	(0.762)	-0.0746	(0.422)
	£100K - £200K	0.1620	(0.073)	-0.0269	(0.781)
	£200K - £300K	0.1685	(0.104)	0.0193	(0.858)
	£300K - £500K	**0.2759**	(0.011)	0.1354	(0.217)
	£500K - £1m	**0.4335**	(0.000)	0.1161	(0.323)
	£1 million	**0.6443**	(0.000)	0.1983	(0.127)
Tourist Trade (Bc – no involvement)	Direct Tourist Trade	**0.7457**	(0.000)	**0.4859**	(0.000)
	Indirect Tourist Trade	**0.2180**	(0.014)	0.1676	(0.065)
Firm Age (Base category – less than 3 years old)	4 - 9 years	0.0260	(0.788)	0.1424	(0.148)
	10 to 19 years	-0.1919	(0.069)	0.1098	(0.340)
	20 or more years	**-0.2683**	(0.020)	0.0597	(0.566)
Entrepreneur's Age (Base category – younger than 35 years)	35 to 44 years old	**-0.2693**	(0.017)	-0.0386	(0.703)
	45 to 54 years old	**-0.2640**	(0.024)	0.0684	(0.522)
	55 to 64 years	-0.1925	(0.156)	0.1774	(0.164)
	Over 65 years old	0.1673	(0.065)	0.0613	(0.484)
Entrepreneur's educational attainment (Base category A-levels)	Postgraduate	0.1033	(0.168)	-0.0332	(0.661)
	Bachelors Degree	-0.0456	(0.525)	-0.0610	(0.413)
	Professional Qualifications	-0.1354	(0.082)	0.0649	(0.442)
	GCSE/O level	**-0.2996**	(0.002)	-0.0872	(0.449)
	Vocational Qualifications	-0.0638	(0.540)	0.1043	(0.346)
	No Formal Qualifications	-0.0069	(0.887)	-0.0662	(0.175)
Gender of owners (Bc – equal male & female)	Male Majority	**-0.1732**	(0.012)	-0.1001	(0.175)
	Female Majority	**-0.2555**	(0.006)	0.1444	(0.196)
Hours committed to business (Bc – 30 to 48 hours)	Less than 30 hours	-0.0281	(0.580)	0.0787	(0.147)
	49 to 60 hours	-0.0282	(0.656)	0.1038	(0.112)
	More than 60 hours	0.1885	(0.071)	0.0867	(0.455)

continued on the following page

Table 5. continued

Change in sales volume over last 12 months (base category – decreased by 0% to 5%)	Decreased by 20%+	0.1427	(0.152)	-0.0203	(0.855)
	Decreased by 10%-20%	0.0363	(0.719)	0.1290	(0.249)
	Decreased by 5%-10%	0.0083	(0.920)	-0.0270	(0.774)
	Increased by 0%-5%	0.0876	(0.308)	-0.0707	(0.466)
	Increased by 5%-10%	0.1027	(0.258)	0.0288	(0.769)
	Increased by 10%-20%	0.1238	(0.195)	0.0998	(0.320)
	Increased by 20%+	**0.6410**	(0.000)	**0.5322**	(0.000)
Objectives for business over next two years (base category – remain same size)	Grow turnover 20%+	**0.4340**	(0.000)	**0.2728**	(0.000)
	Expand up to 20%	-0.0087	(0.937)	0.0492	(0.725)
	Downsize business	-0.0220	(0.781)	0.0999	(0.295)
	Sell or close business	0.2970	(0.072)	0.3352	(0.054)
	Hand on business	0.0293	(0.733)	0.0680	(0.471)
		Full	Censored	Uncensored	
N		5089	1151	3938	

Notes: p-values in parenthesis

GEOGRAPHICAL SCOPE, INTERNATIONALIZATION AND WEB FUNCTIONALITY AND INTEGRATION

A major difficulty faced by SMEs attempting to grow beyond their core market is a lack of knowledge of new markets (Petersen et al., 2002). Whilst particularly important for breaking into international markets, this is also true of moving from a local to regional or national scale (Gorton, 1999). Frequently this can result in the need for partners or intermediaries who possess greater knowledge of the market to be engaged (Johanson and Vahle, 1977). This may result in increased costs and reduced margins plus a continuing principle-agent problem. One of the early expectations of e-commerce was to decrease the cost for both buyers and sellers by the elimination of intermediaries within the electronic value chain (O'Keefe et al., 1998), however, research suggests that intermediaries remain important in providing value-added linkages and are therefore can not be easily substituted by the direct supplier-buyer e-commerce relationship (Howcroft, 2001; Giaglis et al., 2002).

Yet, authors including Lawson et al. (2003); Kula and Tatoglu (2003) and Galloway et al. (2008) have suggested that the Web provides an opportunity to grow beyond local markets and even internationalize client bases at a relatively low cost. In general there has been a reduction in the physical and psychical barriers to commerce allowing for greater internationalization (Wen et al., 2001). So much so that e-commerce has been predicted to increase the linkages between entrepreneurial activity and international trade which was previously the sole domain of large businesses (McDougall and Oviatt, 2000). A couple of notes of caution need to be highlighted, large trans-national corporations may use market power to ensure that e-commerce develops in a fashion, which in turn favours their requirements rather than SMEs (Fariselli et al., 1999; Howcroft, 2001). In addition, although a basic website is relatively cheap to develop a more comprehensive offering is not and leaves SMEs disadvantaged in the global cyber-market place as well as in the conventional market place (Samiee, 1998).

The experience of economic downturns is that often SMEs can be adversely affected by localized business failures, where a more diversified client base would allow the firm to survive. For those firms operating in more peripheral regions being effective beyond the local market is the only way to achieve growth (Gorton, 1999). The reliance on local markets is observable in the FSB data with firms that have no websites reporting that local markets account for 59.2 per cent of sales. This falls to only 32.7 per cent and 34.7 per cent of sales for those firms with on-line sales facilities and fully integrated facilities on their websites, respectively. Non-active websites again tend to be associated with a more confined geographical spread of sales with those only providing contact details relying on local markets for around half their sales (50.1 per cent), whilst advertising products on-line only lowers this reliance to 41.7 per cent.

Many of the characteristics associated with greater website functionality are also likely to be associated with greater geographical spread. For example, larger firms with higher turnover will tend to place less reliance on local markets. This will especially be the case where firms have grown rapidly or intend to grow swiftly; in fact this may be a necessary condition for growth (O'Farrell et al., 1995). Equally those involved in the tourist trade will tend to draw custom from outside the local area, and it is for this reason that the tourist industry is often cited as a possible source of growth for marginalized and peripheral areas (Briedenhann and Wickens, 2004). When moving beyond a core market, human capital has an important role to play, especially the decision-makers' knowledge of internationalization which has been linked to educational attainment (Simpson and Kujawa, 1974) and foreign market experience (Langston and Teas, 1976). The FSB data confirms these characteristics are negatively associated with reliance on the local market when using a multi-

nominal logit of sales from local markets (Table 6) and reliance on sales to local and regional markets (Table 7).

One of the expectations of owner-managers in the late 1990s was that the Internet would allow them increase the geographical scope of their customer bases (Dutta and Evrard, 1999). This is seen as particularly important for growth if the firm is reliant on a thinly spread customer base (Levy et al., 2002). Although attracting new customers was a major incentive for adoption of Internet related activities Daniel and Wilson (2002) found that firms felt e-commerce under performed in terms of achieving this type of benefit. From the FSB data it appears that this is particularly salient for those firms using active rather than non-active websites. For example those with non-active websites are more than 60 per cent more likely to rely on local markets for less than a quarter of their turnover compared to those without websites (relative risk of 1.634), on the other hand, those with active websites are two and half times as likely to have reduced their reliance on local markets to this level compared to those without websites (relative risk of 2.532).

Where the Web is seen as emerging in importance is in terms of breaking into international markets. Whilst SMEs are often felt to be able to grow organically and acquisitively within national markets, they are often felt to be incapable of breaking into international markets (Fariselli et al., 1999). SMEs considering internationalization may not dive in straight away, but rather take a staged approach, with traditional internationalization models such as the Uppsala process suggesting the depth of involvement based upon the extent of market knowledge and commitment (Johanson and Vahle, 1977). Commitment is incrementally increased as market knowledge is deepened moving from no exports through exports via independent agents and offshore sales subsidies to overseas production facilities. The rate of internationalization depends on the speed that market risk falls, which is related to changes in uncertainty

Table 6. Multinominal reliance of customers within local area

		0-25%		26-50%		51-75%	
Website (Bc – No Website)	Non-Active Website	**0.4912**	(0.000)	**0.3560**	(0.005)	**0.5562**	(0.000)
	Active Website	**0.9288**	(0.000)	**0.6347**	(0.000)	**0.4649**	(0.012)
Turnover (Bc – less than £25,000)	£25K - £50K	0.3044	(0.058)	0.1958	(0.321)	0.4039	(0.054)
	£500k - £100K	**0.7549**	(0.000)	0.2272	(0.241)	0.3457	(0.096)
	£100K - £200K	**0.5918**	(0.000)	0.0518	(0.793)	0.2887	(0.165)
	£200K - £300K	**0.7924**	(0.000)	0.1394	(0.536)	**0.5876**	(0.010)
	£300K - £500K	**0.7230**	(0.000)	0.3632	(0.095)	0.3848	(0.100)
	£500K - £1m	**1.2988**	(0.000)	**0.4959**	(0.031)	**0.6873**	(0.004)
	£1 million	**1.8761**	(0.000)	**0.7337**	(0.004)	**0.9216**	(0.000)
Tourist Trade (Bc – none)	Direct	**1.7164**	(0.000)	**1.5659**	(0.000)	**0.6964**	(0.007)
	Indirect	**-0.2547**	(0.048)	**0.4189**	(0.004)	0.1042	(0.488)
Firm Age (Bc – less than 3 years old)	4 - 9 years	0.3073	(0.052)	**0.4812**	(0.020)	0.1397	(0.482)
	10 to 19 years	0.1519	(0.376)	**0.5827**	(0.010)	-0.1177	(0.592)
	20 or more years	-0.1244	(0.519)	0.2788	(0.272)	-0.0153	(0.950)
Entrepreneur's Age (Bc – younger than 35 years)	35 to 44 years old	-0.1451	(0.451)	**-0.4579**	(0.037)	**-0.4208**	(0.051)
	45 to 54 years old	0.2063	(0.275)	-0.3263	(0.131)	-0.3564	(0.094)
	55 to 64 years	**0.5644**	(0.004)	-0.2521	(0.268)	-0.3760	(0.097)
	Over 65 years old	**0.7794**	(0.001)	-0.3893	(0.177)	**-0.7578**	(0.012)
Entrepreneur's educational attainment (Bc A-levels)	Postgraduate	**0.7478**	(0.000)	0.2954	(0.145)	**0.5259**	(0.013)
	Bachelors Degree	0.2082	(0.114)	-0.2805	(0.091)	-0.0550	(0.752)
	Professional	-0.0921	(0.476)	-0.2103	(0.184)	0.0889	(0.589)
	GCSE/O level	0.0159	(0.911)	-0.1636	(0.351)	0.0406	(0.823)
	Vocational	-0.3403	(0.060)	-0.1948	(0.376)	0.1707	(0.442)
	No Formal	**-0.5168**	(0.008)	-0.0541	(0.812)	0.0876	(0.712)
Owners' gender (Bc – equal)	Male Majority	0.0952	(0.260)	**0.2293**	(0.037)	0.1134	(0.304)
	Female Majority	-0.0802	(0.523)	0.1624	(0.301)	0.0699	(0.658)
Hours committed to business (Bc – 30 to 48 hours)	Less than 30 hours	0.1224	(0.477)	-0.2468	(0.304)	-0.2996	(0.251)
	49 to 60 hours	0.0205	(0.822)	-0.0850	(0.464)	0.1561	(0.186)
	More than 60 hours	0.0406	(0.719)	0.0324	(0.818)	0.0443	(0.763)
Objectives for business over next two years (Bc – remain same size)	Grow 20%+	**0.3248**	(0.014)	0.0996	(0.558)	**0.3651**	(0.038)
	Expand up to 20%	0.0989	(0.325)	0.1105	(0.386)	**0.3758**	(0.005)
	Downsize business	-0.0162	(0.939)	-0.0974	(0.728)	-0.0490	(0.872)
	Sell or close	-0.1413	(0.353)	-0.2885	(0.156)	0.0906	(0.657)
	Hand on business	-0.1943	(0.508)	-0.8408	(0.077)	0.2664	(0.470)
N		5056					
R^2		0.117					

Notes: p-values in parenthesis

Table 7. Multinominal logit of reliance of customers within region

		0-25%		26-50%		51-75%	
Website (Bc – No Website)	Non-Active Website	**0.4359**	(0.000)	**0.5555**	(0.000)	0.1610	(0.283)
	Active Website	**1.0101**	(0.000)	**0.8814**	(0.000)	**0.4065**	(0.035)
Turnover (Bc – less than £25,000)	£25K - £50K	0.1212	(0.498)	0.1373	(0.530)	**0.6248**	(0.013)
	£500k - £100K	**0.6399**	(0.000)	**0.5617**	(0.006)	**0.7567**	(0.002)
	£100K - £200K	**0.4640**	(0.007)	0.3657	(0.085)	**0.5215**	(0.040)
	£200K - £300K	**0.4522**	(0.019)	0.3470	(0.154)	**0.9057**	(0.001)
	£300K - £500K	**0.4843**	(0.012)	**0.4713**	(0.048)	**0.7364**	(0.007)
	£500K - £1m	**1.0427**	(0.000)	**0.5393**	(0.030)	**1.1138**	(0.000)
	£1 million	**1.4542**	(0.000)	**1.2079**	(0.000)	**1.2041**	(0.000)
Tourist Trade (Bc – none)	Direct	**1.1606**	(0.000)	**1.7139**	(0.000)	**1.6403**	(0.000)
	Indirect	**-0.4920**	(0.001)	-0.0627	(0.716)	**0.5012**	(0.001)
Firm Age (Bc less than 3 years old)	4 - 9 years	0.2019	(0.231)	-0.0160	(0.938)	0.1720	(0.440)
	10 to 19 years	0.1957	(0.273)	0.0193	(0.930)	0.1473	(0.539)
	20 or more years	-0.0364	(0.856)	-0.1967	(0.444)	-0.0823	(0.762)
Entrepreneur's Age (Bc – younger than 35 years)	35 to 44 years old	-0.1737	(0.388)	0.0732	(0.783)	-0.3282	(0.176)
	45 to 54 years old	0.2123	(0.276)	0.3946	(0.126)	-0.1927	(0.417)
	55 to 64 years	**0.4455**	(0.027)	0.4608	(0.085)	0.1076	(0.661)
	Over 65 years old	**0.7735**	(0.001)	**1.0574**	(0.001)	0.2922	(0.337)
Entrepreneur's educational attainment (Bc A-levels)	Postgraduate	**0.5753**	(0.000)	0.3377	(0.107)	0.2760	(0.185)
	Bachelors Degree	0.1503	(0.264)	0.2747	(0.121)	-0.0694	(0.700)
	Professional	-0.2607	(0.055)	0.0483	(0.783)	-0.2108	(0.228)
	GCSE/O level	-0.1862	(0.208)	-0.0228	(0.907)	**-0.4165**	(0.036)
	Vocational	**-0.8021**	(0.000)	-0.2687	(0.289)	-0.3699	(0.141)
	No Formal	**-0.6607**	(0.001)	-0.4715	(0.090)	-0.3839	(0.142)
Owners' gender (Bc – equal)	Male Majority	-0.0324	(0.709)	0.1490	(0.192)	**0.2600**	(0.030)
	Female Majority	-0.2611	(0.056)	0.1401	(0.395)	-0.0674	(0.720)
Hours committed to business (Bc – 30 to 48 hours)	Less than 30 hours	0.2190	(0.221)	-0.0658	(0.784)	-0.4137	(0.189)
	49 to 60 hours	-0.0602	(0.531)	-0.0918	(0.454)	0.0569	(0.661)
	More than 60 hours	-0.0382	(0.747)	-0.0326	(0.827)	0.0058	(0.971)
Objectives for business over next two years (Bc – remain same size)	Grow 20%+	**0.2932**	(0.030)	0.0828	(0.637)	**0.4371**	(0.020)
	Expand up to 20%	-0.0288	(0.788)	-0.0439	(0.745)	**0.3253**	(0.030)
	Downsize business	0.0228	(0.921)	0.1834	(0.510)	0.1967	(0.530)
	Sell or close	-0.2098	(0.198)	-0.1049	(0.607)	-0.1706	(0.476)
	Hand on business	-0.3966	(0.219)	-0.5689	(0.223)	0.1375	(0.730)
N		5056					
R^2		0.132					

Notes: p-values in parenthesis

and commitment. In spite of this, the process of internationalization may differ between firms depending on their products and characteristics. For example, those with innovative goods and services may prefer to sell to a greater number of markets, whilst maintaining a single source of production for economies of scale. Those firms with less innovative products may not have the margins to cover freight costs, and need to rely on speed of delivery to a greater extent to win customers, and therefore develop production facilities in other countries. It is likely that the Internet will be of aid in internationalizing for both these groups, as far as providing information via a 'sow and reap' approach so firms will have a presence in more countries and can identify those which are most promising for further exploitation (Chetty and Campbell-Hunt, 2003).

The advent of e-commerce and the opportunities to service international markets in different ways might be expected to alter the traditional patterns of internationalization. The relatively low infrastructure costs of entering new markets for example may increase the speed that new markets of a similar nature are entered. Some patterns are found to continue with firms more likely to enter those markets with the lowest psychic distance first, and local partners often are involved in localizing the website (Kim, 2003). This indicates that some barriers such as cultural and language differences still remain even in the Internet age (Jaw and Chen, 2006). Evidence also suggests that entry normally takes the lower risk exporting route as previously, but later stages may be jumped (Jaw and Chen, 2006).

A study of SMEs in the North American hospitality industry found that a large proportion of respondents saw the Internet as being an effective tool to expand their international trade, in spite of this, an early study, like many others, found website functionality to be relatively low (Lituchy and Rail, 2000). This means that often firms will limit themselves to the advantages of advertising internationally without putting the

means to undertaken transactions internationally in place (Poon and Swatman, 1999). The average scale of the firms included in the FSB data means that relatively few sales are obtained overseas, so that the average percentage of all sales that are outside the UK is 7.6 per cent. This varies from 4.6 per cent for those firms which have no website presence to 11.6 per cent of firms with fully integrated websites linking to consumers and suppliers. Nevertheless, these figures if anything, overstate the sales overseas as 66.4 per cent of firms obtain none of their sales from outside the UK. This again varies from 80.7 per cent of firms without websites who make no sales outside the UK, to only 44.3 per cent of firms with fully integrated websites having no non-UK sales. A majority of those firms with just on-line sales facilities are found to obtain some of their sales from outside the UK. Brochure style websites have less influence in increasing international presence as would be expected with 74 per cent of those with just contact details and 64.8 per cent using their websites simply as a method of advertising their products having no international sales. This comes as no surprise given that Sinkovic and Pene (2005) find online transactions to be one of the factors identified when establishing the effectiveness of websites. Firms may not actually intend to internationalize when developing a Web presence, rather it is a side-effect and may lead to the firm receiving its first overseas orders unsolicited (Oviatt and McDougall, 1999). Since unsolicited orders from international markets are found to be one of the strongest stimuli to exporting (Simpson and Kujawo, 1974), the development of websites may increase the likelihood that SMEs will start to internationalize their sales.

Using a multi-nominal logit of the proportion of sales from international markets the FSB data provides evidence that greater website integration is positively associated with increased probability of exporting (Table 8). For the highest level of exports those with non-active websites are half as likely again to belong in this category as those

Table 8. Multinominal logit of sales to customers outside the UK

		1-5%		6-20%		21-100%	
Website (Bc – No Website)	Non-Active Website	**0.5266**	(0.000)	0.2722	(0.059)	**0.4079**	(0.007)
	Active Website	**0.8024**	(0.000)	**0.7216**	(0.000)	**0.7772**	(0.000)
Turnover (Bc – less than £25,000)	£25K - £50K	0.2745	(0.243)	0.0544	(0.797)	0.3939	(0.091)
	£500k - £100K	0.3930	(0.085)	0.3745	(0.058)	**0.8019**	(0.000)
	£100K - £200K	**0.6169**	(0.006)	0.2273	(0.268)	**0.5768**	(0.011)
	£200K - £300K	0.3181	(0.205)	0.0858	(0.712)	0.4805	(0.057)
	£300K - £500K	0.3016	(0.235)	0.2328	(0.309)	**0.7532**	(0.002)
	£500K - £1m	**0.6251**	(0.011)	**0.4514**	(0.047)	**0.9712**	(0.000)
	£1 million	**0.9476**	(0.000)	**0.8693**	(0.000)	**1.2739**	(0.000)
Tourist Trade (Bc – none)	Direct	**1.1599**	(0.000)	**1.4219**	(0.000)	**0.9779**	(0.000)
	Indirect	0.2211	(0.140)	0.1052	(0.501)	-0.0185	(0.913)
Firm Age (Bc – less than 3 years old)	4 - 9 years	0.3735	(0.088)	0.1321	(0.503)	0.2789	(0.215)
	10 to 19 years	**0.7267**	(0.002)	0.0867	(0.682)	**0.6920**	(0.003)
	20 or more years	**0.5457**	(0.038)	0.3293	(0.163)	**0.6671**	(0.012)
Entrepreneur's Age (Bc – younger than 35 years)	35 to 44 years old	-0.1911	(0.388)	-0.1176	(0.612)	0.3097	(0.276)
	45 to 54 years old	-0.2041	(0.348)	-0.0223	(0.921)	**0.6163**	(0.025)
	55 to 64 years	-0.2348	(0.303)	0.0147	(0.950)	**0.7840**	(0.005)
	Over 65 years old	-0.3284	(0.250)	0.4381	(0.108)	**1.1904**	(0.000)
Entrepreneur's educational attainment (Bc A-levels)	Postgraduate	0.3140	(0.103)	**0.7456**	(0.000)	**0.8351**	(0.000)
	Bachelors Degree	0.0495	(0.759)	**0.3717**	(0.029)	**0.3656**	(0.029)
	Professional	-0.2189	(0.174)	0.0611	(0.719)	-0.1906	(0.273)
	GCSE/O level	-0.2899	(0.100)	0.1154	(0.525)	**-0.4444**	(0.025)
	Vocational	-0.3104	(0.192)	0.0413	(0.861)	**-0.6558**	(0.017)
	No Formal	-0.4262	(0.087)	-0.1759	(0.482)	-0.3680	(0.150)
Owners' gender (Bc – equal)	Male Majority	-0.0631	(0.565)	0.1363	(0.210)	0.1645	(0.130)
	Female Majority	0.2104	(0.178)	0.2791	(0.073)	-0.1502	(0.379)
Hours committed to business (Bc – 30 to 48 hours)	Less than 30 hours	-0.1325	(0.593)	-0.1901	(0.425)	**0.5405**	(0.011)
	49 to 60 hours	-0.1224	(0.295)	-0.0272	(0.817)	0.0869	(0.483)
	More than 60 hours	-0.1048	(0.469)	0.0740	(0.598)	0.2520	(0.088)
Objectives for business over next two years (Bc – remain same size)	Grow 20%+	-0.2369	(0.191)	0.1482	(0.369)	0.2360	(0.160)
	Expand up to 20%	0.2076	(0.119)	0.0781	(0.552)	0.0359	(0.791)
	Downsize business	-0.5097	(0.135)	-0.4030	(0.181)	-0.0668	(0.810)
	Sell or close	0.0029	(0.988)	-0.1695	(0.391)	-0.1420	(0.480)
	Hand on business	0.0500	(0.900)	0.3574	(0.294)	-0.2070	(0.626)
N		5056					
R^2		0.124					

Notes: p-values in parenthesis

with no website (relative risk of 1.504). Those with active websites are over twice as likely to be exporting more than 20 per cent of their sales (relative risk of 2.175). This is similar to the results found by Daniel et al. (2002) suggesting that one of the primary discriminants between those at an early 'stage' and those at a later 'stage' of e-commerce adoption was the proportion of sales outside the UK.

Interestingly, the presence of a firm website increases the probability of exporting, but the coefficients do not appear to show the increase in probability for those firms with active websites that might be expected for those categories representing a larger proportion of sales. This means that whilst the Web increases the probability of internationalizing, for UK SMEs at this point in time there is little influence on expanding international sales to a point where they contribute a large proportion of sales. This is likely to be once again a reflection of the relatively low level of reliance on the Internet by UK SMEs, where even those firms using more integrated websites are in general dominated by their bricks and mortar sales.

Obviously the links between website adoption and greater geographical distribution of the customer base may run in both directions. Those firms with customers further from the firm's home base may feel that the Internet may provide an efficient means of communicating with their customers. Similarly the influence of greater integration may in part reflect the requirement to sell to customers further afield, consistent with the findings that a firm's use of the Web will relate to the fit with the firm's existing business model. Consistent with this Arnott and Bridgewater (2002) found that those firms selling to international markets used higher levels of facilities within their websites, but no significant difference was found between those firms using the Web to internationalize and those that internationalized before developing a website.

SHORTAGES OF IT SKILLS AND WEBSITE FUNCTIONALITY AND INTEGRATION

Although website functionality is associated with greater growth ambitions particularly through increased geographical spread of customer bases, websites of UK SMEs remain mainly in the form of electronic brochures with few, if any, interactive functions. Even when firms acknowledge the benefits and potential of the Web for growth and internationalization, the level of functionality is generally low, with a fear of technology leading a suboptimal usage of the Web (Litchy and Rail, 2000).

Research repeatedly indicates that one of the primary barriers to adoption of technology, such as the Internet and the Web, is the lack of capability within the business (Drew, 2003). In the late 1990s a lack of understanding of the potential benefits and costs of new technology was identified as one of the major barriers to full embracement of the Web (Dutta and Evrard, 1999). Once a decision to adopt has been made research also suggests that it is important that relevant skills are in place before implementation, so that staff have the confidence to overcome the barriers they encounter during the implementation process (Love et al., 2001). A lack of website development skills is likely to be common within SMEs preventing inexpensive improvements of website functionality (Darch, and Lucas, 2002; Lawson et al., 2003). This comes as no surprise as most SMEs will be reliant on basic skills of staff specializing in other tasks, with more complex tasks subcontracted to expensive external consultants.

Table 9 shows the raw percentages of firms indicating that they had experienced a shortage of basic and advanced IT skills in relation to their level of website integration. As would be expected those firms with higher levels of website functionality are more likely to have encountered both basic and advanced IT skills shortages. It appears that those firms least likely to encounter shortages are those

Table 9. Shortage of Staff IT Skills by Website Facilitation

		No	Basic Information	Advertise Products	Sell on-line	Link to Suppliers	Sell on-line and link to suppliers	All	Pearson Chi-Square		
Employees younger than 25 years of age	Shortage of Basic IT Skills	6.9%	8.1%	9.3%	9.7%	11.9%	16.3%	8.8%	18.198	[5]	(0.003)
	Shortage of Advanced IT Skills	4.2%	8.9%	8.5%	9.3%	11.9%	17.7%	8.0%	46.327	[5]	(0.000)
Employees older than 25 years of age	Shortage of Basic IT Skills	8.7%	10.5%	12.8%	12.6%	13.6%	19.0%	11.6%	22.580	[5]	(0.000)
	Shortage of Advanced IT Skills	9.1%	12.9%	12.8%	11.7%	13.6%	17.0%	11.9%	15.556	[5]	(0.008)
In potential staff recruits	Shortage of Basic IT Skills	4.4%	8.0%	8.8%	8.4%	15.3%	14.3%	7.8%	35.187	[5]	(0.000)
	Shortage of Advanced IT Skills	3.7%	6.9%	8.3%	7.5%	11.9%	13.6%	7.0%	36.769	[5]	(0.000)
Staff recruitment and training decisions	New staff	22.3%	33.0%	41.7%	34.6%	49.2%	48.3%	34.8%	140.993	[5]	(0.000)
	Increasing in Staff Training	11.7%	18.6%	23.6%	19.5%	28.8%	25.2%	19.4%	74.450	[5]	(0.000)

Notes: degrees of freedom shown in square brackets; p-values in parenthesis

with no websites at all, the group of employees in which shortages of skills are most frequently reported is the older employee group, so that of those firms with no websites 8.7 per cent have reported a shortage of basic IT skills and 9.1 per cent a shortage of advanced IT skills. Less than one in twenty firms with no website reported a shortage of basic and advanced IT skills when considering potential recruits.

At the other end of the spectrum those businesses with fully integrated websites appear to be most likely to encounter IT skills shortages from current and potential employees. Again, it is older workers that are most likely to display IT skills shortages for this group of firms, so much so, that nearly one in five firms (19.0 per cent) reported encountering a shortage of basic IT skills in employees aged over 25 years, with a shortage of advanced IT skills reported by 17.0 per cent of firms with fully integrated websites for this group of workers. For younger workers (those less than 25 years of age) the percentage of fully integrated website firms encountering a shortage of IT skills drops to 16.3 per cent for basic skills and 17.7 per cent for advanced skills. The lower shortages reported regarding recruitment may be in part misleading as many firms may not have attempted to recruit during the last two years.

The need to keep websites updated and relevant makes true e-commerce either impractical or more commonly simply out of the price range of most UK SMEs. Consequently, this has made it highly important that firms ensure that the staff and management receive training in usage of new IT developments (Dutta and Evrard, 1999; Fariselli et al., 1999). For those with fully integrated websites the probability of encountering basic IT shortages when recruiting is doubled (odds ratio = 2.051) compared to those without websites. Interestingly, the probability of encountering a basic IT skills shortage when recruiting for those firms using websites to connect primarily with suppliers is approaching three times that of those without websites (odds ratio = 2.778). This means that those

firms which have moved to the highest levels of website functionality are not able to bring in the talent they require. Knowledge of this is likely to put firms operating with more basic websites off further development unless they already have employees with the skills required.

Using a resource-based theory approach Caldeira and Ward (2003) highlight the importance of IT skills being developed in-house to ensure they fit with the requirements of the firm, where possession of IT skills can form an important competitive advantage in itself. However, when considering advanced IT skills it appears those with more sophisticated websites do not appear to have developed these skills in-house. This is to the extent that those firms with fully integrated websites are three times as likely to encounter advanced IT skills shortages in younger workers than those firms with no websites at all (odds ratio = 3.139). Searching for new talent may not solve the problem either as those with fully integrated websites are twice as likely to encounter advanced IT shortages when attempting to recruit as those with no website (odds ratio = 2.060). Again this appears to be where firms with greater website integration are attempting to bring in employees with the skills that they require, or looking to younger employees to take on responsibilities associated with newer technological advances.

CONCLUSION AND FUTURE RESEARCH DIRECTIONS

Building on existing literature this chapter has used data from a relatively large sample of SMEs from the UK to examine the links between the level of website integration and turnover growth in general, and more specifically through increased geographical scope.

The data examined here has confirmed the findings of previous studies such as Levy and Powell, (2003) and Crespi et al. (2004) in that Internet adoption in general in the UK appears to

Table 10. Shortage of staff IT skills by presence of non-active and active Website

		No Website	Non-Active Website	Active Website	All	Pearson Chi-Square		
Employees younger than 25 years of age	Shortage of Basic IT Skills	6.9%	8.9%	10.7%	8.8%	9.975	[2]	(0.007)
	Shortage of Advanced IT Skills	4.2%	8.6%	10.6%	8.0%	34.122	[2]	(0.000)
Employees older than 25 years of age	Shortage of Basic IT Skills	8.7%	12.1%	13.5%	11.6%	14.128	[2]	(0.001)
	Shortage of Advanced IT Skills	9.1%	12.9%	12.5%	11.9%	12.063	[2]	(0.002)
In potential staff recruits	Shortage of Basic IT Skills	4.4%	8.5%	9.6%	7.8%	25.782	[2]	(0.000)
	Shortage of Advanced IT Skills	3.7%	7.8%	8.6%	7.0%	26.390	[2]	(0.000)
Staff recruitment and training decisions	New Staff	22.3%	38.8%	37.3%	34.8%	104.843	[2]	(0.000)
	Increase in staff training	1.7%	22.0%	20.8%	19.4%	58.877	[2]	(0.000)

Notes: degrees of freedom shown in square brackets; p-values in parenthesis

Table 11. Logits of shortages of basic IT skills encountered

		Younger Employees (Under 25 years)		Older Employees (Under 25 years)		Recruitment	
Website (Bc – No Website)	Non-Active Website	-0.1441	(0.333)	-0.0412	(0.756)	0.2477	(0.155)
	Active Website	-0.0731	(0.701)	0.0029	(0.986)	0.3550	(0.101)
Employment (Bc – owner only)	2 - 4 Employees	**0.6823**	(0.001)	**1.1095**	(0.000)	**0.7632**	(0.001)
	5 - 9 Employees	**1.0305**	(0.000)	**1.5871**	(0.000)	**1.3498**	(0.000)
	10 - 19 Employees	**1.5384**	(0.000)	**1.7826**	(0.000)	**1.5566**	(0.000)
	20+ Employees	**1.8602**	(0.000)	**2.1079**	(0.000)	**2.0074**	(0.000)
Turnover (Bc – less than £25,000)	£25K - £50K	0.2313	(0.487)	0.0299	(0.915)	0.1236	(0.737)
	£500k - £100K	0.3684	(0.244)	0.0958	(0.717)	0.2027	(0.561)
	£100K - £200K	0.4798	(0.133)	0.1904	(0.475)	0.6420	(0.061)
	£200K - £300K	0.5477	(0.106)	0.3255	(0.249)	0.4900	(0.183)
	£300K - £500K	0.6030	(0.077)	0.3170	(0.267)	**0.7236**	(0.048)
	£500K - £1m	0.5265	(0.133)	0.4743	(0.103)	0.6268	(0.095)
	£1 million	0.6834	(0.063)	**0.6062**	(0.049)	**0.8287**	(0.034)
Tourist Trade (Bc – none)	Direct	0.3749	(0.089)	0.0556	(0.785)	-0.1484	(0.564)
	Indirect	0.1182	(0.477)	-0.0596	(0.694)	0.0789	(0.656)
Firm Age (Bc – less than 3 years old)	4 - 9 years	-0.0909	(0.673)	-0.1467	(0.428)	-0.0528	(0.815)
	10 to 19 years	-0.0008	(0.997)	-0.2723	(0.178)	-0.2052	(0.404)
	20 or more years	-0.1336	(0.611)	-0.3187	(0.167)	-0.1952	(0.489)
Entrepreneur's Age (Bc – younger than 35 years)	35 to 44 years old	-0.1366	(0.546)	0.0388	(0.853)	-0.1231	(0.592)
	45 to 54 years old	**-0.4883**	(0.032)	-0.1593	(0.446)	-0.4317	(0.061)
	55 to 64 years	**-0.8060**	(0.001)	**-0.4842**	(0.030)	**-0.7356**	(0.003)
	Over 65 years old	**-0.6577**	(0.030)	-0.4532	(0.104)	-0.5954	(0.067)
Entrepreneur's educational attainment (Bc A-levels)	Postgraduate	0.2185	(0.314)	0.2883	(0.132)	0.2360	(0.280)
	Bachelors Degree	0.1721	(0.354)	**0.3496**	(0.030)	0.1888	(0.316)
	Professional	0.2655	(0.142)	0.1420	(0.382)	0.0089	(0.962)
	GCSE/O level	0.1490	(0.454)	0.0946	(0.591)	-0.0050	(0.981)
	Vocational	0.2611	(0.302)	-0.0206	(0.930)	-0.1170	(0.678)
	No Formal	0.0944	(0.728)	-0.0308	(0.900)	**-0.8054**	(0.028)
Owners' gender (Bc – equal)	Male Majority	-0.0388	(0.742)	0.1643	(0.119)	0.0669	(0.600)
	Female Majority	**0.3557**	(0.036)	**0.4912**	(0.001)	**0.6598**	(0.000)
Hours committed to business (Bc – 30 to 48 hours)	Less than 30 hours	-0.2175	(0.524)	0.3046	(0.220)	-0.1780	(0.634)
	49 to 60 hours	**0.4725**	(0.001)	**0.3178**	(0.010)	**0.4546**	(0.003)
	More than 60 hours	**0.8920**	(0.000)	**0.8231**	(0.000)	**1.0356**	(0.000)
Objectives for business over next two years (Bc – remain same size)	Grow 20%+	0.2641	(0.159)	0.0833	(0.618)	0.3026	(0.135)
	Expand up to 20%	0.1570	(0.312)	0.1292	(0.338)	0.2242	(0.189)
	Downsize business	0.0903	(0.777)	-0.1726	(0.579)	-0.0819	(0.826)
	Sell or close	**0.5270**	(0.012)	0.3126	(0.102)	0.2673	(0.274)
	Hand on business	-0.1238	(0.777)	-0.4759	(0.268)	0.2205	(0.610)

continued on following page

Table 11. continued

N	5056		5056		5056	
R^2	0.105		0.106		0.131	
Hosmer-Lemeshow	10.6	(0.226)	2.88	(0.942)	6.22	(0.623)

Notes: p-values in parenthesis

Table 12. Logit of shortages of advanced IT skills encountered

		Younger Employees (Under 25 years)		Older Employees (Under 25 years)		Recruitment	
Website (Bc – No Website)	Non-Active Website	**0.3384**	(0.050)	0.0272	(0.835)	0.1528	(0.412)
	Active Website	**0.5181**	(0.014)	-0.0551	(0.748)	0.2437	(0.288)
Employment (Bc – owner only)	2 - 4 Employees	**0.7077**	(0.001)	**0.8025**	(0.000)	**0.9060**	(0.000)
	5 - 9 Employees	**1.1395**	(0.000)	**0.8916**	(0.000)	**1.2441**	(0.000)
	10 - 19 Employees	**1.4141**	(0.000)	**0.9907**	(0.000)	**1.4263**	(0.000)
	20+ Employees	**1.7359**	(0.000)	**1.2297**	(0.000)	**1.5788**	(0.000)
Turnover (Bc – less than £25,000)	£25K - £50K	0.4593	(0.171)	0.1441	(0.535)	-0.5228	(0.134)
	£500k - £100K	0.3153	(0.338)	0.0302	(0.894)	-0.2438	(0.435)
	£100K - £200K	**0.6439**	(0.049)	0.1591	(0.491)	0.1542	(0.618)
	£200K - £300K	0.4040	(0.252)	0.0555	(0.830)	-0.0748	(0.827)
	£300K - £500K	0.4929	(0.163)	0.3147	(0.220)	0.2433	(0.471)
	£500K - £1m	0.6552	(0.067)	0.4459	(0.090)	0.4741	(0.166)
	£1 million	0.4852	(0.203)	**0.6631**	(0.019)	0.6179	(0.091)
Tourist Trade (Bc – none)	Direct	-0.0620	(0.810)	0.2301	(0.264)	0.0185	(0.947)
	Indirect	0.0818	(0.641)	0.1477	(0.317)	0.2320	(0.223)
Firm Age (Bc – less than 3 years old)	4 - 9 years	0.0360	(0.874)	-0.1816	(0.309)	0.5359	(0.038)
	10 to 19 years	-0.0523	(0.827)	-0.3079	(0.117)	0.3025	(0.273)
	20 or more years	-0.3220	(0.232)	-0.2488	(0.270)	0.2121	(0.502)
Entrepreneur's Age (Bc – younger than 35 years)	35 to 44 years old	**-0.4500**	(0.043)	-0.0141	(0.943)	-0.3052	(0.205)
	45 to 54 years old	**-0.8542**	(0.000)	-0.3810	(0.054)	-0.3456	(0.146)
	55 to 64 years	**-1.1537**	(0.000)	**-0.7551**	(0.000)	**-0.8436**	(0.001)
	Over 65 years old	**-1.2892**	(0.000)	**-0.7138**	(0.008)	**-0.9879**	(0.006)
Entrepreneur's educational attainment (Bc A-levels)	Postgraduate	**0.6675**	(0.002)	**0.4827**	(0.007)	**0.6941**	(0.003)
	Bachelors Degree	0.3665	(0.057)	**0.3615**	(0.021)	**0.6047**	(0.004)
	Professional	0.2125	(0.270)	0.1055	(0.507)	0.3167	(0.138)
	GCSE/O level	0.0512	(0.811)	-0.1223	(0.498)	0.0170	(0.944)
	Vocational	-0.1002	(0.736)	-0.4228	(0.106)	-0.0042	(0.990)
	No Formal	0.0279	(0.925)	-0.1571	(0.537)	-0.0625	(0.861)

continued on the following page

Table 12. continued

Owners' gender (Bc – equal)	Male Majority	-0.0539	(0.653)	**0.2055**	(0.049)	-0.0005	(0.997)
	Female Majority	-0.0791	(0.683)	**0.3245**	(0.030)	0.3063	(0.117)
Hours committed to business (Bc – 30 to 48 hours)	Less than 30 hours	0.4373	(0.133)	**0.5966**	(0.007)	-0.2685	(0.494)
	49 to 60 hours	**0.3832**	(0.009)	**0.4127**	(0.001)	**0.2947**	(0.057)
	More than 60 hours	**0.8515**	(0.000)	**0.7154**	(0.000)	**0.8315**	(0.000)
Objectives for business over next two years (Bc – remain same size)	Grow 20%+	0.0706	(0.713)	0.3157	(0.053)	**0.5482**	(0.008)
	Expand up to 20%	0.0164	(0.918)	**0.2727**	(0.044)	0.2114	(0.245)
	Downsize business	-0.0629	(0.852)	0.2774	(0.315)	0.1211	(0.749)
	Sell or close	**0.5262**	(0.015)	0.3823	(0.053)	0.3018	(0.264)
	Hand on business	-0.7484	(0.177)	-0.7797	(0.147)	0.2454	(0.608)
N		5056		5056		5056	
R^2		0.112		0.0857		0.1406	
Hosmer-Lemeshow		21.31	(0.006)	2.86	(0.943)	23.05	(0.003)

be high and many firms have their own websites. As in previous studies however, the average level of functionality and integration is low in UK SMEs. Whilst website functionality is not significantly linked to the growth rates achieved by firms over the past two years, it is linked perhaps more tellingly to aspirations of growth, so that those firms whose objectives are to grow in the future are much more likely to develop their websites to have higher levels of facilities.

The percentage of firms adding active elements to their websites is still relatively low, which is surprising given the links found between website functionality and the escape from reliance on local markets. Those firms with greater website functionality are both found to be more likely to export and are less likely to draw a majority of their sales from local markets.

It was suggested that given the importance of IT self-efficacy in adoption of newer technologies (Lee, 2004), a shortage of IT skills was likely to be one of the factors holding back greater website de-

velopment (Drew, 2003). The percentage of firms encountering shortages of basic and advanced IT skills was found to be much higher for those firms with higher levels of website integration. Whilst much of this appears to be related to firm and entrepreneurial characteristics associated with both website adoption and skills shortages it does appear that those firms with the websites of greatest functionality are significantly more likely to be hindered by a lack of availability in advanced IT skills.

Whilst IT skills shortages are most commonly found for older workers it is the skills shortages associated with younger workers and potential employees when attempting to recruit that is linked to website functionality. It does seem therefore that those firms that have brochure style websites are unlikely to naturally follow the stages models of website development (Daniel et al., 2002), if those firms that have already followed this path are frequently baulked in their ambitions by a lack of available talent.

The findings suggest that SMEs that understand the potential of the Web are prepared to embrace the potential of e-commerce. This reduces the reliance on local markets which in times of economic difficulty can be essential. Nonetheless, as has been found previously a large proportion of SMEs do not desire or seek growth (Levy and Powell, 2003). This may reflect differing objectives and ambitions. However, the extent to which firms understand the ramifications of not adopting and embracing technological advances is not clear. Whilst business advice services are provided from a variety of sources, it is likely that all too often owners of SMEs will seek this advice at a point when it is too late to change the course of the firm, and resources are not available. It would appear therefore that trade associations have an important role to play in educating their members to the benefits and threats that technological advancements such as the Web bring. Given that the strategic importance of functionality and integration appears to be recognized by or acted upon by relatively few firms (Lee, 2004), and given the increase in globalization, UK SMEs need to be made aware of these issues to ensure competitiveness is maintained, as the Internet provides not just opportunities but also is a source of threats to existing sales (Drew, 2003).

Against a backdrop of low interest in growth, firms that would gladly use website functionality as a method of not only growing, but also expanding their customer base, even achieving international sales growth, may not be able to do so. A considerable barrier to this may be the lack of IT skills present in the UK labour force. Clearly any scheme to increase the awareness of UK SMEs to the Web will be limited if the skills are not available in the workforce. Whilst training can be provided directly to SMEs the shortage of more advanced IT skills appears to be fairly chronic for those firms with the highest levels of website integration. This would suggest that there needs to be an emphasis on providing IT skills of this level to young people in full time educa-

tion. It is surprising that given the role that IT/IS equipment and applications play in the modern workplace that a vast majority of further and higher education courses are limited to basic PC applications with Web skills learnt in an ad hoc and informal manner.

Website integration may currently be the preserve of those firms wishing to grow rapidly. Given the rapid integration of global markets and growth of online sales this may not remain the case for much longer. The ability of the Web to help firms grow beyond their core local markets will become more and more of necessity for survival. If this is the case it is important that SME owners are educated to make them aware of the threats and opportunities this engenders. Growth orientated firms and more and more frequently those firms with aspirations simply to survive will be hamstrung unless more advanced IT skills are added to curriculum of students as standard.

It is important to acknowledge the limitations of the data in terms of investigating issues relating to e-commerce given the survey's more general purpose and clearly there is a need for further quantitative and qualitative work to be undertaken. For example, firms with websites more fully integrated into their businesses are more likely to be growth orientated but there is no strong link between previous growth and website functionality. Future work needs to ascertain what these growth orientated businesses hope to achieve through their greater integration of their websites, and also why in retrospect this did not occur. Ideally such work would be longitudinal in nature to follow businesses through their adoption, and integration decisions, keeping track of their expectations and desires at all points. Obviously focused research projects such as this could examine the functions of websites to a much greater degree to obtain a fuller and more precise measure of integration. Similarly when looking for explanations as to why a greater number of UK SMEs do not develop their websites beyond basic brochure style websites the FSB data is limited in asking indirect questions in relation to shortages of IT capabilities. Clearly there does seem to be an issue of IT shortages which may hinder growth orientated businesses from increasing their geographical scope, but whether this is the reason for lower levels of commitment to the web by UK SMEs in general needs to be investigated more thoroughly through questionnaire and interview approaches specifically looking to answer these questions. Overall there seems to be an acceptance that although SME website adoption and functionality is relatively low and a number of potential answers to why this might be the case, no conclusive work has so far been conducted. This means that policy responses will have to be made to a large extent in the dark, possibly costing the UK in terms of lost opportunities for growth and employment.

Whilst the work discussed within this chapter has concentrated upon the use of the website for the purposes of e-commerce, the final stage of development is seen as the complete integration of the businesses operations to form an e-business, clearly as time goes on similar issues to those raise above will need to be investigated in terms of full development of e-businesses. Similarly certain under-researched groups such as pure-play Web-based firms need to also be captured in surveys as these are often under-represented in existing data sources, and may provide many of the new opportunities for employment growth in the SME sector in the future.

ACKNOWLEDGMENT

The authors wish to thank the Federation of Small Business for their support and the opportunity to use the data from the "Lifting the Barriers to Growth Survey" of their members. Without this support it would not have been possible to complete the work within this chapter.

REFERENCES

Alonso Mendo, F., & Fitzgerald, G. (2005a). A multidimensional framework for SME e-business progression. *Journal of Enterprise Information Management, 18*(6), 678–696. doi:10.1108/17410390510628382

Alonso Mendo, F., & Fitzgerald, G. (2005b). Theoretical approaches to study SMEs eBusiness progression. *Journal of Computing and Information Technology, 13*(2), 123–136. doi:10.2498/cit.2005.02.04

Arnott, D. C., & Bridgewater, S. (2002). Internet interaction and implications for marketing. *Marketing Intelligence & Planning, 20*(2), 86–95. doi:10.1108/02634500210418509

Audretsch, D. B., & Thurik, A. R. (2001). What is new about the new economy: sources of growth in the managed and entrepreneurial economies. *Industrial and Corporate Change, 10*(1), 17–34. doi:10.1093/icc/10.1.267

Briedenhann, J., & Wickens, E. (2004). Tourism routes as a tool for the economic development of rural areas – vibrant hope or impossible dream? *Tourism Management, 25*(1), 71–79. doi:10.1016/S0261-5177(03)00063-3

Caldeira, M. M., & Ward, J. M. (2003). Using resource-based theory to interpret the successful adoption and use of information systems and technology in manufacturing small and medium-sized enterprises. *European Journal of Information Systems, 12*(2), 127–141. doi:10.1057/palgrave.ejis.3000454

Carree, M., van Stel, A., Thurik, R., & Wennekers, S. (2002). Economic development and business ownership: an analysis using data of 23 OECD countries in the period 1976-1996. *Small Business Economics, 19*(3), 271–290. doi:10.1023/A:1019604426387

Carter, N. M., & Allen, K. R. (1997). Size determinants of women-owned businesses: choice or barriers to resources? *Entrepreneurship and Regional Development*, 9(3), 211–220. doi:10.1080/08985629700000012

Carter, S., & Bennett, D. (2006). Gender and entrepreneurship. In S. Carter & D. Jones-Evans (Eds.), *Enterprise and small business: Principles, practice and policy*. London: FT Prentice-Hall.

Chaffey, D. (2007). *E-business and e-commerce* (3rd Ed.). London: Financial Times Press.

Chetty, S., & Campbell-Hunt, C. (2003). Paths to internationalisation among small- to medium-sized firms: a global versus regional approach. *European Journal of Marketing*, 37(5/6), 796–820. doi:10.1108/03090560310465152

Chuang, T.-T., Nakatani, K., Chen, J. C. H., & Huang, I.-L. (2007). Examining the impact of organisational and owner's characteristics on the extent of ecommerce adoption in SMEs. *International Journal of Business and Systems Research*, 1(1), 61–80. doi:10.1504/IJBSR.2007.014770

Cohen, S., & Kallirroi, G. (2006). e-commerce investments from a SME perspective: costs, benefits and processes. *Electronic Journal of Information Evaluation*, 9(2), 45–56.

Cragg, P., & Zinatelli, N. (1995). The evolution of IS in small firms. *Information & Management*, 29(1), 1–8. doi:10.1016/0378-7206(95)00012-L

Crespi, G., Mahdi, S., & Patel, P. (2004). Adoption of e-commerce technology: do network and learning externalities matter? *Draft Final Report for the Department of Trade and Industry*, London: HMSO.

Damanpour, F. (1991). Organizational innovation: a meta-analysis of effects of determinants and moderators. *Academy of Management Journal*, 34(3), 555–590. doi:10.2307/256406

Daniel, E., & Wilson, H. (2002). Adoption intentions and benefits realised: a study of e-commerce in UK SMEs. *Journal of Small Business and Enterprise Development*, 9(4), 331–348. doi:10.1108/14626000210450522

Daniel, E., Wilson, H., & Myers, A. (2002). Adoption of e-commerce by SMEs in the UK: towards a stage model. *International Small Business Journal*, 20(3), 253–270. doi:10.1177/0266242602203002

Darch, H., & Lucas, T. (2002). Training as an e-commerce enabler. *Journal of Workplace Learning*, 14(40), 148–155. doi:10.1108/13665620210427276

Drew, S. (2003). Strategic uses of e-commerce by SMEs in the East of England. *European Management Journal*, 21(1), 79–88. doi:10.1016/S0263-2373(02)00148-2

Dutta, S., & Evrard, P. (1999). Information technology and organisation within European small enterprises. *European Management Journal*, 17(3), 239–251. doi:10.1016/S0263-2373(99)00003-1

Elliot, S., & Fowell, S. (2000). Expectations versus reality: a snapshot of consumer experiences with Internet retailing. *International Journal of Information Management*, 20(5), 323–336. doi:10.1016/S0268-4012(00)00026-8

Eurostat (1996) *Enterprises in Europe*, Fourth Report.

Fariselli, P., Oughton, C., Picory, C., & Sugden, R. (1999). Electronic commerce and the future for SMEs in a global market-place: networking and public policies. *Small Business Economics*, 12(3), 261–275. doi:10.1023/A:1008029924987

Fichman, R. G., & Kemerer, C. F. (1997). The assimilation of software process innovations: an organizational learning perspective. *Management Science*, 43(10), 1345–1363. doi:10.1287/mnsc.43.10.1345

Fillis, I., Johannson, U., & Wagner, B. (2004). Factors impacting on e-business adoption and development in the smaller firm. *International Journal of Entrepreneurial Behaviour and Research, 10*(3), 178–191. doi:10.1108/13552550410536762

Galloway, L., Deakins, D., & Sanders, J. (2008, November). *The use of Internet portals by Scotland's Rural Business Community.* Paper presented at the 31st Institute for Small Business and Entrepreneurship (ISBE) Conference, Belfast, Northern Ireland.

Giaglis, G. M., Klein, S., & O'Keefe, R. M. (2002). The role of intermediaries in electronic marketplaces: developing a contingency model. *Information Systems Journal, 12*(3), 231–246. doi:10.1046/j.1365-2575.2002.00123.x

Gorton, M. (1999). Spatial variations in markets served by UK-based small and medium sized enterprises (SMEs). *Entrepreneurship and Regional Development, 11*(1), 39–55. doi:10.1080/089856299283281

Grandon, E. E., & Pearson, J. M. (2004). Electronic commerce adoption: an empirical study of small and medium US businesses. *Information & Management, 42*(1), 197–216.

Heckman, J. (1979). Sample selection bias as a specification error. *Econometrica, 47*(1), 153–161. doi:10.2307/1912352

Howcroft, D. (2001). After the goldrush: deconstructing the myths of the dot.com market. *Journal of Information Technology, 16*(4), 195–204. doi:10.1080/02683960110100418

Iacovou, C., Benbasat, I., & Bexter, A. (1995). Electronic Data interchange and small organisations: adoption and impact of technology. *MIS Quarterly, 19*(4), 465–485. doi:10.2307/249629

Irani, Z., Ezingeard, J.-N., & Grieve, R. J. (1997). Integrating the costs of a manufacturing IT/IS infrastructure into the investment decision-making process. *Technovation, 17*(11/12), 695–362. doi:10.1016/S0166-4972(97)00060-6

Jaw, Y.-L., & Chen, C.-L. (2006). The influence of the Internet in the internationalization of SMEs in Taiwan. *Human Systems Management, 25*(3), 167–183.

Johanson, J., & Vahlne, J.-E. (1977). The internationalisation process of the firm. *Journal of International Business Studies, 8*(1), 23–32. doi:10.1057/palgrave.jibs.8490676

Kadlec, P., & Mareš, M. (2003). B2B eCommerce opportunity for SMEs. In *Systems Integration,* Prague, Czech Republic (pp. 537-544).

Kierzkowski, A., McQuade, S., Waitman, R., & Zeisser, M. (1996). Marketing to the digital consumer. *The McKinsey Quarterly, 3,* 5–21.

Kim, D. (2003). The internationalization of US Internet portals: does it fit the process model of internationalization? *Marketing Intelligence & Planning, 21*(1), 23–36. doi:10.1108/02634500310458126

Kleindl, B. (2000). Competitive dynamics and new business models for SMEs in the virtual marketplace. *Journal of Developmental Entrepreneurship, 5*(1), 73–85.

Knight, G., & Cavusgil, T. (1996). The born global firm: a challenge to traditional internationalization theory. In S. T. Cavusgil (Ed.), *Advances in International Marketing* (Vol. 8, pp. 11-26). Greenwich, CT: JAI Press.

Kula, V., & Tatoglu, E. (2003). An exploratory study of internet adoption by SMEs in an emerging market economy. *European Business Review, 15*(5), 324–333. doi:10.1108/09555340310493045

Langston, C. M., & Teas, R. K. (1976). *Export commitment and characteristics of management.* Paper presented at the Annual Meeting of the Midwest Business Association, St Louis, MO.

Lawson, R., Alcock, C., Cooper, J., & Burgess, L. (2003). Factors affecting adoption of electronic commerce technologies by SMEs: an Australian study. *Journal of Small Business and Enterprise Development, 10*(3), 265–276. doi:10.1108/14626000310489727

Lee, J. (2004). Discriminant analysis of technology adoption behaviour: a case of internet technologies in small businesses. *Journal of Computer Information Systems, 44*(4), 57–66.

Levy, M., & Powell, P. (2003). Exploring SME internet adoption: towards a contingent model. *Electronic Markets, 13*(2), 173–181. doi:10.1080/1019678032000067163

Levy, M., Powell, P., & Yetton, P. (1998). SMEs and the gains from IS: from cost reduction to value added. In T. Larsen, L. Levine, & J. De-Gross (Eds.), *Information Systems: Current Issues and Future Changes* (pp. 377-392). Amsterdam: Kluwer Academic Publishers.

Levy, M., Powell, P., & Yetton, P. (2002). The dynamics of SME information systems. *Small Business Economics, 19*(4), 341–354. doi:10.1023/A:1019654030019

Lin, C., Huang, Y.-A., & Tseng, S.-W. (2007). A study of planning and implementation stages in electronic commerce adoption and evaluation: the case of Australian SMEs. *Contemporary Management Research, 3*(1), 83–100.

Lituchy, T. R., & Rail, A. (2000). Bed and breakfasts, small inns, and the internet: the impact of technology on the globalization of small business. *Journal of International Marketing, 8*(2), 86–97. doi:10.1509/jimk.8.2.86.19625

Liu, C., & Arnett, K. P. (2000). Exploring the factors associated with Web site success in the context of electronic commerce. *Information & Management, 38*(1), 23–33. doi:10.1016/S0378-7206(00)00049-5

Love, P., & Irani, Z. (2004). An exploratory study of information technology evaluation and benefits management practices for SMEs in the constructing industry. *Information & Management, 42*(1), 227–242.

Love, P., Irani, Z., Li, H., Cheng, E. W. L., & Tse, R. Y. C. (2001). An empirical analysis of the barriers to implementing e-commerce in small-medium sized construction contractors in the state of Victoria, Australia. *Construction Innovation, 1*(1), 31–41.

Martin, L. (2005). Internet adoption and use in small firms: internal processes, organisational culture and the roles of the owner-manager and key staff. *New Technology, Work and Employment, 20*(3), 190–204. doi:10.1111/j.1468-005X.2005.00153.x

Martin, L. M., & Matlay, H. (2001). "Blanket" approaches to promoting ICT in small firms: some lessons from the DTI ladder adoption model in the UK. *Internet Research, 11*(5), 399–410. doi:10.1108/EUM0000000006118

McConville, A. (2009). *Impact of ICT on SMEs in the South East: Report Prepared for the South East of England Development Agency.* Birmingham: BMG Research.

McDougall, P. P., & Oviatt, B. M. (2000). International entrepreneurship: the intersection of two research paths. *Academy of Management Journal, 43*(5), 902–906. doi:10.2307/1556418

Mehrtens, J., Cragg, P. B., & Mills, A. M. (2001). A model of internet adoption by SMEs. *Information & Management, 39*(3), 165–176. doi:10.1016/S0378-7206(01)00086-6

Mirchandani, A. A., & Motwani, J. (2001). Understanding small business e-commerce adoption: an empirical analysis. *Journal of Computer Information Systems, 41*(3), 70–73.

Napier, H. A., Judd, P. J., Rivers, O. N., & Wagner, S. W. (2001). *Creating a Winning E-Business.* Boston, MA: Course Technology.

O'Farrell, P. N., Hitchens, D. M., & Moffat, L. A. R. (1995). Business service firms in two peripheral economies: Scotland and Ireland. *Tijdschrift voor Economische en Sociale Geografie, 86*(2), 115–128. doi:10.1111/j.1467-9663.1995.tb01351.x

O'Keefe, R. M., O'Connor, G., & Kung, H.-J. (1998). Early adopters of the web as a retail medium: small company winners and losers. *European Journal of Marketing, 32*(7/8), 629–643. doi:10.1108/03090569810224038

Office for National Statistics. (2008). *First Release: E-commerce activity 2007.* Newport: ONS.

Oviatt, P., & McDougal, B. (1999). Accelerated internationalization: why are new and small ventures internationalizing in greater numbers and with increasing speed? In R. Wright, (Ed.) *Research in Global Strategic Management,* (23-40). Stamford, CT: JAI Press.

Petersen, B., Welch, L., & Liesch, P. (2002). The Internet and foreign market expansion by firms. *Management International Review, 42*(2), 207–221.

Poon, S., & Swatman, P. M. C. (1997). Small business use of the internet: findings from Australian case studies. *International Marketing Review, 14*(5), 385–402. doi:10.1108/02651339710184343

Rao, S., Metts, G., & Monge, C. M. A. (2003). Electronic commerce development in small and medium sized enterprises: a stage model and its implications. *Business Process Management Journal, 9*(1), 11–32. doi:10.1108/14637150310461378

Raymond, L., Bergeron, F., & Blili, S. (2005). The assimilation of E-business in manufacturing SMEs: determinants and effects on growth and internationalization. *Electronic Markets, 15*(2), 106–118. doi:10.1080/10196780500083761

Rayport, J., & Jaworski, B. (2001). *E-Commerce.* New York, NY: McGraw-Hill/Irwin.

Robertson, A., & Lockett, N. Brown, D. and Crouchley, R. (2007, November). *Entrepreneur attitude towards the computer and its effect on e-Business adoption,* Paper presented at the 30th Institute for Small Business and Entrepreneurship (ISBE) Conference, Glasgow.

Samiee, S. (1998). Exporting and the Internet: a conceptual perspective. *International Marketing Review, 15*(5), 413–426. doi:10.1108/02651339810236452

Sarosa, S., & Zowghi, D. (2003). Strategy for adopting information technology for SMEs: experience in adopting email within an Indonesian furniture company. *Electronic Journal of Information Systems Evaluation, 6*(2), 165–176.

Simpson, C. L., & Kujawa, D. (1974). The export decision process: an empirical inquiry. *Journal of International Business Studies, 5*(1), 107–117. doi:10.1057/palgrave.jibs.8490815

Sinkovics, R. R., & Pene, E. (2005). Empowerment of SME websites – development of a web-empowered scale and preliminary evidence. *Journal of International Entrepreneurship, 3*(4), 303–315. doi:10.1007/s10843-006-7858-8

Stockdale, R., & Standing, G. (2004). Benefits and barriers of electronic marketplace participation: an SME perspective. *Journal of Enterprise Information Management*, *17*(4), 301–311. doi:10.1108/17410390410548715

Van de Ven, W. P. M. M., & Van Praag, B. M. S. (1981). The demand for deductibles in private health insurance: a probit model with sample selection. *Journal of Econometrics*, *17*(2), 229–252. doi:10.1016/0304-4076(81)90028-2

Walker, E., & Brown, A. (2004). What success factors are important to small business owners? *International Small Business Journal*, *22*(6), 577–594. doi:10.1177/0266242604047411

Wen, H. J., Chen, H.-G., & Hwang, H.-G. (2001). E-commerce Web site design: strategies and models. *Information Management & Computer Security*, *9*(1), 5–12. doi:10.1108/09685220110366713

Williams, D. R. (2004). Effects of childcare activities on the duration of self-employment in Europe. *Entrepreneurship Theory and Practice*, *28*(5), 467–485. doi:10.1111/j.1540-6520.2004.00058.x

Yeung, W. L., & Lu, M.-t. (2004). Functional characteristics of commercial web sites: a longitudinal study in Hong Kong. *Information & Management*, *41*(4), 483–495. doi:10.1016/S0378-7206(03)00086-7

Zhuang, Y., & Lederer, A. L. (2006). A resource-based view of electronic commerce. *Information & Management*, *43*(2), 251–261. doi:10.1016/j.im.2005.06.006

ADDITIONAL READING

Al-Qirin, N. (2005). An empirical investigation of an e-commerce adoption-capability model in small businesses in New Zealand. *Electronic Markets*, *15*(4), 418–437. doi:10.1080/10196780500303136

Beynon-Davies, P. (2007). eBusiness maturity and regional development. *International Journal of Business Science and Applied Management*, *2*(1), 9–20.

Bharati, P., & Chaudhury, A. (2006, July). *Small and medium enterprises (SMEs) adoption of technology along the value chain*. Paper presented at the European and Mediterranean Conference on Information Systems (EMICS), Alicante.

Brynjolfsson, E., & Kahin, B. (Eds.). (2000). *Understanding the Digital Economy*. Cambridge, MA: MIT press.

Bui, T. X., Sankaran, S., & Sebastian, I. M. (2003). A framework for measuring national e-readiness. *International Journal of Electronic Business*, *1*(1), 3–22. doi:10.1504/IJEB.2003.002162

Del Aguila-Obra, A. R., & Padilla-Melendez, A. (2006). Organizational factors affecting Internet technology adoption. *Internet Research*, *16*(1), 94–110. doi:10.1108/10662240610642569

Dos Santos, B. L., & Peffers, K. (1998). Competitor and Vendor influence on the adoption of innovative applications in electronic commerce. *Information & Management*, *34*(3), 175–184. doi:10.1016/S0378-7206(98)00053-6

Hartland, C. M., Cardwell, N. D., Powell, P., & Zheng, J. (2007). Barriers to supply chain information integration: SMEs adrift of e-Lands. *Journal of Operations Management*, *25*(6), 1234–1254. doi:10.1016/j.jom.2007.01.004

Jutla, D., Bodorick, P., & Dhaliwal, J. (2002). Supporting the e-business readiness of small and medium-sized enterprises: approaches and metrics. *Internet Research Electronic Working Applications and Policy*, *12*(2), 139–164. doi:10.1108/10662240210422512

Macgregor, R., & Vrazalic, L. (2005). A basic model of electronic commerce adoption barriers: a study of regional small businesses in Sweden and Australia. *Journal of Small Business and Enterprise Development, 12*(4), 510–527. doi:10.1108/14626000510628199

Marasini, R., Ions, K., & Ahmad, M. (2008). Assessment of e-business adoption in SMEs: A study of manufacturing industry in the UK North East region. *Journal of Manufacturing Technology Management, 19*(5), 627–644. doi:10.1108/17410380810877294

O'Regan, N., Ghobadian, A., & Galler, D. (2006). In search of the drivers of high growth in manufacturing SMEs. *Technovation, 26*(1), 30–41. doi:10.1016/j.technovation.2005.05.004

Parker, C. M., & Castleman, T. (2007). New directions for research on SME-eBusiness: insights from an analysis of journal articles from 2003 to 2006. *Journal of Information Systems and Small Business, 1*(1-2), 21–40.

Pavic, S., Koh, S. C. L., Simpson, M., & Padmore, J. (2007). Could e-business create a competitive advantage in UK SMEs. *Benchmarking: An International Journal, 14*(3), 320–351. doi:10.1108/14635770710753112

Poon, S. (2000). Business environment and internet commerce benefit-small business perspective. *European Journal of Information Systems, 9*(2), 72–81. doi:10.1057/palgrave/ejis/3000361

Quayle, M. (2002). E-commerce: the challenge for UK SMEs in the twenty-first century. *International Journal of Operations & Production Management, 22*(10), 1148–1161. doi:10.1108/01443570210446351

Rickards, R. C. (2007). BSC and benchmark development for an e-commerce SME. *Benchmarking: An International Journal, 14*(2), 222–250. doi:10.1108/14635770710740413

Steinfield, C., & Whitten, P. (1999). Community level socio-economic impacts of electronic commerce. *Journal of Computer-Mediated Communication, 5*(2).

Van Beveren, J., & Thompson, H. (2002). The use of electronic commerce by SMEs in Victoria, Australia. *Journal of Small Business Management, 40*(3), 250–253. doi:10.1111/1540-627X.00054

Wagner, B. A., Fillis, A., & Johannson, U. (2003). E-business and e-supply strategy in small and medium-sized businesses (SMEs). *Supply Chain Management: An International Journal, 8*(4), 343–354. doi:10.1108/13598540310490107

Yasin, M., Czunchy, A., Gonzales, M., & Bayes, P. (2006). E-commerce implementation challenges: Small to medium-sized versus large organisations. *International Journal of Business Information Systems, 1*(3), 256–275. doi:10.1504/IJBIS.2006.008599

DATA APPENDIX: OPERATIONALIZATION OF WEBSITE FUNCTIONALITY

The data used in this study is drawn from the Federation of Small Business (FSB) Lifting the Barriers to Growth Survey 2008. The survey is distributed to the members of the FSB through postal questionnaires and electronically through the FSB website, with the questions identically phrased in the two formats. The questionnaire was originally mailed early in 2008 with a number of reminder emails are sent out directing respondents to the FSB website where the electronic version of the questionnaire was accessible. For the purposes of the work studied here 5089 usable responses were available.

Although the FSB survey was not designed to examine website functionality specifically, it does include a question which allows a measure of understanding of the level of website development by respondent firms:

Does your business have a website, and if yes, what is it used for?

The respondents are asked to select one of the options from those listed below that best describe their current Web presence.

1. No
2. Yes, but only for basic contact information
3. Yes and it is used to advertise our products
4. Yes and it is used to advertise and sell our products on-line
5. Yes and it is used to link to suppliers
6. Yes and it is used to link to suppliers and sell our products on-line

In general the options can be thought of as increasing in Web presence from a complete absence through brochure style non-active websites to e-commerce capable websites with links to customers and suppliers. In terms of ranking responses as lesser or greater website integration it is perhaps only options 4 and 5 which are difficult to rank relative to one another.

As a vast majority of those with websites are in the lower orders of website functionality it is often necessary for analysis to aggregate groups by website functionality into non-adopters (those with no Web presence at all, group 1), non-active website users (those with websites simply providing contact details, or simple brochure websites advertising products, groups 2 and 3), active website users (those using websites for some form of e-commerce, either to link to customers, suppliers, or both, groups 4 to 6).

The more general nature of the FSB survey means that the no specific question is asked linking website adoption or functionality and a lack of IT skills. On the other hand, if a shortage of IT skills is an important barrier to greater functionality it would be expected that those firms with greater functionality would be more likely to report that they had encountered shortages in IT skills in the previous two years. Questions are asked in relation to whether basic and advanced IT skills shortages have been encountered in younger employees (less than 25 years of age), older employees (25 years and over), and when attempting to recruit.

Chapter 9
ICT Opportunities Unlimited:
The International Dimension in Opportunity Development

Ingrid Wakkee
VU University Amsterdam, The Netherlands

Peter van der Sijde
VU University Amsterdam, The Netherlands

ABSTRACT

Previous studies suggest that the majority of global startups have no choice but to operate across borders from day one (e.g., Oviatt and McDougall, 1994) to pursue their opportunities. Yet, few studies have explored how the opportunities for such firms come into existence and drive the emergence of global startups. In this chapter, we describe the process by which such opportunities originate, starting with a universal and fluid idea and moving into an opportunity that is at first moldable but that becomes increasingly coagulated. In addition, we describe how global startups make use of ICT to embed into a global network during this process.

INTRODUCTION

In the last two decades, research on international entrepreneurship focused on recently founded firms and their international activities (e.g., Zahra and George, 2002). A wealth of evidence presented in the literature suggests that the majority of startups or international new ventures have no choice but to operate across borders from day one (e.g., Oviatt and McDougall, 1994) to pursue their opportunities. A major theme in international entrepreneurship according to Dimitratos and Jones (2005) is inter-

national opportunity perception. Yet, to date, few scholars looked beyond the process of inception (Madsen and Servais, 1997; Wakkee, 2004; Kirwan, Van der Sijde, and Groen, 2007) and examined the process opportunity development underlying these (global) ventures. Our contribution will look into the process by which an opportunity scenario unfolds in the context of global startups. We will link theoretical insights on opportunity recognition (see, e.g., Bhave, 1994; Ardichvili, Cardozo, and Ray, 2003; Schwartz and Teach, 2000; Sigrist, 1999) to theoretical insights on international entrepreneurship (Oviatt and McDougall, 2005) and of ICT-supported communication. We will utilize insights

DOI: 10.4018/978-1-60566-998-4.ch009

Box 1. Summary of the cases used in this chapter

TMP / C2V (Elders and Walsh, 1999; Ridder, Van der Sijde, Kirwan, and Elders, 2006): The company started in 1992 as a spin-off of the MESA+ Laboratory of the University of Twente as the Foundation Twente Microproducts. In 1998, it was transformed into a limited company, and the university transferred its intellectual property in the company over to the company. In 2000, it merged with the company BBV, which was established in 1991 in the area of integrated optics and was integrated into Kymata UK. In 2001, Kymata was purchased by Alcatel, and it became the MEMS division of Alcatel. In 2002, there was a management buyout. C2V is, as mentioned on its website, a leading supplier of Microsystems-based solutions from concept to volume (hence the name) production.
Laser ACT (Bant & Meijer, 1999): Laser ACT is the brainchild of three (small) industrial companies (ILT Industrial Laser Applications, DEMAR Laser, and ECO Engineering) and the research group Precision Engineering of the University of Twente. It specializes in laser cutting, welding, cladding, and hardening. It acts as an R&D partner for, primarily, regional industry.
Lemniscates (Van der Sijde, Bliek, and Groen, 2003): A company based on a patent developed by a veterinarian doctor who works the international equestrian circuit. He developed a cure (officially, a medical device class III) for horses with leg problems that are unable to race.
Motion Inc (Wakkee, Groen, and Heerink, 2007): The company was established in 1999 by three students. As running enthusiasts, they were interested in measuring the distance they ran while training, and a technology for doing this was developed: a runners' watch for sports shoes. The company's objective was to sell 14,000 units in 5-years time. As it turned out, it was not successful, but they discovered that the technology was more generic and could be used in other applications. Over a short period, they explored the technology's application in sports, rehabilitation, and finally in "general motion technology" for bio-medical and military applications.

from cases previously published in the global start-up literature to illustrate and conceptualize how entrepreneurs virtually embed themselves (Morse, Fowler, and Lawrence, 2007) and use IT to interact with international contacts throughout this process.

This chapter is structured as follows. First, we present a brief discussion of the global start-up concept as it evolved in the literature over the past two decades. Second, we present a review of contemporary insights on the opportunity recognition process. From this review, we will argue that ideas, which are the basis of any opportunity recognition process, are both "universal" and "fluid," meaning that they can lead to a variety of opportunities to be exploited. Opportunities, in turn, start out as being "moldable," but they become increasingly "coagulated" as the venture in which they will be exploited begins to take shape. The actual exploitation process is beyond the scope of this paper and will not be discussed. Using evidence from previously published cases, we describe the process, starting with an idea via the business opportunity to the opportunity scenario (see Box 1 for an overview). We especially pay attention to the international dimension (markets and resources). Third, we explore how global startups use ICT to support the process from a universal and fluid

idea towards becoming a coagulated opportunity. We end this chapter with a future research agenda and a conclusion. See Box 1.

BACKGROUND: GLOBAL START-UPS IN THE LITERATURE

The term *global start-up* was introduced, but not defined, by two authors (Mamis, 1989; Ray, 1989; 1995). The first author—Mamis—described a French firm (Technomed) involved in international exchange relationships before the first product flowed from the production lines; the company sold its products in more than 28 countries within three years of its first sale both through exports and wholly owned subsidiaries. The second author published a series of four case studies in which he used the term *global start-up*. From these articles, a tentative definition emerged: The original ideas on which the enterprise are built are discovered abroad, and/or the resources, partners, and markets needed to exploit the opportunities cannot be found domestically, i.e., they were globally dispersed.

The article of Mamis (1989) and a series of related events led Patricia McDougall and Ben Oviatt to begin their research into global start-ups

(2005). Eventually, they stated their definition as follows: *"a firm that seeks to derive significant competitive advantage from extensive co-ordination along multiple organisational activities, the location of which is geographically unlimited. Such firms not only respond to globalising market conditions but also proactively act upon opportunities to acquire resources and sell outputs wherever in the world they have the greatest value"* (Oviatt and McDougall 1994, p. 59). Since their seminal article, many authors contributed to this new theme by focusing on early stages of global exploitation of opportunities (e.g., Rasmussen, Madsen, and Evangelista, 1997; Knight, Madsen, and Servais, 2004; Knight and Cavusgil, 1996; Madsen and Servais, 1997). A smaller number of authors (Wakkee, 2004; Kirwan, forthcoming) also explored how global startups actually come into existence. Wakkee (2004) concluded that for many global start-ups, international activities are not so much the result of a strategic decision but an integrative part of the actual opportunity: in order to create value, global business is a necessity. Both Wakkee (2004) and Kirwan (forthcoming) emphasize the importance of international networking from opportunity recognition onwards, which they formulate as one of the six defining characteristics of global start-ups (Kirwan and Wakkee, 2007):

1. Global start-ups are involved in international activities and exchange prior to opportunity exploitation.
2. Global start-ups are driven by the pursuit of opportunities that are truly global in nature.
3. Global start-ups are involved in multiple and significant formal and informal activities across national borders.
4. Global start-ups are embedded in international networks and international exchange relations in multiple countries and multiple regions of the world prior to the exploitation of the opportunity.

5. Global start-ups face unlimited potential for growth and value creation due to the global nature of their opportunity; yet, growth may not be actualized in terms of the strive for the formation of a large corporation or an IPO.
6. Global start-ups have high levels of entrepreneurial orientation

Kirwan, Van der Sijde, and Groen (2006) further show that global start-ups rely on a key partner (an organization that is instrumental in many ways in the foundation of the venture). Kirwan, Van der Sijde, and Groen (2007) write, "The key partners (…) are embedded in international networks and play a vital role in opening up their networks (social capital) allowing the start-up to accumulate the required capitals" (p. 397). Finally, many studies indicated the importance of innovations in IT for explaining the rise of this type of ventures (e.g., Madsen and Servais, 1997) without actually addressing the specific ways and mechanisms that allow global startups to embed themselves virtually (Wakkee, Groenewegen, and Englis, 2008).

FROM IDEA TO OPPORTUNITY SCENARIO

Ideas are Universal and Fluid

Sitting in his bathtub, Archimedes experienced the (first) eureka moment — the sudden moment of insight that gives birth to ideas. In 1754, Horace Walpole coined the accidental discovery process of ideas as serendipity (e.g., Fleming's discovery of penicillin) (Young, Ashdown, Arnold, and Subramonian, 2007). Sometimes, ideas come to life at different places on the globe at the same time (e.g., the discovery of the AIDS virus by French and Canadian researchers—Rawling, 1994); it even happens that ideas need to be reinvented because they were forgotten (map of Antarctica, "klap" skate). Some ideas survive the times (e.g., da Vinci's flying machine that became a helicopter); some ideas are wrong and persistent (the geocentric worldview—Kuhn, 1970; the flat earth—Garwood, 2007). There are useful and useless ideas, but all ideas, right or wrong, have in common that they are universal and the product of human creativity. Ideas have no borders and travel from mind to mind. An idea is knowledge in search of some kind of shape. At its very origin, every idea is in fact fluid (shapeless). An idea cannot be exchanged or otherwise acted upon if it only exists in the mind of the beholder, and it will change shape as a result of any conversation initiated or action undertaken to develop it (such as a river will never be the same after one steps into it). An idea is a notion or thought formed as a result of (conscious) reasoning and reflection after an (sensory) experience. But as Pasteur observed, chance favors only the prepared mind (Young, Ashdown, Arnold, and Subramonian, 2007).

Ideas as Sources of Opportunities

Ideas, thus, are the start of every entrepreneurial endeavor. As Venkataraman (1997) writes, opportunities do not appear in prepackaged forms; they need to be transformed into a business opportunity to enable an entrepreneur to do something with the idea. Ardichvili, Cardozo, and Ray (2003) describe three different ways through which ideas can be shaped into opportunities. First, there is *opportunity perception* that can be described as the process by which opportunities are observed locally. An example of this would be an entrepreneur who realizes that existing resources, such as unused and depreciated army barracks, are underutilized and can be used to create value when being deployed in a new way like a university campus (as happened with former US Army barracks in Germany). Although this local matching of market needs and underutilized resources is an important and probably the most common source for opportunities, we will not consider it in the remainder of

this chapter. The other two types are *opportunity discovery* and *opportunity creation* (Alvarez and Barney, 2005). On a daily basis, many ideas exist in the market, floating around as (abstract) notions of problems or latent market needs for which no solution currently can be found because either the technological or political landscape does not provide the necessary resources for a solution. Therefore, a real opportunity to create value has not yet emerged, and the idea remains fluid for the moment. Only a result of exogenous shocks, such as changes in technology, political/regulatory changes, and social/demographic changes, the opportunity arises to actually solve the problem. At this stage, entrepreneurs step in and begin to make their abstract ideas more tangible. It should be noted that at this stage, the direction it takes is not at all fixed. Even though this type of opportunities largely exists independent of the entrepreneur (e.g., the need for a cleaner environment or a solution for our energy deficiency), several entrepreneurs will usually simultaneously discover various alternative solutions based on the opportunities created by the exogenous shock, each of them focusing on a small niche of the original problem or solution.

Opportunities can also be created, e.g., an (academic) researcher sees value in the results of his studies, and together with an entrepreneur (or alone), he creates opportunities as a spin-off of their research. Shane (2000) illustrates how one specific type of technology, the three-dimensional printing (3DP^tm) developed at MIT, gave rise to (at least) eight different kinds of business opportunities: four of these business opportunities were realized, and companies were founded; four of the business opportunities were abandoned because the market was too small. The company Lemniscates patented a particular molecular chaining technique (Van der Sijde, Bliek, and Groen, 2003). Its founders realized from the start that their originally targeted (equestrian) market was only one of the markets for which they could develop applications, and so they filed for a more generic

Table 1. Global nature of the idea

	Attainable resources	Perceived market needs
TMP	Local	Local
Laser ATC	Local	International
Lemniscates	International	International
Motion Inc.	International	Local

patent. Likewise, the original idea underlying Motion Inc. ultimately proved to be applicable in a broad variety of markets ranging from sports and leisure to health care and revalidation and from robotics to space technology. In turn, in each of these markets, a whole variety of products could be created, all stemming from the same original idea. However, at the start, the entrepreneurs were only aware of the possibility to use their sensor in a running shoe, only searching for other applications when the running-shoe option failed.

Moulding Opportunities: Towards the Opportunity Scenario

Once entrepreneurs perceive a more concrete way to create value from their ideas, the opportunity recognition process begins in earnest (Lumpkin and Lichtenstein, 2005). Although the opportunity recognition process has been modeled in various ways by different authors (Bhave, 1994; De Koning and Muzyka, 1999; Hills, Lumpkin, and Singh, 1997; Lumpkin and Lichtenstein, 2005), the process can be depicted as consisting of a staged process that involves a discovery phase including preparation, incubation, and insight and a formation phase consisting of evaluation and elaboration. As explained by Lumpkin, Hills, and Schrader (2004), the process is highly iterative: insights are contemplated; new information is collected and considered, and knowledge is created over time. In this way, entrepreneurs go back and forth on an idea; in this iterative process, the (fluid) idea obtains some kind of "shape." The entrepreneur continues working on the idea until

it has a more fixed shape that can be molded into its final shape.

Based on a review of the literature, Van Der Veen and Wakkee (2006) conclude that this process involves the *mental matching* of attainable resources and perceived market needs through extensive interactions with other players in the environment, for example, potential lead users (Bhave, 1994; De Koning and Muzyka, 1999).

So far, however, few authors have studied this process in the context of internationalization. Even within the international entrepreneurship literature, it is often implicitly assumed that opportunity recognition takes place in a domestic context where the entrepreneur mainly exchanges ideas with others located in his/her vicinity. In this day and age, however, many entrepreneurs have some kind of international experience; they turn to the Internet to communicate electronically with actors located in other parts of the world. Consequently, it is likely that many opportunities actually are recognized in a cross-border context, and both the attainable resources as well as the perceived market needs can be international. As shown in Table 1, three of the four cases introduced in Box 1 either have the attainable resources and or the perceived market needs as international in nature.

The idea that led to the foundation of TMP (Total Micro Products; Elders & Walsh, 1999) was to make the (local) resources of the University of Twente available for local SMEs in the MEMS (microelectronics and microsystems) business: a business opportunity for a local need and local resources. The idea that founded Laser ACT (Bant & Meijer, 1999) was not very different; the knowledge of the university was combined with the expertise of local companies operating in the domain of laser technology, but what was different was the conception of the perceived market needs. Laser ACT perceived itself operating in an international market because of their resources (knowledge and facilities) and the perceived needs of industry all over the world. Alternatively, Motion Inc.'s founders originally planned to serve the domestic market—even though they could see international growth in the near future—but they could only create value for this market if they would source relevant knowledge and technology internationally. With a medical device for the equestrian world, Lemniscates (Van der Sijde, Bliek & Groen, 2004) is a company with both international perceived market needs and international resources.

Moulding Opportunities into Opportunity Scenario

Even when entrepreneurs begin to prepare for the exploitation of their opportunity, the opportunity is not yet solid. Throughout the formation process, the business opportunity remains moldable while it is obtaining its final shape. In order to work towards this final shape, entrepreneurs create, either consciously or subconsciously, what we call an opportunity scenario. We define an opportunity scenario as the way the entrepreneur or the entrepreneurial team envisions the realization of the opportunity. Such a scenario can take the shape of a business plan, a business model, or any other kind of strategic document that indicates the resources that need to be accessible and how these resources are going to be made accessible to the company as well as the potential market. Lemniscates continues moulding its opportunity: although the registration for medical devices is less difficult than for medicines, it is still an important step to take, and Lemniscates has not taken that step yet. The other companies have coagulated their opportunities. For example, Laser ACT, although

it perceived an international market, decided to concentrate on the local market, while TMP decided to concentrate on forming an opportunity scenario further that involves the development of a concrete business model enabling exchange with the market. This business model incorporates the identification, attraction, and combination of necessary resources (Brush, Greene, Hart, and Haller, 2001), the creation of a (new) organization (Bruyat and Julien, 2001; Gartner, 1985; 1988), the development of products or services and the marketing plan, and gaining legitimacy (e.g., Elfring and Hulsink, 2003; Zukin and DiMaggio, 1990). When this leads to the creation of marketable products or services, exchange processes between the firm and its customers begin to take place. See Figure 1.

"Re-Fluidification" and "Re-Moldification" of the Opportunity

Many science and technology-based ventures form technology platforms for the development of their products. Such platforms (Halman and Keizer, 2004) are characterized by modular architecture, interfaces, and standards that allow these types of ventures to develop new products quickly at reduced cost and with a high quality. One type of platform (Halman and Keizer, 2004) can be defined as a global platform: it contains, for a large part, standardized units, but to meet the local demands and wishes, the product is tailored. In other words, the coagulated opportunity is made "re-moldable" to meet the clients' demands and wishes. Such platforms allow architectural innovations (Halman and Keizer, 2004) by going back to the opportunity scenario. The case of Motion Inc. provides a clear example of "re-fluidification." After being in operation for about a year, this venture returned to its original idea. Its original application in the runners' market and the general sports technology market failed. Still building on the original idea, Motion Inc.'s founders decided that the rehabilitation market could actually be

Figure 1. From idea to opportunity scenario

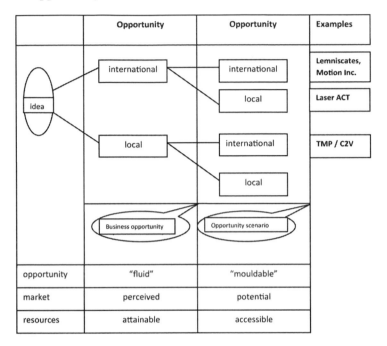

more promising. In pursuing this new market, the entrepreneurs actually discovered wider applications of its original technology, although used and marketed in a different way. Because this new market had its own unique characteristics and required specific resources, Motion Inc. must return to the business opportunity. This example indicates that the process of pursuing opportunities is not a one-way street. In fact, it shows that even after specific resource commitments have been made, entrepreneurs continue to have ample possibilities to make use of the fact that opportunities are not solid but can be remolded into a different shape. This remoulding underpins the non-linearity of the process and the value of the business opportunity and the opportunity scenario. Lemniscates still is in the stage of preparation regarding its "medical device," but in an attempt to raise capital, it decided to start exploiting food supplements for the equestrian market, which is a second idea—not a re-fluidification or re-moldification. The C2V/TMP case, however, is a

case of re-moldification; based on its technology platform as the source of ideas, a new business opportunity was developed.

Virtual Embeddedness, ICT, and the Opportunity Scenario

Global start-ups almost always have a key partner that supports the venture in the first stages of the entrepreneurial process (Kirwan et al., 2006, 2007). This key partner plays a role to "overcome the liabilities of newness" (Stinchcombe, 1965) as well as the liability of foreignness (Zaheer, 1995). Via the key partner(s), the venture can tap into the social capital and other resources of the supporting key partner for its own purposes (with the key partner's approval). Based on the embeddedness with the key partner, the venture has to embed itself further.

Building on the works of Morse (Morse, Fowler, and Lawrence, 2007; Lawrence, Morse, and Fowler, 2005; and Wakkee et al., 2008), we

Table 2. Usage of ICT during opportunity discovery and formation

	info-search/ browsing	e-mail	internet fora, discussion lists
TMP	international	international	international
Laser ATC	international	domestic	-
Lemniscates	international	domestic	-
Motion Inc.	international	domestic	-

argue that IT is essential for a global startup to become globally embedded early in the opportunity recognition process. The widespread use of the Internet has led to additional possibilities for entrepreneurs to connect information that leads to the discovery of new ideas in several ways (Teece, 1998). First, the borderless nature of the Internet has led people to exchange new information with people around the world with whom they would not have shared through other communication channels (Pantelli, 2002). By bridging (previous) structural holes in this manner (Burt, 2004), entrepreneurs are able to connect pieces of information and possibly recognize opportunities to exploit in the real world. Second, well known e-commerce examples have shown that not only can the opportunity recognition process exist in the virtual world, but some opportunities only exist in virtual space, leading to the rise of new industries (i.e., Shapiro and Varian, 1999). See Table 2.

Using the Internet not only enables global startups to discover and/or recognize new ideas and opportunities, but it also enables these entrepreneurs to build legitimacy much more quickly than would be possible in the real world only. By making use of high levels of global connectivity amongst both science-based ventures and their customers, even the smallest and newest organization can make its presence known and recruit others to endorse it (Wakkee et al., 2008).

When looking at the cases, it seems that only TMP/C2V actively used ICT to obtain information and to establish and maintain relationships internationally. The other companies only searched for information online. Given that the Internet is by definition global in nature, this means that they could benefit from the knowledge and insights concerning their technology and products regardless of where these were created, thus expanding the scope of information available. Consequently, the formation of the opportunity was facilitated. The companies used email to communicate with their domestic counterparts during these early stages; they did not use the Internet forums. The main reason that Lemniscates did not use these options was that they actively sought to protect their technology and to operate under the radar at this stage in their development. It is unclear why Laser ATC and Motion Inc. did not participate in forums, but a possible explanation could be that at that moment in time, these were not as widespread as they are today.

FUTURE RESEARCH DIRECTIONS

A focus of future research should be on the processes in which startups return to earlier stages of the entrepreneurial process. Although it is acknowledged that the process from idea to exploitation is an iterative one, hardly any research explores the "return to earlier stages" or the processes that we coined as *re-fluidification* and *re-moldification*. Many consultants in technology transfer offices at universities are aware of this phenomenon; nevertheless, these observations have not lead to research. These processes are important for reasons that we set out in this contribution. A second focus should be on the virtual embeddedness, a direction of research that we are already exploring (Wakkee et al., 2008).

CONCLUSION

Ideas are without borders and are universal; opportunities (business opportunities and opportunity scenarios) are unlimited (but can be limited) when the venture is virtually embedded through the use of electronic technologies (IT). Ideas are shapeless, and in the process of opportunity discovery, they obtain some shape (they morph from a shapeless entity to a "fluid" entity) as the business opportunity. In the process of opportunity discovery, the perceived market needs and attainable resources are inventoried and judged to be feasible either locally or internationally. In the opportunity development process in which the "fluid" business opportunity is "molded" into a coagulated scenario for the development of the venture, the perceived markets should be transformed into potential markets and attainable resources into accessible ones (both either locally or internationally). Every idea has the potential to be the "raw material" for a new international venture; the process of discovery of the business opportunity and the process of development of the business opportunity into an opportunity scenario determines whether the venture turns into a new international venture or a global startup venture. Returning from the exploitation phase to the business opportunity ("re-fluidification") and returning to the opportunity scenario ("re-moldification") are both strategies of new ventures to reframe the exploitation of their activities.

In conclusion, ideas are per definition international. A business opportunity provides a first indication of whether the venture is potentially a new international venture or a global startup. The opportunity scenario yields the strategic direction, an indication of the perceived market with the resources to be attained, and the venture

in developing into: locally or internationally. The pursuit of opportunities is the core activity of any venture, and it often means returning to earlier stages in the process; even an apparent coagulated opportunity (a product or a service) can be made fluid and moldable once again, but in order to be virtually embedded, it is necessary to be able to access future markets and resources.

REFERENCES

Alvarez, S. A., & Barney, J. B. (2005). How do entrepreneurs organize firms under conditions of uncertainty? *Journal of Management*, *31*(5), 776–793. doi:10.1177/0149206305279486

Ardichvili, A., Cardozo, R., & Ray, S. (2003). A theory of entrepreneurial opportunity identification & development. *Journal of Business Venturing*, *18*(1), 105–123. doi:10.1016/S0883-9026(01)00068-4

Bant, P., & Meijer, J. (1999) In P.C. van der Sijde & A. Ridder (Eds.), *Commercialising Knowledge, examples of entrepreneurship at the University of Twente*. Enschede: Twente University Press.

Bhave, M. P. (1994). A process model of entrepreneurial venture creation. *Journal of Business Venturing*, *9*(2), 223–223. doi:10.1016/0883-9026(94)90031-0

Brush, C. G., Greene, P. G., Hart, M. M., & Haller, H. S. (2001). From Initial Idea To Unique Advantage: The Entrepreneurial Challenge Of Constructing A Resource Base. *The Academy of Management Executive*, *15*(1), 64–78.

Bruyat, C., & Julien, P. A. (2001). Defining the field of research in entrepreneurship. *Journal of Business Venturing*, *16*(2), 165–180. doi:10.1016/S0883-9026(99)00043-9

Burt, R. S. (2004). Structural Holes and Good Ideas. *American Journal of Sociology*, *110*(2), 349–399. doi:10.1086/421787

De Koning, A., & Muzyka, D. F. (1999). *Conceptualizing Opportunity Recognition as a Socio-Cognitive Process*. Fontainebleau: Insead (working paper).

Dimitratos, P., & Jones, M. V. (2005). Future directions for international entrepreneurship research. *International Business Review, 14*(2), 119–128. doi:10.1016/j.ibusrev.2004.06.003

Elders, J., & Walsh, S. T. (1999). TMP (Total Micro Products, a micro-electro-mechanical systems company. In P. C. Van Der Sijde & A. Ridder (Eds.), *Commercialising Knowledge, examples of entrepreneurship at the University of Twente*. Enschede: Twente Univeristy Press.

Elfring, T., & Hulsink, W. (2003). Networks in Entrepreneurship: The Case of High-technology Firms. *Small Business Economics, 21*(4), 409–422. doi:10.1023/A:1026180418357

Gartner, W. B. (1985). A conceptual framework for describing the phenomenon of new venture creation. *Academy of Management Review, 10*(4), 696–706. doi:10.2307/258039

Gartner, W. B. (1988). Who is an entrepreneur? Is the wrong question. *American journal of small business, 12*(4), 11-32.

Garwood, C. (2007). *Flat earth, the history of an infamous idea*. London, MacMillan.

Halman, J., & Keizer, J. (2004). Platform gedreven ontwikkeling van productfamilies [Plaform-driven development of productfamilies]. In P. De Weert Nederhof, B. Van Looy & K. Visser (Eds.), *Innovatie(f) organiseren* (pp.71-98). Deventer: Kluwer.

Hills, G. E., Lumpkin, G. T., & Singh, R. P. (1997). Opportunity Recognition: Perceptions and Behaviors of Entrepreneurs. *Frontiers of Entrepreneurship Research, 17*(4), 168–182.

Kirwan, P. (forthcoming). *Early-stage networking in high-tech start-up ventures*. Enschede: Nikos, University of Twente (Ph.D. thesis).

Kirwan, P., Van der Sijde, P., & Groen, A. (2006). Assessing the needs of new technology based firms (NTBFs), an investigation among spin-off companies from six European universities. *The International Entrepreneurship and Management Journal, 2*(2), 173–187. doi:10.1007/s11365-006-8683-1

Kirwan, P., Van der Sijde, P. C., & Groen, A. J. (2007). Early-stage networking: how entrepreneurs use their social capital to establish & develop high-technology start-ups. In J. Ulijn, D. Drillon & F. Lasch (Eds.), *Entrepreneurship, cooperation and the firm – the emergence & survival of high-technology ventures in Europe*. Cheltenham, UK: Edward Elgar.

Kirwan, P., & Wakkee, I. (2007). *An empirical exploration of the global startup concept in an entrepreneurship context*. Paper presented at the Babson Kaufmann Conference on Entrepreneurship.

Knight, G., Madsen, T. K., & Servais, P. (2004). An inquiry into born-global firms in Europe & the USA. *International Marketing Review, 21*(6), 645–665. doi:10.1108/02651330410568060

Knight, G. A. & Cavusgil, S. T. (1996). The born global firm: a challenge to traditional internationalization theory. *Advances in international marketing, 8*, 11-26.

Kuhn, T. (1970). *The structure of scientific revolutions*. IL: University of Chicago Press.

Lawrence, T. B., Morse, E. A., & Fowler, S. W. (2005). Managing your portfolio of connections. *MIT Sloan Management Review, 46*(2), 59–62.

Lumpkin, G. T., Hills, G. E., & Schrader, R. C. (2004). Opportunity recognition. In H. P. Welsch (Ed.), *Entrepreneurship: the way ahead* (pp. 73-90). London: Routledge.

Lumpkin, G. T., & Lichtenstein, B. B. (2005). The role of organizational learning in the opportunity-recognition process. *Entrepreneurship Theory & Practice, 29*(4), 451–472. doi:10.1111/j.1540-6520.2005.00093.x

Madsen, T., & Servais, P. (1997a). The internationalization of born globals—an evolutionary process. *International Business Review, 6*(6), 1–14. doi:10.1016/S0969-5931(97)00032-2

Madsen, T. K., & Servais, P. (1997b). The internationalization of born globals: an evolutionary process? *International Business Review, 6*(6), 561–583. doi:10.1016/S0969-5931(97)00032-2

Mamis, R. A. (1989). Global start-up. *Inc., August, 11*(8), 38-47.

Morse, E., Fowler, S., & Lawrence, T. (2007). The impact of virtual embeddedness on new venture survival: Overcoming the liabilities of newness. *Entrepreneurship Theory & Practice, 31*(2), 139–159. doi:10.1111/j.1540-6520.2007.00167.x

Oviatt, B. M., & McDougall, P. P. (1994). Toward a theory of new international ventures. *Journal of International Business Studies, 25*(1), 45–64. doi:10.1057/palgrave.jibs.8490193

Oviatt, B. M., & McDougall, P. P. (2005). Defining international entrepreneurship & modeling the speed of internationalization. *Entrepreneurship Theory & Practice, 29*(5), 537–554. doi:10.1111/j.1540-6520.2005.00097.x

Pantelli, N. (2002). Richness, power cues, & email text. *Information & Management, 40*, 75–78. doi:10.1016/S0378-7206(01)00136-7

Rasmussen, E. S., Madsen, T. K., & Evangelista, F. (1997). *The founding of the born global company in Denmark & Australia: Sense making and networking.* Odense: Odense University, Department of Marketing.

Rawling, A. (1994). The AIDS virus dispute—Awarding priority for the discovery of the human immunodeficiency virus. *Science, Technology & Human Values, 19*, 342–390. doi:10.1177/016224399401900305

Ray, D. M. (1989). *Entrepreneurial companies 'born' international: four case studies.* Paper presented at the Babson Kaannufm Entrepreneurship Research Conference on Entrepreneurship, June, St Louis.

Ray, D. M. (1995). *Strategic patterns of global start-up ventures: 5 case studies.* Unpublished.

Ridder, A., Van der Sijde, P., Kirwan, P., & Elders, J. (2006). C2V: A global start-up company from Twente. In M. Anderson, P. Van der Sijde & A. Mateos (Eds.), *The Netherlands New strategies for innovation support.* Salamanca: Signum.

Schwartz, R. G., & Teach, R. D. (2000). *A model of opportunity recognition & exploitation: an empirical study of incubator firms.* Atlanta: Georgia Tech Center for International Business Education & Research, Dupree School of Management.

Shane, S. (2000). Prior knowledge & the discovery of entrepreneurial opportunities. *Organization Science, 11*(4), 448–469. doi:10.1287/orsc.11.4.448.14602

Shapiro, C., & Varian, H. R. (1999). *Information rules: A strategic guide to the network economy.* Cambridge, MA: Harvard Business School Press.

Sigrist, B. (1999). *Entrepreneurial opportunity recognition.* Geneva, Switzerland: University of Geneva (Ph.D. thesis)

Stinchcombe, A. L. (1965). Social structure & organizations. In J. G. March (ed.), *Handbook of organizations* (pp. 142-193). Chicago: Rand McNally & Company.

Teece, D. (1998). Capturing value from knowledge assets: The new economy, markets for know-how, and intangible assets. *California Management Review, 40*(3), 55–79.

Van der Sijde, P. C., Bliek, P., & Groen, A. (2003). The exploitation of biotech innovations: a networking model for survival & success. *PRISM Case Ref. 9.3.3*, ECCH No 803-028-1.

Van Der Veen, M., & Wakkee, I. (2006). Understanding the entrepreneurial process. In P. Davidsson (Ed.), *New firm startups*. Cheltenham, UK: Edward Elgar.

Venkataraman, S. (1997). The distinctive domain of entrepreneurship research: An editor's perspective. In Venkataraman (ed.), *Advances in entrepreneurship, firm emergence & growth* (p.119-138). Greenwich, CT: JAI Press.

Wakkee, I. (2004). *Starting global, an entrepreneurship in networks approach*. Enschede, The Netherlands, University of Twente (Ph.D. thesis)

Wakkee, I., Groenewegen, P., & Englis, P. (2008). *Organizational emergence in the digital age*. Paper presented at the Transnational Entrepreneurship and Global Reach Conference, Nexxt Center, Wilfrid Laurier University, Canada.

Wakkee, I. A. M., Groen, A. J., & Heerink, R. (2007). High-tech start-ups & innovation journeys: strategic shifts, culture & networks. In J. Ulijn, D. Drillon & F. Lasch (Eds.), *Entrepreneurship, cooperation & the firm – the emergence & survival of high-technology ventures in Europe*. Cheltenham, UK: Edward Elgar.

Young, G., Ashdown, D., Arnold, A., & Subramonian, K. (2007). Serendipity in urology. *BJU International, 101*(4), 415–416.

Zaheer, S. (1995). Overcoming the liability of foreignness. *Academy of Management Journal, 38*(2), 341–363. doi:10.2307/256683

Zahra, S. A., & George, G. (2002). International entrepreneurship: the current status of the field and future research agenda. In M. Hitt, D. Ireland, D. Sexton & M. Camp (Eds.), *Strategic entrepreneurship: Creating a new mindset* (pp. 255–288) Oxford, UK: Blackwell.

Zukin, S., & DiMaggio, P. (1990). *Structures of capital: The social organization of the economy*. New York: Cambridge University Press.

ADDITIONAL READING

Ardichvili, A., Cardozo, R., & Ray, S. (2003). A theory of entrepreneurial opportunity identification & development. *Journal of Business Venturing, 18*(1), 105–123. doi:10.1016/S0883-9026(01)00068-4

Davidsson, P. (Ed.). *New firm startups*. Cheltenham, UK: Edward Elgar

Morse, E., Fowler, S., & Lawrence, T. (2007). The impact of virtual embeddedness on new venture survival: Overcoming the liabilities of newness. *Entrepreneurship Theory & Practice, 31*(2), 139–159. doi:10.1111/j.1540-6520.2007.00167.x

Oviatt, B. M., & McDougall, P. P. (2005). Defining international entrepreneurship & modeling the speed of internationalization. *Entrepreneurship Theory & Practice, 29*(5), 537–554. doi:10.1111/j.1540-6520.2005.00097.x

Ulijn, J., Drillon, D., & Lasch, F. (Eds.). *Entrepreneurship, cooperation & the firm – The emergence & survival of high-technology ventures in Europe*. Cheltenham, UK: Edward Elgar.

Van Der Veen, M., & Wakkee, I. (2006). Understanding the entrepreneurial process. In P. Davidsson (Ed.), *New firm startups*. Cheltenham, UK: Edward Elgar.

Section 5
E–Business and E–Marketing among Small Business Enterprises

Chapter 10
E–Business among Ethnic Minority Businesses:
The Case of Ethnic Entrepreneurs

Martin Beckinsale
Leicester Business School, UK

ABSTRACT

A small but growing body of evidence (SBS, 2004; Beckinsale & Ram, 2006) has indicated that Ethnic Minority Businesses (EMBs) have not adopted Information Communication Technology (ICT) at comparable rates to their non-EMB counterparts predominantly Small and Medium Sized Enterprises (SMEs). With EMBs accounting for almost 10% of businesses in the UK the economic impact as ICT adoption continues to further develop across mainstream markets could be highly significant. Existing UK ICT policies have also failed to engage with EMBs until the NW ICT Adoption Pilot in 2004. The current, limited body of research is fragmented, provides limited understanding and coherence on reasons of low ICT adoption and lacks exemplars upon which policy considerations may be made. Firstly, the chapter will examine and review the existing body of literature. Secondly, EMB cases that have developed ICT to a degree where they are engaging in eBusiness activity are analysed and discussed. The findings provide a number of options and guidance for EMB owners. Finally, the recommendations point to the need for improved ICT awareness, better business support provision nationally and the importance of generation and education as key drivers.

INTRODUCTION

The role of Information Communication Technology (ICT) is viewed as critical within the economic challenges faced by government and businesses, whether small or large. ICT's importance is often conflated

DOI: 10.4018/978-1-60566-998-4.ch010

with viable and competitive businesses (Levy et al, 2003). Only recently has government policy considered Ethnic Minority Businesses (EMBs) within ICT and economic policy. Most notably the North West ICT Adoption Pilot supported by the DTI, SBS and The North West Development Agency (Beckinsale & Ram, 2006). The pilot confirmed that Ethnic Minority Businesses (EMBs) are not utilising ICT to the same degree as other small businesses (Foley and Ram, 2002; Beckinsale and Ram, 2006). The gap was widest in the area of website adoption and eCommerce suggesting a more potentially significant economic weakness amongst EMBs.

The difficulty for both policy makers and deliverers is the lack of data, detail and understanding of ICT amongst Ethnic Minority Business communities. There have been significant assumptions that the gap in ICT adoption is significantly influenced by culture or language. There is some truth in the fact that these are factors but are only two in a list of factors relevant to all SMEs. Therefore, the chapter reviews existing data (Foley & Ram, 2002; SBS 2004) along with research carried out (Beckinsale & Ram, 2006) across a year-long DTI-supported pilot initiative that aimed to address the lack of utilisation of ICT by EMBs and stimulate the adoption of ICT and electronic commerce (e-commerce) amongst EMBs.

The main objectives of the following discussion and analysis are: to provide a review and critical understanding of Ethnic Minority Business issues in the context of Information Communication Technology (ICT, eCommerce and eBusiness); to discuss those issues in the wider context of SME literature including growth, ICT adoption, new business opportunities and entrepreneurial activity; and to provide simple steps and guidelines developed from a critical examination of identified exemplar entrepreneurial EMBs.

In achieving the objectives the interplay of insights from relevant literatures on ICT, EMBs, entrepreneurship, and actual elements that impact on adoption will be examined. Further to developing the insight is the examination of entrepreneurial EMB owners. The chapter critically examines two cases relating to 2nd or 3rd generation Ethnic Minority Businesses owners that are leaving behind the traditional view of EMB business owners. The cases focused upon have either developed traditional businesses into online brands or operating in sectors not traditionally considered or

perceived to be EMB related and invested in ICT with varying degrees of success. The discussion will examine: How they developed their vision?; What made the entrepreneurs different?; Causal Mechanisms - inhibitors and enablers; Business support and policy engagement; and good practice and why and how this may be applied in a wider EMB context.

BACKGROUND TO ICT ADOPTION AND EBUSINESS

ICT is defined as 'any technology used to support information gathering, processing, distribution and use' (Beynon-Davies, 2004, pp. 7-8). ICT has also become synonymous with the areas of eCommerce and eBusiness and Chaffey (2007) states that ICT is 'used to create eBusiness systems' (p. 14). Chaffey (2007) defines eCommerce as all electronically mediated information exchanges between an organisation and its external stakeholders and significantly distinguishes eBusiness by including additional exchanges within the organization that support a range of business processes (p. 5). The definitions are clear but the ICT adoption literature has generally been viewed as fragmented (Galloway, 2006) and lacking cohesion in the understanding of issues (p. 140) especially relating to SMEs, entrepreneurs and EMBs.

Though wide-ranging, research interest in the use of ICT within SMEs can arguably be classified in four ways although not mutually exclusive. First, there is a stream of research that tends to concentrate upon ICT adoption (Levy & Powell, 2003; Mehrtens et al, 2001; Levy et al, 2005). The ICT adoption literature tends to focus on technology use based upon the purchase of computer hardware, software, data and communications technology. In some instances this has focused upon the differences between adopters and non-adopters (Thong & Yapp, 1995) but government literature tends to be concerned with benchmarking adoption rates in the UK against other G7 countries

(DTI, 2004). A second group of studies examine how ICT is actually used in SMEs (Foley, Watts & Wilson, 1993; Lunati, 2000) concentrating, in particular, on the key factors that influence the success of ICT in SMEs. This research tends to focus on the development of the information system, rather than its effects on the business. Third, studies have also investigated the degree to which ICT is used within SMEs as a strategic tool, with particular reference to the necessary intent, capabilities and structures required within a small firm to exploit the technology (Levy et al, 2005; Beckinsale & Levy, 2002). Finally, and perhaps most pertinently, some studies have endeavoured to embed ICT firmly within the small firm context (Beckinsale et al, 2006; Blackburn & McClure, 1998; Southern & Tilley, 2000). The SME ICT literature has predominantly focused on the stages of Internet adoption. Suggesting SMEs move through various stages of adoption that can be categorised (Chaffey, 2007; Willcocks et al, 2000; Poon & Swatman, 1999). These have their critics (Martin & Matlay, 2001, Storey, 1994). The developed frameworks/models are helpful in classifying the stage or stages at which individual SMEs are currently at the ICT adoption cycle but are far less helpful in moving them forward as circumstances/drivers and influences vary. Tending to be linear models they over simplify a variety of complex issues and over generalise circumstances and economic issues (Fallon & Moran, 2000; Kai-Uwe Brock, 2000). However, this research explicitly recognises the heterogeneity of the small firm sector and questions the presumption that the use of ICT will benefit all businesses, and how, in some inevitable way, all small and micro businesses will profit.

To summarise, the ICT adoption literature provides a number of frameworks to bring mutually exclusive issues for adoption together. Within the ICT adoption literature the factors/drivers for ICT adoption have tended to be focused around: perceived benefits (Dyerson & Harindranath, 2007; Mehrtens et al, 2001; Poon & Swatman,

1999; Windrum & de Berranger, 2003) often focused on efficiency improvements, organisational/ operational effectiveness and new business opportunities (Levy et al, 2005) and SME promotion; organisational readiness (Levy et al, 2005; Levy & Powell, 2003; Merhtens et al, 2001) and external pressures (Merhtens et al, 2001). As Merhtens et al (2001) and Levy et al (2005) point out, these factors along with strategic intent influence the decisions to invest in eBusiness.

The inhibitors are especially prevalent in micro (1-9 employees) and small firms (10-49 employees) as well as limiting development beyond email and basic web sites. The literature (Levy et al, 2005; Poon & Swatman, 1999; Straub et al, 2002; Van Akkeren & Cavaye, 2000) identifies a number of inhibitors including: culture, government policies; cost of implementation; the need for immediate return on investment; considered complexity of technologies like EDI which could require new skills; lack of organisational readiness with many SMEs having limited existing IT resources; a lack of perceived benefits; and a lack of assertiveness by the owner/manager.

The summary of ICT adoption enablers and inhibitors among SMEs since the work of Poon and Swatman (1999) highlights the fragmented nature of the literature and how it has concentrated on generic groups of SMEs, has failed to develop an holistic view of adoption among SMEs and has considered a variety of sectors (Food, Agriculture, IT, Manufacturing ect.). However, one fragment missing, until only recently, has been EMBs. The examination of ICT adoption and eCommerce/eBusiness is documented across a handful of academic papers to varying degrees of understanding and insight.

ICT Adoption and Use by EMBs

The ICT literature (Beckinsale et al, 2006; Levy et al, 2005; Poon and Swatman, 1999) has dealt with SMEs examining the areas or adoption, resources, inhibitors, enablers, commerce, sector and size variations, growth, strategy and entrepreneurial activity. However, the literature relating to SMEs and ICT has a major flaw EMBs have been conspicuous by their absence. According to Deakins & Freel (2006) ethnic immigrants are of importance to the UK's economic development. Through history they have brought new skills, practices and developments in markets and sectors (restaurants and retail) that have been ignored. Figures from Ram and Jones (2008) show, that in 2004, EMBs in the UK contributed at least £15 billion (€19 billion) to the UK economy.

The labour survey for Spring 2004 to Winter 204/5 highlights the variation between full-time and self-employment among various ethnic groups and compared to non-ethnic groups. Across all ethnic groups, including Indian, Pakistani, Bangladeshi, Caribbean, African, and Chinese the rate of self-employment is 16.7%. The highest rate by ethnicity is the Pakistani community with 25.6% and lowest being African at 9.3%. Being self-employed does not in itself indicate growth or entrepreneurial activity. The figures are comparable with the data and findings of the ONS survey (2004). The ONS survey also provides population size by ethnicity. The ONS survey (2004) states that ethnic minorities account for 7.9% of the UK population. That figure suggests a significant economic population that has been ignored in terms of ICT policy development and delivery.

Ram & Smallbone (1999) were, amongst the first researchers to identify a limited use of ICT amongst Ethnic Minority Businesses. They noted that EMBs were significantly less likely to be users of ICT than white owned firms. Only 64% of EMBs used ICT for some purpose (such as for accounts, stock control or 'general purpose' computing) compared with 89% of white owned firms. Their findings also identified 82% of white owned micro enterprises were using computers for some purpose compared with just 54% of EMBs in this size group (Ram & Smallbone, 1999, p.16).

Foley and Ram (2002) undertook the first major study, commissioned by the Small Business Service (SBS), into the use of ICT and EMBs in the UK. Their findings identified a lower adoption rate than in the non-EMB population. The adoption level differed significantly with only 37% of micro EMBs having Internet access compared to 75% of micro non-EMBs. The Small Business Service survey (SBS, 2004), undertook one of the most comprehensive studies comparing almost 5000 EMBs and non-EMBs. However, specific research into industry or sector effects was remiss. The survey noted a smaller disparity with 65.8% of micro EMBs now using ICT compared to 81.9% of non-EMBs. Uniquely, the SBS (2004) survey also identified differences between ethnic groups. African Caribbean businesses adoption rates were comparable to their non-EMB counterparts; but Chinese business owners, at 32.9%, were the least likely to use ICT. Pakistani and Bangladeshi EMBs had a higher rate of use at 57%. Furthermore, ICT use by EMBs was confined to lower level functions such as PC use for word processing or accounts and email. As stated 'Record keeping, accounts, word processing, email communication and research are the five most common uses of ICT among EMBs with employees' (SBS, 2004, p. 2).

Moving from lower to higher-level ICT adoption the gap continues to remain significant. EMBs with a website were in low single figures (Chinese – 3.4%, Pakistani – 3.5% and Bangladeshi – 5.4%) compared to over 22% of non-EMBs. eCommerce is even less evident across the variety of EMBs surveyed by the SBS. In the SBS (2004) survey eCommerce was treated as sales via the Internet or via other e-Networks. As table 1 shows the adoption of eCommerce was highest in Black businesses and in all other ethnic groups was less than 7% for sales via the Internet. In relation to selling via other networks (such as B2B portals and eMarketplaces) the figures dropped even further.

Beckinsale & Ram's (2006) findings, in relation to the NW ICT Adoption Pilot initiative, also

Table 1. Rate of eCommerce amongst ethnic groups (adapted from SBS, 2004)

	Sales via internet- %	Sales via other e-networks - %
Indian	5.6	4.2
Pakistani	6.6	3.3
Other Asian (incl. Bangladeshi)	2.4	3
Black	14.4	0.6
Chinese	0.5	1.7
Other	2.3	0.1
Total (All)	7.6	1.1

support the previous discussed data (SBS, 2004). The pilot, unlike the SBS (2004) survey, focused on two ethnic communities in a single region of the United Kingdom. The two ethnic communities were Chinese and Pakistani EMBs. Table 2 provides a summary of the findings from almost 200 EMBs

Beckinsale & Ram's (2006) examination of ICT beyond basic PC use begins to provide a picture further supporting the SBS (2004) survey. The data did suggest higher levels of email and website adoption compared to the SBS (2004) survey. However, there is a clear pattern of reducing ICT adoption rates and use between PC use and Sales via Internet. Most notable was the extremely limited sales via the Internet and the low adoption of business websites especially in the Pakistani business community. Interestingly however where a website was adopted in the Pakistani community this appeared to develop into selling online especially in the retail sector where as Chinese retail had adopted websites at

the rate of 20% but none of these where converted into online retail.

The gap between EMBs and non-EMB ICT adoption has evidently reduced since 1999. However, the reduction appears to mainly be due to low-level ICT adoption i.e. PC use, record keeping and limited email. This is very much in keeping with evidence from the United States that although not as detailed in terms of ethnic groups, highlights a significant closing of the ICT adoption gap between 2002 and 2007 amongst non-EMBs, Hispanic and African-Americans (Laudon & Traver, 2008 pp. 340-341). International studies that offer a comparable examination are extremely limited. The focus in the UK has been Pakistani, Bangladeshi and Chinese business where as US studies focus on Hispanic and African Americans (Laudon & Traver, 2008). From other areas of the Globe studies focus on Chinese SMEs in China (Yu et al, 2008) and Indian SMEs in India. Therefore, the context is different again making comparisons very problematic.

Table 2. Summary of ICT use in NW ICT adoption pilot

Business Community	PC use	Email	Website	Purchasing	Online Sales
Chinatown	52.5%	45%	27.5%	20%	0%
Retail	15%	12.5%	20%	10%	0%
Restaurant	37.5%	32.5%	7.5%	10%	0%
Rusholme	92.3%	84.6%	6%	5%	3.5%
Retail	69%	69%	3.5%	3.5%	3.5%
Restaurant	23.3%	15.4%	2.5%	1.5%	0%

With Ethnic Minority Businesses (EMBs) accounting for a significant slice of the economic business population and a considerable prominence in government policy towards Small and Medium-sized Enterprises (SMEs) the question still remains as to why EMBs have not played a role in ICT policies delivered and not adopted ICT to the levels of their non-EMB counterparts. Policy makers, according to Ram & Smallbone (2003), are increasingly turning to small firms to tackle myriad economic challenges, from the creation of a 'knowledge-driven economy' to the regeneration of depressed 'inner-cities'. The role of ICT in SMEs is critical within this discourse, since it is often conflated with viable and competitive businesses already engaging in policy. This suggests that to develop policy and detailed understanding champions or exemplars may prove beneficial.

Reason for Lower ICT Adoption among EMBs

The ICT adoption rate variation amongst ethnic groups raises a number of questions that may identify explanations that are in inline with SME findings but also outside the traditional ICT literature view. The studies outlined in the previous section (SBS, 2004; Foley & Ram, 2002; Ram & Smallbone, 1999), have suggested reasons why the ICT adoption disparity between EMBs and non-EMBs may exist but have not examined or explained them. The existing suggestions for the disparity appear to include size, sector, clustering, family support, culture and age of business owner. These possible reasons outlined in the existing studies are examined.

Firstly, Ram & Smallbone (1999) suggest that the lower level of computer use by EMBs could not be explained by their smaller average size. Which taking the general SME ICT literature suggests that firm size is not the predominant issue but may play some role. The research however was not focused on causal effects of ICT adoption

and therefore did not consider other factors or a detailed examination of firm size. It is widely accepted that most EMBs are not just small, but very small firms. ICT adoption may be more difficult for micro-businesses given their shortage of resources (Premkumar & Roberts 1999) and lack of capacity to view ICT strategically (Levy et al, 2001). Therefore, other factors may be at play in influencing or inhibiting ICT adoption. Differences between what are by any definition SMEs go to highlight the possible failings of the ICT adoption literature and support the Windrum & de Berranger (2003) criticism. With the SBS (2004) data showing significant differences between cultural groups this heterogenic view of the factors may have even less credence in the case of EMBs.

Secondly, in respect to EMBs the argument may not simply be age as a factor but generation. Allinson et al (2004) suggest that second generation business owners are more likely to be receptive to ICT than their first generation counterparts; recent surveys of EMBs support this observation (CEEDR, 2001; Ram et al, 2003). The children of immigrant entrepreneurs now tend to shy away from the self-denying life-style demanded by self-employment, with increasing numbers of second generation South Asians opting for higher education and a professional trajectory (Jones & Ram, 2003; Ram et al, 2003). This statement may well indicate a greater awareness by second and third generation business owners of technology, computers and ICT. Where the second generation does opt for business, its members are now increasingly to be found in pioneering areas, higher up the entrepreneurial food chain and far away from the stereotypical corner shop and sweat shop activities that traditionally sustained their parents. (Ram et al, 2003, pp. 5-6). Such changes may also account for the obvious reduction in the ICT gap between the Ram & Smallbone (1999) study and the SBS (2004) study.

Thirdly, the tendency for EMBs to cluster in particular sectors and, as stated by Ram and Jones

(2008, 64), that EMBs are 'lamentably skewed towards a narrowly constricted range of poorly rewarded and fiercely competitive sectors.' is advanced as an explanatory factor as ICT is not seen to be used. Allinson et al (2004), drawing on evidence from focus groups conducted with ethnic minority business owners, points to this as a significant reason for low ICT adoption. The suggestion is that with the focus on traditional businesses such as restaurants there is less inclination by EMB business owners to view ICT as an integral factor to the business. The internal drive of the business owner is viewed as critical to adoption and success amongst EMBs (Levy et al, 2005).

Fourthly, culture, according to Straub et al (2002) can have both positive and negative influences on ICT adoption. Given Yap et al's (1992) identification of social networks as a critical influence to ICT adoption, the expectation is that particular specific cultural traits may influence ICT adoption to varying degrees and vary by ethnicity if culture is a factor. An example of such an influence may relate to finance issues in the Chinese business community where access to investment predominantly is via the family. Therefore, a particular cultural trait to resource and investment is likely to influence ICT adoption investment. Specific ICT research relating to this factor in relation to EMBs is non-existent, although a number of information systems studies have introduced the cultural characteristic (Checchi et al, 2002; Straub et al, 2002). Culture specific beliefs and values, including hierarchical social structures and preference for personal contact (Checchi et al, 2002, p. 7) are viewed to be inhibiting factors where such cultural beliefs are strong. Such a factor may well account for differences between EMB groups.

Finally, Deakins & Freel (2006) point out that the ethnic minority enterprise development literature has tended to point to the accessing of resources (finance and labour), the accessing markets and motivation. The first, accessing of

resources, may well be a significant issues in the context of ICT take-up as well as for policy development. If the use of family and co-ethnic labour is important to EMB development then it may well be that this is the very issue that limits ethnic business owners accessing business support or being aware of the business potential of ICT. The business support issue raises a further question as to whether contextually appropriate support can influence ICT adoption in EMBs. Yap et al (1992) and CLES (2003) addressed this question in relation to non-EMBs concluding that business support can influence adoption but the examination from a contextual and holistic perspective has been limited. Beckinsale & Ram (2006) examined the EMB context. The research findings relating to the North West ICT Pilot found that less than 2% of EMBs had engaged with traditional business support. Importantly 75% of businesses identified business support as important but were unsure of what support was needed other than finance. Awareness of initiatives or areas of support appropriate to ICT development and adoption was non-existent, until the pilot, amongst EMBs.

From the foregoing discussion and existing data, it is clear that EMBs are less likely to utilise ICT than their non-EMB counterparts. A variety of reasons have been identified many of which are represented in the general small firm ICT literature as inhibitors to adoption but also those that are more significant to EMBs. The limitation of this current understanding is the lack of data or as Deakins et al (2003, p. 857) states there is a 'widespread lack of intelligence on the characteristics and needs of EMBs'. This lack of data adds to the consistent difficulty in identifying generalisable causal factors amongst EMBs. As Ram & Smallbone (2002) point out there is an absence of comprehensive, large-scale business databases. The ethnicity variable in current data sets makes it impossible to paint a totally accurate picture. Ram & Jones (2008) suggest that this contributes to the failure of policy development, support and solutions.

Table 3. Summary of Yap et al's (1992) Five Factors (adapted from Windrum and de Berranger, 2003, p. 184-188)

Organisational Characteristics	Organisational Action	System Characteristics	Internal Expertise	External Expertise
The key characteristics highlighted by Yap et al (1992) are company size, ICT experience and in-house capabilities, ICT training, financial resources, managerial resources and time.	The focus is the relationship between the CEO (Business Owner) and support for ICT. Palvia and Palvia (1999) suggested that age and experience are critical factors in ICT adoption success that has been suggested in terms of generation for influencing ICT adoption amongst EMBs.	Examines and identifies the relationship between particular ICT systems and 'decisional and functional problems' (Windrum and de Berranger, 2003, p. 186).	Daft (1998) points to the exploitation of internal expertise such as systems analysts to ensure plans/strategy fit with ICT adoption strategy. However, finding a systems analyst inside many SMEs or EMBs is unlikely.	External expertise can be utilised to overcome internal weaknesses. Yap et al's (1992) research highlighted successful ICT adoption is related to the quality of external advice provided by consultants and social networks.

THEORETICAL FRAMEWORK

To better form solutions and develop intelligence with a focus on ICT adoption, use and development, two exemplar cases (Beckinsale and Ram, 2006) are examined. The cases are examined and analysed utilising Yap et al (1992) framework/schema, developed by Windrum and de Berranger (2003) for the examination of SMEs and ICT adoption. To summarise, the framework clusters successful and limiting adoption factors discussed earlier for ICT in SMEs under a set of five factors. The factors are summarised in table 3.

The Yap et al (1992) schema is potentially useful in understanding the majority of key elements that influence ICT adoption. However, there has been criticism of the frameworks (Windrum and de Berranger, 2003). One of the major criticisms of the use of these factors has been the lack of heterogeneity between SMEs. Especially under the category of SME as highlighted by Windrum and de Berranger (2003) with many studies categorising SMEs based on 'nearly all conceivable dimensions' (Windrum and de Berranger, 2003, p. 186). Another key criticism is the lack of contextually specific categorisations of ICT adoption and a lack of a dynamic understanding of the contextually appropriate enablers and inhibitors. This argument may be most agreeable in

the context of EMBs. Hence, to develop this lack of contextually specific understanding and to go beyond the quantitative approaches of the existing research the focus on more detailed cases offers a qualitative insight and intelligence that is also remiss in the current EMB – ICT literature. The cases where identified as exemplars for reasons that they had begun to adopt and had utilised and engaged with systems, policies that as Deakins et al (2003) and Ram and Jones (2008) suggest are unusual in the examination of EMBs.

CASE STUDIES

Case 1: SimplyIslam Background

Rolex Books (Four Corners) began selling Islamic books to the Islamic community. The business began trading in 1962 from its origins in Bradford and was the very first Islamic/Asian bookstore in the UK. Currently, the business imports goods from across the globe. Countries include: Turkey, Dubai, South Africa, India, Malaysia, Hong Kong and it has offices in Pakistan. In November 2001 Rolex Books began to trade online as SimplyIslam. com (http://www.SimplyIslam.com). The online store offers and continues to offer a broad range of Islamic products including books, tapes and

CDs, clothing and Muslim toothbrushes. These products, as Amazon has proven, can be sold over the Internet.

SimplyIslam ICT Adoption

Rolex Books stood still whilst SimplyIslam made a significant leap into ICT adoption. Importantly the new business and business model was the idea of the Son (< 30 years of age) of the owner of Rolex Books. The Father was happy with the sate of the business prior to the consideration of ICT adoption. However, he was supportive of his Son's ideas. Investment was made in a single PC, email and website development.

The ICT developments that SimplyIslam undertook focussed on software, at the expense of the necessary hardware. Accounting software, stock control packages and web design packages were the main investments along with third party payment services. "We work with an online Internet payment service provider, which deals with all the payments for the goods, but our customer database, and access to our products is vital to our trading. If we lose data, it would be very damaging to our bottom line." The Son added, "The IT system we

had was adequate, but in need of updating, and security was negligible – which was dangerous when you consider we are transacting online," (SimplyIslam.com, Business Owner).

Importantly, SimplyIslam's market went beyond the local community selling globally with its largest market, outside the UK, being the US. Significantly this eCommerce activity was predominantly with customers in the U.S. rather than the UK. Trade was in Islamic goods. Figure 1 plots SimplyIslam's ICT adoption stages.

SimplyIslam ICT Drivers

The Son, a second generation Pakistani, educated to degree level in Computer Science saw an opportunity in growing the business beyond its' local community based market. This drive with the support on his Father was key to ultimately moving Rolex books forward. Marketing undertaken by the Son was also influential in the rapid adoption to eCommerce activity. "Our marketing suggests that in the US there are very few Islamic merchants. Therefore the online store provides an opportunity to offer those wishing to purchase Islamic products a channel to do so." (SimplyIslam,

Figure 1. A summary the ICT adoption stages of SimplyIslam (adapted from Martin and Matlay, 2001, p. 400)

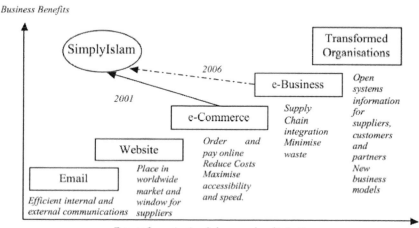

Business Owner). A risk aversion strategy was also adopted. The businesses although based on the same premises trades as a separate organisations. As stated by the Son "The potential risk of failure in 2001 and my Father concerned it could have an adverse effect on the original business meant Simplyislam.com began as a separate business entity and ran parallel to Rolex Books."

The Son was very clear about his reasons for the online element of his business, alluding to a generational gap and the view that business must develop and evolve. "Although I am a business owner I now have a family and enjoy other areas in my life. This business is not the be all and end all. The business potentially could run itself and therefore I would have a lot more time away from the business whilst still reaping the rewards." He continued, "My father has worked tirelessly on his business but it runs his life. I do not want that."

SimplyIslam eBusiness Success and Limitations

The owner was very clear about his reasons for the business and its continued development and evolution. This was notably evident in 2007 when the product offering included the addition of downloads. Achieving this significant business transformation required vision by the owner and importantly knowledge obtained from his education. This was additionally supported by business support advice that the Son had sort in 2002 and 2004 from his local Chamber of Commerce and Business Link. As stated "The support I sort was mainly in the area of general business advice rather than ICT specific."

Although SimplyIslam had invested in an off the shelf customer database, to develop customer relationships, the owner continued to respond to all customer queries himself. There was no automated system in place. A very time consuming activity that as the business continued to grow, the more difficult that personal service response became. Also, suppliers were not fully, e-procurement automated.

There was some spot sourcing e-procurement (Beynon-Davies, 2004) but traditional purchasing methods are the norm due to suppliers not being ready. The majority of suppliers to SimplyIslam.com are EMBs themselves.

In 2005 Simply Islam looked to further business advice and specifically ICT support. When they engaged with the NW ICT pilot initiative the hardware was out-of-date, and no longer capable of dealing with the volume of sales that the business was turning over. The IT system, that is one PC, had everything attached to it, the printers, Internet etc. If anything failed, employees had to stop working. The pilot provided a funding opportunity to move hardware development and improvements providing more robust internal back-office ICT developments, wireless stock control and electronic customer relationship. This now supports the eCommerce activities allowing for new offerings online but also the inclusion of Rolex Books.

Case 2: Tile Mart Background

Tile Mart was founded in 1994 as a family run business. In 10 years it grew to employ 32 staff, providing customers with possibly the largest selection of wall and floor tiles in the North West. Stores are based in Preston, Wigan and Bolton with continued plans to expand. According to the Business Development Manager (< 30 years of age), since 2002, the company had been internally developing its use of ICT to support the businesses processes, providing efficiencies, reducing overheads and supporting the customer. The process of adoption and the growth of knowledge in house involved a lot of research and accessing advice from external sources.

Tile Mart ICT Adoption

Initially two PCs and email were installed and a software based systems were put in place to undertake accounts and stock control. The initial investment was aimed at supporting internally communications of the business. The business then developed, utilising third party web developers, a website (www.tilemart.co.uk) to aid the marketing of Tile Mart and with the potential to sell online. In 2004 the company's web site was launched (http://www.tilemart.co.uk). Since 2005 the business had attempted, to varying success, engage in eProcurement activity. Figure 2 plots Tile Mart's ICT adoption stages.

Tile Mart ICT Drivers

Tile Mart's Business Development Manager, with the support of the business owner, had driven the developments. The decision to develop ICT was focused around clear strategic intent including co-ordination, growth and access to new markets (Levy et al, 2005). This internal support identified early on the need for external help, advice and support. The Business Development Manager made a conscious decision in 2002 to access their local Business Link advisors. They had been contacted via a Business Link outreach advisor, prior to 2002, and followed up this original contact. As stated by the Business Development Manager about the

Outreach Worker "…..he was from and is based in the community."

Advice was taken, by the Business Development Manager, on how to move forward with the development of the web site. Based on a lack of in house web site development skills and a need for a professional online site a third party web design company was approached. The company was one of many on the Business Link preferred provider list. Through the outreach advisor, in 2005 the Business Development Manager was made aware of possible e-procurement activity within the region (Lancashire).

Tile Mart eBusiness Success and Limitations

Prior to Tile Mart's awareness of local council eProcurement opportunities, the Business Development Manager had examined placing bids in local council regeneration projects and had bid and won a contract with Preston North End Football Club. He stated, "The process and submission of the tender was complicated and at times frustrating……… The experience from prior tender failures had helped in understand-

Figure 2. A summary the ICT adoption stages of Tile Mart (adapted from Martin and Matlay, 2001, p. 400)

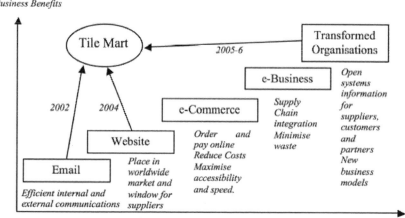
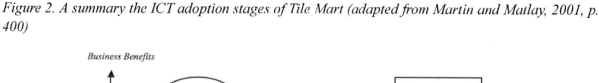

ing the process and delivering improved tender submissions."

The pilot required limited ICT (email and web access only) by the participating firms. Tile Mart had previously developed ICT well in excess of the requirements plus, had a level of skills and knowledge of the potential that ICT could provide the business. The Business Development Manager was trained in accountancy packages and stock control utilising Microsoft Excel. This prior training provided them with the knowledge, tools and a degree of understanding required to make full use of the e-procurement system offered.

Important to engaging with local councils and potentially securing eProcurement contracts was the service and products that fit the council requirements. The potential was identified early on by Tile Mart's Business Development Manager who, having had the opportunity to meet with council procurement managers, understood their eProcurement activity and the requirement of potential sellers, was not planning to let the opportunity slip. Tile Mart is now able to bid for local council contracts and sell and buy products and supplies online through regional and national business-to-business (B2B) online portals.

FRAMEWORK APPLIED TO BOTH CASES

The product portfolio of SimplyIslam supports a positive organisational characteristic for ICT adoption and potential value and benefits to engage with a wider market as argued by Windrum and de Berranger (2003). The understanding and knowledge of the market beyond that of Rolex Books was critical to visioning an opportunity. Further supporting a positive set of organisational characteristics (Yap et al, 1992). The Son also had time unlike his Father who was running Rolex Books day to day (Yap et al, 1992). Tile Mart has moved away from traditional EMB retail markets and provides products and services that are not

ethnically specific. Interestingly, Tile Mart had adopted a Business Development Manager within its small firm structure. The role significantly driving business development focused on growth, efficiency and effective activities that offered opportunities and value through ICT adoption (Windrum and de Berranger, 2003). Importantly, both cases are retail based but in retail where ICT opportunities exist.

SimplyIslam's owner drove organisational action. As CEO he was singularly making the decisions based on Yap et al (1994) and Palvia and Palvia (1999) findings. In terms of leveraging ICT adoption the SimplyIslam findings are supported by Levy et al's (2005) concept of 'strategic intent' in relation to ICT adoption and eBusiness development. Although, unlike Tile Mart there was no formal strategy the vision and objectives of selling Islamic merchandise online supports Yap et al's (1994) and Windrum and de Berranger's (2003) findings. The educational experiences of both differ however their educational experience and 'technological culturation' (Checchi et al, 2002) was significant in identifying potential actions that may benefit the business. Most notably where ICT has not yet been adopted (Rolex Books), IT experience (The Son) through education and training is likely to support adoption and potential success (Windrum and de Berranger, 2003) or as in Tile Mart's case argue for adoption to aid business development.

The system characteristics factor relates to both cases in very differing ways. Positive system characteristics are evident in SimplyIslam. The systems (ICT adoption) being driven by a different way of operating and running of a business compared to the Father. After the initial adoption weaknesses in the initial systems and the day-to-day running of the business outgrew the initial investments meant development was required to continue growth. Functional weaknesses in existing technology drove the owner to identify solutions (Yap et al, 1992) just as in the case of Tile Mart except it was activities rather than technology.

Tile Mart's case the key system characteristics related to a realisation that the business functions in the back office may benefit and add value from the adoption of ICT (Windrum and de Berranger, 2003; Beckinsale et al, 2006).

SimplyIslam's owner appeared to have greater expertise in relation to ICT in comparison to Tile Mart. This internal expertise meant that the owner was able to significantly rely on the knowledge, understanding and any expertise he had in the early adoption stage. Evidently the Father lacked any of these in relation to ICT and its application. Supporting Yap et al (1992) view that a lack or limited internal expertise whether of the owner or of the employees will limit and likely stifle ICT adoption. The Son is the antithesis of his Father and the fact that expertise is evident leads to ICT adoption although not necessarily success. Tile Mart's Business Development Manager had knowledge of back office software packages. His understanding and knowledge was important in identifying the limited internal expertise and stimulating the identification of other sources of expertise.

External expertise relates to a resounding concern amongst EMB scholars (Deakins et al, 2003 and Ram and Jones, 2008). The use of external expertise outside of the family structures is argued to potentially limit business development and possibly ICT adoption. In order to develop organisational learning and therefore internal expertise is can be argued that external sources are required. Both cases, to varying degrees, engaged with external business support with some success. The findings of both cases support the argument that business support can assist the development of the business (Windrum and de Berranger, 2003; Yap et al, 1992) and in this case the ICT infrastructure of the original ICT adoption. Significantly, the role of outreach in the Tile Mart case assisting across a wide spectrum of business issues over time has led to a strong relationship and trust between the two parties.

CRITICAL VIEW OF THE CASES AND SOLUTIONS

The two cases highlight the possibilities of developing and breaking out of the traditional and expected EMB activity to the extent that the business is able to grow and offer new opportunities not available prior to the investment in ICT. Both cases support the findings of Jones and Ram (2003) and the 'technological culturation' theory developed by Checchi et al (2002) that suggests exposure to technology through education and use is likely to act as an enabler to ICT adoption. The introduction to ICT and its potential provides a view of the family business not conceived in the previous generation. A lack of drive and knowledge are two key inhibitors throughout the ICT literature (Poon & Swatman, 1999; Levy et al, 2005) for SMEs but both EMBs have either an Owner or a Champion (Business Development Manager) driving adoption and ICT development.

Strategically, both cases are examples of very different paths to ICT adoption and relative success. The cases highlight the evolutionary/ systematic approach whilst the other is more risk taking and direct. Tile Mart took a more strategic and progressive strategy and SimplyIslam went direct to market. The later reduced the risks to Rolex Books seeing success early with online growth. However, the limited strategic planning (Levy et al, 2005) saw technological problems and significant impact on investment for the owner 4 years on from initial investment. Tile Mart's evolutionary approach has meant planned investment within budget and developments based on actual business benefits.

The tendency for EMBs to utilise business support less than the wider SME population is documented (Deakins et al, 2003). Deakins et al (2003) have argued the case of EMBs to engage with and be engaged by appropriate business support. Evidence, from the Tile Mart case suggests there is an emphasis to developing relationships with ethnic minorities that may have been under-represented among business support clients in the past. From an ICT adoption perspective, Yap et al (1992) first raised the significant issues of appropriate business support or networks. Both cases, although using business support for very different requirements have gained through those relationships. It must be said that SimplyIslam's owner was a rare EMB case in the North West region for seeking business support. Where as in Tile Mart's case business support took a pro-active approach to engagement across SMEs and EMBs. Outreach was common in their particular region and the support agencies in the area undertook significant steps to raise awareness among a wide variety of business including EMBs. Business support in the case of Tile Mart has not only supported ICT awareness raising and advice but acted as an intermediary/broker between local councils and the EMB to facilitate a relationship.

The cases and the findings of the review of ICT adoption amongst EMBs highlights a number of potential opportunities, options and recommendations to consider for EMB owners. Business context will be important in the final decision-making process but understanding and awareness of a number of avenues and options could enable a serious consideration for adopting ICT.

1. With family connections more often than not being the focus for help and advice amongst EMBs the use of increasingly IT and ICT literate children to, at the minimum, build awareness of ICT and possible applications is likely to foster a raising of internal expertise within a business.
2. The strategic perspective seen in case 1 follows a low risk strategy (Chaffey, 2007). Rather than implementing ICT formally in Rolex Books the approach is to have a new business running in parallel therefore reducing the costs and risks to the existing offline brand and importantly allowing a trial or pilot of the business model in an online context. A note in doing this the online context could

develop beyond the existing brand limiting the traditional businesses opportunities. This has not been seen in the cases outlined.
3. The adoption of ICT is not simply about having a web site and selling products on line. EMB owners should be aware that ICT could be utilised to improve the day-to-day performance of business activities. Most notably in cost savings, and efficiencies in areas where paper based systems add time to a process. By identifying those activities decisions can be made on areas of investment (e.g. accounts, stock & inventory control, invoicing and more developed payment systems).
4. Solutions can be obtained through a range of private third party support and solution providers. Case 1 uses Google's own check out system for payments. Reducing the need for complex, costly systems and infrastructure. Be aware to take advice from the experience of other business owners. Where business owner experience is lacking then business support is available. EMB owners must be aware of where their local Chamber of Commerce or Business Link is. A simple phone call (number available in Yellow Pages under business centres, business enterprise agencies) can identify avenues of assistance not just in terms of ICT but other business areas including marketing, finance and law. There are also business support third parties such as Enterprise4all (www.enterprise4all.co.uk) that take a greater EMB focus but are open to all.
5. There is also a need for business support agencies to ensure that EMB owners are aware that they exist. Learning from the Tile Mart case, findings from CLES (2003) and Beckinsale & Ram (2006) offers a precedence supporting personal contact through Outreach that builds relationships between EMBs and traditional business support and can stimulate ICT adoption.

6. The application of the stages model suggests that engagement in business support should not end after ICT adoption. Each business context will differ but the cases highlight that, as time progresses, the original adoption may no longer deliver in relation to its original objectives and new opportunities may well be considered like ecommerce, eMarketing and eProcurement activity. If the case, as the two cases here highlight, business support should be considered seriously as an avenue for ICT and eBusiness development.

FUTURE RESEARCH DIRECTION

Stated early in the chapter ICT has become synonymous with eCommerce and eBusiness. ICT adoption is fragmented. The requirement now of future research and to support policy maker's decisions has to offer an holistic view of ICT adoption and development. Bringing the strands together and supported by developed qualitative research with an action research methodology (Beckinsale & Ram, 2006 and 20082008). An action research approach is ideally suited to the meshing together knowledge of cultural processes, niches within sectors, and informal support networks and diverse sources of expertise, since one of its key characteristics is a 'team-based' approach to investigation involving researchers and practitioners (Eden and Huxham, 1996). Beckinsale and Ram (2006) argue that the action research methodology (Coghlan & Brannick, 2004) not only provides the data and findings but also supports a critical realist (Mingers, 2002) delivery of solutions for EMBs and SMEs.

The family issues amongst EMBs with the addition of transnational supply chains supporting the business activity (Ram & Jones, 2008) as in the case of Simply Islam offers a strand of ICT research not yet tackled. The development and understanding of those relationships, the examination of the technological development and business issues that need to be overcome are crucial to the current eProcurement policies in the UK. This is an area of ICT research in the EMB field that has yet to be examined specifically and would support and provide an additional perspective to the current developments in the area of supplier diversity Migration Policy Group (2002).

Finally, each case highlights the potential opportunities within and beyond the constricted range of markets related to EMBs. The cases 'break-out' of their perceived existing market as well as in a new sector of retail not relating to supermarkets or restaurants and growth and development is enabled through ICT adoption. Further examination across a wider base of markets and consideration of the appropriate approaches to 'breaking out' of the traditional structures through ICT has significant potential. The opportunity here is to develop a body of exemplar entrepreneurial ICT activity within the context of EMBs and applicable also to non-EMBs.

Potentially The Minority Ethnic Enterprise Centre of Expertise project (CREME, 2008) based the West Midlands may act as a catalyst to research that considers a broader holistic view, providing outcomes that not only offer local solutions but national policies to deliver a range of ICT initiatives that are not simply researched focused but 'action research' methodologically focused. Therefore, implementation and delivery being primary outcomes at a national level benefiting all EMBs.

CONCLUSION

The chapter has presented an overview and review of the current ICT literature. The review has provided an insight into the well-developed causal mechanisms for why SMEs adopt ICT as well as the factors that inhibit adoption. The review then indicates the limited insight of EMBs within the

ICT literature but importantly provides unquestionable evidence that EMBs are adopting ICT to a lesser extent than their non-EMBs counterparts. The focus then turned to EMBs and clear indicators as to why the ICT adoption gap currently continues to exist albeit slowly reducing. Evident, is the dearth of qualitative based data and literature. The data have not offered examples or exemplars that are representative of the potential of ICT adoption (Beckinsale & Ram, 2006). For this reason there is a lack of contextually appropriate detailed data and understanding (Deakins et al, 2003).

The examined cases indicate that EMBs can successfully adopt ICT and move beyond the PC Use and email options. Importantly, in understanding factors that are perceived as inhibitors there is evidence they can potentially be enablers. The range of ICT drivers and inhibitors are relevant in the EMB sector. Although not an exhaustive list, the critical drivers in ICT adoption are: the owner; the strategic intent; education; family support; and business support. The experiences reported on here are not unique but, as the data suggests, they are certainly not the norm amongst EMBs. The often-noted reluctance of EMBs to use formal sources of business support (Ram & Smallbone, 2003) was not evident in the two cases. It appears that sufficient time and resources for contextually appropriate awareness-raising activities had been built into local business support activities and programmes. Across the two cases business support was not seen as a choice between family support or a third party support option. They appear to have complemented each other and aid the success of the two EMBs in their adoption, understanding, knowledge and application of ICT. From a policy perspective generation and education are critical to the perceived view of ICT adoption allowing, as EMB owner's Sons and Daughters enter the employment market, to see ICT from a very different perspective. The generation factor is where ICT and eBusiness policy and awareness raising needs to focus, with significant improvements, nationally to business support awareness raising and delivery within EMB sectors.

REFERENCES

Allinson, G., Braidford, P., Grewer, N., Houston, M., Orange, R., Leigh Sear, R., & Stone, I. (2004). *Ethnic minority businesses and ICT, focus group research*, Durham Business School for SBS. Retrieved May 2, 2008, from http://www.sbs.gov.uk/SBS_Gov_files/researchandstats/EMB_and_ICT.pdf

Beckinsale, M. J. J., & Levy, M. (2002). *Hi-tech entrepreneurs and the Internet*. Paper presented at the 10th Annual International Conference High Technology Small Firms Conference, Twente University, 10-11 June 2002, Netherlands

Beckinsale, M. J. J., Levy, M., & Powell, P. (2006). Exploring Internet adoption drivers in SMEs. *Electronic Markets – . International Journal (Toronto, Ont.)*, *16*(4), 361–370.

Beckinsale, M. J. J., & Ram, M. (2006). Delivering ICT to Ethnic Minority Businesses: An Action Research Approach . *Environment and Planning. C, Government & Policy*, *24*(6), 847–867. doi:10.1068/c0559

Beckinsale, M. J. J., & Ram, M. (2008). *SME/EMB action research: A framework for ICT policy driven initiatives* ®. Paper presented at the 31st Institute for Small Business and Entrepreneurship, Nov 5th-Nov 7th, Belfast, Ireland.

Beynon-Davies, P. (2004). *E-business*. New York: Palgrave Macmillan. Blackburn, R., & McClure, R. (1998). *The use of information communication technologies (ICTs) in small business service firms*. Report by Small Business Research Centre, Kingston Business School.

CEEDR. (2001). *Researching business support needs of ethnic minority owned businesses in Coventry and Warwickshire*. Report commissioned by the Coventry and Warwickshire Chamber of Commerce, Training and Enterprise, Centre for Enterprise and Economic Development Research, Middlesex University.

Chaffey, D. (2007). *E-business and e-commerce management* (3rd Ed.). London: Pearson Education.

Checchi, R. M., Sevcik, G. R., Loch, K. D., & Straub, D. D. (2002). An instrumentation process for measuring ICT policies and culture. In *Proceedings of International Conference on Information Technology, Communications and Development*, Kathmandu, Nepal (pp. 1-17).

CLES (Centre for Local Economic Strategies) Consulting. (2003). *EMBs and ICT services*. Retrieved June 14, 2005, from http://cles.live. poptech.coop/C2B/document_tree/ ViewACategory.asp?CategoryID=1

Coghlan, D., & Brannick, T. (2004). *Doing action research in your own organization* (2nd Edition). London: Sage Publications.

CREME. (2009). *The minority ethnic enterprise centre of expertise*. Retrieved February 25, 2009, from http://www.dmu.ac.uk/faculties/business_and_law/business/research/creme/meecoe/index.jsp

Deakins, D., & Freel, M. (2006). *Entrepreneurship and small firms* (4th Ed.). Berkshire: McGraw-Hill Education.

Deakins, D., Ram, M., & Smallbone, D. (2003). Addressing the business support needs of ethnic minority firms in the United Kingdom. *Environment and Planning. C, Government & Policy*, *21*(6), 843–859. doi:10.1068/c0305

DTI. (2004). *International bench marking survey for ICT use*. UK Department of Trade and Industry. Retrieved July 28, 2006, from http://www2.bah.com/dti2004/main/mr_86.htm

Dyerson, R., & Harindranath, G. (2007). *ICT adoption & use by SMEs in the UK: A survey of south east*. Management of Engineering and Technology. *Portland International Center, 5-9*, 1756–1770.

Eden, C., & Huxham, C. (1996). Action research for the study of organisations. In S. Clegg, C. Hardy, & W. Nord. (Eds.) *Handbook of organisation Studies* (pp. 526-542). London: Sage.

ESRC. (2008). *Economic and Social Research Council Society Today – Business engagement scheme for ESRC centres*. Retrieved June 25, 2008, from http://www.esrcsocietytoday.ac.uk/ESRCInfoCentre/opportunities/current_funding_opportunities/business_engagement.aspx?ComponentId=18191&SourcePageId=15428

European Commission. (2007). ICT information and communication technologies – Work Programme 2007-8, Cordis. Retrieved May 3, 2008, from ftp://ftp.cordis.europa.eu/pub/fp7/ict/docs/ict-wp-2007-08_en.pdf

Foley, P., & Ram, M. (2002). *The use of online technology by ethnic minority businesses: A comparative study of the West Midlands and UK*, De Montfort University monograph. Retrieved February 3, 2008, from http://www.sbs.gov.uk/contents/research/EMB-IT.pdf

Foley, P., Watts, H. D., & Wilson, B. (1993). *New technology, skills shortages and training strategies* in P. Swann (Ed.), *New technology and the firm* (pp. 279-289). London: Routledge.

Galloway, L. (2006). Information and communications technologies and e-business. In D. Deakins & M. Freel (Eds.), *Entrepreneurship and small firms* (4th Ed.) (pp. 139-156). Berkshire: McGraw-Hill.

Jones, T., & Ram, M. (2003). South Asian businesses in retreat? The case of the United Kingdom. *Journal of Ethnic and Migration Studies, 29*(3), 485–500. doi:10.1080/13691830305611

Kai-Uwe Brock, J. (2000). Information and technology in the small firm. In S. Carter & D. Jones-Evans (Eds.), *Enterprise and the Small Business* (pp. 384-408). Upper Saddle River, NJ: Prentice Hall, Pearson Education.

Laudon, K. C., & Traver, C. G. (2008). *e-Commerce business, technology, society* (4th Ed). London: Pearson International Edition.

Levy, M., & Beckinsale, M. J. J. (2004). *SMEs and Internet adoption strategy: Who do SMEs listen to?* Paper presented at the 12th European Conference on Information Systems June 14-16. 2004, Turku, Finland

Levy, M., & Powell, P. (2003). Exploring SME Internet adoption: Towards a contingent model . *Electronic Markets, 13*(2), 173–181. doi:10.1080/1019678032000067163

Levy, M., Powell, P., & Worrall, L. (2005). Strategic Intent and e-business in SMEs enablers and inhibitors. *Information Resources Management Journal, 18*(4), 1–20.

Levy, M., Powell, P., & Yetton, P. (2002). SMEs: The dynamics of IS development. *Small Business Economics.*

Lunati, M. (2000). *SMEs and electronic commerce: An overview*. OECD, Directorate for Science. Presented to the Technology and Industry Committee, DST/IND/PME(2000).

Martin, L. M., & Matlay, H. (2001). "Blanket" approaches to promoting ICT in small firms: Some lessons from the DTI ladder adoption model in the UK. *Internet Research, 11*(5), 399–410. doi:10.1108/EUM0000000006118

Mehrtens, J., Cragg, P., & Mills, A. (2001). A model of Internet adoption by SMEs. *Information & Management, 39*, 165–176. doi:10.1016/S0378-7206(01)00086-6

Migration Policy Group. (2002). *Supplier diversity: The case of immigrant and ethnic minority enterprise*. Background paper prepared for the Transatlantic Round Table, Brussels, 15 January 2002.

Mingers, J. (2002). Real-izing information systems: Critical realism as an underpinning philosophy for information systems. In *Proceedings from the International Conference on Information Systems* (pp. 295-303). Barcelona: Association of Information Systems.

Papazafeiropoulou, A., Pouloudi, A., & Doukidis, G. (2002). A framework for best practices in electronic commerce awareness creation. *Business Process Management Journal, 8*(3), 233–245. doi:10.1108/14637150210428943

Poon, S. (2000). Business environment and Internet commerce benefit- Small business perspective. *European Journal of Information Systems, 9*(2), 72–81. doi:10.1057/palgrave/ejis/3000361

Poon, S., & Swatman, P. (1999). An exploratory study of small business Internet commerce issues. *Information & Management, 35*, 9–18. doi:10.1016/S0378-7206(98)00079-2

Premkumar, G., & Roberts, M. (1999). Adoption of new information technologies in rural small businesses. *International Journal of Management Science, 27*(4), 467–484.

Ram, M., Gilman, M., Arrowsmith, J., & Edwards, P. (2003). Once more into the sunset? Asian clothing firms after the national minimum wage. *Environment and Planning. C, Government & Policy, 21*, 71–88. doi:10.1068/c0136

Ram, M., & Jones, T. (2008). *Ethnic minority business: An overview*. Retrieved February 26, 2009, from http://www.oi.acidi.gov.pt/docs/Revista_3_EN/Migr3_Sec1_Art3_EN.pdf

Ram, M., & Smallbone, D. (1999, November). *Ethnic minority enterprises in Birmingham*. Paper presented to the 2nd Ethnic Minority Enterprise Seminar, London.

Ram, M., & Smallbone, D. (2002). Ethnic minority business support in the era of the small business service. *Environment and Planning. C, Government & Policy, 20*(2), 235–249. doi:10.1068/c0050

Ram, M., & Smallbone, D. (2003). Policies to support ethnic minority enterprise: The English experience. *Entrepreneurship and Regional Development, 15*(2), 151–166. doi:10.1080/0898562032000075177

Sanderson, I. (2002). Evaluation, policy learning and evidence-based policy making. *Public Administration, 80*(1), 1–22. doi:10.1111/1467-9299.00292

SBS (Small Business Service). (2004). SBS booster survey. Retrieved July 7, 2005, from http://www.sbs.gov.uk/sbsgov/action/layer?r.l2=7000000243&r.l1=7000000229&r.s=tl&topicId=7000011759

Smallbone, D., Lyon, F., & Li, X. (2006). Trust, co-operation and networking in an immigrant business community: the case of Chinese-owned businesses in the UK. In H. H. Hohmann, & F. Welter (Eds.), *Trust and entrepreneurship: A west-east perspective*. Cheltenham, UK: Edward Elgar.

Southern, A., & Tilley, F. (2000). Small firms and information and communication technologies (ICTs), Toward a typology of ICT usage. *New Technology, Work and Employment, 15*(2), 138–154. doi:10.1111/1468-005X.00070

Straub, D. W., Loch, K. D., Evaristo, R., Karahanna, E., & Strite, M. (2002). Toward a theory-based measurement of culture. *Journal of Global Information Management, 10*(January), 13–23.

Thong, J. Y. L., & Yap, C. S. (1995). CEO characteristics, organisational characteristics and information technology adoption in small businesses. *International Journal of Management Science, 23*(4), 429–442.

Van Akkeren, J. K., & Cavaya, A. L. M. (2000). Factors affecting entry-level Internet technology adoption by small firms in Australia – Evidence from three cases. *Journal of Systems and Information Technology, 3*(2), 33–47.

Windrum, P., & de Berranger, P. (2003). The adoption of e-business technology by SMEs. In O. Jones & F. Tilley (Eds.), *Competitive Advantage in SMEs: Organising for Innovation and Change* (pp. 177-201). Wiley: England.

Yap, C. S., Soh, C. P. P., & Raman, K. S. (1992). Information systems success factors in small businesses. *International Journal of Management Science, 20*(5), 597–609.

Yu, L., Suojapelto, K., Hallikas, J., & Tang, O. (2008). Chinese ICT industry from supply chain perspective - A case study of the major Chinese ICT players. *International Journal of Production Economics, 115*(2), 374. doi:10.1016/j.ijpe.2008.03.011

ADDITIONAL READINGS

Costello, F. J. (2000). An exemplar model of classification in simple and combined categories. In L. R. Gleitman, & A. K. Joshi (Eds.), *Proceedings of the Twenty-Second Annual Conference of the Cognitive Science society* (pp. 95-100). Mahwah, NJ: Erlbaum.

Cragg, P., & King, M. (1993). Small Firm Computing: Motivators and Inhibitors. *MIS Quarterly*, *17*(1), 47–60. doi:10.2307/249509

Fallon, M., & Moran, P. (2000). *Information Communication technology (ICT) and manufacturing SMEs*. Paper presented at The 2000 Small Business and Enterprise Development Conference, Manchester University, Manchester (pp. 100-109).

Fuller, T., & Southern, A. (1999). Small Firms and Information and Communication Technologies: Policy issues and some words of caution. *Environment and Planning. C, Government & Policy*, *17*, 287–302. doi:10.1068/c170287

Jones, T., & Ram, M. (2007). Re-embedding the Ethnic Business Agenda. *Work, Employment and Society*, *21*(3), 439–457. doi:10.1177/0950017007080007

Keindl, B. (2000). Competitive dynamics and new business models for SMEs in the virtual marketplace. *Journal of Developmental Entrepreneurship*, *5*(1), 73–85.

Levy, M., Powell, P., & Yetton, P. (2001, September). SMEs: Aligning IS and the strategic context. *Journal of Information Technology*, *16*, 133–144. doi:10.1080/02683960110063672

Martin, L. M., & Matlay, H. (2001). Blanket approaches to promoting ICT in small firms: Some lessons from the DTI ladder adoption model in the UK. *Internet Research*, *11*(5), 399–410. doi:10.1108/EUM0000000006118

Oc, T., & Tiesdell, S. (1999). Supporting ethnic minority business: a review of business support for ethnic minorities in city challenge areas. *Urban Studies (Edinburgh, Scotland)*, *36*(10), 1723–1746. doi:10.1080/0042098992791

OGC. (2002). *Review of Major Government IT Projects*, Office of Government Commerce. Retrieved July 11, 2005, from http://www.ogc.gov.uk/embedded_object.asp?docid=2634

Papazafeiropoulou, A., Pouloudi, A., & Doukidis, G. (2002). A framework for best practices in electronic commerce awareness creation. *Business Process Management Journal*, *8*(3), 233–245. doi:10.1108/14637150210428943

Ram, M., Edwards, P., & Jones, T. (2007). Staying underground: informal work, small firms and employment regulations in the United Kingdom. *Work and Occupations*, *34*, 318–344. doi:10.1177/0730888407303223

Ram, M., & Jones, T. (1998). *Ethnic minorities in business*. Small Business Research Trust.

Ram, M., Smallbone, D., & Deakins, D. (2002). *The finance and business support needs of ethnic minority firms in Britain*. British Bankers Association Research Report

Saunders, M., Lewis, P., & Thornhill, A. (2007). *Research methods for business students* (4th Ed.). London: Prentice Hall.

Smallbone, D., Lyon, F., & Li, X. (2006). Trust, co-operation and networking in an immigrant business community: the case of Chinese-owned businesses in the UK. In *Small Business and Enterprise Research Group*. Barriers and Drivers for Ethnic Minority Businesses in the East Midlands, De Montfort University, Leicester Business School, Leicester.

Steeples, C. (2004). Using action-oriented or participatory research methods for research on networked learning. In S. Banks, P. Goodyear, V. Hodgson, C. Jones, V. Lally, D. McConnel, & C. Steeples (Eds.), *Proceedings of the Fourth International Conference on networked learning 2004: a research based conference on e-learning in higher education and lifelong learning* (pp. 113-118). Lancaster University and University of Sheffield

Storey, D. (1994). *Understanding the small business sector*. London: Routledge.

Willcocks, L., Sauer, C., et al. (2000). *Moving to e-business: The ultimate practical guide to effective e-business*. New York: Century Press.

Zuber-Skerritt, O. (1996). Emancipatory action research for organisational change and management development. In O. Zuber-Skerritt (Ed.), *New Directions in Action Research* (pp. 83-105). London: Falmer.

Chapter 11
The 'Knock-on' Effect of E-Business upon Graphic Design SMEs in South Wales

Lyndon Murphy
University of Wales Newport, UK

Joanna Jones
University of Wales Newport, UK

Huw Swayne
University of Glamorgan, UK

Brychan Thomas
University of Glamorgan, UK

ABSTRACT

This chapter depicts the current findings of an ongoing longitudinal study pertaining to e-business and the graphic design industry. The research problem can be described as identifying the extent of engagement by graphic designers with e-business. The location of the study is Industrial South Wales: Cardiff, Newport, Swansea and the South Wales Valleys with the particular focus being Small and Medium Size Enterprises (SMEs). For the purpose of the study, the European Commission definitions relating to SMEs have been utilised (last revised 2005).

INTRODUCTION

This chapter depicts the current findings of an ongoing longitudinal study pertaining to e-business and the graphic design industry. The research problem can be described as being: to identify the extent of engagement by graphic designers with e-business. The location of the study is Industrial South Wales: Cardiff, Newport, Swansea and the South Wales Valleys with the particular focus being Small and Medium Size Enterprises (SMEs). For the purpose of the study, the European Commission definitions relating to SMEs have been utilised (last revised 2005), that is:

- **Medium sized enterprises:** Employs fewer than 250 persons and whose annual turnover

DOI: 10.4018/978-1-60566-998-4.ch011

or balance sheet total does not exceed 50 million euro

- **Small enterprises:** Employs fewer than 50 persons and whose annual turnover or annual balance sheet total does not exceed 10 million euro
- **Micro enterprises:** Employs fewer than 10 persons and whose annual turnover or annual balance sheet total does not exceed 2 million euro.

Additionally, it should be noted that the European Commission definition also requires that the enterprises are classed as autonomous.

Since this study commenced in 2001 there has been much academic debate concerning the definitions of, and boundaries between, e-business and e-commerce. For example, in 2000, Turban, Lee, King & Chung considered the term e-commerce and e-business to be broadly equivalent whilst other commentators (Amor 2000; Siegel 1999) believed that e-commerce encompassed a much narrower range of activities than e-business, such as monetary transactions and marketing. It could be argued that not only has this view of e-commerce as a subset of e-business prevailed in text books (e.g. Chaffey 2006; Jelassi & Enders 2008), but also it has proved to be a convenient classification allowing the natural inclusion of subsequent emerging subsets such as m-commerce. Therefore, for the purpose of this chapter, e-commerce is considered to be a constituent element under the umbrella of e-business; with the definition of e-business being taken from Jelassi & Enders (2008) as 'the use of electronic means to conduct an organisation's business internally and/ or externally'. (p 4). This definition can be seen to have evolved from those initially utilised by IBM and UK government agencies; being wide enough to incorporate ICT which is not necessarily internet based. However, it is acknowledged that even in 2008 some authors are still embracing much wider definitions of e-commerce; thus

perpetuating the blur between e-business and e-commerce. For example, Hultman & Eriksson (2008) in their study relating to balancing acts in SME e-commerce development, use the broad and early definition of e-commerce devised by Poon & Swatman (1999); 'the sharing of business information, maintaining business relationships and conducting business transactions by means of internet-based technologies.' (p. 477).

Regardless of definitions, it is an undeniable fact that in the 21st century e-business activities have had a far reaching affect upon commercial organisations, government agencies and consumers. However, there are definite indications that smaller businesses have not embraced or benefited from e-business activities to the same extent as their larger counterparts. In fact, during the course of this study, there was evidence that some small businesses in the UK, having initially embraced e-commerce, were "clicking off". For instance, micro business connectivity fell from 62% in 2001 to 45% in 2003; and small business connectivity fell from 77% in 2001 to 45% in 2003 (DTI, 2003). Despite subsequent improvements in these numbers, more recent figures published by the European Commission (2006) demonstrate that there is no doubt that SMEs in Europe have a lower propensity to adopt e-business activities than larger enterprises. Table 1 summarises data collected for eBusiness W@tch in 2006. The values for the largest enterprises have been normalised to 100 and compared to the results for micro, small and medium enterprises.

Similarly, a 2007 e-commerce survey of UK business (ONS, 2008), confirmed that smaller businesses were less likely to utilise information communication technologies. For example in 2007, of businesses with more than 250 employees, 95.9% had established a website, 80.8% used the internet to interact with public authorities, 67.6% possessed an intranet and 98.6% had a broadband connection: in direct comparison to small businesses where 66.1% had established a

Table 1. E-business index and sub indexes (eBusiness W@tch 2006)

	micro	small	medium	large
ICT Network	41	60	84	100
e-integration of internal processes	23	39	56	100
e-procurement and supply chain integration	34	43	56	100
e-marketing and sales	40	54	67	100
e-business index	34	49	66	100

website, 57.2% used the internet to interact with public authorities, 17.7% possessed an intranet and 78.8% had a broadband connection.

Hultman and Eriksson (2008) emphasised the benefits of longitudinal research when studying SMEs, explaining that much previous research had focussed upon one-off decisions, rather than exploring dilemmas that only occur over time. In this context, the chapter aims to monitor and evaluate longitudinal developments in graphic design SMEs based in South Wales.

Graphic design businesses in South Wales have typically relied upon a staple diet of print-based publicity and packaging material for businesses in a range of sectors. Output varies from producing logos/symbols and associated printed matter such as leaflets, brochures, and annual reports, to magazines, newsletters and paper packaging solutions.

However, much has been written about the 'death' of print and its replacement by web, internet and interactive media. While new technology and the ensuing lower origination and print costs have resulted in the continued proliferation of magazines and newspapers, the increasing presence of online services which duplicate mainstream printed communication is increasingly being felt.

Giffen (2005) evaluated the 'agony and the ecstasy' of the move to digital design and bemoaned that 'at one time the technical process of what designers did was mysterious and complex to outsiders – something that was worth paying for.' (p. 14). This view was shared by Furneaux (2004)

who observed that multimedia tools have lead to a situation where anyone can call themselves a designer, but it is the value of the thinking behind the design message that matters; thus leading to an identity crisis for some graphic designers. During the course of this study, it could be argued that few industries have seen such dramatic consequences of ICT, than graphic design. Perhaps, the best evidence of this was the 2006 name change of the American Institute of Graphic Arts (AIGA). The AIGA had used this name since 1914, but had become concerned that the title, particularly the word 'graphic' did not best describe the wide range of activities (including multimedia) that its members practiced; thus the name was changed to The Professional Association for Design.

SME E-BUSINESS ADOPTION: DRIVERS AND INHIBITORS

Previously in this chapter, it was evidenced that SMEs are less likely to fully embrace e-business, when compared to larger enterprises; although, as will be discussed later in this chapter, graphic design SMEs in South Wales can be seen to counter this trend. Existing research relating to SME e-commerce may help to illuminate this adoption phenomenon.

Chwelos, Benbasat and Dexter (2001), when testing EDI adoption in SMEs, ascertained that there were three main factors that influenced propensity to adopt: perceived benefits, organisational readiness and external pressure. Similarly,

Stockdale and Standing (2006), when devising a classification model to support SME adoption initiatives, devised an "issue" framework which was based upon previous literature. This framework included such issues as: industry sectors and relationships; expectations and realisations of benefits; external factors; technology factors; lack of knowledge and resources.

It is, perhaps, unsurprising that perceived benefits is an important factor for SMEs, particularly as in most 'capital resources as well as intangible assets, such as knowledge, expertise and time are scarce.' (Pool, Parnell, Spillan, Carraher & Lester 2006, p104). Whereas, in the case of graphic design SMEs, external pressure / industry sectors and relationships can be seen as a key impetus to e-business adoption. The degree of ICT adoption of both customers and suppliers has inevitably impacted and perhaps even exerted pressure upon graphic design enterprises when deciding whether to adopt e-business activities. However, it should be noted that previous research (Stockdale and Standing 2003; Mehrtens, Cragg and Mills 2001) indicates that pressure is more likely to come from customers than from suppliers. One facet of the technological barriers for SMEs was initially seen to be relating to connectivity and the digital divide. (Swatman 2000). The Stockdale and Standing research (2006) confirmed that this remains a major issue with respondents being concerned regarding 'connectivity and the ability to access the internet at all times at a reasonable cost.' (p 389.) In the UK, dial up connectivity has been available in most areas since the mid 1990s, mainly on the back of pre-existing telephone networks. However, as Galloway and Mochrie (2005) noted, the telephone wire dial up is no longer appropriate for the volume and sophistication of many business based e-business activities. There is an argument that this connectivity issue may be a contributing factor to the lower take-up of e-business solutions by SMEs already discussed in this chapter. However, it should be noted that other researchers (Caskey & Subirana 2007)

believe that lack of ICT usage in rural SMEs is a psychological or perception issue rather than a connectivity one. Furthermore, the UK Office of Communications - OFCOM (2007) reported that in Wales, rural areas lag urban areas in terms of take up of communication services such as Broadband and 3G mobile. Interestingly OFCOM also reported that perceived service ability was also lower in rural areas of Wales, when compared to urban areas. Nevertheless, it is indubitable that both broadband and mobile take-up in Wales based SMEs is considerably lower than other parts of the UK, that is, 47% having broadband access and 46% mobile access.

Resulting from the inherent industry forces, it will be seen that most graphic design SMEs have adopted e-business activities. However, that is just the beginning of the journey. Hultman and Eriksson (2008) identified three post adoption dilemmas for SMEs that had adopted e-business initiatives:

e-commerce capacity and competence development – outsourcing or finding e-commerce competence in house, e-commerce scope – finding the balance in the use of on and offline communication; and e-commerce development drive- relying on a market driven or an internal, resource driven development. (p. 494)

These post adoption dilemmas can be seen to be particularly relevant to graphic design SMEs and will help in the appraisal of why initial adoption of e-business activities may not necessarily mean continued use of the medium (Simmons, Durkin, McGowan & Armstrong 2007).

Research Methods

The survey undertaken was of the graphic design firms in South Wales: Cardiff, Newport, Swansea and the South Wales Valleys. The firms surveyed were sourced from the Chartered Society of Designers database, and Design Wales: The Welsh

Table 2. Length of time business has been established

	How many years has your business been established? (2003)	How many years has your business been established? (2008)
Less than 18 months	-	-
18 months – 3 years	22.2%	25.0%
3 – 5 years	22.2%	35.0%
5 – 10 years	33.3%	40.0%
10 – 20 years	22.2%	

Design Advisory Service and the Yell.com web-based directory. All graphic design businesses listed in the aforementioned 'directories' were included in the survey. The population of firms included in the survey was 142 in 2003 and 199 in 2008.

To collect the data, a structured questionnaire was employed. The questionnaire rationale was to ascertain the degree to which traditional print-based graphic design firms are engaging in "new media" work, and what effect that work has and will have on the nature of their business, and the type of employees required for business development. The initial survey during 2003 was undertaken by post, of the returns a 23% were complete and able to be analysed. The second survey undertaken during 2008 was distributed by email, of the returns a 20% were complete and able to be analysed.

Findings

Description of Sample

The questionnaire introductory section produced several primary sample statistics. Graphic design businesses with between 1-9 employees accounted for 45% (2003), 60% (2008) of respondents, whilst businesses with between 10-49 employees accounted for 55% (2003), and 40% of the responses received in 2008. The larger business size categories recorded a nil response. The response to the questionnaire, revealed quite an even spread of data relating to the length of time the graphic design businesses had been established – as may be seen in Table 2.

Turnover was also explored in the questionnaire. The volume of turnover for the past year varied from £150,000 to £1.6 million with a mean of £774,000 (2003). A greater variance was experienced in the 2008 survey from £56,000 to £1.7 million (mean £475,200). Both survey samples may be described as having representatives from the two main graphic design organizational size categories. However, both samples may have been more representative, if graphic design firms with less than 18 months experience were among the questionnaire respondents. In terms of turnover data, all respondents in 2003 and most respondents in 2008 are currently experiencing growth in turnover (at date of response).

Further, descriptive elements of the questionnaire probe, into the business use of ICT. As may be seen in Table 3, 79% of respondents considered internet usage to be essential and 88% of respondents consider email usage to be essential (2003). Predictably the 2008 survey recorded internet and email usage to be essential. This is indicative of greater stakeholder usage of email. Further, there is evidence to suggest that the contract approval process is made more efficient and effective. This is achieved via the transmission of draft work to and from the graphic designers' clients.

MEASURING THE 'KNOCK–ON' EFFECT

There are a number of potential methods of measuring the 'knock-on' effect. For instance, the 'knock-on' effect upon workload, recruitment, and expenditure on technology will be explored.

Table 3. ICT usage

Would you consider internet usage to be:	Percentage Response 2003	Percentage Response 2008
Essential Useful Unnecessary	78.8 21.2 -	100.0
Would you consider email usage to be:		
Essential Useful Unnecessary	87.9 12.1	100.0

The location for the undertaking of web/interactive contracts is of interest to both workload and recruitment issues. 21% (2003 survey), 20% (2008 survey) of respondents stated web/interactive contracts were handled entirely in house. See Tables 4. This compares to 78% (2003 survey), 80% (2008 survey) employing a mix of in-house and contracted-out solutions. Of the businesses using a 'mixture', 71% stated, recruiting staff in website design was difficult (2003 survey). All of the business respondents expressed the wish to expand their in-house website design capability in the future (2003 survey). However, given the 'difficulty' in recruiting such staff this may have proved to be problematic. It appears that although graphic design firms still wish to undertake website design in-house (2008 survey) they are still experiencing recruitment difficulties. It should be noted there may be other issues prohibiting in-house website design capability (although 20% respondents during 2008 considered recruiting website designers to be easy); namely, financial constraints, prohibitive operational scale and workload proportion of web-based activity.

The 2003 survey reveals the skill areas most difficult to recruit in are website design (57%), interactive design (67%) and audiovisual design (76%). A stark contrast may be found with more traditional skills. For example, when asked how difficult it is to recruit staff in print based design only 9% of firms considered recruiting staff with these skills to be difficult. This matter was also scrutinized by size of organization (number of employees). When asked to comment upon the ease with which new staff are recruited. All respondents in the size category 1-9 employees stated they had difficulty recruiting staff with website design skills. This result contrasts with the data for recruitment of 'print based staff'. Businesses in the 1-9 employees category consider that it is 'moderately easy' to recruit staff with print based skills. A slightly different synopsis is an outcome of the larger businesses (10-49 employees) response. The larger businesses consider employing print-based staff to be more difficult than smaller organizations. Businesses in the 10-49 employment category consider recruiting website designers slightly easier than their smaller coun-

Table 4. Recruitment

	How difficult is it to recruit staff – print based design		How difficult is it to recruit staff – website design		How difficult is it to recruit staff – interactive design		How difficult is it to recruit staff – audio visual design	
	2003	2008	2003	2008	2003	2008	2003	2008
Easy								
Moderately Easy	57.5%	57.5%	45.5%	20.0%	33.3%	17.5%	24.2%	10.0%
Mod. Difficult	33.3%	42.5%	54.5%	37.5%	66.7%	82.5%	75.8%	77.5%
Difficult	9.2%			42.5%				12.5%

Table 5. Longitudinal workload developments

	2003		2008	
	Mean	Standard Deviation	Mean	Standard Deviation
What percentage of your work is/was in Corporate Identity – 5 years ago?	43.3	5.8	7.5	2.3
What percentage of your work is/was in Corporate Identity – 2 years ago?	38.1	6.5	5.0	2.8
What percentage of your work is/was in Corporate Identity – Today?	36.3	7.4	4.8	1.4
What percentage of your work is/was in Corporate Identity – 2 years from now?	30.0	5.9	3.5	1.1
What percentage of your work is/was in Website Design – 5 years ago?	-	-	72.5	9.8
What percentage of your work is/was in Website Design – 2 years ago?	15.0	7.1	77.8	7.6
What percentage of your work is/was in Website Design – Today?	20.6	7.8	85.0	8.1
What percentage of your work is/was in Website Design – 2 years from now?	31.9	3.7	82.5	8.8

terparts. Given the 'difficulty' rating of recruiting individuals with web/interactive skills, the desire to complete web contracts in-house may not be realised by some firms for some time.

The 2008 survey indicates changes in the skill base of graphic designers. Of the skills that were difficult to recruit in 2003 only print-based design remains in this category. Others, such as website design and audio visual design, are recording scores in the easy to recruit category. This is likely to be the case given the evolution of graphic design education and training. UK based graphic design education and training programmes have responded to the e-business challenge and have equipped graphic designers with e-business related knowledge and skills. However, traditional skills such as print-based design are becoming increasingly difficult to recruit. This may be a further reflection of changes in the graphic design education and training programmes. The recruitment trends indicated by business size in the 2003 survey are not indistinguishable in 2008. Business size does not seem to be a factor

influencing recruitment of specific sector related skills (see Table 5).

Both 2003 and 2008 survey responses reveal several developments in graphic design workload activity distribution. All of the questionnaires returned both identified and forecasted a reduction in requests for the traditional staple diet of graphic design – corporate identity contracts. The 2003 mean data revealed, five years ago 43.3% (standard deviation 5.8) of a graphic designer's workload had a corporate identity core. However, when asked to forecast the proportion of corporate identity work to be undertaken in two years time, the mean response was 30% (standard deviation 5.9). This result is in stark contrast to the 2008 survey, where corporate identity five years ago only scored a mean of 7.5% and in the two years from now category a mean of 3.5%. Clearly the 2003 survey forecasted trend of shrinkage in corporate identity work has been confirmed in the 2008 survey. This development is likely to have been initiated by the graphic designers' clients' customers. Our research reveals that the

Figure 1. Longitudinal workload developments

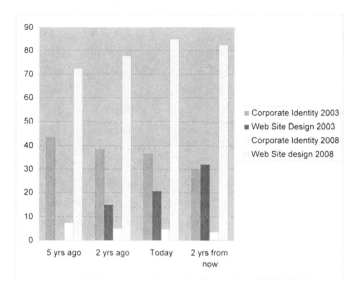

derived demand for graphic designers' work has evolved and is now far more likely to require an e-business input.

A counter trend manifests itself when investigating the importance of website design to graphic design firms. The 2003 survey reveals that in the five years ago category it would appear website design work was non-existent as a function of graphic design. However, the mean data discloses an expeditious growth in website design activities. The percentage of website design work undertaken two years ago was 15% (standard deviation 7.1). The mean figure forecasted two years from now was 31.9% (standard deviation 3.7). The growth in website design forecast in 2003 arguably understated the actual growth. The 2008 figures reveal a greater proportion of website design activity than forecast in 2003. In 2008 the website design score in the five years ago category of 72.5% is indicative of a dramatic shift in workload. However, the growth in website design activity has continued to the present day. In the two years from now category, there is a predicted decline in website design activity. This potential phenomenon may be explained by several respondents stating that requests for newer

technological developments such as Bluetooth, touch screen kiosks and mobile applications are becoming increasingly common. The 2008 survey indicates that in two years time up to 10% of workload could be in the newer technologies. In continuation, the work of Balocco, Mogre and Toletti (2009) highlight the positive outcomes of introducing mobile applications to SMEs. If a greater number of SMEs take advantage of mobile applications then graphic designers' workload could again be reconfigured. The questionnaire responses mapping activity developments are noted in Table 5 and illustrated in Figure 1.

When investigating the 'knock-on' effect of e-commerce upon the graphic design industry it is worth considering the follow-up or after sales service element of website contracts. The issue of maintenance and up-date of websites was raised with graphic designers. The response revealed a clear trend, with 55.6% (22% in 2008) of respondents stating that 'most' of their clients requested quarterly maintenance and up-date of their website. The monthly figure falls to 33.3% (41% in 2008) requesting maintenance and up-date of their website. However, a nil response was recorded for the 'most' category when weekly maintenance and up-date were explored. The 2003 data may have led us to believe that if the future 'knock-on' effect were to be considered, the challenge posed by website 'after-care' may be dramatic. However, the knock-on effect of after sales service has not been identified as an issue (in 2008), even though the volume of website design work has increased substantially. The 2003 forecast of after sale service challenges may not have materialised because of the comparative ease with which website designers may be recruited.

CONCLUSION

One of the leading practitioners in e-commerce education and training Mendleson (2000) holds the opinion that e-commerce cannot be separated from traditional commerce. If this is so, given our research findings graphic designers will continue to work with new media but in a commercial environment with a traditional culture. This proposition is not universally held. Others such as Amor (2000) consider e-commerce as the germination of a sustainable shift in the culture of trade. Romm and Sudweeks (1998) share the revolutionary vision of Amor. They note the asteroid like impact e-commerce is having on upon business.

The work of Siegel (1999) may be considered of particular interest to graphic designers. He refers to the term e-cancer used to encase a host of website negatives. His position in relation to business use of e-commerce has opportunities for graphic designers to add value. He continues by referring to business treating the web as a trade show. This view may provide graphic designers with an opportunity to supply value-added services of creativity in customer focused website design. The 2008 survey results concur with the views of Stockdale and Standing (2003) and Mehrtens, Cragg and Mills (2001). Namely e-business developments are driven by customers rather than suppliers. Indeed, responses to questions exploring e-business activity drivers identify custom-

ers as having the most influence in the extent of e-business adoption amongst graphic design SMEs. The responses also suggest technological advances such as Bluetooth, touch screen kiosks and mobile applications are extending connectivity B-2-B and B-2-C. To more fully exploit such technology customers are co-demanding graphic design output. Therefore to optimize e-business related outcomes it is incumbent on graphic design SMEs to be customer led.

Another feature of e-business optimisation to be considered by graphic designers is that of recruiting individuals with e-business related skills sets. Research outcomes suggest that graphic designers are actively engaging with both educators and trainers. This is especially true of graphic designers' relationships with Higher Education Institutions. Respondents frequently described the active role they play in higher education. Citing examples such as involvement in the assessment of student graphic design projects, attending and evaluating exhibitions of students work and networking with university staff at professional body events.

Given Amor's (2000) proposition, businesses are moving from phase to phase in the e-commerce – e-business evolutionary path. The contribution made by graphic designers has evolved. The survey reveals that trenchant behaviour is not a hallmark of the graphic design industry. However, recruitment and training strategies may have to correlate with the evolution of e-business. There is evidence from our research that graphic designers are managing the evolution of e-business moving to a development phase characterised by mobile applications. Arguably, technological developments may be described as a pseudo customer. In other words technological advances appear to co-demand (in conjunction with business customers) a response from the graphic design industry. Technological developments have been identified by graphic designers and their customers as a factor affecting e-business activity. Therefore, not only do graphic designers need to monitor technology usage/need amongst their customer base but also maintain the currency of their own technology usage. Further, to achieve optimisation, graphic design SMEs need to monitor and maintain an appropriate e-business focused skill set amongst its employees. The implication may be, as considered by Furneaux (2004) and Giffen (2005) that graphic designers may increasingly lament the passing of traditional graphic design qualities and skills.

The e-commerce challenge facing the graphic design industry in South Wales may be summarized by Weisman (2000) referring to the opportunities and threats posed by e-business evolution. The degree of proactivity found in the graphic design industry will dictate whether or not they will be able to survive the turbulence of e-business evolution. It may be stated that to thrive in the e-business environment graphic design SMEs are required to actively engage with customers, technology and network with both trainers and educators. Given the changes in e-business activity identified between 2003 and 2008 it is clear that to at least maintain business survival/ growth expectations graphic design SMEs need to closely monitor the market, technology and education providers. The 2008 survey arguably indicates that the graphic design industry (with the support of education and training providers) is riding the e-business cyclone.

LIMITATIONS OF THE STUDY AND FUTURE RESEARCH

This research project although a longitudinal study remains a 'snap shot' of a dynamic industry. Graphic design SMEs are arguably in the vanguard of e-business change/development. As a consequence an e-business related study of the industry necessitates continuous monitoring. Additionally, in the context of e-business, given the ease with which graphic design SMEs may be established (a laptop computer and an internet connection), the number of graphic design SMEs in the industry changes frequently.

Clearly as identified in the research limitations, there is a need for continuous monitoring of e-business activity in the graphic design industry. It is proposed that future research will focus upon exploring the on-going impact e-business is having on graphic design SMEs.

REFERENCES

Amor, D. (2000). *The e-business revolution*. New York: Prentice Hall.

Balocco, R., Mogre, R., & Toletti, G. (2009). Mobile internet and SMEs: a focus on the adoption. *Industrial Management & Data Systems, 109*(2), 245–261. doi:10.1108/02635570910930127

Caskey, K., & Subirana, B. (2007). Supporting SME e-commerce migration through blended e-learning. *Journal of Small Business and Enterprise Development, 14*(4), 670–688. doi:10.1108/14626000710832767

Chaffey, D., Bocij, P., Greasley, A., & Hickie, S. (2007). *Business information systems – Technology, development & management for e-business* (3rd Ed.). London: Prentice Hall.

Chwelos, P., Benbasat, I., & Dexter, A. S. (2001). Empirical test of an EDI adoption model. *Information Systems Research, 12*(3), 304–321. doi:10.1287/isre.12.3.304.9708

Cutshall, S. (2002). The printing. *Techniques - Association for Career and Technical Education, 77*(3), 26–29.

Department of Trade and Industry. (2003). *International benchmarking study 2003*.

Department of Trade and Industry. (2004). *International benchmarking study 2004*.

European Commission. (2006). *A pocketbook of e-business indicators - A portrait of e-business in 10 sectors of the EU economy.* Retrieved from http://www.ebusiness-watch.org/statistics/pocketbooks.htm

European Commission. (2008). *The European e-business report 2008 - The impact of ICT and e-business on firms, sectors and the economy.* Retrieved from http://www.ebusiness-watch.org/key_reports/synthesis_reports.htm

European Commission. (2008). *E-business guide for SMEs- e-business software and services in the European market.* Retrieved from http://ec.europa.eu/enterprise/e-bsn/ebusiness-solutions-guide/welcome.do

Furneaux, J. (2004). The credibility gap. *Ove Design & Communications.*

Galloway, I. (2007). Supporting SME e-commerce migration through blended e-learning. *Journal of Small Business and Enterprise Development, 14*(4), 641–653. doi:10.1108/14626000710832749

Giffen, P. (2005). Technology's terror & triumphs. *Applied Arts, 20*(2), 8–14.

Hultman, J., & Eriksson, L. T. (2008). The balancing acts in SME e-commerce development: A multiple case study. *Journal of Electronic Business, 6*(5), 476–497. doi:10.1504/IJEB.2008.021183

Jelassi, T., & Enders, A. (2008). *Strategies for e-business- creating value through electronic and mobile commerce* (2nd Ed.). London: Prentice Hall.

Lin, C., Huang, Y., & Tseng, S. (2007). A study of planning and implementation stages in e-commerce adoption and evaluation: A case of Australian SMEs. *Contemporary Management Research, 3*(1), 83–100.

Mehrtens, J., Cragg, P. B., & Mills, A. (2001). A model of internet adoption by SMEs. *Information & Management, 39*(3), 165–176. doi:10.1016/S0378-7206(01)00086-6

Murphy, L., Thomas, B., Swayne, H., Metcalfe, R., & Jones, J. (2007). An exploration of the skill and competence issues of an e-business directed graphic design industry. *International Journal of E-business Management, 1*(1), 22–36. doi:10.3316/IJEBM0101022

Ofcom. (2007). *The communications market 2007 – Nations and regions, Wales.*

Office for National Statistics. (2008). *E-commerce and ICT Activity: 2007 e-commerce survey of business.*

Pool, P. W., Parnell, J. A., Spillan, J. E., Carraher, S., & Lester, D. L. (2006). Are SMEs meeting the challenge of integrating e-commerce into their businesses? A review of the development, challenges and opportunities. *International Journal of Information Technology and Management, 5*(2/3), 97–113.

Poon, S., & Swatman, P. M. C. (1999). An exploratory study of small business internet commerce issues. *Information & Management, 35*(1), 9–18. doi:10.1016/S0378-7206(98)00079-2

Raymond, L., & Bergeron, F. (2008). Enabling the business strategy of SMEs through e-business capabilities: A strategic alignment perspective. *Industrial Management & Data Systems, 108*(5), 577–595. doi:10.1108/02635570810876723

Romm, C. T., & Sudweeks, F. (Eds.). (1998) *Doing business electronically.* London: Springer.

Siegel, D. (1999). *Futurize your enterprise: Business strategy in the age of the e-customer.* New York: Wiley.

Simmons, G. J., Durkin, M. G., McGowan, P., & Armstrong, G. A. (2007). Determinants of internet adoption by SME agri-food companies. *Journal of Small Business and Enterprise Development, 14*(4), 620–640. doi:10.1108/14626000710832730

Stockdale, R., & Standing, C. (2003). The effect of B2B online reverse auctions on buyer-supplier relationships. In *Proceedings of the 14th Australian Conference on Information Systems, Perth, Australia*

Stockdale, R., & Standing, C. (2006). A classification model to support SME e-commerce adoption initiatives. *Journal of Small Business and Enterprise Development, 13*(3), 381–394. doi:10.1108/14626000610680262

Swatman, P. (2000). Internet for SMEs: a new skill road? *International Trade Forum, 3*, 22–24.

Turban, E., & Lee, J. King, D., & Chung, H.M. (2000*). Electronic commerce - a managerial perspective*. Uppder Saddle River, NJ: Prentice Hall.

Vienne, V. (2007). Strong words. *Print, 61*(2), 26–27.

Chapter 12
Electronic Customer Relationship Management and SME Marketing Practice:
Exploring Potential Synergies

Fiona McMahon
University of Ulster, UK

Aodheen O'Donnell
University of Ulster, UK

ABSTRACT

Evidence suggests that small to medium sized enterprises (SMEs) have failed to capitalize on the Internet to facilitate the management of customer relations (e-CRM) and the creation of competitive advantage (Chen & Popovich, 2003; Geiger & Martin, 1999; McGowan et al., 2001; O'Toole, 2001). This is attributed to a lack of influence, time, finance and specialised knowledge, (Carson & Gilmore, 2003) coupled with the reality that most Information Systems and Technology models and tools have been developed from the perspective of the large firm (Maguire et al., 2007; Poon & Swatman, 1999). Despite such constraints, it is posited that by exploring the components of e-CRM in the unique context of SME business and marketing practice that a natural synergy exists between e-CRM and SME marketing in the creation of value propositions. Specifically this is addressed through the two contributing constructs of SME marketing; namely entrepreneurial marketing and network marketing (Carson & Gilmore, 2000).

INTRODUCTION

More than a decade on from the dotcom boom and burst, debate continues as to the influence of e-business and the Internet upon contemporary marketing practice and business performance

DOI: 10.4018/978-1-60566-998-4.ch012

(Brodie et al. 2007; Day & Bens, 2005). Whilst it is accepted that the use of the Internet has become widespread amongst businesses, the *extent* of its use and subsequent impact remains unclear (Drennan & McColl-Kennedy, 2003; Gilmore et al. 2007). Potential benefits including reduced market research and entry costs; customer service efficiencies; and improved customer satisfaction and retention via two-way personalized interactions, are well-documented in the extant literature (Arnott & Bridgewater, 2002; Day & Hubbard, 2003; Ibeh et al., 2005; Martin & Matlay, 2001; Rowley 2004;). Yet there is a dearth of scholarly evidence linking Internet usage to improved sales, profits and customer satisfaction levels (Bitner et al., 2000; Drennan & McColl-Kennedy, 2003; Feinberg & Kadam 2002). Indeed, recent research suggests that in reality, most firms will fail to capitalize on Internet–related opportunities (Day & Bens, 2005). In order to address this dichotomy between theory and practice, there is a need for specific tools and techniques to be developed to help the small firm identify and capitalise upon the opportunities offered by the Internet to create business value (Downie, 2003; Maguire et al. 2007; Sands, 2003). A conceptual framework is therefore proposed that models how particular small firm characteristics might be exploited to counteract the inherent difficulties associated with SME Internet adoption for relational purposes.

For the SME in particular, the ability to successfully engage with and optimise Internet technologies is considered particularly essential. By widening customer access and providing equal exposure to prospects, the efficiency, interactivity and immediacy of the Internet can level the playing field for the smaller organization (Drennan & McColl-Kennedy, 2003; Simmons et al, 2008). The integration of the Internet with strategic thinking is considered critical to SME value propositions, both online and offline and their overall competitiveness (Ab Hamid, 2005; Day & Hubbard, 2003; Martin & Matlay, 2003; Simmons et al. 2008). Competitive advantage is realised through the sustained creation and delivery of customer value (Porter, 2001). The Internet supports this process by providing access to a range of performance and profit-enhancing tools (Drennan & McColl-Kennedy, 2003). Firms that fail to engage are considered to be at a distinct disadvantage (Egan et al. 2003).

Grönroos (2004) contends that the principles of relationship marketing should underpin any value-adding strategy, and the Internet itself has been hailed as the ultimate relationship marketing tool (Geller, 1998; Zineldin, 2000) In relationship marketing, profits are maximised by attaining, maintaining and enhancing mutually beneficial relationships with specific customers and other partners in order to increase their lifetime value (Gummesson, 2004). Establishing and retaining relationships with customers is considered key to profitability, as 'relationship customers' are likely to be less price sensitive, more loyal, and prove less costly to sell to than new customers (Bull, 2003; Reichheld & Sasser, 1990;).

While it is recognised in the literature that the purported benefits of e-CRM are unlikely to be realised through software implementation alone, (Doherty & Lockett, 2008) there is a lack of consensus as to how best to approach e-business adoption from a small firm perspective (van der Veen, 2004). For the small business, typified by inherent resource constraints and their close, personal relationships with customers, (Gilmore & Carson, 1999) it is therefore posited that e-CRM; the use of Internet technologies to facilitate the management of customer relationships (Chanston & Mangles, 2003) may act as a natural complement to SME business and marketing practice. By exploring the components of e-CRM, in the unique context of SME entrepreneurial marketing and network marketing practice, it is proposed by way of a conceptual model that a natural synergy exists between e-CRM and SME marketing in the creation of value propositions.

The proposed conceptual model attempts to align small firm characteristics, resources and practices with the more formal organisational and resource requirements associated with successful e-CRM adoption. By modelling the potential relationships and synergies between e-CRM success factors and SME business and marketing practice, its purpose is to help the SME owner better identify and strategically assess opportunities to leverage their existing capabilities and characteristics in order to successfully implement e-CRM; and to compensate in instances where there are none. It is hoped that this model will help reduce the 'expectations gap' typically experienced by SME owner/managers upon adoption of new technologies (Doherty & Lockett, 2008) by providing a tool which will enable a more strategic and informed approach to e-CRM, resulting in the creation of added value. Suggestions also follow as to how researchers might use this model to support qualitative research into e-CRM practice by SMEs, with the intention of developing an empirically validated model to further inform academia, small business practice and government policy.

BACKGROUND

The Rise of E-CRM

In the last decade, the rapid advancement of e-business technologies have combined with the key concepts of relationship marketing to produce a new 'core communications strategy' typically referred to as customer relationship management (CRM) (Buttle, 2004). CRM is a combination of people, processes and technology intended to increase a firm's competitiveness via increased operational efficiency and improved customer satisfaction and loyalty (Chen & Popovich, 2003). Crucially, technology facilitates the management of customer relationships by linking front and back office business functions and all customer 'touch-points' to provide a unified, enterprise-wide customer view.

CRM traditionally involved the purchase and hosting of specific software (Buttle, 2004). However, the rise in web-based applications has led to the evolution of e-CRM, (Iyer & Bejou, 2003). E-CRM extends connectivity among a business, their customers and stakeholders by integrating Internet technologies with existing e-business applications (Pan & Lee, 2003). The superior analytical, interactive and personalisation capabilities of Internet technologies can offer firms real sources of competitive advantage (Chanston & Mangles, 2003; Kennedy, 2006; Romano & Fjermestad, 2003).

Competitive advantage in e-CRM is realised through the 'dual creation' of both firm and customer value (Boulding et al., 2005). This concept of value creation is derived from relationship marketing; a strategy developed to defend against purely price-based competition (Chanston & Mangles, 2003). Core to e-CRM therefore, are the practice and principles of relationship marketing (Doherty & Lockett, 2008). The relationship marketing paradigm emphasises long-term partnering with customers and other stakeholders as providing more value-adding opportunities than the classic product and sales, transactional, 'marketing mix' approach (Boulding et al. 2005; Grönroos 2004; Gummesson, 2004). Value added by e-CRM includes the provision and management of detailed customer knowledge, more targeted, personalised and real-time customer interaction, cost savings, mass-customisation and customer empowerment (Buttle, 2004: Chen & Chen, 2004; Frieldlein, 2001; Peppers at al 1999).

e-CRM fosters relationship building and customer loyalty in an increasingly competitive and dynamic market by facilitating the effective interactive exchange of information between a firm and its customers (Sands, 2003). The Internet has contributed to heightened customer knowledge and expectations by allowing the easy search, research, and comparison of alternative offerings on a global scale (Ab Hamid & Kassim, 2004; Srirojanant & Creswell, 1998; Zineldin, 2000). Organisations that fail to capitalise on the relational and informational properties of the Internet and pursue a transactional strategy may be at risk of reduced margins, commoditisation of their product range and temporal customer loyalty (Chanston and Mangles, 2003; Day & Hubbard, 2003; Grönroos, 2004).

To date, academic research into e-CRM is fragmented. In particular, the literature refers to the marketing benefits and Information Technology (IT) challenges of e-CRM somewhat independently. As a result, there is an increasing body of research critical of e-CRM's ability to deliver upon the associated benefits of relationship marketing (Adebanjo, 2003; Rigby et al. 2002). This failure is often attributed to an unrealistic expectation on the part of an organisation that technology implementation alone should suffice (Doherty & Lockett, 2008). However, the lack of empirical research exploring both the process and outcome perspectives of e-CRM makes it difficult for organizations to understand how to improve effectiveness in a more holistic manner (Kennedy, 2006; Romano and Fjermestad, 2003). In addition, most IT techniques and business models have been developed from the perspective of the large firm, further highlighting the difficulty for SMEs to leverage e-CRM to gain competitive advantage (Maguire et al., 2007).

SME Marketing

There is growing recognition of the importance of research into SME business activities and practice due to their combined economic weight and unique business context (Hill, 2001). Some literature exists detailing the parallels between relationship marketing and small business practice (Zotanos & Anderson, 2004) and the potential of the Internet within it (Geiger & Martin, 1999; O'Toole, 2001; McGowan et al, 2001). However, there is little firm evidence to suggest that SMEs have managed to utilise the Internet in order to add value and competitive advantage through the management of customer relationships (Pavic et al. 2007). Indeed much of the extant literature points to the small firm failing to capitalise on the Internet by continuing to use it for basic, informational rather than advanced, relational purposes,

which assumes interactivity and data processing opportunities (Ab Hamid, 2004; Bengtsson et al. 2007; Harrigan et al., 2008; Kennedy, 2006).

Despite illustrating that small business relationships can be improved by an electronic dimension, O'Toole (2001) suggests that a relationship approach may not always the most suitable marketing strategy for SMEs. This may be due to SMEs' marketing orientation, which tends to be more operational and concerned with short-term profits (Carson & Gilmore 2000; Gilmore et al., 2006). Interestingly, research is emerging however to suggest that Internet technologies can be used to complement and positively contribute to a transactional marketing strategy (Brodie et al, 2007). Indeed, Thomas (2001) reminds that before a relational strategy can be deployed it is firstly necessary to acquire a customer base. Therefore, customer acquisition and retention are not mutually exclusive (Johnson & Selnes, 2004). Brodie et al. (2007) clearly evidence this link through their empirical research study which demonstrates a positive relationship between the extent of Internet usage and customer acquisition performance; which in turn positively influences retention.

SME marketing practice does not adhere to traditional, large-firm marketing theory, (Blankson & Stokes, 2002; Hill 2001). but rather is limited by inherent resource constraints, and dominated by owner/manager characteristics (Carson & Gilmore, 2000). The small business owner/manager must therefore rely upon, and leverage their unique competencies in an effort to remain competitive, (Gilmore et al, 2006). In recent years a number of concepts have been applied in an attempt to better understand and explain the nature of SME marketing. In order to further explore the potential for e-CRM in SME marketing practice, the two contributing constructs of entrepreneurial marketing and network marketing, (Carson & Gilmore, 2000) are considered.

Entrepreneurial Marketing

While it is acknowledged that entrepreneurial marketing is not exclusive to the small firm, (Runyan et al, 2008) for many, its practice has become 'second-nature' (Collinson & Shaw, 2001). This is due to the flatter, cross-functional structure of the SME; its natural customer intensity and the necessity of an intuitive, creative approach to marketing in order to leverage limited resources and remain competitive (Morris et al. 2002). Despite many small firms not having a specified marketing function, these dual processes of customer intensity and value creation indicate a marketing orientation (Collinson & Shaw, 2001; Jaworski & Kohli, 1993). A marketing orientation, in which firms are closely connected to the needs of their customers, positively contributes to the successful implementation of e-business technologies (van der Veen, 2004). The ability to create value through the innovative exploitation of the Internet opportunity is 'shaped by the adopting organisation' and the extent to which they are entrepreneurial in business practice (van der Veen, 2004, p.18).

A 'hands-on' management approach typifies the entrepreneurial culture and the term 'entrepreneurial marketing' acknowledges the dominating influence of the entrepreneurial owner/manager upon SME marketing activities, (Stokes, 2000) and IT adoption decisions (Riemenschneider et al., 2003). McGowan et al. (2001) characterise entrepreneurs as 'constantly innovative, continuously opportunity focused and comfortable with change' (pg.2). This practice of innovation and change is considered core to entrepreneurial marketing (McGowan & Durkin 2002) and is in keeping with the following definition:

Entrepreneurial marketing is defined as the proactive identification and exploitation for acquiring and retaining profitable customers through innovative approaches to risk management, resource leveraging and value creation. (Morris et al. 2002; p.5)

'Innovative approaches' therefore, do not solely relate to new product development, but rather extend to new ways of doing business (Gilmore et al. 2001; McGowan & Durkin, 2002). Indeed with less bureaucracy than the large organisation and a resulting lack of constraint on creativity, flexibility and responsiveness (Coviello & Munro, 1997; Storey, 1994) the entrepreneurial small firm is ideally placed to inherently incorporate added value across their business and marketing activities to create competitive advantage (Gilmore et al. 1999).

Morris et al. (2002) describe innovative value creation as the focal point of entrepreneurial marketing. Innovation alone however, does not automatically result in value creation (van der Veen, 2004). Rather, it is the 'entrepreneurial perspective' that leads to value-adding opportunities for both firm and customer. This perspective differentiates entrepreneurship from innovation by framing the e-business technology within a specific external market context (van der Veen 2004 p.69). Interestingly, this entrepreneurial concern with creating and eliciting value across all business functions is also in keeping with the relationship marketing perspective (Zontanos & Anderson, 2004). The entrepreneurial small firm, naturally closer to their customers than their larger counterparts, can better identify and understand their customers' needs (Gilmore et al. 1999). This closeness allows SMEs to provide added value through customized offerings (Gilmore et al., 1999) leading to more satisfied, loyal and profitable customers in the long term. Maximising the lifetime value of customers through tailored products and services is an outcome that is associated in the literature with both entrepreneurial marketing (Morris et al. 2002) and relationship marketing (Grönroos, 2004) respectively.

Ragins and Greco (2003) identify industries that have close customer contact, are competitive and innovative as best placed to implement e-CRM; qualities inherent in the entrepreneurial small firm. Morris et al. (2002) identify a number of creative and alternative marketing approaches that have emerged in recent years as being particularly suited to the smaller firm. Radical, viral and buzz marketing, amongst others, naturally complement the tactical, creative and visceral entrepreneurial marketing approach and crucially are enabled by Internet technologies. In a recent investigation into small firm advanced Internet usage, it was the companies that had management, technical and entrepreneurial support which were mostly likely to succeed (Bengtsson et al., 2007).

Network Marketing

Just as the creation of value is integral to small firm marketing activity, networking is also considered an inherent part of this process (Hill and McGowan, 1996; Gilmore & Carson, 1999). McGowan and Durkin, (2002) identify the maintenance of close networked relations by the entrepreneur as key to continuous development and growth of the small firm. Carson et al. (1995) define networking as:

an activity in which the entrepreneurially orientated SME owners build and manage personal relationships with particular individuals in their surroundings. (p.201)

The forging of relationships between the entrepreneur and their networks helps the small firm to compensate for lack of market knowledge by accessing accurate market, technical and scientific information, as well as sharing resources and business opportunities (Shaw, 1999). In order to innovate and remain competitive SMEs increasingly leverage their networks to provide access to market information, know-how and new technologies (Lal, 2002; OECD, 2005). An SME's marketing network extends to both potential and existing customers and suppliers, competitors, business friends and colleagues, government agencies and employees of the firm (O'Donnell, 2004). The innate networking of the small firm

owner/manager is in keeping with relationship marketing practice, whereby the emphasis is upon establishing, developing and maintaining relational exchanges for the creation of added value and attainment of mutual goals (Hunt & Morgan, 1994).

Innovation in both products and processes is a recognised outcome of recurrent interaction between firms and their customers (Håkansson & Snehota, 1995). Small firm owner-managers typically engage in extensive networking with existing and potential customers (O'Donnell, 2004, McGowan & Durkin, 2002). The close customer relationships maintained by small firms can create strategic value and loyalty opportunities in line with relationship marketing principles, whereby a customer becomes a 'co-producer' rather than a receiver of the product or service (Rothwell, 1992; McGowan & Durkin, 2002). As with entrepreneurial marketing, the level of networking activity is related to individual owner/manager characteristics and ability (O'Donnell, 2004; Stokes, 2000).

By identifying conceptual linkages between key elements of SME marketing and business practice and components of e-CRM, the next section endeavours to explore the existence of synergies which may enable SME owner-managers to more fully exploit the interactive potential of the Internet for the creation of added-value for customers and themselves. Competitive advantage may also be gained through the structure of the owner/manager's network and the location of their contacts within it (van der Veen, 2004). Recent research into 'scale-free' networks highlights the potential benefits of dominant 'hubs'; nodes within a network with a disproportionately high ('scale-free') number of connections, to business and marketing practice (Barabasi, 2003).

E-CRM AND SME MARKETING: ISSUES, PROBLEMS, CONTROVERSIES

Successful e-CRM implementation involves the integration of 'hardware, software, processes, applications and management commitment' (Romano & Fjermestad, 2003). However, SMEs' inherent lack of influence, time, finance and specialised knowledge (Carson & Gilmore, 2000) makes them particularly vulnerable when attempting to avail of knowledge management processes such as e-CRM (Maguire et al. 2007). Furthermore, a perceived lack of applicability and uncertain profitability prevents the small firm from adopting and eliciting value from new technologies as readily as their larger counterparts (OECD, 2005; Poon & Swatman, 1999).

The somewhat limited research in this area suggests that in instances where SMEs are implementing e-CRM, their approach is somewhat 'ad hoc' and lacking in strategic planning (Harrigan et al, 2007). While this is typical of the SMEs' more informal, tactical approach to business and marketing management (Carson & Gilmore, 2000; McCole & Ramsey, 2004; McGowan & Durkin, 2002) there is consensus in the literature that a well-planned strategy is a prerequisite to successful e-business practice (Chen & Chen, 2004; Day & Hubbard, 2003; Lin et al. 2006, Pavic et al., 2007). Without prior development of a strategy dedicated to improved identification, understanding and retention of the most profitable customers, purely technical e-CRM application is likely to meet with failure, negatively impacting upon the business as a whole (Lin et al, 2006; Ramsey et al. 2003; Rigby et al, 2002). Without planning, Pavic et al. (2007) contend that 'it is difficult for SMEs to succeed and create competitive advantage in this new virtual environment.' (p.323)

Relating to the above discussion, there is clearly confusion present in the extant literature in relation to e-CRM and its relevance to SMEs in affording competitive advantage. This is not surprising given the lack of empirical research pertaining to the use of the Internet for marketing purposes by SMEs, (Dandridge & Levenburg, 2000) and the generally discursive and dichotomous nature of the literature detailing its importance (Downie, 2003). In addition there is limited, in-depth research into the relevance and practice of CRM by SMEs and the role that technology plays, (McGowan & Durkin, 2002). While some models have been developed detailing the factors that contribute to e-CRM success (Chen & Chen, 2004; Day & Hubbard, 2003; Lin et al. 2006; Romano & Fjermestad, 2003) with the exception of that of Doherty & Lockett (2008) they have been developed with the larger organisation in mind. There is a need, therefore, for 'models, tools, techniques and methodologies' (Maguire et al. 2007) to be developed for the entrepreneurial small firm with its unique characteristics, to help enable it to derive sustainable competitive advantage from e-business strategies such as e-CRM (Downie, 2003; Harrigan et al. 2008; Haynes et al. 1998; Sands, 2003).

A review of the literature pertaining to e-CRM implementation and practice identifies several factors as fundamental to e-CRM success. Romano & Fjermestad (2003) categorise the five key e-CRM influences as: 'Markets, Business Models, Human Factors, e-CRM Technology and Knowledge Management'. Change and knowledge management processes are considered necessary to ensure employee buy-in and a market-orientated organisational culture (Bradshaw and Brash, 2001; Chen & Chen, 2004; Doherty & Lockett, 2008; Lin et al. 2006; Romano & Fjermestad, 2003). Adequate resources and infrastructure are required to support the alignment and integration of e-CRM technologies with existing Information Systems and business strategies (Doherty & Lockett, 2008; Lin et al. 2006, Chen & Chen, 2004; Romano & Fjermestad, 2003; Bradshaw and Brash, 2001). Finally, senior management leadership and commitment is considered core to the success of e-CRM operations (Bengtsson, 2007; Buttle, 2004; Chen & Chen, 2004; Lin et al. 2006).

At first, these proposed frameworks appear to conflict with the characteristics of SME marketing, suggesting that fully integrated e-CRM requires significant competencies and resources and may therefore be beyond the reach of the small firm. For example, the small firm has limited capabilities when it comes to accessing and processing information (McGowan & Durkin, 2002). A recent study by Maguire et al. (2007) cited financial constraints and a lack of technical and business expertise as barriers to SMEs effectively implementing IT/IS strategies to gain competitive advantage.

Much of SME marketing practice is unplanned and deficient of a long-term market-orientated focus (Blankson & Stokes, 2002, pg.49). This somewhat contradicts the formal, planned approach required for e-CRM. In relation to the use of the Internet for relational purposes specifically, McGowan et al, (2001) conclude that even when an owner-manager has technological competence and an awareness of the importance of the Internet, they are often unable to appreciate the valuable contribution it can make to their business relationships and treat it instead as an informational tool.

However, despite these obvious restrictions in relation to the implementation of e-CRM and the practice of marketing in general, SMEs do manage to survive and grow. Indeed the above critique is based upon models mainly developed for large firm practice, which clearly do not make allowances for the unique context of the smaller firm. If taken instead from the perspective of SME marketing; there are natural linkages with relationship marketing (Zotanos & Anderson, 2004; McGowan et al. 2001). Furthermore, while acknowledging the necessity of the adequate provision of resources to develop and support CRM initiatives, Day and Bens (2005) claim that this does not automatically translate into the purchase or pioneering use of Information Technology. Rather, they emphasise that it is companies who already excel at managing customer relationships and whose customers perceive significant differences in their value offering that are best positioned to gain from e-CRM. Those companies with a 'relationship leader' are better not only at anticipating how to exploit the Internet but also deploy it more quickly and effectively. It could be argued, therefore, that the entrepreneurial SME with a marketing orientation (Bengtsson, 2007; Blanskon & Stokes, 2002) will be ideally positioned to gain from the competitive opportunities offered by e-CRM (Baumeister, 2002; Sands, 2003). This is in keeping with Day & Bens' (2005) findings which suggest that smaller firms more readily recognize the Internet as an additional channel with which to reach their customers.

SME/E-CRM Synergy: Opportunities and Implications

While the SME's focus on short term profits could be considered a somewhat transactional approach to marketing, from the above discussion it is apparent that they inherently practice relationship marketing through their entrepreneurial and networking endeavours. E-CRM should therefore be viewed as a natural complement to SME marketing activity. E-CRM provides SMEs with the opportunity to enhance, not replace, existing communications channels and practices by improving the management of customer information and the delivery of value through increasingly personalised, two-way interactions (Kennedy, 2006; Scullin et al. 2004; Swatman, 2000).

In the case of the SME, trust and credibility between external network partners is intrinsically linked to interpersonal interactions (McGowan & Durkin, 2002). Research by Geiger & Martin (1999) suggests a preference on the part of both the small firm owner/manager and their customers for face to face contact. The social relationship with customers differentiates SME business practice from that of the larger firm and can provide them with a competitive edge (Ragins & Greco, 2003). Economic opportunities can be realized through the exchange of knowledge, learning and problem-solving endeavours between inter-firm relationships characterized by trust (Uzzi, 1997). However, SME owner managers should be able to leverage the high levels of intimacy and trust they enjoy as a result of their extensive, proactive networking (O'Donnell, 2004) to introduce an additional electronic dimension to the relationship. Indeed, Bauer et al. (2002) contend that the use of Internet technologies is most appropriate in established face-to-face relationships, where trust is already established. When used creatively, personalisation and on-line interactivity has been shown to help forge emotional connections with customers in ways that no other medium can (Weiss, 1999). Research by Brodie et al. (2007) reveals that despite an increase in Internet penetration amongst businesses, face to face, personal contact remains core to fostering customer relationships and encouraging retention. Recognising and accepting the Internet as a channel to supplement, rather than substitute, existing relationships is therefore crucial. Furthermore, a more in-depth understanding of customer behaviour, buying patterns and profitability as a result of e-CRM technology and practice can inform the allocation of resources, both *off-line* as well as on. (Buttle, 2004)

There are a number of online e-CRM methods and tools that small business managers can use to add value and enhance competitiveness, of which many are tactical in nature (Morris et al., 2002). In addition to a web presence, assessing interest or increasing awareness of products and services can be addressed via on-line mailing lists, participation in discussion groups and the organisation of on-line focus groups (Dandridge and Levenburg, 2000). By participating in online industry forums, browsing competitor web sites or signing-up to government portals, small firms could easily and effectively supplement information that they would normally gather from trade shows and business seminars (Sands, 2003). Existing customer relationships may benefit

from e-bulletins, personalised web pages, or the opportunity to customise products or services online (Sands, 2003). In relationships with potential customers the electronic personalisation of the relationship via relevant and timely emails may help encourage purchase and strengthen relationship ties (Chanston & Mangles, 2003). Such online tools and applications enable small firms to firstly 'experiment' at relatively low cost and risk, in order to learn how e-CRM can contribute to, and augment existing business relationships, before investing resources in specialised database technologies.

Ultimately, the successful integration of online and offline channels in the management of network relationships will rely upon the ability of the entrepreneur to appropriately balance personal relationships with more remote electronic relationships (McGowan & Durkin, 2002). Both the owner/manager and the networks members' acceptance or resistance to online channels could impede first level adoption of the Internet (Howcroft and Durkin, 2000) and consequently its advanced usage for relational, interactive purposes. Prowess with Internet technologies (Day & Hubbard, 2003) or in the case of the small firm an 'Internet champion' (Mehrtens et al., 2001; Bengtsson, 2007) is required if e-CRM is to be successfully integrated with existing business routines. Management leadership and employee support are incremental to e-CRM, with the small firm's close workforce ties considered an added advantage (Bengtsson, 2007; Doherty & Lockett, 2008). Finally, before implementing Internet technologies all firms regardless of size must identify how e-CRM can be utilised to augment their value proposition, by carefully considering the product or service offering and the market environment in which they operate (Day and Hubbard, 2003; Howcroft & Durkin, 2000).

SME/E-CRM Synergy: A Conceptual Model

In light of the above discussion, is posited that there is a synergy between e-CRM and the entrepreneurial and networking components of SME marketing for the creation of added value. While it also acknowledges that there are inherent characteristics of the small firm that conflict with the factors considered to contribute to successful e-CRM integration and implementation; one should not necessarily negate the other.

The following conceptual model (Figure 1) was developed from the extant literature, and interprets the potential synergy between more formal e-CRM approaches and informal SME characteristics. The factors detailed in the literature as critical to the success of e-CRM, (Bengtsson, 2007; Day and Hubbard, 2003; Day & Lockett, Chen & Chen, 2004; Lin et al. 2006, Romano & Fjermestad, 2003) were combined and categorised, and an attempt

made to align them with SME characteristics to illustrate where a natural synergy may or may not exist. 'Conditions' refers to the organisational culture or climate necessary for e-CRM to flourish. 'Processes' recognises the formal business strategies and approaches required for successful e-CRM, and 'resources' identifies the individual resource requirements needed to implement e-CRM. These success factors mostly relate to the larger organization and the implementation of specific e-CRM software. The model therefore attempts to incorporate both the small business context and the potential offered by the Internet, which is comparatively lower risk and lower cost than specific e-CRM software applications.

As discussed in the literature, the 'outcome' of successful e-CRM is added value. Therefore the conditions, processes and resources categorised as formal e-CRM success factors positively contribute to the creation of added value. In the conceptual model this is illustrated by arrows

Figure 1.

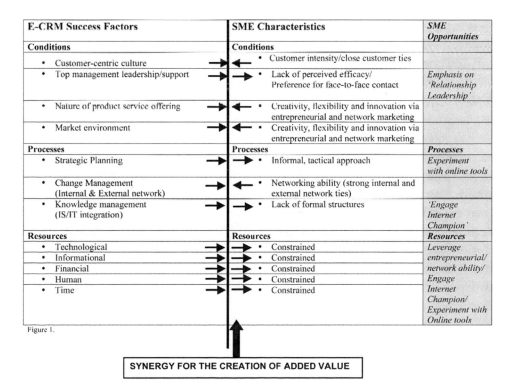

Figure 1.

pointing inwards. In the case of the SME, the characteristics associated with the creation of added value, and which naturally complement the more formal components of successful e-CRM, have also been attributed inward-pointing arrows. In instances whereby SME characteristics conflict with elements of the formal e-CRM approach, and thus hinder the creation of value, the arrows point away from the central line of synergy. The third column makes tentative suggestions, again drawn from the literature reviewed, as to how entrepreneurial capabilities, online tools and additional human resources may be leveraged further by the SME to lessen the potential 'risk' areas associated with small firm e-CRM implementation.

The model goes some way to illustrate where natural synergies, and therefore opportunities, may exist for SMEs to leverage their unique characteristics to optimise the Internet for competitive impact. Furthermore, it highlights the potential 'risk' areas such as lack of perceived efficacy; (OECD, 2005; Poon & Swatman, 1999) preference for face to face contact; (Geiger & Martin, 1999; McGowan & Durkin, 2002) informal, unstructured approach to business processes (Carson & Gilmore, 2000; McCole & Ramsey, 2004) and lack of resources (Maguire et al., 2007) which could perhaps inhibit or undermine the successful implementation of e-CRM in SMEs. There is a suggestion in the literature that existing theoretical frameworks, and the extension thereof, no longer adequately address the competitive complexities of the contemporary marketplace (Morris et al. 2002). In the SME context, Harrigan et al. (2008) suggest that in order to capitalize upon the Internet for the management of customer relationships, small firms must draw upon their own 'entrepreneurial style' to develop suitable strategies. By introducing the constructs of network and entrepreneurial marketing in relation to e-CRM, it is therefore proposed that the more inherent and developed the entrepreneurial and networking ability of the small firm, the better placed they are to develop unique Internet strategies which will positively

impact upon the creation and maintenance of valuable customer relationships (e-CRM).

Finally, it is generally accepted that E-business adoption is a continuous process (Wu et al., 2003). The more a firm engages in Internet activities, even at a tactical level, the greater the perceived performance (Drennan & McColl-Kennedy, 2003; Morris et al.) and the increased likelihood of advanced Internet usage (Dholakia & Kshetri (2004). It is proposed by way of the conceptual model therefore, that the small firm which displays a willingness to experiment by seeking advice from an Internet champion (Bengtsson, 2007; Merhtens et al. 2001) via their networks, or by proactively appointing one, is more likely to overcome the difficulties associated with small firm e-CRM adoption and implementation.

CONCLUSION AND FUTURE RESEARCH

While there is a growing body of literature concerning the use of the Internet as a strategic customer relationship management tool, there is little empirical evidence linking Internet usage amongst small firms with improved customer retention and profitability (Ab Hamid & Kassim, 2004; Dandridge & Levenburg, 2000; Drennan & McColl-Kennedy, 2003). Consequently, this first-stage model is proposed as a means to explore both how, and to what extent SMEs are using the Internet to augment their value proposition and facilitate customer relationships, retention and loyalty.

In particular, this model not only identifies the organisational conditions, processes and resources necessary for successful e-CRM implementation, but also anticipates the small firm characteristics and opportunities that can best support the use of the Internet for advanced relational purposes. It is proposed that this conceptual model can be further developed and used in longitudinal case studies of SMEs to explore if, and how, they leverage their unique capabilities and characteristics to support these 'natural synergies' by incorporating e-CRM into their existing business practices; and compensate in the instances where there are none.

Brodie et al. (2008) call for in-depth, qualitative research with exemplar firms to help better understand how and under what conditions the Internet can optimally influence business and marketing practice. A purposive sample of 'brick and click' SMES is therefore proposed, whereby firms are selected based upon their level of integration of Internet technologies with existing processes. Further, it would be of interest to apply the model to firms from less technologically advanced regions with those from 'first wave' adopter countries, (Fletcher et al. 2004) or to compare firms from differing industry sectors. The desired outcome of such research would be to establish an empirically validated framework, specific to SMEs. This would allow small form owner/managers to understand through the experiences of their peers, Internet usage patterns to become more competitive through the development of successful e-CRM strategies (Downie, 2003; Haynes et al, 1998; Sands 2003).

REFERENCES

Ab Hamid, N. R. (2005). E-CRM: Are we there yet? *The Journal of American Academy of Business*, 6(1), 51–57.

Ab Hamid, N. R., & Kassim, N. (2004). Internet technology as a tool in customer relationship management. *The Journal of American Academy of Business*, 4(1/2), 103–108.

Adebanjo, D. (2003). 'Classifying and selecting e-CRM applications: an analysis-based proposal. *Management Decision, 41*(6), 570–577. doi:10.1108/00251740310491517

Arnott, D. C., & Bridgewater, S. (2002). Internet, interaction and implications for marketing. *Marketing Intelligence & Planning, 20*(2), 86–95. doi:10.1108/02634500210418509

Barabasi, A. L., & Bonabeay, E. (2003). Scale-free networks. *Scientific American, 288*(5), 60–70.

Bauer, H. H., Gretner, M., & Leach, M. (2002). Building customer relations over the Internet. *Industrial Marketing Management, 31*(2), 155–163. doi:10.1016/S0019-8501(01)00186-9

Baumeister, H. (2002, October). Customer relationship management for SMEs, e2000 e-business & e-work. In *Proceedings of the E2002 Conference*, Prague

Bengtsson, M., Boter, H., & Vanyushyn, V. (2007). Integrating the Internet and marketing operations: A study of antecedents in firms of different size. *International Small Business Journal, 25*(1), 27–48. doi:10.1177/0266242607071780

Berry, L.L. (1995). Relationship marketing of services – Growing interest, emerging perspectives. *Journal of Academy of Marketing Science, 23*(fall), 236-245.

Bitner, M. J., Brown, S. W., & Meuter, M. L. (2000). Technology infusion in service encounters. *Journal of the Academy of Marketing Science, 28*(1), 138–149. doi:10.1177/0092070300281013

Blankson, C., & Stokes, D. (2002). Marketing practices in the UK small business sector. *Marketing Intelligence & Planning, 20*(1), 49–61. doi:10.1108/02634500210414774

Boulding, W., Staelin, R., Ehret, M., & Johnston, W. J. (2005). A customer relationship management roadmap: what is known, potential pitfalls, and where to go. *Journal of Marketing, 69*(4), 155–166. doi:10.1509/jmkg.2005.69.4.155

Bradshaw, D., & Brash, C. (2001). Managing customer relationships in the e-business world: how to personalise computer relationships for increased profitability . *International Journal of Retail & Distribution Management, 29*(12), 520. doi:10.1108/09590550110696969

Brodie, R. J., Winklhofer, H., Coviello, N. E., & Johnston, W. J. (2007). Is e-marketing coming of age? An examination of e-marketing and firm performance. *Journal of Interactive Marketing, 21*(1), 2–21. doi:10.1002/dir.20071

Bull, C. (2003). Strategic issues in customer relationship management (CRM) implementation. *Business Process Management Journal, 9*(5), 592–602. doi:10.1108/14637150310496703

Buttle, F. (2004). *Customer relationship management, concepts and tools.* Oxford,UK: Elsevier, Butterworth, Heinemann

Carson, D., Cromie, S., McGowan, P., & Hill, J. (1995). *Marketing and entrepreneurship in SMEs.* Englewood Cliffs, NJ: Prentice-Hall

Carson D., & Gilmore, A. (2000). Marketing at the interface: Not 'what' but 'how'. *Journal of Marketing Theory and Practice, Spring, 8*(2), 1-8.

Chaston, I., & Mangles, T. (2003). Relationship marketing in online business-to-business markets: A pilot investigation of small UK manufacturing firms. *European Journal of Marketing, 37*(5/6), 753–773. doi:10.1108/03090560310465134

Chen, I. J., & Popovich, K. (2003). Understanding customer relationship management (CRM) people, process and technology. *Business Process Management Journal, 9*(5), 672–688. doi:10.1108/14637150310496758

Chen, Q., & Chen H. (2004). Exploring the success factors of eCRM strategies in practice. *Database Marketing & Customer Strategy Management, July, 11*(4), 333-343.

Collinson, E., & Shaw, E. (2001). Entrepreneurial marketing- A historical perspective on development and practice. *Management Decision, 39*(9), 761–766. doi:10.1108/EUM0000000006221

Coviello, N., & Munro, H. (1997). Network relationships and the internationalisation process of the small software firm. *International Business Review, 6*(4), 361–386. doi:10.1016/S0969-5931(97)00010-3

Dandridge, T., & Levenburg, N. M. (2000). High-tech potential? An exploratory study of very small firms' usage of the Internet. *International Small Business Journal, 18*(2), 81–91. doi:10.1177/0266242600182004

Day, G. S., & Bens, K. F. (2005). Capitalizing on the Internet opportunity. *Journal of Business and Industrial Marketing, 20*(4/5), 160–168. doi:10.1108/08858620510603837

Day, G. S., & Hubbard, J. K. (2003). Customer relationships go digital. *Business Strategy Review, 14*(1), 17–26. doi:10.1111/1467-8616.00240

Dholakia, R. R., & Kshetri, N. (2004). Factors impacting the adoption of the Internet among SMEs. *Small Business Economics, 23*(4), 311–322. doi:10.1023/B:SBEJ.0000032036.90353.1f

Doherty, N., & Lockett, N., (2008). Mind the gap: Exploring the links between the expectations of relationship marketing and the reality of electronic-CRM. *International Journal of e-Business Management, 2*(2), 1-17.

Downie, G. (2003). Internet marketing and SMEs. *Management Service Enfield, 47*(7), 8–13.

Drennan, J., & McColl-Kennedy, J. R. (2003). The relationship between Internet use and perceived performance in retail and professional service firms. *Journal of Services Marketing, 17*(3), 295–311. doi:10.1108/08876040310474837

Egan, T., Clancy, S., & O'Toole, T. (2003). The integration of e-commerce tools into the business processes of SMEs. *Irish Journal of Management, 24*(1), 139–153.

Feinberg, R., & Kadam, R. (2002). E-CRM Web service attributes as determinants of customer satisfaction with retail Web-sites. *International Journal of Service Industry Management, 13*(5), 432–451. doi:10.1108/09564230210447922

Fletcher, R., Bell, J., & McNoughton, R. (2004). *International e-business marketing.* London: Thomson

Freidlein, A. (2001, February). CRM meets E-CRM: An executive briefing. *Wheel consultancy.* Retrieved 4th February, 2008 from www.e-consultancy.com

Geiger, S., & Martin, S. (1999). The Internet as a relationship marketing tool – Some evidence from Irish companies. *Irish Marketing Review, 12*(2), 24–35.

Geller, K. (1998). The Internet: The ultimate relationship marketing tool. *Direct Marketing, Garden City, Sep; 61*(5), 36-39.

Gilmore, A., & Carson, D. (1999). Entrepreneurial marketing by networking. *New England Journal of Entrepreneurship, Fall, 2*(2), 31-38.

Gilmore, A., Carson, D., & Grant, K. (2001). SME marketing in practice. *Marketing Intelligence & Planning, 19*(1), 6–11. doi:10.1108/02634500110363583

Gilmore, A., Carson, D., Grant, K., O'Donnell, A., Laney, R., & Pickett, B. (2006). Networking in SMEs: Findings from Australia and Ireland. *Irish Marketing Review, 18*(1/2), 21–29.

Gilmore, A., Carson, D., O'Donnell, A., & Cummins, D. (1999). Added value: A qualitative assessment of SME marketing. *Irish Marketing Review, 12*(1), 27–36.

Gilmore, A., Gallagher, D., & Henry, S. (2007). E-marketing and SMEs: Operational lessons for the future. *European Business Review, 19*(3), 234–247. doi:10.1108/09555340710746482

Grönroos, C. (1994). From marketing mix to relationship marketing: Towards a paradigm shift in marketing. *Management Decision, 32*(2), 4–22. doi:10.1108/00251749410054774

Grönroos, C. (2004). The relationship marketing process: communication, interaction, dialogue, value. *Journal of Business and Industrial Marketing, 19*(2), 99–113. doi:10.1108/08858620410523981

Gummesson, E. (1994). Making relationship marketing operational. *International Journal of Service Industry Management, 5*(5), 5–20. doi:10.1108/09564239410074349

Gummesson, E. (2004). Return on relationships (ROR), the value of relationship marketing and CRM in business-to-business contexts. *Journal of Business and Industrial Marketing, 19*(2), 136–146. doi:10.1108/08858620410524016

Håkansson, H., & Snehota, I. (1995). *Developing relationships in business networks.* London: Routledge.

Harrigan, P., Ramsey, E., & Ibbotson, P. (2008). E-CRM in SMEs: An exploratory study in Northern Ireland. *Marketing Intelligence & Planning, 26*(4), 385–404. doi:10.1108/02634500810879296

Haynes, P. J., Becherer, R. C., & Helms, M. M. (1998). Small and mid-sized businesses and Internet use: unrealized potential? *Internet Research: Electronic Networking Applications and Policy, 8*(3), 229–235. doi:10.1108/10662249810217786

Hill, J. (2001). A multidimensional study of the key determinants of effective SME marketing activity: Part 1. *International Journal of Entrepreneurial Behaviour & Research, 7*(5), 171–204. doi:10.1108/EUM0000000006006

Hill, J., & McGowan, P. (1996). Marketing development through networking: a competency based approach for small firm entrepreneurs. *Journal of Small Business and Enterprise Development, 3*(3), 148–157. doi:10.1108/eb020974

Howcroft, J. B., & Durkin, M. (2000). Reflections on bank-customer interactions in the new millennium. *Journal of Financial Services Marketing, 5*(1), 9–20. doi:10.1057/palgrave.fsm.4770002

Hunt, S. D., & Morgan, R. M. (1994). Relationship marketing in the era of network competition. *Marketing Management, 3*(1), 18–28.

Ibeh, K. I., Luo, Y., & Dinnie, K. (2005). E-branding strategies of internet companies: Some preliminary insights from the UK. *The Journal of Brand Management, 12*(5), 355–373. doi:10.1057/palgrave.bm.2540231

Iyer, R., & Bejou, D. (Eds.). (2003). *Customer relationship management in electronic markets.* Binghamton, NY: Hawthorne Press.

Jaworski, B. J., & Kohli, A. J. (1993). Marketing Orientation: antecedents and consequences. *Journal of Marketing, 57*(3), 53–70. doi:10.2307/1251854

Johnson, M. D., & Selnes, F. (2004). Customer portfolio management: Toward a dynamic theory of exchange relationships. *Journal of Marketing, 68*(2), 1–17. doi:10.1509/jmkg.68.2.1.27786

Kennedy, A. (2006). Electronic customer relationship management (e-CRM): Opportunities and challenges in a digital world. *Irish Marketing Review, 18*(1/2), 58–69.

Lal, K. (2002). E-business and manufacturing sector: A study of small and medium-sized enterprises in India. *Research Policy, 31*, 1199–1211. doi:10.1016/S0048-7333(01)00191-3

Lin, C., Lin, K., Huang, Y., & Kuo, N. (2006). Evaluation of electronic customer relationship management: The critical success factors. *Business Review (Federal Reserve Bank of Philadelphia), 6*(2), 206–212.

Maguire, S., Koh, S. C. L., & Magrys, A. (2007). The adoption of e-business and knowledge management in SMEs. *Benchmarking . International Journal (Toronto, Ont.), 14*(1), 37–58.

Martin, L., & Matlay, H. (2001). "Blanket" approaches to promoting ICT in small firms: Some lessons from the DTI ladder adoption model in the UK. *Internet Research, 11*(5), 399–410. doi:10.1108/EUM0000000006118

Martin, L., & Matlay, H. (2003). Innovative use of the Internet in established small firms: The impact of knowledge management and organisational learning in accessing new opportunities. *Qualitative Market Research: An International Journal, 6*(1), 18–26. doi:10.1108/13522750310457348

McCole, P., & Ramsey, E. (2004). Internet-enabled technology in knowledge-intensive business services: A comparison of Northern Ireland, the Republic of Ireland and New Zealand. *Marketing Intelligence & Planning, 22*(7), 761–779. doi:10.1108/02634500410568

McGowan, P., & Durkin, M. (2002). Toward an Understanding of Internet Adoption at the Marketing/Entrepreneurship Interface. *Journal of Marketing Management, 18*, 361–377. doi:10.1362/0267257022872451

McGowan, P., Durkin, M., Allen, L., Dougan, C., & Nixon, S. (2001). Developing competencies in the entrepreneurial small firm for the use of the Internet in the management of customer relationships. *Journal of European Industry Training, 25*(2/3/4), 126-36.

Mehrtens, J., Cragg, P. B., & Mills, A. M. (2001). A model of Internet adoption by SMEs. *Information & Management, 39*(3), 165–176. doi:10.1016/S0378-7206(01)00086-6

Morris, M. B., Schindehutte, M., & Laforge, R. W. (2002). Entrepreneurial marketing: A construct for integrating emerging entrepreneurship and marketing perspectives. *Journal of Marketing Theory and Practice, 10*(4), 1–19.

O'Donnell, A. (2004). The nature of networking in small firms. *Qualitative Market Research: An International Journal, 7*(3), 206–217. doi:10.1108/13522750410540218

O'Toole, T. (2001). E-relationships – Emergence and the small firm. *Marketing Intelligence & Planning, 21*(2), 115–122. doi:10.1108/02634500310465434

OECD. (2005). *SME and entrepreneurship outlook*. Retrieved November 6, 2007, from http://www.oecd.org

Pan, S.L., & Lee, J. (2003). Using e-CRM for a unified view of the customer. *Communications of the ACM archive, April, 46(4),* 95-99.

Pavic, S., Koh, S. C. L., Simpson, M., & Padmore, J. (2007). Could e-business create a competitive advantage in UK SMEs? *Benchmarking: An International Journal, 14*(3), 320–351. doi:10.1108/14635770710753112

Peppers, D., Rodgers, M., & Dorf, B. (1999). Is your company ready for one-to-one marketing? *Harvard Business Review, 77*(1), 151–160.

Peppers, D., Rodgers, M., & Dorf, B. (1999). Is your company ready for one-to-one marketing? *Harvard Business Review, 77*(1), 151–160.

Poon, S., & Swatman, P. M. C. (1999). An exploratory study of small business Internet commerce issues. *Information & Management, 35*(1), 9–18. doi:10.1016/S0378-7206(98)00079-2

Porter, M. E. (2001). Strategy and the Internet. *Harvard Business Review, 79*(3), 62–78.

Ragins, J. E., & Greco, J. A. (2003). Customer relationship management and e-business: more than a software solution. *Review of Business, 24*(1), 25–30.

Ramsey, E., Ibbotson, P., Bell, J., & Gray, B. (2003). E-opportunities of service sector SMEs: An Irish cross-border study. *Journal of Small Business and Enterprise Development, 10*(3), 250–265. doi:10.1108/14626000310489709

Reichheld, F. F., & Sasser, J. W. E. (1990). Zero defections: Quality comes to services. *Harvard Business Review, 68*(5), 105–111.

Riemenschneider, C. K., Harrison, D. A., & Mykytyn, P. P. Jr. (2003). Understanding IT adoption decisions in small business: Integrating current theories. *Information & Management, 40,* 269–285. doi:10.1016/S0378-7206(02)00010-1

Rigby, D. K., Reichheld, F. F., & Schefter, P. (2002). Avoid the four perils of customer relationship marketing. *Harvard Business Review, 80*(2), 101–199.

Romano, N. C. Jr, & Fjermestad, J. (2003). Electronic commerce customer relationship management: A research agenda. *Information Technology and Management, 4,* 233–258. doi:10.1023/A:1022906513502

Rothwell, R. (1992). Successful industrial innovation: critical factors for the 1990s. *R & D Management, 22*(3), 221–239. doi:10.1111/j.1467-9310.1992.tb00812.x

Rowley, J. (2004). Partnering paradigms? Knowledge management and relationship marketing. *Industrial Management & Data Systems, 104*(2), 149–157. doi:10.1108/02635570410522125

Runyan, R., Droge, C., & Swinney, J. (2008). Entrepreneurial orientation versus small business orientation: What are their relationships to firm performance? *Journal of Small Business Management, 46*(4), 567–588. doi:10.1111/j.1540-627X.2008.00257.x

Sands, M. (2003). Integrating the Web and e-mail into a push-pull strategy. *Qualitative Market Research, 6*(1), 27–37. doi:10.1108/13522750310457357

Scullin, S. S., Fjermestad, J., & Romano, N. C. Jr. (2004). E-relationship marketing: changes in traditional marketing as an outcome of electronic customer relationship management. *The Journal of Enterprise Information Management, 17*(6), 410–415. doi:10.1108/17410390410566698

Shaw, E. (1999). Networks and their relevance to the entrepreneurial/marketing interface: A review of the evidence. *Journal of Research in Marketing & Entrepreneurship, 1*(1), 24–40.

Simmons, G. (2008). Marketing to postmodern consumers: Introducing the Internet chameleon. *European Journal of Marketing, 42*(3/4), 294–310. doi:10.1108/03090560810852940

Simmons, G., Armstrong, G., & Durkin, M. (2008). A conceptualization of the determinants of small business Website adoption. *International Small Business Journal, 26*(3), 351–389. doi:10.1177/0266242608088743

Srirojanant, S., & Cresswell-Thirkell, P. (1998). Relationship Marketing And Its Synergy With Web-based technologies. *Journal of Market Focused Management, 3*, 23–46. doi:10.1023/A:1009790421951

Stokes, D. (2000). Entrepreneurial marketing: a conceptualisation from qualitative research. *Qualitative Market Research: An International Journal, 3*(1), 47–54. doi:10.1108/13522750010310497

Storey, D. J. (1994). *Understanding the small business sector.* London: Routledge.

Subba Rao, S., Metts, G., & Monge, C. A. M. (2003). Electronic commerce development in small and medium sized enterprises. *Business Process Management Journal, 9*(1), 11–33. doi:10.1108/14637150310461378

Swatman, P. (2000). Internet for SMEs: A new silk road? *International Trade Forum, 3*, 22–24.

Uzzi, B. (1997). Social structure and competition in interfirm networks: The paradox of embeddedness. *Administrative Science Quarterly, 42*(1), 35–67. doi:10.2307/2393808

Van der Veen, M. (2004). *Explaining e-business adoption; innovation and entrepreneurship and in Dutch SMEs.* Unpublished doctoral dissertation, University of Twente, Holland.

Weiss, T. J. (1999). Cyber-relationships and brand building. *Integrated Marketing Communications Research Journal, 5*, 19–22.

Wu, F., Mahajan, V., & Balasubramanian, S. (2003). An analysis of e-business adoption and its impact on business performance. *Academy of Marketing Science Journal, 31*(4), 425–448. doi:10.1177/0092070303255379

Zineldin, M. (2000). Beyond relationship marketing; technologicalship marketing. *Marketing Intelligence & Planning, 18*(1), 9–23. doi:10.1108/02634500010308549

Zontanos, G., & Anderson, A. R. (2004). Relationships, marketing and small business: an exploration of links in theory and practice. *Qualitative Market Research: An International Journal, 7*(3), 228–236. doi:10.1108/13522750410540236

Chapter 13

Understanding the Factors Affecting the Adoption of E-Marketing by Small Business Enterprises

Hatem El-Gohary
Bradford University School of Management, UK

Myfanwy Trueman
Bradford University School of Management, UK

Kyoko Fukukawa
Bradford University School of Management, UK

ABSTRACT

The chapter builds on the current body of knowledge in the field of E-Marketing through a survey and organised systematic examination of the published work related to the Technology Acceptance Model (TAM), Innovation Diffusion Theory (IDT) and E-Marketing adoption by Small Business Enterprises. Furthermore, the chapter illustrates that although many E-Marketing adoption factors are driven from the literature of E-Marketing, as well as the technology adoption theories like TAM and IDT, only some of these factors are found to significantly affect the adoption of E-Marketing by Small Business Enterprises. This review and the results of the fieldwork research conducted by the authors will enable entrepreneurs, policy makers, students and practitioners to build a greater understanding of E-Marketing adoption in a small business context. Moreover, the chapter will help researchers and scholars in the field of E-Marketing to have a clearer view towards suitable future research studies in the field of E-Marketing that in turn will contribute to the related accumulated knowledge in the field.

INTRODUCTION

Small Business Enterprises (SBE's) play a one of the main roles in the world economy today, and they are recognised as one of the main contributors to economic development, innovations and employment growth all over the world. According to Mulhern (1995), most of the registered European companies (99% of the total number of companies

DOI: 10.4018/978-1-60566-998-4.ch013

in Europe) are small and medium sized (SME) and had provided 66% of the employment in Europe in the period from 1985-1995. That is also true in Less Developing Countries (LDC's) since small businesses represent a high percentage of the total number of enterprises.

Moreover, the revolution in computer science, the Internet, information technology (IT), media and communications has changed the ways of conduct business today. In the last two decades, growing numbers of companies and enterprises have been using the Internet and other electronic communications to conduct its marketing efforts and activities, giving the chance for Electronic marketing (as a new marketing phenomenon and philosophy) to grow in a dramatic and dynamic way.

From the authors point of view, adopting and implementing E-Marketing effectively and efficiently by small business enterprise can change both the characteristics and nature of SBEs business all over the world. As a result of the increased usage of the Internet and other Electronic marketing tools (i.e.: Intranets, Extranets and Mobile phones) in conducting electronic transactions not only a lot of opportunities for Small Business Enterprises can be created but also this might eliminate many of the threats facing SBE's. From this perspective, the Internet and other electronic media and Electronic marketing tools are playing a vital role in marketing activities within business enterprises regardless of type or size.

On the other hand, the adoption of new technologies has attracted a lot of interest from researchers and practitioners during the last two decades to gain a better understanding of how they can be used more effectively. Unlike new technological innovation, which often appears to occur as a single event or jump, the adoption or diffusion of technology into practice appears as a continuous and rather slow process (Hall and Khan, 2003, p:1). However, there are a number of accepted theoretical frameworks that have been used by researchers to investigate the adoption

and diffusion of information technology and new technologies by the business community. Although there are a lot of theories about technology adoption, only three have been rigorously applied by the research community namely: the Davis (1989) Technology Acceptance Model (TAM), the Rogers (1995) Innovation Diffusion Theory (IDT) and the Decomposed Theory of Planned Behaviour model (TPB) (Looi, 2004).

Moreover, recent research into IT adoption and use has been motivated by the desire to predict factors, which can lead to successful application in a marketing context (Lynn *et al.*, 2002:35; Rose and Straub, 1998:39). But E-Marketing is still a relatively new concept, particularly for Small Business Enterprises that have limited resources and can ill afford to make unwise investments. Therefore, there is a need to have a much clearer understanding of E-Marketing problems as well as its opportunities for SBE's and how these technologies can be used to carry out the marketing process in a more effective way than a reliance on traditional practice.

Depending on that, the chapter aims to explore, analyze and develop a clear and deep understanding about the different factors affecting the adoption of E-Marketing by Small Business Enterprises. This understanding will provide benefits for entrepreneurs, policy makers, students, practitioners, researchers, and educators though providing a clearer view and deep complete understanding for all the aspects related to the adoption of E-Marketing by Small Business Enterprises. The chapter will review the most frequently used new technologies adoption models theories and then examine their potential for an analysis of E-Marketing practice. Because each theory has a different perspective of new technology, a combination of elements from each may provide a more robust model that may be constructive and practical for the analysis of E-Marketing in an SBE context.

BACKGROUND

Small Business Enterprises

Despite of the powerful and important position held by small businesses within today economy, defining it has always been difficult and there is a little agreement on what defines a small business enterprise because the term covers a variety of firms. Therefore it is clear that there is no single optimal definition of a small firm, which is mainly because of the wide diversity of small businesses. Since the late 1970's there have been many various attempts to standardise the definitions of Small Business Enterprises (SBE's) by researchers, practitioners and other interested parties and institutions using many variables such as: the number of employees, annual sales, annual turnover, balance sheet, the value added by the enterprise, the value of the enterprise assets and ownership. But the first two variables are most often used to delimit the category of SBE's.

As a result small businesses have been defined in a mystifying number of different ways according to national and local needs (Theng and Boon 1996; Watson and Everrett 1996). But the SBE definition currently in force in the European Community (EC) low is that one adopted by the European Commission in its Recommendation 2003/361/EC of the sixth of May 2003 (replacing Recommendation 96/280/EC) and addressed to Member states, the European Investment Bank (EIB) and the European Investment Fund (EIF) (European Commission, 2008). This new definition takes into account the economic developments since 1996 and the lessons drawn from the application of the definition.

On the other hand, number of employees is the most frequently used element in determining the category of SBE's in most countries. Furthermore, in most countries (countries of the European Union, Canada – in services -, Mexico and Turkey) a SBE will be defined as an enterprise that employs less than 50 employees. Accordingly and due to the absence of a unique official definition for SBEs, the authors within this chapter will use the European definition for SBEs for the purpose of conducting the current research. According to this definition an enterprise will be considered as a small business if it employs less than 50 employees, have an a annual turnover (or global balance) that is less than 10 million Euros and not exceeding 25% of the enterprise capital or voting rights withheld by one or more companies (or public bodies) which are not themselves SME's.

Electronic Marketing

Electronic marketing can be viewed as a new modern business practice associated with buying and selling goods, services, information and ideas via the Internet and other electronic means. A review of relevant literature revealed that the definitions of Electronic marketing vary according to authors' point of view, background and specialization, as follows:

Achieving marketing objectives through applying digital technologies. (Smith and Chaffey, 2005. p: 11)

The use of electronic data and applications for planning and executing the conception, distribution and pricing of ideas, goods and services to create exchanges that satisfy individual and organizational objectives. (Strauss and Frost, 2001, p: 454)

Any use of technology to achieve marketing objectives. (McDonald and Wilson, 1999, P: 29)

Achieving marketing objectives through use of electronic communications technology. (Chaffey, 2007, P: 339)

The process aimed at facilitating and conducting of business communication and transactions over networks. (Reedy and Schullo, 2004, p: 16)

Figure 1. E-Marketing Concept (Source: Prepared by the authors)

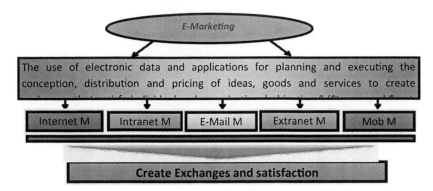

The authors used the Strauss and Frost (2001) definition to conduct the current research since it takes into consideration all the elements of E-Marketing, all types of products and it illustrates the main objective of E-Marketing which is creating the exchanges that satisfy individual and organizational needs. Moreover it is the current official definition for E-Marketing adopted by the American E-Marketing Association. Accordingly, the concept of E- marketing can be illustrated in Figure 1.

Based on the E-Marketing definition adopted within this chapter, E-Marketing will include any electronic form of conducting marketing activities. However, within this chapter the authors will investigate the factors affecting the adoption of five E-Marketing tools (namely Internet Marketing, E-Mail Marketing, Mobile Marketing, Intranet Marketing and extranet Marketing) by Small Business Enterprises.

Adoption of New Technology

The adoption of new technologies has attracted a lot of interest from researchers and practitioners during the last two decades, to gain a better understanding of how they can be used more effectively. However, there are a number of accepted theoretical frameworks that have been used by researchers to investigate the adoption

and diffusion of information technology and new technologies by the business community. Although there are a lot of theories about technology adoption, only three have been rigorously applied by the research community namely: the Davis (1989) Technology Acceptance Model (TAM), the Rogers (1995) Innovation Diffusion Theory (IDT) and the Decomposed Theory of Planned Behaviour model (TPB) (Looi, 2004). Consequently the following parts of the chapter will review all three theories and then examine their potential for an analysis of E-Marketing practice. Because each theory has a different perspective of new technology, a combination of elements from each may provide a more robust model that may be of use for the analysis of E-Marketing in an SBE context.

The Technology Acceptance Model (TAM)

The Technology Acceptance Model (TAM) is proposed by Davis (1989) to explain the acceptance, usage and adoption of information technology. When developing this model, Davis refers to the theory developed by Ajzen and Fishbein (1980) regarding the understanding of attitudes and the predicting of social behaviour. Davis (1989) uses this theory about reasoned action (TRA) to show that beliefs influence attitudes which lead to intentions, and therefore generate behaviours. Moreover this belief–attitude–intention–behavioural relationship can predict user acceptance of IT (Lederer et al, 2000).

Based on that, according to Davis' point of view, IT adoption is affected by prior use-related beliefs. When constructing his model, Davis depended on the following two beliefs to develop his model:

- **Perceived beliefs/usefulness (PU)** which is: *"The degree to which a person believes that using a particular system would enhance his or her job performance" (Davis, 1989p:320)*
- **Perceived ease of use (PEOU)** which refer to: *"The degree to which a person believes that using a particular system would be free of effort" (Davis, 1989p: 320)*

Although the perceived usefulness and the ease of use represent are the main component of TAM, there are two other constructs in the model which are:

- *Attitude towards the use of IT*
- *Behavioural intention to use*

The Technology Acceptance Model has played an important role in the understanding of the acceptance, usage and adoption of information technology. Any review of the literature and scholarly research on Information Technology acceptance and usage will show that TAM has emerged as one of the most significant models in this stream of research. Thus it represents a solid important theoretical contribution toward understanding the usage and acceptance behaviours of IT.

Nevertheless, economic factors or outside influences (such as: suppliers, customers, social influence and competitors) are not specifically addressed in this model, nor the influence of personal control factors on behaviour (Looi, 2004). For that many researchers attempted to test the model.

In this respect, there are a large numbers of studies that had tested the model since it was first presented in 1989. These studies had not only covered a number of deferent technologies and deferent aspects but also while some of it tested all the model components, the rest tested only the two main components of the model (perceived usefulness and ease of use) (Looi, 2004; Grandon and Pearson, 2003; Dembla, Palvia and Krishnan, 2007; Adams et al, 1992; Bagozzi et al, 1992; Chau, 1996; Davis, 1989; Davis et al, 1989; Gefen and Straub, 1997; Haynes and Thies, 1991; Hendrickson and Collins, 1996; Igbaria et al, 1995; Mathieson, 1991; Morris and Dillon, 1997; Straub et al, 1995; Szajna, 1994; Taylor and Todd, 1995; Teo et al, 1999; Thompson, 1998; Lederer et al, 2000).

TAM has provided a very good base to understand the acceptance and usage of new technologies. The model had been tested for more than two decades in many different technologies and had been accepted as a successful model in predicting and explaining behaviour across a wide variety of domains. By reviewing the literature it is noticed that there are a limited number of studies that had been conducted to apply the Technology Acceptance Model (TAM) in the field of E-Marketing. Accordingly, there is a need to conduct more research to investigate the model from an E-Marketing prospective. Which is applicable because: according to Davis *et al.* (1989), TAM is considerably less general than the Theory of Reasoned Action (TRA), but it is designed to apply to computer usage behaviour. Also TAM incorporates findings accumulated from over a decade of IS research, for that it may be especially well-suited for modelling computer application acceptance which include E-Marketing (the subject of this study). Nevertheless, the model ignores some other important factors both within and outside the organization that may have an impact on E-Marketing adoption. For that, when implementing the model to study the adoption of E-Marketing, the model needs to be expanded to include some other factors. These factors might include: economic factors (cost, pressure from suppliers or customers or competitors), and characteristics of the firm (size, sector and status).

The Innovation Diffusion Theory (IDT)

Distinct from the invention of a new technology, which often appears to occur as a single event or jump, the diffusion of that technology usually appears as a continuous and rather slow process (Hall and Khan, 2003, P:1). Accordingly, the implementation problems of any new technology will be - in most cases - related to the diffusion of this technology. For that many researchers in Management, Information Systems and Information Technology had begun to rely on the theories of innovation diffusion to study implementation problems of new technologies.

Innovation Diffusion Theory (IDT) is one of the most popular theories in the diffusion of new technology and appeared to be the most widely accepted model by researchers and is often associated with research into technology innovation. The theory had been introduced by Rogers (1983; 1995) who had identified eight types of diffusion research among it: earliness of knowing about innovation, rate of adoption in different social systems, opinion leadership, diffusion networks, communication channel use and consequences of innovation.

According to Rogers (1995) while diffusion is "the process by which an innovation is communicated through certain channels over time among the members of a social system", innovation is "an idea, practice, or object that is perceived as new by an individual or another unit of adoption" (Rogers, 1995:5).

The innovation decision process developed by Rogers (1995) consists of five stages which start with one's knowledge about the innovation existence. At this stage, expected users are first exposed to the innovation and gain initial understanding of it. In the second stage (persuasion) the expected users will be influenced by the new technology which in turn will lead to the third stages when managers/expected users move from persuasion to the decision of adopting or rejecting the innovation. In the fourth stages managers/ users will implement the new technology, by this usage of the new technology the managers/users in the final stage will confirm or reserve the system from a usefulness or fitness perspective.

The main contribution of the Innovation Diffusion Theory (IDT) is the set of innovation attributes it provides that affect the rate of adoption. These attributes include: relative advantage, compatibility, complexity, trialability, visibility, and observability (Rogers, 1983).

Rogers (1995) defines these attributes as follows:-

1. **Relative advantage:** The degree to which an innovation is perceived as being better than its antecedent
2. **Compatibility:** The degree to which an innovation is perceived as being consistent with the existing values, needs and past experiences of potential adopters.
3. **Complexity:** The degree to which an innovation is perceived as being difficult to use.
4. **Trialability:** The degree to which an innovation may be experimented with before adoption.
5. **Observability:** The degree to which the results of an innovation are observable by others (Rogers, 1995).

Moreover, according to Rogers these five attributes can explain 49 to 87 percent of the variance rate of adoption (Rogers, 1995).

Unsurprisingly, there are a large numbers of studies that had tested the model since it was first presented in 1983. These studies had covered a number of deferent technologies and deferent aspects (Park and Yoon, 2005; Zhu and Kraemer, 2005; Tan and Teo, 2000; Venkatesh, Morris, Davis and Davis, 2003; Wu and Wang, 2005; Roman, 2003; Seyal and Rahman, 2003; Parthasarathy and Bhattacherjee, 1998; Peansupap and Walker, 2005; Rajagopal, 2002).

The IDT model had provided a good contribution toward understanding the acceptance, usage and diffusion of new technologies. The model had been tested in many different technologies and had been accepted as a successful model. By reviewing the literature it is noticed that there are a limited number of studies that had been contacted to apply the IDT in the field of E-Marketing. Accordingly, there is a need to conduct more research to investigate the model from an E-Marketing prospective. Although the model had taken important factors into consideration to illustrate the diffusion of new technologies, it ignores some other important factors both within and outside the organization that may impact on E-Marketing adoption. For that, when implementing the model to study the adoption of E-Marketing, the model needs to be expanded to include some other factors.

The Decomposed Theory of Planned Behaviour Model

An additional IT adoption model which is known as the Decomposed Theory of Planned Behaviour model had been introduced by Taylor and Todd (1995). The model is an extension of the well-known Theory of Planned Behaviour (TPB) and discusses technology adoption in terms of behaviour and social influence. Based on that, the model indicated that a better understanding of the relationships between the belief structures and antecedents of intention requires the decomposition of attitudinal beliefs (Taylor and Todd, 1995).

In this model, technology adoption is a direct function of behavioural intention and perceived behavioural control. The model further suggests that innovation characteristics (e.g. relative advantage, compatibility) help to form intention.

The constructs used in this model are generally based on perceptions, attitudes, beliefs, perceived behavioural control and social influence, together with psychological considerations in determining technology adoption, acceptance and usage.

Taylor and Todd (1995) showed that their model has better explanatory power than the pure Theory of Planned Behaviour (TPB). Since the research in hand is mainly about E-Marketing which is considered as a technological innovation. Thus the decomposed TPB model could give a satisfactory explanation of E-Marketing adoption intention by Small Business Enterprises.

To determine the possibility of depending on the Decomposed Theory of Planned Behaviour in explaining and understanding the adoption of E-Marketing by Small Business Enterprises, the authors examined the literature related to the model. By reviewing this literature it was found that while some studies had found support for the model (e.g. Shih and Fang, 2004; Burnkrant and Page, 1988), there are some other studies that have failed to support the model or to identify a multidimensional structure for it such as: Shimp and Kavas (1984) and Oliver and Bearden (1985).

On the other hand, some of the main constructs used in this model are adopted from the Innovation Diffusion Theory (IDT) - related advantage, complexity and compatibility -. Accordingly, depending on the Innovation Diffusion Theory (IDT) could give a more satisfactory explanation of E-Marketing adoption intention by Small Business Enterprises (especially if the limitations of the model were taken into consideration). In this respect the model has some main limitations. The main limitation is that the model tends to ignore factors both within and outside the organization that might have an impact on new technologies adoption and diffusion, for example, economic factors (like: cost, pressure from suppliers, customers or competitors), and characteristics of the enterprise (size, sector and status).

RESEARCH NICHE

Although the Technology Acceptance Model (TAM), Innovation Diffusion Theory (IDT) and the Decomposed Theory of Planned Behaviour model are among the most effective theories in predicting and explaining innovation diffusion. For the purpose of conducting the research on hand, the authors will take into consideration only the first two models namely Technology Acceptance Model (TAM) and Innovation Diffusion Theory (IDT) for the reasons discussed in the previous section of this chapter.

In this respect, both TAM and IDT are considered to have a solid theoretical foundation and both of them had been tested and proven successful in various studies. Consequently the research on hand explains the possibility of their use to anticipate the different factors that might have an effect on the adoption of E-Marketing among Small Business Enterprises.

Unquestionably, E-Marketing is a new type of end-user information system that is heavily based on telecommunication technologies. Moreover – as illustrated earlier in this chapter - there are a number of studies that tested the TAM model in the acceptance of electronic commercial transactions (Gefen and Straub, 2000; Grandon and Pearson, 2003; Devaraj et al, 2002; Kamel et al, 2003; Wang et al, 2003; Pikkarainen et al, 2004; McCloskey, 2004; Chan and Lu, 2004; Dembla, Palvia and Krishnan, 2007; Looi, 2004).

Some of these studies had found that TAM was appropriate to analyse: the use of websites for product browsing and purchasing (Gefen and Straub, 2000), web-enabled transaction processing by small business organizations (Dembla et al., 2007), Electronic Commerce adoption by Small and Medium Enterprises (Looi, 2004), buying products online (McCloskey, 2004), online shopping and online consumer behaviour (Vijayasarathy, 2004; Gefen, 2003; Gefen et al, 2003 and Koufaris, 2002) and Business to Customer (B2C) satisfaction (Devaraj et al, 2003). Consequently,

using TAM to study small businesses acceptance and adoption of E-Marketing is a highly valid approach.

On the other hand, the Innovation Diffusion Theory (IDT) is a theory that helps to understand how and why a certain innovation is diffused into a social system (Rogers, 1995). Given that E-Marketing is highly considered to be innovative because of its ability to completely change the traditional marketing practice and since E-Marketing still in its infancy stage, a well-researched theory such as the IDT will help us to understand the process of using and adopting E-Marketing by Small Business Enterprises.

Furthermore, there are a number of studies that had used TAM and IDT as a combined tool to investigate the factors affecting the adoption of new technologies (Jie, Peiji and Jiaming, 2007; Yi et al, 2006; Chen, Gillenson and Sherrell, 2002, 2004; Wu and Wang, 2005; Looi, 2004; Lertwongsatien and Wongpinunwatana, 2003). In this respect, in a study to understand the factors that attract consumers to use firm's websites, Chen, Gillenson and Sherrell (2002) applied the Technology Acceptance Model (TAM) and Innovation Diffusion Theory (IDT) to examine consumer behavior in the virtual store context. The findings illustrated that the technology acceptance and innovation diffusion/adoption theories are still valid in explaining and predicting user behaviors (in the business-to-consumer context). Almost the same findings had been reached by: Jie, Peiji and Jiaming (2007), Yi et al (2006), Chen, Gillenson and Sherrell (2004), Wu and Wang (2005), Looi (2004) and Lertwongsatien and Wongpinunwatana (2003).

Based on the previous discussion and the fact that TAM and IDT often compliment each other in research (Eid, 2003); combining both TAM and IDT to study small businesses acceptance and adoption of E-Marketing is a highly valid approach and can lead to fruitful results.

However, researchers and practitioners working with TAM and the IDT have discovered a similar relationship between the two theories. This similarity is clear between "relative advantage" and "complexity" from one side (IDT), and "perceived usefulness" and "perceived ease of use" on the other side (TAM). Although TAM does not use Rogers' constructs "relative advantage" and "complexity", perceived ease of use (PEU) and perceived usefulness (PU) are related and lead to similar results to the diffusion theory outcomes. Consequently, TAM can be viewed as a sub model of the Rogers IDT model.

On the other hand, although that the IDT had been studied by many researchers, it has been reported that the elements of the model have different influences on the adoption of technological innovation. Most of the researchers and scholars found that: relative advantage, compatibility, and complexity are the most important elements in the IDT model that can influences on the adoption of new technological innovation (Al-Qirim, 2007; Al-Qirim, 2006; Lertwongsatien and Wongpinunwatana, 2003; Stockdale and Standing, 2006 and Looi, 2004). This is in line with the findings of Tornatzky and Klein (1982), based of their meta-analysis of 105 studies in innovation diffusion literature, they found that only: relative advantage, compatibility and complexity were strongly related to new innovation adoption and had the most significant relationships with adoption across a broad range of innovation types. Consequently, for the purpose of conducting the research in hand, the authors can reasonably include these variables in the research model.

Moreover, Moore and Benbasat (1991: 197) raised a question about: the appropriate terminology to be use for the "perceived usefulness" construct of the TAM. They suggested instead using the term "Relative Advantage" (Moore and Benbasat, 1991:197). The main logic behind that is that the term usefulness is a broad term while the term "relative advantage" has more significant intuitive appeal, as it is a very generalisable concept (Moore and Benbasat, 1991:198; Tornatzky and Klein, 1982:34).

Accordingly, the main constructs of interest for the research in hand are these three main elements namely:-

1. Perceived ease of use
2. Perceive relative advantage (Usefulness)
3. Perceived compatibility

These three constructs are included in the first part of the research framework that deals with internal factors affecting E-Marketing adoption by small businesses. It also refers to the work of Moore and Benbasat (1991), in which they had developed measurement scales for these attributes that can be applied to any innovation. these measurements depending on a seven-point Likert scale ranging from "extremely disagree" to "extremely agree" as the response format." (Moore and Benbasat; 1991, p: 198)

In fact many researchers have adapted the Moore and Benbasat (1991) measurements in many research studies (e.g. Moore and Benbasat, 1996; Karahanna et al, 1999; Moon and Kim 2001; Pavlou 2003; Eid, 2003; Van Slyke et al. 2004, Carter and Belanger, 2004; Slyke, 2007) which reflect not only its nature as a validated scales but also the high possibility for reusing it to measure the same constructs in future researches. Consequently, for the purpose of conducting this research the authors will adopt the measurements of Moore and Benbasat (1991) to measure the constructs of: perceived ease of use, perceive relative advantage (usefulness) and perceived compatibility of the research model. In this context, in some cases shortened forms of the scales were used in order to control the length of the survey. Also, items were slightly reworded to reflect the current research context (E-Marketing) and the scale items were measured on a seven-point Likert scale with the anchors "strongly disagree" (1) to "strongly agree" (7).

EXTENDING TAM AND IDT

As discussed earlier, many authors and scholars have extended both the TAM and IDT in an attempt to improve the ability of the models to predict new technology use and adoption (Chau, 1996; Igbaria, *et al.*, 1995; Gefen and Straub, 1997, Eid 2003 and Vijayasarathy, 2004). The main logic behind that is, although the two models had taking important factors into consideration to illustrate the acceptance and diffusion of new technologies, they both ignores some other important factors both within and outside the organization that may impact on new technology acceptance, diffusion and adoption.

For that, when implementing the model to study the adoption of E-Marketing, the model needs to be expanded to include some other factors. These factors will include some external and internal variables that might have an impact on E-Marketing adoption by Small Business Enterprises. To determine these factors the authors investigated the literature of new technology adoption from a Small Business Enterprises context to form a clear picture about the factors used by other researchers and scholars to understand the adoption of new technologies by small businesses.

E-Marketing Adoption

Gallagher and Gilmore (2004) indicated that regardless of the enormous opportunities and benefits of employing, adopting and implementing an E-Marketing strategy, small businesses were very slow to respond effectively or efficiently to the different changes brought by the Internet into the business world and were not yet making effective use of it. Whiteley (2000) has shown that, in spite of the fact that technology facilitating improved business practice in terms of developing electronic markets, electronic data interchange and internet commerce, a number of small businesses have not capitalised on this new mode of carrying out business. Moreover, one survey

found extremely low adoption rates of around 10 per cent in the Republic of Ireland and 7 per cent in Northern Ireland (Smyth and Ibbotson, 2001). For that, it is tremendously important to study and investigate the different possible factors or drivers of E-Marketing adoption by Small Business Enterprises.

To conduct such a study – as discussed earlier - the authors will investigate the effect of some factors on the adoption of E-Marketing by Small Business Enterprises. These factors are: Competitive pressures, Government influences, Market trends, Cultural orientation towards E-Marketing, Entrepreneur skills, Organizational culture, SBE resource (financial, human and technical), Type of the product, International orientation of the SBE, Size of the firm, Perceived ease of use Perceive relative advantage (usefulness) and, Perceived compatibility. These factors were chosen to be added to TAM and IDT bearing in mind that in most cases Small Business Enterprises are on the disadvantaged end of the global digital world and might lose the some benefits of E-Marketing (as the traditional literature suggests). But on the other hand, E-Marketing is conceptualized to be a management tool that can lead to huge organizational improvement.

On the other hand, even though the authors see that the different factors and drivers of E-Marketing adoption by Small Business Enterprises can be classified into:

• Pro-active, and
• Reactive factors or drivers

From the authors standpoint it will be more efficient to classify these factors into:

• Environmental Macro factors, and
• Environmental Micro factors or drivers

That can be justified by reviewing the literature. From the literature, several pro-active and reactive factors had been recognized and identified as motivations for SBE's to adopt the internet and E-Marketing activities. In this respect, while Proactive reasons include: the chance to eliminate competitive disadvantages of the SBE, the chance to lower operating and marketing costs, the chance to increase sales and profits, the opportunity to promote the enterprise better and enrich the marketing communications mix (Jeffcoate *et al.*, 2002; Downie, 2002; Poon and Swatman, 1997 and Dann and Dann, 2001), the reactive reasons included: increased competition from local competitors as well as larger firms, shrinkage or lack of domestic markets and the fear of competitive disadvantage (Kardaras and Papathanassiou, 2000; Premkumar and Roberts, 1999; Ching and Ellis, 2004).

But, most of the researchers within the literature had classified these factors into internal or external environmental factors which is more applicable and practical in the same time (e.g. Eid, 2003 and Doolin et al, 2003). Moreover what can be classified as reactive reasons for one industry might be classified as proactive reasons for anther industry. Accordingly, for the purpose of conducting the research in hand, the authors will classify the factors and drivers of E-Marketing adoption by Small Business Enterprises into: Environmental Macro, and Micro factors or drivers.

With respect to the *Environmental macro factors*, the level of competition pressures that the firm faces and the market trends might constitute triggers for E-Marketing adoption. Also, small firms may choose sometimes to adopt E-Marketing, E-Commerce or E-business as a result of external forces and its need to remain competitive, rather than having direct increases in productivity or day to day activities (UNCTAD - United Nations, 2004). In this respect competition, market trends as well as competitive pressure could be one of E-Marketing trigger in cases where small firms find themselves losing their competitive advantage or being out of the competition because the industry competitors are adopting E-Marketing or E-business and gaining both: competitive advantage and business effectiveness and efficiency.

Additionally, according to the literature there are some other triggers for E-Marketing adoption like: the cultural orientation towards E-Marketing, government influences and the favourable climate for Small Business Enterprises adoption of E-Marketing.

On the other hand, the *Environmental Micro triggers* play a major role in E-Marketing adoption by Small Business Enterprises. Both *Environmental Macro* and *Micro* factors for E-Marketing adoption by Small Business Enterprises had been included in the conceptual framework of the research which is illustrated and discussed below.

THE RESEARCH FRAMEWORK

Based on the previous results and discussion the authors constructed the research framework illustrated in Figure 2 to investigate the impact of these previous discussed factors on E-Marketing adoption by Small Business Enterprises. To test the research framework the authors conducted a major survey within the UK and used multiple and single regression to analyse the data collected through the survey. The research population and sample are discussed in the following parts.

RESEARCH HYPOTHESES AND FIELDWORK

Derived from the research framework the following hypotheses were formulated (see Table 1).

The Research Population and Sample

The survey questionnaire targeted a sample of 391 Small Business Enterprises within the UK that had been selected randomly from a population of 1953 Small Business Enterprises within the same region. Since the study was designed

Figure 2. external and internal environmental factors affecting the adoption of e-marketing

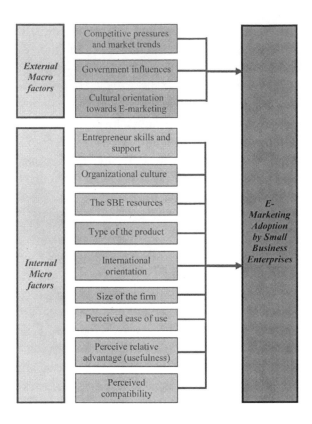

to acquire responses from different industries so that generalisation of the study findings could be gained, the research population were generated from some databases and business directories through searching the enterprises that are based in UK and can satisfy the essential requirement to be considered as Small Business Enterprises (number of employees and annual turnover). The following directories were used in generating the research population: E – Business Directory, Business Directory London, Internet Business Directory, Bizwiki, Freeindex, Countyweb, Business Directory UK, Alibaba Business Directory and FAME Business Directory. The sample was chosen to represent 20% of the population as accepted by most researchers within the field.

391 questionnaires were mailed to the selected Small Business Enterprises. Of the 391 SBEs, a total of 147 questionnaires were returned. This included 14 returned (not completed) with a label stating "Gone Away-Not in this address any more." A further 19 questionnaires were returned with a covering letter explaining why they had not completed the questionnaire. Most of the responses indicated that this was due to the enterprise policy which does not support participating in research surveys or lack of time due to work pressures. Therefore, the number of returned completed questionnaires was 114. Table 2 provides a summary of the response distribution and rate. This response rate was calculated depending on the response rate calculation technique introduced by De Vaus (1991: 99) and was 31.84%.

Based on the descriptive analysis of the data collected through the survey it was found that the majority of SBEs (78.9%) were located in England and only 4.4% of these SBEs were located in Northern Ireland. In addition, the majority of small businesses within the study were trading SBEs with a percentage of 64% of the total number of enterprises participating in the study and 36% of the participating enterprises were manufacturing SBEs. Moreover, the research sample was distributed among eleven different industries with the largest number of small businesses (29) in the computer and IT sector, representing 25.4% of the sample. It was also found that the SBEs within the research sample are classified into three main business classification namely Business to Business (B2B), Business to Consumer (B2C) and both (B2B & B2C). With regards to the number of employees, it was found that the majority of SBEs (64 enterprises with a percentage of 56.1% of the total number of enterprises) fall into the category of enterprises that have between 10 - 19 employees. Moreover, 80.7% of the total number of enterprises had 39 employees or less. Meanwhile, the majority of Small Business Enterprises within the study (21.1%) had less than 250,000 of annual sales (24 SBEs). In addition, the majority of study SBEs (42.1%) had a marketing budget that is less than 10% of total enterprise budget (48

Table 1.

H1A	Adopting E-Marketing by the SBEs is dependent on the entrepreneur skills and support.
H1B	Adopting E-Marketing by the SBEs is dependent on the available resources of the SBE
H1C	Adopting E-Marketing by the SBEs is dependent on the SBEs organizational culture.
H1D	Adopting E-Marketing by the SBEs is dependent on the type of products produced by the SBE.
H1E	Adopting E-Marketing by the SBEs is dependent on the international orientation of the SBE
H1F	Adopting E-Marketing by the SBEs is dependent on the SBE size
H1G	Adopting E-Marketing by the SBEs is dependent on E-Marketing perceived ease of use
H1H	Adopting E-Marketing by the SBEs is dependent on E-Marketing perceived relative advantage (usefulness).
H1I	Adopting E-Marketing by the SBEs is dependent on E-Marketing perceived compatibility
H1J	There is a positive relationship between market trends and competitive pressures and E-Marketing adoption by the SBEs.
H1K	There is a positive relationship between government influence and E-Marketing adoption by the SBEs.
H1L	There is a positive relationship between cultural orientation towards E-Marketing by the SBE customers and E-Marketing adoption by the SBEs.

SBEs) and most of the research SBEs (29.8%) were in business for 11 – 20 years (34 SBE's).

With regards to capital, it was found that the majority of the SBEs (28.1%) were in the category of less than 250,000 pounds as capital (32 SBEs). On the other hand it was found that most of the research SBEs (64.9%) was working nationally (74 SBEs). With reference to the individual participants, it was found that the majority of the individual participants were the small business owners themselves (42.1% of the total), aged between 30 – 40 years (42.1% of the total), worked within their enterprises for 5 – 10 years (43% of the total), participated and were involved in E-Marketing implementation within their enterprises (85.1% of the total) and university graduates (55.3% of the total).

Results of Hypotheses Testing

As mentioned earlier multiple regression analysis was used to test these hypotheses. The multiple regression model can be expressed in a multiple linear regression equation as follows:

E-Marketing *adoption* = Constant + β_1 Entrepreneur skills (H3a) + β_2 Available resources of the SBE (H3b) + β_3 SBE organizational culture (H3c) + β_4 Type of products (H3d) + β_5 International orientation of the SBE (H3e) + β_6 SBE size (H3f) + β_7 E-Marketing perceived ease of use (H3g) + β_8 E-Marketing perceived relative advantage (H3h) + β_9 E-Marketing perceived compatibility (H3i) + β_{10} competitive pressures (H3j) + β_{11} government influence (H3k) + β_{12} cultural orientation towards E-Marketing by the SBE customers (H3l) + ε

Table 2. SBE survey response summary

Total number of questionnaires	391
Number of completed and returned questionnaires	114
Unreachable SBEs	14
Number of SBEs that declined participation	19
Response rate	*31.84%*

To investigate the above hypotheses, all the variables were entered in a single block. The results showed that the proposed model illustrates and explains a significant percentage of variance to indicate the impact of TAM and IDT factors, Small Business Enterprises internal factors and Small Business Enterprises external factors on E-Marketing adoption by these Small Business Enterprises. Table 3 shows that 70.2% of the observed variability in E-Marketing adoption is explained by the twelve independent variables (R^2= 0.733, Adjusted R^2= 0.702). According to Sykes (1993), a high value of R^2 suggests that the regression model explains the variation in the dependent variable well. Based on that and by taking into consideration the value of R^2 resulted from the regression, TAM/IDT factors, internal and external factors explain the variation in E-Marketing in a good way.

To test the equivalent null hypothesis that there is no linear relationship in the research population between the dependent variable and the independent variables, the Analysis of Variance (ANOVA) was used. Table 4 illustrates the results of this Analysis of Variance. As can be seen from the table, the ratio of the two mean squares (F) was 23.131 (F value = 23.131, P<0.001). Since the observed significance level was less than 0.001, the twelve independent variables influence E-Marketing adoption by Small Business Enterprises.

To test the null hypothesis that the research population fractional regression coefficient for a variable is 0, t-statistic and its observed significance level were used. The results are shown in Table 5.

As can be seen from the results in Table 5, the researcher can safely reject the null hypotheses that the coefficients for entrepreneur (owner) skills (B=0.156, t= 1.996, p<0.05), perceived ease of use (B= 0. 215, t= 2.331, p<0.05), perceived relative advantage (B= 0. 318, t= 3.001, p<0.05), the perceived compatibility (B= 0.243, t= 2.596, p<0.05) and cultural orientation (B= 0. 121, t= 1.965, p<0.05) are 0. Multicollinearity between the independent variables was minimal, as shown in Table 5 the values of Tolerance averaged between 0.235 to 0.741 and the variance inflation factor (VIF) averaged between 1.349 and 4.259, indicating that the results are reliable.

However, based of the fact that the fractional coefficient does not contribute significantly to the research model the null hypothesis is accepted for the factors related to the SBE resources (B=-0.047 t= - 0.574, p>0.05), type of product (B= 0.040, t= 0.667, p>0.05), international orientation (B= 0.013, t= 0. 219, p>0.05), size of SBE (B= 0.093, t= 1.556, p>0.05), organisational culture(B= 0.051, t= 0.652, p>0.05), competitive pressures (B= -0.018, t= -0.251, p>0.05) and government influence (B= -0.054, t= -0.753, p>0.05).

The beta weights show that the perceived relative advantage (B= 0. 318) is relatively stronger than the perceived compatibility (B= 0.243), perceived ease of use (B= 0. 215), owner skills (B= 0.156) and cultural orientation (B= 0. 121) in explaining the adoption of E-Marketing by Small Business Enterprises. The results are summarised in the following table.

Although the hypothesis for SBE resources, organizational culture, type of product, interna-

Table 3. Model summary

Model	R	R Square	Adjusted R Square	Std. Error of the Estimate
1	0.856[a]	0.733	0.702	0.32519
a. Predictors: (Constant), compatibility, type of product, size of SBE, international orientation, entrepreneur skills, organisational culture, ease of use, SBE resources, relative advantage, competitive pressures, government influence, cultural orientation towards E-Marketing by the SBE customers.				
b. Dependent Variable: E-Marketing Adoption				

Table 4. Summary of ANOVA[b] results

Model		Sum of Squares	df	Mean Square	F	Sig.
1	Regression	29.354	12	2.446	23.131	**0.000[a]**
	Residual	10.681	101	0.106		
	Total	40.035	113			
a. Predictors: (Constant), compatibility, type of product, size of SBE, international orientation, entrepreneur (owner) skills, organisational culture, ease of use, SBE resources, relative advantage, competitive pressures, government influence, cultural orientation towards E-Marketing by the SBE customers.						
b. Dependent Variable: E-Marketing Adoption						

tional orientation, size of SBE, competitive pressures and government influence are rejected, to support these findings the researcher investigated the individual effect of each of these factors on the adoption of E-Marketing by Small Business Enterprises through conducting simple regression analysis. This is mainly to determine the importance of each independent variable in relation with the dependent variable (E-Marketing adoption). Based on the simple regression analysis it was found that some factors have a positive linear relationship with E-Marketing adoption by the small businesses. In this context; SBE resources, SBE international orientation, organizational culture and competitive pressures alone reveal that they has a significant positive linear relationship with E-Marketing adoption. This suggests that with the other eleven variables in the multiple regression model, the impact of SBE resources, SBE international orientation, organizational culture and competitive pressures on E-Marketing adoption were overshadowed.

Table 5. Results of regression coefficients[a]

Model	Unstandardied Coefficients	Standardized Coefficients	T- value	Sig.	Collinearity Statistics	
	β	Beta			Tolerance	VIF
(Constant)	.001		.003	.998		
Entrepreneur (owner) Skills	.158	.156	1.996	**.049**	**.432**	**2.314**
Organisational Culture	.048	.051	.652	.516	**.427**	**2.343**
SBE resources	-.038	-.047	-.574	.567	**.387**	**2.583**
Type Of Product	.030	.040	.667	.506	**.732**	**1.367**
International Orientation	.009	.013	.219	.827	**.741**	**1.349**
Size Of SBE	.064	.093	1.556	.123	**.741**	**1.350**
Ease Of Use	.190	.215	2.331	**.022**	**.310**	**3.223**
Relative Advantage	.269	.318	3.001	**.003**	**.235**	**4.259**
Compatibility	.210	.243	2.596	**.011**	**.300**	**3.329**
Competitive Pressures	-.014	-.018	-.251	.802	**.527**	**1.899**
Government Influence	-.030	-.054	-.753	.453	**.508**	**1.969**
Cultural orientation towards E-Marketing	.102	.121	1.965	**.005**	**.699**	**1.431**

Table 6. Summary of the results of TAM/IDT, SBE internal and external factors hypotheses

Hypotheses	Results
H1A - Adopting E-Marketing by the SBEs is dependent on the entrepreneur (owner) skills and support.	*Accepted*
H1B - Adopting E-Marketing by the SBEs is dependent on the available resources of the SBE	*Rejected*
H1C - Adopting E-Marketing by the SBEs is dependent on the SBE organizational culture.	*Rejected*
H1D - Adopting E-Marketing by the SBEs is dependent on the type of products produced by the SBE.	*Rejected*
H1E - Adopting E-Marketing by the SBEs is dependent on the international orientation of the SBE	*Rejected*
H1F - Adopting E-Marketing by the SBEs is dependent on the SBE size	*Rejected*
H1G - Adopting E-Marketing by the SBEs is dependent on E-Marketing perceived ease of use	*Accepted*
H1H - Adopting E-Marketing by the SBEs is dependent on E-Marketing perceived relative advantage (usefulness).	*Accepted*
H1I - Adopting E-Marketing by the SBEs is dependent on E-Marketing perceived compatibility	*Accepted*
H1J - There is a positive relationship between market trends and competitive pressures and E-Marketing adoption by the SBEs.	*Rejected*
H1K - There is a positive relationship between government influence and E-Marketing adoption by the SBEs.	*Rejected*
H1L - There is a positive relationship between cultural orientation towards E-Marketing by the SBE customers and E-Marketing adoption by the SBEs.	*Accepted*

FUTURE RESEARCH DIRECTIONS

There are few numbers of studies that have investigated the impact/effect of entrepreneurial skills and top management support on the adoption of new technologies, such as E-Marketing, E-commerce and E-business; consequently there is a need to conduct more research to investigate this impact in an E-Marketing context. On the other hand, there is a small number of studies that have researched the impact/effect of organisational culture on the adoption of E-Marketing or electronic commercial transactions. Accordingly, there is a need to investigate the impact of organisational culture on the adoption of E-Marketing in Small Business Enterprises. The impact of international orientation of the SBE on its adoption of E-Marketing also needs to be investigated. This will lead to a greater and deep understanding of the different factors that affect the adoption of E-Marketing by Small Business Enterprises and will add to the accumulated knowledge in the field of E-Marketing.

CONCLUSION

Generally, the research findings support the research model and the results support most of the hypotheses. Furthermore, the results of the questionnaire help to provide good and deep understanding of the impact of the different environmental factors on the adoption of E-Marketing by small businesses within the UK. Within the study, it has been found that small business internal factors, ease of use, relative advantage and compatibility have a significant positive impact on E-Marketing adoption. The authors were surprised, however, to find that most of the small businesses external factors do not have a powerful impact on E-Marketing adoption by SBEs. The findings stress the important role of the Small Business Enterprises internal factors, ease of use, relative advantage and compatibility in the adoption of E-Marketing and have some important implications for marketing activities within Small Business Enterprises.

REFERENCES

Adams, D. A., Nelson, R. R., & Todd, P. A. (1992). Perceived usefulness, ease of use, and usage of information technology: a replication. *MIS Quarterly*, 227–247. doi:10.2307/249577

Ajzen, I., & Fishbein, M. (1980). *Understanding attitudes and predicting social behavior.* Upper Saddle River, NJ: Prentice-Hall.

AL-Qirim, N. (2007). E-commerce adoption in small businesses: cases from New Zealand. *Journal of Information Technology Case and Application Research, 9,* 28.

Al-Qirim, N. (2006). Personas of e-commerce adoption in small businesses in New Zealand. *Journal of Electronic Commerce in Organizations, 4,* 18–45.

Al-Qirim, N. (2007). Personas of e-commerce adoption in small businesses in New Zealand. *Web Technologies for Commerce and Services Online,* 286.

Bagozzi, R. P., Davis, F. D., & Warshaw, P. R. (1992). Development and test of a theory of technological learning and usage. *Human Relations, 45*(7), 659. doi:10.1177/001872679204500702

Burnkrant, R. E., & Page, T. J. (1988). The structure and antecedents of the normative and attitudinal components of Fishbein's theory of reasoned action. *Journal of Experimental Social Psychology, 24*(1), 66–87. doi:10.1016/0022-1031(88)90044-3

Carter, L., & Belanger, F. (2004). The influence of perceived characteristics of innovating on e-government adoption. *Electronic . Journal of E-Government, 2*(1), 11–20.

Chaffey, D. (2007). *E-business and e-commerce management: Strategy, implementation and practice.* Upper Saddle River, NJ: Prentice Hall.

Chan, S., & Lu, M. (2004). Understanding internet banking adoption and use behavior: A Hong Kong perspective. *Journal of Global Information Management, 12*(3), 21–43.

Chau, P. Y. K. (1996). An empirical assessment of a modified technology acceptance model. *Journal of Management Information Systems, 13*(2), 185–204.

Chen, L., Gillenson, M. L., & Sherrell, D. L. (2002). Enticing online consumers: an extended technology acceptance perspective. *Information & Management, 39*(8), 705–719. doi:10.1016/S0378-7206(01)00127-6

Chen, L., Gillenson, M. L., & Sherrell, D. L. (2004). Consumer acceptance of virtual stores: a theoretical model and critical success factors. *Database, 35,* 8–31.

Ching, H. L., & Ellis, P. (2004). Marketing in cyberspace: what factors drive e-commerce adoption? *Journal of Marketing Management, 20, 3*(4), 409-429.

Dann, S., & Dann, S. (2001). *Strategic Internet marketing.* New York: Wiley.

Davis, F. D. (1989). Perceived usefulness, perceived ease of use, and user acceptance of information technology. *MIS Quarterly,* 319–340. doi:10.2307/249008

Davis, F. D., Bagozzi, R. P., & Warshaw, P. R. (1989). User acceptance of computer technology: a comparison of two theoretical models. *Management Science, 35*(8), 982–1003. doi:10.1287/mnsc.35.8.982

De Vaus, D. A. (1991). *Surveys in social research.* London: Routledge.

Dembla, P., Palvia, P., & Krishnan, B. (2007). Understanding the adoption of Web-enabled transaction processing by small businesses. *Journal of Electronic Commerce Research, 8*(1), 1–16.

Devaraj, S., Fan, M., & Kohli, R. (2002). Antecedents of B2C channel satisfaction and preference: validating e-commerce metrics. *Information Systems Research, 13*(3), 316. doi:10.1287/isre.13.3.316.77

Doolin, B., McLeod, L., McQueen, B., & Watton, M. (2003). Internet strategies for establishing retailers: Four New Zealand case studies. [JITCA]. *Journal of Information Technology Cases and Applications, 5*(4), 3–19.

Downie, G. W. (2002). Internet marketing and SMEs. *Management Services, 14*(7), 8–20.

DTI-news-release. (2008). *National statistics, The Small Business Service (SBS), The British Department of Trade and Industry.* Retrieved October 14, 2008, from http://www.sbs.gov.uk/SBS_Gov_files/researchandstats/SMEStats2004.pdf

Eid, R. (2003). *Business-to-business international internet marketing: adoption, implementation and implications, an empirical study of UK companies.* UK: Bradford University.

Gallagher, D., & Gilmore, A. (2004). The stages theory of SME internationalisation: a Northern Ireland case study. *International Journal of Management Cases, 7*(1), 13–23.

Gefen, D. (2003). TAM or just plain habit: A look at experienced online shoppers. *Journal of End User Computing, 15*(3), 1–13.

Gefen, D., Karahanna, E., & Straub, D. W. (2003a). Inexperience and experience with online stores: The importance of TAM and trust. *IEEE Transactions on Engineering Management, 50*(3), 307–321. doi:10.1109/TEM.2003.817277

Gefen, D., Karahanna, E., & Straub, D. W. (2003b). Trust and TAM in online shopping: An integrated model. *MIS Quarterly, 27*, 51–90.

Gefen, D., & Straub, D. (2000). The relative importance of perceived ease of use in IS adoption: a study of e-commerce adoption. *Journal of the Association for Information Systems, 1*(8), 1–28.

Gefen, D., & Straub, D. W. (1997). Gender differences in the perception and use of e-mail: An extension to the Technology Acceptance Model. *MIS Quarterly, 21*, 389–400. doi:10.2307/249720

Grandon, E., & Pearson, J. M. (2003). Strategic value and adoption of electronic commerce: an empirical study of Chilean small and medium businesses. *Journal of Global Information Technology Management, 6*(3), 22–43.

Hall, B. H., & Khan, B. (2003). Adoption of new technology. *NBER working paper.*

Haynes, R. M., & Thies, E. A. (1991). Management of technology in service firms. *Journal of Operations Management, 10*(3), 388–397. doi:10.1016/0272-6963(91)90075-9

Hendrickson, A. R., & Collins, M. R. (1996). An assessment of structure and causation of IS usage. *The Data Base for Advances in Information Systems, 27*(2), 61.

Igbaria, M., Guimaraes, T., & Davis, G. B. (1995). Testing the determinants of microcomputer usage via a structural equation model. *Journal of Management Information Systems, 11*(4), 87–114.

Jeffcoate, J., Chappell, C., & Feindt, S. (2002). Best practice in SME adoption of e-commerce. *Benchmarking: An International Journal, 9*(2), 122–132. doi:10.1108/14635770210421791

Jie, S., Peiji, S., & Jiaming, F. (2007). *A Model for Adoption of Online Shopping: A Perceived Characteristics of Web as a Shopping Channel View.*

Kamel, S., Hassan, A., & ebrary, I. (2003). *Assessing the introduction of electronic banking in Egypt using the* Technology Acceptance Model: Idea Group.

Karahanna, E., Straub, D. W., & Chervany, N. L. (1999). Information technology adoption across time: a cross-sectional comparison of pre-adoption and post-adoption beliefs. *MIS Quarterly*, *23*183–213. doi:10.2307/249751

Kardaras, D., & Papathanassiou, E. (2000). The development of B2C e-commerce in Greece: Current situation and future potential. *Internet Research: Electronic Networking Applications and Policy*, *10*(4), 284–294. doi:10.1108/10662240010342568

Koufaris, M. (2003). Applying the technology acceptance model and flow theory to online consumer behavior. *Information Systems Research*, *13*(2), 205–223. doi:10.1287/isre.13.2.205.83

Lederer, A. L., Maupin, D. J., Sena, M. P., & Zhuang, Y. (2000). The technology acceptance model and the World Wide Web. *Decision Support Systems*, *29*(3), 269–282. doi:10.1016/S0167-9236(00)00076-2

Lertwongsatien, C., & Wongpinunwatana, N. (2003). E-commerce adoption in Thailand: An empirical study of small and medium enterprises (SMEs). *Journal of Global Information Technology Management*, *6*(3), 67–83.

Looi, H. (2004). A model of factors influencing electronic commerce adoption among SME's in Brunei Darussalam. *International Journal of Information Technology*, *10*, 72–87.

Lynn, G. S., Lipp, S. M., Akgün, A. E., & Cortez, A. (2002). Factors impacting the adoption and effectiveness of the World Wide Web in marketing. *Industrial Marketing Management*, *31*(1), 35–49. doi:10.1016/S0019-8501(00)00104-8

Mathieson, K. (1991). Predicting user intentions: comparing the Technology Acceptance Model with the theory of planned behavior. *Information Systems Research*, *2*(3), 173–191. doi:10.1287/isre.2.3.173

McCloskey, D. (2004). Evaluating electronic commerce acceptance with the Technology Acceptance Model. *Journal of Computer Information Systems*, *44*(2), 49–57.

McDonald, M., & Wilson, H. (1999). E-Marketing Improving marketing effectiveness in a digital world.

Moon, J. W., & Kim, Y. G. (2001). Extending the TAM for a World-Wide-Web context. *Information & Management*, *38*(4), 217–230. doi:10.1016/S0378-7206(00)00061-6

Moore, G. C., & Benbasat, I. (1991). Development of an instrument to measure the perceptions of adopting an information technology innovation. *Information Systems Research*, *2*(3), 192–222. doi:10.1287/isre.2.3.192

Moore, G. C., & Benbasat, I. (1996). Integrating diffusion of innovations and theory of reasoned action models to predict utilization of information technology by end-users. *Diffusion and adoption of information technology*, 132-146.

Morris, M. G., & Dillon, A. (1997). How user perceptions influence software use. *IEEE Software*, *14*(4), 58–65. doi:10.1109/52.595956

Mulhern, A. (1995). The SME sector in Europe: A broad perspective. *Journal of Small Business Management*, *33*(3).

Oliver, R. L., & Bearden, W. O. (1985). Crossover effects in the theory of reasoned action: A moderating influence attempt. *The Journal of Consumer Research*, *12*324–340. doi:10.1086/208519

Park, S., & Yoon, S. H. (2005). Separating early-adopters from the majority: The case of Broadband Internet access in Korea. *Technological Forecasting and Social Change*, *72*(3), 301–325. doi:10.1016/j.techfore.2004.08.013

Parthasarathy, M., & Bhattacherjee, A. (1998). Understanding post-adoption behavior in the context of online services. *Information Systems Research, 9*, 362–379. doi:10.1287/isre.9.4.362

Pavlou, P. A. (2003). Consumer acceptance of electronic commerce: Integrating trust and risk with the Technology Acceptance Model. *International Journal of Electronic Commerce, 7*(3), 101–134.

Peansupap, V., & Walker, D. (2005). Exploratory factors influencing information and communication technology diffusion and adoption within Australian construction organizations: a micro analysis. *Construction Innovation, 5*(3), 135–157.

Pikkarainen, T., Pikkarainen, K., Karjaluoto, H., & Pahnila, S. (2004). Consumer acceptance of online banking: an extension of the Technology Acceptance Model. *Internet Research, 14*(3), 224–235. doi:10.1108/10662240410542652

Poon, S., & Swatman, P. M. C. (1997). Small business use of the Internet. *International Marketing Review, 14*(5), 385–402. doi:10.1108/02651339710184343

Premkumar, G., & Roberts, M. (1999). Adoption of new information technologies in rural small businesses. *Omega, 27*(4), 467–484. doi:10.1016/S0305-0483(98)00071-1

Rajagopal, P. (2002). An innovation—diffusion view of implementation of enterprise resource planning (ERP) systems and development of a research model. *Information & Management, 40*(2), 87–114. doi:10.1016/S0378-7206(01)00135-5

Reedy, J. E., Schullo, S. S., & Zimmerman, K. R. (1999). *Electonic marketing: Integrating electronic resources into the marketing process.* Orlando, FL: Harcourt College Publishers.

Rogers, E. M. (1983). *Diffusion of innovations.* New York: The Free Press.

Rogers, E. M. (1995). *Diffusion of innovations.* New York: Free Press.

Roman, R. (2003). Diffusion of innovations as a theoretical framework for telecenters. *Information Technologies and International Development, 1*(2), 53–66. doi:10.1162/154475203322981969

Rose, G., & Straub, D. (1998). Predicting general IT use: Applying TAM to the Arabic world. *Journal of Global Information Management, 6*(3), 39–46.

Seyal, A. H., & Rahman, M. N. A. (2003). A preliminary investigation of e-commerce adoption in small & medium enterprises in Brunei. *Journal of Global Information Technology Management, 6*(2), 6–26.

Shih, Y. Y., & Fang, K. (2004). The use of a decomposed theory of planned behavior to study Internet banking in Taiwan. *Internet Research, 14*(3), 213–223. doi:10.1108/10662240410542643

Shimp, T. A., & Kavas, A. (1984). The theory of reasoned action applied to coupon usage. *The Journal of Consumer Research, 11*, 795–809. doi:10.1086/209015

Smith, P. R., & Chaffey, D. (2005). *E-marketing excellence.* Oxford, UK: Butterworth-Heinemann.

Smyth, M., & Ibbotson, P. (2001). Internet connectivity in Ireland. *Joint report by the Bank of Ireland and the University of Ulster.* Retrieved from http://www.bankofireland.co. uk/whats_new/item. php

Stockdale, R., & Standing, C. (2006). A classification model to support SME e-commerce adoption initiatives. *Journal of Small Business and Enterprise Development, 13*(3), 381. doi:10.1108/14626000610680262

Straub, D., Limayem, M., & Karahanna-Evaristo, E. (1995). Measuring system usage: implications for IS theory testing. *Management Science, 41*(8), 1328–1342. doi:10.1287/mnsc.41.8.1328

Straus, J., & Frost, R. (2001). *E-markzeting.* Upper Saddle River, NJ: Prentice-Hall.

Szajna, B. (1994). Software evaluation and choice: predictive validation of the technology acceptance instrument. *MIS Quarterly, 18*(3), 319–324. doi:10.2307/249621

Tan, M., & Teo, T. S. H. (2000). Factors influencing the adoption of Internet banking. *Journal of the AIS, 1*(1).

Taylor, S., & Todd, P. (1995). Assessing IT usage: The role of prior experience. *MIS Quarterly, 19*(4), 561–570. doi:10.2307/249633

Taylor, S., & Todd, P. A. (1995b). Understanding information technology usage: A test of competing models. *Information Systems Research, 6*(2), 144. doi:10.1287/isre.6.2.144

Teo, T. S. H., Lim, V. K. G., & Lai, R. Y. C. (1999). Intrinsic and extrinsic motivation in Internet usage. *Omega, 27*(1), 25–37. doi:10.1016/S0305-0483(98)00028-0

Theng, L. G., & Boon, J. L. W. (1996). An exploratory study of factors affecting the failure of local small and medium enterprises. *Asia Pacific Journal of Management, 13*(2), 47–61. doi:10.1007/BF01733816

Thompson, R. (1998). Extending the Technology Acceptance Model with motivation and social factors. In *AMCIS 1998 Proceedings* (pp. 254).

Tornatzky, L. G., & Klein, K. J. (1982). Innovation characteristics and innovation adoption-implementation: A meta-analysis of findings. *IEEE Transactions on Engineering Management, 29*(1), 28–45.

UNCTAD-UN. (2004). *E-commerce and development report 2004.* Retrieved August 9, 2007, from http://www.unctad.org/en/docs/ecdr2004ch2_en.pdf

Van Slyke, C., Belanger, F., & Comunale, C. L. (2004). *Factors influencing the adoption of Web-based shopping: The impact of trust.*

Venkatesh, V., Morris, M. G., Davis, G. B., & Davis, F. D. (2003). User acceptance of information technology: Toward a unified view. *MIS Quarterly, 27*, 425–478.

Vijayasarathy, L. R. (2004). Predicting consumer intentions to use on-line shopping: the case for an augmented Technology Acceptance Model. *Information & Management, 41*(6), 747–762. doi:10.1016/j.im.2003.08.011

Wang, Y. S., Wang, Y. M., Lin, H. H., & Tang, T. I. (2003). Determinants of user acceptance of internet banking: an empirical study. *International Journal of Service Industry Management, 14*(5), 501–519. doi:10.1108/09564230310500192

Watson, J., & Everett, J. E. (1996). Do small businesses have high failure rates? *Journal of Small Business Management, 34*(4), 45–62.

Whiteley, D. (2000). *E Commerce: Strategy, technologies and applications.* New York: McGraw-Hill.

Wu, J. H., & Wang, S. C. (2005). What drives mobile commerce? An empirical evaluation of the revised Technology Acceptance Model. *Information & Management, 42*(5), 719–729. doi:10.1016/j.im.2004.07.001

Yi, M. Y., Jackson, J. D., Park, J. S., & Probst, J. C. (2006). Understanding information technology acceptance by individual professionals: Toward an integrative view. *Information & Management, 43*(3), 350–363. doi:10.1016/j.im.2005.08.006

Zhu, K., & Kraemer, K. L. (2005). Post-adoption variations in usage and value of e-business by organizations: cross-country evidence from the retail industry. *Information Systems Research, 16*(1), 61. doi:10.1287/isre.1050.0045

Section 6
Small Business and Electronic Retailing

Chapter 14
Multichannel Integration for Small and Medium Retailers

Daniela Andreini
University of Bergamo, Italy

ABSTRACT

Channel marketing literature has underlined the importance and the advantages of developing a multichannel integration between virtual and physical marketing channels, but researchers have concentrated their works on retail chains and large infrastructures. This chapter studies the multichannel integration strategies for small and medium retailers, formulating a multichannel integration codification scheme and explaining the barriers and related solutions under these strategic decisions.

INTRODUCTION

Since the development of the internet as a retail channel, marketing literature has acquired new insight in the research field of multichannel retailing for large and small firms. Multichannel consumers are said to be more profitable (Kumar and Venkatesan, 2004) and more loyal than single-channel ones (DoubleClick's, 2005). For this reason, in literature the development of carefully integrated online and offline retail channels has been considered strategic.

Researchers have concentrated their works on retail chains and large infrastructures which have

more possibilities of recovering IT investments, thanks to a consistent territorial presence which is defined by the number of outlets owned. Retailers with just one or a few physical stores seem to be limited in developing an integrated multichannel strategy because they lack a physical presence on the territory.

Contrary to these statements, multichannel integration can be modulated on different levels or strategies according to the retailers' characteristics, type of products and market environment.

The fundamental research questions of this study are:

- Which are the different strategies of multichannel integration?

DOI: 10.4018/978-1-60566-998-4.ch014

- What are the most interesting solutions of integration according to small and medium retailers' characteristics and market conditions?
- What are small and medium retailers' barriers and related responses for each multichannel strategy?

By means of a literature review and explorative research, four strategic models will be presented and measured through a codification scheme developed by Steinfield et al. (2005), and adapted here to small and medium retailers. Moreover, a conceptual model that individualizes the drivers for the development of different multichannel integration strategies does not exist yet. Therefore, a qualitative research approach and case study research have been used (Eisenhardt 1989; Yin, 2003), in order to demonstrate how small and medium retailers can also creatively develop various multichannel integration strategies. Finally, at the end of this paper, drivers and barriers affecting the multichannel integration decisions will be discussed with the relevant solutions.

This work wishes to make a further contribution to theory and empirical research. First it tests the levels of multichannel integration in retailing for SMEs, extending Steinfield's (2005) and Müller-Lankenau's (2005) theoretical insights into different patterns of multichannel integration.

Secondly, it will also help small and medium retailers to consider distinctive multichannel integration strategies.

In the first part of this paper, a brief review of the literature will be presented with empirical and qualitative research into small and medium Italian retailers. In the second part, the research discusses retailers' barriers and solutions for each multichannel strategy, the professional implications and future research.

BACKGROUND

In this paper, multichannel integration is defined as the activity of traditional retailers to combine physical infrastructures (stores) and virtual channels (internet), in order to enhance customer value, and to increase revenues for firms. From the customers' point of view, the integration between physical and virtual channels implies that traditional stores and their websites become interchangeable in selling, communicating and interacting with them. In this case, customers can buy products online and pick them up from the store, or use the same fidelity cards online and offline, or buy products and services online and return them to the store. On the other side, retailers can benefit from this synergy by reducing inventory, post-sales, pre-sales and logistic costs. At the same time, retailers can increase revenues because multichannel customers are said to be more profitable (Kumar and Venkatesan, 2005) than single-channel ones (DoubleClick, 2005).

Nowadays, literature about multichannel retailing presents both a theoretical and an empirical research trend. The theoretical trend emphasises the benefits from integration of a physical presence and e-commerce for consumers. It describes how consumers can communicate and interact in different ways, how they compare prices and trust sounded offline brand names. At the same time, small and medium firms can benefit from the international internet marketplace, and reduce investments and costs in communication and transaction. (Steinfield et al., 1999; Gulati and Garino, 2000; Otto and Chung 2000; Kumar and Venkatesan, 2005).

On the other side, empirical research has demonstrated that strategies of integration between online and offline channels are not so common in practice due to product characteristics, availability of resources, business strategies and environment. Some products need the physical presence of consumers, some enterprises have to invest too many resources in IT infrastructures compared with the ROI of e-commerce activities, and in other cases the environment and local buying behaviour influence the success of integrated multichannel strategies (Saeed et al. 2003, Steinfield et al. 2005, Kabadayi et al. 2007). Many researchers have studied the diffusion of e-commerce by SMEs (Stansfield, 2003; Johnston, 2007; Daesoo, 2008), measuring the type of use. This work wants to pinpoint the level of diffusion, and in particular different strategies for the multichannel integration in small and medium retailers.

METHODOLOGY

In order to verify how small and medium retailers are integrating their activities online and offline, two different research methods have been used.

The first one refers to exploratory research which has been conducted in one of the most industrialized areas of Italy (the province of Bergamo and Milan) in January 2009. The aim of this study is to carry out an initial test of the theory on the most preferred multichannel strategies used by small and medium retailers. For the exploratory research 200 small and medium retailers' websites in the tourism and fashion businesses have been scanned. Tourism and fashion industries have been selected because they are the most developed businesses in the Italian provinces analysed; moreover, they represent two important categories: digital and physical products.

Furthermore, in order to codify retailers' web features according to different multichannel strategies, content analysis has been considered a suitable research method which has already been used for other e-commerce studies (McMillan, 2000; Zhu and Kraemer, 2005; Steinfield et al., 2005). Since innovation in B2C activities are consumer-facing activities, data collection through website analysis is the most appropriate research method in this field. The results of the research are illustrated in the in a later paragraph.

For the second research, case studies have been used (Eisenhardt 1989; Yin, 2003), the aim being to investigate how small and medium retailers use multichannel integration strategies, focusing on the most peculiar examples.

The case study for each multichannel integration strategy was identified and analysed in January 2009 in Italy. The objective was to verify the multichannel strategy usage and to show small and medium retailers' peculiarity in adopting it.

The case studies have been gathered and selected during the above mentioned explorative research and from the annual research report on Italian e-commerce of the B2C Observatory at the Polytechnic of Milan (2007). Due to the relative scarcity of multichannel approaches among small and medium retailers, once a list of firms was compiled, their websites were scanned to identify their multichannel strategy, according to the codification scheme presented in the next paragraph.

The case studies were selected on the basis of the size of the retailers (e.g. multinational retail chains have not been considered) and the originality of the multichannel integration solutions. The information gathered for each case study has been drawn from their websites, trade literature, interviews in popular press articles, and in research reports.

An original case study for each multichannel integration strategy is illustrated and discussed in the following paragraphs.

MULTICHANNEL INTEGRATION STRATEGIES: DEFINITION, CODIFICATION, EXPLORATION AND CASE STUDIES

Multichannel Integration Definition

Many researchers have codified firms' multichannel strategies in different ways. Prasarnphanich and Gillenson (2003) enumerate a variety of hybrid clicks and bricks activities which retailers can develop in order to integrate virtual and physical channels.

Müller-Lankenau et al. (2006) have developed a strategic channel alignment model for the purpose of finding how retailers can align IT and commercial strategies. They have observed the most developed European grocery chains and four strategic models have been formulated: a) offline-dominated strategy: retailers' websites support the core business offline; b) online-dominated strategy: in this case, offline stores support retailers' core business online; c) isolation strategy: offline and online channels present different brand names, in this way, there is no integration and no support between the two marketplaces; d) integration strategy: offline and online channels are used together interchangeably. Müller-Lankenau et al.'s work has been written observing large retail chains; moreover, they do not indicate a scheme capable of categorizing retailers' web activities according to different strategies.

The strategic models proposed in this study have been created through a content analysis of 200 small and medium retailers' websites in Italy and by analysing selected case studies presented in a next paragraph.

The four multichannel integration strategies proposed in this paper enhance Müller-Lankenau et al.'s model, indicating the strategic activities that are able to mix offline and online channels. It has also made an attempt to adapt the multichannel strategy models to small and medium businesses, indicating which web features can facilitate the channel integration process.

Multichannel Integration Strategies

This study has led to four different multichannel strategies: 1. Information supporting strategy; 2. Independent Channels Strategy; 3. Database Integration Strategy; 4. Full-Integrated channels strategy.

Informational Supporting Strategy

In line with the original model (Müller-Lankenau et al., 2006), also for small and medium retailers, the objective of this strategy is a low cost internet presence. Therefore, internet is used only for pre and post-sales information, therefore, on these websites customers can find contact information, product information, store locator systems, news and promotions, but no transactions are allowed. Informational Supporting Strategy is represented by virtual shopping windows which are a cheap way of being present online. These websites are static and provide basic information about the retailer: location, contacts, maps, and opening hours. In the most advanced cases updated catalogues, news and promotions are supplied online. Shopping window websites have very low barriers of implementation, because they require no interaction with customers and scarce updating activity, which facilitate those retailers with little IT knowledge and commitment.

In these cases, the level of multichannel integration is very low because no investments in database or logistical integration are needed. The main benefit for sellers and buyers is the reduction in information costs. Saban and Rau (2005) have discovered that SMEs' websites are used more as shopping windows than as a sales channel because costs and other resources inhibit the use. This strategy is also the strategy used the most by small and medium retailers, because it is less demanding in terms of financial and organizational resources, and the benefits for owners and managers are immediate.

This strategy is also used by small and medium producers who do not want to create conflicts with their traditional resellers. Nevertheless, some SMEs have found a way of supporting their business offline with an informative website and a little interaction activity as is illustrated in the case studies paragraph.

Independent Channels Strategy

In this strategy, retailers create a virtual store independent from the physical one, so that customers can buy both online and/or offline, but they must return or change the products bought using only the channel from which they were purchased. Unlike Müller-Lankenau et al.'s isolation model, when this strategy is developed by small and medium retailers, it is not focused on brand differentiation between online and offline channels, but on their capacity to create a virtual commercial channel beside the offline store using the same brand name. Retailers with a single or few physical stores are limited in the development of an integrated multichannel strategy, because they lack physical presence on the territory. Therefore, if they want to develop an e-commerce activity, they have to implement an independent channel strategy. In this case, the integration of the two channels (virtual and physical) is low, and for small and medium retailers it refers only to brand communication (King et al. 2004; Saeed, 2003). The benefits for small and medium retailers are high especially for niche products (traditional local products, or collectors' items), in terms of expansion of market opportunities, new targets, internationalization, etc.... The barriers derive from the inexperience and lack of knowledge in developing a virtual store. During the explorative and case study research, it has emerged that some small retailers have outsourced the e-commerce website which is managed by a specialized e-commerce partner. This is a good solution for reducing investments in IT platforms and knowledge. On the other hand, the outsourcing of online commercial and communication activities can be very expensive, therefore it may be difficult to find the right e-commerce partner.

Database Integration Strategy

This strategic model has been developed by analysing the research conducted by Steinfield et al. (2005) and it has also been supported by the exploratory research conducted for this paper. Unlike Müller-Lankenau et al.'s study (2006), traditional small and medium retailers do not develop an online-dominated strategy, because their core business is especially offline and the number of outlets does not benefit from this approach. Differently, database integration strategy takes advantage of internet potentiality, as an instrument for gathering information about actual and potential customers. By integrating online and offline databases, retailers enable gift tokens and fidelity cards to be used which allow data on customers' behaviour and preferences to be collected. The advantage for customers is a more integrated buying experience, while firms can limit the multichannel integration investments only to a database platform. This strategy presumes advantages from the integration of online and offline CRM systems, and it is suitable for those retailers whose earnings come from the personalization of products and services. For instance: small retail chains, service retailers and shops for tailor-made products could benefit from this integration strategy. More innovative retailers schedule appointments online for services delivered in the retail outlet (e.g. post-sales services). The exploratory research has shown that few retailers use this strategy, because it entails high implementation costs and considerable involvement by the owners. As a matter of fact, as opposed to the independent channels strategy where small retailers can outsource the e-commerce activity completely, in this case integration between online and offline channels is compulsory. For instance, having received the profile of a potential customer from the website, the retailer has to elaborate this information according to the internal retailing operations. Therefore, the commitment and organizational readiness are serious barriers in developing this strategy.

Full-Integrated Channels Strategy

In line with Müller-Lankenau et al.'s model (2006), with this strategy retailers mirror the physical store in the websites, integrating the two channels with advanced services, for instance: booking or ordering online and picking up offline, returning products to physical stores and searching the inventory in each retail outlet. The objectives are related to added value for customers and to the improvement of the store image. In this case, retailers need the maximum coordination investment in communication, operation and logistic activities in order to create a flexible and agile distribution process (Saeed, 2003) especially for physical products. On one side, a well-coordinated multichannel structure could easily be developed by small and medium retailers thanks to their sizes, but on the other side, the investments in IT infrastructures are a considerable obstacle. During the explorative research, it has been noted that some small and medium retailers have integrated online and offline channels through partnerships with producers or wholesalers, as is illustrated in a later paragraph about the case studies. In this way, very small retailers are also able to develop an e-commerce website fully integrated with their shop, without entailing costs for IT integration. The disadvantage of this solution is that the channel power shifts from the local store towards the producer or the wholesaler because they control the entire process from the online contact to the delivery of the product and they can gather information about store clients.

Codification Scheme

Having individualised which multichannel integration strategies small and medium retailers can develop online, it was important to measure and codify retailers' web features according to each multichannel integration strategy. Starting from the literature review, a codification scheme has been developed and utilised for the exploratory research of the 200 Italian retailers' websites.

Steinfield et al. (2005) have codified the level of multichannel integration in three groups: 1) simple information: corporate websites with basic references to physical stores; 2) complex online/offline activities: corporate websites with an explicit involvement of retail outlets in the transactions; 3) other features: referring to websites with some degree of online expertise, but not necessarily implying click & mortar strategies. Steinfield et al. (2005) was one of the first research studies to have codified and measured different levels of multichannel integration through a content analysis of different retailers' web features. The codification developed in this work is similar to Steinfield et al.'s, but contrary to the version proposed earlier, this scheme does not measure the intensity, but it codifies the web features in the four multichannel integration strategies. Moreover, the click & mortar features on the multichannel retailers' websites have been grouped according to the multichannel strategies presented above. The original codification scheme has been modified and adapted to small and medium retailers, verifying the presence or the absence of the 16 features illustrated in the websites explored (*Table 1*).

This codification is very useful as concrete evidence of online strategic decisions which can be used by retailers to focus on the most effective web features.

As illustrated in *Table 1*, Information Supporting Strategy (ISS) is based on information web features, Database Integration Strategy (DIS) is characterized by interaction with customers, Independent Channel Strategy (ICS) is focused on e-commerce activities and Full-integrated Channels Strategy (FCS) on full-integrated customers' experience and brand image.

Explorative Research

The codification scheme has been used for the initial exploratory research mentioned and 200

Table 1. Codification scheme (Source: exploratory research)

Information Supporting Strategy
1. Contact information of retail outlets
2. Address and Map to retail outlets or driving directions
3. Opening hours of retail outlets
4. Information on retail outlet events or specials
Database Integration Strategy
5. Ability to use store fidelity cards in both channels
6. Allow customers to set up and manage accounts also valid in retail outlets
7. Allow customers to use coupons or gift tokens redeemable in retail outlets or vice versa
8. Ability to make an appointment or reservation for a service in the retail outlet
Independent Channel Strategy
9. E-commerce without logistic support by stores
10. Allow customers to set up and manage accounts only online
11. Allow the status of an online order to be checked without any support by local store
Full-Integrated Channels Strategy
12. E-commerce with logistic support by stores
13. Allow customers to return items purchased online to retail outlets
14. Allow online orders to be picked up at retail outlets
15. Ability to search the inventory of any outlet of the retail chain
16. Allow the status of an online order to be checked with the support of local store

Italian websites in tourism and fashion retailing have been explored by means of a content analysis. This research method has been considered a suitable analysis, since innovation in B2C is a consumer-facing activity. The results of the analysis are summarized in *Table 2*.

According to this exploratory analysis, half of the websites investigated, use the internet for information and database strategy is used especially by small and medium retail chains.7% of the websites analysed has developed an independent e-commerce website and only 1% a full-integrated channel strategy.

Table 2. Results of the exploratory research (Source: Exploratory research)

Strategy	Results of the analysis of 200 websites		
	Adoption	Tourism	Fashion
Information Supporting Strategy	52%	61%	44%
Database Integration Strategy	9%	11%	8%
Independent Channel Strategy	7%	11%	3%
Full-Integrated channels strategy	1%	1%	1%

This is an initial analysis, (the number of firms and sectors must be increased), but these first results are consistent with literature review: internet is used by SMEs especially for pre and post-sales information. Figures concerning the integration of internet technology in database and commercial processes are low; but, as we will see in the next subsection, when SMEs recognize business opportunities online, they are very creative in adopting it.

Moreover, from this analysis it can be observed that there is no single best strategy for retailers, but when SMEs recognize internet as a business opportunity they are very fast and creative in adopting it as a commercial channel. In order to demonstrate how creative small and medium retailers are in integrating online and offline channels, for each strategy model a best Italian practice has been analysed.

Case Studies

This study was conducted in Italy which is considered a difficult market for B2C e-commerce activities. As a matter of fact, in Italy, only 57% of companies have websites or pages (the EU average is 65%), and a large proportion of them are small- and medium sized enterprises. Internet sales are soaring, but they are lower than any other European countries. Research by the Polytechnic of Milan (2007) quoted the value of the business-to-consumer market in Italy at €4bn in 2006. This represents around 1% of total retail sales in Italy, significantly lower than percentages in the United States (10%) and the EU (6%) (The Economist, 2007).

As previously mentioned, the case studies have been gathered and selected during the explorative research and integrated with the case studies presented in the annual research report on Italian B2C e-commerce published by the B2C Observatory at the Polytechnic of Milan (2007). The information gathered for each case study has been drawn from their websites, trade literature, interviews in popular press articles, and in financial and research reports. In this way, an original case study for each multichannel integration strategy has been illustrated and discussed in this section.

Informational Supporting Strategy

Tourism represents 12% of the GDP in Italy and 49% of Italian e-commerce (Polytechnic of Milan, 2007). Nevertheless, only a few tour operators and travel agencies have chosen to sell directly online. According to our exploratory research, only 61% of tourism firms have chosen to develop an informative website and 11% a direct commercial channel. One of them is a very well-known tour operator in Italy: Viaggi del Ventaglio (www. ventaglio.com). Viaggi del Ventaglio is one of the leading Italian outbound and domestic tour operators. Each year more than 540,000 clients travel with Ventaglio around the world. The core business is represented by "all inclusive" holiday resorts which are marketed under the name VentaClub, some of which are directly owned and/or managed by the company. Its most well-developed distribution channel is the traditional travel agency, where "all inclusive" customers usually buy their holidays. Despite the great success of online tourism business, for Viaggi del Ventaglio the decision to sell directly on the internet was affected by strong channel conflicts with travel agencies. Therefore, the strategic decision was to develop an informative website, where potential customers can gather information, ask for quotations and book their holidays. All the requests are sent to the nearest travel agency, which are presented by means of a store locator online. On the other hand, the travel agency chosen by the customer will receive a percentage on the holiday sold online. This strategy has the benefit of reducing potential channel conflicts with traditional resellers, and at the same time provides a really useful informative support online to customers.

Independent Channels Strategy

An emblematic example of this strategy in Italy is Peck (http://www.peck.it). Peck is a family business which produces and sells Italian gastronomic products through a well-known shop in Milan (Italy) and all over the world through its website since 2000. 50% of its business online is developed in Italy and 50% abroad (especially in the USA and in Japan). With its 128 employers, in 2007 the firm achieved revenue of almost 23,000,000 euro online and offline. The website is managed by an external firm which is in charge of all e-commerce processes. The independent channel model does not satisfy multichannel purchase behaviour that has evolved, but it avoids additional logistic costs to retailers and overcomes the knowledge barriers related to the development of IT in SMEs structures. The e-commerce solution company provides: an e-commerce platform, customer service for online orders, search engine positioning and online advertising. The e-commerce platform has been integrated with the shop's accounting system and it permits up-dated product availability to be displayed online. The entire online order process is managed by the external company, which checks the online requests and sends them to Peck's storehouse. Finally a bar code system permits online tracking of the order.

This solution has enabled Peck to take advantage of online market opportunity without spending many resources on the development of competences and resources inside the shop.

Database Integration Strategy

Bottega Verde (www.bottegaverde.it) has been producing and selling its own line of cosmetics and beauty products (only natural ingredients are used, with no animal testing) since 1972. It sells products through three direct channels: catalogues, internet website and more than 210 shops. Its most important markets are: Italy, Spain and Arabia. The website has been the natural commercial

extension of paper catalogues and nowadays, it is the most profitable channel with more than 500,000 online members and 100,000 pages viewed per day. The website is also an important community channel where customers exchange product reviews, participate in online surveys and product tests online. A reserved area allows the web page to be personalised and a virtual shopping assistant helps customers to choose the right products. The integration between the website and the physical stores has been realized through an integrated fidelity card, which can be used both online and offline in order to participate in fidelity reward programs. This strategy has helped Bottega Verde to monitor customers' purchase behaviour, in order to personalize promotions, cross-selling and cross-channel activities.

Full-Integrated Channels Strategy

Esprinet (www.esprinet.it) was set up in 2000 as a wholesaler of PC and electronics with a portfolio of 160 brands, more than 44,000 products and 23,000 clients (small and medium resellers). Its website has evolved over the last ten years: from an e-procurement website, it has become an e-commerce "hub" for its small and medium resellers. Through the Esprinet website, resellers can create their own e-commerce site with the program named "e-Web Club". The websites in this program have independent domain names, but they are integrated with the information system of the wholesaler. News about products, promotions and availability are automatically updated, and a configuration mask enables small and medium resellers to choose which products and promotions will be viewed by their customers. Esprinet also offers a personalized logistic service to its resellers, in order to deliver the products bought on the resellers' website, directly to end consumers with the reseller's brand name on invoices and packaging. In this way, resellers gain in brand image and consumers can choose between two different channels: internet and/or at the local shop. This solution guarantees a strong integration between the online and offline channels and small and medium resellers can benefit from this strategy without investing in expensive IT platforms. On the other hand, the wholesaler gains the resellers' high fidelity and a local widespread partnership for post-sales activities.

The results of the explorative and case study research with the related implications for small and medium retailers are discussed in the next paragraph.

DISCUSSION

In order to examine the results of explorative research and case study analysis, it is important to review the international marketing literature, highlighting the most important drivers and barriers for the adoption of the internet for marketing activities.

Channel Marketing theories indicate that a firm's decision to adopt and assimilate internet as a retailing channel is based on internal strategies, organization and environment, but a sounded theoretical framework about this integration has not yet been developed.

Geyskens et al. (2002) suggest that the decision to integrate physical and virtual channels differs according to the performance of the new entry channel and it depends on: firm characteristics (channel power, direct channel experience, and size); the introduction strategy (they consider two introduction decisions: the order of entry and the level of surrounding publicity); and the marketplace or environment (the growth in demand for the product sold through the internet channel and the growth in demand for the new channel per se). Chatterjee et al. (2002) have studied the organizational assimilation of e-commerce strategies and activities through institutional enablers and they have developed a framework consisting of organizational factors: top management championship

(beliefs and participation), strategic investment rationale and extent of coordination.

These frameworks are complete but too complex for small and medium retailers.

Steinfield et al. (2005) have studied the factors influencing the retailers' decisions to integrate online and offline channels, developing a framework which includes: the type of product, firm structure and resources, but no environmental factors have been included in the framework.

In the European grocery industry, Müller-Lankenau et al.(2005) have found two strategic drivers which explain the diversity of multichannel strategies: the company's retail format strategy and the national market structure, but further enquiries are needed in this field.

Mehrtens et al.'s (2001) research has been identified as the most appropriate starting point for the discussion of the results of the explorative and case study research illustrated in the previous paragraphs. This model refers especially to SMEs and it considers both internal and external factors affecting the decisions to invest in e-business, that for small and medium traditional retailers consists in multichannel integration. The drivers identified by the authors are: external pressure, organisational readiness and perceived benefits (*Figure 1*).

External Pressure

Due to their nature, retail activities are stretched towards the external environment, therefore they are affected by industry characteristics (customers, competition, institutions, legacy, etc…).

Contrary to many B2B businesses, where the external pressure comes from multinational suppliers which require e-supply management platforms to SMEs (Gibbs et al., 2003), in the retail business, the adoption of IT is mostly driven by external pressure: customers and competitors. Retailing strategies are based on competitive advantage, affecting consumers' store choice behaviour, and the

Figure 1. Internet marketing drivers for small and medium retailers (Source: Mehrtens et al.'s, 2001)

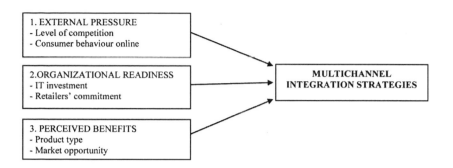

competition is mostly based on price, store format and brand (Cardinali, 2005; Gauri et al., 2008; Gonzalez-Benito et al., 2005; Levy and Barton., 2003). This means that most of the investments are exploited for store and brand image offline, therefore, little is devoted to innovation and IT implementation. Customers' behaviour affects the level of IT innovation of retailers. As previously mentioned, Italian e-commerce represents only 1% of total retail sales, and internet users are only 48% of the Italian population (the European Union average is 60%) (http://www.internetworldstats.com). These figures also explain the low level of internet adoption by Italian firms.

On the other hand, competition has been one of the most studied phenomena in retail marketing literature. In particular, e-commerce research has demonstrated that pure player competitors have pressed traditional retailers to develop their own e-commerce channel (Zhu et al., 2006; King et al. 2004). Consistently with the theory, the initial results of this work confirm that in a very competitive sector, like tourism, small and medium retailers are more likely to develop a presence online (ISS tourism: 61% vs. fashion: 44%); and in particular to develop an e-commerce website (ICS tourism:11% vs. fashion: 3%).

Consequently, an external barrier for traditional small and medium retailers is the number of internet users, but at the same time, the benefit of integrating their channels is related to the level of competition online and offline. As a matter of fact, the case studies illustrated in this work have been drawn from very competitive online markets: tourism, traditional products, consumer electronics and beauty. It seems that competition does not affect only the presence online, but also the multichannel integration solutions developed by firms.

Organizational Readiness

A factor affecting the organizational readiness is the owners' or managers' commitment. IT adoption by SMEs is very similar to IT adoption by individuals (Rogers, 1995), because the owners' and SME managers' predispositions strongly affect small and medium organizations. Companies implementing internet technologies successfully are the ones, whose owners have the role of innovation champion of IT adoption (Levy and Powell, 2002). This work does not investigate this aspect, but from the case studies it can be inferred that an effective multichannel project derives from the definition of a focused strategy. All case studies illustrated in this work are family businesses or single owner firms.

Another aspect of organizational readiness is the retailers' resources for IT development. Some research has demonstrated that organisational resources have no influence on the decision to adopt internet technologies (Mehrtens et al.,

2001). On the contrary, other studies highlight that SMEs cannot afford IT technologies due to limited resources (e.g. finances, time, personnel) and for the fear of making expensive mistakes (EBPG, 2002). This last statement is particularly true in retailing, where many financial resources are devoted to store image, internal operations and personnel. Consequently, many SME managers and owners show a 'wait and see' attitude regarding the adoption of internet technologies and electronic commerce initiatives in order to minimize risks (EBPG, 2002).

Investments in IT implementation are certainly the main barrier in multichannel integration for traditional retailers. From the case study research it has been shown that in order to reduce these costs, small retailers have created partnerships with suppliers (FCS) or they have outsourced e-commerce activities (ICS).

Perceived Benefits

With regard to benefits perceived by retailers, these include increased sales, improved communications with customers, vendors and employees, faster responses to customer enquiries and easier order tracking (Baldwin et al. 2000). According to Johnston et al. (2007), after the adoption of internet technologies by a sample of small and medium retailers and manufactures, a little improvement has been noted in communication and in revenue (actual and expected).

In retailing the "product type" aspect plays an important role in customers' online purchasing behaviour (Thirumalai and Sinha, 2004; Steinfield et al, 2005), like the perceived benefits for a multichannel integration strategy. From this initial exploration, it seems that niche products fit in very well with an independent e-commerce channel (ICS). In this case, multichannel integration investment can be reduced by an outsourcing policy. Personalised products and services, on the other hand, match very well with a database integration strategy (DIS). In these cases, the

perceived benefits are immediate because they are related to online sales.

For SMEs it is more difficult to evaluate intangible benefits such as improved company image, reinforcement of the brand name, and visibility (Marshall et al. 2000). In this case, Lymer et al. (1999) assert that a clear and explicit strategy and careful planning is an essential process for the maximization of internet value and the benefits that it may provide. This is strongly related to owners' commitment and management.

CONCLUSION

In order to summarize the results of this work, *table 3* highlights the main aspects discussed in the previous paragraphs.

The subject of Multichannel is not an easy issue because it involves different corporate processes and activities, and in this context, a simple and structured codification may also be helpful to SMEs' managers in approaching the subject.

> **ISS:** Information Supporting Strategy is the easiest and cheapest way to be present online, but retailers' and customers' perceived benefits derived from an online shopping window are very low. A more advanced informative website can be created in order to link online and offline businesses, as Viaggi del Ventaglio has done by connecting potential customers with local travel agencies. ISS can provide benefits when really useful information is provided online.
> **ICS:** Independent Channel Strategy can be very expensive and often retailers have no competency or commitment in developing it. In this case, small and medium retailers can outsource this activity, gaining market expansion without working on the related activities.

Table 3. Summarising table (Source: Exploratory research and case study analysis)

Strategy	Origin	Company strategy	Case Study	Results of the analysis of 200 websites	Barriers	Solutions
ISS	Müller-Lankenau's (2005)	Informative cost reduction	Viaggi del Ventaglio	52%	Perceived benefits	Advanced informative websites
ICS	Explorative research and Müller-Lankenau's (2005)	Demand and market expansion	Peck	7%	Organizational readiness and implementation costs	Outsourcing
DIS	Explorative research and Steinfield et al. (2005)	Customer interaction	Bottega Verde	9%	Organizational readiness and perceived benefits	Online product personalization and niche product proposal.
FCS	Müller-Lankenau's (2005)	Online customers' Full-experience	Esprinet	1%	Organizational readiness, implementation costs and perceived benefits	Partnerships with wholesalers or producers

DIS: Database Integration Strategy is suitable for personalized and niche products. In these cases, this strategy can be very useful for gathering and elaborating precious customer information.

FCS: Full-integrated Channels Strategy. Previous research has presented the full-integrated model as a successful model for click & mortar retailers (Gulati and Garino, 2000; Saeed et al., 2003; Kumar and Venkatesan 2005, Otto and Chung 2000), underling opportunities and barriers, but without considering the organizational and environmental contexts. In this work we have seen, instead, that for small and medium retailers the full-integrated model may be considered optimal when developed in partnership with wholesalers or producers.

As mentioned, an optimal solution for integrating online and offline channels does not exist, but multichannel integration strategies can be modulated according to the type of product, the marketing strategy decisions (standardisation vs. personalization) and partnerships developed online and offline.

FUTURE RESEARCH DIRECTIONS

This study provides some evidence for the investigation of multichannel integration in small and medium retailers. The usefulness of multichannel integration strategies for small and medium retailers is demonstrated by the recent literature and in this work has illustrated some tentative statements regarding the relative applications for small and medium retailers.

From this present research, there are opportunities for further work especially on the key issues of multichannel strategy adoption and SME managers' perception.

- Future research could repeat the explorative research with a wider sample, also in an international context, to determine the multichannel strategies that are adopted the most by small and medium retailers. The examination of larger data sets would permit more extensive statistical analyses than those conducted in the present study.
- A complete case study analysis with interviews of small and medium retailers would provide more insight into benefits, barriers and solutions for multichannel integration.

REFERENCES

Baldwin, A., Lymer, A., & Johnson, R. (2000). Business impacts of the Internet for small and medium-sized enterprises. In B. Hunt & S. Barnes (Eds.), *Ecommerce and V-Business: Business Models for Global Success* (pp. 103-120). Oxford, UK: Butterworth- Heinemann.

Cardinali, G. C. (2005). *Nuove Traiettorie dell'innovazione nel retailing*. Milano: EGEA.

Chau, P. (2001). Inhibitors to EDI adoption in small businesses: An empirical investigation. *Journal of Electronic Commerce Research*, 2(2), 24–46.

Kim, Daesoo., Ow, Terence T.., & Jun, Minjoon. (2008). SME strategies: An assessment of high vs. low performers. *Communications of the ACM*, 51(11), 113–117. doi:10.1145/1400214.1400237

DoubleClick. (2005, June 28). *Touchpoints III: The Internet's role in the modern purchase process.*

EBPG. (2002). *eEurope go digital: Benchmarking national and regional e-business policies for SMEs.* Final Report of the E-Business Policy Group.

Eisenhardt, K. M. (1989). Building theories from case study research. *Academy of Management Review*, 14, 532–550. doi:10.2307/258557

Gauri, K. G., Trivedi, M., & Grewal, D. (2008). Understanding the determinants of retail strategy: An empirical analysis. *Journal of Retailing*, 84(3), 256–267. doi:10.1016/j.jretai.2008.06.004

Geyskens, I., Gielens, K., & Dekimpe, M. G. (2002). The market valuation of Internet channel additions. *Journal of Marketing*, 66(2), 102–119. doi:10.1509/jmkg.66.2.102.18478

Gibbs, J., Kraemer, K. L., & Dedrick, J. (2003). Environment and policy factors shaping global e-commerce diffusion: A cross-country comparison. *The Information Society*, 19(1), 5–18. doi:10.1080/01972240309472

Gonzalez-Benito, O., Munoz-Gallego, P. A., & Kopalle, P. K. (2005). Asymmetric competition in retail store formats: Evaluating inter- and intra-format spatial effects. *Journal of Retailing*, 81(1), 75–79. doi:10.1016/j.jretai.2005.01.006

Gulati, R., & Garino, J. (2000). Get the right mix of bricks & clicks. *Harvard Business Review*, 78(3), 107–114.

Johnston, D. A., Wade, M., & McClean, R. (2007). Does e-business matter to SMEs? A comparison of the financial impacts of Internet business solutions on European and North American SMEs. *Journal of Small Business Management*, 45(3), 354–361. doi:10.1111/j.1540-627X.2007.00217.x

Kabadayi, S., Eyuboglu, N., & Thomas, G. P. (2007, October). The performance implications of designing multiple channels to fit with strategy and environment. *Journal of Marketing*, 71, 195–211. doi:10.1509/jmkg.71.4.195

King, R. C., Sen, R., & Xia, M. (2004). Impact of Web-based e-commerce on channel strategy in retailing. *International Journal of Electronic Commerce*, 8(3), 103–130.

Koenig, W., & Wigand, R. T. (2004). Globalization and e-commerce: Diffusion and impacts of the internet and e-commerce in Germany. *Digest of Electronic Commerce Policy and Regulation*, 27, 197–227.

Kumar, V., & Venkatesan, R. (2005). Who are the multichannel shoppers and how do they perform? Correlates of multichannel shopping behavior. *Journal of Interactive Marketing*, 19(2), 44–62. doi:10.1002/dir.20034

Levy, M., & Barton, A. W. (2003). *Retail management* (5th Ed.). Chicago: McGraw-Hill/ Irwin.

Levy, M., & Powell, P. (2002, June 17-19). SMEs Internet adoption: Toward a transporter model. In *Proceedings of the Fifteenth Bled Electronic Commerce Conference (Reality: Constructing the Economy)*, (pp. 507–21). Bled, Slovenia.

Lymer, A. (1999). UK business and the information superhighway: The impact of the Internet on SMEs. *ACCA Occasional Research Paper 23.*

Marshall, P., Sor, R., & McKay, J. (2000). An industry case study of the impacts of electronic commerce on car dealerships in Western Australia. *Journal of Electronic Commerce Research, 1*(1), 1–12.

McMillan, S. J. (2000). The microscope and the moving target: The challenge of applying content analysis to the World Wide Web. *Journalism & Mass Communication Quarterly, 77*(1), 80–98.

Mehrtens, J., Cragg, P. B., & Mills, A. M. (2001). A model of Internet adoption by SMEs. *Information & Management, 39,* 165–176. doi:10.1016/S0378-7206(01)00086-6

Müller-Lankenau, C., Wehmeyer, K., & Klein, S. (2005-6). Multichannel strategies: Capturing and exploring diversity in the European retail grocery industry. *International Journal of Electronic Commerce, 10*(2), 85–122. doi:10.2753/JEC1086-4415100204

Otto, J. R., & Chung, Q. B. (2000). A framework for cyber-enhanced retailing: Integrating e-commerce retailing with brick-and-mortar retailing. *Electronic Markets, 10*(3), 185–191. doi:10.1080/10196780050177099

Polytechnic of Milan. (2007). *L'eCommerce B2c in Italia: crescono Servizi e Dot Com* [Research Report]. Milan, Italy: Polytechnic of Milan, B2C Observatory.

Prasarnphanich, P., & Gillenson, M. L. (2003). The hybrid clicks and bricks business strategy. *Communications of the ACM, 46*(12), 178–185. doi:10.1145/953460.953498

Rogers, E. (1995). *Diffusion of innovation* (4th Ed.). New York: The Free Press.

Saban, K., & Rau, S. (2005). The functionality of Websites as export marketing channels. *Electronic Markets, 15*(2), 128–135. doi:10.1080/10196780500083803

Saeed, K. A., Grover, V., & Hwang, Y. (2003). Creating synergy with a clicks and mortar approach. *Communications of the ACM, 46*(12).206–212doi:10.1145/953460.953501

Steinfield, C., Adelaar, T., & Liu, F. (2005). Click and mortar strategies viewed from the Web: A content analysis of features illustrating integration between retailers' online and offline presence. *Electronic Markets, 15*(3), 199–212. doi:10.1080/10196780500208632

Steinfield, C., Bouwman, H., & Adelaar, T. (2002). The dynamics of click-and-mortar electronic commerce: Opportunities and management strategies. *International Journal of Electronic Commerce, 7*(1), 93–119.

Steinfield, C., Mahler, A., & Bauer, J. (1999). Electronic commerce and the local merchant: Opportunities for synergy between physical and Web presence. *Electronic Markets, 9*(1-2), 51–57. doi:10.1080/101967899359247

The Economist Intelligence Unit Limited. (2007). *Country commerce.* Retrieved from http://www.eiu.com

Thirumalai, S., & Sinha, K. K. (2005). Customer satisfaction with order fulfilment in retail supply chains: implications of product type in electronic B2C transactions. *Journal of Operations Management, 23,* 291–303. doi:10.1016/j.jom.2004.10.015

Venkatesan, R., & Kumar, V. (2004). A customer lifetime value framework for customer selection and resource allocation strategy. *Journal of Marketing, 68,* 106–125. doi:10.1509/jmkg.68.4.106.42728

Yin, R. K. (2003). *Case study research-Design and methods.* London: Sage Publications.

Zhu, K., & Kraemer, L. K. (2005). Post-adoption variations in usage and value of e-business by organizations: Cross-country evidence from the retail industry. [f]. *Information Systems Research, 16*(1), 61–84. doi:10.1287/isre.1050.0045

Chapter 15

E–Fulfilment and Offshore Centres:
Economic Policy Implications for Small Business

Simon McCarthy
University of Glamorgan, UK

Brychan Thomas
University of Glamorgan, UK

Geoff Simmons
University of Ulster, UK

ABSTRACT

This chapter introduces the importance of the e-fulfilment industry for offshore centres and in particular the small business and economic policy implications. The extant concepts, research, and experiences the chapter builds on is the literature concerning the e-fulfilment industry. It argues that the key results, evidence, and experience, from the models that have been developed and the specific model formulated for this work, indicate reasons for the development of e-fulfilment in offshore centres with particular reference to the tax advantages provided by the Channel Island of Jersey. The limitations of the results are that they report the early findings of other work and the conceptualisation of the e-fulfilment model in this work and as a result there is a need for empirical evidence. The authors therefore plan to undertake empirical research to support the evidence that has been researched so far. Furthermore, there are important implications of the study for policy makers, small business, practitioners, researchers, and educators for the specific field of e-fulfilment developments in particular and e-commerce in general.

INTRODUCTION

Past research on the development of the e-fulfilment industry has provided understanding of the activity at a time when it has attracted negative publicity. Negative publicity has focused on businesses that have switched their distributions of low value goods such as CD's/DVD's through offshore centres to take advantage of Low Value Consignment Relief (LVCR) which is the European Union (EU) ap-

DOI: 10.4018/978-1-60566-998-4.ch015

proved mechanism for VAT exemption. LVCR allows products in the single parcel to be shipped sales tax/VAT free throughout the EU if the value of the goods is between 10 and 22 Euros (£8 to £18 in the UK). The specific level of the relief is set by individual EU members and the UK limit is £18.

There are basically two types of activity within the e-fulfilment sector, although a number of businesses operate as a hybrid of the two activities. Whole Chain Companies (WCC), such as Play. com, buy and own stock and sell goods to final customers. On the other hand, Third Party Service Providers (3PS) provide logistics or distribution services for other retailers. It is known that some big retail players, such as Tesco, Asda and Amazon, are using agent companies with operations on Jersey to obtain the benefits of LVCR. WCC receive revenues based on the total value of sales whereas 3PS receive revenues based on the service they provide, with sales revenue received by the retail firm.

The key for e-fulfilment businesses operating in Jersey to take advantage of the LVCR relief is to balance the additional package and delivery charges against the increased profits arising from the competitive advantage offered by lower prices due to the VAT free sales prices.

In this chapter we initially consider the literature concerning the e-fulfilment industry and the models that have been developed. This is followed by the conceptualisation of a model of the e-fulfilment industry which is appropriate to offshore centres. We then apply the model to the case study of the island of Jersey which is an offshore jurisdiction in the English Channel off the shores of France. Finally we draw conclusions from the findings of this study and consider the policy implications of the e-fulfilment activities which are taking place.

BACKGROUND

According to Ash and Burn (2003) enterprises over the last fifteen years have had to reconsider their role with regard to Information and Communication Technologies (ICTs) as a support tool for significant business change. Not only has e-business become essential to industries, including financial services and retailing, but to businesses in general. In some situations new e-business opportunities have arisen themselves and a good example of this is e-fulfilment. In fact, the services provided by e-fulfilment have been estimated to be worth US1.006 Trillion in the US alone or 0.1% of their GDP (Rogers, 2002). Twenty one percent of all logistics transactions were expected to be online by 2005 with long term implications for freight companies (Homs, Meringer & Rehkopf, 2001). E-fulfilment has been defined as "everything an online company does to satisfy customer demand within an e-Business framework and includes both supply chain and logistic functions" (Palmer, Kallio & Heck, 2000). A further definition is that "e-Fulfilment defines that part of e-Business which aims at efficiently and effectively integrating a company's back office processes, activities and functions arising from order capture through to final delivery to the customer" (BCI, 2002). The scope of e-fulfilment involves companies with online retailing adapting e-fulfilment applications and the provision of applications and both the Business-to-Business (B2B) and Business-to-Consumer (B2C) market (BCI, 2002). The literature on e-fulfilment, and online retailing, identifies a number of issues that the provider needs to consider and these include location design and systems, packing, customer service, financial transactions, warehouse costs, delivery, transport mechanisms and flows, procurement management, management information systems, front end ordering systems, after sales service, returns and real-time tracking. These are recognised as integrated components which create virtual proximity between e-trader and customer.

Figure 1. A model of staged e-fulfilment transformation (Based on Deise et al, 2000; Burn & Alexander, 2005)

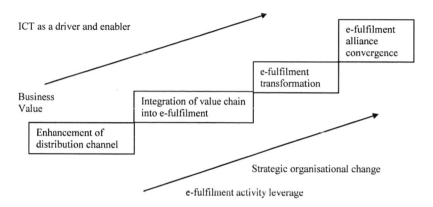

They represent a succession of activities that are for the successful supply of customers and markets. Whereas components can be aligned with existing activities, e-fulfilment requires unique supply chains and distribution networks (DiMaria, 2001). Supply chain and distribution networks are central to the concept of e-fulfilment and since the degree of integration between legacy logistics and delivery and supply chain systems ensures information sharing and end to end co-ordination (Esper & Williams, 2003; Strader, Lin & Shaw, 1999). The nature of delivery zones, customer delivery expectations and product range have changed in online retailing and have caused changes in the supporting supply chains (Rabinovish & Evers, 2003). New issues such as remote payments and product returns need to be addressed by systems.

Previous research provides evidence of staged transformation with regard to e-fulfilment businesses (Alexander, 2002) and this can be linked to a general model of e-business transformation (Burn & Alexander, 2005) based on Deise, Nowikow, King & Wright (2000) (see Figure 1).

The model shows the adoption of ICT with a parent company involving warehousing and transportation enhancing distribution channels through e-commerce, followed by application of ICT across and within value chains extending to e-fulfilment (Burn & Alexander, 2005). Rapid technology uptake, especially online and mobile, has led to fast change that is not incremental but transformational (Alexander, 2002; Anderson & Lee, 2001). Another model is the e-Fulfilment process model which involves more than an Internet enabled front office being established (BCI, 2002). Here there is integration of the Web site front office with back office activities, functions including finance, logistics, marketing and sales, and processes supporting customer order fulfilment resulting in the improvement of logistics efficiencies and a decrease in transportation costs and inventory (BCI, 2002) (Figure 2).

Figure 2 shows the back office processes following clicking the buy button with the sequence of events of order capture (Web order) – stock availability (e-warehousing) and interface to finance house (e-billing) – order confirmation – manufacturing or procurement – order release (picking/packing/shipping) – delivery to consumer (BCI, 2002). Processes can be executed externally or internally and effective integration of functions creates strategic information and data on consumer choice and behaviour and exploitation of this helps forecasting, inventory reduction and cycle times reduced (BCI, 2002).

It is apparent that the e-fulfilment process is strongly interdependent (Dewsnap & Jobber,

Figure 2. e-Fulfilment process model (Source: BCI, 2002)

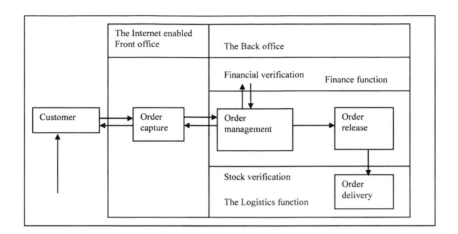

2000). The relationship requires cohesion, co-ordination and co-operation (Shocker, Scrivastava & Reukert, 1994; Urbanski, 1987; Wellman, 1995, Wood & Tandon, 1994). In fact, the process involves a fundamental variety of forces (Bradley, 1998). Through the e-fulfilment process it is possible to marshal these forces and it exists between the supplier and the customer (Sparkes & Thomas, 2000; Sparkes et al, 2001). Due to the limited number of models to provide illustration this chapter attempts to present a fundamental model of e-fulfilment and describes the main factors involved in the process with reference to offshore centres and the Channel Island of Jersey in particular. The thesis of the chapter maintains that if the principal elements are properly integrated in the operation of the e-fulfilment process this will be conducive to efficient online retailing. Vital to the e-fulfilment process between companies and customers (Gray, 1999) are the business-to-business (B2B) and business-to-customer (B2C) activities (Sparkes et al, 2001; BCI, 2002). A problem that can hinder e-fulfilment is that barriers can arise that affect the operation of the process (Cespedes, 1994). It is therefore essential to manage the process in relation to overcoming barriers. Managing this process is becoming increasingly important for e-fulfilment businesses. By doing this it is possible

to build a platform to develop future markets. The sharing of information is therefore a key dimension (Song & Parry, 1993). Since fast changing technologies are involved with e-fulfilment it is necessary to keep pace with these developments for marketing benefits to be realised. Figure 3 provides a conceptual model of the e-fulfilment process appropriate to this research.

The e-fulfilment process illustrated in Figure 3 involves customers making orders over the Internet to the e-retailer who checks stock availability and provides order confirmation before order release from the warehouse (involving selecting, packing and shipping) prior to final delivery to the customer.

Following the conceptualisation of the e-fulfilment process this chapter now introduces the importance of the e-fulfilment industry for offshore centres and the economic policy implications that arise from this through the case study of the Channel Island of Jersey. This has been undertaken by building on the extant concepts, research and experiences in the literature involving the e-fulfilment industry. The key results, evidence and experience, from the models that have been developed, and the specific model formulated for this work, indicate reasons for the development of the e-fulfilment industry in Jersey.

Figure 3. A Conceptual model of the e-fulfilment process

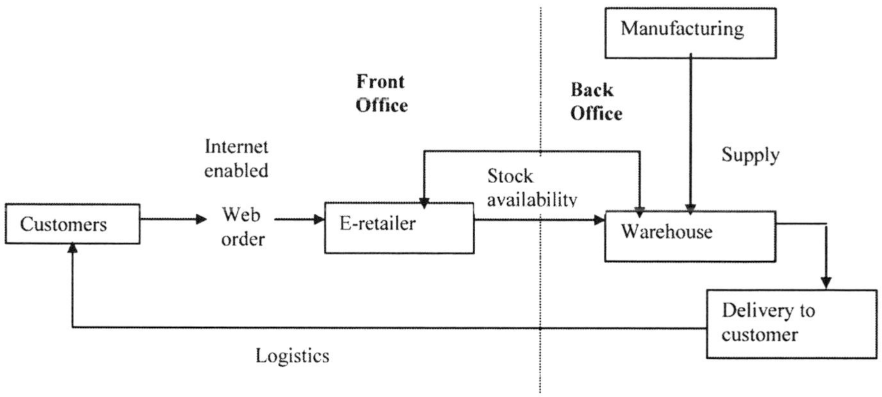

OFFSHORE CENTRES

The origin of the term Offshore Financial Centre (OFC), as applied to Jersey, can be traced to Roberts (1994) and can be defined as a low tax jurisdiction that is moderately regulated which specialises in commercial and corporate infrastructure to facilitate the investment of funds and the formation of offshore structures (they are usually crown dependencies or former British colonies and are titled offshore jurisdictions). Bennett (2001) refers to offshore jurisdictions as providing specific facilities for offshore financial centres. The International Monetary Fund (IMF) (2000) lists three main characteristics of an OFC as (i) centres which provide a number of offshore services (including moderate or light financial regulation, zero or low taxation, anonymity and banking secrecy), (ii) financial systems with external assets and liabilities, and (iii) jurisdictions with a comparatively large number of financial institutions involving business with those who are non residents. In recent years OFCs have attracted considerable attention and there have been initiatives through the International Monetary Fund (IMF) and the Organisation for Economic Co-operation and Development (OECD) (IMF, 2000). As a result OFCs strengthened their key regulated activities and internal regulations and in

a survey of OFCs the Economist (2007) recognised that the global finance system is enhanced by properly run jurisdictions, both off and on shore. Table 1 provides a list of the main OFCs.

Jersey is listed as one of the eight main OFCs and due to its sophistication overshadows jurisdictions such as its near neighbour Guernsey and the Isle of Man which are also well developed and regulated.

The basis of OFCs, such as Jersey, is the creation of offshore structures which involve the formation of offshore companies, offshore partnerships, offshore trusts and private foundations, and these structures are formed for a variety of reasons (Table 2). WCC and 3PS can be considered according to legitimate and illegitimate structures.

Legitimate reasons for the formation of offshore structures include asset holding vehicles, asset protection, avoidance of forced heir-ship provisions, collective investment vehicles, derivatives trading, exchange control trading vehicles, joint venture vehicles, stock market listing vehicles and trade finance vehicles. With regard to asset holding vehicles corporate conglomerates will have a large number of corporate companies with high risk assets and these are parked in different companies to stop legal risk being borne by the main group. Asset protection will involve individuals with wealth living in unstable countries using offshore

Table 1. Offshore Financial Centres (OFCs)

Centre	Description
Bahamas	Considerable number of registered vehicles
Bermuda	Market leader for captive insurance
British Virgin Islands	Largest number of offshore companies
Cayman Islands	Largest value in offshore funds
Gibraltar	Strong presence in most fields
Jersey	Dominant player in the European market
Luxembourg	Market leader in Undertakings for Collective Investments in Transferable Securities
Panama	International maritime centre

Source: Economist (2007)

companies to hold wealth and avoid expropriation or exchange control restrictions. For avoidance of heir-ship provisions assets in an offshore company enable avoidance of succession law in certain countries. In order to enable international distribution mutual funds, hedge funds and unit trusts can be formed offshore through collective investment vehicles. Offshore vehicles can be formed by wealthy individuals to participate in risky investments including derivatives trading. With exchange control trading vehicles exporters form trading vehicles in offshore companies to

Table 2. Formation of offshore structures (legitimate reasons)

Offshore structure	Description
Asset holding vehicles	Corporate conglomerates will have a large number of corporate companies with high risk assets and these are parked in different companies to stop legal risk being borne by the main group.
Asset protection	Individuals with wealth living in unstable countries use offshore companies to hold wealth and avoid expropriation or exchange control restrictions.
Avoidance of heir-ship provisions	Assets in an offshore company enable avoidance of succession law in certain countries.
Collective Investment Vehicles	In order to enable international distribution mutual funds, hedge funds and unit trusts can be formed offshore.
Derivatives trading	Offshore vehicles can be formed by wealthy individuals to participate in risky investments including derivatives trading.
Exchange control trading vehicles	Exporters form trading vehicles in offshore companies to park exports in the offshore vehicles until further investment.
Joint venture vehicles	Joint venture companies are often set up in offshore jurisdictions as either a compromise neutral jurisdiction or (also) to access corporate and commercial laws.
Stock market listing vehicles	Shares are transferred into an offshore vehicle and the offshore vehicle is listed by companies who are unable to obtain a stock market listing.
Trade finance vehicles	Offshore companies are formed by large corporate groups to obtain financing and for the financing to be off the balance sheet through accounting procedures that are applicable.

Table 3. Formation of offshore structures (illegitimate reasons)

Offshore structure	Description
Creditor avoidance	An anonymous offshore company may be set up by a person who is in debt in order to transfer assets and cash.
Market manipulation	Companies may be formed offshore in order to manipulate financial results.
Money laundering	Offshore structures may be set up to facilitate laundering schemes.
Tax evasion	Tax is evaded by not declaring the gains made by offshore vehicles.
Terrorist financing	It is possible that offshore vehicles could be used to finance terrorist activities.

park exports in the offshore vehicles until further investment. Joint venture companies are often set up in offshore jurisdictions as either a compromise neutral jurisdiction or (also) to access corporate and commercial laws. With stock market listing vehicles shares are transferred into an offshore vehicle and the offshore vehicle is listed by companies who are unable to obtain a stock market listing. Finally, through trade finance vehicles offshore companies are formed by large corporate groups to obtain financing and for the financing to be off the balance sheet through accounting procedures that are applicable.

On the other hand illegitimate reasons for forming offshore structures include creditor avoidance (an anonymous offshore company may be set up by a person who is in debt in order to transfer assets and cash), market manipulation (companies may be formed offshore in order to manipulate financial results), money laundering (offshore structures may be set up to facilitate laundering schemes), tax evasion (tax is evaded by not declaring the gains made by offshore vehicles) and terrorist financing (it is possible that offshore vehicles could be used to finance terrorist activities) (Table 3).

According to the above categorisation WCC is a more legitimate structure and 3PS less legitimate especially with regard to VAT exemption. Structures can also be established as trusts or partnerships and offshore jurisdictions can offer specialised versions of these entities as well as setting up companies.

JERSEY E-FULFILMENT AND THE SALES TAX ADVANTAGE

Introduction

In addition to the literature surveyed concerning e-fulfilment the extant concepts, research and experiences the chapter is building on also include surveys into offshore financial centres and reports on OFCs. According to Austin (2002) there are three issues facing businesses in Jersey which are international, industry and Island issues. International issues include those posed by the OECD requirements, EU Savings Tax Directive and the EU Code of Conduct on Business Taxation (requiring the dismantling of the Exempt Tax companies and IBCs) (Bellows, 2002; Jersey Finance, 2005). Industry issues involve problems such as the increasing burden of regulation, high costs, complacency and quality (Austin, 2002). Island issues include the need to balance other demands with the necessary demands of business (Bellows, 2002).

Jersey is the largest, most important and southerly of the Channel Islands in the English Channel (Learmouth et al, 2001; Government of Jersey, 2002; Merret & Walton, 2005). It is located 49 13

Figure 4. Population growth of Jersey (Source: Jersey Census, 2001)

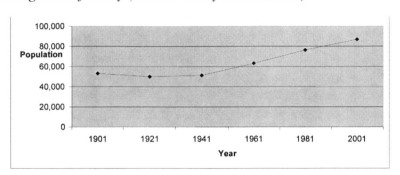

N 2 07 W (WFE, 1990) off the north-west coast of France with Normandy 14 miles to the east, Brittany 30 miles to the south and the nearest point of the English coast 85 miles north (RFR, 1998). The Finance industry has developed from the arrival of the first merchant bank in the 1960s to its present day standing providing 60% of GDP (Jersey Finance, 2006). Finance in Jersey originated to meet the growing demands of predominantly British customers living or working abroad. Initially this consisted of offshore bank accounts followed by a range of tailored financial products and services. The Island has also been successful in offering wealth management services including trusts and estate planning and most recently a successful funds management sector. Innovations in these three areas are ongoing. The Economic Growth Plan (EGP) of the States of Jersey has been set out by the Economic Development Committee with the intention to deliver a target of a 2% annual economic growth rate between 2005 and 2009 (States of Jersey, 2005). Whereas there is concern over the adverse effects that a static or declining work force will have on the main sector of Finance there is also concern over harmful environmental effects through congestion and pollution due to an increase in population (Learmouth et al, 2001). Figure 4 shows the growth in the population of Jersey from 1901 to 2001.

Jersey as an OFC is not part of the UK nor a member of the European Union but is a self governing dependency of the Crown and as such

is not subject to any British or EU laws, however Jersey does have special status (Protocol 3) to obtain favourable trading terms with the EU (Sikka, 2007). The Island therefore has its own administrative, fiscal and legal systems and most laws are made by the States of Jersey as the representative assembly and public services are administered by the committees of the assembly (Merret & Walton, 2005). The successful, strong and stable economy of Jersey is dominated by the largely externally owned high quality financial services industry which provides a high standard of living (Government of Jersey, 2002).

Issues, Controversies and Problems

The States of Jersey have considered the issues, controversies and problems of the e-fulfilment industry by centralising policy to provide direct political support for the industry and promoting diversification through e-commerce activity. This involves the current and potential role of the e-fulfilment industry for the economy of Jersey. The Jersey Competitive Regulations Authority has investigated cross-subsidy between Offshore Solutions Limited (OSL) and Jersey Post International Limited (JPIL). The e-fulfilment industry is seen as the new 4th arm of a diversified economy (States of Jersey, 2006b). And as such the export of CDs/DVDs is the fourth biggest business on the Island of Jersey (Guardian, 2005). In these terms opportunities to promote the industry in the

Figure 5. The e-fulfilment process model appropriate to Jersey

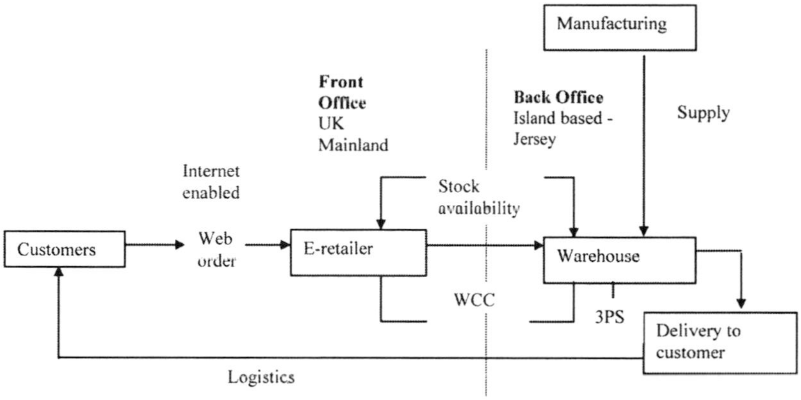

international supply of cheap consumer goods need to be undertaken. Consequently the industry has come under attack from United Kingdom (UK) small business organisations. There has also been confusion and misunderstanding of the policies applied to e-fulfilment.

Solutions and Recommendations

Jersey, and other offshore centres, can benefit from the growth of e-commerce and can maximise its effort for this. It has been recommended that the Economic Development Department of the States centralise policy for the e-fulfilment industry under an e-commerce 'Tsar' to provide more political support for the industry to promote diversification through e-commerce (States of Jersey, 2006b). Prior to 2005 there was no clear indication as to how large the e-fulfilment industry was on the Island. Although Jersey Financial Services Commission (JFSC) holds data on companies in Jersey it does not categorise fulfilment companies as a category since they are itemised as 'retailers'. It is therefore difficult to quantify how many companies are operating. Prior to 2005 data held by the Economic Development Department only counted WCC and 3PS operations and did not

record customers of each 3PS (States of Jersey, 2006b).

In the past the business model of OSL was directed towards the encouragement of branded retailers operating through the Island and Jersey Post. Large UK retailers have been positioned to develop e-fulfilment operations. Businesses have focused on operations for the UK market selling CDs and DVDs with large growth potential. This has been the easiest way for 'pick and pack' custom increasing overseas postings and stamp revenue through Jersey Post. A small business example would be Razamataz, Classic TV & Film, a classic e-fulfilment enterprise which was established in Jersey in 2005.

An important solution will be to have an efficient and properly operated e-fulfilment process on the Island. Taking the conceptual model for the e-fulfilment process (Figure 3) this can be applied to the Jersey e-fulfilment industry as shown in Figure 5.

With regard to Jersey the e-fulfilment process model shows the front office activities which will be based on the UK mainland involving the e-retailer and back office activities based on the Island involving warehousing and delivery to the customer. WCCs will buy in and sell goods to the final customer and 3PS will provide logistics and distribution services for other retailers.

FUTURE RESEARCH DIRECTIONS

The findings presented illustrate that e-fulfilment is an important tool for e-commerce optimisation especially with regard to B2C activities. In these terms the chapter builds on the work of Deise, Nowikow, King and Wright (2000) concerning a research agenda for e-business logistics based on professional opinions, Burn and Alexander (2005) regarding the measurement of e-transformation in the logistics industry and a knowledge capability index and Buck Consultants International (BCI) (2002) outlining e-fulfilment future opportunities for the European Union. It argues that the key results, evidence, and experience, from the models that have been developed and the specific model formulated for this work, indicate reasons for the development of e-fulfilment in offshore centres with particular reference to the case study of the Channel Island of Jersey. The limitations of the results are that they report the early findings of other work and the conceptualisation of the e-fulfilment model in this work and as a result there is a need for empirical evidence. By doing this it will be possible to test the validity of the e-fulfilment model in relation to offshore centres. The authors therefore plan to undertake empirical research to support the evidence that has been researched so far. Pertinent research questions need to be investigated including those relating to the significant demand for employment for the e-fulfilment industry which poses two research questions – will the labour be drawn from the unemployed, new labour market entrants or from other industries and could this labour be allocated to more productive uses? Another important research question to be investigated is - what are the consequences of the value added tax (VAT) loophole which allows e-fulfilment companies in the Channel Islands to sell products worth less than

£18 to the mainland without charging VAT? It is felt by some commentators that if the £18 VAT loophole is not closed it could have considerable negative effects on the music industry, for example (BBC, 2006). It is hoped that by developing these lines of enquiry they will be beneficial to academic researchers in the area of e-commerce and will foster the research community to expand the body of literature in the e-fulfilment field.

CONCLUSION AND POLICY IMPLICATIONS

The Economic Growth Plan (EGP) of Jersey has two key objectives which are to create high value employment for local people and to generate £20 million of additional tax revenue. The important tax contribution of WCC activity and the high value added per employee complement the EGP and therefore need to be supported by the States of Jersey. The activity of 3PS, however, contributes less to the two objectives of the EGP and there is therefore a need to be careful with this type of activity. On the basis of the operation of the EGP there is a strong case not to permit the growth of 3PS activity but to support the activity of WCC. Furthermore, e-fulfilment issues need to be considered on the basis of the international reputation of Jersey. With 3PS activity the selling structure of the retailer has involved the vendor, and vendor parent company, together with the purchaser being located in the United Kingdom (UK). Goods from the UK are shipped to Jersey for selling and are then shipped back to the UK for delivery to the customer. Appropriate policy that is in accordance with the EGP and will protect Jersey's international reputation requires the support of WCC and new WCC, and high value added hybrid companies that do not involve UK businesses diverting business through Jersey trading in CD and DVD's to the UK market. Some UK businesses operating in the CD and DVD market though 3PS are required to apply for licences and those that have not need to do so. Since there is no basis for refusing licences such businesses that are operating contrary to policy should be given time limited licences so that they can reduce and discontinue activities if required. 3PS activities should only be allowed to grow where they are consistent with the EGP and policy (States of Jersey of Jersey, 2006a).

REFERENCES

Alexander, P. R. (2002). *What's driving e-fulfilment: new aims, new frames.* Paper presented at the 3rd International We-B Conference, Perth, Western Australia.

Anderson, D., & Lee, H. (2001). *New supply chain business models – The opportunities and challenges.* Paper presented at the Keynote – the Achieving Supply Chain Through Excellence (ASCET) project.

Ash, C. G., & Burn, J. M. (2003). Assessing the benefits from e-business transformation through effective enterprise management. *European Journal of Information Systems, 12*(4), 297–308. doi:10.1057/palgrave.ejis.3000476

Austin, P. (2002). *The key issues facing Jersey's finance industry.* A review of the talk by Phil Austin on October 09, Société-Jersiaise, St. Helier, 1-3.

Bellows, A.M. (2002). *Finance, after the war: Essays of Jersey history: 1946-2002,* Société-Jersiaise, St. Helier, 1-3.

Bennett, T. (2001). Glossary Terms. *Tolley's international initiatives affecting financial havens,* London.

Bradley, F. (1998). From Clashmore containers to value relationships in the business system. *Irish Review of Marketing, 11*(1), 78–84.

British Broadcasting Authority (BBC). (2006). Talking Jersey: Music will be "less diverse." Retrieved from http://www.bbc.co.uk/jersey/content/articles/2006/03/20/fullfilment

Buck Consultants International (BCI). (2002). *E-thematic final report e-fulfilment future opportunities.* Information Society Technologies Programme, European Union.

Burn, J., & Alexander, P. (2005, June 6-8). Measuring e-transformation in the logistics industry: A knowledge capability index. In *18th Bled eConference eIntegration in Action,* Bled, Slovenia.

Cespedes, F. W. (1994). Industrial marketing: Managing new requirements. *Sloan Management Review, 35*(3), 45–63.

Deise, M. V., Nowikow, C., King, P., & Wright, A. (2000). Research agenda for e-business logistics based on professional opinions. *International Journal of Physical Distribution and Logistics Management, 32*(7), 513–532.

Dewsnap, B., & Jobber, D. (2000). The sales-marketing interface in consumer packaged-goods companies: A conceptual framework. *Journal of Personal Selling & Sales Management, 20*(2), 109–119.

DiMaria, F. (2001). FAQs: Is international e-commerce really for you? *World Trade, 14*(9), 36–38.

Economist. (2007). *Survey of offshore financial centres.* Retrieved from http://www.economist.com/surveys

Esper, T. L., & Williams, L. R. (2003). The value of collaborative transportation management (CTM): Its relationship to CPFR and information technology. *Transportation Journal, 42*(4), 5.

Government of Jersey. (2002). Introduction, Jersey, Ref 670.0389. In *Jersey Island Plan Final Draft* (pp. 1-9). Retrieved from http://www.planning.gov.je

Gray, R. (1999, September). Using the voice at the end of the line. *Marketing, 16*, 29–30.

Guardian. (2005). *Have turned in to Channel Island discs?* London: Guardian Newspapers.

Homs, C., Meringer, J., & Rehkopf, F. (2001). *Europe's online logistics push.* Retrieved from http://www.forester.com

International Monetary Fund (IMF). (2000). *Report in offshore finance centres.* Washington, DC: IMF.

Jersey Finance. (2005). *Jersey in figures.* Jersey, UK: States of Jersey.

Jersey Finance. (2006). *Jersey – A back to basic introduction to the island.* UK: States of Jersey.

Learmouth, D., McGregor, P. G., Swales, J. K., Turner, K. R., & Yin, Y. P. (2001). *Modelling the economic and environmental impacts of population policy in Jersey: A multi-period computable general equilibrium analysis.* Fraser of Allander Institute, Department of Economics, Glasgow: University of Strathclyde, 1-21.

Merret, S., & Walton, N. (2005). *Nitrate pollution on the Island of Jersey: Managing water quality within European community directives.* Retrieved from http://www.dgroups.org/groups/worldbank/MENA-Water/

Palmer, J., Kallio, J., & Heck, E. (2000). Online grocery shopping around the World: Examples of key business models. *Communications of the Association for Information Systems, 4*(3), 1–34.

Rabinovich, E., & Evers, P. T. (2003). Product fulfilment in supply chains supporting internet-retailing operations. *Journal of Business Logistics, 24*(2), 205.

Review of Financial Regulation (RFR). (1998). *Review of financial regulation in the Crown Dependencies – Part 2.* Retrieved from http://www.archive.official-documents.co.uk/document/cm41/4109/b-chap03.htm

Roberts, R. (1994). *Offshore financial centres.* Cheltenham, UK: Edward Elgar.

Rogers, D. S. (2002). *Reverse logistics: Trends and practices.* Sao Paulo, Brasil: Centre for Logistics Management.

Shocker, A. D., Srivatava, R. K., & Reukert, R. W. (1994, May). Challenges and opportunities facing brand management: An introduction to the special issue. *JMR, Journal of Marketing Research, 31*, 49–158. doi:10.2307/3152190

Sikka, P. (2007). Globalization and its discontents: Accounting firms buy limited liability partnership legislation in Jersey. *Accounting, Auditing & Accountability Journal, 21*(3), 398–426. doi:10.1108/09513570810863987

Song, X. M., & Parry, M. E. (1993). How the Japanese manage the R&D-marketing interface. *Research and Technology Management, 36*(4), 32–42.

Sparkes, A., & Thomas, B. (2001). The use of the Internet as a critical success factor for the marketing of Welsh agri-food SMEs in the 21st century. *British Food Journal, 103*(5), 331–347. doi:10.1108/00070700110395368

States of Jersey (2005). *Growing Jersey's economy: An economic growth plan.* The Economic Development Committee, 1-72.

States of Jersey. (2006a). *Policy for the fulfilment industry.* Economic Development Department, Jersey, February, (pp. 1-3).

States of Jersey. (2006b). *Fulfilment industry policy.* In *Jersey Economic Affairs Scrutiny Panel*, 17th November (pp. 1-7).

Strader, T. J., Lin, F.-R., & Shaw, M. J. (1999). The impact of information sharing on order fulfilment in divergent differentiation supply chains. *Journal of Global Information Management, 7*(1), 16.

Urbanski, A. (1987). Repackaging the brand manager. *Sales and Marketing Management, April,* 42-45.

Webster's Family Encyclopaedia (WFE). (1990). *Jersey.* New York: Arrow.

Wellman, D. (1995). Brand management report: People and management. *Food and Beverage Marketing,* January, 16-18.

Wood, V. R., & Tandon, S. (1994). Key components in product management success (and Failure), A model of product managers' job performance and job satisfaction in the turbulent 1990s and beyond. *Journal of Product and Brand Management, 3*(1), 19–38. doi:10.1108/10610429410053068

ADDITIONAL READING

Agatz, N. A. H., Fleischmann, M., & van Nunen, J. A. E. E. (2007). E-fulfilment and multi-channel distribution – A review. *European Journal of Operational Research, 187,* 339–356. doi:10.1016/j.ejor.2007.04.024

Bayles, D. L. (2001). *E-commerce logistics and e-fulfilment: From click to clutch.* London: Prentice Hall.

Joyce, P., Green, R., & Winch, G. (2006). A new construct for visualising and designing e-fulfilment systems for quality healthcare delivery. *The TQM Magazine, 18*(6), 638–651. doi:10.1108/09544780610707129

KEY TERMS AND DEFINITIONS

3PS: Provide distribution services or logistics to other retailers.

Back Office: Components and processes behind the scenes which support the front office.

Cross Border E-Fulfilment: E-fulfilment involving delivery and payment across borders of nations.

E-Business: Internet use to sell, buy or exchange services or products.

E-Fulfilment: The integration of a business's back office activities, functions and processes from order capture to customer delivery.

E-Market Place: An electronic market place that allows buyers and sellers to communicate online.

Front Office: The customer interface enabling data to be communicated between a customer/computer or computer/customer.

Fulfilment: A process leading to the consumption of a service or product.

Hybrids: Fulfilment related businesses that are not WCC or 3PS and have activities, either all or some of them, in the Island which include customer service, finance, head office, marketing, purchasing.

Information and Communication Technology (ICT): Communications and computer information systems processing, storing and transmitting information and data.

Legacy Systems: Operating systems, hardware and software that have considerable value to a business which operate with standard controls from origin to consumption.

Tracking and Tracing: The recoding and monitoring of the movement of shipments from the origin to a destination.

Whole Chain Companies (WCC): Buy and sell goods to customers and receive revenue on total of sales.

APPENDIX A

LIST OF ABBREVIATIONS

3PS - Third Party Service Providers
CD - Compact Disk
DVD - Digital Video Disk
EU - European Union
GDP - Gross Domestic Product
IBC - International Business Centre
ICT - Information and Communication Technology
IMF - International Monetary Fund
LVCR - Low Value Consignment Relief
OECD - Organisation for Economic Co-operation and Development
OFC - Offshore Financial Centre
UK - United Kingdom
US - United States
VAT - Value Added Tax
WCC - Whole Chain Companies

Compilation of References

Ab Hamid, N. R. (2005). E-CRM: Are we there yet? *The Journal of American Academy of Business, 6*(1), 51–57.

Ab Hamid, N. R., & Kassim, N. (2004). Internet technology as a tool in customer relationship management. *The Journal of American Academy of Business, 4*(1/2), 103–108.

Adams, D. A., Nelson, R. R., & Todd, P. A. (1992). Perceived usefulness, ease of use, and usage of information technology: a replication. *MIS Quarterly,* 227–247. doi:10.2307/249577

Adebanjo, D. (2003). 'Classifying and selecting e-CRM applications: an analysis-based proposal. *Management Decision, 41*(6), 570–577. doi:10.1108/00251740310491517

Adomi, E. E. (2007). African Web portals. In A. Tatnall (Ed.), *Encyclopedia of portal technologies and applications,* (Vol. 1, pp. 41-46). Hershey, PA: Information Science Publishing.

Agatz, N. A. H., Fleischmann, M., & van Nunen, J. A. E. E. (2007). E-fulfilment and multi-channel distribution – A review. *European Journal of Operational Research, 187,* 339 356. doi:10.1016/j.ejor.2007.04.024

Ajzen, I., & Fishbein, M. (1980). *Understanding attitudes and predicting social behavior.* Upper Saddle River, NJ: Prentice-Hall.

Akhter, S. H. (2003). Digital divide and purchase intention: Why demographic psychology matters? *Journal of Economic Psychology, 24*(3), 321–327. doi:10.1016/S0167-4870(02)00171-X

Alam, S. S., & Ahsan, M. N. (2007). ICT adoption in Malaysian SMEs from services sectors: Preliminary findings. *Journal of Internet Banking and Commerce, 12*(3). Retrieved May 12, 2009, from http://www.arraydev.com/commerce/jibc/2007-12/Syed_accepted.pdf

Alam, S. S., Ahmad, I., Abdullah, Z., & Ishak, N. A. (2007). ICT usage in SMEs: Empirical study of service sectors in Malaysia. In *Proceedings of the 4th SMEs in a Global Economy Conference,* Shah Alam, Malaysia.

Alam, S. S., Khatibi, A., Sayyed Ahmad, M. I., & Ismail, H. (2007). Factors affecting e-commerce adoption in the electronic manufacturing companies in Malaysia. *International Journal of Commerce and Management, 17*(1/2), 125–139. doi:10.1108/10569210710776503

Alexander, P. R. (2002). *What's driving e-fulfilment: new aims, new frames.* Paper presented at the 3rd International We-B Conference, Perth, Western Australia.

Allan, C., Annear, J., Beck, E., & Beveren, J. (2003). *A framework for the adoption of ICT and security technologies by SMEs.* Retrieved January 11, 2005, from http://www.cecc.com.au/programs/resource_manager/accounts/seaanz_papers/62AnnearetalFinal.pdf

Allinson, G., Braidford, P., Grewer, N., Houston, M., Orange, R., Leigh Sear, R., & Stone, I. (2004). *Ethnic minority businesses and ICT, focus group research,* Durham Business School for SBS. Retrieved May 2, 2008, from http://www.sbs.gov.uk/SBS_Gov_files/researchandstats/EMB_and_ICT.pdf

Alonso Mendo, F., & Fitzgerald, G. (2005). A multidimensional framework for SME e-business progression.

Journal of Enterprise Information Management, 18(6), 678–696. doi:10.1108/17410390510628382

Alonso Mendo, F., & Fitzgerald, G. (2005). Theoretical approaches to study SMEs eBusiness progression. *Journal of Computing and Information Technology, 13*(2), 123–136. doi:10.2498/cit.2005.02.04

Al-Qirim, N. (2003). A framework for electronic commerce research in small to medium-sized enterprises. In: N. Al-Qirim, N. (Ed.), *Electronic commerce in small to medium-sized enterprises: Frameworks, issues and implications* (pp. 1-16). Hershey, PA: IGI Global Publishing.

Al-Qirim, N. (2006). Personas of e-commerce adoption in small businesses in New Zealand. *Journal of Electronic Commerce in Organizations, 4,* 18–45.

AL-Qirim, N. (2007). E-commerce adoption in small businesses: cases from New Zealand. *Journal of Information Technology Case and Application Research, 9,* 28.

Al-Qirim, N. A. Y. (Ed.). (2004). *Electronic commerce in small to medium-sized enterprises: Frameworks, issues and implications.* Hershey, PA: IGI Global Publishing.

Al-Qirin, N. (2005). An empirical investigation of an e-commerce adoption-capability model in small businesses in New Zealand. *Electronic Markets, 15*(4), 418–437. doi:10.1080/10196780500303136

Alvarez, S. A., & Barney, J. B. (2005). How do entrepreneurs organize firms under conditions of uncertainty? *Journal of Management, 31*(5), 776–793. doi:10.1177/0149206305279486

Alzougool, B., & Kurnia, S. (2008). Electronic commerce technologies adoption by SMEs: A conceptual study. In *Proceedings of the 19th Australasian Conference on Information Systems*, Christchurch, New Zealand.

Amor, D. (2000). *The e-business revolution.* New York: Prentice Hall.

Analoui, F., & Karami, A. (2003). *Strategic management in SMEs.* London: Thomson Learning.

Andersen, A., & National Small Business United. (1998). *Survey of Small and Medium-sized Businesses.*

Anderson, D., & Lee, H. (2001). *New supply chain business models – The opportunities and challenges.* Paper presented at the Keynote – the Achieving Supply Chain Through Excellence (ASCET) project.

Ang, C., Davies, M., & Finlay, P. (2001). An empirical model of IT usage in the Malaysian public sector. *The Journal of Strategic Information Systems, 10,* 159–174. doi:10.1016/S0963-8687(01)00047-6

Ardichvili, A., Cardozo, R., & Ray, S. (2003). A theory of entrepreneurial opportunity identification & development. *Journal of Business Venturing, 18*(1), 105–123. doi:10.1016/S0883-9026(01)00068-4

Arnott, D. C., & Bridgewater, S. (2002). Internet interaction and implications for marketing. *Marketing Intelligence & Planning, 20*(2), 86–95. doi:10.1108/02634500210418509

Ash, C. G., & Burn, J. M. (2003). Assessing the benefits from e-business transformation through effective enterprise management. *European Journal of Information Systems, 12*(4), 297–308. doi:10.1057/palgrave.ejis.3000476

Audretsch, D. B., & Thurik, A. R. (2001). What is new about the new economy: sources of growth in the managed and entrepreneurial economies. *Industrial and Corporate Change, 10*(1), 17–34. doi:10.1093/icc/10.1.267

Auger, P. (2005). The impact of interactivity and design sophistication on the performance of commercial websites for small businesses. *Journal of Small Business Management, 43*(2), 119–137.

Austin, P. (2002). *The key issues facing Jersey's finance industry.* A review of the talk by Phil Austin on October 09, Société-Jersiaise, St. Helier, 1-3.

Baggozi, R., & Lee, K. H. (1999). Consumer resistance to, and acceptance of, innovations. *Advances in Consumer Research. Association for Consumer Research (U. S.), 26,* 218–225.

Bagozzi, R. P., Davis, F. D., & Warshaw, P. R. (1992). Development and test of a theory of technological learning and usage. *Human Relations*, *45*(7), 659. doi:10.1177/001872679204500702

Baida, Z., Liu, J., & Tan, Y.-H. (2007). Towards a methodology for designing e-government control procedures. *Electronic Government*, 4646, 56-67. Berlin/Heidelberg: Springer.

Baida, Z., Rukanova, B., Liu, J., & Tan, Y. H. (2007, June 3-6). Rethinking EU trade procedures - The beer living lab. In *Proceedings of the 20th Bled eConference: eMergence*. Bled, Slovenia.

Baker & McKenzie. (2001). *Doing e-commerce in Europe*. Hong Kong: Baker and McKenzie.

Bakry, S. H. (2004). Development of e-Government: a STOPE View. *International Journal of Network Management*, *14*(5), 339–350. doi:10.1002/nem.529

Baldwin, A., Lymer, A., & Johnson, R. (2000). Business impacts of the Internet for small and medium-sized enterprises. In B. Hunt & S. Barnes (Eds.), *Ecommerce and V-Business: Business Models for Global Success* (pp 103-120). Oxford, UK: Butterworth- Heinemann.

Balocco, R., Mogre, R., & Toletti, G. (2009). Mobile internet and SMEs: a focus on the adoption. *Industrial Management & Data Systems*, *109*(2), 245–261. doi:10.1108/02635570910930127

Bant, P., & Meijer, J. (1999) In P.C. van der Sijde & A. Ridder (Eds.), *Commercialising Knowledge, examples of entrepreneurship at the University of Twente*. Enschede: Twente University Press.

Bantel, K. A., & Jackson, S. E. (1989). Top management and innovations in banking: Does the composition of the top management team make a difference? *Strategic Management Journal*, *10*, 107–124. doi:10.1002/smj.4250100709

Baourakis, G., Kourgiantakis, M., & Migdalas, A. (2002). The impact of e-commerce on agro-food marketing: The case of agricultural co-operatives, firms and consumers in Crete. *British Food Journal*, *104*(8), 580–590. doi:10.1108/00070700210425976

Barabasi, A. L., & Bonabeay, E. (2003). Scale-free networks. *Scientific American*, *288*(5), 60–70.

Barlette, Y., & Fomin, V. (2008). Exploring the suitability of IS security management standards for SMEs. In *Proceedings of the 41st Hawaii International Conference on System Sciences*, 2008. Retrieved May 24, 2008, from http://csdl2.computer.org/comp/proceedings/hicss/2008/3075/00/30750308.pdf

Bauer, H. H., Gretner, M., & Leach, M. (2002). Building customer relations over the Internet. *Industrial Marketing Management*, *31*(2), 155–163. doi:10.1016/S0019-8501(01)00186-9

Baumeister, H. (2002, October). Customer relationship management for SMEs, e2000 e-business & e-work. In *Proceedings of the E2002 Conference*, Prague

Bayles, D. L. (2001). *E-commerce logistics and e-fulfilment: From click to clutch*. London: Prentice Hall.

Beaver, G. (2007). The strategy payoff for smaller enterprises. *The Journal of Business Strategy*, *28*(1), 11–17. doi:10.1108/02756660710723161

Beckinsale, M. J. J., & Levy, M. (2002). *Hi-tech entrepreneurs and the Internet*. Paper presented at the 10th Annual International Conference High Technology Small Firms Conference, Twente University, 10-11 June 2002, Netherlands

Beckinsale, M. J. J., & Ram, M. (2006). Delivering ICT to Ethnic Minority Businesses: An Action Research Approach . *Environment and Planning. C, Government & Policy*, *24*(6), 847–867. doi:10.1068/c0559

Beckinsale, M. J. J., & Ram, M. (2008). *SME/EMB action research: A framework for ICT policy driven initiatives ®*. Paper presented at the 31st Institute for Small Business and Entrepreneurship, Nov 5th-Nov 7th, Belfast, Ireland.

Beckinsale, M. J. J., Levy, M., & Powell, P. (2006). Exploring Internet adoption drivers in SMEs. *Electronic*

Markets – . International Journal (Toronto, Ont.), 16(4), 361–370.

Bellows, A.M. (2002). *Finance, after the war: Essays of Jersey history: 1946-2002,* Société-Jersiaise, St. Helier, 1-3.

Bengtsson, M., Boter, H., & Vanyushyn, V. (2007). Integrating the Internet and marketing operations: A study of antecedents in firms of different size. *International Small Business Journal, 25*(1), 27–48. doi:10.1177/0266242607071780

Bengtsson, M., Boter, H., & Vanyushyn, V. (2007). Integrating the Internet and marketing operations. *International Small Business Journal, 25*(1), 27–48. doi:10.1177/0266242607071780

Bennett, T. (2001). Glossary Terms. *Tolley's international initiatives affecting financial havens,* London.

BERR. (2009). *Enterprise directorate analytical unit frequently asked questions.* Retrieved May 4, 2009, from http://www.berr.gov.uk/whatwedo/enterprise/enterprisesmes/research-and-statistics/statistics/page38573.html

Berry, L.L. (1995). Relationship marketing of services – Growing interest, emerging perspectives. *Journal of Academy of Marketing Science, 23*(fall), 236-245.

Beynon-Davies, P. (2004). *E-business.* New York: Palgrave Macmillan. Blackburn, R., & McClure, R. (1998). *The use of information communication technologies (ICTs) in small business service firms.* Report by Small Business Research Centre, Kingston Business School.

Beynon-Davies, P. (2007). eBusiness maturity and regional development. *International Journal of Business Science and Applied Management, 2*(1), 9–20.

Beynon-Davies, P., Evans, S., & Owens, I. (2000). Electronic commerce and small and medium enterprises. In *Proceedings of 10th Business Information Technology Conference (BIT),* Manchester Metropolitan University, UK.

Bharadwaj, P. N., & Soni, R. G. (2007). E-commerce usage and perception of e-commerce issues among small firms: Results and implications from an empirical study. *Journal of Small Business Management, 45*(4), 501–521. doi:10.1111/j.1540-627X.2007.00225.x

Bharati, P., & Chaudhury, A. (2006, July). *Small and medium enterprises (SMEs) adoption of technology along the value chain.* Paper presented at the European and Mediterranean Conference on Information Systems (EMICS), Alicante.

Bhave, M. P. (1994). A process model of entrepreneurial venture creation. *Journal of Business Venturing, 9*(2), 223–223. doi:10.1016/0883-9026(94)90031-0

Bitner, M. J., Brown, S. W., & Meuter, M. L. (2000). Technology infusion in service encounters. *Journal of the Academy of Marketing Science, 28*(1), 138–149. doi:10.1177/0092070300281013

Bjørn-Andersen, N., Razmerita, L. V., & Henriksen, H. Z. (2007). The streamlining of cross-border taxation using IT: The Danish eExport solution. In J. Makolm & G. Orthofer (Eds.), *E-Taxation: State & perspectives: E-government in the field of taxation: Scientific Basis, Implementation Strategies, Good Practice Examples* (pp. 195-206). Linz, Austria: Trauner Verlag.

Black, J. (2001). *Managing discretion.* Unpublished manuscript, London School of Economics, UK.

Blackburn, R., & Athayde, R. (2000). Making the connection: The effectiveness of Internet training in small business. *Education and Training, 42*(4/5), 289–299. doi:10.1108/00400910010373723

Blakeley, C. J., & Matsuura, J. H. (2001). E-Government: An Engine to Power e-Commerce Development. In *Proceedings of the European Conference on e-Government, Trinity College; Dublin, Ireland,* September 27-28.

Blankson, C., & Stokes, D. (2002). Marketing practices in the UK small business sector. *Marketing Intelligence & Planning, 20*(1), 49–61. doi:10.1108/02634500210414774

Blili, S., & Raymond, L. (1993). Information technology: Threats and opportunities for small and medium sized enterprises. *International Journal of Information Management, 13*(6), 439–448. doi:10.1016/0268-4012(93)90060-H

Bolongkikit, J., Obit, J. H., Asing, J. G., & Tanakinjal, G. H. (2006). An exploratory research of the usage level of e-commerce among SMEs in the West Coast of Sabah, Malaysia. *Journal of Internet Banking and Commerce, 11*(2).

Boulding, W., Staelin, R., Ehret, M., & Johnston, W. J. (2005). A customer relationship management roadmap: what is known, potential pitfalls, and where to go. *Journal of Marketing, 69*(4), 155–166. doi:10.1509/jmkg.2005.69.4.155

Boyd, S. L., Hobbs, J. E., & Kerr, W. A. (2003). The impact of customs procedures on business to consumer e-commerce in food products. *Supply Chain Management: An International Journal, 8*(3), 195–200. doi:10.1108/13598540310484591

Bradley, F. (1998). From Clashmore containers to value relationships in the business system. *Irish Review of Marketing, 11*(1), 78–84.

Bradshaw, D., & Brash, C. (2001). Managing customer relationships in the e-business world: how to personalise computer relationships for increased profitability. *International Journal of Retail & Distribution Management, 29*(12), 520. doi:10.1108/09590550110696969

Briedenhann, J., & Wickens, E. (2004). Tourism routes as a tool for the economic development of rural areas – vibrant hope or impossible dream? *Tourism Management, 25*(1), 71–79. doi:10.1016/S0261-5177(03)00063-3

British Broadcasting Authority (BBC). (2006). Talking Jersey: Music will be "less diverse." Retrieved from http://www.bbc.co.uk/jersey/content/articles/2006/03/20/fullfilment

Brodie, R. J., Winklhofer, H., Coviello, N. E., & Johnston, W. J. (2007). Is e-marketing coming of age? An examination of e-marketing and firm performance. *Journal of Interactive Marketing, 21*(1), 2–21. doi:10.1002/dir.20071

Brooksbank, D., Morse, L., & Thomas, B. (2000). *Learning Chamber Report 'Towards a Learning Strategy.* Cardiff: Cardiff Chamber of Commerce, 92. Retrieved from http://www.cardiffchamber.co.uk/

Brooksbank, D., Quayle, M., & Thomas, B. (2001). Project looks at the effects of e-commerce on SMEs. *The Western Mail*, Wednesday, September 19.

Brown, R. (1994). Theory and practice of regulatory enforcement: Occupational health and safety regulation in British Colombia. *Law & Policy, 16*, 63–71. doi:10.1111/j.1467-9930.1994.tb00117.x

Brunner, C., & Bennett, D. (1998). Technology perceptions by gender. *Education Digest*, (February): 56–58.

Brush, C. G., Greene, P. G., Hart, M. M., & Haller, H. S. (2001). From Initial Idea To Unique Advantage: The Entrepreneurial Challenge Of Constructing A Resource Base. *The Academy of Management Executive, 15*(1), 64–78.

Bruyat, C., & Julien, P. A. (2001). Defining the field of research in entrepreneurship. *Journal of Business Venturing, 16*(2), 165–180. doi:10.1016/S0883-9026(99)00043-9

Brynjolfsson, E., & Kahin, B. (Eds.). (2000). *Understanding the Digital Economy*. Cambridge, MA: MIT press.

Buck Consultants International (BCI). (2002). *E-thematic final report e-fulfilment future opportunities*. Information Society Technologies Programme, European Union.

Buhalis, D., & Main, H. (1998). Information technology in peripheral small and medium hospitality enterprises: Strategic analysis and critical factors. *International Journal of Contemporary Hospitality Management, 10*(5), 198–202. doi:10.1108/09596119810227811

Bui, T. X., Sankaran, S., & Sebastian, I. M. (2003). A framework for measuring national e-readiness. *International Journal of Electronic Business, 1*(1), 3–22. doi:10.1504/IJEB.2003.002162

Bull, C. (2003). Strategic issues in customer relationship management (CRM) implementation. *Business Process Management Journal, 9*(5), 592–602. doi:10.1108/14637150310496703

Burn, J., & Alexander, P. (2005, June 6-8). Measuring e-transformation in the logistics industry: A knowledge capability index. In *18ᵗʰ Bled eConference eIntegration in Action*, Bled, Slovenia.

Burn, J., & Robins, G. (2003). Moving towards e-government: A case study of organisational change process. *Logistics Information Management, 16*(1), 25–35. doi:10.1108/09576050310453714

Burnkrant, R. E., & Page, T. J. (1988). The structure and antecedents of the normative and attitudinal components of Fishbein's theory of reasoned action. *Journal of Experimental Social Psychology, 24*(1), 66–87. doi:10.1016/0022-1031(88)90044-3

Burrows, T. (2004). Making Web site compliance easy. *ITWeb*. Retrieved September 4, 2005, from http://www.itweb.co.za/sections/internet/2004/0409 220806.asp?A=COV&S=Cover

Burt, R. S. (2004). Structural Holes and Good Ideas. *American Journal of Sociology, 110*(2), 349–399. doi:10.1086/421787

Buttle, F. (2004). *Customer relationship management, concepts and tools.* Oxford,UK: Elsevier, Butterworth, Heinemann

Buys. (2007). *Records management guide*, Buys IT Law Consulting (Pty) Ltd. Retrieved October 14, 2008, from http://www.buys.co.za/gbDownloads.asp?field=file&RID=517

Caldeira, M. M., & Ward, J. M. (2003). Using resource-based theory to interpret the successful adoption and use of information systems and technology in manufacturing small and medium-sized enterprises. *European Journal of Information Systems, 12*(2), 127–141. doi:10.1057/palgrave.ejis.3000454

Cardinali, G.C. (2005). *Nuove Traiettorie dell'innovazione nel retailing.* Milano: EGEA.

Carina, I., Monika, M., Ada, S., & Virpi Kristiina, T. (2003). SME barriers to electronic commerce adoption: Nothing changes-everything is new. In *Managing IT in government business & communities* (pp. 147-163). Hershey, PA, USA: IGI Publishing.

Carree, M., van Stel, A., Thurik, R., & Wennekers, S. (2002). Economic development and business ownership: an analysis using data of 23 OECD countries in the period 1976-1996. *Small Business Economics, 19*(3), 271–290. doi:10.1023/A:1019604426387

Carson D., & Gilmore, A. (2000). Marketing at the interface: Not 'what' but 'how'. *Journal of Marketing Theory and Practice, Spring, 8*(2), 1-8.

Carson, D., Cromie, S., McGowan, P., & Hill, J. (1995). *Marketing and entrepreneurship in SMEs.* Englewood Cliffs, NJ: Prentice-Hall

Carter, L., & Belanger, F. (2004). The influence of perceived characteristics of innovating on e-government adoption. *Electronic . Journal of E-Government, 2*(1), 11–20.

Carter, N. M., & Allen, K. R. (1997). Size determinants of women-owned businesses: choice or barriers to resources? *Entrepreneurship and Regional Development, 9*(3), 211–220. doi:10.1080/08985629700000012

Carter, S., & Bennett, D. (2006). Gender and entrepreneurship. In S. Carter & D. Jones-Evans (Eds.), *Enterprise and small business: Principles, practice and policy.* London: FT Prentice-Hall.

Caskey, K., & Subirana, B. (2007). Supporting SME e-commerce migration through blended e-learning. *Journal of Small Business and Enterprise Development, 14*(4), 670–688. doi:10.1108/14626000710832767

CEEDR. (2001). *Researching business support needs of ethnic minority owned businesses in Coventry and Warwickshire.* Report commissioned by the Coventry and Warwickshire Chamber of Commerce, Training and Enterprise, Centre for Enterprise and Economic Development Research, Middlesex University.

Cespedes, F. W. (1994). Industrial marketing: Managing new requirements. *Sloan Management Review, 35*(3), 45–63.

Chaffey, D. (2007). *E-business and e-commerce management: Strategy, implementation and practice.* Upper Saddle River, NJ: Prentice Hall.

Chaffey, D., Bocij, P., Greasley, A., & Hickie, S. (2007). *Business information systems – Technology, development & management for e-business* (3rd Ed.). London: Prentice Hall.

Chan, S., & Lu, M. (2004). Understanding internet banking adoption and use behavior: A Hong Kong perspective. *Journal of Global Information Management, 12*(3), 21–43.

Chaston, I., & Mangles, T. (2003). Relationship marketing in online business-to-business markets: A pilot investigation of small UK manufacturing firms. *European Journal of Marketing, 37*(5/6), 753–773. doi:10.1108/03090560310465134

Chau, P. (2001). Inhibitors to EDI adoption in small businesses: An empirical investigation. *Journal of Electronic Commerce Research, 2*(2), 24–46.

Chau, P. Y. K. (1996). An empirical assessment of a modified technology acceptance model. *Journal of Management Information Systems, 13*(2), 185–204.

Chau, P. Y. K. (2001). Determinants of small business EDI adoption: An empirical investigation. *Journal of Organizational Computing and Electronic Commerce, 11*(4), 229–252. doi:10.1207/S15327744JOCE1104_02

Checchi, R. M., Sevcik, G. R., Loch, K. D., & Straub, D. D. (2002). An instrumentation process for measuring ICT policies and culture. In *Proceedings of International Conference on Information Technology, Communications and Development,* Kathmandu, Nepal (pp. 1-17).

Chen, I. J., & Popovich, K. (2003). Understanding customer relationship management (CRM) people, process and technology. *Business Process Management Journal, 9*(5), 672–688. doi:10.1108/14637150310496758

Chen, L., Gillenson, M. L., & Sherrell, D. L. (2002). Enticing online consumers: an extended technology acceptance perspective. *Information & Management, 39*(8), 705–719. doi:10.1016/S0378-7206(01)00127-6

Chen, L., Gillenson, M. L., & Sherrell, D. L. (2004). Consumer acceptance of virtual stores: a theoretical model and critical success factors. *Database, 35*, 8–31.

Chen, Q., & Chen H. (2004). Exploring the success factors of eCRM strategies in practice. *Database Marketing & Customer Strategy Management, July, 11*(4), 333-343.

Chen, S. (2005). *Strategic management of e-business* (2nd ed.). Chichester, UK: John Wiley & Sons.

Chetty, S., & Campbell-Hunt, C. (2003). Paths to internationalisation among small- to medium-sized firms: a global versus regional approach. *European Journal of Marketing, 37*(5/6), 796–820. doi:10.1108/03090560310465152

Cheung, W. (1998). The use of the World Wide Web for commercial purposes. *Industrial Management & Data Systems, 98*(4), 172–177. doi:10.1108/02635579810219345

Ching, H. L., & Ellis, P. (2004). Marketing in cyberspace: what factors drive e-commerce adoption? *Journal of Marketing Management, 20, 3*(4), 409–429.

Chuang, T. T., Nakatani, K., Chen, J. C. H., & Huang, I. L. (2007). Examining the impact of organisational and owner's characteristics on the extent of e-commerce adoption in SMEs. *Int. J. Business and Systems Research, 1*(1), 61–80. doi:10.1504/IJBSR.2007.014770

Chuang, T. T., Rutherford, M. W., & Lin, B. (2007). Owner/manager characteristics, organisational characteristics and IT adoption in small and medium enterprises. *International Journal of Management and Enterprise Development, 4*(6), 619–634. doi:10.1504/IJMED.2007.014985

Chuang, T.-T., Nakatani, K., Chen, J. C. H., & Huang, I.-L. (2007). Examining the impact of organisational and owner's characteristics on the extent of ecommerce adoption in SMEs. *International Journal of Business and Systems Research, 1*(1), 61–80. doi:10.1504/IJBSR.2007.014770

Chwelos, P., Benbasat, I., & Dexter, A. S. (2001). Empirical test of an EDI adoption model. *Information Systems Research, 12*(3), 304–321. doi:10.1287/isre.12.3.304.9708

CLES (Centre for Local Economic Strategies) Consulting. (2003). *EMBs and ICT services.* Retrieved June 14, 2005, from http://cles.live.poptech.coop/C2B/document_tree/ViewACategory.asp?CategoryID=1

Coghlan, D., & Brannick, T. (2004). *Doing action research in your own organization* (2nd Edition). London: Sage Publications.

Cohen, S., & Kallirroi, G. (2006). e-commerce investments from a SME perspective: costs, benefits and processes. *Electronic Journal of Information Evaluation, 9*(2), 45–56.

Coleman, S., Fararo, T., & Zey, M. (1993). Rational choice theory: Advocacy and critique. *Social Forces, 72*(1), 273–275. doi:10.2307/2580174

Collinson, E., & Shaw, E. (2001). Entrepreneurial marketing- A historical perspective on development and practice. *Management Decision, 39*(9), 761–766. doi:10.1108/EUM0000000006221

Computer Business Review. (2004). Website compliance survey. *Computer business review.* Retrieved September 20, 2006, from http://www.cbr.co.za/article.aspx?pklArticleId=3246&pklCategoryId=384

Costello, F. J. (2000). An exemplar model of classification in simple and combined categories. In L. R. Gleitman, & A. K. Joshi (Eds.), *Proceedings of the Twenty-Second Annual Conference of the Cognitive Science society* (pp. 95-100). Mahwah, NJ: Erlbaum.

Costello, P., Sloane, A., & Moreton, R. (2007). IT evaluation frameworks – Do they make a valuable contribution? A critique of some of the classic models for use by SMEs. *Electronic Journal of Information systems . Evaluation, 10*(1), 57–64.

Courtney, P., & Brydon, J. (2001, November). *Differential economic performance: Experience from two Scottish regions.* Paper presented at RICS Research Foundation Rural Research Conference, London.

Coviello, N., & Munro, H. (1997). Network relationships and the internationalisation process of the small software firm. *International Business Review, 6*(4), 361–386. doi:10.1016/S0969-5931(97)00010-3

Cragg, P. B., & King, M. (1993). Small-firm computing: motivators and inhibitors. *MIS Quarterly, 17*(1), 47–60. doi:10.2307/249509

Cragg, P., & Zinatelli, N. (1995). The evolution of IS in small firms. *Information & Management, 29*(1), 1–8. doi:10.1016/0378-7206(95)00012-L

CREME. (2009). *The minority ethnic enterprise centre of expertise.* Retrieved February 25, 2009, from http://www.dmu.ac.uk/faculties/business_and_law/business/research/creme/meecoe/index.jsp

Crespi, G., Mahdi, S., & Patel, P. (2004). Adoption of e-commerce technology: do network and learning externalities matter? *Draft Final Report for the Department of Trade and Industry,* London: HMSO.

Curran, J., & Blackburn, R. A. (2001). *Researching the small enterprise.* SAGE Production, London.

Cutshall, S. (2002). The printing. *Techniques - Association for Career and Technical Education, 77*(3), 26–29.

Dahlan, N., Ramayah, T., & Koay, A. H. (2002). Data mining in the banking industry: An exploratory study. In *Proceedings of the International Conference, Internet Economy and Business,* Kuala Lumpur, Malaysia.

Damanpour, F. (1991). Organizational innovation: a meta-analysis of effects of determinants and moderators. *Academy of Management Journal, 34*(3), 555–590. doi:10.2307/256406

Damanpour, F. (2001). E-business e-commerce evolution: perspective and strategy. *Managerial Finance, 27*(7), 16–33. doi:10.1108/03074350110767268

Dandridge, T., & Levenburg, N. M. (2000). High-tech potential? An exploratory study of very small firms' usage of the Internet. *International Small Business Journal, 18*(2), 81–91. doi:10.1177/0266242600182004

Daniel, E. M., Wilson, H., & Myers, A. (2002). Adoption of e-commerce by SMEs in the UK: Towards a stage model. *International Small Business Journal, 20*(3), 253–270. doi:10.1177/0266242602203002

Daniel, E., & Wilson, H. (2002). Adoption intentions and benefits realised: a study of e-commerce in UK SMEs. *Journal of Small Business and Enterprise Development, 9*(4), 331–348. doi:10.1108/14626000210450522

Dann, S., & Dann, S. (2001). *Strategic Internet marketing.* New York: Wiley.

Darch, H., & Lucas, T. (2002). Training as an e-commerce enabler. *Journal of Workplace Learning, 14*(40), 148–155. doi:10.1108/13665620210427276

Dasgupta, S., Agarwal, D., Ioannidis, A., & Gopalakrishnan, S. (1999). Determinants of information technology adoption: An extension of existing models to firms in a developing country. *Journal of Global Information Management, 7*(3), 30–40.

Davidsson, P. (Ed.). *New firm startups.* Cheltenham, UK: Edward Elgar

Davis, C., & Vladica, F. (August 2004). *Adoption of Internet technologies and e-business solutions by small and medium enterprises (SMEs) in New Brunswick.* Saint John, Canada: University of New Brunswick Saint John, Electronic Commerce Centre.

Davis, C., Lin, C., & Vladica, F. (2005). *State of e-Business in SMEs in Atlantic Canada in 2005.* Paper presented at the annual Atlantic Schools of Business conference, Halifax, N.S., Canada.

Davis, F. D. (1989). Perceived usefulness, perceived ease of use, and user acceptance of information technology. *MIS Quarterly,* 319–340. doi:10.2307/249008

Davis, F. D., Bagozzi, R. P., & Warshaw, P. R. (1989). User acceptance of computer technology: a comparison of two theoretical models. *Management Science, 35*(8), 982–1003. doi:10.1287/mnsc.35.8.982

Day, G. S., & Bens, K. F. (2005). Capitalizing on the Internet opportunity. *Journal of Business and Industrial Marketing, 20*(4/5), 160–168. doi:10.1108/08858620510603837

Day, G. S., & Hubbard, J. K. (2003). Customer relationships go digital. *Business Strategy Review, 14*(1), 17–26. doi:10.1111/1467-8616.00240

De Koning, A., & Muzyka, D. F. (1999). *Conceptualizing Opportunity Recognition as a Socio-Cognitive Process.* Fontainebleau: Insead (working paper).

De Vaus, D. A. (1991). *Surveys in social research.* London: Routledge.

Deakins, D., & Freel, M. (2006). *Entrepreneurship and small firms* (4th Ed.). Berkshire: McGraw-Hill Education.

Deakins, D., Galloway, L., & Mochrie, R. (2003). *The use and effect of ICT on Scotland's rural business community.* Scotecon Report.

Deakins, D., Ram, M., & Smallbone, D. (2003). Addressing the business support needs of ethnic minority firms in the United Kingdom. *Environment and Planning. C, Government & Policy, 21*(6), 843–859. doi:10.1068/c0305

Deise, M. V., Nowikow, C., King, P., & Wright, A. (2000). Research agenda for e-business logistics based on professional opinions. *International Journal of Physical Distribution and Logistics Management, 32*(7), 513–532.

Del Aguila-Obra, A. R., & Padilla-Melendez, A. (2006). Organizational factors affecting Internet technology adoption. *Internet Research, 16*(1), 94–110. doi:10.1108/10662240610642569

Dembla, P., Palvia, P., & Krishnan, B. (2007). Understanding the adoption of Web-enabled transaction processing by small businesses. *Journal of Electronic Commerce Research, 8*(1), 1–16.

Department for Business Enterprise & Regulatory Reform of UK. (2007). *Small and medium enterprise statistics for the UK and regions.* Retrieved May 8, 2009, from http://stats.berr.gov.uk/ed/sme/

Department of Statistics Malaysia. (2005). *Census of establishments and enterprises 2003.* The Secretariat, Research & Development Division, Department of Statistics, Federal Government Administrative Centre, Putrajaya, Malaysia.

Department of Trade and Industry. (2003). *International benchmarking study 2003.*

Department of Trade and Industry. (2004). *International benchmarking study 2004.*

Dev, C.S., & Schultz, D.E. (2005, January/February). In the mix: A customer focused approach can bring the current marketing mix into the 21st century. *Marketing Management, 14*(1).

Devaraj, S., Fan, M., & Kohli, R. (2002). Antecedents of B2C channel satisfaction and preference: validating e-commerce metrics. *Information Systems Research, 13*(3), 316. doi:10.1287/isre.13.3.316.77

Dewsnap, B., & Jobber, D. (2000). The sales-marketing interface in consumer packaged-goods companies: A conceptual framework. *Journal of Personal Selling & Sales Management, 20*(2), 109–119.

Dholakia, R. R., & Kshetri, N. (2004). Factors impacting the adoption of the Internet among SMEs. *Small Business Economics, 23*(4), 311–322. doi:10.1023/B:SBEJ.0000032036.90353.1f

Dillman, D. (2000) *Mail and Internet surveys: The tailored design method* (2nd Ed.). New York: John Wiley and Sons.

DiMaria, F. (2001). FAQs: Is international e-commerce really for you? *World Trade, 14*(9), 36–38.

Dimitratos, P., & Jones, M. V. (2005). Future directions for international entrepreneurship research. *International Business Review, 14*(2), 119–128. doi:10.1016/j.ibusrev.2004.06.003

Doherty, N., & Lockett, N., (2008). Mind the gap: Exploring the links between the expectations of relationship marketing and the reality of electronic-CRM. *International Journal of e-Business Management, 2*(2), 1-17.

Doolin, B., McLeod, L., McQueen, B., & Watton, M. (2003). Internet strategies for establishing retailers: Four New Zealand case studies. [JITCA]. *Journal of Information Technology Cases and Applications, 5*(4), 3–19.

Dos Santos, B. L., & Peffers, K. (1998). Competitor and Vendor influence on the adoption of innovative applications in electronic commerce. *Information & Management, 34*(3), 175–184. doi:10.1016/S0378-7206(98)00053-6

DoubleClick. (2005, June 28). *Touchpoints III: The Internet's role in the modern purchase process.*

Downie, G. (2003). Interactive marketing and SMEs. *Management Services, 47*(7), 8-13.

Drennan, J., & McColl-Kennedy, J. R. (2003). The relationship between Internet use and perceived performance in retail and professional service firms. *Journal of Services Marketing, 17*(3), 295–311. doi:10.1108/08876040310474837

Drew, S. (2003). Strategic uses of e-commerce by SMEs in the East of England. *European Management Journal, 21*(1), 79–88. doi:10.1016/S0263-2373(02)00148-2

DTI. (2004) *UK National Broadband Strategy.* Retrieved April 24, 2005, from http://www.dti.gov.uk/industry_files/pdf/uknational_broadband_strategy.pdf

DTI. (2004). *Business in the information age, international benchmarking study 2004.* A report prepared by Booz, Allen, Hamilton. eCIC (2005). *eCommerce in Welsh SMEs: The State of the Nation report 2005/6.* eCommerce Innovation Centre, Cardiff Business School, Cardiff University.

DTI. (2004). *International bench marking survey for ICT use.* UK Department of Trade and Industry. Retrieved July 28, 2006, from http://www2.bah.com/dti2004/main/mr_86.htm

DTI-news-release. (2008). *National statistics, The Small Business Service (SBS), The British Department of Trade and Industry.* Retrieved October 14, 2008, from http://www.sbs.gov.uk/SBS_Gov_files/researchandstats/SMEStats2004.pdf

Dun & Bradstreet. (1998, February 19). *17 Annual D&B small business study.* Retrieved from http://www.dnb.com/newsview/0217news4.htm

Dutta, S., & Evrard, P. (1999). Information technology and organisation within European small enterprises. *European Management Journal, 17*(3), 239–251. doi:10.1016/S0263-2373(99)00003-1

Dwelly, T., Maguire, K., & Truscott, F. (2005). *Under the radar: Tracking and supporting rural home based businesses.* Live Network Report to the Commission for Rural Communities.

Dwivedi, Y. K., Selamat, M. H., Abd Wahab, M. S., Mat Samsudin, M. A., & Lal, B. (2008). Examining factors influencing the behavioral intention to adopt broadband in Malaysia. In León, G., Bernardos, A., Casar, J., Kautz (Eds), *Open IT-based innovation: Moving towards cooperative IT transfer and knowledge diffusion* (pp. 325-342). Boston: Springer.

Dyerson, R., & Harindranath, G. (2007). *ICT adoption & use by SMEs in the UK: A survey of south east.* Management of Engineering and Technology . *Portland International Center, 5-9*, 1756–1770.

EBPG. (2002). *eEurope go digital: Benchmarking national and regional e-business policies for SMEs.* Final Report of the E-Business Policy Group.

Economist. (2007). *Survey of offshore financial centres.* Retrieved from http://www.economist.com/surveys

ECT Act (2002). Electronic Communications and Transactions Act. 2002. *Acts Online.* Retrieved March 30, 2005, from http://www.acts.co.za/ect_act/

Eden, C., & Huxham, C. (1996). Action research for the study of organisations. In S. Clegg, C. Hardy, & W. Nord. (Eds.) *Handbook of organisation Studies* (pp. 526-542). London: Sage.

Egan, T., Clancy, S., & O'Toole, T. (2003). The integration of e-commerce tools into the business processes of SMEs. *Irish Journal of Management, 24*(1), 139–153.

Eid, R. (2003). *Business-to-business international internet marketing: adoption, implementation and implications, an empirical study of UK companies.* UK: Bradford University.

Eisenhardt, K. M. (1989). Building theories from case study research. *Academy of Management Review, 14*, 532–550. doi:10.2307/258557

Elbeltagi, I. (2007). E-commerce and globalization: An exploratory study of Egypt. *Cross Cultural Management: An International Journal, 14*(3), 196–201. doi:10.1108/13527600710775748

ELC. (2003). Legalising electronic communications - electronic billing. *Electronic Law Consultancy.* Re-

trieved February 24, 2006, from http://elc.co.za/article.php?subaction=showfull&id=1052909342&archive=&start_from=&ucat=3&.

Elders, J., & Walsh, S. T. (1999). TMP (Total Micro Products, a micro-electro-mechanical systems company. In P. C. Van Der Sijde & A. Ridder (Eds.), *Commercialising Knowledge, examples of entrepreneurship at the University of Twente.* Enschede: Twente Univeristy Press.

Electronic Commerce Research & Training Centre (ECRTC). (2008). *Marketing on the Internet training program.* University of New Brunswick Saint John, Saint John, N.B., Canada.

Elfring, T., & Hulsink, W. (2003). Networks in Entrepreneurship: The Case of High-technology Firms. *Small Business Economics, 21*(4), 409–422. doi:10.1023/A:1026180418357

Elliot, S., & Fowell, S. (2000). Expectations versus reality: a snapshot of consumer experiences with Internet retailing. *International Journal of Information Management, 20*(5), 323–336. doi:10.1016/S0268-4012(00)00026-8

Engelbrecht, L. (2008, April 18). Fraud flies in Q1 2008 ITWeb 2008. Retrieved April 20, 2008 from http://www.itweb.co.za/sections/business/2008/0804181100.asp

Esper, T. L., & Williams, L. R. (2003). The value of collaborative transportation management (CTM): Its relationship to CPFR and information technology. *Transportation Journal, 42*(4), 5.

ESRC. (2008). *Economic and Social Research Council Society Today – Business engagement scheme for ESRC centres.* Retrieved June 25, 2008, from http://www.esrcsocietytoday.ac.uk/ESRCInfoCentre/opportunities/current_funding_opportunities/business_engagement.aspx?ComponentId=18191&SourcePageId=15428

European Commission. (1987). Council Regulation (EEC) No 2658/87 of 23 July 1987 on the Tariff and Statistical Nomenclature and on the Common Customs Tariff [Electronic Version]. *Official Journal of the European Communities, L256.* Retrieved April 8, 2009, from http://www.eugbc.net/files/52_129_447309_23.07.1987-CombinedNomenclature.pdf

European Commission. (1992). Council Regulation (EEC) No 2913/92 of 12 October 1992 establishing the Community Customs Code [Electronic Version]. *Official Journal of the European Communities, L253*. Retrieved April 8, 2009, from http://eur-lex.europa.eu/LexUriServ/LexUriServ.do?uri=CONSLEG:1992R2913:20070101:EN:PDF

European Commission. (1999). Directive 1993/93/EC of the European parliament and of the Council [Electronic Version]. *Official Journal of the European Communities, L13/12*. Retrieved April 8, 2009, from http://portal.etsi.org/esi/Documents/e-sign-directive.pdf

European Commission. (2000b). Directive 2000/31/EC of the European Parliament and of the Council of 8 June 2000 on certain legal aspects of information society services, in particular electronic commerce, in the Internal Market (Directive on electronic commerce) [Electronic Version]. *Official Journal of the European Communities, L178/1*. Retrieved April 8, 2009, from http://eur-lex.europa.eu/LexUriServ/LexUriServ.do?uri=OJ:L:2000:178:0001:0016:EN:PDF

European Commission. (2003). Commission Recommendation 2003/361/EC of 6 May 2003 Concerning the Definition of Micro, Small and Medium-Sized Enterprises [Electronic Version]. *Official Journal of the European Union, L 124*, 36. Retrieved April 8, 2009, from http://eur-lex.europa.eu/LexUriServ/LexUriServ.do?uri=OJ:L:2003:124:0036:0041:EN:PDF

European Commission. (2004). Internationalisation of SMEs [Electronic Version]. *Obervatory of European SMEs 2003, 4*. Retrieved April 9, 2009, from http://ec.europa.eu/enterprise/enterprise_policy/analysis/doc/smes_observatory_2003_report4_en.pdf

European Commission. (2005). Regulation (EC) No 648/2005 of the European Parliament and of the Council of 13 April 2005 amending Council Regulation (EEC) No 2913/92 establishing the Community Customs Code [Electronic Version]. *Official Journal of the European Union, L 117*. Retrieved April 8, 2009, from http://eur-lex.europa.eu/LexUriServ/LexUriServ.do?uri=CELEX:32005R0648:en:HTML

European Commission. (2006). *A pocketbook of e-business indicators - A portrait of e-business in 10 sectors of the EU economy*. Retrieved from http://www.ebusiness-watch.org/statistics/pocketbooks.htm

European Commission. (2006). *Annex to the Proposal on the Community Programme Customs2013 – Impact Assessment*. Retrieved February 10, 2009, from http://ec.europa.eu/taxation_customs/resources/documents/Customs2013_impact.pdf.

European Commission. (2006). *Authorized economic operators*. Retrieved March 16, 2009, from http://www.ifcba.org/UserFiles/File/SP0218E1(2).doc

European Commission. (2007). ICT- information and communication technologies – Work Programme 2007-8, Cordis. Retrieved May 3, 2008, from ftp://ftp.cordis.europa.eu/pub/fp7/ict/docs/ict-wp-2007-08_en.pdf

European Commission. (2007a). *Electronic Customs Multi-Annual Strategic Plan, 2007 Yearly Revision (MASP 8)*. Retrieved March 16, 2009, from http://ec.europa.eu/taxation_customs/resources/documents/customs/policy_issues/e-customs_initiative/MASP_rev7.pdf.

European Commission. (2007b). *Proposal for a Regulation of the European Parliament and of the Council laying down the Community Customs Code (Modernized Customs Code)*. Retrieved February 10, 2009, from http://ec.europa.eu/taxation_customs/resources/documents/customs/procedural_aspects/general/community_code/mccc_en.pdf.

European Commission. (2008). *E-business guide for SMEs- e-business software and services in the European market*. Retrieved from http://ec.europa.eu/enterprise/e-bsn/ebusiness-solutions-guide/welcome.do

European Commission. (2008). *The European e-business report 2008 - The impact of ICT and e-business on firms, sectors and the economy*. Retrieved from http://www.ebusiness-watch.org/key_reports/synthesis_reports.htm

European Commission. (2008). Decisions Adopted Jointly by the European Parliament and the Council:

Decision No 70/2008/EC of the European Parliament and the of the Council of 15 January 2008 on a paperless environment for customs and trade [Electronic Version]. *Official Journal of the European Union, L 23/21 - L23/26*. Retrieved April 8, 2009, from http://eur-lex.europa.eu/LexUriServ/LexUriServ.do?uri=OJ:L:2008:023:0021:0026:EN:PDF

European Commission. (2008). *Legislation Proposed or Adopted*. Retrieved February 10, 2009, from http://ec.europa.eu/taxation_customs/customs/policy_issues/electronic_customs_initiative/electronic_customs_legislation/index_en.htm.

European Commission. (2008). *Synthesis Report on Consumer and Business Attitudes to Cross-Border Sales and Consumer Protection in the Internal Market*. Retrieved February 10, 2009, from http://ec.europa.eu/consumers/strategy/docs/eurobar_298_synthrep_oct2008_en.pdf.

European Strategic Program on Research in Information Technology. (1997). *ESPRIT and ACTS projects related to Electronic Commerce*. Retrieved May 8, 2009, from http://cordis.europa.eu/esprit/src/ecomproj.htm

Eurostat (1996) *Enterprises in Europe*, Fourth Report.

Evans, D., & Yen, D. C. (2006). E-government: Evolving relationship of citizens and government, domestic, and international development. *Government Information Quarterly, 23*(2), 207–235. doi:10.1016/j.giq.2005.11.004

Fallon, M., & Moran, P. (2000). Information Communications Technology (ICT) and manufacturing SMEs. In *Proceedings of the 2000 Small Business and Enterprise Development Conference*, University of Manchester (pp. 100–109).

Fariselli, P., Oughton, C., Picory, C., & Sugden, R. (1999). Electronic commerce and the future for SMEs in a global market-place: networking and public policies. *Small Business Economics, 12*(3), 261–275. doi:10.1023/A:1008029924987

Feinberg, R., & Kadam, R. (2002). E-CRM Web service attributes as determinants of customer satisfaction with retail Web-sites. *International Journal of Service Industry Management, 13*(5), 432–451. doi:10.1108/09564230210447922

Fichman, R. G., & Kemerer, C. F. (1997). The assimilation of software process innovations: an organizational learning perspective. *Management Science, 43*(10), 1345–1363. doi:10.1287/mnsc.43.10.1345

Field, A. (2005) *Discovering Statistics Using SPSS* (2nd Ed.). London: Sage Publications.

Fielden, S., Davidson, M., & Makin, P. (2000). Barriers encountered during micro and small business start-up in North West England. *Journal of Small Business and Enterprise Development, 7*(4), 295–304. doi:10.1108/EUM0000000006852

Fillis, I., & Wagner, B. (2005). E-business development: an explanatory investigation of the small firm. *International Small Business Journal, 23*(6), 604–634. doi:10.1177/0266242605057655

Fillis, I., Johannson, U., & Wagner, B. (2004). Factors impacting on e-business adoption and development in the smaller firm. *International Journal of Entrepreneurial Behaviour and Research, 10*(3), 178–191. doi:10.1108/13552550410536762

Fillis, I., Johanson, U., & Wagner, B. (2003). E-business development: a conceptual model of the smaller firm. *Journal of Small Business and Enterprise Development, 10*(3), 336–345. doi:10.1108/14626000310489808

Fink, D., & Disterer, G. (2006). International case studies – To what extent is ICT infused into the operations of SMEs? *Journal of Enterprise Information Management, 19*(6), 608–624. doi:10.1108/17410390610708490

Fleet, G. (November 2008). *Export and the role of the Internet for SMEs in Atlantic Canada*. Paper presented at the International Council for Small Business (ICSB) 2008 World Conference, Halifax, N.S., Canada.

Fletcher, R., Bell, J., & McNoughton, R. (2004). *International e-business marketing*. London: Thomson

Foley, P., & Ram, M. (2002). *The use of online technology by ethnic minority businesses: A comparative study of the West Midlands and UK*, De Montfort University monograph. Retrieved February 3, 2008, from http://www.sbs.gov.uk/contents/research/EMB-IT.pdf

Foley, P., Watts, H. D., & Wilson, B. (1993). *New technology, skills shortages and training strategies* in P. Swann (Ed.), *New technology and the firm* (pp. 279-289). London: Routledge.

Folstand, A., Jorgensen, H. D., & Krogstie, J. (2004). User involvement in e-government development projects. In *Proceedings of the Third Nordic Conference on Human-Computer Interaction* (Vol. 82, pp. 217-224). New York: ACM.

Forman, C., Goldfarb, A., & Greenstein, S. (2005). How did location affect adoption of the commercial internet? Global village vs. urban leadership. *Journal of Urban Economics, 58*, 389–420. doi:10.1016/j.jue.2005.05.004

Forrester Research. (1998, November 19). *Growth spiral in online retail sales will generate $108 billion in revenues by 2003*. Retrieved from http://www.forrester.com.

Forrester Research. (2007, May 11). *Five immediate opportunities for ecommerce improvement*. Retrieved from http://www.forrester.com.

Frambach, R., & Schillweaert, N. (2002). Organizational innovation adoption: A multi-level framework of determinants and opportunities for future research. *Journal of Business Research, 55*(2), 163–176. doi:10.1016/S0148-2963(00)00152-1

Freidlein, A. (2001, February). CRM meets E-CRM: An executive briefing. *Wheel consultancy*. Retrieved 4th February, 2008 from www.e-consultancy.com

Friedman, T. (April 2005). *The world is flat: A brief history of the 21st century*. New York: Farrar, Straus & Giroux.

Froehlich, G., Hoover, H. J., Liew, W., & Sorenson, P. G. (1999). Application framework issues when evolving business applications for electronic commerce. *Information Systems, 24*(6), 457–473. doi:10.1016/S0306-4379(99)00027-7

Fulford, H. (2007). A local community web portal and small business. In A. Tatnall (Ed.), *Encyclopedia of por-*

tal technologies and applications. (Vol. 1, pp. 559-563). Hershey, PA: Information Science Publishing.

Fuller, T., & Southern, A. (1999). Small Firms and Information and Communication Technologies: Policy issues and some words of caution. *Environment and Planning. C, Government & Policy, 17*, 287–302. doi:10.1068/c170287

Furneaux, J. (2004). The credibility gap. *Ove Design & Communications*.

Gallagher, D., & Gilmore, A. (2004). The stages theory of SME internationalisation: a Northern Ireland case study. *International Journal of Management Cases, 7*(1), 13–23.

Galloway, I. (2007). Supporting SME e-commerce migration through blended e-learning. *Journal of Small Business and Enterprise Development, 14*(4), 641–653. doi:10.1108/14626000710832749

Galloway, L. (2006). Information and communications technologies and e-business. In D. Deakins & M. Freel (Eds.), *Entrepreneurship and small firms* (4th Ed.) (pp. 139-156). Berkshire: McGraw-Hill.

Galloway, L. (2007). Can broadband access rescue the rural economy? *Journal of Small Business and Enterprise Development, 14*(4), 641–653. doi:10.1108/14626000710832749

Galloway, L., & Mochrie, R. (2005). The use of ICT in rural firms: a policy orientated literature review. *Info, 7*(3), 33–46. doi:10.1108/14636690510596784

Galloway, L., & Mochrie, R. (2006). Entrepreneurial motivation, orientation and realisation in rural economies: A study of rural Scotland. *International Journal of Entrepreneurship and Innovation, 7*(3), 173–184.

Galloway, L., Deakins, D., & Sanders, J. (2008, November). *The use of Internet portals by Scotland's Rural Business Community*. Paper presented at the 31st Institute for Small Business and Entrepreneurship (ISBE) Conference, Belfast, Northern Ireland.

Galloway, L., Deakins, D., & Sanders, J. (2008, November). *The use of Internet portals by Scotland's rural business community.* Paper presented at Institute for Small Business & Entrepreneurship Conference, Belfast, Northern Ireland.

Galloway, L., Mochrie, R., & Deakins, D. (2004). ICT-enabled collectivity as a positive rural business strategy. *International Journal of Entrepreneurial Behaviour and Research, 10*(4), 247–259. doi:10.1108/13552550410544213

Gartner, W. B. (1985). A conceptual framework for describing the phenomenon of new venture creation. *Academy of Management Review, 10*(4), 696–706. doi:10.2307/258039

Gartner, W. B. (1988). Who is an entrepreneur? Is the wrong question. *American journal of small business, 12*(4), 11-32.

Garwood, C. (2007). *Flat earth, the history of an infamous idea.* London, MacMillan.

Gauri, K. G., Trivedi, M., & Grewal, D. (2008). Understanding the determinants of retail strategy: An empirical analysis. *Journal of Retailing, 84*(3), 256–267. doi:10.1016/j.jretai.2008.06.004

Gefen, D. (2003). TAM or just plain habit: A look at experienced online shoppers. *Journal of End User Computing, 15*(3), 1–13.

Gefen, D., & Straub, D. (2000). The relative importance of perceived ease of use in IS adoption: a study of e-commerce adoption. *Journal of the Association for Information Systems, 1*(8), 1–28.

Gefen, D., & Straub, D. W. (1997). Gender differences in the perception and use of e-mail: An extension to the Technology Acceptance Model. *MIS Quarterly, 21,* 389–400. doi:10.2307/249720

Gefen, D., Karahanna, E., & Straub, D. W. (2003). Inexperience and experience with online stores: The importance of TAM and trust. *IEEE Transactions on Engineering Management, 50*(3), 307–321. doi:10.1109/TEM.2003.817277

Gefen, D., Karahanna, E., & Straub, D. W. (2003). Trust and TAM in online shopping: An integrated model. *MIS Quarterly, 27,* 51–90.

Geiger, S., & Martin, S. (1999). The Internet as a relationship marketing tool – Some evidence from Irish companies. *Irish Marketing Review, 12*(2), 24–35.

Geller, K. (1998). The Internet: The ultimate relationship marketing tool. *Direct Marketing, Garden City, Sep; 61*(5), 36-39.

Geyskens, I., Gielens, K., & Dekimpe, M. G. (2002). The market valuation of Internet channel additions. *Journal of Marketing, 66*(2), 102–119. doi:10.1509/jmkg.66.2.102.18478

Giaglis, G. M., Klein, S., & O'Keefe, R. M. (2002). The role of intermediaries in electronic marketplaces: developing a contingency model. *Information Systems Journal, 12*(3), 231–246. doi:10.1046/j.1365-2575.2002.00123.x

Gibbs, J., & Kraemer, K. (2004). A Cross-country investigation of the determinants of scope of E-Commerce use: an institutional approach. *Electronic Markets, 14*(2), 124–137. doi:10.1080/10196780410001675077

Gibbs, J., Kraemer, K. L., & Dedrick, J. (2003). Environment and policy factors shaping global e-commerce diffusion: A cross country comparison. *The Information Society, 19*(1), 5–18. doi:10.1080/01972240309472

Giffen, P. (2005). Technology's terror & triumphs. *Applied Arts, 20*(2), 8–14.

Gilmore, A., & Carson, D. (1999). Entrepreneurial marketing by networking . *New England Journal of Entrepreneurship, Fall, 2*(2), 31-38.

Gilmore, A., Carson, D., & Grant, K. (2001). SME marketing in practice. *Marketing Intelligence & Planning, 19*(1), 6–11. doi:10.1108/02634500110363583

Gilmore, A., Carson, D., Grant, K., O'Donnell, A., Laney, R., & Pickett, B. (2006). Networking in SMEs: Findings from Australia and Ireland. *Irish Marketing Review, 18*(1/2), 21–29.

Gilmore, A., Carson, D., O'Donnell, A., & Cummins, D. (1999). Added value: A qualitative assessment of SME marketing. *Irish Marketing Review, 12*(1), 27–36.

Gilmore, A., Gallagher, D., & Henry, S. (2007). E-marketing and SMEs: Operational lessons for the future. *European Business Review, 19*(3), 234–247. doi:10.1108/09555340710746482

Gonzalez-Benito, O., Munoz-Gallego, P. A., & Kopalle, P. K. (2005). Asymmetric competition in retail store formats: Evaluating inter- and intra-format spatial effects. *Journal of Retailing, 81*(1), 75–79. doi:10.1016/j.jretai.2005.01.006

Goode, A., & Stevens, K. (2000). An analysis of the business characteristics of adopters and non-adopters of World Wide Web technology. *Information Technology and Management, 1*, 129–154. doi:10.1023/A:1019112722593

Google investor relations – Financial tables. (2008). Retrieved March 18, 2009, from http://investor.google.com/fin_data.html

Gorton, M. (1999). Spatial variations in markets served by UK-based small and medium sized enterprises (SMEs). *Entrepreneurship and Regional Development, 11*(1), 39–55. doi:10.1080/089856299283281

Government of Jersey. (2002). Introduction, Jersey, Ref 670.0389. In *Jersey Island Plan Final Draft* (pp. 1-9). Retrieved from http://www.planning.gov.je

Grandon, E. E., & Pearson, J. M. (2004). Electronic commerce adoption: an empirical study of small and medium US businesses. *Information & Management, 42*(1), 197–216.

Grandon, E., & Pearson, J. M. (2003). Strategic value and adoption of electronic commerce: an empirical study of Chilean small and medium businesses. *Journal of Global Information Technology Management, 6*(3), 22–43.

Gray, C. (2004). Entrepreneurship: Links between growth, ICT-adoption and innovation. In *Proceedings of the 27th ISBA Conference*, Newcastle, Gateshead.

Gray, C., & Lawless, N. (2000). Innovations in the distance development of SME management. *European Journal of Open and Distance Learning.* Retrieved May 16, 2002, from http://www1.nks.no/eurodl/shoen/Gray.html

Gray, R. (1999, September). Using the voice at the end of the line. *Marketing, 16*, 29–30.

Gribbins, M., & King, R. (2004). Electronic retailing strategies: A case study of small businesses in the gifts & collectibles industry. *Electronic Markets, 14*(2), 138–152. doi:10.1080/10196780410001675086

Grimm, C. M., & Smith, K. G. (1991). Management and organizational change: a note on the railroad industry. *Strategic Management Journal, 12*, 557–562. doi:10.1002/smj.4250120708

Grönroos, C. (1994). From marketing mix to relationship marketing: Towards a paradigm shift in marketing. *Management Decision, 32*(2), 4–22. doi:10.1108/00251749410054774

Grönroos, C. (2004). The relationship marketing process: communication, interaction, dialogue, value. *Journal of Business and Industrial Marketing, 19*(2), 99–113. doi:10.1108/08858620410523981

Grossman, D., & Zaelke, D. 2005. An introduction to theories of why states and firms do (and do not) comply with law. INECE Conference Proceedings. *INECE*. Retrieved September 10, 2006, from www.inece.org/conference/7/vol1/index.html.

Grunert, K. G., & Ramus, K. (2005). Consumers' willingness to buy food through the internet. *British Food Journal, 107*(6), 381–403. doi:10.1108/00070700510602174

Guardian. (2005). *Have turned in to Channel Island discs?* London: Guardian Newspapers.

Gulati, R., & Garino, J. (2000). Get the right mix of bricks & clicks. *Harvard Business Review, 78*(3), 107–114.

Gummesson, E. (1994). Making relationship marketing operational. *International Journal of Service Industry Management, 5*(5), 5–20. doi:10.1108/09564239410074349

Gummesson, E. (2004). Return on relationships (ROR), the value of relationship marketing and CRM in business-to-business contexts. *Journal of Business and Industrial Marketing, 19*(2), 136–146. doi:10.1108/08858620410524016

Hahn, J., & Kauffman, R. (2003). Measuring what you could never measure: A new science of Web site design performance evaluation. In *Revolutionary Strategies and*

Tactics in Research Design and Data Collection for E-Business Management Research Workshop in association with the International Conference on Electronic Commerce (ICEC 2003), Pittsburgh, PA, September 2003.

Håkansson, H., & Snehota, I. (1995). *Developing relationships in business networks*. London: Routledge.

Hall, B. H., & Khan, B. (2003). Adoption of new technology. *NBER working paper*.

Halman, J., & Keizer, J. (2004). Platform gedreven ontwikkeling van productfamilies [Plaform-driven development of productfamilies]. In P. De Weert Nederhof, B. Van Looy & K. Visser (Eds.), *Innovatie(f) organiseren* (pp.71-98). Deventer: Kluwer.

Hambrick, D. C., & Mason, P. A. (1984). Upper echelons: The organization as a reflection of it's top managers. *Academy of Management Review, 9*, 193–206. doi:10.2307/258434

Hamel, G. (2000). *Leading the revolution*. Boston: Harvard Business School Press.

Hansemark, O. C. (1998). The effects of an entrepreneurship programme on need for achievement and locus of control of reinforcement. *International Journal of Entrepreneurial Behaviour and Research, 4*(1), 28–50. doi:10.1108/13552559810203957

Harrigan, P., Ramsey, E., & Ibbotson, P. (2008). E-CRM in SMEs: An exploratory study in Northern Ireland. *Marketing Intelligence & Planning, 26*(4), 385–404. doi:10.1108/02634500810879296

Hartland, C. M., Cardwell, N. D., Powell, P., & Zheng, J. (2007). Barriers to supply chain information integration: SMEs adrift of e-Lands. *Journal of Operations Management, 25*(6), 1234–1254. doi:10.1016/j.jom.2007.01.004

Hashim, N. A. (2006). E-commerce adoption issues in Malaysian SME. In *Proceedings of International Conference on E-commerce (ICoEC)*, Penang, Malaysia.

Hay, M., & Kamshad, K. (1994). Small firm growth: intentions, implementation and impediments. *Business Strategy Review, 5*(3), 49–68. doi:10.1111/j.1467-8616.1994.tb00166.x

Haynes, P. J., Becherer, R. C., & Helms, M. M. (1998). Small and mid-sized businesses and Internet use: unrealized potential? *Internet Research: Electronic Networking Applications and Policy, 8*(3), 229–235. doi:10.1108/10662249810217786

Haynes, R. M., & Thies, E. A. (1991). Management of technology in service firms. *Journal of Operations Management, 10*(3), 388–397. doi:10.1016/0272-6963(91)90075-9

Heckman, J. (1979). Sample selection bias as a specification error. *Econometrica, 47*(1), 153–161. doi:10.2307/1912352

Hedman, J., & Borell, A. (2005). Broadening information systems evaluation through narratives. *Electronic Journal of Information Systems Evaluation, 8*(2), 115–122.

Hempell, T. (2006). Diffusion of information and communication technology. In U. Schmoch, C. Rammer & H. Legler (Eds.), *National systems of innovation in comparison* (pp. 169-184). New York: Springer.

Hendrickson, A. R., & Collins, M. R. (1996). An assessment of structure and causation of IS usage. *The Data Base for Advances in Information Systems, 27*(2), 61.

Henriksen, H. Z., & Rukanova, B. (2008, April 23-25). Barriers and drivers of ecustoms implementation: Never mind IT. In *Proceedings of the 6th Eastern European eGovernment Days*, Prague, Czech Republic.

Henriksen, H. Z., Rukanova, B., & Tan, Y.-H. (2008). Pacta Sunt Servanda but where is the agreement? The complicated case of eCustoms. In M. A. Wimmer, H. J. Scholl & E. Ferro (Eds.), *EGOV 2008* (pp. 13-24). Berlin Heidelberg: Springer-Verlag.

Henriques, I., & Sadorsky, P. (1996). The determinants of an environmentally responsive firm: An empirical approach. *Journal of Environmental Economics and Management, 30*, 381–384. doi:10.1006/jeem.1996.0026

Hill, J. (2001). A multidimensional study of the key determinants of effective SME marketing activity: Part 1. *International Journal of Entrepreneurial Behaviour & Research, 7*(5), 171–204. doi:10.1108/EUM0000000006006

Hill, J., & McGowan, P. (1996). Marketing development through networking: a competency based approach for small firm entrepreneurs. *Journal of Small Business and Enterprise Development, 3*(3), 148–157. doi:10.1108/eb020974

Hill, S. (2000). *Changing Wales Report*. Cardiff, Wales.

Hills, G. E., Lumpkin, G. T., & Singh, R. P. (1997). Opportunity Recognition: Perceptions and Behaviors of Entrepreneurs. *Frontiers of Entrepreneurship Research, 17*(4), 168–182.

Hisrich, R., & Peters, M. (1998). *Entrepreneurship* (4th Ed.). Boston: McGraw Hill.

Hoffman, D. L., Novak, T. P., & Schlosser, A. E. (2000). The evolution of the digital divide: How gaps in Internet access may impact Electronic commerce. *Journal of Computer-Mediated Communication, 5*(3).

Hoi, J., Shim, J. P., & Yin, A. (2003). Current progress of e-commerce adoption: SMEs in Hong Kong. *Communications of the ACM, 46*(9).

Homs, C., Meringer, J., & Rehkopf, F. (2001). *Europe's online logistics push*. Retrieved from http://www.forester.com

Houghton, K. A., & Winklhofer, H. (2002). Internet adoption in exporting SMEs: development of a conceptual model. *American Marketing Association, Conference Proceedings, Chicago, 13*, 504.

Howcroft, D. (2001). After the goldrush: deconstructing the myths of the dot.com market. *Journal of Information Technology, 16*(4), 195–204. doi:10.1080/02683960110100418

Howcroft, J. B., & Durkin, M. (2000). Reflections on bank-customer interactions in the new millennium. *Journal of Financial Services Marketing, 5*(1), 9–20. doi:10.1057/palgrave.fsm.4770002

Hudson, J. (2003). RIAS and private sector development: Some thoughts from the South African context. *Centre on Regulation and Competition*. Retrieved January 4,

2007, from http://www.competition-regulation.org.uk/conferences/mcrria03/conf8.pdf.

Huggins, R., & Izushi, H. (2002). The digital divide and ICT learning in rural communities: Examples of good practice service delivery. *Local Economy, 17*(2), 111–122. doi:10.1080/02690940210129870

Hultman, J., & Eriksson, L. T. (2008). The balancing acts in SME e-commerce development: A multiple case study. *Journal of Electronic Business, 6*(5), 476–497. doi:10.1504/IJEB.2008.021183

Hunt, S. D., & Morgan, R. M. (1994). Relationship marketing in the era of network competition. *Marketing Management, 3*(1), 18–28.

Hunter, K., & Kemp, S. (2004). The personality of e-commerce investors. *Journal of Economic Psychology, 25*(4), 529–537. doi:10.1016/S0167-4870(03)00050-3

Hussin, H., & Mohamad Noor, R. (2005). Innovating business through e-commerce: Exploring the willingness of Malaysian SMEs. Retrieved: March 3, 2009, from http://www.it-innovations.ae/iit005/proceedings/articles/I_4_IIT05_Hussin.pdf

Huy, L. V., & Filiatrault, P. (2006). The adoption of e-commerce in SMEs in Vietnam: A study of users and prospectors. *In Proceedings of the 10th Pacific Asia Conference on Information Systems*, Kuala Lumpur, Malaysia (pp. 1335-44).

Iacovou, C., Benbasat, I., & Dexter, A. (1995). Electronic data interchange and small organisations: Adoption and impact of technology. *MIS Quarterly, 19*(4), 465–485. doi:10.2307/249629

Ibeh, K. I., Luo, Y., & Dinnie, K. (2005). E-branding strategies of internet companies: Some preliminary insights from the UK. *The Journal of Brand Management, 12*(5), 355–373. doi:10.1057/palgrave.bm.2540231

Ibls -Internet Business Law. (2007). *Overview of e-commerce in South Africa*. Retrieved January 20, 2008, from http://www.ibls.com/internet_law_news_portal_view.aspx?s=sa&id=1098

Igbaria, M., Guimaraes, T., & Davis, G. B. (1995). Testing the determinants of microcomputer usage via a structural equation model. *Journal of Management Information Systems, 11*(4), 87–114.

Inland Revenue. (1998). Chapter 1 - Encouraging the growth of e-commerce, *Electronic Commerce: The UKs Taxation Agenda.* http://www.inlandrevenue.gov.uk/taxagenda/ecom1.htm.

International Data Corporation (IDC). (1998). *Small business embraces the Internet.* http://www.idc.com/F/HNR/071398.htm.

International Monetary Fund (IMF). (2000). *Report in offshore finance centres.* Washington, DC: IMF.

Internet World Stats. (2007). *Internet usage growth.* Retrieved from http://www.internetworldstats.com

Internet World Stats. (2008). *Internet usage statistics.* Retrieved February 10, 2009, from http://www.internetworldstats.com/stats.htm

Irani, Z., Ezingeard, J.-N., & Grieve, R. J. (1997). Integrating the costs of a manufacturing IT/IS infrastructure into the investment decision-making process. *Technovation, 17*(11/12), 695–362. doi:10.1016/S0166-4972(97)00060-6

Isle of Man Government. (IoMG) (2000, July, 25). *E-commerce strategy – A report by the council of ministers.* Douglas, Isle of Man.

Iyer, R., & Bejou, D. (Eds.). (2003). *Customer relationship management in electronic markets.* Binghamton, NY: Hawthorne Press.

Jack Myers media business report: US advertising forecast. (November 2007). Retrieved November 2008 from http://www.jackmyers.com

Jantan, M., Ismail, N., Ramayah, T., & Mohamed Salehuddin, A. H. (2001). The CEO and AMT adoption in Malaysian small and medium scale manufacturing industries. In *Proceedings of the International Conference on Information Technology,* Lausanne, Switzerland.

Jarboe, G. (March 16, 2007). *Boosting PR results with SEO and RSS.* Retrieved March 18, 2009 from www.ipressroom.com/pr/SchwartzmanPR/info/document/JarboeBulldogChicago2007.ppt

Jarillo, J. C. (1995). *Strategic networks: Creating the borderless organization.* Woburn, MA: Butterworth-Heinemann.

Jaw, Y.-L., & Chen, C.-L. (2006). The influence of the Internet in the internationalization of SMEs in Taiwan. *Human Systems Management, 25*(3), 167–183.

Jaworski, B. J., & Kohli, A. J. (1993). Marketing Orientation: antecedents and consequences. *Journal of Marketing, 57*(3), 53–70. doi:10.2307/1251854

Jeffcoate, J., Chappell, C., & Feindt, S. (2002). Best practice in SME adoption of e-commerce. *Bench marking: An International Journal, 9*(2), 122–132. doi:10.1108/14635770210421791

Jelassi, T., & Enders, A. (2008). *Strategies for e-business creating value through electronic and mobile commerce* (2nd Ed.). London: Prentice Hall.

Jenamani, M., Zhong, Y., & Bhargava, B. (2007). Cheating in online auction – Towards explaining the popularity of English auction. *Electronic Commerce Research and Applications, 6,* 53–62. doi:10.1016/j.elerap.2005.12.002

Jensen, J. (2004). *Issues facing SMEs in their adoption of electronic commerce.* Retrieved February 24, 2005, from http://www.crf.dcita.gov.au/papres03/ jensenpaper12final.pdf

Jersey Finance. (2005). *Jersey in figures.* Jersey, UK: States of Jersey.

Jersey Finance. (2006). *Jersey – A back to basic introduction to the island.* UK: States of Jersey.

Jie, S., Peiji, S., & Jiaming, F. (2007). *A Model for Adoption of Online Shopping: A Perceived Characteristics of Web as a Shopping Channel View.*

Jobber, D. (1991). Choosing a survey method in management research. In N.G. Smith, & P. Dainty (Eds.), *The management research handbook* (pp. 174-179). London: Routledge.

Johanson, J., & Vahlne, J.-E. (1977). The internationalisation process of the firm. *Journal of International Business Studies*, *8*(1), 23–32. doi:10.1057/palgrave.jibs.8490676

Johnson, M. D., & Selnes, F. (2004). Customer portfolio management: Toward a dynamic theory of exchange relationships. *Journal of Marketing*, *68*(2), 1–17. doi:10.1509/jmkg.68.2.1.27786

Johnston, D. A., Wade, M., & McClean, R. (2007). Does e-business matter to SMEs? A comparison of the financial impacts of Internet business solutions on European and North American SMEs. *Journal of Small Business Management*, *45*(3), 354–361. doi:10.1111/j.1540-627X.2007.00217.x

Jones, C., Hecker, R., & Holland, P. (2003). Small firm internet adoption: opportunities forgone, a journey not begun. *Journal of Small Business and Enterprise Development*, *10*(3), 287–298. doi:10.1108/14626000310489763

Jones, J. (2004). Training and development, and business growth: A study of Australian manufacturing small-medium sized enterprises. *Asia Pacific Journal of Human Resources*, *42*(1), 96–121. doi:10.1177/1038411104041535

Jones, P., Beynon-Davies, P., & Muir, E. (2003). E-business barriers within the SME sector. *The Journal of Systems and Information Technology*, *7*(1), 1–26.

Jones, T., & Ram, M. (2003). South Asian businesses in retreat? The case of the United Kingdom. *Journal of Ethnic and Migration Studies*, *29*(3), 485–500. doi:10.1080/13691830305611

Jones, T., & Ram, M. (2007). Re-embedding the Ethnic Business Agenda. *Work, Employment and Society*, *21*(3), 439–457. doi:10.1177/0950017007080007

Jones-Evans, D. (2001). Creating an entrepreneurial Wales – Growing our indigenous enterprises. *The Gregynog papers, Institute of Welsh Affairs*, *3*(1). Cardiff: Welsh Academic Press.

Joubert, J., & Van Belle, J. P. (2004). *Compliance of South African E-Commerce Websites with Legislation to protect consumer rights.* Retrieved March 14, 2007, from http://www.commerce.uct.ac.za/InformationSystems/Staff/PersonalPages/jvbelle/pubs/IBIMA04.doc

Joyce, P., Green, R., & Winch, G. (2006). A new construct for visualising and designing e-fulfilment systems for quality healthcare delivery. *The TQM Magazine*, *18*(6), 638–651. doi:10.1108/09544780610707129

Jutla, D., Bodorick, P., & Dhaliwal, J. (2002). Supporting the e-business readiness of small and medium-sized enterprises: approaches and metrics. *Internet Research Electronic Working Applications and Policy*, *12*(2), 139–164. doi:10.1108/10662240210422512

Kabadayi, S., Eyuboglu, N., & Thomas, G. P. (2007, October). The performance implications of designing multiple channels to fit with strategy and environment. *Journal of Marketing*, *71*, 195–211. doi:10.1509/jmkg.71.4.195

Kadlec, P., & Mareš, M. (2003). B2B eCommerce opportunity for SMEs. In *Systems Integration,* Prague, Czech Republic (pp. 537-544).

Kai-Uwe Brock, J. (2000). Information and technology in the small firm. In S. Carter & D. Jones-Evans (Eds.), *Enterprise and the Small Business* (pp. 384-408). Upper Saddle River, NJ: Prentice Hall, Pearson Education.

Kalakota, R., & Whinston, A. (1996). *Frontiers of electronic commerce.* London: Addison-Wesley.

Kalakota, R., Oliva, R. A., & Donath, B. (1999). Move Over, e-Commerce. *Marketing Management*, *8*(3), 22–32.

Kalember, R. (2004). *Compliance Essentials: standard method of fulfilling requirements,* storage & security journal. Retrieved September 20, 2006 from World Wide Web: http://issj.sys-con.com/47516.htm

Kamel, S., Hassan, A., & ebrary, I. (2003). *Assessing the introduction of electronic banking in Egypt using the* Technology Acceptance Model: Idea Group.

Karagozoglu, N., & Lindell, M. (2004). Electronic commerce strategy, operations, and performance in small and medium-sized enterprises. *Journal of Small Business and Enterprise Development, 11*(3), 290–301. doi:10.1108/14626000410551555

Karahanna, E., Straub, D. W., & Chervany, N. L. (1999). Information technology adoption across time: a cross-sectional comparison of pre-adoption and post-adoption beliefs. *MIS Quarterly, 23*183–213. doi:10.2307/249751

Kardaras, D., & Papathanassiou, E. (2000). The development of B2C e-commerce in Greece: Current situation and future potential. *Internet Research: Electronic Networking Applications and Policy, 10*(4), 284–294. doi:10.1108/10662240010342568

Kasteler, J. M., Gay, R. M., & Caruth, M. J. (1968). Involuntary relocation of the elderly. *The Gerontologist, 8*(4), 276–279.

Kathmandi. (2000). *Commerce and LDCs – challenges for enterprises and governments*. Retrieved January 12, 2007 from http://r0.unctad.org/ecommerce/event_docs/kathmandu_background.pdf

Keen, C. A., Wetzels, M. B., De Ruyter, c., & Feinberg, D. R. (2004). Marketing on the web - behavioural, strategy and practices and public policy: E-tailers versus retailers, which factors determine consumer preferences. *Journal of Business Research, 57*(7), 685–695. doi:10.1016/S0148-2963(02)00360-0

Keen, P. (1999). E-commerce: Chapter 2. *Computerworld, 33*(37), 48.

Keindl, B. (2000). Competitive dynamics and new business models for SMEs in the virtual marketplace. *Journal of Developmental Entrepreneurship, 5*(1), 73–85.

Keller, W. (2004). International technology diffusion. *Journal of Economic Literature, 42*(3), 752–782. doi:10.1257/0022051042177685

Kennedy, A. (2006). Electronic customer relationship management (e-CRM): Opportunities and challenges in a digital world. *Irish Marketing Review, 18*(1/2), 58–69.

Kierzkowski, A., McQuade, S., Waitman, R., & Zeisser, M. (1996). Marketing to the digital consumer. *The McKinsey Quarterly, 3*, 5–21.

Kim, D. (2003). The internationalization of US Internet portals: does it fit the process model of internationalization? *Marketing Intelligence & Planning, 21*(1), 23–36. doi:10.1108/02634500310458126

Kim, Daesoo., Ow, Terence T., & Jun, Minjoon. (2008). SME strategies: An assessment of high vs. low performers. *Communications of the ACM, 51*(11), 113–117. doi:10.1145/1400214.1400237

King, R. C., Sen, R., & Xia, M. (2004). Impact of Web-based e-commerce on channel strategy in retailing. *International Journal of Electronic Commerce, 8*(3), 103–130.

Kirwan, P. (forthcoming). *Early-stage networking in high-tech start-up ventures*. Enschede: Nikos, University of Twente (Ph.D. thesis).

Kirwan, P., & Wakkee, I. (2007). *An empirical exploration of the global startup concept in an entrepreneurship context*. Paper presented at the Babson Kaufmann Conference on Entrepreneurship.

Kirwan, P., Van der Sijde, P. C., & Groen, A. J. (2007). Early-stage networking: how entrepreneurs use their social capital to establish & develop high-technology start-ups. In J. Ulijn, D. Drillon & F. Lasch (Eds.), *Entrepreneurship, cooperation and the firm – the emergence & survival of high-technology ventures in Europe*. Cheltenham, UK: Edward Elgar.

Kirwan, P., Van der Sijde, P., & Groen, A. (2006). Assessing the needs of new technology based firms (NTBFs), an investigation among spin-off companies from six European universities. *The International Entrepreneurship and Management Journal, 2*(2), 173–187. doi:10.1007/s11365-006-8683-1

Kleindl, B. (2000). Competitive dynamics and new business models for SMEs in the virtual marketplace. *Journal of Developmental Entrepreneurship, 5*(1), 73–85.

Knight, G., & Cavusgil, T. (1996). The born global firm: a challenge to traditional internationalization theory. In S. T. Cavusgil (Ed.), *Advances in International Marketing* (Vol. 8, pp. 11-26). Greenwich, CT: JAI Press.

Knight, G., Madsen, T. K., & Servais, P. (2004). An inquiry into born-global firms in Europe & the USA. *International Marketing Review, 21*(6), 645–665. doi:10.1108/02651330410568060

Koenig, W., & Wigand, R. T. (2004). Globalization and e-commerce: Diffusion and impacts of the internet and e-commerce in Germany. *Digest of Electronic Commerce Policy and Regulation, 27*, 197–227.

Koh, S., & Maguire, S. (2004). Identifying the adoption of e-business and knowledge management within SMEs. *Journal of Small Business and Enterprise Development, 11*(3), 338–348. doi:10.1108/14626000410551591

Kohlberg, L. (1969). *Stage and sequence: the cognitive-development approach to socialization.* In Goslin, DA. (Ed.), Handbook of Socialisation Theory and Research, Rand McNally, New York, NY

Koufaris, M. (2003). Applying the technology acceptance model and flow theory to online consumer behavior. *Information Systems Research, 13*(2), 205–223. doi:10.1287/isre.13.2.205.83

Kuhn, T. (1970). *The structure of scientific revolutions.* IL: University of Chicago Press.

Kuiper, E. J. (2007). *Convergence by cooperation in IT – The EU's customs and fiscalis programmes* [Electronic Version]. Master's Thesis, Delft University of Technology. Retrieved April 8, 2009, from http://www.itaide.org/forms/document.asp?Q=7771

Kula, V., & Tatoglu, E. (2003). An exploratory study of internet adoption by SMEs in an emerging market economy. *European Business Review, 15*(5), 324–333. doi:10.1108/09555340310493045

Kumar, V., & Venkatesan, R. (2005). Who are the multichannel shoppers and how do they perform? Correlates of multichannel shopping behavior. *Journal of Interactive Marketing, 19*(2), 44–62. doi:10.1002/dir.20034

Kumar, V., Maheshwari, B., & Kumar, U. (2002). ERP systems implementation: Best practices in canadian government organizations. *Government Information Quarterly, 19*(2), 147–172. doi:10.1016/S0740-624X(02)00092-8

Kyobe, M. E. (2008, November 5-7) Evaluating information security within SMEs engaged in e-commerce in South Africa. In *Proceedings of the 31st Institute for Small Business & Entrepreneurship Conference,* Belfast, N. Ireland.

Kyobe, M. E. (2009). Factors influencing SME compliance with government regulation on use of IT. *Journal of Global Information Management, 17*(2), 30–59.

Labbé, M. (2007). The role of government in the promotion of e-commerce [Electronic Version]. *Workshop on Potential of e-Commerce.* Retrieved February 10, 2009, from http://www.intracen.org/e-trade/docs/trainiran/ITC_IROST_e-government_JUN07v3.ppt#257,2,Putting EC into perspective

Lal, K. (2002). E-business and manufacturing sector: A study of small and medium-sized enterprises in India. *Research Policy, 31*, 1199–1211. doi:10.1016/S0048-7333(01)00191-3

Langston, C. M., & Teas, R. K. (1976). *Export commitment and characteristics of management.* Paper presented at the Annual Meeting of the Midwest Business Association, St Louis, MO.

Lau, G. T., & Voon, J. (2004). Factors affecting the adopting of electronic commerce among small and medium enterprises in Singapore. *Journal of Asian Business., 20*(1), 1–26.

Laudon, K. C., & Traver, C. G. (2008). *e-Commerce business, technology, society* (4th Ed). London: Pearson International Edition.

Lawrence, T. B., Morse, E. A., & Fowler, S. W. (2005). Managing your portfolio of connections. *MIT Sloan Management Review, 46*(2), 59–62.

Lawson, R., Alcock, C., Cooper, J., & Burgess, L. (2003). Factors affecting adoption of electronic commerce technologies by SMEs: an Australian study. *Journal of Small Business and Enterprise Development, 10*(3), 265–276. doi:10.1108/14626000310489727

Learmouth, D., McGregor, P. G., Swales, J. K., Turner, K. R., & Yin, Y. P. (2001). *Modelling the economic and environmental impacts of population policy in Jersey: A multi-period computable general equilibrium analysis.* Fraser of Allander Institute, Department of Economics, Glasgow: University of Strathclyde, 1-21.

Leatherman, J. C. (2000). Internet-based commerce: Implications for rural communities. *Reviews of Economic Development Literature and Practice, 5.* US Economic Development Administration, Washington, USA.

Lederer, A. L., Maupin, D. J., Sena, M. P., & Zhuang, Y. (2000). The technology acceptance model and the World Wide Web. *Decision Support Systems, 29*(3), 269–282. doi:10.1016/S0167-9236(00)00076-2

Lederer, A., & Sethi, A. (1988). The implementation of strategic information systems planning methodologies. *MIS Quarterly, 12*(3), 445–461. doi:10.2307/249212

Lee, C. B. P., & Lei, U. L. E. (2007). Adoption of e-government services in Macao. In *ACM International Conference Proceeding Series* (Vol. 232, pp. 217-220). New York: ACM.

Lee, J. (2004). Discriminant analysis of technology adoption behaviour: a case of internet technologies in small businesses. *Journal of Computer Information Systems, 44*(4), 57–66.

Leebaert, D. (1998). *The future of electronic market place.* Cambridge, MA, USA: MIT Press.

Lertwongsatien, C., & Wongpinunwatana, N. (2003). E-commerce adoption in Thailand: An empirical study of small and medium enterprises (SMEs). *Journal of Global Information Technology Management, 6*(3), 67–83.

Levy, M., & Barton, A. W. (2003). *Retail management* (5th Ed.). Chicago: McGraw-Hill/ Irwin.

Levy, M., & Beckinsale, M. J. J. (2004). *SMEs and Internet adoption strategy: Who do SMEs listen to?* Paper presented at the 12th European Conference on Information Systems June 14-16. 2004, Turku, Finland

Levy, M., & Powell, P. (2002, June 17-19). SMEs Internet adoption: Toward a transporter model. In *Proceedings of the Fifteenth Bled Electronic Commerce Conference*

(Reality: Constructing the Economy), (pp. 507–21). Bled, Slovenia.

Levy, M., & Powell, P. (2003). Exploring SME Internet adoption: Towards a contingent model. *Electronic Markets, 13*(2), 173–181. doi:10.1080/1019678032000067163

Levy, M., Powell, P., & Worrall, L. (2005). Strategic Intent and e-business in SMEs enablers and inhibitors. *Information Resources Management Journal, 18*(4), 1–20.

Levy, M., Powell, P., & Yetton, P. (1998). SMEs and the gains from IS: from cost reduction to value added. In T. Larsen, L. Levine, & J. DeGross (Eds.), *Information Systems: Current Issues and Future Changes* (pp. 377-392). Amsterdam: Kluwer Academic Publishers.

Levy, M., Powell, P., & Yetton, P. (2001, September). SMEs: Aligning IS and the strategic context. *Journal of Information Technology, 16,* 133–144. doi:10.1080/02683960110063672

Levy, M., Powell, P., & Yetton, P. (2002). SMEs: The dynamics of IS development. *Small Business Economics.*

Levy, M., Powell, P., & Yetton, P. (2002). The dynamics of SME information systems. *Small Business Economics, 19*(4), 341–354. doi:10.1023/A:1019654030019

Lewis, R., & Cockrill, A. (2002). Going global—remaining local: the impact of e-commerce on small retail firms in Wales. *International Journal of Information Management, 22*(3), 195–209. doi:10.1016/S0268-4012(02)00005-1

Liew, V. K. (2002). *The prospect of e-commerce for the small and medium enterprises in Malaysia.* Kuala Lumpur: University of Malaya.

Lim, T. M. (2006). *Outsourcings to ensure successful ICT systems implementation and maintenance.* School of Information Technology, Monash University. Retrieved March 20, 2008, from http://www.infotech.monash.edu.my/news/media.html

Lin, C., Huang, Y.-A., & Tseng, S.-W. (2007). A study of planning and implementation stages in electronic commerce adoption and evaluation: the case of Australian SMEs. *Contemporary Management Research, 3*(1), 83–100.

Lin, C., Lin, K., Huang, Y., & Kuo, N. (2006). Evaluation of electronic customer relationship management: The critical success factors. *Business Review (Federal Reserve Bank of Philadelphia), 6*(2), 206–212.

Lituchy, T. R., & Rail, A. (2000). Bed and breakfasts, small inns, and the internet: the impact of technology on the globalization of small business. *Journal of International Marketing, 8*(2), 86–97. doi:10.1509/jimk.8.2.86.19625

Liu, C., & Arnett, K. P. (2000). Exploring the factors associated with Web site success in the context of electronic commerce. *Information & Management, 38*(1), 23–33. doi:10.1016/S0378-7206(00)00049-5

Lockett, N., & Brown, D. (2003b). *The investigation of e-business engagement by SMEs with reference to strategic networks and aggregation: The dairy farming industry.* Lancaster University Management School Working Paper, 19.

Looi, H. (2004). A model of factors influencing electronic commerce adoption among SME's in Brunei Darussalam. *International Journal of Information Technology, 10,* 72–87.

Love, P., & Irani, Z. (2004). An exploratory study of information technology evaluation and benefits management practices for SMEs in the constructing industry. *Information & Management, 42*(1), 227–242.

Love, P., Irani, Z., Li, H., Cheng, E. W. L., & Tse, R. Y. C. (2001). An empirical analysis of the barriers to implementing e-commerce in small-medium sized construction contractors in the state of Victoria, Australia. *Construction Innovation, 1*(1), 31–41.

Love, P., Irani, Z., Standing, C., Lin, C., & Burn, J. (2005). The enigma of evaluation: benefits, costs and risks of IT in Australian small-medium-sized enterprises. *Information & Management, 42*(7), 947–964. doi:10.1016/j.im.2004.10.004

Lumpkin, G. T., & Lichtenstein, B. B. (2005). The role of organizational learning in the opportunity-recognition

process. *Entrepreneurship Theory & Practice, 29*(4), 451–472. doi:10.1111/j.1540-6520.2005.00093.x

Lumpkin, G. T., Hills, G. E., & Schrader, R. C. (2004). Opportunity recognition. In H. P. Welsch (Ed.), *Entrepreneurship: the way ahead* (pp. 73-90). London: Routledge.

Lunati, M. (2000). *SMEs and electronic commerce: An overview.* OECD, Directorate for Science. Presented to the Technology and Industry Committee, DST/IND/PME(2000).

Lymer, A. (1999). UK business and the information superhighway: The impact of the Internet on SMEs. *ACCA Occasional Research Paper 23.*

Lynch, J. (2005). Identity theft in cyberspace: Crime control methods and their effectiveness in combating phishing attacks. *Berkeley Technology Law Journal, 20,* 259–300.

Lynn, G. S., Lipp, S. M., Akgün, A. E., & Cortez, A. (2002). Factors impacting the adoption and effectiveness of the World Wide Web in marketing. *Industrial Marketing Management, 31*(1), 35–49. doi:10.1016/S0019-8501(00)00104-8

MacGregor, R. C. (2004). The role of small business strategic alliances in the adoption of E-commerce in small-medium enterprises (SMEs). Retrieved June 6, 2008, from http://ro.uow.edu.au/cgi/viewcontent.cgi?article=1303&context=theses

MacGregor, R. C., & Hodgkinson, A. (2007). *Small business clustering technologies: Applications in marketing, management, IT and economics.* Hershey, PA: Idea Group Inc (IGI).

MacGregor, R. C., & Vrazalic, L. (2005). A basic model of electronic commerce adoption barriers: A study of regional small businesses in Sweden and Australia. *Journal of Small Business and Enterprise Development, 12*(4), 510–527. doi:10.1108/14626000510628199

MacGregor, R. C., & Vrazalic, L. (Eds.). (2008). *E-commerce in regional small to medium enterprises.* Hershey, PA: IGI Global Publishing.

Macgregor, R., & Vrazalic, L. (2005). A basic model of electronic commerce adoption barriers: a study of regional small businesses in Sweden and Australia. *Journal of Small Business and Enterprise Development, 12*(4), 510–527. doi:10.1108/14626000510628199

Madsen, T. K., & Servais, P. (1997b). The internationalization of born globals: an evolutionary process? *International Business Review, 6*(6), 561–583. doi:10.1016/S0969-5931(97)00032-2

Maes, P., Guttman, R., & Moukas, A. (1999). Agents that buy and sell. *Communications of the ACM, 42*(3), 81–91. doi:10.1145/295685.295716

Maguire, S., Koh, S. C. L., & Magrys, A. (2007). The adoption of e-business and knowledge management in SMEs. *Benchmarking . International Journal (Toronto, Ont.), 14*(1), 37–58.

Malloy, T. F. (2003). Compliance and the firm. *Temple Law Review, 76*, 451–457.

Mamis, R. A. (1989). Global start-up. *Inc., August,* 11(8), 38-47.

Marasını, R., Ions, K., & Ahmad, M. (2008). Assessment of e-business adoption in SMEs: A study of manufacturing industry in the UK North East region. *Journal of Manufacturing Technology Management, 19*(5), 627–644. doi:10.1108/17410380810877294

Marshall, P., Sor, R., & McKay, J. (2000). An industry case study of the impacts of electronic commerce on car dealerships in Western Australia. *Journal of Electronic Commerce Research, 1*(1), 1–12.

Martin, L. (2005). Internet adoption and use in small firms: internal processes, organisational culture and the roles of the owner-manager and key staff. *New Technology, Work and Employment, 20*(3), 190–204. doi:10.1111/j.1468-005X.2005.00153.x

Martin, L. M., & Matlay, H. (2001). "Blanket" approaches to promoting ICT in small firms: Some lessons from the DTI ladder adoption model in the UK. *Internet Research, 11*(5), 399–410. doi:10.1108/EUM0000000006118

Martin, L., & Matlay, H. (2003). Innovative use of the Internet in established small firms: The impact of knowledge management and organisational learning in accessing new opportunities. *Qualitative Market Research: An International Journal, 6*(1), 18–26. doi:10.1108/13522750310457348

Mathieson, K. (1991). Predicting user intentions: comparing the Technology Acceptance Model with the theory of planned behavior. *Information Systems Research, 2*(3), 173–191. doi:10.1287/isre.2.3.173

Matlay, H. (2000). Training in the small business sector of the British economy. In S. Carter & D. Jones (Eds.), *Enterprise and small business: Principles, policy, and practice.* London: Addison Wesley Longman.

Matlay, H., & Westhead, P. (2005). Virtual teams and the rise of e-entrepreneurship in Europe. *International Small Business Journal, 23*(3), 279–302. doi:10.1177/0266242605052074

Mayne, M. (2006). How are businesses facing up to the compliance challenge? *SC Magazine Australia.* Retrieved November 30, 2006, from http://www.scmagazine.com.au/feature/how-are-businesses-facing-up-to-the-compliance-challenge.aspx

Mazzarol, T., Volery, T., Doss, N., & Thein, V. (1999). Factors influencing small business start-ups. *International Journal of Enterpreneurial Behaviour and Research, 5*(2), 48–63. doi:10.1108/13552559910274499

McCarthy, E. J. (1960). *Basic marketing: A managerial approach.* Homewood, IL: Irwin.

McCloskey, D. (2004). Evaluating electronic commerce acceptance with the Technology Acceptance Model. *Journal of Computer Information Systems, 44*(2), 49–57.

McCole, P., & Ramsey, E. (2004). Internet-enabled technology in knowledge-intensive business services: A comparison of Northern Ireland, the Republic of Ireland and New Zealand. *Marketing Intelligence & Planning, 22*(7), 761–779. doi:10.1108/02634500410568

McConnell, J. (1994). *National Training Standard for Information System Security.* Retrieved March 12 2007, from http://security.isu.edu/pdf/4011.pdf

McConville, A. (2009). *Impact of ICT on SMEs in the South East: Report Prepared for the South East of England Development Agency.* Birmingham: BMG Research.

McDonald, M., & Wilson, H. (1999). E-Marketing Improving marketing effectiveness in a digital world.

McDougall, P. P., & Oviatt, B. M. (2000). International entrepreneurship: the intersection of two research paths. *Academy of Management Journal, 43*(5), 902–906. doi:10.2307/1556418

McGowan, P., & Durkin, M. (2002). Toward an Understanding of Internet Adoption at the Marketing/Entrepreneurship Interface. *Journal of Marketing Management, 18*, 361–377. doi:10.1362/0267257022872451

McGowan, P., Durkin, M., Allen, L., Dougan, C., & Nixon, S. (2001). Developing competencies in the entrepreneurial small firm for the use of the Internet in the management of customer relationships. *Journal of European Industry Training, 25*(2/3/4), 126-36.

McMillan, S. J. (2000). The microscope and the moving target: The challenge of applying content analysis to the World Wide Web. *Journalism & Mass Communication Quarterly, 77*(1), 80–98.

Mehling, H. (1998). Survey Says: E-commerce is crucial to success - Small businesses are eager to sell wares on the Web. *Computer Reseller News,* May 4, 787.

Mehrtens, J., Cragg, P. B., & Mills, A. M. (2001). A model of Internet adoption by SMEs. *Information & Management, 39*(3), 165–176. doi:10.1016/S0378-7206(01)00086-6

Merret, S., & Walton, N. (2005). *Nitrate pollution on the Island of Jersey: Managing water quality within European community directives.* Retrieved from http://www.dgroups.org/groups/worldbank/MENA-Water/

Meziane, F., & Kasiran, M. (2008). Evaluating trust in electronic commerce: A study based on information provided on merchant's Websites. *The Journal of the Operational Research Society, 59*(4), 464–472. doi:10.1057/palgrave.jors.2602430

Michalson, L., & Hughes, B. (2005). Guide to the ECT Act, *Michalsons Attorneys.* Retrieved September 20, 2006, from http://www.michalson.com

Migration Policy Group. (2002). *Supplier diversity: The case of immigrant and ethnic minority enterprise.* Background paper prepared for the Transatlantic Round Table, Brussels, 15 January 2002.

Mingers, J. (2002). Real-izing information systems: Critical realism as an underpinning philosophy for information systems. In *Proceedings from the International Conference on Information Systems* (pp. 295-303). Barcelona: Association of Information Systems.

Mirchandani, A. A., & Motwani, J. (2001). Understanding small business e-commerce adoption: an empirical analysis. *Journal of Computer Information Systems, 41*(3), 70–73.

Mitchell, S., & Clark, D. (1999). Business adoption of information and communications technologies in the two tier rural economy: some evidence from South Midlands. *Journal of Rural Studies, 15*(4), 447–455. doi:10.1016/S0743-0167(99)00012-1

Mithal, M. (2000). Illustrating B2C complaints in the online environment. In *The Joint Conference of the OECD, HCOPIL, ICC: Building Trust in the Online Environment: Business to Consumer Dispute Resolution, The Hague.* Retrieved from http://www1.oecd.org/dsti/sti/it/secur/act/online_trust/presentations.htm

Moon, J. W., & Kim, Y. G. (2001). Extending the TAM for a World-Wide-Web context. *Information & Management, 38*(4), 217–230. doi:10.1016/S0378-7206(00)00061-6

Moore, G. C., & Benbasat, I. (1991). Development of an instrument to measure the perceptions of adopting an information technology innovation. *Information Systems Research, 2*(3), 192–222. doi:10.1287/isre.2.3.192

Moore, G. C., & Benbasat, I. (1996). Integrating diffusion of innovations and theory of reasoned action models to predict utilization of information technology by end-users. *Diffusion and adoption of information technology,* 132-146.

Morris, M. B., Schindehutte, M., & Laforge, R. W. (2002). Entrepreneurial marketing: A construct for integrating emerging entrepreneurship and marketing perspectives. *Journal of Marketing Theory and Practice, 10*(4), 1–19.

Morris, M. G., & Dillon, A. (1997). How user perceptions influence software use. *IEEE Software, 14*(4), 58–65. doi:10.1109/52.595956

Morris, M., & Ventakesch, V. (2000). Age differences in technology adoption decisions: Implications for a changing work force. *Personnel Psychology, 53*(2), 375–403. doi:10.1111/j.1744-6570.2000.tb00206.x

Morse, E., Fowler, S., & Lawrence, T. (2007). The impact of virtual embeddedness on new venture survival: Overcoming the liabilities of newness. *Entrepreneurship Theory & Practice, 31*(2), 139–159. doi:10.1111/j.1540-6520.2007.00167.x

Müller-Lankenau, C., Wehmeyer, K., & Klein, S. (2005-6). Multichannel strategies: Capturing and exploring diversity in the European retail grocery industry. *International Journal of Electronic Commerce, 10*(2), 85–122. doi:10.2753/JEC1086-4415100204

Mulhern, A. (1995). The SME sector in Europe: A broad perspective. *Journal of Small Business Management, 33*(3).

Mullon, P. (2006). The six elements of legally acceptable electronic documents. *Computer Business Review, Technews.* Retrieved December 05, 2006, from http://cbr.co.za/article.aspx?pklArticleId=3972&pklIssueId=447&pklCategoryId=384

Murphy, L., Thomas, B., Swayne, H., Metcalfe, R., & Jones, J. (2007). An exploration of the skill and competence issues of an e-business directed graphic design industry. *International Journal of E-business Management, 1*(1), 22–36. doi:10.3316/IJEBM0101022

Mustaffa, S., & Beaumont, N. (2002). The Effect of Electronic Commerce on Small Australian Enterprises. *Technovation, 24*(2), 85–95. doi:10.1016/S0166-4972(02)00039-1

MyBroadband. (2008). *South Africa's email risk.* Retrieved December 20, 2008, from http://mybroadband.co.za/news/General/6355.html

Napier, H. A., Judd, P. J., Rivers, O. N., & Wagner, S. W. (2001). *Creating a Winning E-Business.* Boston, MA: Course Technology.

National Economic Development Strategy (NEDS). (2001). *A Winning Wales – the National Economic Development strategy of the Welsh Assembly Government.* Retrieved December 10, 2005, from http://www.wales.gov.uk/themesbudgetandstrategic/content/neds/awinningwales-0302-c.pdf

National SME Development Council of Malaysia. (2005). *Definitions for small and medium enterprises in Malaysia.* Secretariat to National SME Development Council, Bank Negara Malaysia, Kuala Lumpur. Retrieved May 3, 2009, from http://www.smeinfo.com.my/pdf/smc_definitions_ENGLISH.pdf

Ng, H.-I., Pan, Y. G., & Wilson, T. D. (1998). Business use of the World Wide Web: A report on further investigations. *International Journal of Information Management, 18*(5), 291–314. doi:10.1016/S0268-4012(98)00021-8

Nicol, C. (2003). ICT Policy: *A beginner's handbook. The Association for Progressive Communications (APC), South Africa.* Internet and ICT for Social Justice and Development.

Niitamo, V. P., Kulkki, S., Eriksson, M., & Hribernik, K. A. (2006). State-of-the-art and good practice in the field of living labs. In *Proceedings of the 12th International Conference on Concurrent Enterprising: Innovative Products and Services through Collaborative Networks,* Milan, Italy, June 26-28.

NOP. (2000). *Small Business in Wales – An NOP study in the ICT and advice needs of SMEs based on their market orientation and attitude towards growth.* NOP research group.

Normah, M. A. (2006). *SMEs: Building blocks for economic growth.* Paper presented at the National Statistical Conference, Kuala Lumpur, Malaysia.

O'Donnell, A. (2004). The nature of networking in small firms. *Qualitative Market Research: An International Journal, 7*(3), 206–217. doi:10.1108/13522750410540218

O'Farrell, P. N., Hitchens, D. M., & Moffat, L. A. R. (1995). Business service firms in two peripheral economies: Scotland and Ireland. *Tijdschrift voor Economische en Sociale Geografie, 86*(2), 115–128. doi:10.1111/j.1467-9663.1995.tb01351.x

O'Keefe, R. M., O'Connor, G., & Kung, H.-J. (1998). Early adopters of the web as a retail medium: small company winners and losers. *European Journal of Marketing, 32*(7/8), 629–643. doi:10.1108/03090569810224038

O'Regan, N., Ghobadian, A., & Galler, D. (2006). In search of the drivers of high growth in manufacturing SMEs. *Technovation, 26*(1), 30–41. doi:10.1016/j.technovation.2005.05.004

O'Toole, T. (2001). E-relationships – Emergence and the small firm. *Marketing Intelligence & Planning, 21*(2), 115–122. doi:10.1108/02634500310465434

Oc, T., & Tiesdell, S. (1999). Supporting ethnic minority business: a review of business support for ethnic minorities in city challenge areas. *Urban Studies (Edinburgh, Scotland), 36*(10), 1723–1746. doi:10.1080/0042098992791

OECD. (2002). *OECD small and medium enterprise outlook - 2002 Edition.* Paris: OECD Publishing.

OECD. (2005). *OECD SME and entrepreneurship outlook - 2005 Edition.* Paris: OECD Publishing.

OECD. (2005). *SME and entrepreneurship outlook.* Retrieved November 6, 2007, from http://www.oecd.org

OECD. (2007). *Key ICT indicators: Internet penetration by size class.* Retrieved February 10, 2009, from http://www.oecd.org/dataoecd/20/23/37442795.xls

OECD. (2007). *Key ICT indicators: Internet selling and purchasing by industry.* Retrieved February 10, 2009, from http://www.oecd.org/dataoecd/20/22/34083121.xls

Ofcom. (2007). *The communications market 2007 – Nations and regions, Wales.*

Office for National Statistics. (2008). *E-commerce and ICT Activity: 2007 e-commerce survey of business.*

Office for National Statistics. (2008). *First Release: E-commerce activity 2007.* Newport: ONS.

OGC. (2002). *Review of Major Government IT Projects,* Office of Government Commerce. Retrieved July 11, 2005, from http://www.ogc.gov.uk/embedded_object.asp?docid=2634

Ogunlana, E. A. (2004). The technology adoption behavior of women farmers: The case of alley farming in Nigeria. *Renewable Agriculture and Food Systems, 19,* 57–65. doi:10.1079/RAFS200057

Oliver, R. L., & Bearden, W. O. (1985). Crossover effects in the theory of reasoned action: A moderating influence attempt. *The Journal of Consumer Research, 12*324–340. doi:10.1086/208519

Onwubiko, C., & Lenaghan, A. (2007). Managing security threats and vulnerabilities for small to medium enterprises. In *5th IEEE International Conference on Intelligence and Security Informatics, IEEE ISI 2007,* IEEE Press, May, New Jersey, USA.

Orford, J., Herrington, M., & Wood, E. (2004). *South African Report Global Entrepreneurship Monitor.* Retrieved January 22, 2005, from www.gsb.uct.ac.za/gsbwebb/userfiles/GEM_2004.pdf

Organisation for Economic Co-operation and Development. (1997). *Globalisation and small and medium enterprises (SMEs).* Paris, France: OECD Publications Service.

Organisation for Economic Co-operation and Development. (2004). *SME statistics: Towards a more systematic statistical measurement of SME behaviour.* Background report for the 2nd OECD Conference of Ministers Responsible for Small and Medium Enterprises (SMEs), Istanbul, Turkey. Retrieved May 3, 2009, from http://www.oecd.org/dataoecd/6/6/31919286.pdf

Organisation for Economic Co-operation and Development. (2005). *OECD SME and Entrepreneurship Outlook - 2005 Edition.* Paris, France: OECD Publications

Service. Retrieved May 3, 2009, from http://www.oecd. org/document/15/0,2340,en_2649_33956792_35096847 _1_1_1_1,00.html

Otto, J. R., & Chung, Q. B. (2000). A framework for cyber-enhanced retailing: Integrating e-commerce retailing with brick-and-mortar retailing. *Electronic Markets*, *10*(3), 185–191. doi:10.1080/10196780050177099

Oviatt, B. M., & McDougall, P. P. (1994). Toward a theory of new international ventures. *Journal of International Business Studies*, *25*(1), 45–64. doi:10.1057/palgrave. jibs.8490193

Oviatt, B. M., & McDougall, P. P. (2005). Defining international entrepreneurship & modeling the speed of internationalization. *Entrepreneurship Theory & Practice*, *29*(5), 537–554. doi:10.1111/j.1540-6520.2005.00097.x

Oviatt, B. M., & McDougall, P. P. (2005). Defining international entrepreneurship & modeling the speed of internationalization. *Entrepreneurship Theory & Practice*, *29*(5), 537–554. doi:10.1111/j.1540-6520.2005.00097.x

Oviatt, P., & McDougal, B. (1999). Accelerated internationalization: why are new and small ventures internationalizing in greater numbers and with increasing speed? In R. Wright, (Ed.) *Research in Global Strategic Management*, (23-40). Stamford, CT: JAI Press.

Palmer, J., Kallio, J., & Heck, E. (2000). Online grocery shopping around the World: Examples of key business models. *Communications of the Association for Information Systems*, *4*(3), 1–34.

Palvia, P., & Palvia, S. (1999). An examination of the IT satisfaction of small-business users. *Information & Management*, *35*(3), 127–137. doi:10.1016/S0378-7206(98)00086-X

Pan, S.L., & Lee, J. (2003). Using e-CRM for a unified view of the customer. *Communications of the ACM archive, April, 46(4)*, 95-99.

Pantelli, N. (2002). Richness, power cues, & email text. *Information & Management*, *40*, 75–78. doi:10.1016/ S0378-7206(01)00136-7

Papazafeiropoulou, A., Pouloudi, A., & Doukidis, G. (2002). A framework for best practices in electronic commerce awareness creation. *Business Process Management Journal*, *8*(3), 233–245. doi:10.1108/14637150210428943

Park, S., & Yoon, S. H. (2005). Separating early-adopters from the majority: The case of Broadband Internet access in Korea. *Technological Forecasting and Social Change*, *72*(3), 301–325. doi:10.1016/j.techfore.2004.08.013

Parker, C. M., & Castleman, T. (2007). New directions for research on SME-eBusiness: insights from an analysis of journal articles from 2003 to 2006. *Journal of Information Systems and Small Business*, *1*(1-2), 21–40.

Parthasarathy, M., & Bhattacherjee, A. (1998). Understanding post-adoption behavior in the context of online services. *Information Systems Research*, *9*, 362–379. doi:10.1287/isre.9.4.362

Patterson, H., & Henderson, D. (2003). What is really different about rural and urban firms? Some evidence from Northern Ireland. *Journal of Rural Studies*, *19*(4), 477–490. doi:10.1016/S0743-0167(03)00027-5

Pavic, S., Koh, S. C. L., Simpson, M., & Padmore, J. (2007). Could e-business create a competitive advantage in UK SMEs? *Benchmarking: An International Journal*, *14*(3), 320–351. doi:10.1108/14635770710753112

Pavlou, P. A. (2003). Consumer acceptance of electronic commerce: Integrating trust and risk with the Technology Acceptance Model. *International Journal of Electronic Commerce*, *7*(3), 101–134.

Peansupap, V., & Walker, D. (2005). Exploratory factors influencing information and communication technology diffusion and adoption within Australian construction organizations: a micro analysis. *Construction Innovation*, *5*(3), 135–157.

Pease, W., & Rowe, M. (2005, July). *Use of information technology to facilitate collaboration and co-opetition between tourist operators in tourist destinations*. Paper presented at the Technology Enterprise Strategies: Thriving and Surviving in an Online Era Conference, Melbourne, Australia.

Pease, W., Rowe, M., & Cooper, M. (2005, August). *Regional tourist destinations – The role of information and communications technology in collaboration amongst tourism providers.* Paper presented at the ITS Africa-Asia-Australasia Regional Conference, Perth, Australia.

Peppers, D., Rodgers, M., & Dorf, B. (1999). Is your company ready for one-to-one marketing? *Harvard Business Review, 77*(1), 151–160.

Petersen, B., Welch, L., & Liesch, P. (2002). The Internet and foreign market expansion by firms. *Management International Review, 42*(2), 207–221.

Pflughoeft, K. A., Ramamurthy, K., Soofi, E. S., Yasai-Ardekani, M., & Fatemah, M. (2003). Multiple conceptualizations of small business Web use and benefit. *Decision Sciences, 34*(3), 467–513. doi:10.1111/j.1540-5414.2003.02539.x

Pikkarainen, T., Pikkarainen, K., Karjaluoto, H., & Pahnila, S. (2004). Consumer acceptance of online banking: an extension of the Technology Acceptance Model. *Internet Research, 14*(3), 224–235. doi:10.1108/10662240410542652

Piris, L., Fitzgerald, G., & Serrano, A. (2004). Strategic motivators and expected benefits from E-Commerce in traditional organisations. *International Journal of Information Management, 24*(6), 489–506. doi:10.1016/j.ijinfomgt.2004.08.008

Pollard, C., & Hayne, S. (1998). The changing face of information systems issues in small firms. *International Small Business Journal, 16*(3), 70–87. doi:10.1177/0266242698163004

Pollman, A., W., & Johnson, A. C. (1974). Resistance to change, early retirement and managerial decisions. *Industrial Gerontology, 1*(1), 33–41.

Polytechnic of Milan. (2007). *L'eCommerce B2c in Italia: crescono Servizi e Dot Com* [Research Report]. Milan, Italy: Polytechnic of Milan, B2C Observatory.

Pool, P. W., Parnell, J. A., Spillan, J. E., Carraher, S., & Lester, D. L. (2006). Are SMEs meeting the challenge of integrating e-commerce into their businesses? A review of the development, challenges and opportunities. *International Journal of Information Technology and Management, 5*(2/3), 97–113.

Poon, S. (2000). Business environment and Internet commerce benefit- Small business perspective. *European Journal of Information Systems, 9*(2), 72–81. doi:10.1057/palgrave/ejis/3000361

Poon, S., & Swatman, P. (1999). An exploratory study of small business Internet commerce issues. *Information & Management, 35*, 9–18. doi:10.1016/S0378-7206(98)00079-2

Poon, S., & Swatman, P. M. C. (1997). Small business use of the internet: findings from Australian case studies. *International Marketing Review, 14*(5), 385–402. doi:10.1108/02651339710184343

Poon, S., & Swatman, P. M. C. (1999). An exploratory study of small business Internet commerce issues. *Information & Management, 35*(1), 9–18. doi:10.1016/S0378-7206(98)00079-2

Porter, M. E. (2001). Strategy and the Internet. *Harvard Business Review, 79*(3), 62–78.

Prasarnphanich, P., & Gillenson, M. L. (2003). The hybrid clicks and bricks business strategy. *Communications of the ACM, 46*(12), 178–185. doi:10.1145/953460.953498

Premkumar, G., & Roberts, M. (1999). Adoption of new information technologies in rural small businesses. *Omega, 27*(4), 467–484. doi:10.1016/S0305-0483(98)00071-1

Pricewaterhouse Coopers (1998, November 3). Economic outlook appears bright for technology businesses, especially smaller ones. *Trendsetter Barometer Report.*

Pricewaterhouse Coopers (1999). *Asia Pacific Economic Cooperation (APEC): SME Electronic Commerce Study - Final Report September 24, 1999.* Retrieved May 12, 2009, from http://www.apec.org/apec/publications/free_downloads/1999.MedialibDownload.v1.html?url=/etc/medialib/apec_media_library/downloads/working-groups/telwg/pubs/1999.Par.0001.File.v1.1

PublicTechnology.net. (2008). *Cybercrime syndicate scoops millions from South African government.* Retrieved June 13, 2008, from http://www.publictechnology.net/modules.php?op=modload&name=News&file=article&side=16110

Quayle, M. (2001). *E-commerce: The challenge for Welsh small and medium size enterprises.* Business Week in Wales Lecture, Cardiff . *Cardiff International Arena, 16*(May), 14.

Quayle, M. (2002). E-commerce: the challenge for UK SMEs in the twenty-first century. *International Journal of Operations & Production Management, 22*(10), 1148–1161. doi:10.1108/01443570210446351

Rabinovich, E., & Evers, P. T. (2003). Product fulfilment in supply chains supporting internet-retailing operations. *Journal of Business Logistics, 24*(2), 205.

Ragins, J. E., & Greco, J. A. (2003). Customer relationship management and e-business: more than a software solution. *Review of Business, 24*(1), 25–30.

Rajagopal, P. (2002). An innovation—diffusion view of implementation of enterprise resource planning (ERP) systems and development of a research model. *Information & Management, 40*(2), 87–114. doi:10.1016/S0378-7206(01)00135-5

Ram, M., & Jones, T. (1998). *Ethnic minorities in business.* Small Business Research Trust.

Ram, M., & Jones, T. (2008). *Ethnic minority business: An overview.* Retrieved February 26, 2009, from http://www.oi.acidi.gov.pt/docs/Revista_3_EN/Migr3_Sec1_Art3_EN.pdf

Ram, M., & Smallbone, D. (1999, November). *Ethnic minority enterprises in Birmingham.* Paper presented to the 2nd Ethnic Minority Enterprise Seminar, London.

Ram, M., & Smallbone, D. (2002). Ethnic minority business support in the era of the small business service. *Environment and Planning. C, Government & Policy, 20*(2), 235–249. doi:10.1068/c0050

Ram, M., & Smallbone, D. (2003). Policies to support ethnic minority enterprise: The English experience.

Entrepreneurship and Regional Development, 15(2), 151–166. doi:10.1080/0898562032000075177

Ram, M., Edwards, P., & Jones, T. (2007). Staying underground: informal work, small firms and employment regulations in the United Kingdom. *Work and Occupations, 34*, 318–344. doi:10.1177/0730888407303223

Ram, M., Gilman, M., Arrowsmith, J., & Edwards, P. (2003). Once more into the sunset? Asian clothing firms after the national minimum wage. *Environment and Planning. C, Government & Policy, 21*, 71–88. doi:10.1068/c0136

Ram, M., Smallbone, D., & Deakins, D. (2002). *The finance and business support needs of ethnic minority firms in Britain.* British Bankers Association Research Report

Ramayah, T., Dahlan, N., Mohamad, O., & Siron, R. (2002). Technology usage among owners/managers of SME's: The role of demographic and motivational variables. In *Proceedings of the 6th Annual Asian-Pacific Forum for Small Business on Small and Medium Enterprises Linkages, Networking and Clustering*, Kuala Lumpur, Malaysia.

Ramsey, E., Ibbotson, P., Bell, J., & Gray, B. (2003). E-opportunities of service sector SMEs: An Irish cross-border study. *Journal of Small Business and Enterprise Development, 10*(3), 250–265. doi:10.1108/14626000310489709

Rao, S., Metts, G., & Monge, C. M. A. (2003). Electronic commerce development in small and medium sized enterprises: a stage model and its implications. *Business Process Management Journal, 9*(1), 11–32. doi:10.1108/14637150310461378

Rasmussen, E. S., Madsen, T. K., & Evangelista, F. (1997). *The founding of the born global company in Denmark & Australia: Sense making and networking.* Odense: Odense University, Department of Marketing.

Raus, M., Flügge, B., & Boutellier, R. (2008). Innovation steps in the diffusion of e-customs solutions. In S. A. Chun, M. Janssen & J. R. Gil-Garcia (Eds.), *ACM International Conference Proceeding Series* (Vol. 289, pp. 315-324). Montréal, Canada: Digital Government Society of North America.

Raus, M., Flügge, B., & Schumacher, R. (2008). Neue Zollabwicklung in der Schweiz. *Swiss Export, 4. Quartal, 2008*, 39–41.

Raus, M., Kipp, A., & Boutellier, R. (2008). Diffusion of e-government IT innovation: A case of failure? In P. Cunningham & M. Cunningham (Eds.), *Collaboration and the knowledge economy: Issues, applications, case studies*. Amsterdam: IOS Press.

Rawling, A. (1994). The AIDS virus dispute—Awarding priority for the discovery of the human immunodeficiency virus. *Science, Technology & Human Values, 19*, 342–390. doi:10.1177/016224399401900305

Ray, D. M. (1989). *Entrepreneurial companies 'born' international: four case studies*. Paper presented at the Babson Kaannufm Entrepreneurship Research Conference on Entrepreneurship, June, St Louis.

Ray, D. M. (1995). *Strategic patterns of global start-up ventures: 5 case studies*. Unpublished.

Raymond, L. (2001). Determinants of Web site implementation in small business. *Internet Research, 11*(5), 411–424. doi:10.1108/10662240110410363

Raymond, L., & Bergeron, F. (2008). Enabling the business strategy of SMEs through e-business capabilities: A strategic alignment perspective. *Industrial Management & Data Systems, 108*(5), 577–595. doi:10.1108/02635570810876723

Raymond, L., Bergeron, F., & Blili, S. (2005). The assimilation of E-business in manufacturing SMEs: determinants and effects on growth and internationalization. *Electronic Markets, 15*(2), 106–118. doi:10.1080/10196780500083761

Rayport, J., & Jaworski, B. (2001). *E-Commerce*. New York, NY: McGraw-Hill/Irwin.

Reedy, J. E., Schullo, S. S., & Zimmerman, K. R. (1999). *Electonic marketing: Integrating electronic resources into the marketing process*. Orlando, FL: Harcourt College Publishers.

Reichheld, F. F., & Sasser, J. W. E. (1990). Zero defections: Quality comes to services. *Harvard Business Review, 68*(5), 105–111.

Remenyi, D., Williams, B., Money, A., & Swartz, E. (1998). *Doing research in business and management – An introduction to process and method*. London: Sage Publications.

Review of Financial Regulation (RFR). (1998). *Review of financial regulation in the Crown Dependencies – Part 2*. Retrieved from http://www.archive.official-documents. co.uk/document/cm41/4109/b-chap03.htm

Reynolds, W., Savage, W., & Williams, A. (1994). *Your own business: A practical guide to success*. New York: Thomson Learning Nelson.

Rickards, R. C. (2007). BSC and benchmark development for an e-commerce SME. *Benchmarking: An International Journal, 14*(2), 222–250. doi:10.1108/14635770710740413

Ridder, A., Van der Sijde, P., Kirwan, P., & Elders, J. (2006). C2V: A global start-up company from Twente. In M. Anderson, P. Van der Sijde & A. Mateos (Eds.), *The Netherlands New strategies for innovation support*. Salamanca: Signum.

Riemenschneider, C. K., Harrison, D. A., & Mykytyn, P. P. Jr. (2003). Understanding IT adoption decisions in small business: Integrating current theories. *Information & Management, 40*, 269–285. doi:10.1016/S0378-7206(02)00010-1

Rigby, D. K., Reichheld, F. F., & Schefter, P. (2002). Avoid the four perils of customer relationship marketing. *Harvard Business Review, 80*(2), 101–199.

Roberts, R. (1994). *Offshore financial centres*. Cheltenham, UK: Edward Elgar.

Roberts, S. (2002). *Key drivers of economic development and inclusion in rural areas*. Initial scoping study for the socio-economic evidence base for DEFRA.

Roberts, V. (1999). Information technology sector to lead US economy's continuing growth in 1999. *Economic*

Outlook, January 27(17). http://www.newsstand.k-link.com/.

Robertson, A., & Lockett, N. Brown, D. and Crouchley, R. (2007, November). *Entrepreneur attitude towards the computer and its effect on e-Business adoption*, Paper presented at the 30th Institute for Small Business and Entrepreneurship (ISBE) Conference, Glasgow.

Robertson, T. S. (1971). *Innovative behavior and communication*. New York: Holt, Rinehart and Winston, Inc.

Rodgers, J. A., Yen, D. C., & Chou, D. C. (2002). Developing e-business: A strategic approach. *Information Management & Computer Security*, *10*(4), 184–192. doi:10.1108/09685220210436985

Rogers, D. S. (2002). *Reverse logistics: Trends and practices*. Sao Paulo, Brasil: Centre for Logistics Management.

Rogers, E. M. (1983). *Diffusion of innovations*. New York: The Free Press.

Roman, R. (2003). Diffusion of innovations as a theoretical framework for telecenters. *Information Technologies and International Development*, *1*(2), 53 66. doi:10.1162/154475203322981969

Romano, N. C. Jr, & Fjermestad, J. (2003). Electronic commerce customer relationship management: A research agenda. *Information Technology and Management*, *4*, 233–258. doi:10.1023/A:1022906513502

Romm, C. T., & Sudweeks, F. (Eds.). (1998) *Doing business electronically*. London: Springer.

Rose, G., & Straub, D. (1998). Predicting general IT use: Applying TAM to the Arabic world. *Journal of Global Information Management*, *6*(3), 39–46.

Rothwell, R. (1992). Successful industrial innovation: critical factors for the 1990s. *R & D Management*, *22*(3), 221–239. doi:10.1111/j.1467-9310.1992.tb00812.x

Rowe, M., Pease, W., & McLeod, P. (2007). Web portals as an exemplar for tourist destinations. In A. Tatnall (Ed.), *Encyclopedia of portal technologies and applications*, (Vol. 2, pp. 1157-1160). Hershey, PA: Information Science Publishing.

Rowley, J. (2004). Partnering paradigms? Knowledge management and relationship marketing. *Industrial Management & Data Systems*, *104*(2), 149–157. doi:10.1108/02635570410522125

Roztocki, N., & Weistroffer, H. (2006). Stock Price Reaction to Investments in Information Technology: The Relevance of Cost Management Systems. *The Electronic Journal Information Systems Evaluation*, *9*(1), 27–30.

Runyan, R., Droge, C., & Swinney, J. (2008). Entrepreneurial orientation versus small business orientation: What are their relationships to firm performance? *Journal of Small Business Management*, *46*(4), 567–588. doi:10.1111/j.1540-627X.2008.00257.x

Saban, K., & Rau, S. (2005). The functionality of Websites as export marketing channels. *Electronic Markets*, *15*(2), 128–135. doi:10.1080/10196780500083803

Sadowski, B. M., Maitland, C., & Van Dongen, J. (2002). Strategic use of the Internet by small- and medium-sized companies: an exploratory study. *Information Economics and Policy*, *14*(1), 75–93. doi:10.1016/S0167-6245(01)00054-3

Saeed, K. A., Grover, V., & Hwang, Y. (2003). Creating synergy with a clicks and mortar approach. *Communications of the ACM*, *46*(12).206–212doi:10.1145/953460.953501

Sagi, J. (2004). ICT and business in the new economy: Globalization and attitudes towards eCommerce. *Journal of Global Information Management*, *12*(3), 44–65.

Samiee, S. (1998). Exporting and the Internet: a conceptual perspective. *International Marketing Review*, *15*(5), 413–426. doi:10.1108/02651339810236452

Sanderson, I. (2002). Evaluation, policy learning and evidence-based policy making. *Public Administration*, *80*(1), 1–22. doi:10.1111/1467-9299.00292

Sands, M. (2003). Integrating the Web and e-mail into a push-pull strategy. *Qualitative Market Research*, *6*(1), 27–37. doi:10.1108/13522750310457357

Sarosa, S., & Underwood, J. (2005). Factors affecting IT adoption within Indonesian SMEs: manager's perspectives. In *Proceedings of the 9ᵗʰ Pacific Asia Conference on Information Systems*, Bangkok, Thailand.

Sarosa, S., & Zowghi, D. (2003). Strategy for adopting information technology for SMEs: experience in adopting email within an Indonesian furniture company. *Electronic Journal of Information Systems Evaluation*, *6*(2), 165–176.

Saunders, M., Lewis, P., & Thornhill, A. (2007). *Research methods for business students* (4th Ed.). London: Prentice Hall.

SBP – Strategic business partnership for growth in Africa (2003). *Is South Africa a good place to do business?* SME Alert. Retrieved January, 15, 2006, from World Wide Web: http://www-za.sbp.org.za/docs/SME_Alert_Nov_2003.pdf

SBS (Small Business Service). (2004). SBS booster survey. Retrieved July 7, 2005, from http://www.sbs.gov.uk/sbsgov/action/layer?r.l2=7000000243&r.l1=7000000229&r.s=tl&topicId=7000011759

Schindehutte, M., & Morris, M. H. (2001). Understanding strategic adaptation in small firms. *International Journal of Entrepreneurial Behaviour and Research*, *7*(3), 84–107. doi:10.1108/EUM0000000005532

Schneider, G., & Perry, J. (2001). *Electronic commerce* (2nd Ed.). Andover: Thomson.

Schwartz, R. G., & Teach, R. D. (2000). *A model of opportunity recognition & exploitation: an empirical study of incubator firms.* Atlanta: Georgia Tech Center for International Business Education & Research, Dupree School of Management.

Scullin, S. S., Fjermestad, J., & Romano, N. C. Jr. (2004). E-relationship marketing: changes in traditional marketing as an outcome of electronic customer relationship management. *The Journal of Enterprise Information Management*, *17*(6), 410–415. doi:10.1108/17410390410566698

Scupola, A. (2003). The adoption of Internet commerce by SMEs in the South of Italy: An environmental, technological and organizational perspective. *Journal of Global Information Technology Management*, *6*(1), 52–71.

Seldon, A. (2004). E-business in South Africa, a matter of trust. *Netdotwork*. Retrieved February, 20, 2006, from http://netdotwork.co.za/article.aspx?pklArticleId=3081

Sellitto, C., & Burgess, S. (2007). A study of a wine industry internet portal. In A. Tatnall (Ed.), *Encyclopedia of portal technologies and applications* (Vol. 2, pp. 979-984). Hershey, PA: Information Science Publishing.

Sengupta, A., Mazumdar, C., & Barik, M. S. (2005). E-commerce security: A life cycle approach, in Sadhana. *Journal of the Indian Academy of Sciences*, *30*(2 & 3), 119–140.

Sexton, R. S., Johnson, R. A., & Hignite, M. A. (2002). Predicting Internet/EC use. *Internet Research: Electronic Networking Application and Policy*, *12*(5), 402–410. doi:10.1108/10662240210447155

Seyal, A. H., & Rahman, M. N. A. (2003). A preliminary investigation of e-commerce adoption in small & medium enterprises in Brunei. *Journal of Global Information Technology Management*, *6*(2), 6–26.

Shackleton, P., Fisher, J., & Dawson, L. (2004, January 5-8). Evolution of local government e-services: The applicability of e-business maturity models. In *Proceedings of the 37ᵗʰ Annual Hawaii International Conference on System Sciences*, Waikoloa, Big Island, HI.

Shane, S. (2000). Prior knowledge & the discovery of entrepreneurial opportunities. *Organization Science*, *11*(4), 448–469. doi:10.1287/orsc.11.4.448.14602

Shapiro, C., & Varian, H. R. (1999). *Information rules: A strategic guide to the network economy.* Cambridge, MA: Harvard Business School Press.

Shaw, E. (1999). Networks and their relevance to the entrepreneurial/marketing interface: A review of the evidence. *Journal of Research in Marketing & Entrepreneurship*, *1*(1), 24–40.

Shih, Y. Y., & Fang, K. (2004). The use of a decomposed theory of planned behavior to study Internet banking in Taiwan. *Internet Research*, *14*(3), 213–223. doi:10.1108/10662240410542643

Shimp, T. A., & Kavas, A. (1984). The theory of reasoned action applied to coupon usage. *The Journal of Consumer Research, 11*, 795–809. doi:10.1086/209015

Shocker, A. D., Srivatava, R. K., & Reukert, R. W. (1994, May). Challenges and opportunities facing brand management: An introduction to the special issue. *JMR, Journal of Marketing Research, 31*, 49–158. doi:10.2307/3152190

Shrader, C., Mulford, C., & Blackburn, V. (1989). Strategic and operational planning, uncertainty, and performance in small firms. *Journal of Small Business Management, 27*(4), 45–60.

Siegel, D. (1999). *Futurize your enterprise: Business strategy in the age of the e-customer.* New York: Wiley.

Sigrist, B. (1999). *Entrepreneurial opportunity recognition.* Geneva, Switzerland: University of Geneva (Ph.D. thesis)

Sikka, P. (2007). Globalization and its discontents: Accounting firms buy limited liability partnership legislation in Jersey. *Accounting, Auditing & Accountability Journal, 21*(3), 398–426. doi:10.1108/09513570810863987

Simmons, G. (2008). Marketing to postmodern consumers: Introducing the Internet chameleon. *European Journal of Marketing, 42*(3/4), 294–310. doi:10.1108/03090560810852940

Simmons, G. J., Armstrong, G. A., & Durkin, M. G. (2008). A conceptualization of the determinants of small business Website adoption: Setting the research agenda. *International Small Business Journal, 26*(3), 351–389. doi:10.1177/0266242608088743

Simmons, G. J., Durkin, M. G., McGowan, P., & Armstrong, G. A. (2007). Determinants of internet adoption by SME agri-food companies. *Journal of Small Business and Enterprise Development, 14*(4), 620–640. doi:10.1108/14626000710832730

Simmons, G., Armstrong, G., & Durkin, M. (2008). A conceptualisation of the determinants of small business Website adoption. *International Small Business Journal, 26*(3), 351–389. doi:10.1177/0266242608088743

Simons, J. (1999, January 26). States chafe as Web shopper ignore sales taxes. *The Wall Street Journal,* B1.

Simpson, C. L., & Kujawa, D. (1974). The export decision process: an empirical inquiry. *Journal of International Business Studies, 5*(1), 107–117. doi:10.1057/palgrave.jibs.8490815

Simpson, M., & Docherty, A. J. (2004). E-commerce adoption support and advice for UK SMEs. *Journal of Small Business and Enterprise Development, 11*(3), 315–328. doi:10.1108/14626000410551573

Sinkovics, R. R., & Pene, E. (2005). Empowerment of SME websites – development of a web-empowered scale and preliminary evidence. *Journal of International Entrepreneurship, 3*(4), 303–315. doi:10.1007/s10843-006-7858-8

Slovic, P. (1966). Risk-taking in children: Age and sex difference. *Child Development, 37*, 169–176. doi:10.2307/1126437

Small Business Service (SBS). (2005). *SME statistics 2004 UK.* Retrieved October 16, 2005, from http://www.sbs.gov.uk/SBS_Gov_files/researchandstats/SMEStatsUK2004.xls.

Smallbone, D., Lyon, F., & Li, X. (2006). Trust, co-operation and networking in an immigrant business community: the case of Chinese-owned businesses in the UK. In H. H. Hohmann, & F. Welter (Eds.), *Trust and entrepreneurship: A west-east perspective.* Cheltenham, UK: Edward Elgar.

Smallbone, D., North, D., Baldock, R., & Ekanem, I. (2002). *Encouraging and supporting enterprise in rural areas.* Centre for Enterprise and Economic Development Research, Middlesex University Business School, London, Report to the Small Business Service.

Smith, J. A. (1998). Strategies for start-ups. *Long Range Planning, 31*(6), 857–872. doi:10.1016/S0024-6301(98)80022-8

Smith, P. R., & Chaffey, D. (2005). *E-marketing excellence.* Oxford, UK: Butterworth-Heinemann.

Smyth, M., & Ibbotson, P. (2001). Internet connectivity in Ireland. *Joint report by the Bank of Ireland and the University of Ulster*. Retrieved from http://www.bankofireland.co. uk/whats_new/item. php

Sohal, A. S., & Ng, L. (1998). The role and impact of information technology in Australian Business. *Journal of Information Technology*, *13*, 201–217. doi:10.1080/026839698344846

Song, X. M., & Parry, M. E. (1993). How the Japanese manage the R&D-marketing interface. *Research and Technology Management*, *36*(4), 32–42.

Southern, A., & Tilley, F. (2000). Small firms and information and communication technologies (ICTs), Toward a typology of ICT usage. *New Technology, Work and Employment*, *15*(2), 138–154. doi:10.1111/1468-005X.00070

Sparkes, A., & Thomas, B. (2001). The use of the Internet as a critical success factor for the marketing of Welsh agri-food SMEs in the 21ˢᵗ century. *British Food Journal*, *103*(5), 331–347. doi:10.1108/00070700110395368

Sparling, L., Toleman, M., & Cater-Steel, A. (2007). SME Adoption of e-Commerce in the Central Okanagan Region of Canada. *In Proceedings of the 18ᵗʰ Australasian Conference on Information Systems*, Toowoomba, Australia (pp. 1046-1059).

Srirojanant, S., & Cresswell-Thirkell, P. (1998). Relationship Marketing And Its Synergy With Web-based technologies. *Journal of Market Focused Management*, *3*, 23–46. doi:10.1023/A:1009790421951

States of Jersey (2005). *Growing Jersey's economy: An economic growth plan*. The Economic Development Committee, 1-72.

States of Jersey. (2006). *Policy for the fulfilment industry*. Economic Development Department, Jersey, February, (pp. 1-3).

States of Jersey. (2006). *Fulfilment industry policy*. In *Jersey Economic Affairs Scrutiny Panel*, 17ᵗʰ November (pp. 1-7).

Steeples, C. (2004). Using action-oriented or participatory research methods for research on networked learning. In S. Banks, P. Goodyear, V. Hodgson, C. Jones, V. Lally, D. McConnel, & C. Steeples (Eds.), *Proceedings of the Fourth International Conference on networked learning 2004: a research based conference one-learning in higher education and lifelong learning* (pp. 113-118). Lancaster University and University of Sheffield

Steinfield, C., & Whitten, P. (1999). Community level socio-economic impacts of electronic commerce. *Journal of Computer-Mediated Communication*, *5*(2).

Steinfield, C., Adelaar, T., & Liu, F. (2005). Click and mortar strategies viewed from the Web: A content analysis of features illustrating integration between retailers' online and offline presence. *Electronic Markets*, *15*(3), 199–212. doi:10.1080/10196780500208632

Steinfield, C., Bouwman, H., & Adelaar, T. (2002). The dynamics of click-and-mortar electronic commerce: Opportunities and management strategies. *International Journal of Electronic Commerce*, *7*(1), 93–119.

Steinfield, C., Mahler, A., & Bauer, J. (1999). Electronic commerce and the local merchant: Opportunities for synergy between physical and Web presence. *Electronic Markets*, *9*(1-2), 51–57. doi:10.1080/101967899359247

Sterrett, C., & Shah, A. (1998). Going global on the information super highway. *S.A.M. Advanced Management Journal, Winter*, *63*(1), 43-47.

Stinchcombe, A. L. (1965). Social structure & organizations. In J. G. March (ed.), *Handbook of organizations* (pp. 142-193). Chicago: Rand McNally & Company.

Stockdale, R., & Standing, C. (2003). The effect of B2B online reverse auctions on buyer-supplier relationships. In *Proceedings of the 14ᵗʰ Australian Conference on Information Systems, Perth, Australia*

Stockdale, R., & Standing, C. (2004). Benefit and barriers of electronic marketplace participation: an SME perspective. *The Journal of Enterprise Information Management*, *17*(4), 301–311. doi:10.1108/17410390410548715

Stockdale, R., & Standing, C. (2004). Benefits and barriers of electronic marketplace participation: an SME perspective. *Journal of Enterprise Information Management, 17*(4), 301–311. doi:10.1108/17410390410548715

Stockdale, R., & Standing, C. (2006). A classification model to support SME e-commerce adoption initiatives. *Journal of Small Business and Enterprise Development, 13*(3), 381–394. doi:10.1108/14626000610680262

Stokes, D. (2000). Entrepreneurial marketing: a conceptualisation from qualitative research. *Qualitative Market Research: An International Journal, 3*(1), 47–54. doi:10.1108/13522750010310497

Storey, D. J. (1994). *Understanding the small business sector.* London: Routledge.

Strader, T. J., Lin, F.-R., & Shaw, M. J. (1999). The impact of information sharing on order fulfilment in divergent differentiation supply chains. *Journal of Global Information Management, 7*(1), 16.

Strassmann, P. A. (1985). *Information Payoff: The Transformation of work in electronic age.* New York: Free Press.

Straub, D. W., Loch, K. D., Evaristo, R., Karahanna, E., & Strite, M. (2002). Toward a theory-based measurement of culture. *Journal of Global Information Management, 10*(January), 13–23.

Straub, D., Limayem, M., & Karahanna-Evaristo, E. (1995). Measuring system usage: implications for IS theory testing. *Management Science, 41*(8), 1328–1342. doi:10.1287/mnsc.41.8.1328

Straus, J., & Frost, R. (2001). *E-markzeting.* Upper Saddle River, NJ: Prentice-Hall.

Subba Rao, S., Metts, G., & Monge, C. A. M. (2003). Electronic commerce development in small and medium sized enterprises. *Business Process Management Journal, 9*(1), 11–33. doi:10.1108/14637150310461378

Sunday Times. (2002). Dozens of threats beset your data. *Sunday Times Surveys.* Retrieved October 5, 2004, from http://www.sundaytimes.co.za/business/surveys/internet/survey10.asp

Swan, J., Newell, S., Scarbrough, H., & Hislop, D. (1999). Knowledge management and innovation: networks and networking. *Journal of Knowledge Management, 3*(4), 262–275. doi:10.1108/13673279910304014

Swatman, P. (2000). Internet for SMEs: A new silk road? *International Trade Forum, 3*, 22–24.

Swiss Federal Customs Administration. (2008). *E-dec.* Retrieved February 10, 2009, from http://www.ezv.admin.ch/themen/00476/00494/index.html?lang=en

Swiss Federal Customs Administration. (2008). *IDEE - Handbuch für Kunden / Firmen.* Retrieved February 10, 2009, from http://www.ezv.admin.ch/themen/00476/02278/02376/index.html?lang=de&download=M3wBPgDB/8ull6Du36WenojQ1NTTjaXZnqWfVpzLhmfhnapmmc7Zi6rZnqCkk1N4fn97bKbXrZ6lhuDZz8mMps2gpKfo&typ=.pdf

Swiss Federal Customs Administration. (2008, May, 2008). *Talks with the EU on amending the agreement on the carriage of goods (24-hour rule).* Retrieved February 10, 2009, from http://www.ezv.admin.ch/zollinfo_firmen/verzollung/02302/index.html?lang=en

Szajna, B. (1994). Software evaluation and choice: predictive validation of the technology acceptance instrument. *MIS Quarterly, 18*(3), 319–324. doi:10.2307/249621

Tabor, S. W. (2005). Achieving significant learning in e-commerce education through small business consulting projects. *Journal of Information Systems Education, 16*(1).

Tan, K. S., & Chong, S., C., Lin, B., & Eze, U. C. (2009). Internet-based ICT adoption: Evidence from Malaysian SMEs. *Industrial Management & Data Systems, 109*(2), 224–244. doi:10.1108/02635570910930118

Tan, M., & Teo, T. S. H. (2000). Factors influencing the adoption of Internet banking. *Journal of the AIS, 1*(1).

Tax Foundation (1998). Mismatch between old tax and new E-commerce has Governments scrambling. *Tax Features, 42*(10), 4,8.

Taylor, M. J., McWilliam, J., England, D., & Akomode, J. (2004). Skills required in developing electronic commerce for small and medium enterprises: Case based generalization approach. *Electronic Commerce Research and Applications, 3*(3), 253–265. doi:10.1016/j.elerap.2004.04.001

Taylor, S., & Todd, P. (1995). Assessing IT usage: The role of prior experience. *MIS Quarterly, 19*(4), 561–570. doi:10.2307/249633

Taylor, S., & Todd, P. A. (1995b). Understanding information technology usage: A test of competing models. *Information Systems Research, 6*(2), 144. doi:10.1287/isre.6.2.144

Technews. (2004). 2004 Website compliancy survey. *Computer Business Review.* Retrieved January 15, 2005, from http://cbr.co.za/article.aspx

Teece, D. (1998). Capturing value from knowledge assets: The new economy, markets for know-how, and intangible assets. *California Management Review, 40*(3), 55–79.

Telford, R. (2006, October). *Small businesses in rural areas – How are they different?* Paper presented at the 26th ISBE Conference, Cardiff, Wales.

Teo, T. S. H. (2001). Demographic and motivational variables associated with Internet usage activities. *Internet Research: Electronic Networking Applications and Policy, 11*(2), 125–137. doi:10.1108/10662240110695089

Teo, T. S. H., & Lim, V. K. G. (2000). Gender differences in Internet usage and task preferences. *Behaviour & Information Technology, 19*(4), 283–295. doi:10.1080/01449290050086390

Teo, T. S. H., & Tan, M. (1998). An empirical study of adopters and non-adopters of Internet in Singapore. *Information & Management, 34*, 339–345. doi:10.1016/S0378-7206(98)00068-8

Teo, T. S. H., Lim, V. K. G., & Lai, R. Y. C. (1999). Intrinsic and extrinsic motivation in Internet usage. *Omega, 27*(1), 25–37. doi:10.1016/S0305-0483(98)00028-0

Teofilovic, N. (2002). The reality of innovation in government. *Innovation Journal*, 1-30.

Tetteh, E., & Burn, J. (2001). Global strategies for SME-business: Applying the SMALL framework. *Logistics Information Management, 14*(1-2), 171–180. doi:10.1108/09576050110363202

The Economist Intelligence Unit Limited. (2007). *Country commerce.* Retrieved from http://www.eiu.com

The Presidency. (2003). No 26 of 2003: National Small Business Amendment Act, 2003, South Africa. Retrieved March 30, 2005, from http://www.info.gov.za/view/DownloadFileAction?id=68002

Theng, L. G., & Boon, J. L. W. (1996). An exploratory study of factors affecting the failure of local small and medium enterprises. *Asia Pacific Journal of Management, 13*(2), 47–61. doi:10.1007/BF01733816

Thirumalai, S., & Sinha, K. K. (2005). Customer satisfaction with order fulfilment in retail supply chains: implications of product type in electronic B2C transactions. *Journal of Operations Management, 23*, 291–303. doi:10.1016/j.jom.2004.10.015

Thomas, B., Sparkes, A., Brooksbank, D., & Williams, R. (2002). Social aspects of the impact of information and communication technologies on agri-food SMEs in Wales. *Outlook on Agriculture, 31*(1), 35–41.

Thomas, F. (2002). Business: Oriented testing in e-commerce. In *Software Quality and Software Testing in Internet Times* (pp. 117-137). New York: Springer-Verlag Inc.

Thompson, R. (1998). Extending the Technology Acceptance Model with motivation and social factors. In *AMCIS 1998 Proceedings* (pp. 254).

Thong, J. Y. L. (1999). An integrated model of information systems adoption in small businesses. *Journal of Management Information Systems, 15*(4), 187–214.

Thong, J. Y. L., & Yap, C. S. (1995). CEO characteristics, organisational characteristics and information technology adoption in small businesses. *International Journal of Management Science, 23*(4), 429–442.

Thong, J. Y. L., & Yap, C. S. (1995). CEO characteristics, organizational characteristics and information technology adoption in small business. *Omega . International Journal of Management Science, 23*(4), 429–442.

Tiessen, J., Wright, R., & Turner, I. (2001). A model of E-commerce use by internationalizing SMEs. *Journal of International Management, 7*, 211–233. doi:10.1016/S1075-4253(01)00045-X

Tornatzky, L. G., & Klein, K. J. (1982). Innovation characteristics and innovation adoption-implementation: A meta-analysis of findings. *IEEE Transactions on Engineering Management, 29*(1), 28–45.

Turban, E., King, D., Lee, K. J., & Viehland, D. (2004). *Electronic commerce: A managerial perspective.* New Jersey: Pearson Prentice Hall.

Turban, E., McLean, E., & Wetherbe, J. (2004). *Information technology for management: Transforming organizations in the digital economy.* Hoboken, NJ: John Wiley & Sons.

Tyler, T. R. (1990). *Why people obey the Law.* New Haven, CT: Yale University Press.

Uhl, K., Anrus, R., & Poulson, L. (1970). How are laggards different? An empirical inquiry. *JMR, Journal of Marketing Research, 7*, 51–54. doi:10.2307/3149506

Ulijn, J., Drillon, D., & Lasch, F. (Eds.). *Entrepreneurship, cooperation & the firm – The emergence & survival of high-technology ventures in Europe.* Cheltenham, UK: Edward Elgar.

UNCTAD UN. (2004). *E commerce and development report 2004.* Retrieved August 9, 2007, from http://www.unctad.org/en/docs/ecdr2004ch2_en.pdf

United Nations Development Programme. Malaysia. (2007). *Small and medium enterprises: Building an enabling environment.* Retrieved May 12, 2009, from http://www.undp.org.my/uploads/UNDP_SME_Publication.pdf

United Nations Economic Commission for Europe. (2005). *Recommendation and guidelines on establishing a single window - recommendation No. 33.* Retrieved March 16, 2009, from http://www.unece.org/cefact/recommendations/rec33/rec33_trd352e.pdf

United States Department of Commerce (USDoC). (1998). *The emerging digital economy.* Washington, DC: USDOC.

United States Department of Commerce (USDoC). (2002). *A nation online: How Americans are expanding their use of the Internet.* Washington, DC: USDOC.

Upfold, C. T., & Sewry, D. A. (2005). *An investigation of Information security in small and medium enterprises (SMEs) in Eastern Cape.* Retrieved September 20, 2006, from http://icsa.cs.up.ac.za/issa/2005/Proceedings/Research/082_Article.pdf

Urbanski, A. (1987). Repackaging the brand manager. *Sales and Marketing Management, April*, 42-45.

US-CERT. (2004). *US-CERT Technical Cyber Security Alert TA04-2939A 2004.* Retrieved December 12, 2004, from http://www.us-cert.gov/cas/techalerts/TA04-2939A

Uzoka, F. M. E., Seleka, G. G., & Khengere, J. (2007). E-commerce adoption in developing countries: A case analysis of environmental and organizational inhibitors. *International Journal of Information Systems and Change Management, 2*(3), 232–260. doi:10.1504/IJISCM.2007.015598

Uzzi, B. (1997). Social structure and competition in interfirm networks: The paradox of embeddedness. *Administrative Science Quarterly, 42*(1), 35–67. doi:10.2307/2393808

Vaessen, P., & Keeble, D. (1995). Growth-oriented SMEs in unfavourable regional environments. *Regional Studies, 29*, 489–505. doi:10.1080/00343409512331349133

Vakoufaris, H., Spilanis, I., & Kizos, T. (2007). Collective action in the Greek agrifood sector: Evidence from the North Aegean region. *British Food Journal, 109*(10), 777–791. doi:10.1108/00070700710821322

Van Akkeren, J. K., & Cavaya, A. L. M. (2000). Factors affecting entry-level Internet technology adoption by small firms in Australia – Evidence from three cases. *Journal of Systems and Information Technology, 3*(2), 33–47.

Van Beveren, J., & Thompson, H. (2002). The use of electronic commerce by SMEs in Victoria, Australia. *Journal of Small Business Management, 40*(3), 250–253. doi:10.1111/1540-627X.00054

Van de Ven, W. P. M. M., & Van Praag, B. M. S. (1981). The demand for deductibles in private health insurance: a probit model with sample selection. *Journal of Econometrics, 17*(2), 229–252. doi:10.1016/0304-4076(81)90028-2

Van der Sijde, P. C., Bliek, P., & Groen, A. (2003). The exploitation of biotech innovations: a networking model for survival & success. *PRISM Case Ref. 9.3.3*, ECCH No 803-028-1.

Van der Veen, M. (2004). *Explaining e-business adoption; innovation and entrepreneurship and in Dutch SMEs.* Unpublished doctoral dissertation, University of Twente, Holland.

Van Der Veen, M., & Wakkee, I. (2006). Understanding the entrepreneurial process. In P. Davidsson (Ed.), *New firm startups.* Cheltenham, UK: Edward Elgar.

Van Ketel, M., & Nelson, T. D. (1998 May 18). *E-commerce.* Retrieved from http://www.whatis.com/

Van Ketel, M., & Nelson, T. D. (2003). *E-commerce, USA,* http://searchcio.techtarget.com/.

Van Niekerk, L., & Labaschagne, L. (2005). The Peculium Model: Information security risk management for the South African SMME. In *ISSA Conference*, Gauteng, South Africa, June 29th – 1 July, 2005. Retrieved January 14, 2007 from http://icsa.cs.up.ac.za/issa/2006/Proceedings/Full/12_Paper.pdf

Van Slyke, C., Belanger, F., & Comunale, C. L. (2004). *Factors influencing the adoption of Web-based shopping: The impact of trust.*

Van Smith, J., & Webster, L. (2000). The knowledge economy and SMEs: A survey of skills requirements. *Business Information Review, 17*(3), 138–146. doi:10.1177/0266382004237656

Venkataraman, S. (1997). The distinctive domain of entrepreneurship research: An editor's perspective. In Venkataraman (ed.), *Advances in entrepreneurship, firm emergence & growth* (p.119-138). Greenwich, CT: JAI Press.

Venkatesan, R., & Kumar, V. (2004). A customer lifetime value framework for customer selection and resource allocation strategy. *Journal of Marketing, 68,* 106–125. doi:10.1509/jmkg.68.4.106.42728

Venkatesh, V., & Morris, M. G. (2000). Why don't men ever stop to ask for directions? Gender, social influence, and their role in technology acceptance and usage behavior. *MIS Quarterly, 24*(1), 115–139. doi:10.2307/3250981

Venkatesh, V., Morris, M. G., Davis, G. B., & Davis, F. D. (2003). User acceptance of information technology: Toward a unified view. *MIS Quarterly, 27,* 425–478.

Vienne, V. (2007). Strong words. *Print, 61*(2), 26–27.

Vijayasarathy, L. R. (2004). Predicting consumer intentions to use on-line shopping: the case for an augmented Technology Acceptance Model. *Information & Management, 41*(6), 747–762. doi:10.1016/j.im.2003.08.011

von Goeler, K. (1998, November 8). *Internet commerce by degrees: Small business early adopters.* Retrieved from http://instat.com

Wagner, B. A., Fillis, A., & Johannson, U. (2003). E-business and e-supply strategy in small and medium-sized businesses (SMEs). *Supply Chain Management: An International Journal, 8*(4), 343–354. doi:10.1108/13598540310490107

Wakkee, I. (2004). *Starting global, an entrepreneurship in networks approach.* Enschede, The Netherlands, University of Twente (Ph.D. thesis).

Wakkee, I. A. M., Groen, A. J., & Heerink, R. (2007). High-tech start-ups & innovation journeys: strategic shifts, culture & networks. In J. Ulijn, D. Drillon & F. Lasch (Eds.), *Entrepreneurship, cooperation & the firm – the emergence & survival of high-technology ventures in Europe.* Cheltenham, UK: Edward Elgar.

Wakkee, I., Groenewegen, P., & Englis, P. (2008). *Organizational emergence in the digital age.* Paper presented at the Transnational Entrepreneurship and Global Reach Conference, Nexxt Center, Wilfrid Laurier University, Canada.

Walker, E., & Brown, A. (2004). What success factors are important to small business owners? *International Small Business Journal*, *22*(6), 577–594. doi:10.1177/0266242604047411

Wang, Y. S., Wang, Y. M., Lin, H. H., & Tang, T. I. (2003). Determinants of user acceptance of internet banking: an empirical study. *International Journal of Service Industry Management*, *14*(5), 501–519. doi:10.1108/09564230310500192

Warden, S., & Motjolopane, I. M. (2007). E-commerce adoption factors: supporting cases from South Africa. In *Information Resource management Association conference*, Vancouver, Canada. Retrieved from http://www.stuartwarden.com/Warden_Motjolopane_eCommerce-AdoptionFactors_IRMA2007.pdf

Warden, S., & Remenyi, D. (2005). *E-commerce in an SME. A case study of a South African low cost or "no frills" airline"*. Paper delivered at ZA-WWW (World Wide Web) 2005 Conference, Cape Town, South Africa 29 to 31 August.

Watson, J., & Everett, J. E. (1996). Do small businesses have high failure rates? *Journal of Small Business Management*, *34*(4), 45–62.

WCO. (2006). *Authorized economic operator*. Retrieved February 10, 2009, from http://www.ifcba.org/UserFiles/File/SP0218E1(2).doc.

Webster's Family Encyclopaedia (WFE). (1990). *Jersey*. New York: Arrow.

Weiss, T. J. (1999). Cyber-relationships and brand building. *Integrated Marketing Communications Research Journal*, *5*, 19–22.

Wejnert, B. (2002). Integrating models of diffusion of innovations: A conceptual framework. *Annual Review of Sociology*, *28*, 297–326. doi:10.1146/annurev.soc.28.110601.141051

Wellman, D. (1995). Brand management report: People and management. *Food and Beverage Marketing*, January, 16-18.

Welsh Assembly Government (WAG). (2003). *Wales for innovation – The Welsh assembly government's action plan for innovation*. Retrieved February 5, 2006, from http://www.wda.co.uk/resources/action-e.pdf

Welsh Assembly Government (WAG). (2005). *Wales: A vibrant economy, the Welsh assembly government's strategic framework for economic development*. Consultation Document, November. Retrieved December 10, 2005, from http://www.wales.gov.uk/subitradeindustry/content/wave/wave-report-e.pdf

Welsh Economic Research Unit (WERU). (2005). *The Welsh economy*. Retrieved October 17, 2005, from http://www.weru.org.uk/economy.html

Wen, H. J., Chen, H. G., & Hwang, H. G. (2001). E-commerce Web site design: Strategies and models. *Information Management & Computer Security*, *9*(1), 5–12. doi:10.1108/09685220110366713

Whiteley, D. (2000). *E-Commerce: Strategy, technologies and applications*. New York: McGraw-Hill.

Wiersema, M. F., & Bantel, K. A. (1992). Top management team demography and corporate strategic change. *Academy of Management Journal*, *35*, 91–121. doi:10.2307/256474

Wigand, R. T. (1997). Electronic commerce: Definition, theory, and context. *The Information Society*, *13*(1), 1–16. doi:10.1080/019722497129241

Willcocks, L., Sauer, C., et al. (2000). *Moving to e-business: The ultimate practical guide to effective e-business*. New York: Century Press.

Williams, D. R. (2004). Effects of childcare activities on the duration of self-employment in Europe. *Entrepreneurship Theory and Practice*, *28*(5), 467–485. doi:10.1111/j.1540-6520.2004.00058.x

Williams, V., & Phillips, B. D. (1999). *E-commerce: Small businesses venture online*. Report, Office of Advocacy, US Small Business Administration, Washington, DC, July. Retrieved from http://www.sba.gov/advo/stats/e_comm.pdf

Windrum, P., & de Berranger, P. (2003). The adoption of e-business technology by SMEs. In O. Jones & F. Tilley (Eds.), *Competitive Advantage in SMEs: Organising for Innovation and Change* (pp. 177-201). Wiley: England.

Wood, V. R., & Tandon, S. (1994). Key components in product management success (and Failure), A model of product managers' job performance and job satisfaction in the turbulent 1990s and beyond. *Journal of Product and Brand Management, 3*(1), 19–38. doi:10.1108/10610429410053068

Wu, F., Mahajan, V., & Balasubramanian, S. (2003). An analysis of e-business adoption and its impact on business performance. *Academy of Marketing Science Journal, 31*(4), 425–448. doi:10.1177/0092070303255379

Wu, J. H., & Wang, S. C. (2005). What drives mobile commerce? An empirical evaluation of the revised Technology Acceptance Model. *Information & Management, 42*(5), 719–729. doi:10.1016/j.im.2004.07.001

Xiao, J. J., Alhabeeb, M. J., Hong, G. S., & Haynes, G. W. (2001). Attitude toward risk and risk-taking behavior of business-owning families. *The Journal of Consumer Affairs, 35*(2), 307–325.

Yankee Group (YG). (1998, November 17). Yankee group finds small and business market missing the Internet commerce opportunity: Market unsatisfied with current Internet solution provider offerings. *YG Communication.*

Yankee Group (YG). (2002, January 1). Application Infrastructure and Software Platforms. *YG Communication.*

Yap, C. S. (1990). Distinguishing characteristics of organizations using computers. *Information & Management, 18*(2), 97–107. doi:10.1016/0378-7206(90)90056-N

Yap, C. S., Soh, C. P. P., & Raman, K. S. (1992). Information systems success factors in small businesses. *International Journal of Management Science, 20*(5), 597–609.

Yap, C. S., Soh, C. P. P., & Raman, K. S. (1992). International systems success factors in small business. *Omega International Journal of Management Science, 5*(6), 597–609. doi:10.1016/0305-0483(92)90005-R

Yasin, M., Czunchy, A., Gonzales, M., & Bayes, P. (2006). E-commerce implementation challenges: Small to medium-sized versus large organisations. *International Journal of Business Information Systems, 1*(3), 256–275. doi:10.1504/IJBIS.2006.008599

Yeung, W. L., & Lu, M.-t. (2004). Functional characteristics of commercial web sites: a longitudinal study in Hong Kong. *Information & Management, 41*(4), 483–495. doi:10.1016/S0378-7206(03)00086-7

Yi, M. Y., Jackson, J. D., Park, J. S., & Probst, J. C. (2006). Understanding information technology acceptance by individual professionals: Toward an integrative view. *Information & Management, 43*(3), 350–363. doi:10.1016/j.im.2005.08.006

Yildiz, M. (2007). E-government research: Reviewing the literature, limitations, and ways forward. *Government Information Quarterly, 24*(3), 646–665. doi:10.1016/j.giq.2007.01.002

Yin, R. K. (2003). *Case study research-Design and methods.* London: Sage Publications.

Young, G., Ashdown, D., Arnold, A., & Subramonian, K. (2007). Serendipity in urology. *BJU International, 101*(4), 415–416.

Yu, L., Suojapelto, K., Hallikas, J., & Tang, O. (2008). Chinese ICT industry from supply chain perspective - A case study of the major Chinese ICT players. *International Journal of Production Economics, 115*(2), 374. doi:10.1016/j.ijpe.2008.03.011

Zaheer, S. (1995). Overcoming the liability of foreignness. *Academy of Management Journal, 38*(2), 341–363. doi:10.2307/256683

Zahra, S. A., & George, G. (2002). International entrepreneurship: the current status of the field and future research agenda. In M. Hitt, D. Ireland, D. Sexton & M. Camp (Eds.), *Strategic entrepreneurship: Creating a new mindset* (pp. 255–288) Oxford, UK: Blackwell.

Zalud, B. (1999). E-commerce obstacles, solutions for small businesses. *Security Distributing and Marketing, January.*

Zantsi, N., & Eloff, M. (2003). *Guide to South African Law*. Retrieved 20 February, 2007, from http://icsa.cs.up.ac.za/issa/2003/Publications/001.doc

Zappala, S., & Gray, C. (Eds.). (2006). *Impact of e-commerce on consumers and small firms*. Aldershot: Ashgate.

Zhang, C., Cui, L., Huang, L., & Zhang, C. (2007). Exploring the role of government in information technology diffusion: An empirical study of IT usage in Shanghai Firms. In *Organizational dynamics of technology-based innovation: Diversifying the research agenda* (vol. 235/2007, pp. 393-407). Boston: Springer.

Zhao, F. (Ed.). (2008). *Information technology entrepreneurship and innovation*. Hershey, PA: Information Science Reference.

Zhu, K., & Kraemer, L. K. (2005). Post-adoption variations in usage and value of e-business by organizations: Cross-country evidence from the retail industry. [f]. *Information Systems Research*, *16*(1), 61–84. doi:10.1287/isre.1050.0045

Zhu, K., Kraemer, K., & Xu, S. (2003). Electronic business adoption by European firms: A cross-country assessment of the facilitators and inhibitors. *European Journal of Information Systems*, *12*(4), 251–268. doi:10.1057/palgrave.ejis.3000475

Zhuang, Y., & Lederer, A. L. (2006). A resource-based view of electronic commerce. *Information & Management*, *43*(2), 251–261. doi:10.1016/j.im.2005.06.006

Zineldin, M. (2000). Beyond relationship marketing; technologicalship marketing. *Marketing Intelligence & Planning*, *18*(1), 9–23. doi:10.1108/02634500010308549

Zontanos, G., & Anderson, A. R. (2004). Relationships, marketing and small business: an exploration of links in theory and practice. *Qualitative Market Research: An International Journal*, *7*(3), 228–236. doi:10.1108/13522750410540236

Zorz. (2003). Small firms 'shun' PC security, *BBC NEWS*. Retrieved October 15, 2004, from http://www.net_security.org/news:php?id=2650

Zuber-Skerritt, O. (1996). Emancipatory action research for organisational change and management development. In O. Zuber-Skerritt (Ed.), *New Directions in Action Research* (pp. 83-105). London: Falmer.

Zukin, S., & DiMaggio, P. (1990). *Structures of capital: The social organization of the economy*. New York: Cambridge University Press.

About the Contributors

Brychan Thomas is a Senior Research Fellow in Small Business and Innovation and Deputy Leader of the Welsh Enterprise Institute at the University of Glamorgan Business School, UK. His main research interests lie in innovation and small business, SMEs and technology transfer networks, technology transfer and internet adoption in the agri-food industry, higher education spinout enterprises, and science communication and education. As such he has been involved in a number of projects examining technology transfer and small firms in Wales. He has a science degree and an MSc in the Social Aspects of Science and Technology from the Technology Policy Unit at Aston University and a PhD in Science and Technology Policy, CNAA/University of Glamorgan. He has produced over 250 publications in the area of science communication, innovation and small business policy, including the book "Triple Entrepreneurial Connection", and is on the Editorial Advisory and Review Board of the International Journal of E-Business Management, the Editorial Review Board of the International Journal of E-Entrepreneurship and Innovation and the Editorial Advisory Board of IMJ – International Management Journals. During the academic year 2008/2009 he has been on secondment as a Fellow of the Advanced Institute of Management at the Centre for Technology Management, University of Cambridge.

Geoff Simmons is a Lecturer in Electronic Marketing within the Department of Marketing, Entrepreneurship and Strategy at the University of Ulster. Geoff lectures on a range of undergraduate and postgraduate marketing programmes. He graduated from the University of Ulster with a BA (Hons) MA and PhD. Geoff's PhD studied the area of small business Internet adoption. His main research interests are in this field and in the Internet branding field. Geoff has published in these areas in leading international academic Journals such as: *European Journal of Marketing, Journal of Strategic Marketing, International Small Business Journal* and the *Journal of Small Business and Enterprise Development*. Geoff lectures at under and postgraduate levels on E-Commerce and has consulted widely in the area particularly with small businesses.

* * *

Daniela Andreini is assistant professor and researcher in the department of business and administration at the University of Bergamo (Italy) and she holds a doctorate in marketing from "La Sapienza" University of Rome. Her research on marketing has included the introduction of e-commerce channel in the commerce of Italian typical products and the return of investment in internet marketing activities. Her current research and teaching activities concern the development of multichannel commerce, branding online for B2C commerce and virtual communities.

Martin Beckinsale is a Senior Lecturer & Researcher in Strategy and Management at Leicester Business School (DMU). As a module leader, his teaching focus relates to EBusiness, Service Operations and Business Research Issues and Analysis. He is a research team member of CREME (Centre for Research in Ethnic Minority Entrepreneurship). His academic background began in Strategic Technology Management, Small Firms and Innovation. Currently, he specializes in Information Communication Technology (ICT), EBusiness, Ethnic Minority Businesses (EMBs) and SMEs. Recent funding, through the ESRC Business Placement Fellows Scheme, sees his research focusing on the development of Ethnic Minority Business Support. The primary objective is in the area of ICT and eProcurement capacity building amongst Ethnic Minority Businesses. A critical aspect of his research focus is the development of the 'action research methodology' assisting and enabling policy development and delivery.

Paul Beynon-Davies is professor of business informatics at Cardiff Business School, Cardiff University. Before taking up an academic post, Professor Beynon-Davies worked for several years in the Informatics industry in the UK both in the public and private sectors. He still regularly acts as a consultant to the public and private sector particularly in the area of ICT and its impact on organisational performance. He has published widely in the field having 11 books and over seventy academic papers to his name. Professor Beynon-Davies has engaged in a number of government-funded projects related to the impact of ICT on the economic, social and political spheres. He was seconded part-time to the National Assembly for Wales (NAfW) as an evaluator of its Cymru-ar-Lein/Information Age strategy for Wales and was director of the eCommerce Innovation Centre at Cardiff University from 2006-2008. This centre was the home of the Broadband Observatory for Wales.

Roman Boutellier is a professor and Chair for Technology and Innovation Management at the Department of Management, Technology and Economics (D-MTEC) at ETH Zurich since 2004. Since 1999 Prof. Boutellier has been a titular professor at the University of St. Gallen (HSG). In 1979 he received his PhD in Mathematics and worked as a postdoctoral fellow at Imperial College in London. His work has appeared in R&D Management, Harvard Business Manager, ZFO and Drug Discovery Today. Roman Boutellier has held several leading positions in industry and has been a member of the management of Leica, Heerbrugg as well as CEO and delegate of the board of directors of the SIG Holding AG, Neuhausen. He is a member of the board of directors of several Swiss large-scale enterprises. The focus of his research is the management of technology driven enterprises with a specific focus on innovation.

David Deakins holds a Chair in enterprise Development and is Director of Dumfries Campus at the University of the West of Scotland. He is now responsible for strategic development at the Dumfries campus whilst maintaining his research interests and conferences connected with enterprise development and entrepreneurship. David's research interests include the finance of small firms, rural enterprise and ethnic minority enterprise. He co-authors a successful textbook on Entrepreneurship and Small Firms, published by McGraw-Hill and now in its 5th edition which was published in February 2009. He will take up a Chair in Small Business Management and Entrepreneurship at Massey University, NZ from 1st September 2009 and retain a Visiting Professorship at UWS.

Daniel Doiron is a professor in the Faculty of Business at the University of New Brunswick Saint John, Canada, where for the past six years he has been teaching in the areas of Management Information Systems, New Venture Development, Small Business Management, Competitive Strategy and Managing

Innovation at both the undergraduate and graduate levels. He also serves as the Director of the Electronic Commerce Research and Training Centre. Daniel has been involved in founding four technology startups, the most recent of which is a company which provides a GIS based Marine Electronics solution to the global in-shore fisheries market. Daniel began his career in the telecommunications industry in 1984 following graduation from the University of New Brunswick where he received a Bachelor degree in Electrical Engineering. In 1991, Daniel received a Masters Degree in the Management of Technology from the Sloan School of Management at MIT.

Hatem El-Gohary is a Lecturer in Marketing and Business and a Marketing researcher at Bradford University School of Management (Bradford, West Yorkshire, UK) and Cairo University Business School (Cairo, Egypt). He has more than 14 years of experience in academia and worked as the marketing director of a multinational company, a general manager for an Egyptian company and as a marketing consultant for a number of national and multinational companies. His research interests include: Electronic Marketing, Electronic Business, Electronic Commerce, Internet Marketing and Small Business Enterprises. He has published in journals such as the Journal of Business and Public Policy, Journal of International Business and Finance, International Business & Technology Review and the International Journal of Business Science and Applied Management.

Kyoko Fukukawa is a Senior Lecturer in Marketing at Bradford University School of Management, UK. Her research interests include ethical decision-making in consumption and business practices, and corporate social responsibility of MNCs concerning their policies and strategic communication. Her publications have appeared in the Journal of Business Ethics, Journal of Corporate Citizenship, and others.

Laura Galloway is a lecturer in entrepreneurship at Heriot-Watt University, Edinburgh. She recently introduced a new undergraduate degree in Management with Enterprise to the university, and leads and teaches various modules on entrepreneurship and enterprise. Her research interests include rural entrepreneurship, electronic business, entrepreneurship education and minority entrepreneurship. She publishes in a variety of peer reviewed journals and books on entrepreneurship and enterprise.

Jo Jones is a senior lecturer specialising in e-business, information systems and general management. She has been lecturing at the Newport Business School since 1997. Jo is jointly responsible for the management of the Undergraduate Business Programmes and is the course tutor for all first year full time Business degree and HND students. Jo recently played an instrumental part in the revalidation of all undergraduate Business Programmes, which included the introduction of degrees in Accounting, Business and Economics, Accounting and Economics and Business Studies. Before commencing her career as a lecturer, Jo worked in industry for ten years. Her final role was as a Business Analyst in a Business Development Division of a leading utility; specialising in spreadsheet modelling. Jo studied part time for an HNC in Business and Finance, a Postgraduate Diploma in Business Administration (Distinction) and a Masters in Business Administration at the University of Wales, Newport. She then completed a P.G.C.E. at the University of Wales, Newport and has recently completed a M.Sc. in E-commerce (Business) at Swansea Institute of Higher Education. Jo's research interests include Strategic Implications of E-Business (she has published several conference papers in this field) and Learning and Teaching. She is currently engaged in research with Ruth Gaffney-Rhys that considers the implications of the National Student Surveys 2005 and 2006, both of which highly ranked the B.Sc./BA Business Courses.

Paul Jones is currently Divisional Head of Enterprise and Economic Development at the University of Glamorgan Business School and has worked in higher education for over 17 years. He has had 18 journals published in refereed journals, given over 40 conference papers and several book chapters in edited books. His areas of research interest include information technology usage in the small enterprise sector, entrepreneurship education, business incubation and e-learning. He is currently the Track Advisor on the E-business Track within the annual ISBE conference having been Track leader for several years. He is a guest lecturer in several European higher education institutions in France, Germany, Poland and the Czech Republic.

Michael Kyobe is an Associate Professor of Information Systems at the University of Cape Town, South Africa. He holds a PhD in Computer Information Systems and a Master's degree in Business Administration. Prior to joining academia, Michael worked in the IT industry for a number of years. He has consulted extensively with the public and small business sectors in Information systems management, IT development & evaluation and Computer security. His research interests include: SMEs, Strategic alignment; Strategic Information Systems Planning; Computer Auditing & Security; IT resource utilization & Knowledge management.

Bee Theng Lau is a lecturer in the School of Computing and Design at Swinburne University of Technology, Sarawak Campus, Malaysia. She received a PhD in Computer Science and Information Technology from the University Malaysia Sarawak. Her research interests include e-commerce; face image processing, facial expressions pattern recognition, and communication application for disabled children and adults. She has presented at a number of national and international conferences and published numerous papers in international journals.

Simon McCarthy is Head of Professional Programmes at the University of Glamorgan Business School and is also the ACCA programme leader. His role involves teaching on the Accounting and Finance degree (which is where the online summative assessment of his research interests has practical application), and various Masters and professional programmes. He is also the person responsible for professional body accreditations. His main research areas include: Business Angel Networks, Small Business Finance and Marketing, Sports Finance, and the use of Online assessment on accounting courses. He has undertaken consultancy work for the Knowledge Exploitation Fund (KEF) in Wales, Industrial Society, Welsh Water, WDA and a Work Based Learning Project. He has published and presented conference papers in the areas of Small Business, Economics and Accountancy.

Fiona McMahon is a Lecturer in Advertising at the University of Ulster. She has 10 years experience working in advertising and marketing from both a client and agency perspective. The majority of her career has been spent working for and consulting with small businesses. In 2006 she obtained an MSc with Distinction in Industrial Practice, with particular emphasis on small firm internet adoption. She is currently undertaking doctoral research investigating how small firms can optimise new media technologies to create customer value and increase competitiveness.

Christopher Miller is a Principal Lecturer in Small Business Management/Head of Consultancy and Deputy Leader of the Welsh Enterprise Institute at the University of Glamorgan Business School. He is also scheme leader for the MSc International Business and Enterprise at the Glamorgan Business School. Dr. Miller's areas of expertise include Small Business Management, Innovation Generation, Business Planning, Business Growth and Enterprise Education. He has more than 30 research papers published in international refereed journals and some 30 published conference proceedings papers. He is a Fellow of the Higher Education Academy and a member of the Institute for Small Business and Entrepreneurship.

Lyndon Murphy originates from Ystrad, in the Rhondda Valley, South Wales. He was educated at Tonypandy Grammar School and the University College of Wales Aberystwyth. He is currently an Academic Leader at Newport Business School. In collaboration with Jo Jones and Huw Swayne, Lyndon has published several journal articles and conference papers in ebusiness. Further, he has worked with the Welsh Assembly Government to develop case studies exploring the impact of broadband accessibility on Welsh business performance. Lyndon's current research interests focus upon innovation policy in Wales. This research evaluates both business and social innovation policy outcomes.

Aodheen O'Donnell is a Senior Lecturer in Communication and Advertising. Her PhD research was in the area of small firm marketing, with a particular focus on how small firm owner-managers build networks and use the process of networking to further their businesses. In addition, Aodheen has engaged in research within the tourism and financial services sectors. A particular research interest is the relationship between face-to-face communication and remote, technologically based communication in a financial services context.

Gary Packham is Director for Enterprise for the University of Glamorgan and Head of Programmes for the Glamorgan Business School. He recently managed the prestigious Federation of Small Business' Lifting the Barriers Survey and acts as the Institute of Small Business and Entrepreneurship's regional champion for Wales. Previously, Dr Packham was Head of Division for Enterprise and Economic Development and was academic delivery manager for the circa £14 million ESF project - e-College Wales. He has published widely in the areas of enterprise and small business management and has extensive experience of developing and delivering enterprise and management education. Dr Packham is a Member of the Chartered Management Institute, the Institute for Leadership and Management and a Fellow of the Higher Education Academy. He is also a director of Age Concern Morgannwg Ltd.

David Pickernell is Head of the Welsh Enterprise Institute and Professor in Economic Development Policy at the University of Glamorgan Business School. He is also Adjunct Professor in the School of Management at Queensland University of Technology in Brisbane Australia. He has had over 50 articles published in refereed journals, given over 30 conference papers and had a number of chapters in edited books. His research areas encompass Foreign Direct Investment and Local-Global interactions, Economic Integration, Clusters and Networks, Regional Economic Development Policy, Construction, Universities and economic development, innovation, festivals and events in social enterprise and capital building, as well as socio-economic effects of gambling. He has also undertaken research and consultancy for a range of organisations, including the OECD, EU, Welsh Assembly Government, Queensland Government,

Victoria Government (Australia), Welsh Development Agency, Cardiff Council, Council of Mortgage Lenders, Associated British Ports, Shaw Trust, and the Federation of Small Business.

Modapothala Jashua Rajesh is a Lecturer in the School of Business and Enterprise at Swinburne University of Technology, Sarawak Campus, Malaysia. He received a PhD in Commerce from Sri Krishnadevaraya University, India. His research interests include strategic use of information technologies/systems, data mining, corporate social responsibility and environmental related studies. He has presented at a number of national and international conferences (inclusive of IEEE) and has a good publishing record.

Marta Raus works as a research associate with the Chair of Technology and Innovation Management at the Department of Management, Technology and Economics (D-MTEC) at ETH Zurich and at SAP Research Lab Zurich since 2006. She is a PhD candidate in Management with a focus on Business Innovation at the University of St. Gallen (HSG). Her research focuses on diffusion of IT innovations and value assessment models in the field of e-government at European level. Marta gained her MSc in managerial and production sciences at ETH Zurich with emphasis on integrated product development and technology and innovation management.

John Sanders is a lecturer in strategic management in the School of Management and Languages at Heriot-Watt University. He teaches strategic management courses to both undergraduate and post-graduate students. In addition, he teaches a small business management course to final year undergraduate students. Previously he held a lecturing position at Massey University, New Zealand, and taught International Business and General Management courses. His research efforts focus on organisational alignment, small firms and innovation management. His PhD investigated strategic fit within a University setting. Beyond research and teaching, he provides academic and administrative support for Heriot-Watt University's distance-learning and International Management and Languages (IML) programmes.

Chia Hua Sim is a lecturer in the School of Business and Enterprise at Swinburne University of Technology, Sarawak Campus, Malaysia. Her research interests include entrepreneurship, small businesses research, and e-commerce. She has presented at national and international conferences on topics related to ICTs and E-commerce.

Huw Swayne is Divisional Head of Design at the Cardiff School of Creative & Cultural Industries at the University of Glamorgan's new ATRiuM Campus at the heart of Wales Capital City. Huw manages provision that includes BA (Hons) programmes in Animation, Graphic Communication Interior Design, Fashion Design and Promotion, as well as a range of taught Masters Awards. Previously as a Principal Lecturer in Design he wrote, delivered and led the highly successful MA Graphic Communication which attracted a large EU development grant. Prior to this he developed many Undergraduate and Foundation Level Awards in Design subject areas seeing the subject area grow from a 60 student base, to over 600 in the past 10 years. Highly active in University Quality Assurance activities he has chaired over 30 validation events for a large number of internal panels and external bodies. A Member of NSEAD; National Society for Art & Design Education, his research interests include curriculum design and course development, skills gaps in Graphic Design SMEs, Entrepreneurship in design, and impact of ebusiness on graphic design providers, publishing a number of conference papers in the process. Personal interests include creating a range of learning resources for Welsh Medium Education, and pursuing interests in traditional/digital image manipulation. Previously he has held a range of lecturing and managerial posts in HE, FE and the Design Industry.

Piers Thompson is a lecturer in economics at the Cardiff School of Management within the University of Wales Institute, Cardiff (UWIC). Prior to this he worked on the Welsh component of the Global Entrepreneurship Monitor (GEM) project, the world's largest international study of entrepreneurial activity and attitudes. His research interests are in small firm finance, ethnic entrepreneurship and macroeconomic investment patterns. His work on topics relating to small business and firm start-up activity has been published at a number of international conferences.

Myfanwy Trueman is a Lecturer in Innovation and Marketing at Bradford University School of Management. Her research focus is on how design and visual evidence of change can enhance city brands. This work is grounded upon a series of ongoing projects with the local business community and Bradford's landscape planning department. Previous work examined how design can add brand value and reduce risk in new product development. She has published in journals such as the Journal of Marketing Management, Journal of Brand Management, Journal of Place Branding and public Diplomacy, Long Range Planning, Product Innovation Management, Corporate Communications: An International Journal, Design Studies and World Class Design to Manufacture.

Peter van der Sijde read (educational and theoretical) psychology at the VU University Amsterdam and after a short period as educational consultant he obtained a Ph.D. position at the University of Twente. After his Ph.D. he worked as research coordinator for educational research. He then moved to the domain of technology transfer and entrepreneurship at the same university and was co-founder in 2001 of the Dutch Institute for Knowledge Intensive Entrepreneurship (Nikos). In 2008 he moved to the VU University as an associate professor. His research interests are research spin-offs and the interaction between university and industry. He serves on the editorial boards of several journals (Industry & Higher Education, International Journal of Entrepreneurship & Innovation, International Journal of Globalization and the Small Business, International Journal of Innovation and Regional Development).

Ingrid Wakkee obtained a Ph.D. in international entrepreneurship from the Institute of Knowledge Intensive Entrepreneurship (Nikos) at the University of Twente in 2004, and is currently working as Assistant Professor at the VU University, The Netherlands. Her research interests lie within the field of entrepreneurship and (social) networks. In particular she has studied born global firms and high tech startups. Further to this, virtualization of business and networking has been an important element in her research. Her current research interests continue to involve the role of social and virtual networks in innovative ventures including the role of embedded ties in new venture creation, and market-driven social entrepreneurship. As a sideline Ingrid also conducted several studies in the field of entrepreneurship education. Her research has been published or is forthcoming in the *International Small Business Journal, International Entrepreneurship Journal, International Journal of Knowledge Management Studies,* and several edited books by Edward Elgar.

Robbie Williams is a researcher based at NEO. Previous assignments include working on the Welsh element of the Global Entrepreneurship Monitor (GEM) project, which is recognized as the world's largest international study of entrepreneurial activity. His research interests are in small rural firm's entrepreneurship, capability and interaction with government rural development policy. Present research focus is on the role and impact of Social Enterprise in deprived areas of Wales. His work on topics relating to small rural business, social enterprise activity and enterprise education has been published at a number of international and national conferences.

Index

A

Abbyshot Clothiers 131, 133, 134, 135
activity based costing (ABC) 55
after-care 216
Aiden's Deep Sea Fishing 118, 119, 123, 124, 131
ANOVA 75, 76
authorised economic operator 3, 4, 15
automated export system (AES) 3, 8
automated import system (AIS) 3

B

biotechnology 141
bounce rate 127
brochure-ware 89
business churn 102
business development manager 196, 197, 198, 199
business, enterprise and regulatory reform (BERR) 101, 113
Business Enterprise & Regulatory Reform (BERR) 68
Business Link 196, 197, 200
business models 140, 142, 168
business processes 188, 230, 233
business-to-business (B2B) 268, 276, 278
business-to-consumer (B2C) 261, 265, 266, 273, 276, 278, 284

C

causal mechanisms 188, 201
chi square 100, 107, 108

Chi-square 76, 77, 78
click & mortar 264, 271
coagulated scenario 182
codification scheme 259, 260, 261, 264
cognitive capabilities 54
commoditisation 222
competitive advantage 220, 222, 223, 224, 226, 227, 235
conceptual model 221, 229, 230, 260, 278, 283
confidentiality, integrity and availability (CIA) 58, 59
core business 262, 263, 266
core communications strategy 222
cost reduction 48
cross-border 2, 3, 5, 14, 15, 16, 17
cross-functional 224
cross-tabulations 100, 107
cryptography 49
customer empowerment 222
customer relationship management (CRM) 220, 222, 230, 231, 232, 234, 235, 236
Customs Code 1, 3, 6, 7, 15, 16, 18
customs regulations 1, 5, 6, 14, 15, 16, 17
cyber-attacks 48, 52, 58
cyber-risks 47
cycle times 277

D

database integration strategy 263, 267, 270
data collection 12, 13, 27, 28, 29
decision-makers 153
delivery problems 15

Breinigsville, PA USA
22 September 2010
245510BV00003BG/2/P

9 781605 669984